Nanotechnology for Drug Delivery and Pharmaceuticals

Nanotechnology for Drug Delivery and Pharmaceuticals

Edited by

RAVINDRA PRATAP SINGH

Department of Biotechnology, Faculty of Science, Indira Gandhi National Tribal University, Amarkantak, Madhya Pradesh, India

KSHITIJ RB SINGH

Department of Chemistry, Institute of Science, Banaras Hindu University, Varanasi, Uttar Pradesh, India

JAY SINGH

Department of Chemistry, Institute of Science, Banaras Hindu University, Varanasi, Uttar Pradesh, India

CHARLES OLUWASEUN ADETUNJI

Applied Microbiology, Biotechnology and Nanotechnology Laboratory, Department of Microbiology, Edo University Iyamho, Auchi, Edo

ELSEVIER

ACADEMIC PRESS

An imprint of Elsevier

Academic Press is an imprint of Elsevier
125 London Wall, London EC2Y 5AS, United Kingdom
525 B Street, Suite 1650, San Diego, CA 92101, United States
50 Hampshire Street, 5th Floor, Cambridge, MA 02139, United States
The Boulevard, Langford Lane, Kidlington, Oxford OX5 1GB, United Kingdom

ISBN: 978-0-323-95325-2

For Information on all Academic Press publications
visit our website at https://www.elsevier.com/books-and-journals

Publisher: Stacy Masucci
Acquisitions Editor: Andre G. Wolff
Editorial Project Manager: Timothy J. Bennett
Production Project Manager: Fahmida Sultana
Cover Designer: Mark Rogers

Typeset by MPS Limited, Chennai, India

Dedication

We, as the editors of this book, would like to dedicate it to those who care, conserve, protect but do not spoil or destroy the beauty and unique characteristics of Kshit (Earth), Jal (Water), Pawak (Fire), Gagan (Sky), and Sameera (Air).

Contents

Section 2 Pharmaceuticals

List of contributors

CO Adetunji
Applied Microbiology, Biotechnology and Nanotechnology Laboratory, Department of Microbiology, Edo State University Uzairue, Edo State, Nigeria

Ankit
School of Pharmaceutical Sciences, Lovely Professional University, Phagwara, Punjab, India

Hira Aslam
Department of Physics, University of Agriculture Faisalabad, Faisalabad, Pakistan

MO Bamigboye
Department of Chemical Sciences, Kings University, Odeomu, Osun State, Nigeria

Najla Bentrad
Faculty of Biological Sciences, Department of Biology and Physiology of Organisms, University of Sciences and Technology Houari Boumediene, Bab Ezzouar, Algeria

Swati Bhati
Department of Life Sciences, School of Basic Sciences and Research, Sharda University, Greater Noida, Uttar Pradesh, India

Monika Bhattu
University Centre for Research and Development, Chandigarh University, Mohali, Punjab, India

Dheeraj Bisht
Department of Pharmaceutical Sciences, Sir J.C. Bose Technical Campus Bhimtal, Kumaun University, Nanital, Uttarakhand, India

Kemal Çetin
Department of Biomedical Engineering, Necmettin Erbakan University, Konya, Turkey; Science and Technology Research and Application Center (BITAM), Necmettin Erbakan University, Konya, Turkey

Anik Kumar Das
Department of Pharmacology, School of Pharmaceutical Sciences, Shoolini University, Solan, Himachal Pradesh, India

Adil Denizli
Department of Chemistry, Hacettepe University, Ankara, Turkey

Santanu Dhara
Biomaterial and Tissue Engineering Laboratory (BMTE), Indian Institute of Technology Kharagpur, Kharagpur, West Bengal, India

Kamal Dua
Discipline of Pharmacy, Graduate School of Health, University of Technology Sydney, Ultimo, NSW, Australia; Faculty of Health, Australian Research Centre in Complementary and Integrative Medicine, University of Technology, Sydney, Ultimo, NSW, Australia

CA Eziukwu
Department of Chemistry, Edo State University Uzairue, Edo State, Nigeria

Hareem Fatima
Department of Physics, University of Agriculture Faisalabad, Faisalabad, Pakistan

Anshuman Gaurav
School of Pharmaceutical Sciences, Shoolini University, Solan, Himachal Pradesh, India

Deepak K Gupta
Department of Pharmacy, Indira Gandhi National Tribal University, Amarkantak, Madhya Pradesh, India

Humaira Hussain
Department of Chemistry, University of Okara, Okara, Pakistan

A Inobeme
Department of Chemistry, Edo State University Uzairue, Edo State, Nigeria

Suyambulingam Jone Kirubavathy
Department of Chemistry, PSGR Krishnammal College for Women, Coimbatore, India

Shikha Kapil
University Institute of Biotechnology, Chandigarh University, Mohali, Punjab, India

Deepika Kathuria
University Centre for Research and Development, Chandigarh University, Mohali, Punjab, India

T Kelani
Department of Chemistry, Edo State University Uzairue, Edo State, Nigeria

Anglina Kisku
NeuroPharmacology Research Laboratory (NPRL), Department of Pharmacy, Indira Gandhi National Tribal University, Amarkantak, Madhya Pradesh, India

Deepak Kumar
Department of Pharmaceutical Chemistry, School of Pharmaceutical Sciences, Shoolini University, Solan, Himachal Pradesh, India

Krishan Kumar
Physical Chemistry Research Laboratory, Department of Chemistry, D.C.R. University of Science and Technology, Sonipat, Haryana, India

Suneel Kumar
Department of Biomedical Engineering, Rutgers, The State University of New Jersey, Piscataway, NJ, United States

Cansu İlke Kuru
Graduate School of Natural and Applied Sciences, Department of Biotechnology, Ege University, Izmir, Turkey; Buca Municipality Science and Art Center, Izmir, Turkey

Kalpana Madgula
RiKarbon Inc., Newark, DE, USA; St. Francis College for Women, Hyderabad, Telangana, India

M Maliki
Department of Chemistry, Edo State University Uzairue, Edo State, Nigeria

Padmavati Manchikanti
Plant Metabolic Pathway Laboratory, Rajiv Gandhi School of Intellectual Property Law (RGSOIPL), Biomaterial and Tissue Engineering Laboratory (BMTE), Indian Institute of Technology Kharagpur, Kharagpur, West Bengal, India

JT Mathew
Department of Chemistry, Ibrahim Badamasi Babangida University, Lapai, Niger State, Nigeria

Sayan Mukherjee
Biomaterial and Tissue Engineering Laboratory (BMTE), Indian Institute of Technology Kharagpur, Kharagpur, West Bengal, India

Gunjan Nagpure
Department of Biotechnology, Faculty of Science, Indira Gandhi National Tribal University, Amarkantak, Madhya Pradesh, India

Arunadevi Natarajan
Department of Chemistry, PSGR Krishnammal College for Women, Coimbatore, India

Vanya Nayak
Department of Chemistry, Institute of Science, Banaras Hindu University, Varanasi, Uttar Pradesh, India

Muhammad Yasin Naz
Department of Physics, University of Agriculture Faisalabad, Faisalabad, Pakistan

E Olori
Department of Chemistry, Edo State University Uzairue, Edo State, Nigeria

BI Onyeachu
Department of Chemistry, Edo State University Uzairue, Edo State, Nigeria

Ajay Pal
School of Medicine, Temple University, Philadelphia, PA, United States

Nirmalya Pal
University Institute of Biotechnology, Chandigarh University, Mohali, Punjab, India

Rishi Paliwal
Nanomedicine and Bioengineering Research Laboratory (NBRL), Department of Pharmacy, Indira Gandhi National Tribal University, Amarkantak, Madhya Pradesh, India

Mrituanjay D Pandey
Department of Chemistry, Institute of Science, Banaras Hindu University, Varanasi, Uttar Pradesh, India

Sadanand Pandey
Department of Chemistry, College of Natural Sciences, Yeungnam University, Gyeongsan, Gyeongbuk, South Korea

Jhansi Lakshmi Parimi
Plant Metabolic Pathway Laboratory, Rajiv Gandhi School of Intellectual Property Law (RGSOIPL), Biomaterial and Tissue Engineering Laboratory (BMTE), Indian Institute of Technology Kharagpur, Kharagpur, West Bengal, India; Biomaterial and Tissue Engineering Laboratory (BMTE), Indian Institute of Technology Kharagpur, Kharagpur, West Bengal, India

Shruthy D. Pattathil
Gulbarga University, Kalaburagi, Karnataka, India; Bhavan's Vivekananda College of Science, Humanities & Commerce, Secunderabad, Telangana, India

Lakshmi Madhuri Peddada
St. Francis College for Women, Hyderabad, Telangana, India; GITAM Deemed to be University, Hyderabad, Telangana, India

Ekta Poonia
Physical Chemistry Research Laboratory, Department of Chemistry, D.C.R. University of Science and Technology, Sonipat, Haryana, India

Rishi Raj
Department of Applied Chemistry and Polymer Technology, Delhi Technological University, New Delhi, Delhi, India

Narender Ranga
Nanomaterials Research Laboratory, Department of Physics, D.C.R. University of Science and Technology, Sonipat, Haryana, India

Rohit Ranga
Physical Chemistry Research Laboratory, Department of Chemistry, D.C.R. University of Science and Technology, Sonipat, Haryana, India

Nadia Razdan
Department of Life Sciences, School of Basic Sciences and Research, Sharda University, Greater Noida, Uttar Pradesh, India

Soumi Sadhu
Department of Life Sciences, School of Basic Sciences and Research, Sharda University, Greater Noida, Uttar Pradesh, India

Arpit Sand
Department of Chemistry, Manav Rachna University, Faridabad, India

Akshansh Sharma
Department of Pharmaceutical Chemistry, School of Pharmaceutical Sciences, Shoolini University, Solan, Himachal Pradesh, India

Ishan Sharma
Department of Pharmacology, School of Pharmaceutical Sciences, Shoolini University, Solan, Himachal Pradesh, India

Monu Kumar Shukla
Department of Pharmaceutical Chemistry, School of Pharmaceutical Sciences, Shoolini University, Solan, Himachal Pradesh, India

Shazia Shukrullah
Department of Physics, University of Agriculture Faisalabad, Faisalabad, Pakistan

Anita Singh
Department of Pharmaceutical Sciences, Sir J.C. Bose Technical Campus Bhimtal, Kumaun University, Nanital, Uttarakhand, India

Jay Singh
Department of Chemistry, Institute of Science, Banaras Hindu University, Varanasi, Uttar Pradesh, India

Kshitij RB Singh
Department of Chemistry, Institute of Science, Banaras Hindu University, Varanasi, Uttar Pradesh, India

Ravindra Pratap Singh
Department of Biotechnology, Faculty of Science, Indira Gandhi National Tribal University, Amarkantak, Madhya Pradesh, India

Sachin Kumar Singh
School of Pharmaceutical Sciences, Lovely Professional University, Phagwara, Punjab, India

Kunjbihari Sulakhiya
NeuroPharmacology Research Laboratory (NPRL), Department of Pharmacy, Indira Gandhi National Tribal University, Amarkantak, Madhya Pradesh, India

Houcine Touati
Institute of Chemistry of Environments and Materials, National School of Engineers of Poitiers (ENSI), University of Poitiers—UMR CNRS 7285, Poitiers Cedex 9, France

Jaya Tuteja
Department of Chemistry, Manav Rachna University, Faridabad, India

Fulden Ulucan-Karnak
Ege University, Institute of Health Sciences, Medical Biochemistry Department, Izmir, Turkey

Meenakshi Verma
University Centre for Research and Development, Chandigarh University, Mohali, Punjab, India

Aparna Vyas
Department of Mathematics, Manav Rachna University, Faridabad, India

Yashraj Yadav
Department of Pharmacology, Acropolis Institute of Pharmaceutical Education and Research, Indore, Madhya Pradesh, India

Koray Şarkaya
Department of Chemistry, Pamukkale University, Denizli, Turkey

About the editors

Dr. Ravindra Pratap Singh did his BSc from Allahabad University, India and his MSc and PhD in biochemistry from Lucknow University, India. He is currently working as an assistant professor in the Department of Biotechnology, Indira Gandhi National Tribal University, Amarkantak, Madhya Pradesh, India. He has previously worked as a scientist at various esteemed laboratories globally, namely Sogang University, IGR Paris, etc. His work and research interests include biochemistry, biosensors, nanobiotechnology, electrochemistry, material sciences, and biosensor applications in biomedical, environmental, agricultural, and forensics. He has to his credit several reputed national and international honors/awards. Dr. Singh has authored over 60 articles in international peer-reviewed journals and more than 50 book chapters of international repute and has edited 8 books. He serves as a reviewer of many reputed international journals and is also a member of many international societies. He is currently also involved in editing various books, which will be published in internationally reputed publication houses, namely IOP Publishing, CRC Press, Elsevier, and Springer Nature. Moreover, he is a book series editor of "Emerging Advances in Bionanotechnology," CRC Press, Taylor and Francis Group. He is also actively involved in guest-editing special issues (SI) for reputed international journals, and one of the latest edited SI by Dr. Singh is "Smart and Intelligent Nanobiosensors: Multidimensional Applications" for Materials Letters, Elsevier.

Mr. Kshitij RB Singh is a postgraduate in biotechnology from Indira Gandhi National Tribal University, Amarkantak, Madhya Pradesh, India. He is currently working in the laboratory of Dr. Jay Singh, Department of Chemistry, Institute of Science, Banaras Hindu University, Varanasi, Uttar Pradesh, India. He has more than 40 peer-reviewed publications to his credit, has edited 7 books, and has authored more than 30 book chapters published in the internationally reputed press, namely Elsevier, IOP Publishing, Springer Nature, Wiley, and CRC Press. He is currently also involved in editing books with international publishing houses, including CRC Press, IOP Publishing, Elsevier, Wiley, and Springer Nature. His research interests include biotechnology, biochemistry, epidemiology, nanotechnology, nanobiotechnology, biosensors, and materials science.

Dr. Jay Singh is currently working as an assistant professor at the Department of Chemistry, Institute of Sciences, Banaras Hindu University, Varanasi, Uttar Pradesh, since 2017. He received his Ph.D. degree in polymer science from Motilal Nehru National

Institute of Technology in 2010 and did MSc and BSc from Allahabad University, Uttar Pradesh, India. He had a postdoctoral fellow at National Physical Laboratory, New Delhi, Chonbuk National University, South Korea, and Delhi Technological University, Delhi. Dr. Jay has received many prestigious fellowships such as CSIR (RA), DST-Young Scientist Fellowship, DST-INSPIRE Faculty Award, etc. He is actively engaged in the development of nanomaterial (CeO_2, NiO, rare-earth metal oxide, Ni, $Nife_2O_4$, Cu_2O, graphene, RGO, etc.)-based nanobiocomposite, conducting polymer, and self-assembled monolayer-based clinically important biosensors for estimation of bioanalaytes such as cholesterol, xanthine, glucose, pathogens, and pesticides/toxins using DNA and antibodies. Dr. Jay has published more than 80 international research papers with total citations more than 3500 and an h-index being 34. He has completed/running various research projects in different funding agencies. He has many edited/authored books (under pipeline) and has authored more than 20 book chapters of internationally reputed press for publications, namely Elsevier, Springer Nature, IOP, Wiley, and CRC. He is actively engaged in fabricating metal oxide-based biosensors for clinical diagnosis, food packaging applications, drug delivery, and tissue engineering applications. His research has contributed significantly toward the fundamental understanding of interfacial charge transfer processes and sensing aspects of metal nanoparticles.

Professor Charles Oluwaseun Adetunji is presently a faculty member at the Microbiology Department, Faculty of Sciences, Edo State University Uzairue (EDSU), Edo State, Nigeria, where he utilized the application of biological techniques and microbial bioprocesses for the actualization of sustainable development goals and agrarian revolution, through quality teaching, research, and community development. He is currently the Ag Dean for the Faculty of Science and the Head of the Department of Microbiology at EDSU. He is a visiting professor and the executive director for the Center of Biotechnology, Precious Cornerstone University, Ibadan. He has won several scientific awards and grants from renowned academic bodies. He has published many scientific journal articles and conference proceedings in refereed national and international journals with over 370 manuscripts. He was ranked among the top 500 prolific authors in Nigeria between 2019 till date by SciVal/SCOPUS. His research interests include microbiology, biotechnology, postharvest management, and nanotechnology. He was recently appointed as the President and Chairman Governing Council of the Nigerian Bioinformatics and Genomics Network Society. He is presently the General/Executive Secretary of the Nigerian Young Academy. He is presently a series editor with Taylor and Francis, United States editing several textbooks on agricultural biotechnology, nanotechnology, pharmafoods, and environmental sciences. He is an editorial board member of many international journals and serves as a reviewer for many double-blind peer-reviewed journals such as Elsevier, Springer, Francis and Taylor, Wiley, PLOS One, Nature, American Chemistry Society, and Bentham Science Publishers.

Preface

The technology is updating and modernizing day by day. Nanotechnology has played a novel role in creating revolutionary changes in various life sciences domains, such as drug delivery, diagnostics, and food. The development from using bulk ointments to developing nanofilms and nanocomposites on the burnt skin is an impressive example that describes nanotechnology's commendable journey from microbiology. Nanotechnology is a branch of science and technology aiming to develop nanosized materials or devices. It mainly gained a lot of interest and attention because of its unique size, ranging from 1 to 100 nm. These exhibit various unique chemical, physical, biological, optical, and electrical properties that differentiate them from bulk materials. The idea of producing nanoscale products that are capable of mimicking the same functions as that of the cell has been the major driving force in the development of nanotechnology in the biomedical fields, along with the growing demand for science and technology for the growth in the areas of medicines and environment has given rise to the advancement of nanotechnology, which is one of the six key enabling technologies. Although metal oxide and nanoparticles produced by physical and chemical routes show toxicity toward the environment and the living cells, they are less preferred in the biomedical domain. Green synthesis has been proved as a sustainable method to produce metal oxide and nanoparticles as they are less toxic, cost-effective, and eco-friendly and follow a simple methodology. Nanotechnology has been very useful in targeted drug delivery and therapeutics for disease prevention, diagnosis, and treatment. It is a highly beneficial and revolutionary technique as it specifically delivers the drug at the targeted site for the better uptake of less soluble drugs, which can be further used in therapeutic and diagnostic applications. This book briefly presents various drug-delivery techniques that utilize nanotechnology in the biomedical domain, highlighting the therapeutic and diagnostic applications. The book also provides important facts and detailed studies on different promising nanocarriers such as liposomes, polymeric nanocarriers, micelles, dendrimers, hydrogels, metallic nanocarriers, quantum dots, ceramic-base nanocarriers, carbon-based nanocarriers, exosomes, and virus-based nanocarriers.

Moreover, these nanocarriers' utilization in the therapeutic applications of various diseases such as cancer, inflammation, neurodegenerative disorders such as Huntington's disease, and Alzheimer's disease, human immunodeficiency virus, and inflammatory bowel disease is also briefly highlighted in this book. A detailed discussion is also laid on passive and active targeting strategies utilizing various conjugation methods and ligands. The book also presents a brief overview of each drug delivery system's multiple advantages and disadvantages caused by each drug-delivery system and describes the most appropriate clinical applications and future clinical trials. Recent research related to drug delivery and targeting has also been covered in this book. The book is one of its kind as, to the best of our knowledge, it provides a detailed description of nanotechnology and its applications in drug delivery and covers the role of nanotechnology in pharmaceuticals. The book describes how nanotechnology has efficiently overtaken the conventional dosage forms and provided comfort and ease to the patient. The pharmaceutical nanoparticle can be described as the sub-nanosized structures containing drugs or bioactive substances made up of several tens or hundreds of atoms or molecules in needles, spherical, crystalline, or amorphous morphologies.

Moreover, this book provides the reader the knowledge about pharmaceutical nanoparticles in a very simple and easy way. The book also efficiently covers the recent development in the pharmaceutical industries by highlighting their old market strategies, such as minimizing the development costs of drugs, enhancing production costs, various types of competition faced by generic manufacturers, and increased failure rates, which can cause pressure on the pharmaceutical business sector, and how the development of pharmaceutical nanoparticle has efficiently revolutionized the pharmaceutical industry and also improved the market profits. Some of the merits and demerits of pharmaceutical nanoparticles are also discussed in this book. Relevant information regarding market trends, patents, and social-economic factors are also provided in this book. The book also majorly highlights the future perspectives and safety issues for both drug-delivery and pharmaceutical applications. Hence, the major facets on which the book is focused are mentioned below pointwise:

- Details about both drug-delivery applications and pharmaceutical applications of nanotechnology.
- A brief description of the utilization of nanotechnology in the drug-delivery domain has been explained.
- Properties of nanocarriers are majorly highlighted for the convenience of the reader.
- Detailed facts about various nanocarriers are provided and discussed with different strategies employed by the nanocarriers.
- Major facts and research regarding various diseases and how they are treated with nanocarriers' help are also highlighted. It also briefly covers the nanocarriers' diagnostic and imaging applications and their potential role in clinical diagnosis.
- Along with the current developments, it also focuses on future developments and possibilities, allowing the reader to enhance and explore the remaining gaps.
- Provides a detailed analysis of nanotechnology's role in pharmaceuticals and will be the only book to cover pharmaceutical potential along with the drug-delivery applications briefly.

- Detailed information is gathered on the market analysis of the nanotechnological products utilized in both drug delivery and pharmaceuticals.
- A detailed analysis of the advantages and disadvantages of the role of nanotechnology in drug delivery and pharmaceuticals is also covered.
- The basic safety regulations are also provided.

Ravindra Pratap Singh
Kshitij RB Singh
Jay Singh
Charles Oluwaseun Adetunji

Acknowledgments

It gives us immense pleasure to acknowledge Professor Shri Prakash Mani Tripathi, Honorable Vice-Chancellor of Indira Gandhi National Tribal University, Amarkantak, India, Professor Sudhir K Jain, Honorable Vice-Chancellor, Banaras Hindu University, Varanasi, Uttar Pradesh, India, Professor Emmanuel O. Aluyor, Vice-Chancellor, Edo State University, Uzairue, Nigeria, and Professor Julius Kola Oloke, Precious Cornerstone University, Ibadan, Nigeria for providing constant assistance in all the possible ways. It is also our great pleasure to acknowledge and express our enormous debt to all the contributors who have provided their quality material to prepare this book. We are grateful to our beloved family members (Dr. Babita Singh, Dr. Juliana Bunmi Adetunji, Dr. Ranjana Verma, Miss Aparajita RB Singh, Mr. Emmanuel Ayomiposi Adetunji, Miss Taiwo Jesugbemi Adetunji, Miss Kehinde Jesugbemi Adetunji, and Miss Shanvi Singh), who joyfully supported and stood with us in many hours of our absence to finish this book project. Thanks are also due to Linda Versteeg-Buschman, Timothy Bennett, and the entire publishing team for their patience and extra care in publishing this book.

Ravindra Pratap Singh
Kshitij RB Singh
Jay Singh
Charles Oluwaseun Adetunji

SECTION 1

Targeted drug delivery

CHAPTER 1

Introduction to drug-delivery techniques based on nanotechnological approaches

Kshitij RB Singh[1], Gunjan Nagpure[2], Jay Singh[1] and Ravindra Pratap Singh[2]
[1]Department of Chemistry, Institute of Science, Banaras Hindu University, Varanasi, Uttar Pradesh, India
[2]Department of Biotechnology, Faculty of Science, Indira Gandhi National Tribal University, Amarkantak, Madhya Pradesh, India

Introduction

Nanotechnology is a multidisciplinary subject dealing with nanosized materials (1−100 nm) and has encountered its profound use in various domains like electronics, chemistry, biotechnology, engineering, and physical and material science. Moreover, nanoscale materials can be a system or device, or these could be composites, complexes, or supramolecular structures (Wilkinson, 2003). In addition to the developments in other scientific fields like engineering and electronics, nanotechnology also shows significant advancements in conventional biomedical applications, including drug delivery, gene therapy, imaging, and novel drug discovery techniques (Choi & Montemagno, 2016). Moreover, with one dimension, nanoparticles (NPs) with <100 nm in the range consist of different biodegradable materials like natural and synthetic polymers. Other than larger micro molecules, NPs are bounded up by the cells more efficiently and, therefore, can be explored as effective in drug development, drug delivery, and treating several disorders, as illustrated in Fig. 1.1 (Sahu et al., 2021). However, for therapeutic applications, drugs can either be attached to the particle's surface or assimilated to the matrix of the particle. A drug targeting system should be able to control the consequences of a drug entering the biological environment (Liu et al., 2009).

Furthermore, nano-drug technologies represent a crucial tool for enlightening drug markets in the pharmaceutical industry. It has been reported that novel drug delivery systems (DDSs) can substantially contribute to global pharmaceutical sales. According to strategy, about 13% of the recent global pharmaceutical market is marked by sales of products accumulating a DDS (Mohanty et al., 2017; Swamy & Sinniah, 2016). Currently, many new pharmaceutical industries offer advanced pharma products and adorning their efforts toward developing more efficient, adequate, and performance-based new DDSs. With this

Nanotechnology for Drug Delivery and Pharmaceuticals
DOI: https://doi.org/10.1016/B978-0-323-95325-2.00010-9

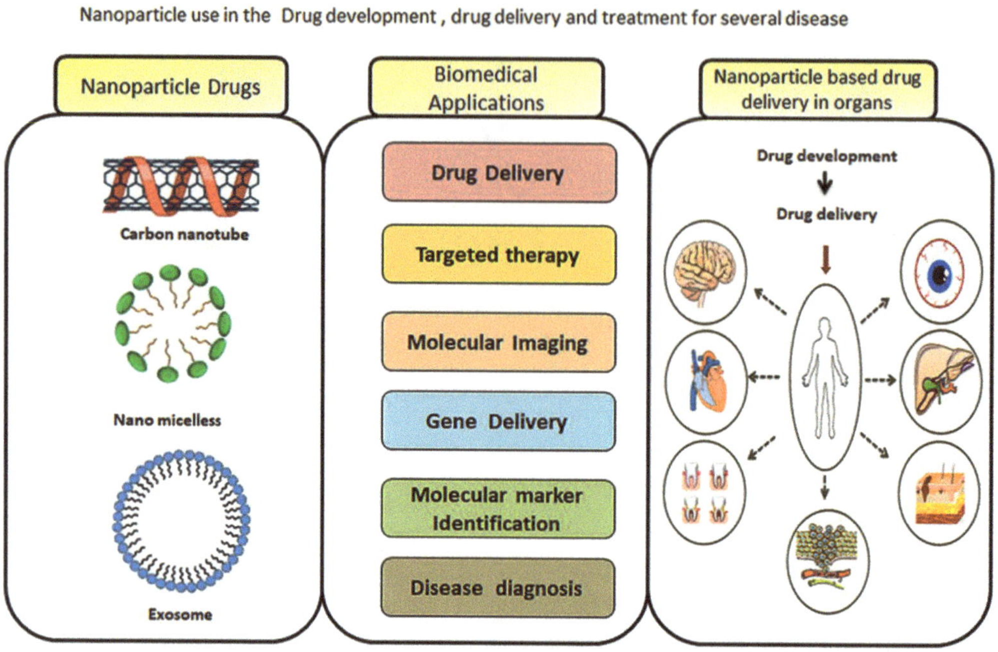

Figure 1.1 The schematic illustration of the use of nanoparticles in the biomedical domain. *Reproduced with permission of Sahu, T., Ratre, Y. K., Chauhan, S., Bhaskar, L. V. K. S., Nair, M. P., & Verma, H. K. (2021). Nanotechnology based drug delivery system: Current strategies and emerging therapeutic potential for medical science.* Journal of Drug Delivery Science and Technology, 63, *102487. https://doi.org/10.1016/j.jddst.2021.102487.*

development, the demand for DDSs is rising gradually due to its advancements over the conventional approach (Thilakarathna & Rupasinghe, 2013). Nanomaterials (NMs) have shown their influential role in drug delivery at the targeted disease site to enhance the uptake of poorly soluble drugs. Moreover, polylactic acid (PLA)- and polylactic/glycolic acid (PLGA)-based NPs have been successfully formulated to encapsulate dexamethasone. Furthermore, nanocarriers have also shown promising advancements in targeted DDSs. Owning to the high surface area to volume ratio, nanocarriers offer the capability to alter the bioactivity and basic properties of drugs. Furthermore, nanotechnology has emerged as a powerful tool in evading conventional DDSs (Kamal et al., 2012).

This book chapter entitled "Introduction to drug-delivery techniques based on nanotechnological approaches" intends to highlight the utility of nanotechnological approaches in DDSs in the biomedical domain. Further, this book will elaborate on the method for fabricating and biologically synthesizing nanocarriers for targeted DDSs in Chapters 2 and 3. Chapter 4 discusses nanomedicines and nanocarriers in cancer treatment. Furthermore, Chapter 5 discusses the role of nanocarrier in inflammation treatment. Chapters 6 and 7 deal with the potentialities of nanocarriers and nanomedicines for treating infectious diseases and neurodegenerative disorders, followed by Chapter 8, which deals with the utility of recent plant-based nanomedicine and nanocarriers for cancer treatments. Chapter 9 deals with the utility of nanomedicines and nanocarriers for treating noninfectious diseases. Chapter 10 discusses the passive and active targeted drug delivery strategies. Chapter 11 deals with the utility of various DDSs and their advantages and disadvantages. Moreover, Chapter 12 deals with clinical applications and future clinical trials of DDSs. Chapter 13 deals with the advantages of nano-drug targeting conventional dosage systems. At last, Chapter 14 deals with the risk assessment of various NMs, along with health safety and perspective.

Synthesis of nanocarriers and nanomedicines for targeted drug delivery

A nanocarrier is a NM ranging in a diameter between 1 and 1000 nm used as a transport element for another substance, such as a drug (Wang et al., 2012). Furthermore, nanocarriers have provided advanced benefits in the biotechnology and biomedical domains and play a unique role in the area of nanoscience and technology (Singh & Lillard, 2009). Moreover, nanocarriers exhibit several advanced characteristics that integrate into drug delivery, including protection against active drug degradation, a decrease in the intensity of undesirable toxic side effects, and improved and more efficient concentration in the target tissues (Hallan et al., 2016; How et al., 2013). It shows unique advancements in the biomedical domain; therefore it is essential to synthesize the nanocarriers. On the other hand, nanomedicines offer a DDS at the nanoscale; the branch of medicines provides the knowledge and tools of nanotechnology to prevent and treat the disease. Nanomedicines use nanoscale materials, such as nanorobots and biocompatible NPs, for living organisms' delivery, diagnosis, and sensing purposes (Soares et al., 2018). This section mainly focuses on synthesizing nanocarriers and nanomedicines via biological and physiochemical approaches.

Biological synthesis

Nowadays, biological approaches are preferable compared to other synthesis approaches due to their various advanced properties. They are convenient, easy, cost-effective, eco-friendly, and minimize the use of toxic chemicals. Biological methods comprise the utilization of various living organisms, such as plants, yeast, and animals. Moreover, various other natural components are also utilized, such as pectin, honey, chitosan, glucose, and starch. Plants extract has been used to synthesize the various NPs-based nanocarriers, such as metal- and metal-oxide-based NPs are used as nanocarriers to deliver drugs in the targeted region, as illustrated in

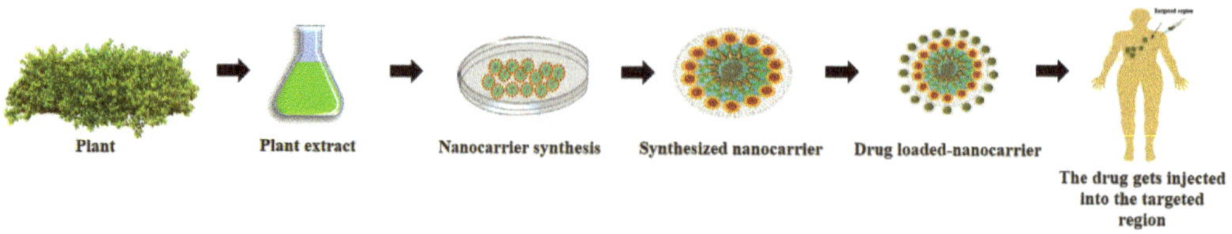

Figure 1.2 This figure illustrates the utility of green synthesized nanocarriers in targeted drug delivery.

Fig. 1.2 (Singh et al., 2021). Moreover, to synthesize various nanocarriers biologically, selecting the correct plant or microorganism is necessary as different plants show the difference in terms of biochemical processing, enzyme activity, phytochemical constituents, and so on.

Akbarian et al. (2020) studied the biological synthesis of novel chitosan-coated ZnO nanocarrier using ethanolic extract of *Camellia sinensis* (green tea) loaded with an anticancer drug paclitaxel (PTX) for selective drug delivery in MCF-7 cell line. Chitosan is an essential polymer obtained from the chitin's deacetylation carrying a positive charge. As solid tumors have a negative charge, chitosan carrying a positive charge can be attracted by these cells and facilitates drug delivery. Moreover, mechanical properties, film-forming, chemical modifications, cost-effectiveness, and high permeability toward water are some of the characteristics that have introduced this polymer as a stabilizing agent in NPs. PTX is an alkaloid, a chemotherapeutic compound derived from plants that show its antitumor activity against prostate, breast, and cervical cancer. As a result, the study reveals that ZnO–Ch–PTX NPs with low cytotoxic effects show promising effects in the DDS. Zafar et al. (2021) studied a green synthesized chitosan-coated cerium oxide nanocarrier derived from the seed extract of *Amomum subulatum* (aka black cardamom) loaded with drug ciprofloxacin, which shows the cytotoxic effect against methicillin-resistant *Staphylococcus aureus*-induced mastitis diagnosed in dairy cattle. Globally, cancer is reported as the significant cause of mortality, with 18.1 million new cases. It has been reported that hematite (Fe_2O_3) shows a good effect in cancer therapy. Ansari et al. (2022) studied a green synthesized porous magnetic iron nanocarrier loaded with an anticancer drug derived from fresh *Nepeta cataria* L. leaves extract, showing cytotoxic activity against human cancer cell line. Oliveira et al. (2018) studied the biological synthesis of carbon-based magnetic nanocarrier derived from the methanolic extract of *Rubus ulmifolius* Schott flowers showing potential effects in drug delivery. Studies reported that carbon-based magnetic nanocarriers functionalized with Pluronic F-68 show a synergistic impact on drug delivery to treat cancer patients. Moreover, Ojha and Das reported, previous studies investigated that microbial biopolyesteric nanocarrier (MBPNc) [poly(3-hydroxybutyrate-*co*-3-

hydroxyvalerate] (P(3HB-*co*-3HV) was fabricated using corn steep liquor, sugarcane molasses, and palm oil derived from yeast, *Wickerhamomyces anomalus* VIT-NN_{01} under stress (sound wave) condition and optimized nutrient. Further, the same copolymer (P(3HB-*co*-3HV) was utilized to synthesize MBPNc that is used as a biodegradable and biocompatible nanocarrier for constant delivery of drug levofloxacin and amoxicillin. Further, the MBPNc loaded with drug levofloxacin and amoxicillin exhibits diverse advantages to minimize the bacterial resistance incidence and for controlled delivery of antibiotic in future at targeted site (Ojha & Das, 2021). Furthermore, one study reports that naturally derived protein, silk fibroin from *Bombyx mori* silkworm, shows promising results in the synthesis of protein-based nanocarriers due to its flexibility, biodegradability, biocompatibility, and mechanical toughness which are further utilized for tissue engineering and wound healing process (Jacob et al., 2018; Numata & Kaplan, 2010; Samrot et al., 2020).

Moreover, green synthesized nanomedicines have also received considerable attention from researchers in biomedical domains, such as diagnosing, monitoring, control, prevention, and disease treatment. Nanomedicines utilize biocompatible NMs for therapeutic purposes to treat various diseases. According to recent reports, phytochemicals, such as flavonoids, alkaloids, phenols, alcohols, terpenoids, sugars, and proteins, present in plants are involved in the stabilization and reduction of metal ions. Flavonoids are used to treat many pathological disorders like cancer, Alzheimer's sickness, atherosclerosis, neurodegenerative disease, and macrophage oxidation. Total flavonoids present in the *Coriandrum sativum* and *Alternanthera tenella* leaf extracts are majorly involved in the silver NPs (AgNPs) synthesis and show clinical applications in curing antidandruff, antiacne, and antibreast cancer, which offers excellent efficiency against *Malassezia furfur*, *Propionibacterium acnes*, and human breast adenocarcinoma cells, respectively, as reported by Sathishkumar et al. (2018). Raghunandan et al. (2010, 2009, 2011) studied green synthesized Ag and gold (Au) NPs derived from aqueous soaked clove buds (*Syzygium aromaticum*) and antimalignant guava (*Psidium guajava*) leaf extract show anticancer efficacy against four different cancer cell lines, human kidney, bone marrow, human cervix, leukemia, and so on. Sabaratnam et al. (2013) studied green synthesized AgNPs derived from *Ganoderma neo-japonicum* imazeki used as a disinfectant and antimicrobial agents show cytotoxic effects against MDA-MB-231 human breast cancer cells. Moreover, Priyadarshini et al. studied the anisotropic AgNPs synthesis derived from *Bacillus flexus* strain possess eco-friendly nature shows promising antimicrobial property against multidrug-resistant human pathogens. Further studies reveal that strains of *S. aureus*, *Enterobacter cloacae*, *Lactobacillus acidophilus*, *Bacillus licheniformis*, *Bacillus cereus*, *Pseudomonas aeruginosa*, and *Bacillus subtilis* could also induce AgNPs synthesis (Priyadarshini et al., 2013; Shivaji et al., 2011).

Physiochemical synthesis

Physiochemically synthesized nanocarriers possess unique properties, due to which it offers relevant application in biomedical science, followed by functionalized DDSs. Various types of nanocarriers are synthesized via different physiochemical methods.

Solid lipid nanocarriers, with sizes 50–100 nm, were synthesized via hot homogenization, high shear homogenization, ultrasonication, cold homogenization, spray drying, and microemulsions. The synthesized nanocarriers show the most advanced applications like targeted drug delivery to solid tumors, in vivo and in vitro drug delivery to solid tumors, followed by antitubercular chemotherapy due to its unique properties like they exhibit better stability, are biodegradable, act as a colloidal carrier, as well as better upgradeability (Kingsley et al., 2006). Moreover, quantum dot nanocarriers with size 2–10 nm synthesized via e-beam lithography, X-ray lithography, ion plantation, molecular beam epitaxy, and luminescence features carry unique electronic properties, high light stability, self-assembly followed by chemical reduction, and continuous absorption spectra that displays bioimaging and biomarker detection applications (Freeman et al., 2011; Geißler et al., 2010). Further, magnetic nanocarriers with sizes 1–100 nm are synthesized via glass crystallization, citrate gel process, and metal alkoxide hydrolysis method, which carries novel properties like high colloidal stability and superparamagnetic chemical stability that reveals biosensing, imaging, and functionalized AuNP-improved drug delivery applications (Hallan et al., 2016). Furthermore, carbon nanotubes–based nanocarriers with 0.4–3 nm in size exhibit unique electrical and elastic properties and possess crystalline nature that manifests various applications like peptide delivery, gene, and drug delivery, tissue engineering, cancer cell identification as well as artificial implantation (Müller et al., 2000). Moreover, polymer-based nanocarriers with 10–100 nm size synthesize via emulsification/solvent diffusion method, polymerization, nanoprecipitation, salting out process, solvent evaporation, and dialysis method that carries unique properties like are biodegradable, effective cell membrane permeation that possesses active and passive drug delivery, high concentration of drug delivery as well as maintains volatile pharmaceutical agent stability (López-Moreno et al., 2010).

However, different NMs are synthesized biologically and physiochemically, and it plays a significant role in nanoscience and technology. Furthermore, physiochemically synthesized nanomedicines play an essential role in biomedical science. Silicon-based biomaterial serves as a carrier for DDSs. Silicon exhibits biocompatible, biodegradable, eco-friendly, and nontoxic properties, showing promising clinical potential in the biomedical domain. Silicon materials, 2D silicene differing from silicon materials, such as silica or pSi, displaying unique physiochemical advantages like giant magnetoresistance, quantum-spin hall effect, and chiral superconductivity by its unique low-buckled topography. Silicene material is manufactured by physical vapor deposition method on

Ag (111) surface and achieved on ZrC (111), Ir (111), MoS_2 (111), and ZB (001) substrates under ultrahigh vacuum ambiance. Hence, high intrinsic biocompatibility of silicon components, high photothermal therapeutic capacity, and advantageous biodegradative nature of the 2D nature of silicene promise to broaden the clinical and biomedical use of silicon-based nanoplatforms (Lin et al., 2019). Moreover, cerium oxide NPs (CeO_2-NPs) have shown their potential efficiency in different domains, including nanomedicine (Mortazavi Milani et al., 2017). Hosseini et al. (2020) studied that CeO_2-NPs are physiochemically synthesized via sol−gel method using poly(allylamine) as stabilizing agent/capping agent. The CeO_2-NPs exhibit cytotoxic and biocompatible properties against cancer cell lines and serve as the best candidates for biomedical applications, such as cancer therapy. Moreover, poly(ethylene glycol)−poly (ε-caprolactone) copolymers (PEG−PCL) play an essential role in improved drug delivery. Grossen et al. (2017) studied that PEG−PCL-based nanomedicines are prepared via the emulsification method and show a biocompatible, biodegradable, and stable property. PEG−PCL-based nanomedicines are good candidates showing their advanced efficiency in multicomponent therapies and drug delivery.

Utility of nanocarriers

A nanocarrier is a NM ranging in diameter from 1 to 1000 nm used as a transport element for another substance, such as a drug. Nanocarriers are known as colloidal drug carrier systems owing to their high surface area. They exhibit their potential efficiency in the biomedical domain, which can change drugs' bioactivity and basic properties (Neubert, 2011). Moreover, decreased toxicities, improved biodistribution and pharmacokinetics, controlled release, and enhanced stability and solubility are the few properties that nanocarriers can assimilate into DDSs. Furthermore, the physicochemical properties of nanocarriers can be regulated by changing their surface properties, shapes, surface charge, sizes, and compositions (ud Din et al., 2017). As a result, the nanocarrier-based platform has received much attention from researchers in delivering drugs at the targeted zone of action to cure various disorders, including tumors and neurodegenerative diseases, with common side effects, as depicted in Fig. 1.3.

Tumors

A tumor refers to the abnormal growth of body tissues, mainly caused by mutation. Moreover, tumor suppressor genes are responsible for stimulating programmed cell death (apoptosis) or liable for determining cell differentiation and proliferation. These mutated genes lead to metastatic tumors that possess distinctive features of unlimited cell growth, the capability to seize distant and adjacent tissues, the absence of apoptosis, and the inability to turn off the excessive cell division (Javier & Butel, 2008). Tumors grow and behave differently depending upon whether they are cancerous

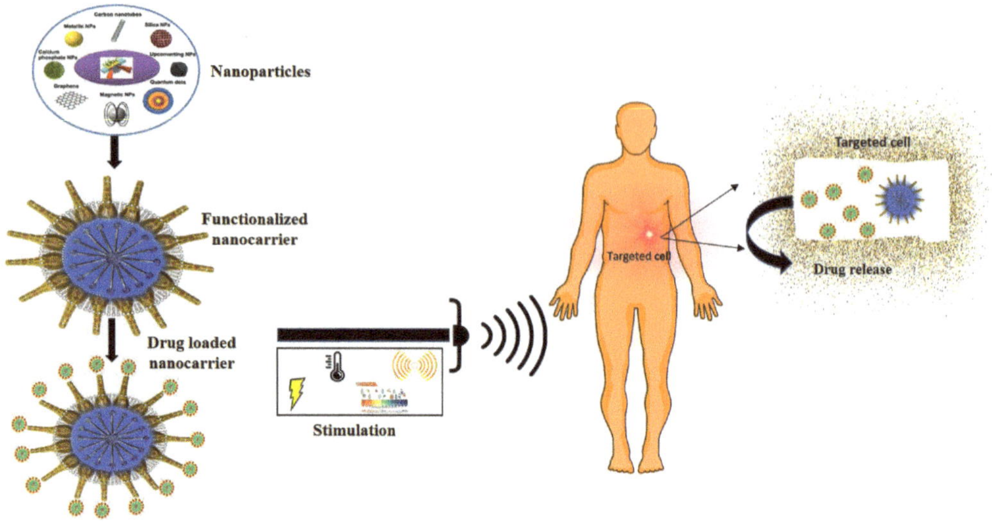

Figure 1.3 This figure represents drug-loaded nanocarriers in targeted drug delivery system.

(malignant), precancerous, or noncancerous (benign). Several risk factors are associated with genetic mutations, including physical irritants, carcinogens, heredity, and viruses. Further, traditional chemotherapies are acclimatized for tumor treatment and management that possess many toxic side effects, such as renal, cardiac, hepatic, gastrointestinal, bone marrow, and pulmonary toxicities. Moreover, researchers are trying to limit the chemotherapeutics drug doses by targeting different tumor cells. Furthermore, nanocarriers show good advantages in enhancing the safety profile and therapeutic effectiveness of traditional angiogenic agents. Moreover, these drug-loaded nanocarriers show their potential effects in antitumor chemotherapeutical delivery to the tumor sites either by decorating them with site-specific ligands or exploiting tumor pathogenesis (Hassanpour & Dehghani, 2017). Due to high mortality rates and worldwide popularity, tumors are classified into pancreatic, breast, and lung tumors. The distinct advantages of relative nanocarriers for treating these tumors are analyzed here.

Pancreatic tumor is reported as the fourth leading cause of cancer deaths, that is estimated about 62,210 genders (29,240 women and 32,970 men) are diagnosed with a pancreatic tumor, and about 49,830 genders (23,860 women and 25,970 men) deaths are reported due to pancreatic cancer. It has been reported that, through surgical procedures, only 10%–15% of cases of pancreatic tumors are resolved. There are several risk factors for this malignant disease has been suggested that including a family history of chronic pancreatitis, smoking, male sex, advancing age, non-O blood group, diabetes mellitus, obesity, occupational exposures (nickel, chlorinated hydrocarbon solvents), a high-fat diets, African–American ethnic origin, low diets in vegetable and folate as well as high diets in meat and possibly periodontal disease and *Helicobacter pylori* infection (Rawla et al., 2019). Family history and cigarette smoking are reported as prime risk factors leading to a multifactorial and complex pancreatic tumor compared to these risk factors. Moreover, two types of tumors that grow in the pancreas are reported: neuroendocrine tumors and exocrine tumors. About 7% of the total neuroendocrine tumors, also known as islet cell tumors, are analyzed, and the rest, 93% of all pancreatic tumors, are exocrine tumors. The most common type of pancreatic cancer is known as adenocarcinoma. Similarly, when most common type begins in the pancreatic ducts, it is known as ductal adenocarcinoma (Halfdanarson et al., 2014). Furthermore, it was estimated that chemotherapy is a widely used method for treating metastatic pancreatic adenocarcinoma and localized advanced-stage pancreatic tumors. For example, gemcitabine is the best therapeutic drug employed to treat pancreatic tumors. Reports suggested that gemcitabine-based therapy replacing FOLFLRINOX, a chemotherapy regimen provides a better survival rate of 11.1 months than the preceding 6.8 months. But according to reports, none of the gemcitabine-based therapy or FOLFLRINOX is proved to be a better result against metastatic pancreatic or advanced tumors in their clinical trials (Lambert et al., 2019).

Nanotechnology has gained considerable attention from biomedical science researchers as nanosize ranged particles are best for visualizing tumors, diagnosis, and localized delivery. Nanocarriers have shown their relevant efficiency in targeting tumor cells. It is also used for enhancing the dose efficiency of imaging and therapeutic contrast agents by increasing their bioavailability and decreasing the toxic effects of angiogenic agents. A solid-lipid NPs-based nanocarrier shows synergistic effects in delivering methotrexate drugs to cure pancreatic tumors (Mitchell et al., 2021). Cucinotto et al. (2013) reported that albumin-obligated PTX-loaded nanocarriers show their potential clinical efficiency in treating the pancreatic tumor. Cabral et al. (2013) prepared a chemotherapeutic drug, oxaliplatin-loaded nanoparticulate micelles, which offer an antitumor effect against the pancreatic tumor. Spadavecchia et al. (2016) reported dicarboxylic acid–terminated polyethylene glycol (PEG)–gold NPs (AuNPs) and doxorubicin-loaded PEG–AuNPs employed as nanocarriers show their potential efficiency in treating Parkinson's disease (PD) via unique targeting strategy.

Moreover, hypoxia-inducible factor 1a (HIF1a) has emerged over the past decades as a relevant new target for treating pancreatic cancer by enhancing the drug resistance of the angiogenic drug gemcitabine (Gem). Zhao et al. (2015) reported biocompatible lipid-polymer hybrid NPs encapsulating Gem and si-HIF1α were synthesized for treating pancreatic cancer and explored their synergistic antitumor effects in orthotopic and subcutaneous models.

Breast tumor emerges in the epithelium cells of the lobules (15%) or ducts (85%) in the breast's glandular tissue. From approximately 2016–18 data, it has been reported that there is a risk of approx. 12.9% of women will be diagnosed with female breast cancer at some point in their lifetime (DeSantis et al., 2015). In 2018 it was estimated that about 3,676,262 women are residing with female breast cancer in the United States. In 2020 it was reported that about 2.3 million women were diagnosed with breast cancer, and globally about 685,000 deaths occurred. As of the end of 2020, it has been reported that about 7.8 million women who were alive have been diagnosed with breast cancer in the last five years, making it the world's most prevalent tumor. For these infected patients, accepted treatments involve neoadjuvant therapy followed by chemotherapy, hormone therapy, and radiation therapy, which aims to diminish tumor size and weight localized within that area to minimize the surgical process, allowing breast protection in various cases (Stoltenberg et al., 2020). As a result, neoadjuvant therapy plays a crucial role in shrinking a tumor before the primary surgery. Examples of neoadjuvant therapy include radiation therapy, hormone therapy, and chemotherapy, which also show potential advantages in preventing additional metastatic spread of the disease (Ginsburg et al., 2020).

Moreover, many antitumor drug-loaded nanocarriers have been reported, which are used as a novel technique for the targeted drug delivery via locoregional lymphatics, which targets tumorous cells and leads to drug delivery with low safety toxicity while accommodating systemic therapeutic levels (Yao et al., 2020). Chawla and Amiji (2002) developed biodegradable poly(epsilon-caprolactone) NPs that are employed to enhance the provincial applications of the drug tamoxifen (Nolvadex or Soltamox), which is used to treat hormone receptor-positive breast tumors. Further studies show that tamoxifen, a selective estrogen receptor prepared by NPs, shows enhanced therapeutic efficiency by carrying the drug in the specific zone of the estrogen receptor.

Lung tumor is the second most prevalent and detected tumor in both men and women and the leading cause of cancer death among both men and women, making up almost 25% of all cancer deaths. American Cancer Society (ACS) estimates lung cancer in the United States for 2022, about 236,740 new cases (117,910 in men and 118,830 in women) and 130,180 death cases (68,820 in men and 61,360 in women). Further, the development of lung tumor cells to a secondary location comparatively to the pancreas and breast leads to more tumor deaths and offers a significant threat to cancer treatments. Studies have shown that inadequate specificity and efficiency is the major problem with chemotherapy techniques. Thus it is essential to evolve targeted and site-specific therapies to accomplish common side effects and adequate efficacy. Moreover, conservative diagnostic methods are reported as inappropriate tumor screening and treatment choices due to their inaccuracy and inexpensive procedures (Cersosimo, 2002).

As a result, nanotechnology shows its potential clinical effects in diagnosing and treating lung tumors. Sensor-based gold NPs (AuNPs) received much attention from researchers due to their cost-effective properties and show their relevant effects in diagnosing lung tumors. Nanocarriers also showed greater antitumor efficiency with sustained drug delivery applications. Tang et al. (2022) studied polyglutamine-based nanocarriers (PGS) utilize the glutamine (Gln) transporter SLC1A5 to deliver therapeutic gene regulator siRNAs to Gln addicted cancer cells. Studies proved that Gln metabolism could be used as a gene/DDS to deliver drugs in targeted lung tumors.

On the other hand, metal–organic frameworks (MOFs) emerged as the most relevant class of functional materials for drug delivery in oncology. MOFs are crystalline porous materials consisting of metal ions or clusters coordinated with organic ligands to form three-dimensional (3D) structures. MOFs have received much attention from researchers due to their large surface areas, excellent chemical and thermal stabilities, mesoporous and 3D structures, and the potential for functionalization. Meng et al. (2021) reported the potentialities of functional MOF-based nanocarriers that show great potential for gene/drug delivery to tumors. The study indicates that MOF-based nanocarriers offer remarkable efficiency in suppressing the growth of the primary 4T1 breast tumors and inhibiting lung metastasis from increasing the survival rate.

Neurodegenerative diseases

Diseases that are related to the brain are referred to as neurodegenerative diseases. Globally, neurodegenerative diseases affect millions of people, which occur when the brain's nerve cell or the peripheral nervous system loses its function overtime, and at last, it ultimately dies. Neurodegenerative diseases, including Alzheimer's disease (AD), PD, and Huntington's disease (HD), throw a heavy burden on society and family. It has been reported that neurodegenerative disorders are incurable, clinical treatments are limited, and also slow down the disease progress. As a result, nanodelivery technology brings hope for neurodegenerative disorders. Nanocarriers act as a powerful vehicle to control the blood–brain barrier (BBB) in curing neurodegenerative disorders.

Moreover, PD is reported as an accelerating nervous system disorder that affects movements and leads to stiffness, shaking, and difficulty in balance, walking, and coordination. Although PD is incurable, medicines might remarkably improve the symptoms. Hence according to a different strategy, nanocarriers have created new opportunities for targeting the diseases and developing disease-modifying therapies and novel treatment approaches. A DDS serves as a powerful vehicle for drugs to attack the zone of interest, prevent harmful side effects, increase drug bioavailability, and minimize drug loss and degradation. There are multiple treatment options available, including rivastigmine, donepezil, and galantamine, which are commonly prescribed drugs to enhance the bioavailability of acetylcholine by inhibiting its breakdown. But these drugs do not show much efficiency in treating PD. Recently, siRNA-loaded nanocarriers developed for treating NDs ensure easy cell delivery with the help of a natural or synthetic polymer as it shows enhanced nuclease stability. Targeted physiochemical modifications and encapsulated siRNA enhances the drug delivery (Wilkinson et al., 2004).

Furthermore, AD is a brain-related disorder that slowly destroys thinking skills and memory and causes the brain to shrink (atrophy) and brain cells to die. It is the common cause of dementia. However, the BBB is involved in the pathogenesis of AD. BBB inhibits foreign objects from entering the brain tissues, whereas it also impedes the transportation of toxic substances and drugs into the brain for protection. Moreover, it is essential to overcome these brain-related issues, and medicines also should be introduced to solve this major issue. Recently, lipid-based nanocarriers received much attention and have been widely reported to treat brain diseases (Huynh & Mohan, 2017). Meng et al. (2015) studied the potentialities of a novel low-density lipoprotein (LDL) that stimulates nanostructured lipid carrier loaded with curcumin (Cur) and modified with lactoferrin (Lf) was evaluated for brain-targeted delivery. LDL is long-circulating, nonimmunogenic, that possesses the innate ability to bind both hydrophilic and hydrophobic molecules. The natural LDL is extracted from human serum, the quantity of which is deficient, and due to the variable size and composition, it is challenging to isolate LDL in large amounts. Moreover, Lf is found in milk and is a naturally occurring iron-binding cationic glycoprotein. It possesses antifungal, antibacterial, antiviral, and anticancer activity. Cur is a phytochemical that exhibits antiinflammatory, antioxidant, antidepressant, and anticancer properties with low toxicity. Moreover, Silva-Abreu et al. (2018) studied antiinflammatory, antiangiogenic, antitumor, and antifibrotic potential effect of peroxisome proliferator-activated receptor-gamma (PPAR-γ) agonist loaded with pioglitazone—PEG (PEG—PLGA) nanocarriers shows potential advantages in treating AD. PGZ has evolved to normalize cerebral blood flow, reduce oxidative stress, increase glucose uptake, enhance neural activity, and positively affect cerebrovascular functions in patients infected with AD.

HD is an inherited disease that causes degeneration of nerve cells in the brain, which causes emotional problems, uncontrolled movements, and cognition effects. It is incurable, but treatment may help to overcome this disorder. Furthermore, nanocarriers utilize their potential efficiency in treating HD disease. Godinho et al. (2013) investigated the utility of oligosaccharide-based molecules and modified amphiphilic β-cyclodextrin NPs as novel siRNA delivery vectors for RNAi-based therapies for treating HD.

Utility of nanomedicines

Nanomedicine is an advanced field of nanotechnology that implements the use of techniques and knowledge of nanoscience and technology and shows its efficient advantages in disease remediation and prevention. It utilizes nanodimensional materials, including nanosensors for diagnosis and sensory purposes, nanorobots, and actuates materials in live cells. Recently, nano-based medicines are an excellent branch of medicine because nanostructures could be used as drug delivery agents by encapsulating and attaching therapeutic drugs with controlled release and delivering them to target tissues more precisely (Soares et al., 2018). In addition, nanostructures help forbid drugs from being oxidized in the gastrointestinal region and provide water-soluble drugs to their addressed location. Moreover, nanostructures reside in the blood circulatory system for an extended period, and as per dose, it enables the release of potent drugs. Furthermore, nanomedicine-based therapeutic applications show potential in the biomedical domain and have become more widely accepted for improving treatment efficiency by reducing side effects in diseased patients.

Breast cancer is reported as the most common type of cancer among women. About 70%–80% of individuals with nonmetastatic disease can be cured early. Mutations cause breast cancer in the progesterone/estrogen receptors, and traditional methods are used to treat the emerging condition. However, conventional treatments like chemotherapy, radiotherapy, and surgery are not reported as efficient for the treatment that pertains to low cellular uptake, low bioavailability, adverse toxicities, and emerging resistance. Nanomedicines show their potential advantages in treating breast cancer (Yersal, 2014). Lipid-based nanocarriers had the most relevant outcomes of all nanocarriers. However, an amalgamation of synthetic chemotherapeutic agents with an herbal anticancer bioactive molecule can resolve the cancer stem cells and drug resistance issues. Researchers mainly focused on the solid-lipid nanocarriers employing a combinative method in the coming decades (Tagde et al., 2022). Furthermore, ovarian cancer (OC) is the most prevalent tumor of female reproductive organs. It has been noted that malignant edema of OC is the outcome of metastasis and peritoneal infiltration of tumor cells, which seriously destroys the patient's life and leads to death. As a result, Alendronate–calcium–THZ_1 (ACaT), a multifunctional carrier-free nanomedicine, due to its biocompatible and antitumor property, shows promising efficacy in treating OC in females. Moreover, chronic lymphocytic leukemia (CLL) is also reported as a type of cancer in which bone marrow makes too many white blood cells (lymphocytes). It is referred to as B-lymphoproliferative disorder exhibiting a divergent growth of $CD_5/CD_{19}/CD_{20}/CD_{23}$ positive lymphocytes. ACS estimated about 21,250 new cases of CLL in 2021, with an approximately 20.3% estimated mortality rate (Awan & Byrd, 2018; Bosch & Dalla-Favera, 2019; Nisticò et al., 2020; Rawstron et al., 2018, 2019). A surplus of drugs was approved for treating CLL, including alkylating agents like chlorambucil, bendamustine, and cyclophosphamide, followed by anti-CD20 antibody rituximab. Several drugs were introduced to inhibit the immune escape of CLL malignant cells and to regulate the microenvironmental interaction.

Further, besides the advancements of various targeted treatments and chemo-immunotherapy, the targeted drug delivery proved efficient for treating and improving the toxicity/effectiveness of both new and conventional drugs. As a result, nanomedicines offered the opportunity to deliver cytotoxic drugs to lymph nodes, bone marrow even the tumor cell (Zoulikha & He, 2022). Lipid-based drug carriers have shown their potential advantages in delivering drugs at the targeted site due to their high loading capacity, sustained and controlled drug release, low production cost, biocompatible nature, and so on (García-Pinel et al., 2019; Kukkar et al., 2021; Yang & Merlin, 2020). Lipid-based approved nanomedicines, such as Onpattro and Doxil for treatment, show potential effects in delivering antileukemic drugs (Thi et al., 2021). Further, Marqibo, a conventional sphingosine/cholesterol liposome loaded with vincristine, is accepted for treating acute lymphoblastic leukemia (Silverman & Deitcher, 2013), whereas a liposome, Vyxeos, is coloaded with cytarabine and daunorubicin for treating acute myeloid leukemia (Krauss et al., 2019).

Moreover, nanomedicine-based approaches have also shown significant advancements in treating neurodegenerative disorders, such as AD, PD and HD. Transition metals like Cu, Zn, and Fe are involved in the functioning of metalloenzymes, and they are present relatively at high concentrations in the brain and used for detecting biomarkers. Metal NPs are fabricated differently by altering surface charges, adjusting particle size, modifying shapes, and combining various surface ligands, which shows its good advantages in drug delivery of NDs. Furthermore, Yang et al. (2016) developed novel gold NP-capped mesoporous silica (MSN-AuNPs)-based H_2O_2-accessible controlled release system for targeted drug clioquinol (CQ) delivery for AD treatment. Moreover, MSNs have gained considerable attention in biomedical applications owing to their well-defined structures, controllable functionalities, and excellent biocompatible nature. Due to tunable porosity, large surface area, and large pore volumes, MSNs play therapeutic roles in delivering drugs to treat neurogenerative disorders (Mendiratta et al., 2019). Furthermore, recent studies reveal that NPs covered Fe_3O_4 protein and Cds showed tremendous advantages in disaggregating and inhibiting Tau in AD disease (Sonawane et al., 2019). Moreover, lipid-based NPs offer significant benefits in developing theragnostic agents for treating various NDs disorders. Recent reports investigate that lipid-based nanocurcumin, developed with enhanced solubility and stability, inhibits the neuronal loss in PD, AD, and HD. Moreover, PEGylated immunoliposomes comprising antibodies directed to transferrin receptors and insulin were successfully utilized as carriers for gene replacement therapy in the PD model (Tapeinos et al., 2017). Furthermore, hydrogels are hydrophilic polymers, with a 3D network, which significantly proved functional in providing neuroprotection; additionally, hydrogel formulations are fabricated for comprehensive drug administration into the brain to obtain targeted action in NDs (Narayanaswamy & Torchilin, 2019). Currently, Li et al. (2016) demonstrated the neuroprotective role of activin B-loaded hydrogels shows potential efficiency in treating PD. Moreover, polymeric NPs emerged as effective diagnostic imaging agents and developed as a carrier of drugs for NDs. Further investigation reveals that curcumin-loaded PLGA with reduced inflammation and oxidative stress enhances drug delivery applications for treating AD. Another study demonstrates ascorbic acid and gallocatechin-3-gallate-loaded PEGylated PLGA NPs displayed potential therapeutic efficiency in the AD model (Yavarpour-Bali et al., 2019).

Targeted drug delivery

Targeted drug delivery is a term also known as drug targeting or sometimes called innovative drug delivery, but it differs from targeted therapy that is generally involved in drug discovery. It is a method that is frequently used in delivering a medicinal drug to a patient's affected body parts that enhances the concentration of the therapeutic drug in the affected area relative to others (Torchilin, 2000). Targeted drug delivery indicates the primary accumulation of drugs within a targeted area independent of the route and the method of drug administration. Different techniques, such as a catheter, direct injection, and gene gun methods, deliver drugs within the targeted site (Dunaevsky, 2013; Kleinstreuer et al., 2012). On the other hand, targeted therapy denotes a specific association between a drug and its receptor at the biological level. Whereas retain, evade, target, and release are four critical requirements of DDS fabrication that are essential for the overall performance and function of the system (Mills & Needham, 1999).

Moreover, NPs have also shown their efficiency in treating solid tumors, oral delivery of therapeutic proteins as well as in single-dose vaccination. NPs are colloidal, solid particles of macromolecular substances ranging from 10 to 1000 nm (Kreuter, 2007). Nanocapsules are vesicular systems where a drug gets compacted into the cavity enclosed by a polymer membrane. In contrast, nanospheres are matrix systems in which the drug is uniformly and physically gets dispersed. Although particles less than 200 nm are not heavily followed, nanomedicines often refer to devices greater than 200 nm (Barratt, 2000). Generally, the drug of interest is entrapped, dissolved, adsorbed, attached, and encapsulated onto a nanomatrix. Depending on the preparation method, NPs, nanocapsules, or nanospheres can be fabricated to release characteristics for the best delivery and possess different properties of therapeutic agents. Furthermore, biodegradable NPs regulated from PLA and PLGA have shown their practical advantages in sustained drug delivery and efficiency toward drugs with the intracellular target (Pitt et al., 1981). Hence, NPs offer their novel functional properties as nanocarriers in delivering drugs to target location as illustrated in Fig. 1.3.

Strategies of targeted drug delivery system

Strategies of drug targeting systems are divided into the "passive" and "active" categories. In "passive targeting," physiochemical properties of drug carrier complex are used so that it escapes the body's defense mechanisms and gets accumulated in the target tissue. It utilizes the natural course of biodistribution of the carrier system through which it eventually gets accumulated in the targeted organs. Moreover, passive targeting is obtained from the body's natural immune system, in which the drug is targeted to the systemic circulation (Torchilin, 2011). As in tumors cells or infected cells, there are leaky capillaries and inflamed tissues in which pores get formed with enhanced permeability and increased retention; therefore discontinuous endothelium occurs, whereas, in normal tissues, the endothelium is continuous (Arap et al., 1998). As a result, passive targeting is also known as enhanced permeability and retention (EPR), and in this, the particle's surface is not altered or modified. Hence, passive targeting is only achieved through the mechanisms of EPR (Kobayashi et al., 2014). According to a recent strategy, compared to normal organs, the EPR effect provides preferably modest tumor specificity with a 20%–35% increase in delivery. The EPR effect is highly dependent on intrinsic tumor biology. Various factors, such as intratumor pressure, angiogenesis and lymphangiogenesis, the degree of perivascular tumor, and the density of the stromal response with physicochemical characteristics of nanocarriers, determine its drug delivery efficacy (Fang et al., 2011). Some of these nanocarriers, like the marketed Caelyx and Doxil, are successfully used in clinics, and the EPR effect shows novel advantages in fabricating passive tumor-targeted systems. Active targeting has led to its potential efficiency in delivering genes, drugs, and theragnostic to the location of interest by avoiding the normal tissues and enhancing the therapeutic efficacy, therefore limiting the side effects. As compared to free drugs or passively targeted nanosystems, active targeting can improve the quality of drugs delivered to the target cell (Danhier et al., 2010). Active targeting represents the specific interaction between target cells and drug/drug carriers, usually through specific ligand–receptor interactions. The term "active targeting" means a particular interaction between ligand and receptors for intracellular localization that only occurs after extravasation and blood circulation. Here in active targeting, surface alternation or modification occurs (Patil et al., 2009). In drugs, coating the surface could be done with either a bioadhesive, specific cells or tissue antibodies, nonionic surfactants, or albumin protein (Muhamad et al., 2018).

Pros of nano-based targeted drug delivery

NMs and NPs are materials with at least one nanoscale dimension ranging between 1 and 100 nm. Owning to increased surface area and decreased size, NMs and NPs possess mechanical, physiochemical, electrical, and biological properties (Jeevanandam et al., 2018). Recently, nanomedicines have received much attention from researchers as it utilizes nanostructures and NMs in DDSs. Drugs can be physically encapsulated or chemically conjugated in nanocarriers, which deliver drugs to target tissues in a controlled release manner. The high surface area and small-sized NMs allow drugs to enter cells and easily combine with macromolecules (Torchilin, 2011). As a result, bioavailability, stability, and improved absorption features of NPs reveal to be most efficient in drug delivery. Moreover, the release rate of the drug depends on the NP's matrix degradation/erosion, desorption of the surface-bound/adsorbed drug, the solubility of the drug, and the combination of diffusion/erosion process. Hence, the matrix's biodegradation, solubility, and diffusion process govern the release process (Wilczewska et al., 2012).

Nanosized structured delivery carriers show their utility in protecting enclosed drugs from in vivo degradation. The widely preferred nano-based delivery carriers are micelles, including carbon nanotubes, liposomes, dendrimers, quantum dots, and polymeric nanomicelles. Nanoliposomes are bilayer lipids with an aqueous reservoir and are known as a versatile DDS (Su & Kang, 2020). Nanoliposomes exhibit various biocompatibility, stability, and biodegradability applications and serve as promising candidates in the nanobiotechnology and nanomedicine domains. Some nanoliposome-based formulations are utilized in DDSs, including Depocyt, DOXIL, Myocet, CPX-1, and CPX-571 (Yingchoncharoen et al., 2016). Furthermore, some commonly known polymeric micelles used in the nanomicelles composition are PLA, PLGA, chitosan, and PCL, which show drug delivery applications in treating cancer. Recently, Genexol PM, NK_{012}, NK_{105}, NK_{911}, and NC6004 are some of the reported polymeric micelles integrated with anticancer under clinical evaluation (Makadia & Siegel, 2011).

Furthermore, nano-based DDSs show significant advantages in drug delivery over conventional-based DDSs. Conventional DDSs of chemotherapeutical agents confer several critical issues related to poor specificity, acute toxicity, and drug resistance induction, which sensitively diminishes the therapeutic efficacy of many drugs system (Lombardo et al., 2019). Conventionally, drugs are taken via injection or orally, which causes severe harm to the cells, tissues, or organs. Conventional drug delivery requires high doses to fabricate bioavailability. On the other hand, a nanoscale DDS carries various advantages in that it offers compliance and comfort to the patients and enhances the therapeutic performance of the drug. It prolongs the half-life of systemic circulation of the drug by diminishing immunogenicity and improving the solubility of poorly water-soluble drugs. A critical factor for preserving the drug is that the drug should be incorporated into the system without a chemical reaction. These novel advantages of nano-based DDSs make them unique compared to conventional ones.

Toxicity of nanomaterials used for targeted drug delivery applications

NPs have revolutionized their fascinating properties like target site-specificity and systemic specificity in the biomedical domain, especially in DDSs. Toxicological study of three widely used NPs, like metal, lipid, and protein NPs, has been evaluated in DDS. FDA approved that superparamagnetic iron oxide (SPIONS) NPs are widely used in therapeutic and diagnostic applications, such as magnetic drug delivery, hyperthermia, and treating anemia. Recent studies evaluated that SPIONS has expanded its potential efficiency in DDSs to cure cancer and other diseases. Still, the SPIONS toxicity has somewhat bounded their uses in medical imaging, which is a significant concern. The FDA approved some of the SPIONs, such as Gastromark, Feridex, and Umirem, used as imaging agents.

On the other hand, ferumoxytol or Feraheme of AMAG pharmaceuticals is reported as an authorized drug involved in treating anemic patients. According to strategy, it has been evaluated that coating agents play an essential role in inhibiting the toxicity of SPIONS. Moreover, Ferretti et al. (2021) studied biocompatible magnetic NPs coated with zwitterionic ferrite NPs (ionic ligand) with unexpected renal clearance that can be functionalized to achieve targeted drug delivery. However, studies show that about 40 liposome-based drugs have been approved for market use and clinical trials. Some negatively charged PEG-liposome formulations often lead to hypersensitivity reactions (HSRs), anaphylactoid reactions, cardiopulmonary distress, and complement activation. However, FDA-approved PEGylated liposome-based drug Doxil serves to help treat the tumor.

Furthermore, Szebeni et al. (Tarhini et al., 2017) conducted a study that evaluated that Tc-HYNIC and doxorubicin (Doxil) PEG liposomes were reported to induce HSRs in susceptible patients. Moreover, recently, protein-based NPs also received attention due to their advanced properties, such as easy biodegradability, biocompatibility, reduced toxicity, and amphiphilicity. Gelatin, albumin, fibrin, casein, and ferritin are a few known protein-based NPs employed for drug delivery (Mariam et al., 2016; Zeeshan et al., 2021). Human serum albumin (HSA) is a flexible protein used to prepare albumin-based nanocarriers for cancer treatment. Byeon et al. (Rahimizadeh et al., 2020) studied HSA-coupled TRAIL delivery can be used as a promising therapy for chronic autoimmune disease, rheumatoid arthritis manifested by joint destruction and synovial hyperplasia. Casein, due to its excellent physiochemical and good structural features, shows its relevant efficiency in drug delivery. Gandhi and Roy (2019) studied casein NPs loaded with anticancer doxorubicin (DOX), which delivers better cytotoxicity against human pancreatic carcinoma cell lines (PANC 1 cells). Moreover, gelatin is considered a natural, biodegradable, biocompatible protein employed to provide medications that include doxorubicin, cycloheximide, and resveratrol for tumor therapy. Moreover, their minimal antigenicity and low-cost show potential applications in various formulations (Chou et al., 2018; Nahar et al., 2008).

Conclusion

A targeted DDS delivers the drugs directly to the patient's affected body area to overcome the toxic effect of the conventional DDS. According to today's scenario, nano-based targeted

DDSs received more attention due to their enhancing properties, such as biocompatibility, solubility, bioavailability, and controlled release of drugs. NPs, nanocapsules, and nanospheres are also involved in drug delivery applications. Nanocarriers exhibit some fascinating advantages, such as improved biodistribution and pharmacokinetics, decreased toxicities, site-specific delivery of therapeutic agents, controlled release, and improved stability and solubility integrated into DDSs. Moreover, nanomedicines also show practical advantages in disease remediation and prevention. It offers its potential to improve treatment efficiency and show diagnostics and therapeutic applications. This chapter highlights the advancements of nano-based DDSs and describes the utility of nanocarriers in DDSs and the toxicological aspects of NMs in DDSs.

References

Akbarian, M., Mahjoub, S., Elahi, S. M., Zabihi, E., & Tashakkorian, H. (2020). Green synthesis, formulation and biological evaluation of a novel ZnO nanocarrier loaded with paclitaxel as drug delivery system on MCF-7 cell line. *Colloids Surfaces B Biointerfaces*, *186*, 110686. Available from https://doi.org/10.1016/j.colsurfb.2019.110686.

Ansari, M. J., Jasim, S. A., Taban, T. Z., Bokov, D. O., Shalaby, M. N., Al-Gazally, M. E., Kzar, H. H., Qasim, M. T., Mustafa, Y. F., & Khatami, M. (2022). Anticancer drug-loading capacity of green synthesized porous magnetic iron nanocarrier and cytotoxic effects against human cancer cell line. *Journal of Cluster Science*. Available from https://doi.org/10.1007/s10876-022-02235-4.

Arap, W., Pasqualini, R., & Ruoslahti, E. (1998). Cancer treatment by targeted drug delivery to tumor vasculature in a mouse model. *Science*, *279*, 377–380. Available from https://doi.org/10.1126/science.279.5349.377.

Awan, F. T., & Byrd, J. C. (2018). *Chronic lymphocytic leukemia. Hematology* (pp. 1244–1264). Elsevier. Available from https://doi.org/10.1016/B978-0-323-35762-3.00077-9.

Barratt, G. M. (2000). Therapeutic applications of colloidal drug carriers. *Pharmaceutical Science & Technology Today*, *3*, 163–171. Available from https://doi.org/10.1016/S1461-5347(00)00255-8.

Bosch, F., & Dalla-Favera, R. (2019). Chronic lymphocytic leukaemia: From genetics to treatment. *Nature Reviews Clinical Oncology*, *16*, 684–701. Available from https://doi.org/10.1038/s41571-019-0239-8.

Cabral, H., Murakami, M., Hojo, H., Terada, Y., Kano, M. R., Chung, U., Nishiyama, N., & Kataoka, K. (2013). Targeted therapy of spontaneous murine pancreatic tumors by polymeric micelles prolongs survival and prevents peritoneal metastasis. *Proceedings of the National Academy of Sciences of the United States of America*, *110*, 11397–11402. Available from https://doi.org/10.1073/pnas.1301348110.

Cersosimo, R. J. (2002). Lung cancer: A review. *American Journal of Health-System Pharmacy*, *59*, 611–642. Available from https://doi.org/10.1093/ajhp/59.7.611.

Chawla, J. S., & Amiji, M. M. (2002). Biodegradable poly(ε-caprolactone) nanoparticles for tumor-targeted delivery of tamoxifen. *International Journal of Pharmaceutics*, *249*, 127–138. Available from https://doi.org/10.1016/S0378-5173(02)00483-0.

Choi, H.-J., & Montemagno, C. D. (2016). *Convergence of nanotechnology and biotechnology. Handbook of science and technology convergence* (pp. 253–277). Cham: Springer International Publishing. Available from https://doi.org/10.1007/978-3-319-07052-0_65.

Chou, M.-J., Yu, H.-Y., Hsia, J.-C., Chen, Y.-H., Hung, T.-T., Chao, H.-M., Chern, E., & Huang, Y.-Y. (2018). Highly efficient intracellular protein delivery by cationic polyethyleneimine-modified gelatin nanoparticles. *Materials (Basel)*, *11*, 301. Available from https://doi.org/10.3390/ma11020301.

Cucinotto, I., Fiorillo, L., Gualtieri, S., Arbitrio, M., Ciliberto, D., Staropoli, N., Grimaldi, A., Luce, A., Tassone, P., Caraglia, M., & Tagliaferri, P. (2013). Nanoparticle albumin bound paclitaxel in the treatment of human cancer: Nanodelivery reaches prime-time? *Journal of Drug Delivery*, *2013*, 1–10. Available from https://doi.org/10.1155/2013/905091.

Danhier, F., Feron, O., & Préat, V. (2010). To exploit the tumor microenvironment: Passive and active tumor targeting of nanocarriers for anti-cancer drug delivery. *Journal of Controlled Release: Official Journal of the Controlled Release Society*, *148*, 135–146. Available from https://doi.org/10.1016/j.jconrel.2010.08.027.

DeSantis, C. E., Bray, F., Ferlay, J., Lortet-Tieulent, J., Anderson, B. O., & Jemal, A. (2015). International variation in female breast cancer incidence and mortality rates. *Cancer Epidemiology, Biomarkers & Prevention: A Publication of the American Association for Cancer Research, Cosponsored by the American Society of Preventive Oncology*, *24*, 1495–1506. Available from https://doi.org/10.1158/1055-9965.EPI-15-0535.

Dunaevsky, A. (2013). The gene-gun approach for transfection and labeling of cells in brain slices. *Methods in Molecular Biology*, *1018*, 111–118. https://doi.org/10.1007/978-1-62703-444-9_11.

Fang, J., Nakamura, H., & Maeda, H. (2011). The EPR effect: Unique features of tumor blood vessels for drug delivery, factors involved, and limitations and augmentation of the effect. *Advanced Drug Delivery Reviews*, *63*, 136–151. Available from https://doi.org/10.1016/j.addr.2010.04.009.

Ferretti, A. M., Usseglio, S., Mondini, S., Drago, C., La Mattina, R., Chini, B., Verderio, C., Leonzino, M., Cagnoli, C., Joshi, P., Boraschi, D., Italiani, P., Li, Y., Swartzwelter, B. J., Sironi, L., Gelosa, P., Castiglioni, L., Guerrini, U., & Ponti, A. (2021). Towards bio-compatible magnetic nanoparticles: Immune-related effects, in-vitro internalization, and in-vivo bio-distribution of zwitterionic ferrite nanoparticles with unexpected renal clearance. *Journal of Colloid and Interface Science*, *582*, 678–700. Available from https://doi.org/10.1016/j.jcis.2020.08.026.

Freeman, R., Liu, X., & Willner, I. (2011). Chemiluminescent and chemiluminescence resonance energy transfer (CRET) detection of DNA, metal ions, and aptamer–substrate complexes using hemin/G-quadruplexes and CdSe/ZnS quantum dots. *Journal of the American Chemical Society*, *133*, 11597–11604. Available from https://doi.org/10.1021/ja202639m.

Gandhi, S., & Roy, I. (2019). Doxorubicin-loaded casein nanoparticles for drug delivery: Preparation, characterization and in vitro evaluation. *International Journal of Biological Macromolecules*, *121*, 6–12. Available from https://doi.org/10.1016/j.ijbiomac.2018.10.005.

García-Pinel, B., Porras-Alcalá, C., Ortega-Rodríguez, A., Sarabia, F., Prados, J., Melguizo, C., & López-Romero, J. M. (2019). Lipid-based nanoparticles: Application and recent advances in cancer treatment. *Nanomaterials*, *9*, 638. Available from https://doi.org/10.3390/nano9040638.

Geißler, D., Charbonnière, L. J., Ziessel, R. F., Butlin, N. G., Löhmannsröben, H.-G., & Hildebrandt, N. (2010). Quantum dot biosensors for ultrasensitive multiplexed diagnostics. *Angewandte Chemie International Edition*, *49*, 1396–1401. Available from https://doi.org/10.1002/anie.200906399.

Ginsburg, O., Yip, C., Brooks, A., Cabanes, A., Caleffi, M., Dunstan Yataco, J. A., Gyawali, B., McCormack, V., McLaughlin de Anderson, M., Mehrotra, R., Mohar, A., Murillo, R., Pace, L. E., Paskett, E. D., Romanoff, A., Rositch, A. F., Scheel, J. R., Schneidman, M., Unger-Saldaña, K., . . . Anderson, B. O. (2020). Breast cancer early detection: A phased approach to implementation. *Cancer*, *126*, 2379–2393. Available from https://doi.org/10.1002/cncr.32887.

Godinho, B. M. D. C., Ogier, J. R., Darcy, R., O'Driscoll, C. M., & Cryan, J. F. (2013). Self-assembling modified β-cyclodextrin nanoparticles as neuronal siRNA delivery vectors: Focus on Huntington's disease. *Molecular Pharmaceutics*, *10*, 640–649. Available from https://doi.org/10.1021/mp3003946.

Grossen, P., Witzigmann, D., Sieber, S., & Huwyler, J. (2017). PEG-PCL-based nanomedicines: A biodegradable drug delivery system and its application. *Journal of Controlled Release: Official Journal of the Controlled Release Society*, *260*, 46–60. Available from https://doi.org/10.1016/j.jconrel.2017.05.028.

Halfdanarson, T. R., Bamlet, W. R., McWilliams, R. R., Hobday, T. J., Burch, P. A., Rabe, K. G., & Petersen, G. M. (2014). Risk factors for pancreatic neuroendocrine tumors. *Pancreas*, *43*, 1219–1222. Available from https://doi.org/10.1097/MPA.0000000000000234.

Hallan, S. S., Kaur, P., Kaur, V., Mishra, N., & Vaidya, B. (2016). Lipid polymer hybrid as emerging tool in nanocarriers for oral drug delivery. *Artificial Cells, Nanomedicine, and Biotechnology*, *44*, 334–349. Available from https://doi.org/10.3109/21691401.2014.951721.

Hassanpour, S. H., & Dehghani, M. (2017). Review of cancer from perspective of molecular. *Journal of Cancer Research and Practice*, *4*, 127–129. Available from https://doi.org/10.1016/j.jcrpr.2017.07.001.

Hosseini, M., Amjadi, I., Mohajeri, M., & Mozafari, M. (2020). Sol–gel synthesis, physico-chemical and biological characterization of cerium oxide/polyallylamine nanoparticles. *Polymers (Basel)*, *12*, 1444. Available from https://doi.org/10.3390/polym12071444.

How, C. W., Rasedee, A., Manickam, S., & Rosli, R. (2013). Tamoxifen-loaded nanostructured lipid carrier as a drug delivery system: Characterization, stability assessment and cytotoxicity. *Colloids Surfaces B Biointerfaces*, *112*, 393–399. Available from https://doi.org/10.1016/j.colsurfb.2013.08.009.

Huynh, R. A., & Mohan, C. (2017). Alzheimer's disease: Biomarkers in the genome, blood, and cerebrospinal fluid. *Frontiers in Neurology*, *8*. Available from https://doi.org/10.3389/fneur.2017.00102.

Jacob, J., Haponiuk, J. T., Thomas, S., & Gopi, S. (2018). Biopolymer based nanomaterials in drug delivery systems: A review. *Materials Today Chemistry*, *9*, 43–55. Available from https://doi.org/10.1016/j.mtchem.2018.05.002.

Javier, R. T., & Butel, J. S. (2008). The history of tumor virology. *Cancer Research*, *68*, 7693–7706. Available from https://doi.org/10.1158/0008-5472.CAN-08-3301.

Jeevanandam, J., Barhoum, A., Chan, Y. S., Dufresne, A., & Danquah, M. K. (2018). Review on nanoparticles and nanostructured materials: History, sources, toxicity and regulations. *Beilstein Journal of Nanotechnology*, *9*, 1050–1074. Available from https://doi.org/10.3762/bjnano.9.98.

Kamal, M. A., Jabir, N. R., Tabrez., Ashraf., Shakil., & Damanhouri. (2012). Nanotechnology-based approaches in anticancer research. *International Journal of Nanomedicine*, 4391. Available from https://doi.org/10.2147/IJN.S33838.

Kingsley, J. D., Dou, H., Morehead, J., Rabinow, B., Gendelman, H. E., & Destache, C. J. (2006). Nanotechnology: A focus on nanoparticles as a drug delivery system. *Journal of Neuroimmune Pharmacology: The Official Journal of the Society on NeuroImmune Pharmacology*, *1*, 340–350. Available from https://doi.org/10.1007/s11481-006-9032-4.

Kleinstreuer, C., Basciano, C. A., Childress, E. M., & Kennedy, A. S. (2012). A new catheter for tumor targeting with radioactive microspheres in representative hepatic artery systems. Part I: Impact of catheter presence on local blood flow and microsphere delivery. *Journal of Biomechanical Engineering*, *134*. Available from https://doi.org/10.1115/1.4006684.

Kobayashi, H., Watanabe, R., & Choyke, P. L. (2014). Improving conventional enhanced permeability and retention (EPR) effects; what is the appropriate target? *Theranostics*, *4*, 81–89. Available from https://doi.org/10.7150/thno.7193.

Krauss, A. C., Gao, X., Li, L., Manning, M. L., Patel, P., Fu, W., Janoria, K. G., Gieser, G., Bateman, D. A., Przepiorka, D., Shen, Y. L., Shord, S. S., Sheth, C. M., Banerjee, A., Liu, J., Goldberg, K. B., Farrell, A. T., Blumenthal, G. M., & Pazdur, R. (2019). FDA approval summary: (Daunorubicin and Cytarabine) Liposome for injection for the treatment of adults with high-risk acute myeloid leukemia. *Clinical Cancer Research: An Official Journal of the American Association for Cancer Research*, *25*, 2685–2690. Available from https://doi.org/10.1158/1078-0432.CCR-18-2990.

Kreuter, J. (2007). Nanoparticles—A historical perspective. *International Journal of Pharmaceutics*, *331*, 1–10. Available from https://doi.org/10.1016/j.ijpharm.2006.10.021.

Kukkar, D., Kukkar, P., Kumar, V., Hong, J., Kim, K.-H., & Deep, A. (2021). Recent advances in nanoscale materials for antibody-based cancer theranostics. *Biosensors & Bioelectronics*, *173*, 112787. Available from https://doi.org/10.1016/j.bios.2020.112787.

Lambert, A., Schwarz, L., Borbath, I., Henry, A., Van Laethem, J.-L., Malka, D., Ducreux, M., & Conroy, T. (2019). An update on treatment options for pancreatic adenocarcinoma. *Therapeutic Advances in Medical Oncology*, *11*. Available from https://doi.org/10.1177/1758835919875568, 175883591987556.

Li, J., Darabi, M., Gu, J., Shi, J., Xue, J., Huang, L., Liu, Y., Zhang, L., Liu, N., Zhong, W., Zhang, L., Xing, M., & Zhang, L. (2016). A drug delivery hydrogel system based on activin B for Parkinson's disease. *Biomaterials*, *102*, 72–86. Available from https://doi.org/10.1016/j.biomaterials.2016.06.016.

Lin, H., Qiu, W., Liu, J., Yu, L., Gao, S., Yao, H., Chen, Y., & Shi, J. (2019). Silicene: Wet-chemical exfoliation synthesis and biodegradable tumor nanomedicine. *Advanced Materials*, *31*, 1903013. Available from https://doi.org/10.1002/adma.201903013.

Liu, Z., Tabakman, S., Welsher, K., & Dai, H. (2009). Carbon nanotubes in biology and medicine: In vitro and in vivo detection, imaging and drug delivery. *Nano Research*, *2*, 85–120. Available from https://doi.org/10.1007/s12274-009-9009-8.

Lombardo, D., Kiselev, M. A., & Caccamo, M. T. (2019). Smart nanoparticles for drug delivery application: Development of versatile nanocarrier platforms in biotechnology and nanomedicine. *Journal of Nanomaterials*, *2019*, 1–26. Available from https://doi.org/10.1155/2019/3702518.

López-Moreno, M. L., de la Rosa, G., Hernández-Viezcas, J. A., Peralta-Videa, J. R., & Gardea-Torresdey, J. L. (2010). X-ray absorption spectroscopy (XAS) corroboration of the uptake and storage of CeO_2 nanoparticles and assessment of their differential toxicity in four edible plant species. *Journal of Agricultural and Food Chemistry*, *58*, 3689–3693. Available from https://doi.org/10.1021/jf904472e.

Makadia, H. K., & Siegel, S. J. (2011). Poly lactic-*co*-glycolic acid (PLGA) as biodegradable controlled drug delivery carrier. *Polymers (Basel)*, *3*, 1377–1397. Available from https://doi.org/10.3390/polym3031377.

Mariam, J., Sivakami, S., & Dongre, P. M. (2016). Albumin corona on nanoparticles – A strategic approach in drug delivery. *Drug Delivery*, *23*, 2668–2676. Available from https://doi.org/10.3109/10717544.2015.1048488.

Mendiratta, S., Hussein, M., Nasser, H. A., & Ali, A. A. A. (2019). Multidisciplinary role of mesoporous silica nanoparticles in brain regeneration and cancers: From crossing the blood–brain barrier to treatment. *Particle & Particle Systems Characterization*, *36*, 1900195. Available from https://doi.org/10.1002/ppsc.201900195.

Meng, F., Asghar, S., Gao, S., Su, Z., Song, J., Huo, M., Meng, W., Ping, Q., & Xiao, Y. (2015). A novel LDL-mimic nanocarrier for the targeted delivery of curcumin into the brain to treat Alzheimer's disease. *Colloids Surfaces B Biointerfaces*, *134*, 88–97. Available from https://doi.org/10.1016/j.colsurfb.2015.06.025.

Meng, Z., Huang, H., Huang, D., Zhang, F., & Mi, P. (2021). Functional metal–organic framework-based nanocarriers for accurate magnetic resonance imaging and effective eradication of breast tumor and lung metastasis. *Journal of Colloid and Interface Science*, *581*, 31–43. Available from https://doi.org/10.1016/j.jcis.2020.07.072.

Mills, J. K., & Needham, D. (1999). Targeted drug delivery. *Expert Opinion on Therapeutic Patents*, *9*, 1499–1513. Available from https://doi.org/10.1517/13543776.9.11.1499.

Mitchell, M. J., Billingsley, M. M., Haley, R. M., Wechsler, M. E., Peppas, N. A., & Langer, R. (2021). Engineering precision nanoparticles for drug delivery. *Nature Reviews. Drug Discovery*, *20*, 101–124. Available from https://doi.org/10.1038/s41573-020-0090-8.

Mohanty, S. K., Swamy, M. K., Sinniah, U. R., & Anuradha, M. (2017). *Leptadenia reticulata* (Retz.) Wight & Arn. (Jivanti): Botanical, agronomical, phytochemical, pharmacological, and biotechnological aspects. *Molecules (Basel, Switzerland)*, *22*, 1019. Available from https://doi.org/10.3390/molecules22061019.

Mortazavi Milani, Z., Charbgoo, F., & Darroudi, M. (2017). Impact of physicochemical properties of cerium oxide nanoparticles on their toxicity effects. *Ceramics International*, *43*, 14572–14581. Available from https://doi.org/10.1016/j.ceramint.2017.08.177.

Muhamad, N., Plengsuriyakarn, T., & Na-Bangchang, K. (2018). Application of active targeting nanoparticle delivery system for chemotherapeutic drugs and traditional/herbal medicines in cancer therapy: A systematic review. *International Journal of Nanomedicine*, *13*, 3921–3935. Available from https://doi.org/10.2147/IJN.S165210.

Müller, R. H., Mäder, K., & Gohla, S. (2000). Solid lipid nanoparticles (SLN) for controlled drug delivery – A review of the state of the art. *European Journal of Pharmaceutics and Biopharmaceutics: Official Journal of Arbeitsgemeinschaft fur Pharmazeutische Verfahrenstechnik e.V*, *50*, 161–177. Available from https://doi.org/10.1016/S0939-6411(00)00087-4.

Nahar, M., Mishra, D., Dubey, V., & Jain, N. K. (2008). Development, characterization, and toxicity evaluation of amphotericin B–loaded gelatin nanoparticles. *Nanomedicine: Nanotechnology, Biology and Medicine*, *4*, 252–261. Available from https://doi.org/10.1016/j.nano.2008.03.007.

Narayanaswamy, R., & Torchilin, V. P. (2019). Hydrogels and their applications in targeted drug delivery. *Molecules (Basel, Switzerland)*, *24*, 603. Available from https://doi.org/10.3390/molecules24030603.

Neubert, R. H. H. (2011). Potentials of new nanocarriers for dermal and transdermal drug delivery. *European Journal of Pharmaceutics and Biopharmaceutics: Official Journal of Arbeitsgemeinschaft fur Pharmazeutische Verfahrenstechnik e.V*, *77*, 1–2. Available from https://doi.org/10.1016/j.ejpb.2010.11.003.

Nisticò, N., Maisano, D., Iaccino, E., Vecchio, E., Fiume, G., Rotundo, S., Quinto, I., & Mimmi, S. (2020). Role of chronic lymphocytic leukemia (CLL)-derived exosomes in tumor progression and survival. *Pharmaceuticals*, *13*, 244. Available from https://doi.org/10.3390/ph13090244.

Numata, K., & Kaplan, D. L. (2010). Silk-based delivery systems of bioactive molecules. *Advanced Drug Delivery Reviews*, *62*, 1497–1508. Available from https://doi.org/10.1016/j.addr.2010.03.009.

Ojha, N., & Das, N. (2021). Green formulation of microbial biopolyesteric nanocarriers toward in vitro drug delivery and its characterization. *Current Microbiology*, *78*, 2061–2070. Available from https://doi.org/10.1007/s00284-021-02464-2.

Oliveira, J., Rodrigues, R., Barros, L., Ferreira, I., Marchesi, L., Koneracka, M., Jurikova, A., Zavisova, V., & Gomes, H. (2018). Carbon-based magnetic nanocarrier for controlled drug release: A green synthesis approach. *C – Journal of Carbon Research*, *5*, 1. Available from https://doi.org/10.3390/c5010001.

Patil, Y., Sadhukha, T., Ma, L., & Panyam, J. (2009). Nanoparticle-mediated simultaneous and targeted delivery of paclitaxel and tariquidar overcomes tumor drug resistance. *Journal of Controlled Release: Official Journal of the Controlled Release Society*, *136*, 21–29. Available from https://doi.org/10.1016/j.jconrel.2009.01.021.

Pitt, G., Gratzl, M., Kimmel, G., Surles, J., & Sohindler, A. (1981). Aliphatic polyesters II. The degradation of poly (DL-lactide), poly (ε-caprolactone), and their copolymers in vivo. *Biomaterials*, *2*, 215–220. Available from https://doi.org/10.1016/0142-9612(81)90060-0.

Priyadarshini, S., Gopinath, V., Meera Priyadharsshini, N., MubarakAli, D., & Velusamy, P. (2013). Synthesis of anisotropic silver nanoparticles using novel strain, *Bacillus flexus* and its biomedical application. *Colloids Surfaces B Biointerfaces*, *102*, 232–237. Available from https://doi.org/10.1016/j.colsurfb.2012.08.018.

Raghunandan, D., Mahesh, B. D., Basavaraja, S., Balaji, S. D., Manjunath, S. Y., & Venkataraman, A. (2011). Microwave-assisted rapid extracellular synthesis of stable bio-functionalized silver nanoparticles from guava (*Psidium guajava*) leaf extract. *Journal of Nanoparticle Research*, *13*, 2021–2028. Available from https://doi.org/10.1007/s11051-010-9956-8.

Raghunandan, D., Bedre, M. D., Basavaraja, S., Sawle, B., Manjunath, S. Y., & Venkataraman, A. (2010). Rapid biosynthesis of irregular shaped gold nanoparticles from macerated aqueous extracellular dried clove buds (*Syzygium aromaticum*) solution. *Colloids Surfaces B Biointerfaces*, *79*, 235–240. Available from https://doi.org/10.1016/j.colsurfb.2010.04.003.

Raghunandan, D., Basavaraja, S., Mahesh, B., Balaji, S., Manjunath, S. Y., & Venkataraman, A. (2009). Biosynthesis of stable polyshaped gold nanoparticles from microwave-exposed aqueous extracellular anti-malignant guava (*Psidium guajava*) leaf extract. *NanoBiotechnology*, *5*, 34–41. Available from https://doi.org/10.1007/s12030-009-9030-8.

Rahimizadeh, P., Yang, S., & Lim, S. I. (2020). Albumin: An emerging opportunity in drug delivery. *Biotechnology and Bioprocess Engineering*, *25*, 985–995. Available from https://doi.org/10.1007/s12257-019-0512-9.

Rawla, P., Sunkara, T., & Gaduputi, V. (2019). Epidemiology of pancreatic cancer: Global trends, etiology and risk factors. *World Journal of Oncology*, *10*, 10–27. Available from https://doi.org/10.14740/wjon1166.

Rawstron, A. C., Kreuzer, K.-A., Soosapilla, A., Spacek, M., Stehlikova, O., Gambell, P., McIver-Brown, N., Villamor, N., Psarra, K., Arroz, M., Milani, R., de la Serna, J., Cedena, M. T., Jaksic, O., Nomdedeu, J., Moreno, C., Rigolin, G. M., Cuneo, A., Johansen, P., ... Montserrat, E. (2018). Reproducible diagnosis of chronic lymphocytic leukemia by flow cytometry: An European Research Initiative on CLL (ERIC) & European Society for Clinical Cell Analysis (ESCCA) Harmonisation project. *Cytometry Part B – Clinical Cytometry*, *94*, 121–128. Available from https://doi.org/10.1002/cyto.b.21595.

Rawstron, A.C., de Tute, R.M., Owen, R.G., & Hillmen, P. (2019). *Laboratory diagnosis of chronic lymphocytic leukaemia* (pp. 21–35). https://doi.org/10.1007/978-3-030-11392-6_2.

Sabaratnam, V., Gurunathan, S., Raman, J., Abd Malek, S. N., & John, P. (2013). Green synthesis of silver nanoparticles using *Ganoderma neo-japonicum* Imazeki: A potential cytotoxic agent against breast cancer cells. *International Journal of Nanomedicine*, 4399. Available from https://doi.org/10.2147/IJN.S51881.

Sahu, T., Ratre, Y. K., Chauhan, S., Bhaskar, L. V. K. S., Nair, M. P., & Verma, H. K. (2021). Nanotechnology based drug delivery system: Current strategies and emerging therapeutic potential for medical science. *Journal of Drug Delivery Science and Technology*, *63*, 102487. Available from https://doi.org/10.1016/j.jddst.2021.102487.

Samrot, A. V., Sean, T. C., Kudaiyappan, T., Bisyarah, U., Mirarmandi, A., Faradjeva, E., Abubakar, A., Ali, H. H., Angalene, J. L. A., & Suresh Kumar, S. (2020). Production, characterization and application of nanocarriers made of polysaccharides, proteins, bio-polyesters and other biopolymers: A review. *International Journal of Biological Macromolecules*, *165*, 3088–3105. Available from https://doi.org/10.1016/j.ijbiomac.2020.10.104.

Sathishkumar, P., Gu, F. L., Zhan, Q., Palvannan, T., & Mohd Yusoff, A. R. (2018). Flavonoids mediated 'Green' nanomaterials: A novel nanomedicine system to treat various diseases – Current trends and future perspective. *Materials Letters*, *210*, 26–30. Available from https://doi.org/10.1016/j.matlet.2017.08.078.

Shivaji, S., Madhu, S., & Singh, S. (2011). Extracellular synthesis of antibacterial silver nanoparticles using psychrophilic bacteria. *Process Biochemistry*, *46*, 1800–1807. Available from https://doi.org/10.1016/j.procbio.2011.06.008.

Silva-Abreu, M., Calpena, A. C., Andrés-Benito, P., Aso, E., Romero, I. A., Roig-Carles, D., Gromnicova, R., Espina, M., Ferrer, I., García, M. L., & Male, D. (2018). PPARγ agonist-loaded PLGA-PEG nanocarriers as a potential treatment for Alzheimer’s disease: In vitro and in vivo studies. *International Journal of Nanomedicine*, *13*, 5577–5590. Available from https://doi.org/10.2147/IJN.S171490.

Silverman, J. A., & Deitcher, S. R. (2013). Marqibo® (vincristine sulfate liposome injection) improves the pharmacokinetics and pharmacodynamics of vincristine. *Cancer Chemotherapy and Pharmacology*, *71*, 555–564. Available from https://doi.org/10.1007/s00280-012-2042-4.

Singh, K. R., Nayak, V., & Singh, R. P. (2021). *Introduction to bionanomaterials: An overview. Bionanomaterials*. IOP Publishing. Available from https://doi.org/10.1088/978-0-7503-3767-0ch1.

Singh, R., & Lillard, J. W. (2009). Nanoparticle-based targeted drug delivery. *Experimental and Molecular Pathology*, *86*, 215–223. Available from https://doi.org/10.1016/j.yexmp.2008.12.004.

Soares, S., Sousa, J., Pais, A., & Vitorino, C. (2018). Nanomedicine: Principles, properties, and regulatory issues. *Frontiers in Chemistry*, *6*. Available from https://doi.org/10.3389/fchem.2018.00360.

Sonawane, S. K., Ahmad, A., & Chinnathambi, S. (2019). Protein-capped metal nanoparticles inhibit tau aggregation in Alzheimer's disease. *ACS Omega*, *4*, 12833–12840. Available from https://doi.org/10.1021/acsomega.9b01411.

Spadavecchia, J., Movia, D., Moore, C., Manus Maguire, C., Moustaoui, H., Casale, S., Volkov, Y., & Prina-Mello, A. (2016). Targeted polyethylene glycol gold nanoparticles for the treatment of pancreatic cancer: From synthesis to proof-of-concept in vitro studies. *International Journal of Nanomedicine*, 791. Available from https://doi.org/10.2147/IJN.S97476.

Stoltenberg, M., Spence, D., Daubman, B., Greaves, N., Edwards, R., Bromfield, B., Perez-Cruz, P. E., Krakauer, E. L., Argentieri, M. A., & Shields, A. E. (2020). The central role of provider training in implementing resource-stratified guidelines for palliative care in low-income and middle-income countries: Lessons from the Jamaica Cancer Care and Research Institute in the Caribbean and Universidad Católica in La. *Cancer*, *126*, 2448–2457. Available from https://doi.org/10.1002/cncr.32857.

Su, S., & Kang, P. M. (2020). Recent advances in nanocarrier-assisted therapeutics delivery systems. *Pharmaceutics*, *12*, 837. Available from https://doi.org/10.3390/pharmaceutics12090837.

Swamy, M. K., & Sinniah, U. R. (2016). Patchouli (*Pogostemon cablin* Benth.): Botany, agrotechnology and biotechnological aspects. *Industrial Crops and Products*, *87*, 161–176. Available from https://doi.org/10.1016/j.indcrop.2016.04.032.

Tagde, P., Najda, A., Nagpal, K., Kulkarni, G. T., Shah, M., Ullah, O., Balant, S., & Rahman, M. H. (2022). Nanomedicine-based delivery strategies for breast cancer treatment and management. *International Journal of Molecular Sciences*, *23*, 2856. Available from https://doi.org/10.3390/ijms23052856.

Tang, E., Liu, S., Zhang, Z., Zhang, R., Huang, D., Gao, T., Zhang, T., & Xu, G. (2022). Therapeutic potential of glutamine pathway in lung cancer. *Frontiers in Oncology*, *11*. Available from https://doi.org/10.3389/fonc.2021.835141.

Tapeinos, C., Battaglini, M., & Ciofani, G. (2017). Advances in the design of solid lipid nanoparticles and nanostructured lipid carriers for targeting brain diseases. *Journal of Controlled Release: Official Journal of the Controlled Release Society*, *264*, 306–332. Available from https://doi.org/10.1016/j.jconrel.2017.08.033.

Tarhini, M., Greige-Gerges, H., & Elaissari, A. (2017). Protein-based nanoparticles: From preparation to encapsulation of active molecules. *International Journal of Pharmaceutics*, *522*, 172–197. Available from https://doi.org/10.1016/j.ijpharm.2017.01.067.

Thi, T. T. H., Suys, E. J. A., Lee, J. S., Nguyen, D. H., Park, K. D., & Truong, N. P. (2021). Lipid-based nanoparticles in the clinic and clinical trials: From cancer nanomedicine to COVID-19 vaccines. *Vaccines*, *9*, 359. Available from https://doi.org/10.3390/vaccines9040359.

Thilakarathna, S., & Rupasinghe, H. (2013). Flavonoid bioavailability and attempts for bioavailability enhancement. *Nutrients*, *5*, 3367–3387. Available from https://doi.org/10.3390/nu5093367.

Torchilin, V. (2011). Tumor delivery of macromolecular drugs based on the EPR effect. *Advanced Drug Delivery Reviews*, *63*, 131–135. Available from https://doi.org/10.1016/j.addr.2010.03.011.

Torchilin, V. P. (2000). Drug targeting. *European Journal of Pharmaceutical Sciences: Official Journal of the European Federation for Pharmaceutical Sciences*, *11*, S81–S91. Available from https://doi.org/10.1016/S0928-0987(00)00166-4.

ud Din, F., Aman, W., Ullah, I., Qureshi, O. S., Mustapha, O., Shafique, S., & Zeb, A. (2017). Effective use of nanocarriers as drug delivery systems for the treatment of selected tumors. *International Journal of Nanomedicine*, *12*, 7291–7309. Available from https://doi.org/10.2147/IJN.S146315.

Wang, S., Sun., Zhu., Du., Liu., & Qian, W.-Y. (2012). pH-sensitive strontium carbonate nanoparticles as new anticancer vehicles for controlled etoposide release. *International Journal of Nanomedicine*, 5781. Available from https://doi.org/10.2147/IJN.S34773.

Wilczewska, A. Z., Niemirowicz, K., Markiewicz, K. H., & Car, H. (2012). Nanoparticles as drug delivery systems. *Pharmacological Reports*, *64*, 1020–1037. Available from https://doi.org/10.1016/S1734-1140(12)70901-5.

Wilkinson, D. G., Francis, P. T., Schwam, E., & Payne-Parrish, J. (2004). Cholinesterase inhibitors used in the treatment of Alzheimer's disease. *Drugs & Aging*, *21*, 453–478. Available from https://doi.org/10.2165/00002512-200421070-00004.

Wilkinson, J. M. (2003). Nanotechnology applications in medicine. *Medical Device Technology*, *14*, 29–31. Available from http://www.ncbi.nlm.nih.gov/pubmed/12852120.

Yang, C., & Merlin, D. (2020). Lipid-based drug delivery nanoplatforms for colorectal cancer therapy. *Nanomaterials*, *10*, 1424. Available from https://doi.org/10.3390/nano10071424.

Yang, L., Yin, T., Liu, Y., Sun, J., Zhou, Y., & Liu, J. (2016). Gold nanoparticle-capped mesoporous silica-based H_2O_2-responsive controlled release system for Alzheimer's disease treatment. *Acta Biomaterialia*, *46*, 177–190. Available from https://doi.org/10.1016/j.actbio.2016.09.010.

Yao, Y., Zhou, Y., Liu, L., Xu, Y., Chen, Q., Wang, Y., Wu, S., Deng, Y., Zhang, J., & Shao, A. (2020). Nanoparticle-based drug delivery in cancer therapy and its role in overcoming drug resistance. *Frontiers in Molecular Biosciences*, 7. Available from https://doi.org/10.3389/fmolb.2020.00193.

Yavarpour-Bali, H., Ghasemi-Kasman, M., & Pirzadeh, M. (2019). Curcumin-loaded nanoparticles: A novel therapeutic strategy in treatment of central nervous system disorders. *International Journal of Nanomedicine*, *14*, 4449–4460. Available from https://doi.org/10.2147/IJN.S208332.

Yersal, O. (2014). Biological subtypes of breast cancer: Prognostic and therapeutic implications. *World Journal of Clinical Oncology*, *5*, 412. Available from https://doi.org/10.5306/wjco.v5.i3.412.

Yingchoncharoen, P., Kalinowski, D. S., & Richardson, D. R. (2016). Lipid-based drug delivery systems in cancer therapy: What is available and what is yet to come. *Pharmacological Reviews*, *68*, 701–787. Available from https://doi.org/10.1124/pr.115.012070.

Zafar, N., Uzair, B., Niazi, M. B. K., Menaa, F., Samin, G., Khan, B. A., Iqbal, H., & Menaa, B. (2021). Green synthesis of ciprofloxacin-loaded cerium oxide/chitosan nanocarrier and its activity against MRSA-induced mastitis. *Journal of Pharmaceutical Sciences*, *110*, 3471–3483. Available from https://doi.org/10.1016/j.xphs.2021.06.017.

Zeeshan, F., Madheswaran, T., Panneerselvam, J., Taliyan, R., & Kesharwani, P. (2021). Human serum albumin as multifunctional nanocarrier for cancer therapy. *Journal of Pharmaceutical Sciences*, *110*, 3111–3117. Available from https://doi.org/10.1016/j.xphs.2021.05.001.

Zhao, X., Li, F., Li, Y., Wang, H., Ren, H., Chen, J., Nie, G., & Hao, J. (2015). Co-delivery of HIF1α siRNA and gemcitabine via biocompatible lipid-polymer hybrid nanoparticles for effective treatment of pancreatic cancer. *Biomaterials*, *46*, 13–25. Available from https://doi.org/10.1016/j.biomaterials.2014.12.028.

Zoulikha, M., & He, W. (2022). Targeted drug delivery for chronic lymphocytic leukemia. *Pharmaceutical Research*. Available from https://doi.org/10.1007/s11095-022-03214-0.

CHAPTER 2

Methods of fabricating various nanocarriers for targeted drug delivery

Rishi Raj[1], Gunjan Nagpure[2], Kshitij RB Singh[3], Jay Singh[3] and Ravindra Pratap Singh[2]

[1]Department of Applied Chemistry and Polymer Technology, Delhi Technological University, New Delhi, Delhi, India
[2]Department of Biotechnology, Faculty of Science, Indira Gandhi National Tribal University, Amarkantak, Madhya Pradesh, India
[3]Department of Chemistry, Institute of Science, Banaras Hindu University, Varanasi, Uttar Pradesh, India

Introduction

The delivery of medicinal compounds into the desired region shows significant challenges in treating various disorders. Moreover, conventional methods, such as chemotherapy, radiation therapy, and surgery, have been employed in past decades as a crucial solution for curing lethal diseases like cancers. But according to reports, these methods have resulted in multiple side effects due to unfavorable side effects, poor distribution, lack of selectivity, and limited effectiveness, including opposite action of the drug to the active cells and burst release (Senapati et al., 2018). Therefore developing a confined structure that enables a sustained release of drug at a targeted location with a solid pharmacological response and reduced side effects is essential. Nanotechnology shows diverse applications in multiple domains, such as cosmetics, biomedical, nutraceuticals, and environmental research fields (Baskar et al., 2017; Chamundeeswari et al., 2010).

Moreover, due to nano size structure, distinct nanostructure forms, including nanocomposites, nanoparticles (NPs), nanotubes, and nanofibers, show promising results as a carrier molecules or act as transporters for drugs, vaccines, proteins, enzymes, and genes (Baskar et al., 2018; Verma et al., 2016; Verma, Barrow, et al., 2013; Verma, Chaudhary, et al., 2013; Verma, Naebe, et al., 2013). Furthermore, while targeting a specific disease site, it is crucial to know about the nature of the drug, such as biocompatibility, biological obstacle, or biological relation of material at the target zone. As a result, nanocarriers possess excellent physiochemical properties, such as shape, surface, and composition, the modification of which can increase their activity with minimum side effects. Nanocarriers are simply colloidal NP consisting of submicron size ranging between 1 and 100 nm in diameter that is being utilized as a transporter of other substances or therapeutic agents to a targeted location (Peer et al., 2007; Zhan et al., 2012). Moreover, with advanced properties, nanocarriers also

Nanotechnology for Drug Delivery and Pharmaceuticals
DOI: https://doi.org/10.1016/B978-0-323-95325-2.00008-0

possess extraordinary features, such as enhanced solubility, improved stability, sustained and targeted drug delivery, reduced toxicity, and enhanced biodistribution and pharmacokinetics. Thus it generates an excess of impact in the zone of drug delivery (How et al., 2013; Mishra et al., 2010). Therefore, it is essential to fabricate the various nanocarriers that show their promising advancements in the drug delivery system. This concise chapter will discuss different nanocarriers and their fabrication methods that are utilized to target the drug at the specific desired location with minimum side effects.

Various nanocarriers for drug delivery

According to recent research, it has been studied that there is a broad range of nanocarriers evolved, but only an isolated one shows the exceptional capability to transport the drug to the addressed location. Furthermore, due to high surface area to volume, various nanocarriers, such as polymer-based NPs, dendrimers, magnetic NPs, carbon-based materials for nanocarriers, micelles-based nanocarriers, liposome-based nanocarriers, and nanocomposites based nanocarriers, are utilized in delivering hydrophobic and hydrophilic drugs to the targeted site as illustrated in Fig. 2.1.

Polymeric nanocarriers are solid, colloidal NPs manufactured from biodegradable polymers (Bamrungsap et al., 2012). Polymeric nanocarriers can be a nanocapsule (reservoir type) that dissolves the drug molecules in the matrix-type nanospheres, or a polymeric core that entangles drug molecules inside the polymer matrix. Both types

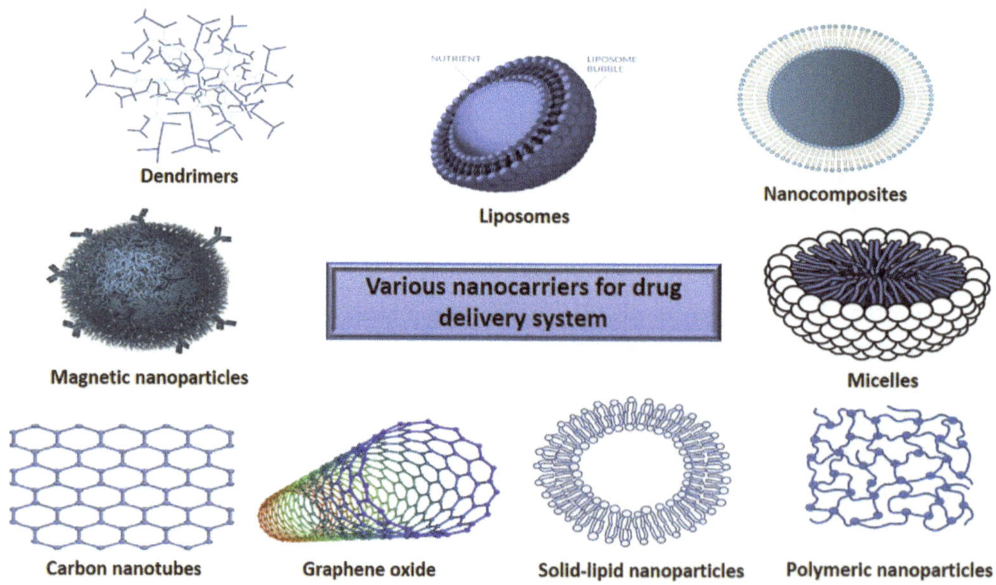

Figure 2.1 This figure represents various nanocarriers for drug delivery system.

can also absorb chemically or conjugate the drug on their surface (Joshi et al., 2015). Moreover, biodegradation of the polymeric nanocarriers generates monomers inside the human body that simply can be degraded by the metabolic pathways (Mishra et al., 2010). Moreover, the polymeric nanocarriers can be derived from both synthetic polymers [polycaprolactone, polyethylene glycol, and polyglutamic acid, poly(lactic-*co*-glycolic acid)] and natural (gelatin, collagen, chitosan, albumin, alginate, etc.) (Wang et al., 2009). As a result, polymer-based nanocarriers offer significant advantages over other nanocarriers in terms of drug payload, higher stability, sustained drug release, and half-life time in the systemic circulation. However, doxorubicin, the anti-cancer drug, is trapped within the polymer-based nanocarrier to target cancer-causing cells. Moreover, by modifying the physicochemical properties of the polymeric source, the controlled drug release could be improved (Cheng et al., 2018). It is feasible to give rise to versatile polymeric nanocarriers that facilitate the incorporation of different drugs in it.

Dendrimers are nanosized three-dimensional monodisperse, homogeneous structures developed from the synthetic polymeric macromolecules consisting of tree-like branches or arms (Abbasi et al., 2014). It consists of the central core and different functional groups on the surface that enhances their functionalities and make them biocompatible and multifunctional (Tomalia, 2005). Their exceptional properties, such as high degree branching, open internal cavities, water-solubility, nanoscale uniform size, polyvalency, and suitable synthesis methods mold them into favorable agents for drug delivery applications. Among various nanomaterials, dendrimers have received considerable attention from researchers. Moreover, dendrimers can be utilized as a carrier system or efficient drug delivery system for therapeutic agents and can be used for compressing the toxicity of drugs and improving their efficiencies (Sherje et al., 2018). However, it is possible to encapsulate the drug molecules within the branches due to unfolded nature of the dendritic armature. Nonbonding interactions and physical entrapment with a definite dendrimer structure can be used as drug encapsulation methods (Pasut et al., 2005). According to research, dendrimers should be nonimmunogenic and nontoxic when utilized in drug delivery applications. Moreover, multiple anticancer drugs, including doxorubicin and cisplatin, are substantially linked with the dendrimer to improve anticancerous activity (Ha et al., 2020; Xu et al., 2013). The dendrimer can be utilized in gene delivery, vaccine delivery, and antiviral and magnetic resonance imaging (MRI) (Stiriba et al., 2002).

During the last few decades, liposomes have gained considerable attention as a drug delivery system for antitumor drugs in biomedical domain. It exhibits a great advantage, such as improved drug delivery, efficient treatment with reduced systemic toxicity including cost-effective expensive drugs formulations and enhanced performance features of the product (Lee et al., 2015). Moreover, as compared to free drugs, drugs integrated with liposomes have markedly modified their pharmacokinetics.

Liposomes containing an aqueous core are spherical vesicles enclosed by lipid bilayers. Furthermore, liposomes' biocompatible and biodegradable composition made them promising therapeutic carriers. Their unique ability to accommodate both lipid-soluble agents and water-soluble in their hydrated central part or lamellae has improved their utility in formulating biomedicines (Deshpande et al., 2013). Moreover, the preparation of drug-loaded liposomes administers the drug distribution within the plasma, leading to enhanced pharmacokinetics and biodistribution of drugs. However, liposomes can also be associated with ligands or antibodies to increase the target specificity (Torchilin, 2005). As a result, liposomes are often used as model cells or carriers for delivering multiple bioactive agents, such as vaccines, drugs, nutraceuticals, and cosmetics.

Micelles are aqueous, nanosized self-aggregates of amphiphilic molecules, competent for solubilizing nonpolar molecules with a hydrophobic core. Moreover, through self-assembly effects, polymeric micelles are built from amphiphilic polymers. Owning to small size and adjustable surface and core—shell structure, polymeric micelles have been extensively explored as nanoscale drug delivery carriers. As a result, corresponding systems may enhance drug solubility and show possible applications in gene therapy and tumor targeting (Qiu et al., 2007). Polymeric micelles increase the bioavailability of the hydrophobic drugs, solubilize hydrophobic drugs, and, thus, protect the drug from inactivation in the biological environment (Jhaveri & Torchilin, 2014).

Carbon-based nanomaterials include graphene oxide (GO), carbon nanotubes, and carbon dots that possess extraordinary thermal, mechanical, electrical, and optical properties, making them attractive candidates for various biomedical applications, such as nanomedicines and drug delivery carriers. Graphene is a one-atom-thick planer sheath of carbon atoms arranged like a honeycomb lattice in two-dimensional space. GO is an oxidized derivative of graphene, which contains functional groups carrying oxygen, such as hydroxyl and carboxyl groups (Chen et al., 2016; Sotirelis & Chrysikopoulos, 2017). These oxidized derivatives of graphene possess superior mechanical properties, excellent thermal and electrical conductivities, and optical properties (Elhissi et al., 2012). GO nanoparticles are utilized in various applications, from high energy storage batteries to electrochemistry, nanomedicines, and delivering the drug to supercapacitor industries. Moreover, carbon nanotubes are cylindrical nanomaterials made by rolled graphene sheets. They are classified into single-walled carbon nanotubes (SWCNTs) and multiwalled CNTs (MWCNTs). SWCNTs are a single layer of graphene rolled up into tube-like structures that form bundles that are not fully dispersed, unlike MWCNTs. Whereas MWCNTs are multilayer graphene structures, the multiple layers of graphene are rolled up in a concentric tube-like structure. Unlike SWCNTs, they do not form bundles while synthesizing and are found to be homogeneously dispersed (Elhissi et al., 2012). Due to their exceptional physical, chemical, mechanical, and electrical properties, CNTs have been currently utilized as nanocarriers and show diverse applications in therapeutics, diagnostics, tissue engineering, and drug delivery (Beg et al., 2011; Bianco et al., 2005; Sinha & Yeow, 2005). Moreover, Luo et al. (2011) developed the MWCNTs reservoirs by functionalization, employing polypyrrole films to control the drug dexamethasone. However, to prevent drug leakage and controlled release of drug delivery, the open ends in MWCNTs were fixed with polypyrrole film. Madaeni et al. (2012) developed the drug delivery tablets coated with a membrane that employs MWCNTs functionalized with carboxyl for the constant therapeutic action of drug indomethacin. Furthermore, carbon dots are the novel class of zero-dimensional, photoluminescent quantum dots with an appropriate size equal to or less than 20 nm (Fernando et al., 2015; Sun et al., 2006). Carbon dots have been utilized as a drug delivery system to enhance half-life, the solubility of the drug, accumulation at the tumorous site, increase bioavailability and tolerance of drugs, and minimize drug side effects (Cheng et al., 2013; Torchilin, 2011). Moreover, nanocomposites are composites that exhibit dimensions in the nanometer range (10^{-9}), further deposited in ceramic, metal, or polymer matrix (Henrique et al., 2009). Moreover, based on cellulose nanofibers, nanocellulose and micro- or nano-fibrillar serve as a novel generation nanomaterial that exhibits a broad range of applications in the area of the pharma industry, biosensors, tissue engineering, microfluidics elements, medicines, drug delivery, and materials for microencapsulation and act as a boundary to save mucosal tissue (Galkina et al., 2015; Ioelovich & Figovsky, 2008; Sannino et al., 2007; Schexnailder & Schmidt, 2009; Zhou et al., 2013). Moreover, multiple biodegradable and nondegradable nanocomposites and polymer–inorganic composites have been studied, including poly(vinyl alcohol)-montmorillonite clay (Kokabi et al., 2007), poly(methyl methacrylate) or polydimethylsiloxane associated with polycaprolactone–graphene (Wan & Chen, 2011), poly(lactide-*co*-glycolides), silicates (Arcos & Vallet-Regí, 2010), including hydroxyapatite, calcium phosphates, or bioactive glass (Lin et al., 2007). Further, numerous composites have been investigated for the controlled release of antibiotic ceftazidime (Costache et al., 2013; Elsner et al., 2010) or other therapeutics, such as aspirin (Rezwan et al., 2006). These nanocomposites possess promising properties, such as enhanced chemical reactivity, high mechanical durability, specific high surface area, nontoxicity, biodegradability, biocompatibility, and controlled drug release, making them ideal candidates for drug release applications. Rasoulzadeh and Namazi (2017) studied the carboxymethylcellulose/GO nanocomposites to deliver doxorubicin, an anticancer drug, whereas Pathania et al. (2016) reported that nanocomposite chitosan-g-poly(acrylamide)/CuS (CPA/CS) nanocomposite efficiency for controlled delivery of a drug, ofloxacin. Magnetic NPs have existed in the form of clusters of micro-nanoparticles or single NPs. Due to the nature of the magnetic fields and the magnetic moment of the network unit, MNPs are explosively altered by the external magnetic field. Further, external magnetic fields behave as inactive particles when they disappear. Moreover, superparamagnetic and single domains are the main characteristics of magnetic NPs. Furthermore, MNPs exhibit a promising role in the biomedical domain due to ease of surface modification, magnetic properties, and biocompatibility. It offers numerous medical applications, such as MRI, cell isolation, purification and macromolecules, transport of needed species mainly, drugs, genes, proteins, stem cells and antibodies to target cells and tissues, biosensors, enzyme immobilization, ability to track in vitro and in vivo particles via MRI and immunocytochemical tests.

Fabrication methods/formulation method of nanocarriers

NPs often show multiple thermal, magnetic, electrical, and optical properties due to limited quantum mechanical effects and high surface area. Moreover, NPs as drug carriers exhibit crucial technological advantages, such as high carrier capacity, high stability, the feasibility of variable routes of administration, such as inhalation and oral applications, and the feasibility of incorporating hydrophobic and hydrophilic substances (Gelperina et al., 2005). Therefore it is essential to fabricate or formulate the various nanocarriers as it shows major applications in the targeted drug delivery system. Solid lipid NPs (SLNPs) have usually had a spherical shape known as colloidal lipid carriers, with a diameter ranging between 50 and 1000 nm that remains solid at human body temperature and room temperature (Mukherjee et al., 2009). Solid lipid nanocarriers show unique features that make them fascinating as drug delivery systems for oral and parental delivery for systemic effects or pulmonary, topical, and ocular delivery to minimize the systemic complexities and improve the efficacy of local treatments. Thus, fabrication methods are important for the size and function of NPs and should be examined simultaneously in fabricating particles to acquire the optimal drug efficacy and absorption, mainly for primary treatments (Mu & Holm, 2018). Musielak et al. (2022) studied the synthesis of SLNPs, encapsulated with hydrophobic polyphenol plant-derived substance curcumin. Curcumin is an active ingredient, and over the past decades, its derivatives have received strong attention due to its multifunctional antiinflammatory, anticancer, and antioxidant properties (Nagahama et al., 2016). Globally, it is used as conventional medicine to treat several inflammatory disorders, and for centuries, it has been used as a drug for curing many infections and fungal diseases (Oppenheimer, 1937). Additionally, the most effective and efficient method used for the synthesis of SLNPs is the high-pressure homogenization (HPH) method, including other strongly known methods, is a microemulsion, solvent evaporation, or ultrasonic methods (Pooja et al., 2016). Moreover, encapsulation of curcumin into SLNPs has proved a perfect method to enhance its efficacy and stability. The study showed that optimizing using HPH technique is crucial to develop the novel adequate semisolid drug formulation for the synthesis of SLNPs. On the other hand, magnetic

NPs can be utilized as photothermal and hyperthermia therapy and as MRI contrast agents (superparamagnetic iron oxide, paramagnetic gadolinium ion complexes) to enhance the diagnostic images of diseases and broadly utilized as artificial core (Hayashi et al., 2017; Ribeiro et al., 2021; Wan et al., 2020). Moreover, Zohreh et al. (2022) formulated the pH-sensitive two-core—shell-containing polymeric shell magnetic nanocarriers through the Fe_3O_4 magnetic NPs modification by utilizing polyoxyethylene glycol PEGylated critical micelle concentration (CMC) and hyperbranched polyglycerol (HPG). HPG is a favorable candidate with advantageous biomedical features, such as biocompatibility and low toxicity, with feasible molecular weight (Rahman et al., 2021; Zafar, 2004; Zhou et al., 2018). Moreover, it has been noted that the hydroxyl group in HPG facilitates the surface alternation with amine (Wan et al., 2019), amide (Wan et al., 2019), vinyl (Hu et al., 2012; Wan et al., 2019), and carboxyl (Du et al., 2016) end groups. Further, then the two polymeric shells together combined by utilizing borax. Moreover, in the structure of the polyglycerol-based hydrogel, borax is utilized as a significant cross-linker nontoxic material, the effect of which is also considered on pH sensitivity, drug loading amount, and amount of drug-releasing (Gosecki et al., 2016; Gosecki et al., 2017; Thombare et al., 2017; Wang et al., 2020; Zaibudeen & Philip, 2018). Further, the result investigated those two types of Fe_3O_4-core/polyglycerol-PEGylated-CMC (Fe_3O_4@PEG) shell nanocarrier developed for delivery of drug doxorubicin. Furthermore, the results showed that due to the boronic ester cross-linkages formation between carboxylate and OH groups of CMC, doxorubicin, and polyglycerol, the use of borax enhances the amount of doxorubicin up to 20% and PEGylated CMC content of nanocarriers. The capability of high HeLa tumor cell inhibition, blood compatibility, and nontoxicity of the nanocarrier to normal cells, the significant ability of MRI contrast agent usage, simple fabrication from inexpensive materials under simple reaction conditions along with improved targeting accumulation of the drug doxorubicin around the nucleus exhibits the excellent possibilities of nanocarriers as a better candidate for versatile and precise diagnosis and treatment of cancer-related issues. Moreover, hollow silica NPs (HSNs) with low density, high pore volumes, significant biocompatibility, excellent stability, and low density have received considerable attention for their and biological applications. Recent studies demonstrate that HSNs serve as an effective carrier for numerous therapeutic agents (Chen et al., 2011; Luo et al., 2013; Ma et al., 2013; Shen et al., 2014; Shi et al., 2013; Yang et al., 2012). Along with HSNs, disulfide bond, due to its instability under reduced glutathione (GSH), offers great interest among numerous redox-sensitive drug delivery systems (Navath et al., 2008). Wang et al. (2014) reported a single-hole GSH-receptive degradable HSNs (G-DHSNs) synthesis by instigating a type of disulfide bond crossover silane (BTOCD) to G-DHSNs for intracellular efficient drug delivery as illustrated in Fig. 2.2. However, the single-hole G-DHSNs were successfully fabricated by imprinting the polystyrene (PS)-based nanospheres core

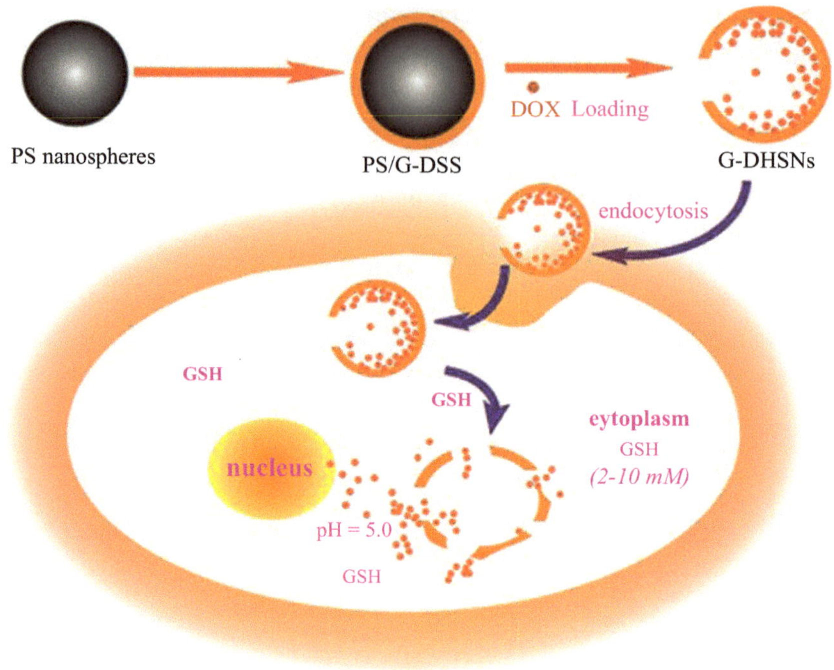

Figure 2.2 This figure represents G-DHSNs fabrication and its drug release mechanism in cancer cells. *G-DHSNs*, Glutathione-receptive degradable hollow silica nanoparticles. *Reproduced with permission of Wang, D., Xu, Z., Chen, Z., Liu, X., Hou, C., Zhang, X., & Zhang, H. (2014). Fabrication of single-hole glutathione-responsive degradable hollow silica nanoparticles for drug delivery.* ACS Applied Materials & Interfaces, 6, *12600–12608. https://doi.org/10.1021/am502585x.*

coated with GSH-responsive degradable silica shell (PS/G-DSS). Further, the drug doxorubicin (DOX) is loaded in G-DHSNs (DOX-G-DHSNs) that are further used as nanocarriers, carried out with DOX release into the nuclei of cancer cells by cleaving the disulfide bond with the decomposition of coinciding G-DHSNs via pH and GSH stimulation. Furthermore, G-DHSNs with accessible hollow structure, excellent colloidal stability, and good biocompatibility reported to be functional for controlled delivery drug. It also have been noted that DOX-G-DHSN shows excellent results by inhibiting the TCA8113 cell growth (Wang et al., 2014).

Conclusion and prospects

Nanocarriers have received a considerable attention of researchers due to its excellent advantages in the pharmaceutical industry. During past decades, as compared to conventional techniques, it showed its enormous exploration in the drug delivery application. Therefore it is crucial to formulate or fabricate the cost-effective nanocarriers with excellent laboratory approaches, which serves as promising agent for the drug delivery functions. This chapter mainly focuses upon the various types of nanocarriers and its fabrication methods. There is need to explore and develop more composite or hybrid or multifunctional nanocarriers that can improve the diagnostic and therapeutic efficacy of the individual nanocarrier.

References

Abbasi, E., Aval, S. F., Akbarzadeh, A., Milani, M., Nasrabadi, H. T., Joo, S. W., Hanifehpour, Y., Nejati-Koshki, K., & Pashaei-Asl, R. (2014). Dendrimers: Synthesis, applications, and properties. *Nanoscale Research Letters*, *9*, 247. Available from https://doi.org/10.1186/1556-276X-9-247.

Arcos, D., & Vallet-Regí, M. (2010). Sol–gel silica-based biomaterials and bone tissue regeneration. *Acta Biomaterialia*, *6*, 2874–2888. Available from https://doi.org/10.1016/j.actbio.2010.02.012.

Bamrungsap, S., Zhao, Z., Chen, T., Wang, L., Li, C., Fu, T., & Tan, W. (2012). Nanotechnology in therapeutics: A focus on nanoparticles as a drug delivery system. *Nanomedicine: Nanotechnology, Biology, and Medicine*, *7*, 1253–1271. Available from https://doi.org/10.2217/nnm.12.87.

Baskar, G., Bikku George, G., & Chamundeeswari, M. (2017). Synthesis and characterization of asparaginase bound silver nanocomposite against ovarian cancer cell line A2780 and lung cancer cell line A549. *Journal of Inorganic and Organometallic Polymers and Materials*, *27*, 87–94. Available from https://doi.org/10.1007/s10904-016-0448-x.

Baskar, G., Garrick, B. G., Lalitha, K., & Chamundeeswari, M. (2018). Gold nanoparticle mediated delivery of fungal asparaginase against cancer cells. *Journal of Drug Delivery Science and Technology*, *44*, 498–504. Available from https://doi.org/10.1016/j.jddst.2018.02.007.

Beg, S., Rizwan, M., Sheikh, A. M., Hasnain, M. S., Anwer, K., & Kohli, K. (2011). Advancement in carbon nanotubes: Basics, biomedical applications and toxicity. *The Journal of Pharmacy and Pharmacology*, *63*, 141–163. Available from https://doi.org/10.1111/j.2042-7158.2010.01167.x.

Bianco, A., Kostarelos, K., Partidos, C. D., & Prato, M. (2005). Biomedical applications of functionalised carbon nanotubes. *Chemical Communications*, 571. Available from https://doi.org/10.1039/b410943k.

Chamundeeswari, M., Sobhana, S. S. L., Jacob, J. P., Kumar, M. G., Devi, M. P., Sastry, T. P., & Mandal, A. B. (2010). Preparation, characterization and evaluation of a biopolymeric gold nanocomposite with antimicrobial activity. *Biotechnology and Applied Biochemistry*, *55*, 29–35. Available from https://doi.org/10.1042/BA20090198.

Chen, X., Hai, X., & Wang, J. (2016). Graphene/graphene oxide and their derivatives in the separation/isolation and preconcentration of protein species: A review. *Analytica Chimica Acta*, *922*, 1–10. Available from https://doi.org/10.1016/j.aca.2016.03.050.

Chen, Y., Chen, H., Ma, M., Chen, F., Guo, L., Zhang, L., & Shi, J. (2011). Double mesoporous silica shelled spherical/ellipsoidal nanostructures: Synthesis and hydrophilic/hydrophobic anticancer drug delivery. *Journal of Materials Chemistry*, *21*, 5290. Available from https://doi.org/10.1039/c0jm04024j.

Cheng, Q., Wei, T., Jia, Y., Farbiak, L., Zhou, K., Zhang, S., Wei, Y., Zhu, H., & Siegwart, D. J. (2018). Dendrimer-based lipid nanoparticles deliver therapeutic FAH mRNA to normalize liver function and extend survival in a mouse model of hepatorenal tyrosinemia type I. *Advanced Materials*, *30*, 1805308. Available from https://doi.org/10.1002/adma.201805308.

Cheng, R., Meng, F., Deng, C., Klok, H.-A., & Zhong, Z. (2013). Dual and multi-stimuli responsive polymeric nanoparticles for programmed site-specific drug delivery. *Biomaterials*, *34*, 3647–3657. Available from https://doi.org/10.1016/j.biomaterials.2013.01.084.

Costache, M. C., Vaughan, A. D., Qu, H., Ducheyne, P., & Devore, D. I. (2013). Tyrosine-derivedpolycarbonate-silica xerogel nanocomposites for controlled drug delivery. *Acta Biomaterialia*, *65*, 44–52.

Deshpande, P. P., Biswas, S., & Torchilin, V. P. (2013). Current trends in the use of liposomes for tumor targeting. *Nanomedicine: Nanotechnology, Biology, and Medicine*, *8*, 1509–1528. Available from https://doi.org/10.2217/nnm.13.118.

Du, F., Hönzke, S., Neumann, F., Keilitz, J., Chen, W., Ma, N., Hedtrich, S., & Haag, R. (2016). Development of biodegradable hyperbranched core-multishell nanocarriers for efficient topical drug delivery. *Journal of Controlled Release: Official Journal of the Controlled Release Society*, *242*, 42–49. Available from https://doi.org/10.1016/j.jconrel.2016.06.048.

Elhissi, A. M. A., Ahmed, W., Hassan, I. U., Dhanak, V. R., & D'Emanuele, A. (2012). Carbon nanotubes in cancer therapy and drug delivery. *Journal of Drug Delivery*, *2012*, 1–10. Available from https://doi.org/10.1155/2012/837327.

Elsner, J. J., Shefy-Peleg, A., & Zilberman, M. (2010). Novel biodegradable composite wound dressings with controlled release of antibiotics: Microstructure, mechanical and physical properties. *Journal of Biomedical Materials Research, Part B: Applied Biomaterials*, *93B*, 425–435. Available from https://doi.org/10.1002/jbm.b.31599.

Fernando, K. A. S., Sahu, S., Liu, Y., Lewis, W. K., Guliants, E. A., Jafariyan, A., Wang, P., Bunker, C. E., & Sun, Y.-P. (2015). Carbon quantum dots and applications in photocatalytic energy conversion. *ACS Applied Materials & Interfaces.*, 7, 8363–8376. Available from https://doi.org/10.1021/acsami.5b00448.

Galkina, O. L., Ivanov, V. K., Agafonov, A. V., Seisenbaeva, G. A., & Kessler, V. G. (2015). Cellulose nanofiber–titania nanocomposites as potential drug delivery systems for dermal applications. *Journal of Materials Chemistry B*, *3*, 1688–1698. Available from https://doi.org/10.1039/C4TB01823K.

Gelperina, S., Kisich, K., Iseman, M. D., & Heifets, L. (2005). The potential advantages of nanoparticle drug delivery systems in chemotherapy of tuberculosis. *American Journal of Respiratory and Critical Care Medicine*, *172*, 1487–1490. Available from https://doi.org/10.1164/rccm.200504-613PP.

Gosecki, M., Kazmierski, S., & Gosecka, M. (2017). Diffusion-controllable biomineralization conducted in situ in hydrogels based on reversibly cross-linked hyperbranched polyglycidol. *Biomacromolecules*, *18*, 3418–3431. Available from https://doi.org/10.1021/acs.biomac.7b01071.

Gosecki, M., Zgardzinska, B., & Gosecka, M. (2016). Temperature-induced changes in the nanostructure of hydrogels based on reversibly cross-linked hyperbranched polyglycidol with B(OH) 4 ⊖ ions. *The Journal of Physical Chemistry C*, *120*, 18323–18332. Available from https://doi.org/10.1021/acs.jpcc.6b06365.

Ha, J., Lee, J. H., & Moon, H. R. (2020). Alterations to secondary building units of metal–organic frameworks for the development of new functions. *Inorganic Chemistry Frontiers*, 7, 12–27. Available from https://doi.org/10.1039/C9QI01119F.

Hayashi, K., Sato, Y., Sakamoto, W., & Yogo, T. (2017). Theranostic nanoparticles for MRI-guided thermochemotherapy: "Tight" clustering of magnetic nanoparticles boosts relaxivity and heat-generation power. *ACS Biomaterials Science & Engineering*, *3*, 95–105. Available from https://doi.org/10.1021/acsbiomaterials.6b00536.

Henrique, P., Camargo, C., Gundappa, K., Satyanarayana, F., & Wypyc, H. (2009). Nanocomposites: Synthesis, structure, properties and new application opportunities. *Materials Research*, *12*, 1–39.

How, C. W., Rasedee, A., Manickam, S., & Rosli, R. (2013). Tamoxifen-loaded nanostructured lipid carrier as a drug delivery system: Characterization, stability assessment and cytotoxicity. *Colloids Surfaces B Biointerfaces*, *112*, 393–399. Available from https://doi.org/10.1016/j.colsurfb.2013.08.009.

Hu, M., Chen, M., Li, G., Pang, Y., Wang, D., Wu, J., Qiu, F., Zhu, X., & Sun, J. (2012). Biodegradable hyperbranched polyglycerol with ester linkages for drug delivery. *Biomacromolecules*, *13*, 3552–3561. Available from https://doi.org/10.1021/bm300966d.

Ioelovich, M., & Figovsky, O. (2008). Nano-cellulose as promising biocarrier. *Advanced Materials Research*, *47–50*, 1286–1289. Available from https://doi.org/10.4028/http://www.scientific.net/AMR.47-50.1286.

Jhaveri, A. M., & Torchilin, V. P. (2014). Multifunctional polymeric micelles for delivery of drugs and siRNA. *Frontiers in Pharmacology*, *5*. Available from https://doi.org/10.3389/fphar.2014.00077.

Joshi, M. D., Patravale, V., & Prabhu, R. (2015). Polymeric nanoparticles for targeted treatment in oncology: Current insights. *International Journal of Nanomedicine*, 1001. Available from https://doi.org/10.2147/IJN.S56932.

Kokabi, M., Sirousazar, M., & Hassan, Z. M. (2007). PVA–clay nanocomposite hydrogels for wound dressing. *European Polymer Journal*, *43*, 773–781. Available from https://doi.org/10.1016/j.eurpolymj.2006.11.030.

Lee, W.-H., Loo, C.-Y., Traini, D., & Young, P. M. (2015). Nano- and micro-based inhaled drug delivery systems for targeting alveolar macrophages. *Expert Opinion on Drug Delivery*, *12*, 1009–1026. Available from https://doi.org/10.1517/17425247.2015.1039509.

Lin, M., Wang, H., Meng, S., Zhong, W., Li, Z., Cai, R., Chen, Z., Zhou, X., & Du, Q. (2007). Structure and release behavior of PMMA/silica composite drug delivery system. *Journal of Pharmaceutical Sciences*, *96*, 1518–1526. Available from https://doi.org/10.1002/jps.20809.

Luo, X., Matranga, C., Tan, S., Alba, N., & Cui, X. T. (2011). Carbon nanotube nanoreservior for controlled release of anti-inflammatory dexamethasone. *Biomaterials*, *32*, 6316–6323. Available from https://doi.org/10.1016/j.biomaterials.2011.05.020.

Luo, Z., Ding, X., Hu, Y., Wu, S., Xiang, Y., Zeng, Y., Zhang, B., Yan, H., Zhang, H., Zhu, L., Liu, J., Li, J., Cai, K., & Zhao, Y. (2013). Engineering a hollow nanocontainer platform with multifunctional molecular machines for tumor-targeted therapy in vitro and in vivo. *ACS Nano*, *7*, 10271–10284. Available from https://doi.org/10.1021/nn404676w.

Ma, X., Zhao, Y., Ng, K. W., & Zhao, Y. (2013). Integrated hollow mesoporous silica nanoparticles for target drug/siRNA co-delivery. *Chemistry—A European Journal*, *19*, 15593–15603. Available from https://doi.org/10.1002/chem.201302736.

Madaeni, S. S., Derakhshandeh, K., Ahmadi, S., Vatanpour, V., & Zinadini, S. (2012). Effect of modified multi-walled carbon nanotubes on release characteristics of indomethacin from symmetric membrane coated tablets. *Journal of Membrane Science*, *389*, 110–116. Available from https://doi.org/10.1016/j.memsci.2011.10.021.

Mishra, B., Patel, B. B., & Tiwari, S. (2010). Colloidal nanocarriers: A review on formulation technology, types and applications toward targeted drug delivery,. *Nanomedicine: Nanotechnology, Biology and Medicine*, *6*, 9–24. Available from https://doi.org/10.1016/j.nano.2009.04.008.

Mu, H., & Holm, R. (2018). Solid lipid nanocarriers in drug delivery: Characterization and design. *Expert Opinion on Drug Delivery*, *15*, 771–785. Available from https://doi.org/10.1080/17425247.2018.1504018.

Mukherjee, S., Ray, S., & Thakur, R. (2009). Solid lipid nanoparticles: A modern formulation approach in drug delivery system. *Indian Journal of Pharmaceutical Sciences*, *71*, 349. Available from https://doi.org/10.4103/0250-474X.57282.

Musielak, E., Feliczak-Guzik, A., & Nowak, I. (2022). Optimization of the conditions of solid lipid nanoparticles (SLN) synthesis. *Molecules (Basel, Switzerland)*, *27*, 2202. Available from https://doi.org/10.3390/molecules27072202.

Nagahama, K., Utsumi, T., Kumano, T., Maekawa, S., Oyama, N., & Kawakami, J. (2016). Discovery of a new function of curcumin which enhances its anticancer therapeutic potency. *Scientific Reports*, *6*, 30962. Available from https://doi.org/10.1038/srep30962.

Navath, R. S., Kurtoglu, Y. E., Wang, B., Kannan, S., Romero, R., & Kannan, R. M. (2008). Dendrimer-drug conjugates for tailored intracellular drug release based on glutathione levels. *Bioconjugate Chemistry*, *19*, 2446–2455. Available from https://doi.org/10.1021/bc800342d.

Oppenheimer, A. (1937). Turmeric (Curcumin) in biliary diseases. *Lancet*, *229*, 619–621. Available from https://doi.org/10.1016/S0140-6736(00)98193-5.

Pasut, G., Scaramuzza, S., Schiavon, O., Mendichi, R., & Veronese, F. M. (2005). PEG-epirubicin conjugates with high drug loading. *Journal of Bioactive and Compatible Polymers*, *20*, 213–230. Available from https://doi.org/10.1177/0883911505053377.

Pathania, D., Gupta, D., Kothiyal, N. C., Sharma, G., Eldesoky, G. E., & Naushad, M. (2016). Preparation of a novel chitosan-*g*-poly(acrylamide)/Zn nanocomposite hydrogel and its applications for controlled drug delivery of ofloxacin. *International Journal of Biological Macromolecules*, *84*, 340–348. Available from https://doi.org/10.1016/j.ijbiomac.2015.12.041.

Peer, D., Karp, J. M., Hong, S., Farokhzad, O. C., Margalit, R., & Langer, R. (2007). Nanocarriers as an emerging platform for cancer therapy. *Nature Nanotechnology*, *2*, 751–760. Available from https://doi.org/10.1038/nnano.2007.387.

Pooja, D., Tunki, L., Kulhari, H., Reddy, B. B., & Sistla, R. (2016). Optimization of solid lipid nanoparticles prepared by a single emulsification-solvent evaporation method. *Data Br*, *6*, 15–19. Available from https://doi.org/10.1016/j.dib.2015.11.038.

Qiu, L., Zheng, C., Jin, Y., & Zhu, K. (2007). Polymeric micelles as nanocarriers for drug delivery. *Expert Opinion on Therapeutic Patents*, *17*, 819–830. Available from https://doi.org/10.1517/13543776.17.7.819.

Rahman, M., Alrobaian, M., Almalki, W. H., Mahnashi, M. H., Alyami, B. A., Alqarni, A. O., Alqahtani, Y. S., Alharbi, K. S., Alghamdi, S., Panda, S. K., Fransis, A., Hafeez, A., & Beg, S. (2021). Superbranched polyglycerol nanostructures as drug delivery and theranostics tools for cancer treatment. *Drug Discovery Today*, *26*, 1006–1017. Available from https://doi.org/10.1016/j.drudis.2020.11.007.

Rasoulzadeh, M., & Namazi, H. (2017). Carboxymethyl cellulose/graphene oxide bio-nanocomposite hydrogel beads as anticancer drug carrier agent. *Carbohydrate Polymers*, *168*, 320–326. Available from https://doi.org/10.1016/j.carbpol.2017.03.014.

Rezwan, K., Chen, Q. Z., Blaker, J. J., & Boccaccini, A. R. (2006). Biodegradable and bioactive porous polymer/inorganic composite scaffolds for bone tissue engineering. *Biomaterials*, *27*, 3413–3431. Available from https://doi.org/10.1016/j.biomaterials.2006.01.039.

Ribeiro, M., Boudoukhani, M., Belmonte-Reche, E., Genicio, N., Sillankorva, S., Gallo, J., Rodríguez-Abreu, C., Moulai-Mostefa, N., & Bañobre-López, M. (2021). Xanthan-Fe_3O_4 nanoparticle composite hydrogels for non-invasive magnetic resonance imaging and magnetically assisted drug delivery. *ACS Applied Nano Materials*, *4*, 7712–7729. Available from https://doi.org/10.1021/acsanm.1c00932.

Sannino, A., Pappadà, S., Giotta, L., Valli, L., & Maffezzoli, A. (2007). Spin coating cellulose derivatives on quartz crystal microbalance plates to obtain hydrogel-based fast sensors and actuators. *Journal of Applied Polymer Science*, *106*, 3040–3050. Available from https://doi.org/10.1002/app.25899.

Schexnailder, P., & Schmidt, G. (2009). Nanocomposite polymer hydrogels. *Colloid and Polymer Science*, *287*, 1–11. Available from https://doi.org/10.1007/s00396-008-1949-0.

Senapati, S., Mahanta, A. K., Kumar, S., & Maiti, P. (2018). Controlled drug delivery vehicles for cancer treatment and their performance. *Signal Transduction and Targeted Therapy*, *3*, 7. Available from https://doi.org/10.1038/s41392-017-0004-3.

Shen, J., Song, G., An, M., Li, X., Wu, N., Ruan, K., Hu, J., & Hu, R. (2014). The use of hollow mesoporous silica nanospheres to encapsulate bortezomib and improve efficacy for non-small cell lung cancer therapy. *Biomaterials*, *35*, 316–326. Available from https://doi.org/10.1016/j.biomaterials.2013.09.098.

Sherje, A. P., Jadhav, M., Dravyakar, B. R., & Kadam, D. (2018). Dendrimers: A versatile nanocarrier for drug delivery and targeting. *International Journal of Pharmaceutics*, *548*, 707–720. Available from https://doi.org/10.1016/j.ijpharm.2018.07.030.

Shi, S., Chen, F., & Cai, W. (2013). Biomedical applications of functionalized hollow mesoporous silica nanoparticles: Focusing on molecular imaging. *Nanomedicine: Nanotechnology, Biology, and Medicine*, *8*, 2027–2039. Available from https://doi.org/10.2217/nnm.13.177.

Sinha, N., & Yeow, J. T.-W. (2005). Carbon nanotubes for biomedical applications. *IEEE Transactions on Nanobioscience*, *4*, 180–195. Available from https://doi.org/10.1109/TNB.2005.850478.

Sotirelis, N. P., & Chrysikopoulos, C. V. (2017). Heteroaggregation of graphene oxide nanoparticles and kaolinite colloids. *The Science of the Total Environment*, *579*, 736–744. Available from https://doi.org/10.1016/j.scitotenv.2016.11.034.

Stiriba, S.-E., Frey, H., & Haag, R. (2002). Dendritic polymers in biomedical applications: From potential to clinical use in diagnostics and therapy. *Angewandte Chemie International Edition*, *41*, 1329–1334, https://doi.org/10.1002/1521-3773(20020415)41:8 < 1329::AID-ANIE1329 > 3.0.CO;2-P.

Sun, Y. P., Zhou, B., Lin, Y., Wang, W., Fernando, K. A. S., Pathak, P., Meziani, M. J., Harruff, B. A., Wang, X., Wang, H., Luo, P. G., Yang, H., Kose, M. E., Chen, B., Veca, L. M., & Xie, S. Y. (2006). Quantum-sized carbon dots for bright and colorful photoluminescence. *Journal of the American Chemical Society*. Available from https://doi.org/10.1021/ja062677d.

Thombare, N., Jha, U., Mishra, S., & Siddiqui, M. Z. (2017). Borax cross-linked guar gum hydrogels as potential adsorbents for water purification. *Carbohydrate Polymers*, *168*, 274–281. Available from https://doi.org/10.1016/j.carbpol.2017.03.086.

Tomalia, D. A. (2005). Birth of a new macromolecular architecture: Dendrimers as quantized building blocks for nanoscale synthetic polymer chemistry. *Progress in Polymer Science*, *30*, 294–324. Available from https://doi.org/10.1016/j.progpolymsci.2005.01.007.

Torchilin, V. (2011). Tumor delivery of macromolecular drugs based on the EPR effect. *Advanced Drug Delivery Reviews*, *63*, 131–135. Available from https://doi.org/10.1016/j.addr.2010.03.011.

Torchilin, V. P. (2005). Recent advances with liposomes as pharmaceutical carriers. *Nature Reviews. Drug Discovery*, *4*, 145–160. Available from https://doi.org/10.1038/nrd1632.

Verma, M. L., Barrow, C. J., & Puri, M. (2013). Nanobiotechnology as a novel paradigm for enzyme immobilisation and stabilisation with potential applications in biodiesel production. *Applied Microbiology and Biotechnology*, *97*, 23–39. Available from https://doi.org/10.1007/s00253-012-4535-9.

Verma, M. L., Chaudhary, R., Tsuzuki, T., Barrow, C. J., & Puri, M. (2013). Immobilization of β-glucosidase on a magnetic nanoparticle improves thermostability: Application in cellobiose hydrolysis. *Bioresource Technology*, *135*, 2–6. Available from https://doi.org/10.1016/j.biortech.2013.01.047.

Verma, M. L., Naebe, M., Barrow, C. J., & Puri, M. (2013). Enzyme immobilisation on amino-functionalised multi-walled carbon nanotubes: Structural and biocatalytic characterisation. *PLoS One*, *8*, e73642. Available from https://doi.org/10.1371/journal.pone.0073642.

Verma, M. L., Puri, M., & Barrow, C. J. (2016). Recent trends in nanomaterials immobilised enzymes for biofuel production. *Critical Reviews in Biotechnology*, *36*, 108–119. Available from https://doi.org/10.3109/07388551.2014.928811.

Wan, C., & Chen, B. (2011). Poly(ε-caprolactone)/graphene oxide biocomposites: Mechanical properties and bioactivity. *Biomedical Materials (Bristol, England)*, *6*, 055010. Available from https://doi.org/10.1088/1748-6041/6/5/055010.

Wan, L., Chen, Z., Deng, Y., Liao, T., Kuang, Y., Liu, J., Duan, J., Xu, Z., Jiang, B., & Li, C. (2020). A novel intratumoral pH/redox-dual-responsive nanoplatform for cancer MR imaging and therapy. *Journal of Colloid and Interface Science*, *573*, 263–277. Available from https://doi.org/10.1016/j.jcis.2020.04.026.

Wan, W., Ouyang, H., Long, W., Yan, W., He, M., Huang, H., Yang, S., Zhang, X., Feng, Y., & Wei, Y. (2019). Direct surface functionalization of cellulose nanocrystals with hyperbranched polymers through the anionic polymerization for pH-responsive intracellular drug delivery. *ACS Sustainable Chemistry & Engineering*, *7*, 19202–19212. Available from https://doi.org/10.1021/acssuschemeng.9b05231.

Wang, D., Xu, Z., Chen, Z., Liu, X., Hou, C., Zhang, X., & Zhang, H. (2014). Fabrication of single-hole glutathione-responsive degradable hollow silica nanoparticles for drug delivery. *ACS Applied Materials & Interfaces*, *6*, 12600–12608. Available from https://doi.org/10.1021/am502585x.

Wang, X., Wang, Y., Chen, Z. G., & Shin, D. M. (2009). Advances of cancer therapy by nanotechnology. *Cancer Research and Treatment*, *41*, 1. Available from https://doi.org/10.4143/crt.2009.41.1.1.

Wang, Y., Huang, H., Wu, J., Han, L., Yang, Z., Jiang, Z., Wang, R., Huang, Z., & Xu, M. (2020). Ultrafast self-healing, reusable, and conductive polysaccharide-based hydrogels for sensitive ionic sensors. *ACS Sustainable Chemistry & Engineering*, *8*, 18506–18518. Available from https://doi.org/10.1021/acssuschemeng.0c06258.

Xu, P., Zeng, G., Huang, D., Hu, S., Feng, C., Lai, C., Zhao, M., Huang, C., Li, N., Wei, Z., & Xie, G. (2013). Synthesis of iron oxide nanoparticles and their application in *Phanerochaete chrysosporium* immobilization for Pb(II) removal. *Colloids and Surfaces A: Physicochemical and Engineering Aspects*. Available from https://doi.org/10.1016/j.colsurfa.2012.10.061.

Yang, P., Gai, S., & Lin, J. (2012). Functionalized mesoporous silica materials for controlled drug delivery. *Chemical Society Reviews*, *41*, 3679. Available from https://doi.org/10.1039/c2cs15308d.

Zafar Razzacki, S. (2004). Integrated microsystems for controlled drug delivery. *Advanced Drug Delivery Reviews*, *56*, 185–198. Available from https://doi.org/10.1016/j.addr.2003.08.012.

Zaibudeen, A. W., & Philip, J. (2018). Temperature and pH sensor based on functionalized magnetic nanofluid. *Sensors and Actuators B: Chemical*, *268*, 338–349. Available from https://doi.org/10.1016/j.snb.2018.04.098.

Zhan, C., Wei, X., Qian, J., Feng, L., Zhu, J., & Lu, W. (2012). Co-delivery of TRAIL gene enhances the anti-glioblastoma effect of paclitaxel in vitro and in vivo. *Journal of Controlled Release: Official Journal of the Controlled Release Society*, *160*, 630–636. Available from https://doi.org/10.1016/j.jconrel.2012.02.022.

Zhou, C., Shi, Q., Guo, W., Terrell, L., Qureshi, A. T., Hayes, D. J., & Wu, Q. (2013). Electrospun bio-nanocomposite scaffolds for bone tissue engineering by cellulose nanocrystals reinforcing maleic anhydride grafted PLA. *ACS Applied Materials & Interfaces*, *5*, 3847–3854. Available from https://doi.org/10.1021/am4005072.

Zhou, X., Xu, L., Xu, J., Wu, J., Kirk, T. B., Ma, D., & Xue, W. (2018). Construction of a high-efficiency drug and gene co-delivery system for cancer therapy from a pH-sensitive supramolecular inclusion between oligoethylenimine-graft -β-cyclodextrin and hyperbranched polyglycerol derivative. *ACS Applied Materials & Interfaces.*, *10*, 35812–35829. Available from https://doi.org/10.1021/acsami.8b14517.

Zohreh, N., Karimi, N., Hosseini, S. H., Istrate, C., & Busuioc, C. (2022). Fabrication of a magnetic nanocarrier for doxorubicin delivery based on hyperbranched polyglycerol and carboxymethyl cellulose: An investigation on the effect of borax cross-linker on pH-sensitivity. *International Journal of Biological Macromolecules*, *203*, 80–92. Available from https://doi.org/10.1016/j.ijbiomac.2022.01.150.

CHAPTER 3

Biologically synthesized nanocarriers for targeted drug delivery applications

Kalpana Madgula[1,2], Lakshmi Madhuri Peddada[2,3] and Shruthy D. Pattathil[4,5]
[1]RiKarbon Inc., Newark, DE, USA
[2]St. Francis College for Women, Hyderabad, Telangana, India
[3]GITAM Deemed to be University, Hyderabad, Telangana, India
[4]Gulbarga University, Kalaburagi, Karnataka, India
[5]Bhavan's Vivekananda College of Science, Humanities & Commerce, Secunderabad, Telangana, India

Introduction

Nanotechnology is a broad phenomenon that ranges from traditional device physics to cutting-edge techniques based on self-assembly of molecules, developing nanoscale materials, and so on. It is an emerging area that is being used to investigate a variety of medical applications (Parveen & Deshpande, 2018) and healthcare. For the synthesis of nanoparticles (NPs), the precise control of size, content, shape, and stability, along with the utilization of environmentally friendly processes, are particularly desirable. Unicellular and multicellular microorganisms have been found to create inorganic compounds with nanoscale dimensions, either intracellularly or extracellularly. Viruses, bacteria, and fungus evolve into unique, distinctive, and structurally intriguing forms that have been employed by many researchers for the self-organization of inorganic materials as templates with the goal of achieving functional macrostructures. The intrinsic regularity of biological structures can be merged with the functional features of inorganic NPs in such assemblages (Dasarat Rao Sawle Balaji et al., 2008; Madgula & Sreenivas Puli, 2021). Although nanotechnology has many promising future applications, it also raises a number of issues, such as those that arise when a new technology is introduced, such as concerns about the toxic impact of nano-residues on the environment and their global-economic consequences, which have prompted many hypothetical scenarios. Governments and intellectuals debated the necessity of bringing a specific regulation for nanotechnology as a result of these concerns (Webster et al., 2004). Green chemistry is a trailblazing research approach that incorporates an application component for product design and development, allowing for more efficient production of goods with less health-hazardous components. In terms of bio, organic, inorganic, analytical, and even physical chemistry areas, the focus of green chemistry solely on large-scale applications (Zovinka Edward & Stock Anne, 2010) is environmentally beneficial. The goal of this green nanotechnology is to minimize human

Nanotechnology for Drug Delivery and Pharmaceuticals
DOI: https://doi.org/10.1016/B978-0-323-95325-2.00009-2

health risks and environmental pollution. Nanomaterials' manufacturing and usage necessitate the replacement of older nano-based products with novel or improved nano-based products that can be advantageous in this regard (Rejeski & Lekas, 2008).

Nanoscience and technology are being given the utmost attention, with a zeal never seen before, because of their tremendous potential to virtually change any field of study where they are applied. As a result, it has sparked the interest of researchers who want to employ nanocarriers in drug delivery systems (DDSs) (Suri et al., 2007). When it comes to safety, the pharmaceutical and biotech industries take great caution when using these novel DDSs as active ingredients, components, or excipients. As a result, it is critical to conduct extensive research into the systemic safety criteria related with the use of novel bio-synthesized nanomaterials. Only minor improvements in medication or delivery system parameters, as is done traditionally, will not make future formulations worthwhile. However, nanotechnology has the potential to positively reverse the situation because it improves efficacy and safety by orders of magnitude. Functionalized gold NPs, for example, are efficiently employed as a contrast agent for diagnosis, treatment, and as a carrier for other drugs from the entry site to the site of action. Nanotechnology has shown to have numerous applications in medication delivery systems, all of which can be very beneficial. When we focus on manufacturing and fabrication of materials with the right technique, the nanotechnology-oriented medication delivery system will grow quickly in contrast to traditional methods (Papazoglou & Parthasarathy, 2007).

Cancer is the world's most lethal human disease. Surgery, immunotherapy, radiation, and chemotherapy are the four main cancer treatment procedures utilized around the world. The primary disadvantages of conventional cancer therapies are toxicity caused by the drugs, poor oral bioavailability, lack of solubility in water, low therapeutic indices, irregularity in circulation, nonspecific biodistribution, and delivery of an anticancer medication to both normal and malignant cells. As a result, innovative, safe, and effective treatments are urgently required to reduce this alarmingly high mortality and morbidity rates (Soni & Yadav, 2015).While there are many improved medications available today, effective drug administration is still difficult. This is due to the fact that the first-pass action of drug metabolism reduces its bioavailability in the blood. As a result, the dosage of the drug could fall less than its therapeutic efficiency, making it ineffective. An overdose, on the other hand, could result in toxic effects if the concentration is too high. As a result, there has been a greater emphasis on controlled DDSs to ensure a delayed and controlled release of the drug at prescribed rates in order to maximize the medicine's intended effects. The short half-lives of peptides in humans add to the difficulty. Controlled drug delivery has progressed from macroscopic to microscopic and eventually to the nanoscopic age (Li et al., 2016; Xian & Jun, 2007).

To combat the exponential rise in the chronic diseases over the last decades, it is inevitable to design an efficient DDS. Traditional drug delivery methods suffer multiple negatives, such as no specific targeting, poor drug stability and bio distribution, accumulation of the drug resulting in the toxic effect (Aminu et al., 2020). With the latest advancements, nanotechnology has become a powerful tool catering to the needs of clinical drug delivery options. It provides numerous alternatives to the delivery of medicines such reduction in the dosage of drug, governing the release of drug at the targeted site (Prasanna et al., 2021). In spite of few limitations in nanotechnology, medical firms have already abided to the medical nanotechnology, especially in the administration of chemotherapeutic drugs (Sahu et al., 2021). For the targeted delivery usually, drugs are encapsulated in natural or synthetic polymers or adsorbed on the surface of the nanocarriers. To ensure that the drug molecules are engulfed by the targeted cells the surface of the nanocarriers is modified, so that they are identified at the targeted site (Sun et al., 2021). The charged nanocarriers are responsible for the electrostatic attraction influenced targeting. The charge on these nanocarriers makes them stable in the blood circulation and helps in the accumulation of the drug at the targeted site. By specific stimulation at the target site, such as pH, light, heat, and stimuli responses, the charge reversal on the nanocarriers is achieved. Such charge reversal DDSs are highly target selective and are mostly employed in administering anticancer drugs (Fang et al., 2020).

Nanotechnology has shown tremendous promise in successful drug delivery because it has the potential to overcome existing drug delivery issues, such as the inability of the drug, to pass through the barriers due to its big size or incompatible surface characteristics. Nanotechnology has improved the encapsulation and functionalization of drug carriers for targeted distribution and controlled release by using nanocarriers (Eleni et al., 2019; Trucillo et al., 2020), such as NPs, micelles, liposomes, and vesicles as seen in the Fig. 3.1.

In this chapter, we discussed the types of biogenic nanocarriers as well as the discovery and development of methods that are used to optimize the delivery of pharmaceutical or active agents to their target areas, in order to increase efficacy, safety, and therapeutic response and to meet some of the goals in drug delivery development. These biogenic nanocarriers include plant virus NPs (PVNPs) and virus-like particles (VLPs), bacteria and bacterial spores, extracellular vesicles (EVs), cyclodextrins (CDs), as well as the biomimetic, and polymer- and plant protein—based nanocarriers. Furthermore, a brief description of their physicochemical properties plant protein based nanocarriers for targeted DDS. Finally, a brief review on smart nanocarriers that are intended for achieving targeted release and increasing absorption and modifying the pharmacokinetic profile of pharmaceuticals with different additives, transporters, and medical devices (Real et al., 2021) for clinical interventions and translation is also presented.

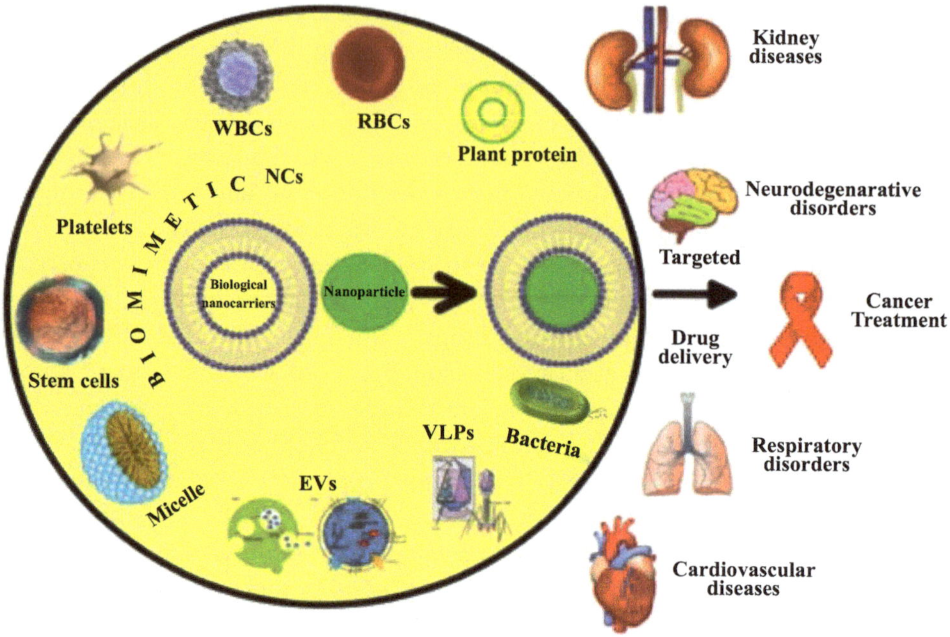

Figure 3.1 Sketch depicting the nanoparticles encapsulated biologically synthesized nanocarriers involved in the treatment of numerous ailments.

Biogenic nanocarriers employed in drug delivery

Plant-based virus nanoparticles and virus-like particles

Researchers and clinicians are keen in technological tools constructed on plant-based VNPs and VLPs, which are biocompatible, biodegradable, noninfectious in mammals, which are easily manipulated chemically as well as genetically to deliver medications (Masarapu et al., 2017).

Plant-based VNPs are very useful as biomedicals because of their biocompatibility and biodegradable nature; on top of this the humans or other mammals are not infected by plant-based viruses (Wen et al., 2015). Unlike mammalian viruses, these plant-based viruses have an RNA or DNA as genetic material, a capsid, and, rarely, a lipid envelope obtained from the cell from which they are produced. Plant viruses come in a variety of forms, including icosahedron, rod, and spiral (Shahgolzari et al., 2020). Due to their dimensions, geometry, and physical and chemical properties, plant-based viruses are categorized as biological nanomaterials. PVNPs have a low risk of causing direct toxicity in humans (Shahgolzari et al., 2021). These properties minimize the toxicity even when the dosages are high (up to 100 mg/kg), which indicate a safe in vivo use of PVNP (Kaiser et al., 2007). By assembling, infusing, or modifying the internal surface of VNPs, they can carry numerous materials in their inner cavity, such as various NPs, drug molecules, and imaging agents, and for tissue-specific delivery, the exterior surface can be altered by attaching targeting ligands (Mateu, 2016; Steinmetz & Mottle, 2017). Many of the challenges posed by NPs previously have been overcome by PVNPs. Many researchers have established PVNPs based on cowpea mosaic virus, physalis mottle virus, tobacco mosaic virus, cowpea chlorotic mottle virus, Potato virus X, and Brome mosaic virus are now being tested (Czapar & Steinmetz, 2017; Steele et al., 2017; Wen & Steinmetz, 2016). VLPs are a subtype of VNPs that are devoid of the infectious viral genetic material and self-build into cage-like structures from viral proteins. Many distinct structural proteins derived from different species of virus, such as *Escherichia coli* (Singh et al., 2006), insect virus (Huang et al., 2017), yeasts (Alberto et al., 2020), and mammalian cells (Kim & Kim, 2017), form VLPs. The VLPs synthesized in this way resemble native virus particles structurally and morphologically, with identical cell engraftment, absorption, and intracellular trafficking. PVNPs' immune-stimulating capabilities promote their application in delivering antigens for tumor and vaccines, making them effective anticancer agents. PVNPs have adjuvant capabilities that are naturally inherited, but they can also be utilized to deliver other supplements to boost immune responses. When PVNP are used as in situ vaccinating reagents and injected into tumors without external antigens, they can simulate antitumor immunity (Wu et al., 2010).

VLPs are nontoxic, nano-sized, self-assembled particles that mimic the morphology and development of the original virus but lack the infectious viral DNA (Sahu et al., 2021). Viral proteins are used to make VLPs in the lab. Many viruses' structural proteins are employed to make VLPs, including hepatitis B and HIV (Agnese et al., 2015). The most promising candidate among the VLP nanocarriers has been hepatitis B virus (HBc) core particles. The HBc virus particles can be bioengineered for in vivo distribution and selective attack on solid tumors (Saha et al., 2020). They are made by putting together the proteins of one or more viruses. VLPs are divided into two categories based on whether or not they have a lipid coating on their surface. Protein capsules can be single-layer or multi-layered (Chung et al., 2020). VLPs will be easily recognized by the immune system because they resemble the highly organized structure of infections and elicit immunological responses in the host (Pushko et al., 2013). VLPs are widely used for targeted drug delivery as well as tumor tissue imaging due to their interior cavity (Nooraei et al., 2021). VLPs can be adapted as an innovative and encouraging nanocarriers for the efficient drug delivery. To ease the formulation of novel material with improved solubility, biocompatibility, and efficiency, they were modified externally and internally to take the drug and deliver it in a timely manner (Alvandi et al., 2022). By chemical cross-linking, functionalization of the outer and inner surfaces of VLPs with heterologous antigens can be achieved, which increases their immunogenicity by engaging multiple pathogen recognition receptors (Manolova et al., 2008). On the surface of VLPs, protein fusion also can be done to give them new specificity and tropism, as well as physical characteristics (Masaaki et al., 2013).

Such surface alterations performed on VLPs make them more target specific in drug delivery, allowing for a wider range of applications in the future. Current advancements in the delivery of targeted medication using VLPs are showing a lot of promise. Even though VLPs exhibit superiority over the other NP-based delivery vehicles, they can still be improved in terms of selectivity, solubility, biocompatibility, and other factors are few key considerations to keep in mind while constructing VLPs as delivery vehicles (Franco et al., 2009). VLPs are widely employed in vaccine delivery because they have numerous advantages over traditional vaccine administration methods. Because of their specific interaction in a similar manner to their mother infections, triggering both hormonal and cell-mediated immune responses, owing to their repeated structural design that matches the native viruses. Because of their ability to induce a possible immunological response via MHC-I and MHC-II molecules, many VLPs have been employed as vaccines. These VLP vaccination candidates are termed "self-adjuvants" because they contain components that encourage professional antigen-presenting cells (APCs) to pick them up (Kim et al., 2019). VLP vaccines are made using a variety of expression platforms, including prokaryotic and eukaryotic systems, including mammalian cells, plants, bacteria, and yeast (Syomin & Ilyin, 2019). VLPs are efficient delivery vehicles, but they have a few disadvantages when it comes to using them as a gene or medication carriers. The preexisting immunity to common viruses in most people is a key concern when using VLPs as medicine carriers (Mohsen et al., 2017). Polyethylene glycol is used as an immune masking agent to reduce the immunogenicity of VLPs in this circumstance. Another disadvantage when VLPs are employed in the treatment is the need for repeated injections, which is mostly avoided except in cancer immunotherapy.

Bacteria and bacterial spores

Bacterial spores are explored as simple inert nanocarriers capable of generating substantial safety with single dosage might be beneficial if exploited as vaccine vehicles (Mohsen et al., 2017). Bacterial spores are dormant form of life, with a significant level of resistance. Bacterial spore coatings have barrier properties and are an example of unique and fascinating structures found in microorganisms. Various protein layers cover the spores in a secure and permeable shell in these nanostructures (Suffian & Al-Jamal, 2021). Self-assembling protomers and the potential to construct and transport foreign molecules are two important properties that are relevant for blending with the areas of nanobiotechnology (Oggion et al., 2003). In fact, the spore-coat could be used as a source of innovative self-assembling biomolecules as well as a delivery vehicle for diverse compounds (Errington, 1993). The coat can be used to deliver heterologous antigens and provide prophylactic immunization. In fact, the spore-coat could be used as a source of innovative self-assembling biomolecules as well as a delivery vehicle for diverse compounds. The coat can be used to deliver heterologous antigens and provide preventive immunization (Duc et al., 2003).

Bacillus spores have a variety of characteristics that make them ideal candidates for vaccination vehicles. Vaccination can be done using two different methods (Casula & Cutting, 2002). The first method involves amalgamation of the spore-coat gene with the antigen sequence to construct an epitope on the spore-coat. By blending the antigen gene with an appropriate bacillus gene, the antigen is produced constitutively in the vegetative cell (Hoa et al., 2001). Spores containing this modified gene are administered orally and proliferate in the gastrointestinal (GI) tract. As a result, the spore has unique characteristics for nanovaccine production, which could result in the better public health in both developing and developed nations (Aronson & Fitz-James, 1976).

Bacteria are amongst the most important groups of organisms that has a dynamic role in the evolution of human health and disease. Bacteria were used as an emerging delivery tool for various applications, especially in the field of medicine, thanks to the integration of chemical biotechnology (Duc et al., 2004). Bacterial-based transport systems have stimulated interest in the detection and treatment of a numerous ailments, particularly malignancy, infectious diseases, renal disorders, and so on, due to their inherent biocompatibility and motility (Li et al., 2021a); a lot of research has begun at the intersection of chemical biotechnology and microorganisms, creating a promising frontier in biological administration (Siamak et al., 2020). The design concepts for bacteria-based transport systems, germ regulation, and clinical adaptations are studied with a special priority on emerging improvements in diagnostic and treatment (Pan et al., 2021).

Bacteria exhibit some unique characteristics, including their ability of recombination with plasmids; certain bacteria possess the ability to penetrate solid tumors and display anticancer action. As a result, they are explored as "strengthy prospective therapeutic agents" (Rafaela & María, 2022). *Clostridium histolyticum*, *Pseudoalteromonas marina*, *Bifidobacterium bifidum*, *Streptococcus pneumoniae*, *Salmonella typhimurium*, *E. coli*, and *Listeria monocytogenes* have all been employed in the therapy of cancer so far (Brader et al., 2008; Cronin et al., 2010; Dietrich et al., 1998; Fu et al., 2008). Similarly, the use of oncolytic bacteria has been greatly strengthened as more bacterial strains with stronger selectivity for cancer cells have been discovered (Pérez & María, 2021). However, potential concerns associated with bacterial-based cancer therapeutic techniques include persistent infection, disruption of immunity, inadequate tumor lysis, and barriers related to bacterial entity distribution to target tissues (Solomon et al., 2015). But designing considerably more efficient living bacteria against cancer is now possible because of the introduction of new opportunities in synthetic biology and genetic engineering (Gill, 2013).

Bacteria could be used as carriers for medicinal substances to boost drug disposal at the illness site and improve treatment potency, or directly given to cure symptoms, such as probiotics-mediated treatment for ulcerative colitis (Gan et al., 2021). Bacteria are frequently delivered directly to the target site via per oral administration, which necessitates protecting bacteria from the stomach's acidic pH and the harsh environment of the GI tract (Bitto & Kaparakis-Liaskos, 2017). Meanwhile, addressing the pathogenicity and immunogenicity of bacteria is crucial for bacteria-based delivery methods to avoid unwanted adverse effects. Although there are advantages, such as easy industrialization, when compared to eukaryotic cells, efficient transport of drug, effortless surface tempering and diagnosing bacterial poisoning at the same time vague mechanism, biosafety, time-consuming isolation process are some of the challenges for the potential use of bacteria as nanocarriers (Aschtgen et al., 2016).

Extracellular vesicles

Because of their potential to encapsulate and transport essential biomolecules to target cells, EVs have attracted a lot of attention as biological carriers for medication administration (Liu et al., 2021). The most intriguing part of EVs is their load, regardless of where they come from. Lipids, proteins, nucleic acids like mRNA, and many bioactive substances are all carried by EVs (Ren et al., 2016). EVs contribute in cell-to-cell communication by either delivering cargo to the acceptor cell or activating them by surface expression ligands. EVs are produced by diverse cells that are found in bodily fluids and plant cells (Wu et al., 2019). Their study would reveal the physiological status of the cells that release them, as well as any potential consequences for other cells (Chen et al., 2022). Although blood is one of the richest sources of EVs originating many cell types, the majority of those seen in plasma are from platelets. Inflammatory diseases could benefit by the utilization of EVs as noninvasive biomarkers (Nieuwland et al., 2018). EVs are membrane-bound lipid bilayered vesicles of size from 40 to 1000 nm. Microvesicles and exosomes are two types of EVs. Exosomes are tiny EVs that are produced by the plasma membrane budding inward, resulting in the capture of both membrane and cellular molecules (Sharma et al., 2021a). In the process of exosomal vesicles formation by the inward sprouting of early endosomal membranes, multivesicular bodies are formed (Gurung et al., 2021). Exosomes have the ability to travel and connect with distant target cells, releasing their contents and inducing physiological changes in the target cells. They are potentially harmless and so can be employed in treatments (Pariset et al., 2017). Microvesicles are generated by the cell's plasma membrane bursting outward and subsequently being released into the cellular space. Oncosomes, apoptotic particles, and other EVs are examples of microvesicles (Chao et al., 2017).

Isolation of EVs—The isolation and characterization methodologies must be refined and standardized in order to generate more reliable and economical diagnostic and therapeutic solutions using EVs. Exosomes were first separated using methods based on ultracentrifugation, which is an old standard method; alternative approaches have evolved to overcome ultracentrifugation's limitations (Bose et al., 2021). These alternative methods are established on the isolation of exosome by their dimension, expression of immunoefficacy, and procedures for precipitating exosomes. Nevertheless, all these techniques are not completely successful and generally yield complicated mixes of EVs along with additional extracellular space ingredients. This is owing to the complexities of the bodily liquids involved in the extraction of exosomes, the significant overlapping of the physico-biochemical effects of exosomes and various EVs, and the diverseness of exosomes (Malhotra et al., 2021). As a result, developing isolation strategies can identify the various varieties of EVs in the extracellular fluid quickly, competently, and in a clinically viable manner remains a challenge (Chris et al., 2016). Furthermore, using numerous isolation procedures like ultracentrifugation, density gradient, precipitation kits, ExoChip, immunoprecipitation, Exo Search Chip, and acoustic nanofilter in a row to enrich the exosomal content of a single isolation has been done, but this increases the expense, time spent, and technical education, making it clinically disadvantageous.

Every isolation method and analysis approach (shown in Fig. 3.2) has advantages and disadvantages of its kind, and it was shown that the procedures employed for isolation to recover exosomes from the same type of cell result in diverse proteome profiles, further confusing the situation (Maria et al., 2014). Rather than focusing on the development of exosomal or nonexosomal protein markers produced by all types of cells, regardless of methods employed in separation, it may probably be more fruitful to concentrate on developing exosomal or nonexosomal protein markers for a specific type of cell, independent of method employed in isolation, or a set of exosomal or nonexosomal protein markers for all exosomes, irrespective of their emergence, and specific method employed in isolation. When conducting and publishing EV-related research, it is critical to evaluate and include the guidelines from the minimal information to increase the rigor and repeatability of detected EV markers (Deun et al., 2014).

However, the isolation of EVs and the absence of target-specific content delivery are two fundamental obstacles to their employment as nanocarriers (Aixue et al., 2021; Dominik et al., 2021). EVs are combined with a variety of designed nanostructures to solve these drawbacks as shown in the Fig. 3.3. The combination provides EVs with enhanced features, such as higher permeability across membranes, increased capsule stability, increased drug loading, and target-specific binding capability, allowing for more efficient and safe drug administration (Bryant et al., 2020). In order to extend their systemic circulation and avoid immune cell uptake a new EV-based nanoformulation based on PEG-functionalization was synthesized which could effectively deliver doxorubin to melanoma (Sharma et al., 2021b).

Despite recent success in research investigating the potential of EVs for premature illness identification, curative application, and drug administration, determining the

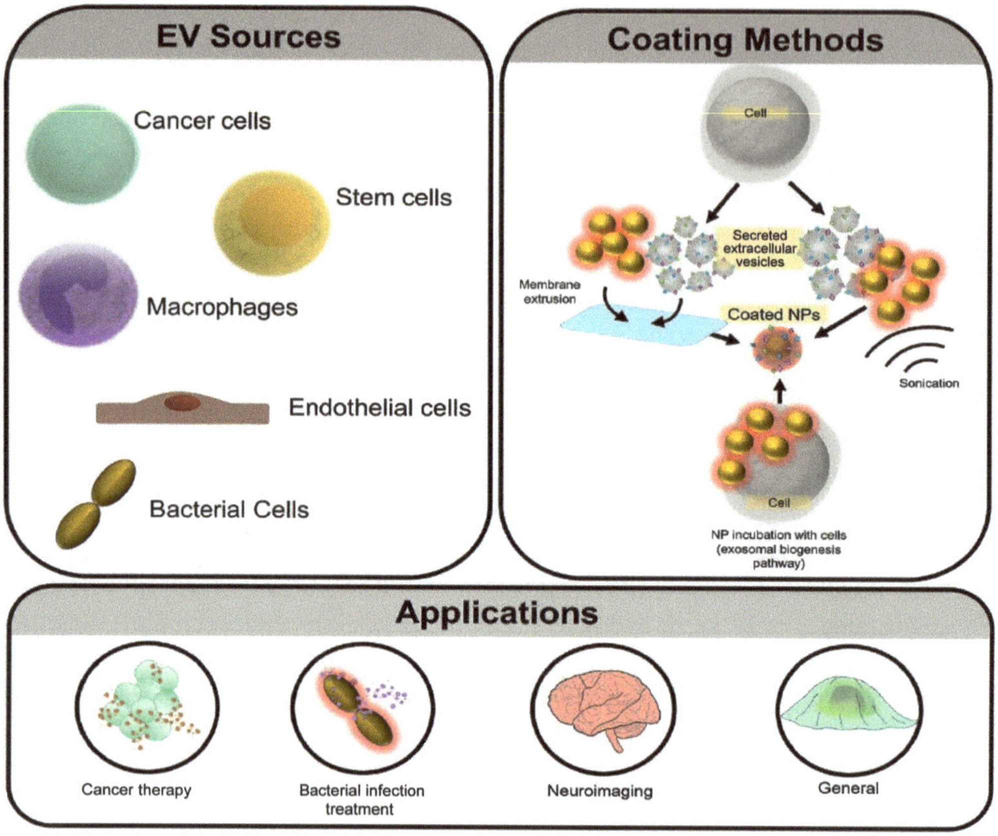

Figure 3.2 Schematic diagram showing various types of nanomaterials that can be coated with extracellular vesicles (EVs) to form hybrid systems (Fathi et al., 2021). *EVs*, Extracellular vesicles. *Reproduced with permission from Fathi, P., Rao, L., & Chen, X. (2021). Extracellular vesicle-coated nanoparticles,* View, *2, 20200187. https://doi.org/10.1002/VIW.20200187. © 2021 The Author(s) CC BY 4.0.*

optimal depository conditions for EVs has proven difficult. The consequences of storage conditions on EVs before and after separation are currently poorly understood. EVs' size, number, contents, functions, and behaviors may be affected by storage. Biofluids and isolated EVs appear to be best preserved at 80°C, and the isolated EVs can be stocked at 4°C for a brief time. Lyophilization appears to be a potential method for storing EV goods. The understanding of storage-mediated diseases is still a work in progress (Li et al., 2021b).

Cyclodextrins

One of the common methods adopted these days for overcoming the drawbacks of conventional DDSs is to form inclusion compounds with CDs. An amalgamation of CDs complexation and nanotechnology is considered a novel approach in DDSs

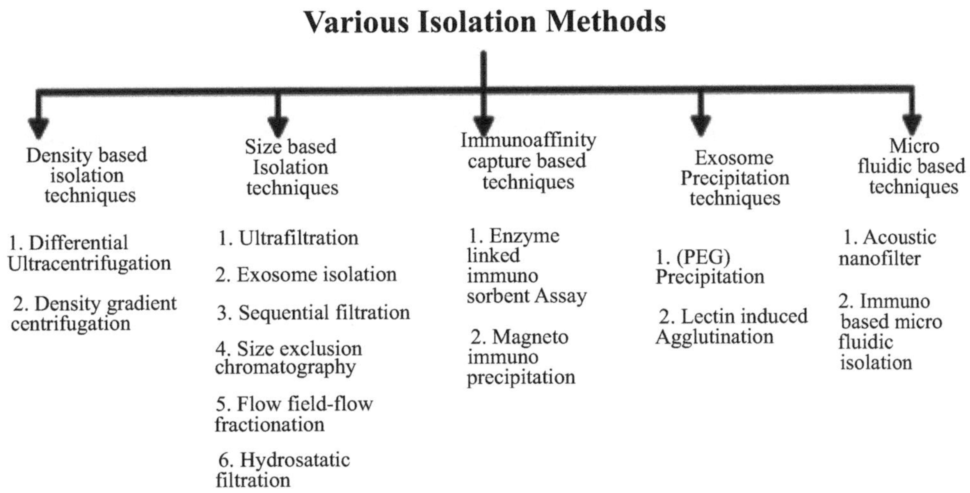

Figure 3.3 Various isolation techniques employed to separate extracellular vesicles.

development. CDs are cyclic oligosaccharides with a distinctive truncated cone form made up of units of D-glucopyranose linked by 1−4 glycosidic linkages that are obtained naturally and are safe. Enzymatic breakdown of starch produces CDs, which are chemically and physically stable macromolecules. They have a outer layer that shows strong affinity for water and a inner layer that easily dissolves in lipids, making them water soluble and biocompatible (Patras et al., 2022). The three most prevalent CD kinds are α, β and γ that differ in the number of units, solubility, diameters, and melting point. From a structural view point, the −OH (hydroxyl) groups face outward, while the hydrogen and oxygen(glycosidic) linkages face inside, giving the cone outside layer that shows great affinity for water and an inner layer that is hydrophobic. As a result, this macromolecule works as a host, engaging with species with a hydrophobic region and appropriate dimensions via soft bonds while remaining soluble in water. This phenomenon leads to the formation of inclusion complex. Even when CD is part of polymers, nanosponges, or NPs, the host−guest complexation process, is straightforward phenomenon, with all these factors and forces (noncovalent) involved (Gidwani & Vyas, 2015; Loftsson et al., 2004; Yuan et al., 2021) as shown in the Fig. 3.4 (Gidwani & Vyas, 2015) for different CD-based nanocarriers employed for the treatment of cancer. Also, Fig. 3.5 (Real et al., 2021) depicts different routes of administration of CD-based nanocarriers for drug delivery with improved bioavailability.

Shringirishi et al. (Szejtli, 2004) investigated the bioavailability and release characteristics of nifedipine, a drug used for the treatment of angina pectoris and hypertension by loading it in CD-based nanosponges in an attempt to improve treatment. The nanosystem's loading efficiency was 78%, and its size was 430 nm. In simulated stomach fluid, drug release was tested with an intense release for the first 4 h and then

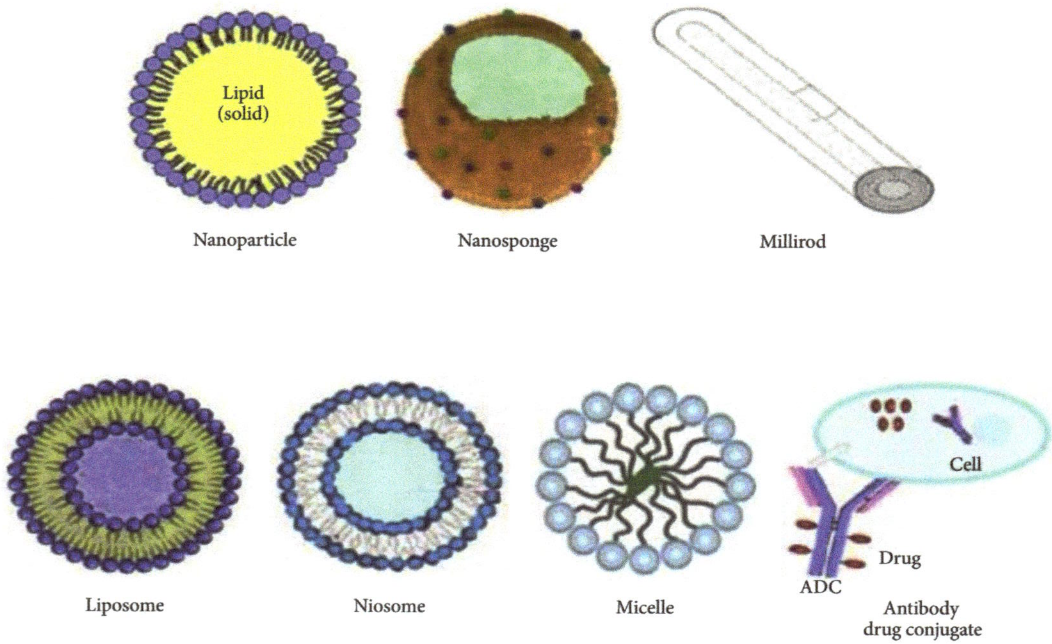

Figure 3.4 Different CD-based nanocarriers with increased bioavailability for the treatment of cancer. *CD*, Cyclodextrin. *Reproduced with permission from Gidwani, B. & Vyas, A. (2015). A comprehensive review on cyclodextrin-based carriers for delivery of chemotherapeutic cytotoxic anticancer drugs.* BioMed Research International, 2015. *https://doi.org/10.1155/2015/198268. © 2015.*

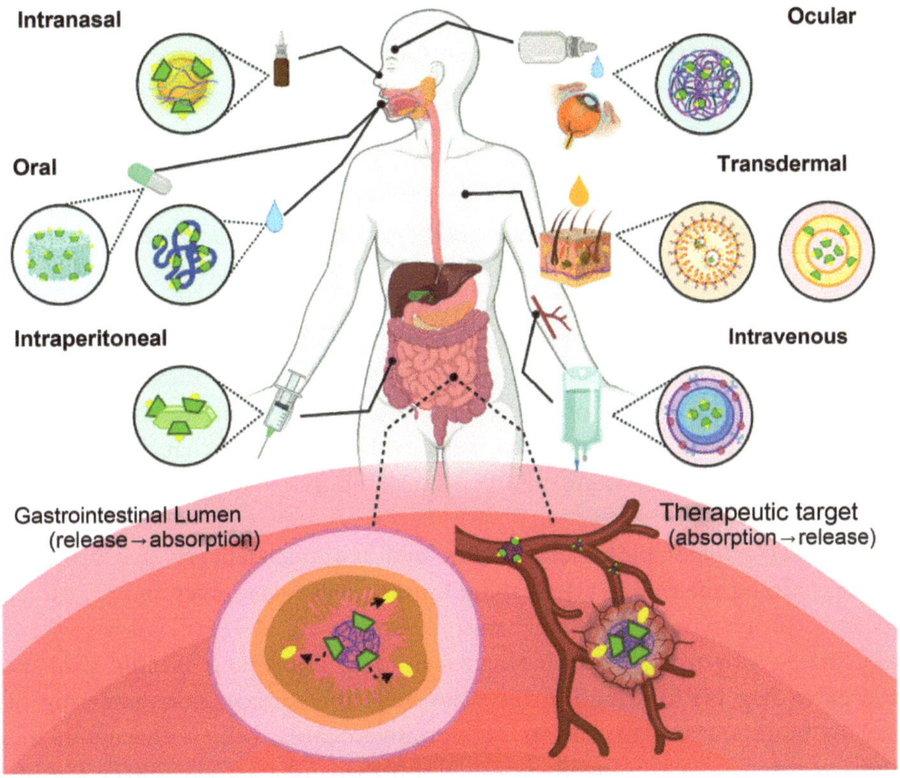

Figure 3.5 Different routes of administration of CD-based nanocarriers for drug delivery with improved bioavailability. *CD*, Cyclodextrin. *Reproduced with permission from Real, D. A., Bolaños, K., Priotti, J., Yutronic, N., Kogan, M. J., Sierpe, R., Donoso-González, O. (2021). Cyclodextrin-modified nanomaterials for drug delivery: Classification and advances in controlled release and bioavailability.* MDPI, 13, *2131. https://doi.org/10.3390/pharmaceutics13122131. © 2021 by the authors. Licensee MDPI, Basel, Switzerland.*

shifted to a regulated distribution continuously for the next few hours. Its oral bioavailability was higher than the formulation in in vivo tests, and it had appropriate stability for 6 months. Zhang et al. created (Han et al., 2018) a CD-functionalized hyperbranching polyglycerol (HPG-CD) of paclitaxel. The produced NPs were biocompatible and demonstrated to be a viable hydrophobic drug delivery method. This helped them achieve good solubility in aqueous media and drug loading capacity. Zidan et al. (Shringirishi et al., 2017) worked on atorvastatin, a drug used for the treatment of cholesterol and triglyceride levels. They looked at the oral bioavailability and therapeutic effect of atorvastatin calcium loaded on CD-based nanosponges. Carbonyl diimidazole was used to make the polymers in various ratios. With a size of 420 nm, the sponges had a maximum drug-loading capacity of 34%. The in vitro release investigation also revealed a biphasic pattern, with a quick release of 58% after

1 h and a longer release of 6 h, which was better than the dissolution time. Fig. 3.4 depicts different routes of administration of CD-based nanocarriers for drug delivery with improved bioavailability.

Biomimetic nanocarriers

To curb the constraints of the prevailing DDSs, a biomimetic synthetic drug carrier system was developed, which was inspired by the distinct behavior of diverse cells in human bodies (Zhang et al., 2011). Native cells, with their built-in functional groups on the surface, may easily bypass biological obstacles and reach their destination (Zidan et al., 2018). With the latest advancements, nanotechnology offers a vast spectrum of synthetic NPs in the form of micelles, liposomes, and polymeric spheres among many, tailored particularly to target sick cells, and so illustrates that they are potential instruments for the unmet demands of clinical transport of drugs (Moloudizargari et al., 2021).

NPs meet two major biological hurdles after systemic delivery that hinders them from accomplishing their goal: (1) escaping kupffer cells in the liver and (2) the blood's mononuclear phagocyte defense mechanism (Patra et al., 2018a; Tiwari et al., 2012). The key strategy for overcoming biological hurdles, improving specific tissue attacking, and extending NP distribution time has been the surface bioengineering of NP. In order to build and design this set of biomimetic NPs, cells with certain inherent biological features were employed as inspiration (Sadauskas et al., 2007) The synthesized organic or inorganic NPs are enclosed in a layer of native cell membrane in cell membrane coating technology, and the resulting nanocarriers carrying synthetic NPs contain the inherent complex features of the parent cell (Gustafson et al., 2015).The fabrication principle for this technique is based on the therapeutic cargo being delivered; one should decide the NP skeleton and modify the surface to include the natural functional moieties that allow original cells to overcome the biological barriers and make it to the target. The cellular membranes of various cells, such as red blood cells (RBCs), immunological cells, platelets, and cancerous cells, can be exploited to mask medicines or NPs depending on the condition being treated (Fig. 3.6) (Dominik et al., 2021).

The basic manufacturing process is similar, and it entails extracting the cell membrane, preparing the nanocore and assembling the "shell-core."

1. Extraction of cell membrane: Cells interact with their surroundings to accomplish a variety of complicated processes in the body, with the functional protein moieties on the surface, which handle major responsibilities. As the characteristics of the proteins be altered smoothly on the membrane, meticulous extraction and separation of the cell membrane is required. For the extraction of cellular membranes, hypotonic solution is needed, which causes cell disintegration; however,

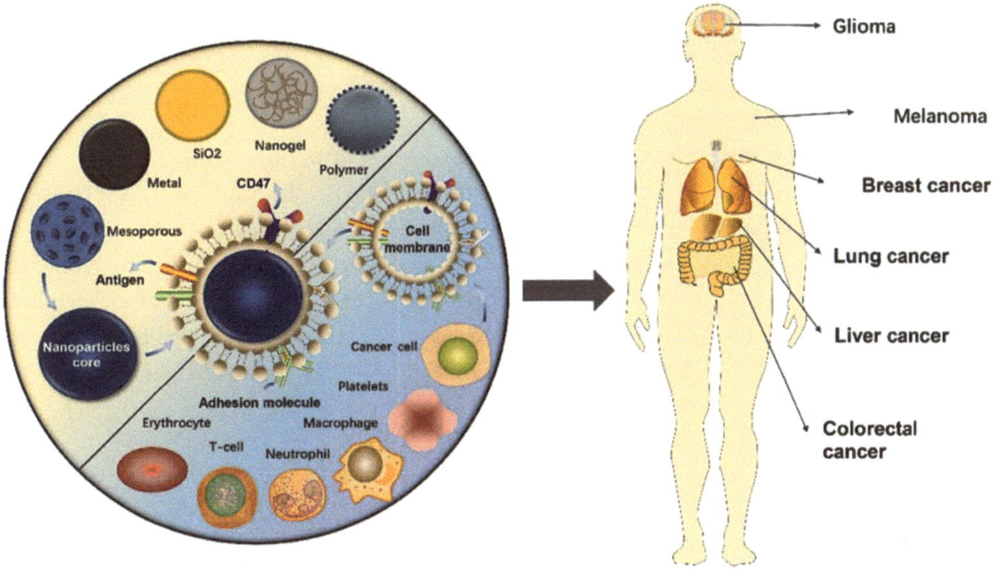

Figure 3.6 Nanoparticles with cell membrane coatings for cancer treatment. Cell membranes derived from various types of cells are employed to encapsulate the diverse nanoparticles. *Reproduced with permission from Dominik, B., Veronika, M., & James, B. B. (2021). Separation, characterization, and standardization of extracellular vesicles for drug delivery applications.* Advanced Drug Delivery Reviews, 174, *348–368. https://doi.org/10.1016/j.addr.2021.04.027. © 2021 The Author(s) CC BY 4.0.*

the process is different for prokaryotic and eukaryotic cells. The enucleated cells are immediately segregated from the blood, and the cell membranes detach from the mixture by centrifugation after the disintegration of the cells. Eukaryotic cells, such as cancerous cells, RBCs, and white blood cells, are lysed in a hypotonic solution initially, and their constituents are subsequently fully detached from the membrane using ultrasound technique. At last, by using high-speed differential centrifugation, pure cell membranes are removed. Extraction of membrane should be carried out in the controlled environment so that the proteins present on the cellular membrane retain their indigenous task (Zinger et al., 2021).

2. Merging of cell membrane with the NPs: The NPs are packed by the membrane in a variety of ways, all with the purpose of maintaining the integrity of the core. Fusion of the shell and the core is attained by exposing the proteins and orienting the membrane in the appropriate way for communication on the membrane. Initially, a physical extrusion process was used, in which the membrane structure can be destroyed by force, causing it to rupture and, thus, wrapping the NPs (Chen et al., 2021). Treatment with ultrasonic waves is also a viable option. Cellular membrane spontaneously rearranges on the NPs when subjected to ultrasonic energy. Ultrasonic therapy has the same outcome as that of physical thermos-formation, but

it utilizes a very small amount of the crude material and can be scaled up effortlessly, implying that the application possibilities are more promising (Fang et al., 2018).

Aside from intricate surface contacts, the shape and flexibility of cells like erythrocytes, leukocytes, and thrombocytes have an impact on their biological functions, which can be duplicated by NPs to mimic those functions (Hu et al., 2015). Researchers began to use a range of cell membranes to disguise NPs, such as the immune cell membrane, platelet membrane, and even cancer cell membrane, for varied application goals because the function of the cell membrane differs by cell type (CCM).To summarize, surface bioengineering combined with imitation of erythrocyte, leukocyte, or thrombocyte morphology appears to improve targeting efficacy compared to surface bioengineering alone (Copp et al., 2014; Zhang et al., 2022).

Polymer-based nanocarriers

Polymeric NPs are particularly interesting for cancer treatment because they can pass through cell membranes via endocytosis. Owing to smaller size of NPs, the cancer cells can internalize them than normal cells at an increased rate. The phenomenon has been frequently used in cancer therapy to selectively accumulate particles at tumor locations for passive targeted administration. To improve the effectiveness and disease specificity drugs, polymeric nanocarriers can be successfully fabricated with folates, peptides, and sugars that are cell specific for specific targeting at the cell. Because chemotherapeutic agents have low solubility and side effects, whereas biological compounds have good permeability, targeted delivery is critical for reducing adverse effects. The popularity of polymeric NPs has expanded substantially, prompting research in this field to improve their drug delivery factors, such as bioavailability, encapsulation, and side effects (Gu et al., 2021).

A group of polyesters known as polyhydroxyalkanoates (PHAs) that can be formed naturally by microorganisms in the presence of an unbalanced nutritional environment. PHA granules are commonly detected as insoluble spherical inclusions. They are made up of a polyester core and an outline of different proteins, or PHA granules. PHAs are known for their high biodegradability and biocompatibility, which makes them appealing for biomedical applications. NPs-based DDSs have benefited from their versatility. When compared to alternative polymeric materials, PHA-based delivery carriers have shown to have much improved encapsulation rates, distribution, and degradation products that are less toxic (Fan et al., 2017; Li and Loh).

PHA granules have been studied for therapeutic drug administration because of their ability to pass many barriers. Because the body rejects hydrophobic particles, it is only natural that the surfaces of many NPs can be modified with polymers showing affinity to water and even targeting ligands. NPs have a stronger affinity for cancerous locations due to the enhanced permeability and retention phenomenon, which is caused by increased intrusion into blood arteries and a lack of lymphatic drainage. Furthermore, the potential of PHA-based NPs to encapsulate highly toxic and poorly water-soluble cancer drugs is a significant aspect in their use (Masood, 2016).

Yao et al. used PHA granule−related amphiphilic proteins to establish receptor-mediated targeted DDS. They employed *Pichia pastoris* GS115 and *E. coli* BL21 (DE3) to express phasin P (PhaP) genes coupled with hAGP and hEGF ligands, respectively. The fusion proteins rhAGP−PhaP and rhEGF−PhaP were then purified and interacted with Rhodamine B isothiocyanate (RBITC)-containing PHA-NPs. During in vitro investigations, targeted tumor cells consumed a significant amount of ligand-containing PhaP−PHA NPs complexes. Furthermore, hEGF−PhaP−NPs containing RBITC suppressed the growth of cancer cells in a mice with promising findings (Danhier et al., 2012).

Controlled release technology (CRT) is used to keep a chemical from leaking out of a polymeric carrier device for as long as possible. The drug is frequently included into a polymer network that acts as a drug carrier in these devices. Since its discovery, when it was initially developed for oral sustained release drugs, this technique has been a success (Yao et al., 2008). The most well-known and commonly used polymer in (CRT) is poly-lactic-*co*-glycolic-acid (PLGA). Because it is biocompatible, biodegradable and has desirable release kinetics, this synthetic polymer has seen a lot of success, but it also has some stability issues for protein delivery. Earlier PLGA was used for surgical sutures, following their success in this area, their usage as polymeric biomaterials has grown. Since then, PLGA is the most successful and extensively researched polymer for use in CRT. Small molecule pharmaceuticals, peptides, and proteins, such as fertility regulating hormones, growth hormones, insulin, and vaccines, have all been released using PLGA. PLGA is very easy to process into injectable micro-/nano-spheres, compared to other members of the same family that have been studied for CRT (Langer & Peppas, 2006).

PLGA NPs studded were used for lung cancer treatment (anti-EGFR, cetuximab). The NPs-based formulation was found to have a high binding affinity for EGFR-expressing cells in A549-luc-C8 lung cancers. Furthermore, after intravenous administration, the proposed combination effectively reduced tumor growth in mice (SCID-bg) used for study with no accumulation or residual NPs at the site of action (Jain, 2000).

Physicochemical properties of nanocarriers for their use in targeted drug delivery systems

As previously mentioned, various forms of nanocarriers have been employed to efficiently carry drugs to their target areas. Several of these systems' features, such as surface charge, and size, were developed to give intended capabilities to improve encapsulated drugs' permeability and bioavailability.

Not only the size and overall surface area of NPs, but also the shape has an impact on NPs receptor engagement and protein adsorption. The shape of nanoformulation impacts biological effectiveness, such as volume of distribution, circulation stability, cell absorption, as well as transport features of nanocarriers, such as particle velocity, diffusion and adhesion to blood vessel walls, and contact with cells. Using an in vitro blood–brain barrier (BBB) model, several morphologies and surface properties of mesoporous silica nanocarriers were examined for drug carriers to the brain by Baghirov et al. In 100-nm region, uncoated and coated with a block copolymer (PEG–PEI) mesoporous silica nanocarriers were examined. When compared to uncoated particles, copolymer-coated nanocarriers had a more robust and reliable absorption (Karra et al., 2013).

Particle size is one of the most important factors to consider when building nanocarriers because it has a big impact on cellular absorption, biodistribution, and clearance. The permeability coefficient (P(app)) is used to determine the permeability of nanocarriers. Generally, the smaller the particle size of nanocarriers (less than 200 nm), the more efficient they are in crossing the barrier, although this must be reviewed on a situation basis because size affects drug encapsulation and release of drugs and must be tuned suitably. In a mouse model of orthotopic glioblastoma multiforme, the effect of the size of nanocarrier on fluorescence-labeled gold NP permeability across the blood–brain tumor barrier was examined. The smallest 10-nm nanocarriers were found throughout the brain tumor tissue, while the larger nanocarriers were found around blood vessels (Baghirov et al., 2016).

The elasticity of nanocarriers aids in their targeting, endocytosis, and phagocytosis processes. Because macrophages distort softer particles into geometries that are more difficult to ingest, softer particles remain in the blood for longer time and have higher organ deposition. Recent research has found that particle elasticity affects NP cell uptake, circulation, targeting ability, and biodistribution greatly. Furthermore, innovations in particle production have aided studies into the role of particle elasticity in regulating the efficacy of various drug delivery methods (Kang et al., 2019).

When nanocarriers are employed for drug delivery particle, size, shape, morphology, and drug release process all have an impact on therapeutic effectiveness. The efficiency of a delivery system is determined not only by its therapeutic constituent but also by its solubility and diffusion. Controlling the size of nanocarrier can thus be used to regulate therapeutic release rates. In general, smaller the size of the nanoparticle, the greater the surface area-to-volume ratio; hence, the majority of the drug is at or near the surface of NPs, resulting in quicker drug release. Larger particles, on the other hand, have larger cores, allowing for more drug encapsulation and long-term release. If medications are weakly attached to the surface of the nanocarrier, they may release as a burst followed by a persistent release profile. pH, temperature, solubility of the drug, diffusion through the matrix, template expansion and dissolution, nanocarriers interaction with biological systems, and a combination of these activities all affect drug release from nanoformulations. Furthermore, ionic interactions between the drug and the matrix of nanocarrier may limit or impede drug release (Myerson et al., 2016).

Plant protein–based nanocarriers for targeted drug delivery system

Zein is a plant protein (water insoluble) consisting of amino acids that are nonpolar, such as alanine, leucine, phenylalanine, and proline, generated from maize. It is classified as alpha, beta, and gamma based on its solubility. Due to its unique structure, they form globules and a many different forms in vivo; it has the ability to carry drug molecules while avoiding interactions with hydrophilic structures in the human body. Because its N-terminus interacts with the cell membrane, gamma form can deliver therapeutics through the cell membrane. Hydroxypropyl trimethyl ammonium chloride derivatized chitosan loaded in zein scaffold, which was incorporated with mesoporous silica SBA-15, and recombinant human bone morphogenetic protein-2 showed good inhibition against few bacterial strains.

Legumin is another group of plant proteins found in peas, which has shown good results in targeted DDSs especially for antitumor drugs. The solubility of these proteins is dependent on pH and ionic strength. Lectin is another group of glycoproteins used for drug delivery applications. Lectin NPs conjugates have shown good results in drug delivery applications. Use of these plant protein results in low toxicity, easy structural modifications, availability, and low-cost making them a suitable candidate for drug delivery applications (Karimi et al., 2016; Rizvi & Saleh, 2018).

Smart nanocarriers in clinical interventions and translation for targeted therapies or disease treatments

Smart nanocarrier systems that are engineered for precision applications with either encapsulated active agents or stimuli responsive drug carriers had a substantial progress in improving diagnosis and personalized treatment specifics. Smart nanocarriers are designed to address the significant limitations of biodistribution to miniscule barriers for targeting specific cells o organelles involved in the molecular or intracellular transport and, hence, can be effective to deliver drug components to the site of action. NPs can enhance stability and solubility of encapsulated components by improving safety and efficacy so that they can be transported across membranes with long circulation times (Khan et al., 2016). Even though extensive studies are being carried out in both in vitro and in animal models, their potential clinical application has barriers when comes to human translation. Some of the drawbacks being in understanding physiological and pathological heterogeneity that exist in humans as compared to animal models and, thus, influencing the efficacy of nanomedicines application in the body. To enhance the delivery of cargos or drugs, NPs are engineered with intricate architectures, bio-based and bio-responsive moieties, and targeting agents by controlled synthesis (Mitragotri et al., 2017). Smart nanocarriers designed for targeted delivery is to tackle the complex systems that can modify pathways, increase the therapeutic potential for specific macromolecules, intended to specific stages in cell cycle or to overcome drug resistance mechanisms. The opportunities for NP-based precision therapies in clinical translations are particularly studied for cancer nanomedicine immunotherapy and in vivo gene editing.

Lipid-based NPs are typical spheres one internal aqueous compartment surrounded by at least one lipid bilayer. Due to their efficiency to carry high payloads with a broad range of physicochemical features with advantages like simple formulation, self-assembly approaches a large number of lipid-based NPs are approved (Wagner et al., 2018; Zhou et al., 2018). In addition, first generation of nanocarrier therapeutics comprised lipid systems, for example, liposomes and micelles that are now approved by FDA (Ventola, 2017), and these can sometimes combine with organic (including polymeric micelles and vesicles, liposomes, dendrimers, and hydrogels) and inorganic (including quantum dots, gold, magnetic and mesoporous silica NPs) materials to improve drug delivery, or imaging and therapeutic functionalities. Smart nanocarriers can be engineered to alter the compositions, size, shapes, and various surface functionalization strategies like PEGylation, surface coating, and conjugation to arrive at desired properties (Patra et al., 2018b). To control and target drug delivery, stimuli-responsive DDS is offering promising approaches (Mitchell et al., 2021). For example, when DDS is directed, it activates the drug release and is modulated by the external action/stimuli to control the dose, duration, and target. Stimuli-activated drug release can be by physical means (magnetic, electric, ultrasound, temperature, and osmotic pressure) or by chemical means (e.g., change in pH, ionic strength, and glucose concentrations) and biological ways (enzymatic and endogenous receptor mediated) (Lopes et al., 2013; Zhou et al., 2018).

Conclusions and future prospects

Results have shown that nanocarrier-based targeted drug delivery reduces the possibility of drug resistance while also increasing drug solubility and stability, making formulation easier and less hazardous. They do not, however, prevent all side effects and have their own set of drawbacks, such as lack of targeting, time-consuming and complex production procedure, limited drug encapsulation efficiency, instability issues, and health and safety issues. In this regard, research work is going on in this field to overcome these drawbacks and to prevent the degradation of these drugs and improve its delivery and diffusion (Cheng et al., 2020).

Given the advantages of nanocarrier-based DDS and the large range of diseases that they potentially cure, particularly malignancies, there are currently very few drugs of this class in the market. Researchers are looking into new directions that have the potential to shift ideas or address this need. However, in most situations, in vivo and clinical investigations on innovative systems do not appear to be worthwhile. Clinical trials are almost exclusively focused on novel compounds, while those comparing components are few. Nanocarrier excipients like the types explored in this chapter will take time to find their way into clinics. Finally, while the pharmaceutical industry is responsible for developing new nanocarriers and pharmaceutical formulations, it must not lose sight of the primary goal of boosting bioavailability and efficacy while minimizing side effects. Building interdisciplinary teams made up of researchers with different points of view and experience working on different stages of innovative and design projects will aid in the development of carriers with a high potential for translation into clinics. There are very few success stories of promising preclinical techniques to clinical trials using nanocarriers-based targeted drug delivery for treatments. The delivery of minute doses of a therapeutic agent to the site of action, the limited selection of ligand—receptor interactions, the overexpression of targeted surface markers cells, the accumulation of NPs in nontargeted areas via extravasation, and nanotoxicology are all key aspects that must be considered during the development of targeted DDSs.

References

Agnese, B., Chiara, L., Selene, B., Lanfranco, B., Carlo, C., Paolo, B., & Luca, S. (2015). In vitro and in vivo toxicity evaluation of plant virus nanocarriers. *Colloids and Surfaces B: Biointerfaces*, *129*, 130—136. Available from https://doi.org/10.1016/j.colsurfb.2015.03.039.

Aixue, L., Yunan, Z., Yixiu, L., Liangdi, J., Yongwei, G., & Jiyong, L. (2021). Cell-derived biomimetic nanocarriers for targeted cancer therapy: Cell membranes and extracellular vesicles. *Drug Delivery*, *28*(1), 1237—1255. Available from https://doi.org/10.1080/10717544.2021.1938757.

Alberto, B., Roger, C.-G., & Lomonossoff George, P. (2020). High stability of plant-expressed virus-like particles of an insect virus in artificial gastric and intestinal fluids. *European Journal of Pharmaceutics and Biopharmaceutics*, *155*, 103—111. Available from https://doi.org/10.1016/j.ejpb.2020.08.012.

Alvandi, N., Rajabnejad, M., Taghvaei, Z., & Neda, E. (2022). New generation of viral nanoparticles for targeted drug delivery in cancer therapy. *Journal of Drug Targeting*, *30*, 151—165. Available from https://doi.org/10.1080/1061186X.2021.1949600.

Aminu, N., Bello, I., Umar, N. M., Tanko, N., Aminu, A. M., & Audu, M. M. (2020). The influence of nanoparticulate drug delivery systems in drug therapy. *ScienceDirect*. Available from https://doi.org/10.1016/j.jddst.2020.101961.

Aronson, A. I., & Fitz-James, P. (1976). Structure and morphogenesis of the bacterial spore coat. *Bacteriological Reviews*, *40*, 360—402.

Aschtgen, M. S., Lynch, J. B., Koch, E., Schwartzman, J., McFall-Ngai, M., & Ruby, E. (2016). Rotation of Vibrio fischeri flagella produces outer membrane vesicles that induce host development. *Journal of Bacteriology*, *198*, 2156—2165.

Baghirov, H., Karaman, D., Viitala, T., Duchanoy, A., Lou, Y. R., Mamaeva, V., Pryazhnikov, E., Khiroug, L., de Lange Davies, C., Sahlgren, C., & Rosenholm, J. M. (2016). Feasibility study of the permeability and uptake of mesoporous silica nanoparticles across the blood-brain barrier. *PLoS One, 11*, e0160705. Available from https://doi.org/10.1371/journal.pone.0160705.

Bitto, N.J., & Kaparakis-Liaskos, M. (2017). The therapeutic benefit of bacterial membrane vesicles. *MDPI.*

Bose, R. J., Kumar, U. S., Garcia-Marques, F., Zeng, Y., Habte, F., McCarthy, J. R., Pitteri, S., Massoud, T. F., & Paulmurugan, R. (2021). *Engineered cell-derived vesicles displaying targeting peptide and functionalized with nanocarriers for therapeutic microRNA delivery to triple-negative breast cancer in mice* (p. 2101387) *Wiley*. Available from https://doi.org/10.1002/adhm.202101387.

Brader, P., Stritzker, J., Riedl, C. C., Zanzonico, P., Cai, S., Burnazi, E. M., Ghani, E. R., Hricak, H., Szalay, A. A., Fong, Y., & Blasberg, R. (2008). *Escherichia coli* Nissle 1917 facilitates tumor detection by positron emission tomography and optical imaging. *American Association for Cancer Research, 14*, 2295–2302.

Bryant, C. N., Samantha, M., Ionita, C. G., Jennifer, C. J., Paul, C. D., Elzafir, E., Wyatt, N. V., & Lili, W. (2020). Measurement and standardization challenges for extracellular vesicle therapeutic delivery vectors. *Nanomedicine, 15*, 2149–2170. Available from https://doi.org/10.2217/nnm-2020-0206.

Casula, G., & Cutting, S. M. (2002). *Bacillus* probiotics: Spore germination in the gastrointestinal tract. *American Society for Microbiology., 68*, 2344–2352.

Chao, L., Haiyan, G., Peng, L., Jingyi, L., & Gang, L. (2017). *Extracellular vesicles as an efficient nanoplatform for the delivery of therapeutics* (13, pp. 2678–2687). Taylor & Francis, 11.

Chen, M., Cui, Y., Hao, W., Fan, Y., Zhang, J., Liu, Q., Jiang, M., Yang, Y., Wang, Y., & Gao, C. (2021). Ligand-modified homologous targeted cancer cell membrane biomimetic nanostructured lipid carriers for glioma therapy. *Drug Delivery, 28*(1), 2241–2255. Available from https://doi.org/10.1080/10717544.2021.1992038.

Chen, A., He, B., & Jin, H. (2022). *Isolation of extracellular vesicles from* Arabidopsis (2, p. e352). Wiley. Available from http://doi.org/10.1002/cpz1.352.

Cheng, Q., Wei, T., Farbiak, L., Johnson, L. T., Dilliard, S. A., & Siegwart, D. J. (2020). Selective organ targeting (SORT) nanoparticles for tissue-specific mRNA delivery and CRISPR–Cas gene editing. *Nature Nanotechnology, 15*, 313–320. Available from https://doi.org/10.1038/s41565-020-0669-6.

Chris, G., Dolores, D. V., Susmita, S., Clotilde, T., Kenneth, W. W., Marca, W., & Andrew, F. H. (2016). Techniques used for the isolation and characterization of extracellular vesicles: Results of a worldwide survey. *Journal of Extracellular Vesicles, 5*, 1. Available from https://doi.org/10.3402/jev.v5.32945.

Chung, Y. H., Cai, H., & Steinmetz, N. F. (2020). Viral nanoparticles for drug delivery, imaging, immunotherapy, and theranostic applications. *Advanced Drug Delivery Reviews, 156*, 214–235. Available from https://doi.org/10.1016/j.addr.2020.06.024.

Copp, J. A., Fang, R. H., Luk, B. T., Hu, C-M. J., Gao, W., Zhang, K., & Zhanga, L. (2014). Clearance of pathological antibodies using biomimetic nanoparticles. *Proceedings of the National Academy of Sciences of the United States of America, 111*, 13481–13486.

Cronin, M., Morrissey, D., Rajendran, S., El Mashad, S. M., van Sinderen, D., O'Sullivan, G. C., & Tangney, M. (2010). Orally administered bifidobacteria as vehicles for delivery of agents to systemic tumors. *Cell Press, 18*, 1397–1407.

Czapar, A. E., & Steinmetz, N. F. (2017). Plant viruses and bacteriophages for drug delivery in medicine and biotechnology. *Current Opinion in Chemical Biology, 38*, 108–116. Available from https://doi.org/10.1016/j.cbpa.2017.03.013.

Danhier, F., Ansorena, E., Silva, J. M., Coco, R., Breton, A. L., & Préat, V. (2012). *Journal of Controlled Release, 161*(2), 505–522.

Dasarat Rao Sawle Balaji, S. B., Deshpande Raghunandan, D. R. B. M., & Belawadi Krishnamurthy Prabhakar, V. A. (2008). Biosynthesis and stabilization of Au and Au–Ag alloy nanoparticles by fungus, *Fusarium semitectum*. *Science and Technology of Advanced Materials*. Available from https://doi.org/10.1088/1468-6996/9/3/035012.

Deun, J. V., Mestdagh, P., Sormunen, R., Cocquyt, V., Vermaelen, K., Vandesompele, J., Bracke, M., De Wever, O., & Hendrix, A. N. (2014). The impact of disparate isolation methods for extracellular vesicles on downstream RNA profiling. *Journal of Extracellular Vesicles*, *3*(1). Available from https://doi.org/10.3402/jev.v3.24858.

Dietrich, G., Bubert, A., Gentschev, I., Sokolovic, Z., Simm, A., Catic, A., Kaufmann, S. H., Hess, J., Szalay, A. A., & Goebel, W. (1998). Delivery of antigen-encoding plasmid DNA into the cytosol of macrophages by attenuated suicide *Listeria monocytogenes*. *Nature*, *16*, 181–185.

Dominik, B., Veronika, M., & James, B. B. (2021). Separation, characterization, and standardization of extracellular vesicles for drug delivery applications. *Advanced Drug Delivery Reviews*, *174*, 348–368. Available from https://doi.org/10.1016/j.addr.2021.04.027.

Duc, L. H., Hong, H. A., Fairweather, N., Ricca, E., & Cutting, S. M. (2003). Bacterial spores as vaccine vehicles. *Infection and Immunity.*, *71*, 2810–2818.

Duc, L. H., Hong, H. A., Uyen, N. Q., & Cutting, S. M. (2004). Immunogenicity and intracellular fate of *B. subtilis* spores. *Vaccine*, *22*, 1873–1885.

Eleni, D., Story Harriet, E., Robin, B., Hailes Helen, C., Tabor Alethea, B., & Xavier, G. J. (2019). American Chemical Society.

Errington, J. (1993). *Bacillus subtilis* sporulation: Regulation of gene expression and control of morphogenesis. *American Society for Microbiology*, *57*, 1–33.

Fan, X., Zhang, W., Hu, Z., & Li, Z. (2017). *Journal of Materials Chemistry B*, *5*, 1062. Available from https://doi.org/10.1039/C6TB02234K.

Fang, R. H., Kroll, A. V., Gao, W., & Zhang, L. (2018). Cell membrane coating nanotechnology. *Advanced Materials*, *30*, e1706759. Available from https://doi.org/10.1002/adma.201706759.

Fang, Z., Pan, S., Gao, P., Sheng, H., Li, L., Shi, L., Zhang, Y., & Cai, X. (2020). *Stimuli-responsive charge-reversal nano drug delivery system: The promising targeted carriers for tumor therapy* (575, p. 118841). Elsevier. Available from https://doi.org/10.1016/j.ijpharm.2019.118841.

Fathi, P., Rao, L., & Chen, X. (2021). Extracellular vesicle-coated nanoparticles. *View*, *2*, 20200187. Available from https://doi.org/10.1002/VIW.20200187.

Franco, M. B., Maria Lina, T., & Luigi, B. (2009). *Virus-like particle vaccines and adjuvants: The HPV paradigm* (8, pp. 1379–1398). Taylor & Francis, 10.

Fu, W., Lan, H., Li, S., Han, X., Gao, T., & Ren, D. (2008). Synergistic antitumor efficacy of suicide/ePNP gene and 6-methylpurine 2'-deoxyriboside via Salmonella against murine tumors. *Nature*, *15*, 474–484.

Gan, Y., Li, C., Peng, X., Wu, S., Li, Y., Tan, J. P. K., Yang, Y. Y., Yuan, P., & Ding, X. (2021). Fight bacteria with bacteria: Bacterial membrane vesicles as vaccines and delivery nanocarriers against bacterial infections. *Nanomedicine: Nanotechnology, Biology and Medicine*, *35*, 102398. Available from https://doi.org/10.1016/j.nano.2021.102398.

Gidwani, B., & Vyas, A. (2015). A comprehensive review on cyclodextrin-based carriers for delivery of chemotherapeutic cytotoxic anticancer drugs. *BioMed Research International*, *2015*. Available from https://doi.org/10.1155/2015/198268.

Gill, P. (2013). Nanocarriers, nanovaccines, and nanobacteria as nanobiotechnological concerns in modern vaccines. *Scientia Iranica*, *20*, 1003–1013. Available from https://doi.org/10.1016/j.scient.2013.05.012.

Gu, X., Gao, Y., Wang, P., Wang, L., Peng, H., He, Y., Liu, Y., & Feng, N. (2021). Nano-delivery systems focused on tumor microenvironment regulation and biomimetic strategies for treatment of breast cancer metastasis. *Journal of Controlled Release*, *333*, 374–390. Available from https://doi.org/10.1016/j.jconrel.2021.03.039.

Gurung, S., Perocheau, D., Touramanidou, L., & Baruteau, J. (2021). The exosome journey: From biogenesis to uptake and intracellular signalling. *Biomedical Central*, *19*, 47. Available from https://doi.org/10.1186/s12964-021-00730-1.

Gustafson, H. H., Holt-Casper, D., Grainger, D. W., & Ghandehari, H. (2015). Nanoparticle uptake: The phagocyte problem. *Nano Today*, *10*, 487–510. Available from https://doi.org/10.1016/j.nantod.2015.06.006.

Han, Y., Liu, W., Huang, J., Qiu, S., Zhong, H., Liu, D., Liu, J. (2018), *Hindawi*, *10*, 271.

Hoa, T. T., Duc, L. H., Isticato, R., Baccigalupi, L., Ricca, E., Van, P. H., & S.M. (2001). Cutting, Fate and dissemination of *Bacillus subtilis* spores in a murine model. *American Society for Microbiology*, *67*, 3819–3823.

Hu, C. M., Fang, R. H., Wang, K. C., Luk, B. T., Thamphiwatana, S., Dehaini, D., Nguyen, P., Angsantikul, P., Wen, C. H., Kroll, A. V., Carpenter, C., Ramesh, M., Qu, W., Patel, S. H., Zhu, J., Shi, W., Hofman, F. M., Chen, T. C., Gao, W., Zhang, K., Chien, S., & Zhang, L. (2015). Nanoparticle biointerfacing by platelet membrane cloaking. *Nature, 526*, 118–121. Available from https://doi.org/10.1038/nature15373.

Huang, X., Wang, X., Zhang, J., Xia, N., & Zhao, Q. (2017). *Escherichia coli*-derived virus-like particles in vaccine development. *NPJ Vaccines, 2*, 3. Available from https://doi.org/10.1038/s41541-017-0006-8.

Jain, R. A. (2000). The manufacturing techniques of various drug loaded biodegradable poly(lactide-*co*-glycolide) (PLGA) devices. *Biomaterials, 21*(23), 2475–2490. Available from https://doi.org/10.1016/s0142-9612(00)00115-0.

Kaiser, C. R., Flenniken, M. L., Gillitzer, E., Harmsen, A. L., Harmsen, A. G., Jutila, M. A., Douglas, T., & Young, M. J. (2007). *Biodistribution studies of protein cage nanoparticles demonstrate broad tissue distribution and rapid clearance in vivo*. Dove Medical Press.

Kang, J. H., Cho, J., & Ko, Y. T. (2019). Investigation on the effect of nanoparticle size on the blood-brain tumour barrier permeability by in situ perfusion via internal carotid artery in mice. *Journal of Drug Targeting, 27*(1), 103–110. Available from https://doi.org/10.1080/1061186X.2018.1497037.

Karimi, M., SahandiZangabad, P., Ghasemi, A., Amiri, M., Bahrami, M., Malekzad, H., Asl, H. G., Mahdieh, Z., Bozorgomid, M., Ghasemi, A., Boyuk, M. R. R. T., & Hambli, M. R. (2016). Temperature-responsive smart nanocarriers for delivery of therapeutic agents: Applications and recent advances. *ACS Applied Materials & Interfaces, 8*, 21107–21133. Available from https://doi.org/10.1021/acsami.6b00371.

Karra, N., Karra, N., Nassar, T., Ripin, A. N., Schwob, O., Borlak, J., & Benita, S. (2013). Antibody conjugated PLGA nanoparticles for targeted delivery ofpaclitaxel palmitate: Efficacy and biofate in a lung cancer mouse model. *Small (Weinheim an der Bergstrasse, Germany), 9*, 4221–4236.

Khan, H., Shukla, R. N., & Bajpai, A. K. (2016). Genipin-modified gelatine nanocarriers as swelling controlled drug delivery system for in vitro release of cytarabine. *Materials Science and Engineering C, 61*, 457–465. Available from https://doi.org/10.1016/j.msec.2015.12.085.

Kim, H., Choi, H., Bae, Y., & Kang, S. (2019). *Development of target-tunable P22 VLP-based delivery nanoplatforms using bacterial superglue* (116, pp. 2843–2851). Wiley. Available from https://doi.org/10.1002/bit.27129.

Kim, H. J., & Kim, H. J. (2017). Yeast as an expression system for producing virus-like particles: What factors do we need to consider? *Letters in Applied Microbiology, 64*, 111–123. Available from https://doi.org/10.1111/lam.12695.

Langer, R., & Peppas, N. (2006). Chemical and physical structure of polymers as carriers for controlled release of bioactive agents: A review. *Journal of Macromolecular Science, Part C: Polymer Reviews, 23*(1), 61–126. Available from https://doi.org/10.1080/07366578308079439.

Li, Z., & Loh, X.J. *Chemical Society Reviews, 44*, 2865. Available from https://doi.org/10.1039/C5CS00089K.

Li, S. R., Man, Q. W., Gao, X., Lin, H., Wang, J., Su, F. C., Wang, H. Q., Bu, L. L., Liu, B., & Chen, G. (2021b). Tissue-derived extracellular vesicles in cancers and non-cancer diseases: Present and future. *Journal of Extracellular Vesicles, 10*, e12175. Available from https://doi.org/10.1002/jev2.12175.

Li, Z., Wang, Y., Liu, J., Rawding, P., Bu, J., Hong, S., & Hu, Q. (2021a). Chemically and biologically engineered bacteria-based delivery systems for emerging diagnosis and advanced therapy. *Advanced Materials, 33*, 2102580.

Li, Z., Ye, E., David., Lakshminarayanan, R., & Loh, X. J. (2016). *Recent advances of using hybrid nanocarriers in remotely controlled therapeutic delivery*. Wiley. Available from https://doi.org/10.1002/smll.201601129.

Liu, H., Zhang, Q., Wang, S., Weng, W., Jing, Y., & Su, J. (2021). *Bacterial extracellular vesicles as bioactive nanocarriers for drug delivery: Advances and perspectives*. Elsevier. Available from https://doi.org/10.1016/j.bioactmat.2021.12.006.

Loftsson, T., Brewster, M. E., & Másson, M. (2004). *The American Journal of Drug Delivery, 2*, 261–275.

Lopes, J. R., Santos, G., Barata, P., Oliveira, R., & Lopes, C. M. (2013). Physical and chemical stimuli-responsive drug delivery systems: Targeted delivery and main routes of administration. *Current Pharmaceutical Design, 19*(41), 7169–7184. Available from https://doi.org/10.2174/13816128113199990698.

Madgula, K., & Sreenivas Puli, V. (2021). *Concept of nanomedicine in Bionanomaterials: Fundamentals and biomedical applications* (pp. 6-1–6-20). IOP Publishing Ltd. Available from https://www.researchgate.net/profile/Venkata-Sreenivas/publication/351591250_Bionanomaterials_Concept_of_nanomedicine/links/6112b1971e95fe241ac261d1/Bionanomaterials-Concept-of-nanomedicine.pdf.

Malhotra, S., Amin, Z. M., Dobhal, G., Cottam, S., Nann, T., & Goreham, R. V. (2021). *Novel devices for isolation and detection of bacterial and mammalian extracellular vesicles* (188, p. 139). Springer Nature. Available from https://doi.org/10.1007/s00604-021-04790-5.

Manolova, V., Flace, A., Bauer, M., Schwarz, K., Saudan, P., & Bachmann, M. (2008). Nanoparticles target distinct dendritic cell populations according to their size. *American Association of Immunologists, 38*, 1404–1413. Available from https://doi.org/10.1002/eji.200737984.

Maria, T. A., Tiina, Ö., Tuula, A. N., Saara, L., Mikaela, G., & Pia, R.-M. S. (2014). Isolation and characterization of platelet-derived extracellular vesicles. *Journal of Extracellular Vesicles, 3*, 1. Available from https://doi.org/10.3402/jev.v3.24692.

Masaaki, K., Masanori, M., & Hiroshi, H. (2013). *SV40 virus-like particles as an effective delivery system and its application to a vaccine carrier* (12, pp. 199–210). Taylor & Francis, 2.

Masarapu, H., Bindi, K. P., Chariou Paul, L., Hu, H., Gulati Neetu, M., Carpenter Bradley, L., Ghiladi Reza, A., Shukla, S., Steele, J. F. C., Peyret, H., Saunders, K., Castells-Graells, R., Marsian, J., Meshcheriakova, Y., & Lomonossoff, G. P. (2017). *Synthetic Plant Virology for Nanobiotechnology and Nanomedicine*. Wiley.

Masood, F. (2016). Polymeric nanoparticles for targeted drug delivery system for cancer therapy. *Materials Science and Engineering: C, 60*, 569–578. Available from https://doi.org/10.1016/j.msec.2015.11.067.

Mateu, M. G. (2016). Assembly, engineering and applications of virus based protein nanoparticles. *Advances in Experimental Medicine and Biology, 940*, 83–120. Available from https://doi.org/10.1007/978-3-319-39196-0_5.

Mitchell, M. J., Billingsley, M. M., Haley, R. M., Wechsler, M. E., Peppas, N. A., & Langer, R. (2021). Engineering precision nanoparticles for drug delivery. *Nature Reviews, Drug Discovery, 20*, 101–124. Available from https://doi.org/10.1038/s41573-020-0090-8.

Mitragotri, S., Lammers, T., Bae, Y. H., Schwendeman, S., De Smedt, S., Leroux, J. C., Peer, D., Kwon, I. C., Harashima, H., Kikuchi, A., Oh, Y. K., Torchilin, V., Hennink, W., Hanes, J., & Park, K. (2017). Drug delivery research for the future: Expanding the nano horizons and beyond. *Journal of Controlled Release: Official Journal of the Controlled Release Society, 246*, 183–184. Available from https://doi.org/10.1016/j.jconrel.2017.01.011.

Mohsen, M.O., Zha, L., Cabral-Miranda, G., & Bachmann, M.F. (2017). Major findings and recent advances in virus–like particle (VLP)-based vaccines. Seminars in Immunology, 34, 123–132, Available from https://doi.org/10.1586/erv.09.81.

Moloudizargari, M., Asghari, M. H., & Goel, A. (2021). The therapeutic triad of extracellular vesicles: As drug targets, as drugs, and as drug carriers. *Biochemical Pharmacology, 192*, 114714. Available from https://doi.org/10.1016/j.bcp.2021.114714.

Myerson, J. W., Anselmo, A. C., Liu, Y., Mitragotri, S., Eckmann, D. M., & Muzykantov, V. R. (2016). Non-affinity factors modulating vascular targeting of nano- and microcarriers. *Advanced Drug Delivery Reviews, 99*, 97–112. Available from https://doi.org/10.1016/j.addr.2015.10.011.

Nieuwland, R., Falcon-Perez, J. M., Soekmadji, C., Boilard, E., Carter, D., & Buzas, E. I. (2018). *Essentials of extracellular vesicles: Posters on basic and clinical aspects of extracellular vesicles* (7, p. 1548234). Wiley. Available from https://doi.org/10.1080/20013078.2018.1548234.

Nooraei, S., Bahrulolum, H., Hoseini, Z. S., Katalani, K., Hajizade, A., Easton, A. J., & Ahmadian, G. (2021). Virus-like particles: Preparation, immunogenicity and their roles as nanovaccines and drug nanocarriers. *Journal of Nanobiotechnology, 19*, 59. Available from https://doi.org/10.1186/s12951-021-00806-7.

Oggion, M. R., Ciabattini, A., Cuppone, A. M., & Pozzi, G. (2003). Bacillus spores for vaccine delivery. *Vaccine, 21*, S96–S101.

Pan, H., Zheng, M. B., Ma, A. Q., Liu, L. L., & Cai, L. T. (2021). Cell/bacteria-based bioactive materials for cancer immune modulation and precision therapy. *Advanced Materials, 33*, 2100241. Available from https://doi.org/10.1002/adma.202100241.

Papazoglou, E. S., & Parthasarathy, A. (2007). Bio nanotechnology synthesis lectures on biomedical engineering. *Morgan & Claypool*. Available from https://doi.org/10.2200/S00051ED1V01Y200610BME007.

Pariset, E., Agache, V., & Millet, A. (2017). *Extracellular vesicles: Isolation methods*, *1*, 1700040. Available from https://doi.org/10.1002/adbi.201700040.

Parveen, A., & Deshpande, R. (2018). *Phytotoxicity of nanoparticles nanobiotechnology in the health care: The game and the goal* (pp. 395–407). Cham: Springer. Available from https://doi.org/10.1007/978-3-319-76708-6.

Patra, J. K., Das, G., Fraceto, L. F., Campos, E. V. R., Rodriguez-Torres, M. d P., Acosta-Torres, L. S., Diaz-Torres, L. A., Grillo, R., Swamy, M. K., Sharma, S., Habtemariam, S., & Shin, H.-S. (2018b). Nano based drug delivery systems: Recent developments and future prospects. *Journal of Nanobiotechnology*, *16*(71), 1–33. Available from https://doi.org/10.1186/s12951-018-0392-8.

Patra, J. K., Das, G., Fraceto, L. F., Campos, E. V. R., del Pilar Rodriguez-Torres, M., Acosta-Torres, L. S., Diaz-Torres, L. A., Grillo, R., Kumara Swamy, M., Sharma, S., Habtemariam, S., & Shin, H.-S. (2018a). Nano based drug delivery systems: recent developments and future prospects. *Journal of Nanobiotechnology*, *16*(1). Available from https://doi.org/10.1186/s12951-018-0392-8.

Patras, L., Ionescu, A. E., Munteanu, C., Hajdu, R., Kosa, A., Porfire, A., Licarete, E., Rauca, V. F., Sesarman, A., Luput, L., Bulzu, P., Chiroi, P., Tranca, R. A., Meszaros, M.-S., Negrea, G., Barbu-Tudoran, L., Potara, M., Szedlacsek, S., & Banciu, M. (2022). Trojan horse treatment based on PEG-coated extracellular vesicles to deliver doxorubicin to melanoma *in vitro* and *in vivo*. *Cancer Biology & Therapy*, *23*, 1–16. Available from https://doi.org/10.1080/15384047.2021.2003656.

Pérez, J.M. M., & María, V.-R. (2021). GIBI. Bacteria and cells as "cabs" for drug-loaded nanoparticles. https://www.youtube.com/watch?v = Wsbcpt-cE3E.

Prasanna, P., Kumar, P., Kumar, S., Rajana, V. K., Kant, V., Prasad, S. R., Mohan, U., Ravichandiran, V., & Mandal, D. (2021). *Current status of nanoscale drug delivery and the future of nano-vaccine development for leishmaniasis – A review*. Elsevier.

Pushko, P., Pumpens, P., & Grens, E. (2013). Development of virus-like particle technology from small highly symmetric to large complex virus-like particle structures. *Intervirology*, *56*, 141–165. Available from https://doi.org/10.1159/000346773.

Rafaela, G.-Á., & María, V.-R. (2022). *Bacteria and cells as alternative nano-carriers for biomedical applications* (19, pp. 103–118). Taylor & Francis, 1.

Real, D. A., Bolaños, K., Priotti, J., Yutronic, N., Kogan, M. J., Sierpe, R., & Donoso-González, O. (2021). Cyclodextrin-modified nanomaterials for drug delivery: Classification and advances in controlled release and bioavailability. *MDPI*, *13*, 2131. Available from https://doi.org/10.3390/pharmaceutics13122131.

Rejeski, D., & Lekas, D. (2008). *Nanotechnology field observations: Scouting the new industrial west* (p. 16) Elsevier.

Ren, Y., Mu, Y., Jiang, L., Yu, H., Yang, S., Zhang, Y., Wang, J., Zhang, H., Sun, H., Xiao, C., Peng, H., Zhou, Y., & Lu, W. (2016). *Multifunctional TK-VLPs nanocarrier for tumor-targeted delivery* (502, pp. 249–257). Elsevier. Available from https://doi.org/10.1016/j.ijpharm.2016.02.037.

Rizvi, S. A. A., & Saleh, A. M. (2018). Applications of nanoparticle systems in drug delivery technology. *Saudi Pharmaceutical Journal*, *26*, 64–70. Available from https://doi.org/10.1016/j.jsps.2017.10.012.

Sadauskas, E., Wallin, H., Stoltenberg, M., Vogel, U., Doering, P., Larsen, L., & Danscher, G. (2007). Kupffercells are central in the removal of nanoparticles from the organism, Biomed Central. *Particle and Fibre Toxicology*, *4*, 1–7. Available from https://doi.org/10.1186/1743-8977-4-10.

Saha, G., Saudagar, P., & Dubey, V. K. (2020). Virus-like particles: Nano-carriers in targeted therapeutic. In *Encapsulation of Active Molecules and their Delivery System*, (pp. 197–210). Elsvier. Available from https://doi.org/10.1016/B978-0-12-819363-1.00012-0.

Sahu, T., Ratre, Y. K., Chauhan, S., Bhaskar, L. V. K. S., Nair, M. P., & Verma, H. K. (2021). Nanotechnology based drug delivery system. *ScienceDirect*. Available from https://doi.org/10.1016/j.jddst.2021.102487.

Shahgolzari, M., Dianat-Moghadam, H., & Fiering, S. (2021). *Multifunctional plant virus nanoparticles in the next generation of cancer immunotherapies*. Elsevier.

Shahgolzari, M., Pazhouhandeh, M., Milani, M., Yari Khosroushahi, A., & Fiering, S. (2020). *Plant viral nanoparticles for packaging and in vivo delivery of bioactive cargos*. Wiley.

Sharma, S., Masud, M. K., Kaneti, Y. V., Rewatkar, P., Koradia, A., Hossain, Md. S. A., Yamauchi, Y., Popat, A., & Salomon, C. (2021a). *Extracellular vesicle nanoarchitectonics for novel drug delivery applications* (17, p. 2102220). Wiley-VCH. Available from https://doi.org/10.1002/smll.202102220.

Sharma, S., Masud, M. K., Kaneti, Y. V., Rewatkar, P., Koradia, A., Hossain, M. S., Yusuke Yamauchi, A., Popat, A., & Salomon, C. (2021b). Extracellular vesicle nanoarchitectonics for novel drug delivery applications. *Small (Weinheim an der Bergstrasse, Germany)*, 2102220. Available from https://doi.org/10.1002/smll.202102220.

Shringirishi, M., Mahor, A., Gupta, R., Prajapati, S. K., Bansal, K., & Kesharwani, P. (2017). Fabrication and characterization of nifedipine loaded cyclodextrin nanosponges: An in vitro and in vivo evaluation. *Journal of Drug Delivery Science and Technology*, *41*, 344–350.

Siamak, A., Abolghasem, E., Abolfazl, B., Mohammad, A. R., & Yadollah, O. (2020). Bioengineered smart bacterial carriers for combinational targeted therapy of solid tumours. *Journal of Drug Targeting*, *28*, 700–713. Available from https://doi.org/10.1080/1061186X.2020.1737087.

Singh, P., Gonzalez, M. J., & Manchester, M. (2006). Viruses and their uses in nanotechnology. *Drug Development Research*, *67*, 23–41. Available from https://doi.org/10.1002/ddr.20064.

Solomon, B. J., Desai, J., Rosenthal, M., McArthur, G. A., Pattison, S. T., Pattison, S. L., MacDiarmid, J., Brahmbhatt, H., & Scott, A. M. (2015). A first-time-in-human phase I clinical trial of bispecific antibody-targeted, paclitaxel-packaged bacterial minicells. *PLoS One*, *10*, e0144559.

Soni, G., & Yadav, K. S. (2015). *Applications of nanoparticles in treatment and diagnosis of leukemia*. Elsevier.

Steele, J.F. C., Peyret, H., Saunders, K., Castells-Graells, R., Marsian, J., Meshcheriakova, Y., Lomonossoff, G.P. (2017). 9:e1447. Available from https://doi.org/10.1002/wnan.1447.

Steinmetz, N. F., & Mottle, P. (2017). Virus-like particles as nanocarriers for imaging reagents and drugs. *American Chemical Society*, *18*(12), 4141–4153. Available from https://doi.org/10.1021/acs.biomac.7b01196.

Suffian, I. F. B. M., & Al-Jamal, K. T. (2021). *Bioengineering of virus-like particles as dynamic nanocarriers for in vivo delivery and targeting to solid tumours* (180, p. 114030). Elsevier. Available from https://doi.org/10.1016/j.addr.2021.114030.

Sun, S., Shang, E., Ju, A., Li, Y., Wu, Q., Li, Q., Yang, Y., Guo, Y., Yang, D., & Shaowa, L. V. (2021). *Tumor-targeted hyaluronic acid-mPEG modified nanostructured lipid carriers for cantharidin delivery: An in vivo and in vitro study* (155, p. 105033). Elsevier. Available from https://doi.org/10.1016/j.fitote.2021.105033.

Suri, S. S., Fenniri, H., & Singh, B. (2007). *Nanotechnology-based drug delivery systems*. Springer nature.

Syomin, B. V., & Ilyin, Y. V. (2019). *Virus-like particles as an instrument of vaccine production*. Springer. Available from https://doi.org/10.1134/S0026893319030154.

Szejtli, J. (2004). Past, present, and future of cyclodextrin research. *Pure and Applied Chemistry. Chimie Pure et Appliquee*, *76*, 1825–1845. Available from https://doi.org/10.1351/pac200476101825.

Tiwari, G., Tiwari, R., Srivastava, B., Bhati, L., Pandey, S., Pandey, P., & Bannerjee, S. K. (2012). Drug delivery systems: An updated review. *International Journal of Pharmaceutical Investigation*, *2*, 2. Available from https://doi.org/10.4103/2230-973X.96920.

Trucillo, P., Ferrari, P. F., Campardelli, R., Reverchon, E., & Perego, P. (2020). *The Journal of Supercritical Fluids*. Elsevier.

Ventola, C. L. (2017). Progress in nanomedicine: Approved and investigational nanodrugs. *Pharmacy and Therapeutics*, *42*, 742–755.

Wagner, A. M., Gran, M. P., & Peppas, N. A. (2018). Designing the new generation of intelligent biocompatible carriers for protein and peptide delivery. *Acta Pharmaceutica Sinica B*, *8*, 147–164. Available from https://doi.org/10.1016/j.apsb.2018.01.013.

Webster, T. J., Waid, M. C., McKenzie, J. L., Price, R. L., & Ejiofor, J. U. (2004). *Nanotechnology*, *15*.

Wen, A. M., Cho, C. F., Lewis, J. D., & Steinmetz, N. F. (2015). *The application of plant viral nanoparticles in tissue-specific imaging. Nanotechnology for biomedical imaging and diagnostics: From nanoparticle design to clinical applications* (1st edition). Wiley.

Wen, A. M., & Steinmetz, N. F. (2016). Design of virus-based nanomaterials for medicine. *Biotechnology, and Energy*, *45*, 4074–4126. Available from https://doi.org/10.1039/C5CS00287G.

Wu, A. Y., Ueda, K., & Lai, C. P. (2019). *Proteomic analysis of extracellular vesicles for cancer diagnostics* (19, p. 1800162). Elsevier. Available from https://doi.org/10.1002/pmic.201800162.

Wu, C. Y., Yeh, Y. C., Yang, Y. C., Chou, C., Liu, M. T., Wu, H. S., Chan, J. T., & Hsiao, P. W. (2010). Mammalian expression of virus-like particles for advanced mimicry of authentic influenza virus. *PLos One*, *5*, e9784. Available from https://doi.org/10.1371/journal.pone.0009784.

Xian, J. L., & Jun, L. (2007). *Biodegradable thermosensitive copolymer hydrogels for drug delivery*. Taylor and Francis. Available from https://doi.org/10.1517/13543776.17.8.965.

Yao, Y.-C., Zhan, X.-Y., Zhang, J., Zou, X.-H., Wang, Z.-H., Xiong, Y.-C., Chen, J., & Chen, G.-Q. (2008). A specific drug targeting system based on polyhydroxyalkanoate granule binding protein PhaP fused with targeted cell ligands. *Biomaterials*, *29*, 4823–4830. Available from https://doi.org/10.1016/j.biomaterials.2008.09.008.

Yuan, F., Li, Y.-M., & Wang, Z. (2021). Preserving extracellular vesicles for biomedical applications: Consideration of storage stability before and after isolation. *DrugDelivery*, *28*, 1501–1509. Available from https://doi.org/10.1080/10717544.2021.1951896.

Zhang, W., Zhao, M., Gao, Y., Cheng, X., Liu, X., Tang, S., Peng, Y., Wang, N., Hu, D., Peng, H., Zhang, J., & Wang, Q. (2022). Biomimetic erythrocytes engineered drug delivery for cancer therapy. *Chemical Engineering Journal*, *433*, 133498. Available from https://doi.org/10.1016/j.cej.2021.133498.

Zhang, X., Zhang, X., Wu, Z., Gao, X., Cheng, C., Wang, Z., & Li, C., Xuejiao Zhang, Xinge Zhang, Zhongming Wu, Xiujun Gao, Cui Cheng, Zhen Wang, Chaoxing Li. (2011). A hydrotropic β-cyclodextrin grafted hyperbranched polyglycerol co-polymer for hydrophobic drug delivery. *Acta Biomaterialia*, 7, 585–592.

Zhou, J., Wang, M., Ying, H., Su, D., Zhang, H., Lu, G., & Chen, J. (2018). Extracellular matrix component shelled nanoparticles as dual enzyme-responsive drug delivery vehicles for cancer therapy. *ACS Biomaterials Science & Engineering*, *4*, 2404–2411. Available from https://doi.org/10.1021/acsbiomaterials.8b00327.

Zidan, M. F., Ibrahim, H. M., Afouna, M. I., & Ibrahim, E. A. (2018). In vitro and in vivo evaluation of cyclodextrin-based nanosponges for enhancing oral bioavailability of atorvastatin calcium. *Drug Development and Industrial Pharmacy*, *44*, 1243–1253. Available from https://doi.org/10.1080/03639045.2018.1442844.

Zinger, A., Cooke, J. P., & Taraballi, F. (2021). Biomimetic nano drug delivery carriers for treating cardiovascular diseases. *Nanomedicine: Nanotechnology, Biology and Medicine*, *33*, 102360. Available from https://doi.org/10.1016/j.nano.2021.102360.

Zovinka Edward, P., & Stock Anne, E. (2010). 87 American Chemical Society, United States.

CHAPTER 4

Nanomedicine and nanocarriers for cancer treatment

Arunadevi Natarajan and Suyambulingam Jone Kirubavathy
Department of Chemistry, PSGR Krishnammal College for Women, Coimbatore, India

Introduction

Cancer is the disease in which cell multiples uncontrollably and spread throughout the body. It is kind of genetic disease and triggered by development of cell divisions and variations which controls all our body functioning Fig. 4.1. This genetic disease may be due to damage in DNA, inherited from ancestor and error in cell division. Generally, human body has tendency to eliminate the damaged DNA at earlier ages but the removal rate is slow for aged people, thereby the cell multiples at faster rate Fig. 4.2.

It is very dangerous disease in current century, and millions of people died every year with severe symptoms like abnormal weight loss, extended cough, and change in bowel movements. The statistics shows the cancer incidence for new cases are is 442.4/100,000 people per year (Bharali & Mousa, 2010). Cancer, a malignant tumor has been mediated by numerous methods depending on type of cancer and level of spreading in the body Fig. 4.3. Instead of single treatment, the combined treatment like radiation therapy with chemotherapy will be positive solution to this carcinodes. Different types of treatments in practical use are as follows:

1. Biomarker testing
2. Chemotherapy—uses chemical drugs to kill cells
3. Hormone therapy—stops development of prostate cancer
4. Immune therapy—by heating the body tissue to higher temperature to kill the cells
5. Photodynamic therapy—uses activated light
6. Targeted therapy—concentrating and giving treatment only to cancer cells
7. Radiation therapy—uses high energy radiation
8. Surgery—removes affected organs/area
9. Stem cell transport—restoration of stem cells.

Nanotechnology for Drug Delivery and Pharmaceuticals
DOI: https://doi.org/10.1016/B978-0-323-95325-2.00001-8

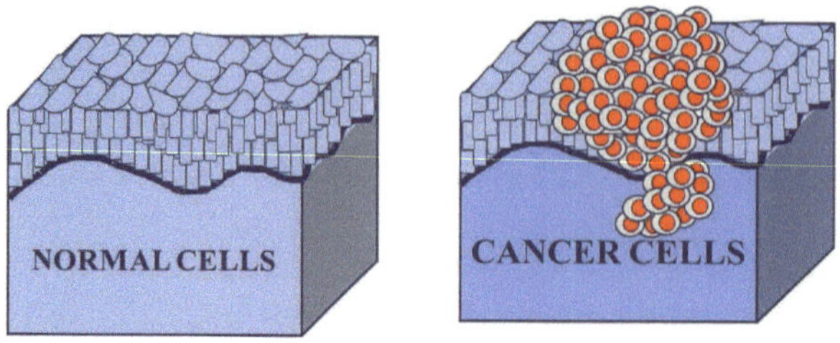

Figure 4.1 Pictorial image of normal cells and cancer cells.

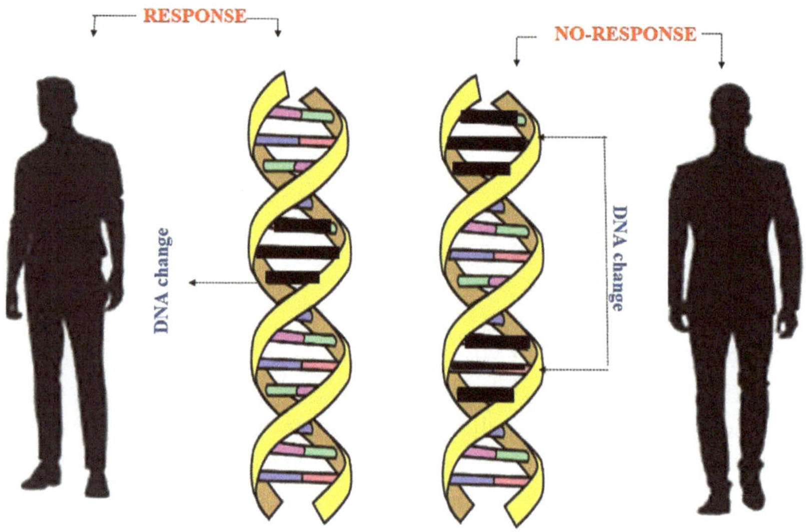

Figure 4.2 DNA change in young and aged person.

All the abovementioned treatments affect the healthy organs and causes constipation, hair loss, anemia, vitamin deficiency, memory loss, vomiting, incurable throat infections, urinary and sleep problems (Jabir et al., 2012).

The research on carcinogen cells makes us to recognize how the cell multiplication process takes place and issues responsible for this disease and thereby helps to prevent and treat in advanced manner. Different approaches used are given in Table 4.1.

Due to complication in genetic levels, the treatment has medical diverseness and curative resistance. All the approaches are good for the treatment of certain type of cancer cells but it has limitations and accompanied with severe side effects. Major reason is non-existence of anticancer drugs for precise delivery. The use of antineoplastic drugs leads to long-term side effects like nerve disorder, lung damage, and heart problems. Hence, the only therapy which helps to overcome the carcinogens is targeted delivery system.

Figure 4.3 Main causes for cancer.

Table 4.1 Different approaches used in cancer cell.

S. no.	Approaches used	Examples	Outcomes
1	Basic cancer cell biology	Study on genes and their interactions	Propose the mechanism physically, chemically, or biologically
2	Genetic analysis	Exome sequencing	Study the genetic change
3	Epidemiological analysis	Cohort study, genomic study	Identify the cause and risk pattern in huge population

Nanotechnology in cancer therapy

Cancer therapies currently in usage are surgical treatment, radiation therapy, and chemotherapy. These approaches have high possibility to affect healthy DNA Fig. 4.4 or partial suppression of damaged cells. Nanotechnology provides a new pathway of direct and targeted therapy to carcinogens and neoplasms. It is purposefully used to recognize the carcinogenic cell, since different cell tissues possess similar properties. This permits the targeted drugs to reach the damaged cells without disturbing the healthier one. The use of nanocarriers will improve therapeutic index of radiation therapy and other treatments procedures, circulation of drugs and thereby increases the efficiency of regimens.

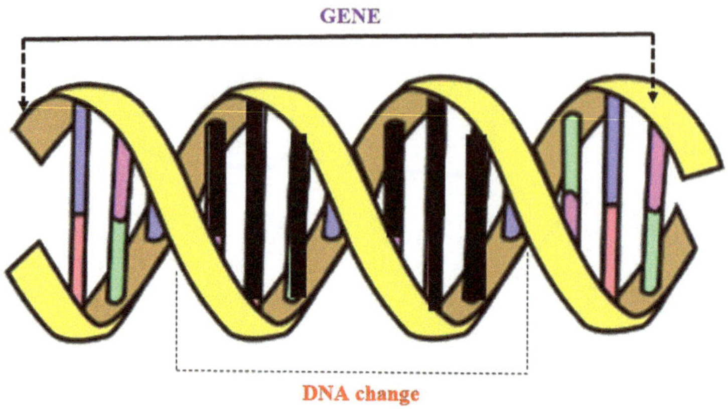

Figure 4.4 DNA change in cancer cells.

In addition to that, it has high carrier capacity, reduced side effects, enhanced targeting ability, and improved pharma physical properties (Aslan et al., 2013). As a whole, this technology will suppress the risk and enhance the life time of the patients. Apart from the creation of new drug delivery (DD) system, nanotechnology develops new therapeutics with the help of extraordinary properties of nanomaterials. Though the size of the nanocarriers is less than cells, it has capacity to encapsulate the carcinogens quickly to avoid multiplication. In addition to that, nanoparticles (NPs) coordinate with metal ions, ligands like aptamers, amino acids, proteins, and antibodies due to its bulky surface area. These properties facilitate combined modality treatment like diagnostic and DD in single therapeutic named "theranostic," action. Theranostic NPs are well intended for targeted preventive medicine by merging diagnostic and therapeutic applications into unique NP platform.

Advanced development of biocompatible NP composites and therapeutic constituents explores a wider range of active medicines to enhance the pharmokinetic properties. The addition of various cargo compounds, surface modification, and surface coatings will modify immune response in order to enhance the life period of NPs and thereby increases effectiveness and precision of DD to target areas. The surface variations will develop "sneaking" NPs that are very active, precise targeting nature, and superfluous functionality. These advantages can be accomplished only by the modification of NPs with proteins, cell membrane coatings, and carbohydrates (Malachowski & Hassel, 2020).

Nanomedicines for cancer treatment

The practice of nanotechnology/nanocarriers for diagnosis and therapeutic use of carcinogens is yet in developing stage. Even though, in commercial market, nano-based drugs are available for medical trials. The practice of nanotechnology in medicinal field comprises the usage of apparent engineered constituents for the development of advanced therapies

Table 4.2 Nanotechnology-based drug therapies.

S. No.	Name of the drug	Nanoparticle	Type of cancer
1	Abraxane (paclitaxel)	Nanoparticle-bound albumin	Breast and lung cancer
2	DepoCyt (cytosine arabinoside)	Liposome	Acute myeloid leukemia
3	Lipodox (doxorubicin)	Liposome encapsulated doxorubicin	Breast and lung cancer
4	Genexol-PM	Polymeric micelle	Breast cancer
5	Myocet	Liposomal, in combination with cyclophosphamide	Metastatic breast cancer
6	Doxil (adriamycin)	Encapsulated in a closed lipid sphere	Bladder cancer, ovarian cancer, and acute lymphocytic leukemia
7	Nanotherm	Iron oxide nanoparticle	Solid tumors
8	Mepact	Activates white blood cells	Osteosarcoma
9	Marqibo (eurocristine)	Sulfate-based chromosome	Hodgkin's disease and lung cancer
10	Onivyde (camptosar)	Liposome	Colon cancer and lung cancer

and medicinal devices with good efficacy and reduced toxicity. The consequences of nanotechnology in cancer treatment may lead to earlier detection, prevention, and treatment. Doxil and Abraxane are the first nanotechnology-based carrier drugs under regulatory bodies. In recent decades, many Investigational New Drugs has approved for nano-coatings, nano-formulations, and preclinical trials for several cancer types. The few permitted nanotechnology-based drug therapies are presented in Table 4.2.

he NPs actively accumulate in cancer cells due to hypervasculature, penetrability to macromolecules, and recovery through lymphatic vessels. This kind of accumulation is seen after intravenous (IV) injection of NPs. Tumor blood vessels are entirely varied from normal one by having irregular structure and functions. These abnormalities have greater penetrability for macromolecules and named as "Enhanced permeability and retention—EPR." This consequence, associated with the transfer of macromolecular nanocarriers like lipid, macro polymers, and liposomes into the damaged DNA, is the trademark of tumor vasculature. This kind of macromolecular compounds is thus superlative for targeted DD system (Maeda et al., 2006). Enhanced efficiency and lower side effects are added advantages for EPR phenomenon.

In addition to tumor vasculature, the potential nanomedicine targets are metastatic cells and stroma. Targeted tumor-associated macrophages (TAMs) will develop immunosuppressant tumor microenvironment by triggering immune proteins. TAMs are more precise method because of the availability of macrophages and it is considered a distinctive method for more aggressive carcinogens (Anchordoquy et al., 2017). Information about the addition of a macrophage-exhausting drug (alendronate) in doxorubicin liposomes significantly improved healing properties in immunocompetent with targeted macrophages (Shmeeda et al., 2016).

Nanotechnology to nanomedicine

To quicken the conflict on cancer treatment, the National Cancer Institute was introduced for the Association for Nanotechnology in Cancer in the year 2004. Huge research funding was allocated for the advanced enhancement of innovative nanotechnologies to minimize the cancer mortality rate. Merging of nanotechnology with drugs or medicine newly led to an interdisciplinary field for researches. Nanomedicinal field collectively brings researchers from physics, chemistry, biotechnology, and engineering to develop or design the instruments for the earlier detection and treatment for cancer. Significant developments in targeted DD (Butcher et al., 2016), tissue regeneration (Bayford et al., 2017; Johari et al., 2016), and therapeutic treatment (Kargozar et al., 2018; Samadikuchaksaraei, 2001) have been taken as nanotechnology achievements in medicinal field. Around 50 nanomedicines was approved and numerous nanocarriers are in clinical trials. Almost all nanomedicines are the combination of polymer composites, liposomes, and nanomaterials. But special consideration has been given to construct more multifaceted materials containing micelles, NPs with protein, and inorganic and metallic compounds (Dobrovolskaia, 2015).

Traditionally, gene transfer can be done physically, chemically, and virally. With the help of nanotechnology and NPs, it is very convenient to deliver biomolecules like DNA and protein. A huge variety of nanocarriers are used for gene delivery process like lipid based, polymer based, inorganic particles, nanocrystals, nanofibers, and nanospheres. Amongst these nanomaterials-based gene delivery systems, the targeted kinds of drugs are more challenging one due to their maintenance of gene delivery properties in DNA-affected tissues (Riley & Vermerris, 2017). Though there is more necessity for treatment of genetic and tumor diseases with the help of NP-based gene delivery system, FDA was not approved any gene delivery system due to extended toxicity and less efficiency in gene transfection.

The important factor in diagnosis and treatment of tumor cells is high resolution images of repaired DNA moiety. Based on this numerous imaging techniques was developed in past decades, which includes X-ray, MRI, and nuclear medicine imaging systems. Advanced molecular imaging requires sophisticated probes to detect biochemical and cellular process. Gadolinium complexes, iron oxide, and gold NPs are considered more prominent MRI contrast agents due to its exceptional light scattering patterns, improved image contrast, facile surface modification, and high payloads (Bharali & Mousa, 2010).

They have been used to detect blood leakage in brain and to study flow dynamics. Clinically proven MRI contrast agent is Ferumoxytol, at the same time it is used for the anemia treatment. But the contrast effectiveness of this Fe-based NPs is below optimal level because of size and crystallinity (Lu et al., 2010).

Emerging vaccine nanotechnology

In 1798, Dr. Edward J. laid the foundation for vaccine world for the small pox treatment. Deprived of vaccines, all the disease will create side effects, and thus the invention of vaccine has created extraordinary breakthrough in medical field, since they connect immune system with pathogens. Recent vaccines successively work with two essential mechanisms that kindle active immunes toward pathogens and deliver immunity to already existing antibodies. During the pandemic period (COVID-19), vaccination is the only efficient treatment that fights against virus. For vaccine technology, a promising factor is proper deliver of antigen to the target area in immune system. Antigen delivery process comprises spatiotemporal relations of cells like T cells, macrophages, and B-cells. Moreover, these types of interactions will take place at particular location further confuses the antigen delivery. Thus, numerous challenging approaches have been applied to construct and design nano vaccines, like crossing the biological barrier, the controlled release of antigen, and cross-presentation. The key factor in vaccination technology is extended persistence or degradation of antigen within shorter duration will improve immune response. Hence, researchers in nanocarriers field were dedicated to increase the extended persistence of antigens at the affected DNA sites, either by conjugating/encapsulating the target antigens in NPs (Moon et al., 2012).

Many viruses and bacteria have similar structures, and this should be considered while designing vaccine. It is proven that multivalency effect provokes a protective humoral and cellular immune response in self-assembled polycomposite NPs, and other polyvalent assemblies. Furthermost promisingly, nanotechnology/nanomedicine has an complete benefit in employing antigen density and structural orientation, thereby leads a new eyeopener for exploring the multivalency mechanism. The various types of nanomaterial-based vaccine is shown in Fig. 4.5.

In addition to the process of designing nanocarriers, the growth of new, innovative immunogens is much needed for infectious diseases, whereas for carcinogenic treatment, the designed nano vaccines should be safety, enhanced targeting capacity, and effective vaccination stream is vibrant for treatment. Immunogenicity and harmfulness are main problems regarding protection of nano vaccine. Once the vaccine is administrated, NPs will stimulate the immune response (Feng et al., 2022).

Patient-centric therapy for cancer treatment is one of the major tasks in clinical field. Combining one or more therapy has more outcome and advantageous. Basically, the drugs are classified into immuno, chemo, and hormonal therapy Fig. 4.6.

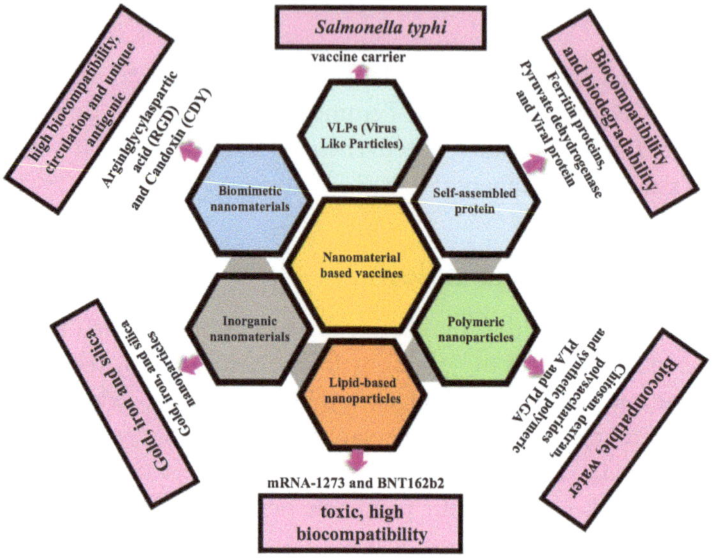

Figure 4.5 Nanomaterial-based vaccines.

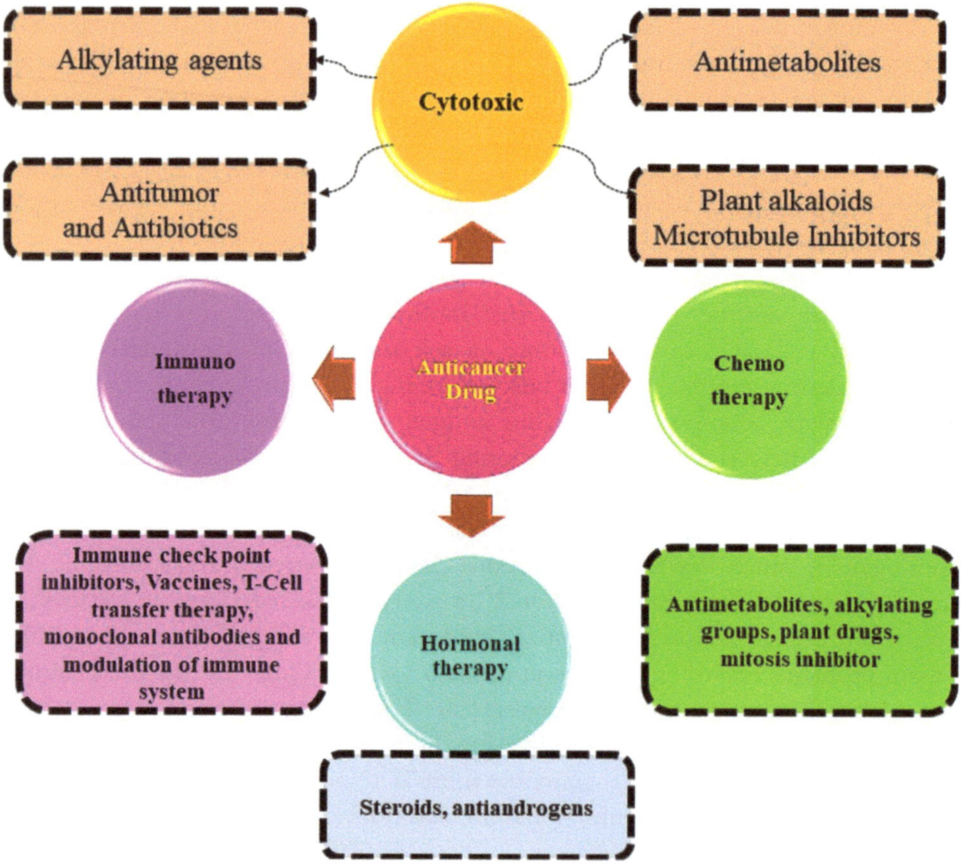

Figure 4.6 Classification of anticancer drugs.

1. Immunotherapy—Immune check point inhibitors, vaccines, T-Cell transfer therapy, monoclonal antibodies, and modulation of immune system
2. Chemotherapy—Antimetabolites, alkylating groups, plant drugs, mitosis inhibitor
3. Hormonal therapy—Steroids, antiandrogens.

In the mechanism of anticancer drug, the resistance between immune, and nonimmune, host cell plays a foremost role. At different growth stages, the normal interactions between the cells will be altered by tumor cells (Krutovskikh, 2002). The homeostasis, self-regulatory process among host cells, and tumor cells might be changed by drugs. All anticancer drugs fight against tumor cells and immune system but few noncytotoxic drugs will modify the reaction between drugs and host and tumor cells. Based on this, Xiong-Zhi Wu et al. (Wu, 2006) made a novel category that depends on drugs and modifiers. Modifiers are again classified into (1) cell biological modifier, (2) biological response modifier, and (3) biochemical modifier.

Cell biological modifier has tendency to converse the biological behavior of carcinogenic cells. Example, Gleevec drug. Biological response modifier controls the host cell by edged effects, namely, suppression and progression by mutagenesis. Example, osteoprotogerin drugs. Biochemical modulator can improve the healing action and decrease the opposing effect by altering metabolic pathway of anticancer drugs. Main clusters of this class are chemo sensitizer and chemo protectant. Example, calcium folinate, daxrazoxane, and uracil-based drugs.

Enhancing drug delivery to the tumor

In usual conventional methods the anticancer drugs will distribute uniformly to both affected and healthier cells. Encapsulation of drugs in NPs/nanocarriers will have more enhanced transfer of therapeutic agents to carcinogenic cells without affecting healthy cells (Decuzzi, 2016). In addition, the encapsulation method has additional advantages like remarkable permeability and retention. The efficacy of the particular DD to the patients depends on penetrating capacity of NP into the carcinogenic cells, their interaction and cell affinity, and time to time drug release. But recent advancement in NPs requires a lot of manufacturing, safety and physiological barriers to be appreciated like opsonization, immune system and side effects. The smart DD system has excellent properties like enhanced activity, minimized side effects and has targeted delivery. This type of drugs depends mainly on physiochemical changes between normal and affected cells, reactivity of functional groups. The mechanism of DD includes adsorption, chemical reaction, bond breakage, and transfer of anticancer drug to affected cells. Combination of multifunctional molecules in a single carrier and even more sophisticated anticancer drugs can also be fabricated nowadays.

Multifunctional nanomedicines display excellent actions at biological atmospheres. It is recognized that nanocarriers after injecting into patient body usually involves five steps Fig. 4.7, namely, mixing in blood, accumulation, tissue penetration, cellular

Figure 4.7 Biological actions of nanocarriers in cancer cells.

internalization, and finally, intracellular drug release (Sun et al., 2017). All steps require specific properties, and DDs should be firm enough to clasp the drugs strongly till the drugs should be released to target moiety. The specific properties of DD system includes hydrophilic nature and neutral charge for extended time period, and the target moiety should be protected throughout the circulation, whereas at tumor spot, the ligands should be exposed to enable the binding between ligands and cells. The size of nanocarriers should be roughly around 100 nm for active agglomeration, but it should be less than 30 nm for penetration. Sequential variation of many stimuli moiety into a single nanocarrier can encourage advanced response of the carriers to diverse cancer cells. Therefore, a rational association of numerous groups to engineer the novel, a multitargeting carrier, will respond many tumor sites and lead to real-time self-controlled anticancer drug release at the target location with an accurate concentration.

Principles involved in the development of nanomedicine

All nanomedicines have capacity to overcome the difficulty raised during solubility and stability than compared to traditional therapeutic agents. Due to their deprived water solubility nature, the commercial availability of drugs was limited in earlier decades (Gao & Hu, 2010; Wicki et al., 2015). The fundamental issues to be addressed before the commercialization of nanomedicines are

1. Many drugs development was stopped due to its solubility issue and chemical instability. This limitation was overcome by synthesizing the anticancer drug in hydrophilic environment, which will also increase the chemical stability. Lipid-based, albumin-based nanocarriers have tendency to enhance the stability and pharmacokinetic properties of drugs (Karve et al., 2012; Minchinton & Tannock, 2006).
2. Secondly, nanocarriers have ability to protect the drugs from deprivation or removal of drugs through deprivation and, thus, increase its reactivity. This can be

attained by the encapsulation of anticancer drugs with nanomedicines or linking biodegradable composites to biologically synthesized polymers.

3. In addition to that, targeting and circulation of anticancer drugs to the blood stream was increased with the help of nanotechnology. The penetrating capacity of drug depends on functional groups, and it varies from drug to drug. Owing to this, design of nanodrugs should be based on its penetration and its reactivity toward target molecule (Rasool et al., 2022).
4. Nanomedicines should be designed in such a way that it should have immediate response on triggering. Trigging process may include change in pH, temperature, and pressure. In general, nanotechnology-based medicines have extended circulation of drug along with drug release, which may lead to less resistance of carcinogenic cells toward nanodrugs.

Opportunities: advanced functionalities

In traditional based therapeutic for cancer treatment, there will equal benefits and ill effects to the patients. The purpose of nanocarriers/medicines should move this equilibrium to more benefits. The improvement in the anticancer drugs are deliberated below:

1. Passive targeting tumor cell
2. Active targeting toward the cancer cells
3. Stimulation of active nanocarriers relief on internal or external triggers by loading
   Tumor endothelium
   Nanocarriers ligand-modified
   There are trio strategies of doxorubicin encumbered liposomes were illustrated.

1. Radiolabeled liposomes in tumor cell to increase the long-circulating, such as Doxil tissue, which produce the leaky vasculature like face and arm.
2. EGFR (Epidermal Growth Factor Receptor) is an active targeting drug on the cancer cell on PEGylated liposomal Doxorubicin (PLD).
3. Waterfall plot represent the modification in the size of tumor patient after treating with the ant-EGFR-ILs is a clinical trial.
4. Intervascular relief from doxorubicin red from thermosensitive liposomes corresponds to the thermodox ensuing on mild hyperthermia (+HT), which was injected on nude mice. The releasing of drug was detected using the intravital confocal microscopy (Mamot et al., 2012).

Tumor targeting via enhanced permeability and retention

The EPR effect was first exposed by Maeda and their team in tumors. The mechanisms of injection of NPs along with anticancer drugs was difficult process, the healthier cells around the tumor cells acts as carrier and transport the drugs to tumor cells. EPR-assisted tumor accumulation is expected to result from lengthier NPs with a high hydrodynamic diameter and can erupt from leaky tumor vessels. But current research has explored many methods to spread the conventional method of EPR-based tumor therapy. EPR enforced in many applications but, particularly, it promotes the biodistribution of NPs in human blood vessels and high level in the solid tumors (Subhan et al., 2021).

Passive targeting or physical targeting

Passive targeted nanoparticles are first clinically approved (e.g., DOXIL) before 22 years due to its exceptional characteristic toward tumor cells and permits nanoparticles to accumulate in tumor cells. This type of process was first defined by Matsumura and Maeda in the year 1986 and commonly referred as the EPR effect. A few of passively targeted nanocarriers, which are in therapeutic use, are Abraxane, Marqibo, Onivyde, Genexol-PM, and all clinically available drugs (first generation drugs). These drugs mainly depend on its distribution, physical, chemical, and pharmacokinetic properties, and few increases therapeutic efficiency and survival rate. Pathophysiological features of carcinogenic cells and its surrounding have been conquered for passive targeting. This type of targeting depends on drug synthesis along with body mechanism like excretion, penetration, and biodegradation of drugs. Its penetrating power depends on pH, size, solvents, temperature, and pressure. This effect is focused on the occurrence of leaky blood vessels, in which endothelium is inserted in the openings of size between 100 and 500 nm. The functioning of affected tissues, based on various pathological circumstances, is exploited in these drugs. Nanocarriers used for therapeutic treatment should have capacity to mix with blood vessels and escape from macrophages stuck in liver and spleen, i.e., reticuloendothelial system. Since the average size of the sinusoid in the endothelial lining of the liver and gap joint between endothelial cells of the leaky blood vessels is around 125–600 nm, the average size of the nanocarriers should in the range of 100 nm in order to spread tumor cells with the help of these vascular bodies (Golden et al., 1998).

Heterogeneity factors, like hypoxic gradient of the tumor cells, have severe influence on the effectiveness of anticancer drugs brought by passive targeting. This will result in the lower penetration of the drug to tumor tissues. Current research aims on the regularization of tumor node lymph earlier starting treatment and with the help of EPR effect. Consequently, the progress of future-generation nanocarrier drugs with cutting-edge functionalities is definitely needed, and it will be based on active targeting with stimuli responsive. Numerous second-generation nanocarrier drugs have been established at a preclinical and early clinical stage, but till now it was not approved by regulatory bodies (Farokhzad & Langer, 2006; Prabhakar et al., 2013; Zwicke et al., 2012).

Active targeting

In active targeting, a chelating ligand is linked to the anticancer drug where the ligand forms bond particularly to the receptor molecule Fig. 4.8. Delivery of the drugs depends on affinity of selected ligand to the target moiety. An extensive variety of ligands have been utilized for these purposes, which includes both micro- and macromolecules, such as peptides, carbohydrates, and folic acid. The ligand should have capacity to bound with target tissues easily without affecting the healthy cells. For effectual targeting, ligands (nanocarriers) should avoid untimely release and degradation in the blood vessels. Likewise, extended drug circulation is important to prevent undesirable exchange of drug with immune system-opsonization. Hence, optimization of ligand is important to uphold properties and prevents the recognition by the reticuloendothelial system.

As stated, functioning of active targeting is based on the nature of a target molecule and coordinating ligand. But it is correspondingly significant to enhance the density of targeting ligands in order to attain maximum targeting efficiency (Bareford & Swaan, 2007). For example, different mechanisms will occur by using gold NPs with varied densities of carcinogenic cells (Bhattacharyya et al., 2010).

Drawbacks like anatomical, pharmacokinetic, and physiological barriers are also important because it will prevent direct interaction of tumor cells with nanocarriers, and care should be given to these properties. Active targeting of tumor neovascularization can control these boundaries. In conclusion, the main objective of nanotechnology in therapeutic field is to achieve a good deal between ligand and nanocarrier. All targeted

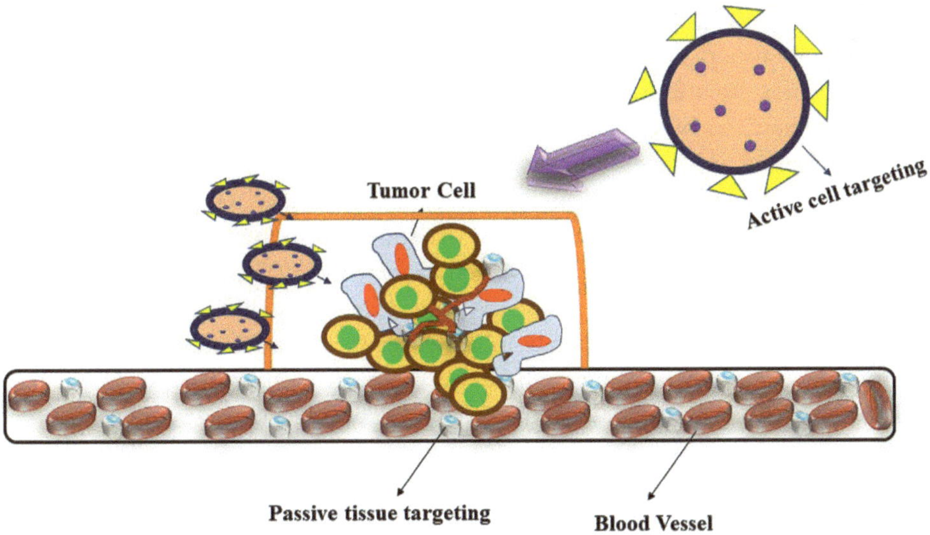

Figure 4.8 Passive and active tumor targeting.

Table 4.3 Difference between active and passive targeting.

S. no.	Passive targeting	Active targeting
1	Enhanced penetration of NPs within the tumor cells	Activates the vigorous uptake of NPs by the tumor cells without adding any external agent
2	Leaky vasculature	Carbohydrate target
3	Local application through IV	Antibody targeting
4	Works with EPR effect	No EPR
5	Technically less challenging	Technically more challenging
6	Based on size, shape of nano particles	Based on ligand, its binding, antigen, antibody
7	Amount of drug required is more, so high cost	Amount of drug required is less so low cost

EPR, Enhanced permeability and retention; *IV*, intravenous; *NPs*, nanoparticles.

NPs will contain a significant quantity of drug per unit. This is another variance between nanomedicines and drug. Actively targeted nanoparticulate delivery can improve drug retention period owing to improved cellular binding, low nonspecific uptake, and mechanisms of resistance (van der Meel et al., 2013). The difference between active and passive targeting is tabulated in Table 4.3.

Stimuli-responsive systems/triggered release

The recent research has been emphasized on stimuli-responsive system, and it has many applications in the field of DD, bioengineering, biosensor, and textiles. Many polymers are determinedly found in pharmaceutical research due to its remarkable chemical and physical properties, such as light, electricity, pH, magnetic field, ion concentration, and temperature. They can be used as chemically or physically in the form of cross-linked hydrogel compound and mixed with various bioactive compounds, such as nucleic acid, carbohydrates, organic molecules, and peptides. Nanocarriers are also used in vesicles, particles, and micelles in combination with the stimuli-responsive polymer and used in the wound healing tissues and cancer chemotherapeutics. Stimuli-responsive systems depend on physical, chemical, or biological triggers, which will increase the penetration of drugs by reacting with the NPs. Stimuli-responsive systems are alike to the feedback mechanism of biological systems, where biochemical signaling procedures depends on variation of physicochemical factors. The benefit of stimuli-responsive systems is noticeable that the drug will be released from nanoparticle only by triggering neoplastic cells, thus diminishing exposure as shown in Fig. 4.9 (Indermun et al., 2018; Wei et al., 2017).

The two types of stimuli responsive systems are internal and external stimuli system.

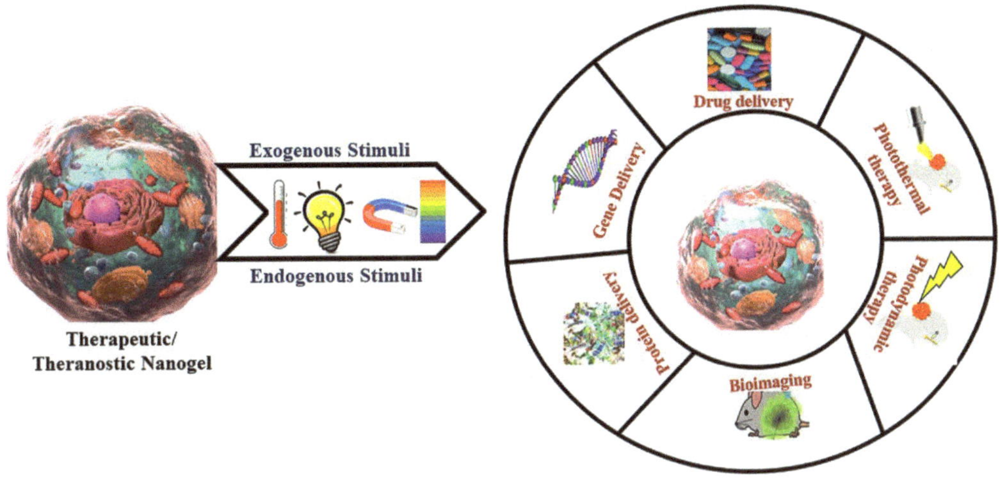

Figure 4.9 Stimuli-responsive systems/triggered release.

Internally responsive drug delivery

Internal stimuli comprise variations in pH, strength, and redox properties (Holme et al., 2012). For example, in tumors, the extracellular cells are more acidic than the systemic cells (Jhaveri et al., 2014). Likewise, there is a pH variation between intracellular organelles and cytoplasm. This disorder can be utilized to develop intracellular penetration of anticancer drugs from nanomedicines.

Thermo-responsive delivery

All Pathophysiological factors will arise only at lower pH and high temperature. The temperature range of affected tissue is high than normal one which will create physiological changes in tumor cells. For example, hyperthermia (40°C–45°C) makes a larger blood flow in the cancer cells and advances the vasculature penetrability than normal tissues (35°C) (Zhu & Torchilin, 2013).

Thus the research about the function of vasculature in existence of hyperthermia has broadened and leads pathway for the use of low temperatures drug along with high temperature nonlabile anticancer drugs. Temperature-independent active polymers will also accumulate in hyperthermia environment due to improved penetrability in such areas. To create temperature variation between normal and damaged cells, some external heating sources like laser, electromagnetic radiation are used. Thermosensitive nanodrugs are considered effective DD systems nowadays due to its synergistic effects. Lipids with proper transition temperatures are used to design thermosensitive based drugs, which will release the drug only at high temperatures (Kono, 2001). Most frequently used lipid-based drug is dipalmitoylphosphatidylcholine with crystalline transition temperature range of 35°C–40°C.

pH-responsive delivery

In the era of medicine, pH variation is the important tool for targeted DD. Mainly, this type of drugs was used in gastrointestinal system because pH varies from acidic to basic along the tract. This factor has been utilized to attain the synthesis of target delivery drugs in therapeutic field. The pH of affected cells will have low value (pH = 6) along with inflammation than the healthier tissue (pH = 8); this feature helps to distinguish normal and tumor cells (Mura et al., 2013). In carcinogenic cells, there is a possibility of two different pH groups:

1. pHe—Acidic, extracellular pH
2. pHi—Neutral, intracellular pH.

The vigorous proliferation of carcinogenic cells is due to its low pH value; hence, vasculature growth is incapable to perform the requirements of the fast isolating cells to nurture the increasing tumor cells.

Malnutrition and poor oxygen intake will form hypoxia, produce a build-up of lactic acid from higher quantity of glycolysis, and finally leads to energy deficient environment (Fleige et al., 2012). Though pH-responsive factor is indirect, it signifies a authoritative strategy for transport of drugs to carcinogenic cells (Ganta et al., 2008). The irregular biochemical characteristics of tumors cells can be utilized for active DD.

This was achieved by using ionizable polymers containing active groups, which will undergo a solubility modification in pH environmental and results in delivering of bioactive molecules from the targeting ligands. Usually pH-responsive systems are used in gastrointestinal areas and current research concentrates in hydrogels to determine their pH effectiveness of targeting moiety in gastrointestinal. Similar result was determined in gum Arabic–modified molecule, which produces effective target molecules (Alsehli, 2020).

Extensive varieties of nanomedicine like liposomes and nanogels have capacity to form the earlier said pH–drugs and have good active target delivery, high efficacy for anticancer agents. Numerous nanocarriers of this type are extremely sophisticated by integrating any two drugs in the similar system and have greater combined results (combination therapy) for distinctly active carcinogenic treatment.

Enzyme-responsive delivery

Initiating and catalyzing are the two important roles of enzymes physiological reaction. The enzymes and its structure will vary from tissue to tissue and is greater in cancer cells (Alsehli, 2020). Due to its specific nature, it is used for framing target-oriented nanomedicines, which will respond more if there is a change in gradient.

MMPs (matrix metalloproteinase) are the group of 23 zinc and calcium endopeptidases, which is the main reason for the deprivation and remodeling of matrix (El Hour et al., 2010). Tumor cells are linked with four main processes that comprise migration, invasion, metastasis, and angiogenesis. These features rely on atmosphere around tumor tissue. The MMPs significantly impact the properties of tumors, because it is engaged in breaking down process, at the same time cell adhesion molecules disturbs cell–cell interactions and the cell–extracellular matrix. Extracellular matrix proteinases, MMP—are found to be the main intermediaries for variations in the tumor atmosphere (Meers, 2001).

Inflammation-responsive delivery

Inflammation-responsive delivery targets on physiological changes in the body temperatures, pH, and enzyme. Cell mediators identify the damage in the cellular including proteolytic enzymes, arachidonic acid metabolites, and reactive oxygen metabolites. There are various cell mediators that have been successfully applied for stimuli-responsive release at an inflammatory site. Example—the inflammation-responsive polymer, a hyaluronic acid, which produce cross-linked product with a glycidyl ether is shown to degrade on exposure to hydroxyl radicals.

Redox-responsive delivery

The largely attracted DD system is redox responsive in intracellular cells than compared with extracellular compartment. The reducing property is due to the occurrence of large amount of the glutathione tripeptide in subcellular compartments (3–9 mM), which are about 1000 times more than extracellular compartment (Schafer & Buettner, 2001). This is due to fast enzymatic decomposition of glutathione in human plasma. It should be noted that levels of glutathione tripeptide are too higher in carcinogenic cells than compared with normal cell. Several polymers have developed by integrating a thiol-reducible bond or by cross-linking reducible bonds in their basic structure in order to form biocompatible systems, which has target delivery in high redox potential location like cancer cell cytosol (Goldenbogen et al., 2011). In addition to this, redox responsive DD systems are very sensitive to hypoxic tumor cells. A better understanding of the reducing behavior of tumor cells will lead to advanced research on redox–drug systems. Many nanomedicines have been synthesized by utilizing redox-responsive compounds for the delivery of anticancer drugs in a target specific cell, and newly these systems are used in combination therapy also.

Externally responsive drug delivery

External stimuli are most appropriate for DD and cancer treatment. The treatment depends on the patient health, nature of cancer, and pathological situations (Mi, 2020). External stimuli DDs are works in controlled and well-organized way throughout the treatment. The triggered nanocarriers in this method deliver progressed site-specific DD, along with speedy payload release (Yao et al., 2016). But, external triggering systems require the employment of sophisticated instruments to perform the function. Several external stimulants were used in cancer treatment, like light, temperature, and magnetic particles. Externally responsive DD focuses on responsive, targeted DD systems. These systems show potential to increase the therapeutic in patients' health in a large quantity in pathological conditions. Due to their physiological properties, its benefits occur in wider applications.

Photo-responsive delivery

Due to its outstanding remote spatial—temporal, (ability to solve multiple problems in one solution) photo-responsive external DD is attracted many researchers in medical field. In 1994, the photo-responsive drug has been officially approved by FDA- (Food and Drug Administration), and there after initiation of photo-responsive DD has created excellent effect on the arena of cancer therapy (Fleige et al., 2012). A large number of photo-responsive system having their characteristic wavelength in IR, and visible radiation has been designed to provoke the release of drugs to affected area. Owing to its absorption in tissues ultraviolet rays cannot able to penetrate inside the tumor cells but near IR radiation has good penetrating power to the cells without affecting the healthier one (Fleige et al., 2012).

Azobenzene and cinnamic acid molecules are commonly used photo-responsive groups. UV—visible photoisomerization will takes place at double bond. UV irradiation alters apolar trans isomer to the polar cis isomer, which can be reconverted to the trans isomer by visible light. Possible mechanisms in photo-responsive DD comprises photo-degradation, photo-isomerization, photo-decrosslinking, and crosslinking, and photosensitization.

Thermo-responsive delivery

Thermo-responsive delivery is a specially made component that contains nanocarrier material, and delivery system is designed in such way that it can hold load and deliver drug at heated cancer cells. This application is externally applied on thermal source, such as changes in the temperature. Among the available delivery systems, thermo-responsive delivery system has good versatility in fabrication, high drug targeting, and reduced side effects (Mura et al., 2013).

Magnetic response delivery

Magnetic response DD system comprises incorporation of magnetically active compound to anticancer drug (Yao et al., 2016). The working procedure for these types of drugs involves the use of external magnetic field or alternating magnetic field to trigger the drug and thereby increases the temperature. In magnetic response DD, the

Table 4.4 Types of drug delivery system in Internal and external responsive stimuli.

	Types of drug delivery system	Reactions
Internally responsive stimuli	Thermo-responsive delivery	hyperthermia, makes a larger blood flow in the cancer cells
	pH-responsive delivery	This affects the synthesis of target delivery drugs in therapeutic field
	Enzyme-responsive delivery	MMP are found to be the main intermediaries for variations in the tumor
	Inflammation-responsive delivery	The inflammation-responsive polymer is a hyaluronic acid which produce cross-linked with a glycidyl ether
	Redox-responsive delivery	Redox-responsive compounds for the delivery of anticancer drugs in a target specific cell
Externally responsive stimuli	Photo-responsive delivery	Azobenzene and cinnamic acid molecules is commonly used photo-responsive
	Thermo-responsive delivery	Piroxicam these particles were detected at higher temperatures
	Magnetic-response delivery	SPIONs have been utilized widely in MRI application for instantaneous imaging and drug delivery

MMP, Matrix metalloproteinases; *SPIONs*, superparamagnetic Fe oxide NPs.

magnetically active nanoparticles loaded with antidrugs are triggered and penetrated to the pathological spot with the help of external magnet (Santhosh & Ulrih, 2013). Hyperthermia causes irreversible damage, increases the penetration of drugs to the tumor cells without affecting normal cells. Usually nano−iron oxide in the form of magnetite is used for this purpose, because it has good magnetic behavior and does not leave any residual magnetism inside the body (Shi et al., 2017). Therefore, these NPs are signified as superparamagnetic Fe oxide NPs—SPIONs. SPIONs are normally used for medical demands like magnetic hyperthermia, drug targeting, magnetofection, and bioseparations. SPIONs have been utilized widely in MRI application for instantaneous imaging and DD. The types of drugs used in internal and external responsive stimuli is shown in Table 4.4.

Multifunctionality/theranostics

Multistimuli-responsive DD systems is a group of internal tumor stimuli to release drugs from the nanocarriers. Related to drug release from single stimuli, the response from multistimuli is high and designed in a controlled programmable manner. Apart from the first and second generations of nanomedicine drugs that have single

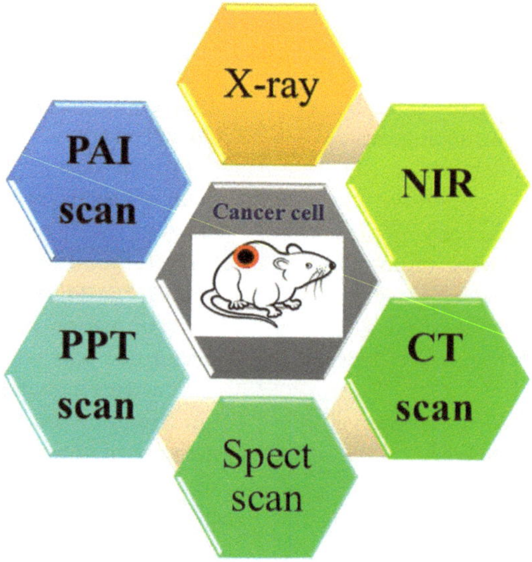

Figure 4.10 Multifunctionality/theranostic.

functionality, multifunctional nanomedicines are anticipated to arrive clinical treatment very shortly. Multifunctional anticancer drugs have the ability to attain numerous functions at same time, such as delivery of drugs, multitargeted delivery, and diagnosis and active therapy. Newly, many types of multifunctional nanomedicines were developed at the preclinical level shown in Fig. 4.10.

Multiple drugs, such as doxorubicin and paclitaxel, composed with DNA or siRNA, will produce effective approach against cancer. The NPs loaded with doxorubicin and DNA shows more apparent in destruction of tumor growth than compared to single dose. Another biodegradable polymer, which coloaded with doxorubicin and paclitaxel, are more effective than normal drugs. Similarly, multifunctional PEGylated liposomes were also used with the P-glycoprotein to avoid multidrug resistance in affected cells (Guo et al., 2013).

Cutting-edge multifunctional nanocarrier drugs have been established by combination of targeted delivery with multistimuli-responsive systems. For example, in micelles, drugs were loaded in hydrophobic part and hydrophilic section is utilized for targeting ligand. These stimuli increases the selectivity and efficiency of drugs (Guo et al., 2013).

Theranostics is an emerging subdivision of multistimuli nanomedicine groups. It delivers the both analysis and treatment in nanoform. Theranostic agents will focus on penetration of drugs at target site, distribution and therapeutic efficacy. It also deals with tumor array; meanwhile it indicates both the presence and location of target drug in the body. The advanced perceptions and approaches of theranostics were not fully assessed in medical trials (Blanco et al., 2009).

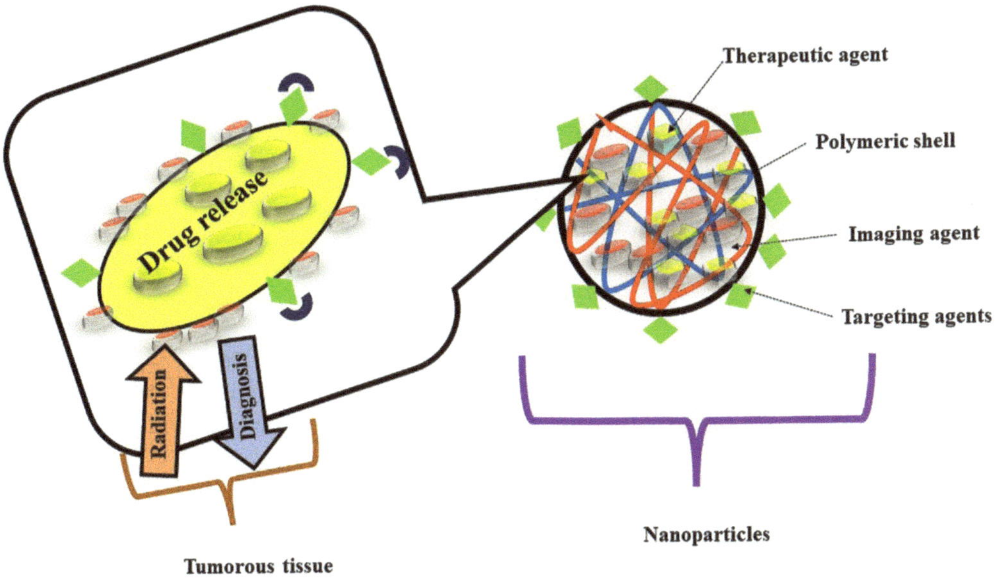

Figure 4.11 Antibody-mediated targeting drug delivery system.

Antibody-mediated targeting

Targeted antibodies are a kind of tumor immunotherapy treatment, which will interrupt cell activity of damaged cells and triggers the immune system to eradicate the carcinogenic cells.

The choice of a suitable target is very important, and it depends on tumor specificity and acceptance level. Few anticancer drugs have been evaluated for their efficacy in targeted antibody-mediated DD, and they have similar features. The efficiency of target antigen on carcinogenic cells is the key factor in antibody mediated delivery. The injected antibody should have the capacity to target and bind the tumor cells more effectively without affecting the healthier cells. The efficacy of many anticancer drugs is directly proportional to the amount of antigen that binds on cells Fig. 4.11. Antibody-targeted DD payloads will functions intracellularly (like receptor-mediated endocytosis) and deliver directly to lysosome where degradation takes place, and, hence, it reduces the toxicity to the patients (Tam et al., 2019).

Antiangiogenesis

The development of new blood vessel is commonly known as angiogenesis and shown in Fig. 4.12. Normally tumor cells require good nutrients and plenty of oxygen, which triggers the growth of new blood vessels. Antiangiogenic treatment is an traditional method to kill carcinogenic cells by stopping the nutrient and oxygen supply to the affected cells through the reduction of the vascular link and the eliminating development

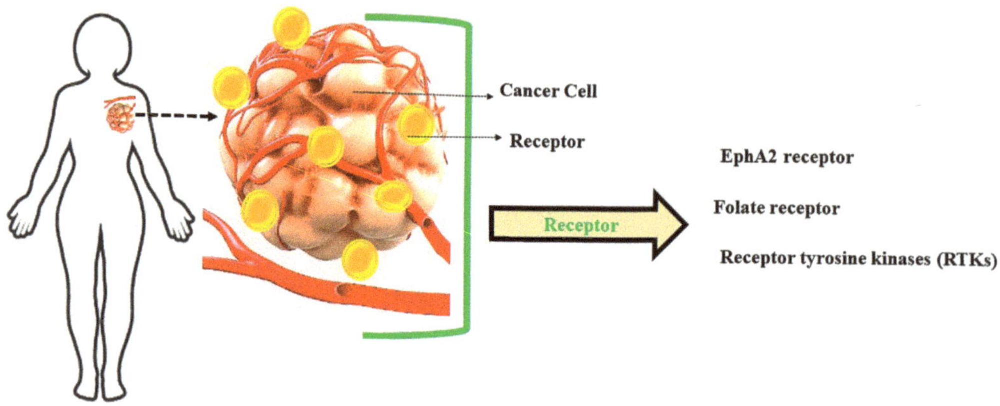

Figure 4.12 Antiangiogenesis.

of new blood vessels. Many antiangiogenic drugs permitted by FDA for therapeutic treatment depends on vascular endothelial growth factor. These drugs have dual role, namely, controlling new blood vessels and performs immunosuppressive functions.

Few examples of angiogenesis inhibitors are shown below

Axitinib—Treatment for kidney cancer.

Bevacizumab—It is used in colorectal, kidney, and lung cancers.

Lenalidomide—It is a multiple myeloma produced by antibodies and mantle cell lymphoma. It is a type of non-Hodgkin lymphoma.

Pazopanib—Advanced soft tissue sarcoma in kidney cancer.

Ramucirumab—Used in stomach cancer, such as gastroesophageal junction adenocarcinoma, and located in stomach joins.

Regorafenib—Treatment for gastrointestinal stromal tumors.

Sorafenib—Used for kidney, liver, and thyroid cancers.

Vandetanib—Used for medullary thyroid cancer.

Ziv-aflibercept—Used for treatment of colorectal cancer.

Nanomedicine in cancer treatment

The use of nanotechnology in cancer diagnosis and treatment is becoming very much advantageous since the toxicity of the drug is greatly reduced, increased solubility, target specific, increased life time to its receptors, and decreased side effects. The advancements in the synthetic strategies of the drug at the nano level greatly influence the researchers to study on different architectures, self-assembled supramolecular structures, many functional materials, led to the advancements in their physical and chemical properties, and also their application in cancer diagnosis and treatment, especially, as DD vehicles. This part explains the different types of nanocarriers for the cancer treatment.

Viral nanoparticles for cancer therapy

Design of efficient tools for delivery of cytotoxic drugs into cells is a challenging task in the field of biotechnology and nanomedicine. Many synthetic nanocarriers have been reported in the literature but the disadvantages lies in the efficiency of the delivery of drug into the cells (Zhang et al., 2020), carriers with good delivery performance, low toxicity, and safety. Viral mimicking nanocarriers and NPs have enhancing physical and chemical characteristics that will help in the cellular uptake and the efficient carrying ability. In the process of revolutionizing medicine in the field of drug carriers, the use of virus mimicking nanocarriers are also form an important part. Virus-based nanocarriers involve the self-assembly of protein molecules that are mainly virus. The advantages of virus like particles are shown in Fig. 4.13.

The types of plant viruses that are used for nanocarriers are presented in Table 4.5.

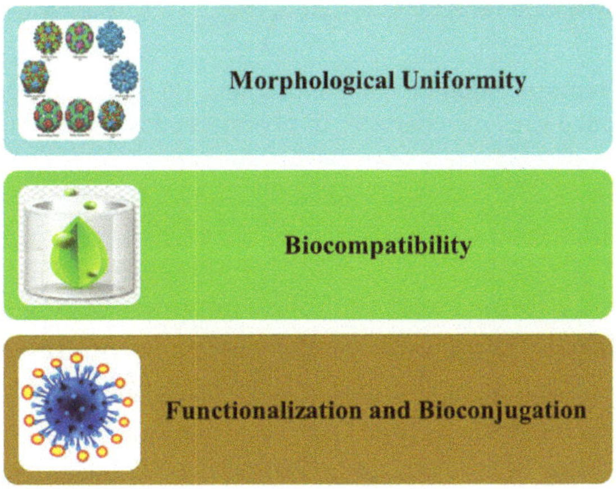

Figure 4.13 Virus-based nanocarriers involves self-assembling of protein molecules.

Table 4.5 Types of plant viruses that are used for nanocarriers

S. no.	Name of the virus used as nanocarrier	Abbreviation	Application
1	Cowpea chlorotic mottle virus	CCMV	Useful in encapsulation
2	Red clover necrotic mosaic virus	RCNMV	Used in packaging drug molecules
3	Cowpea mosaic virus	CPMV	Excellent Stability
4	Qβ	Qβ	Highly stable to make genetic alterations
5	M13	M13	Utilized for phage display and bioconjugation

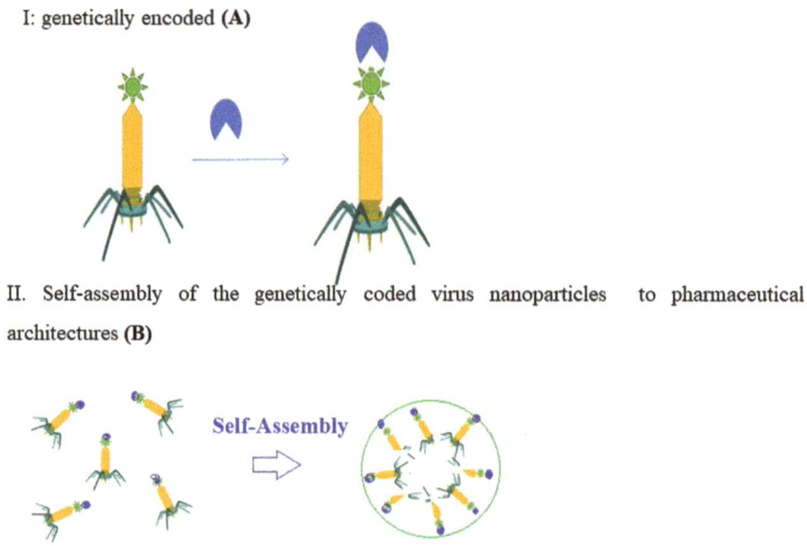

Figure 4.14 Schematic representation of viral nanocarriers. (A) Genetically encoded. (B) Self assembly of the genetically coded virus nanoparticles to pharmaceutical architectures.

Viral nanocarriers are formed after the following processes Fig. 4.14.

Usage of viral NPs as drug vehicles for the treatment of dreadful diseases like cancers is becoming significant because they are available from natural sources, safe to human, and biodegradable. The new strategies that are developed and the existing methodologies in the research reports should be taken into further development, which will possibly bring a great advancement in the field of DD engineering.

Organic nanocarriers for cancer therapy

Recently, cancer research studies focus on the usage of organic nanocarriers for cancer DD. Nanocarriers, such as organic vesicular nanocarriers (liposomes and micelles), are much studied due to their less toxic nature and the versatile nature to carry all types of drugs. Theranostics is the potential to combine the drug and the carrier that takes the hydrophobic formulations into the body. These nanocarriers enhance permeability of the drug to the active site and also have less side effects. There is an active research to encourage the increase of permeability, biomimic character and targeting the active site to act as active nontoxic carrier (Ma et al., 2012; Steinmetz, 2013).

Drug conjugates

Nowadays targeting the affected area through drug conjugates becomes an important area of research. Some of the types of drug conjugates are peptide-drug conjugates, antibody SiRNA drug conjugates, and drug-dye conjugates.

1. Peptide drug conjugates: Peptide drug conjugates are the type of coupled drugs which are a combination of three elements—cytotoxic drug, peptide, and a linker. The drug conjugate containing these three elements deliver the cytotoxic effect of the drug to the diseased tissues and thereby reducing the adverse effect of the tissues (Cho et al., 2022; Shang et al., 2022; Xu et al., 2022). The peptide drug conjugates are shown in Fig. 4.15.

The original cytotoxic drug is unable to differentiate cancer cells from the normal cells. The effective delivery to the tumor tissues lies in their carrier ability as highly hydrophobic enhancing their pharmacokinetic potential. Some of the cytotoxic agents Fig. 4.16 used for the construction are gemcitabine, doxorubicin, daunorubicin, paclitaxel, and camptothecin.

The choice of linker is also very important as it depends on the hydrophobicity/hydrophilicity, functional groups, their release mechanisms, and so on. Some of the challenges are their life time, improve their efficacy, optimizing their formulations, bio compatibility, limited toxicity, and low protein absorption. Currently there are only 2 Protein drug conjugates as FDA-approved drugs and research is going on to increase the number (Wang et al., 2017, 2020).

2. Antibody drug conjugates: Antibody drug conjugates are a new class of pharmaceutical entities that contain three components—monoclonal antibody, linker, and the cytotoxic agent. The schematic representation of antibody drug conjugate is shown in Fig. 4.17.

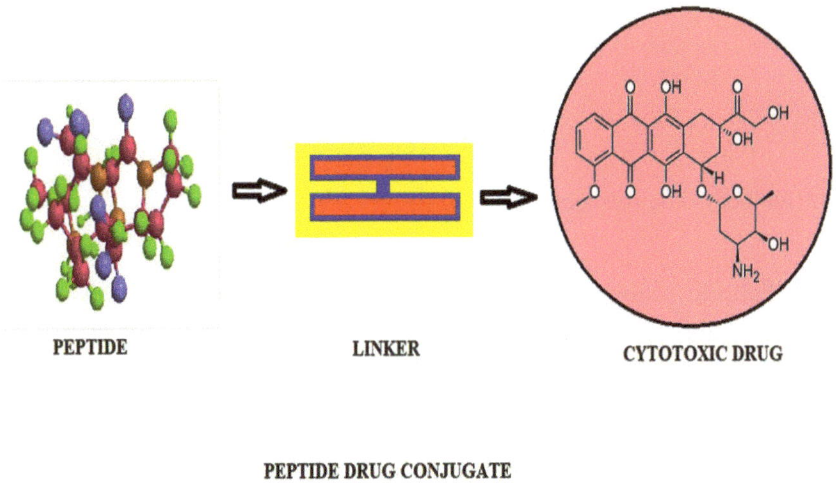

Figure 4.15 Peptide-drug conjugate.

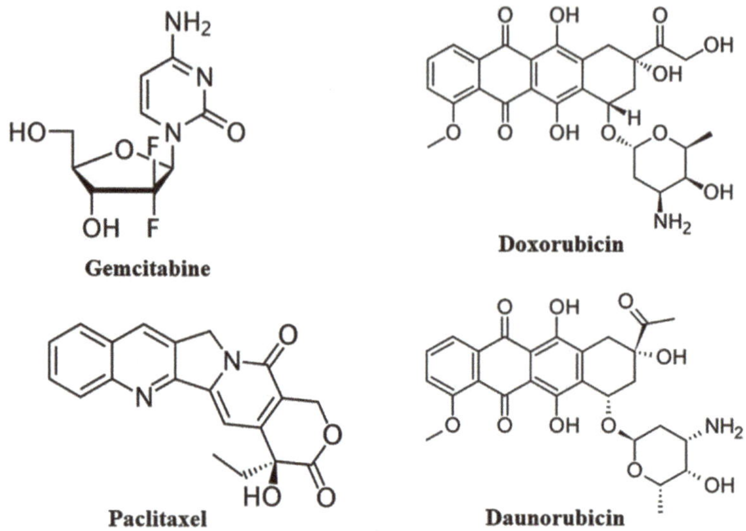

Figure 4.16 Structures of cytotoxic drugs.

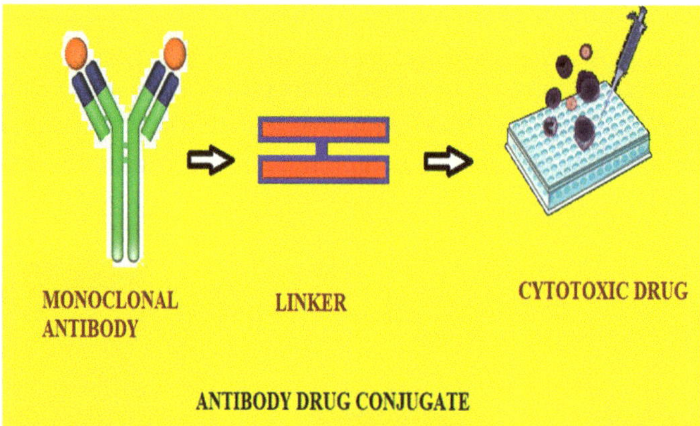

Figure 4.17 Antibody drug conjugate.

The mechanistic action of the antibody drug conjugate is (1) selective covalent bonding of the monoclonal antibody to tumor cells, (2) effective internalization through chemical linking strategies, (3) lysosome-induced protein degradation, and (4) effective release of the cytotoxic drug to the affected cells (Cao et al., 2022; Yao et al., 2021).

3. Drug dye conjugates: The usage of fluorescent dye in cancer treatment is significant since it helps in targeted DD to the infected cells. It contains the components like cytotoxic drug, linker, and fluorescent dye. These fluorescent tracers can help

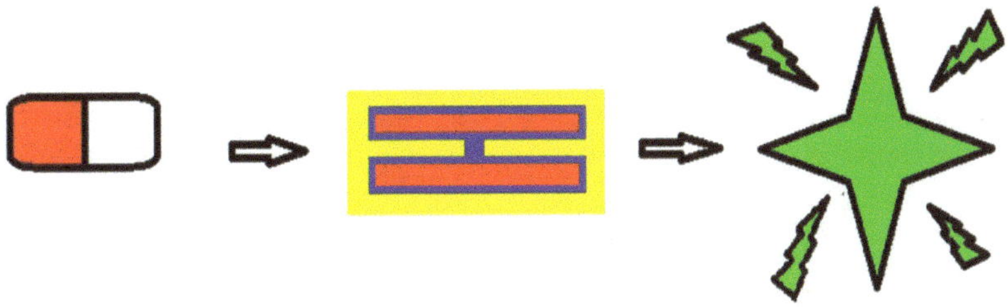

Figure 4.18 Formation of drug-dye conjugate.

in identifying the tumor cells and chemotherapy. The whole DD process can be monitored and combination of these drugs will work out even with inorganic nanocarriers (Choi et al., 2022) Fig. 4.18.

Lipid-based nanocarriers

The oral administration of drugs into the body should cross many metabolic pathways, different pH, enzymatic regions and reach the affected area to get rid of the disease. Therefore the development of significant carriers, which are nontoxic and with increased delivering capability should be studied. Since the peptides and the proteins can form lipophilic base formulations, lipid-based nanocarriers become very challenging and the needed one. There are many barriers for the lipid nanocarriers; they are enzymatic barrier, sulphahydryl barrier, mucus barrier, and epithelial barrier (García-Pinel et al., 2019; Haddadzadegan et al., 2022; Puri et al., 2009). The strategy used for increasing the lipophilic character is the "hydrophobic ion pair." The formation of lipid nanocarrier is shown in Fig. 4.19.

The type of lipid nanocarrier are the following: (1) self-emulsifying drug NPs, (2) solid–liquid NPs/nanostructured NPs; (3) liposomes; and (4) micelles. The significance of the above nanocarriers are (1) even organic molecules, the solubility of which is less can be used as drug because some of the pharmaceutically active molecules are not soluble in aqueous systems; (2) colloidal drug carriers; and (3) they even carry hydrophobic or lipophilic drugs.

Liposomes

Liposomes are much-studied lipid-based nanostructures that have high biodegradability and biocompatibility. These are phospholipids with well-organized bilayers and have amphoteric character (both hydrophilic and lipophilic properties). Along with the

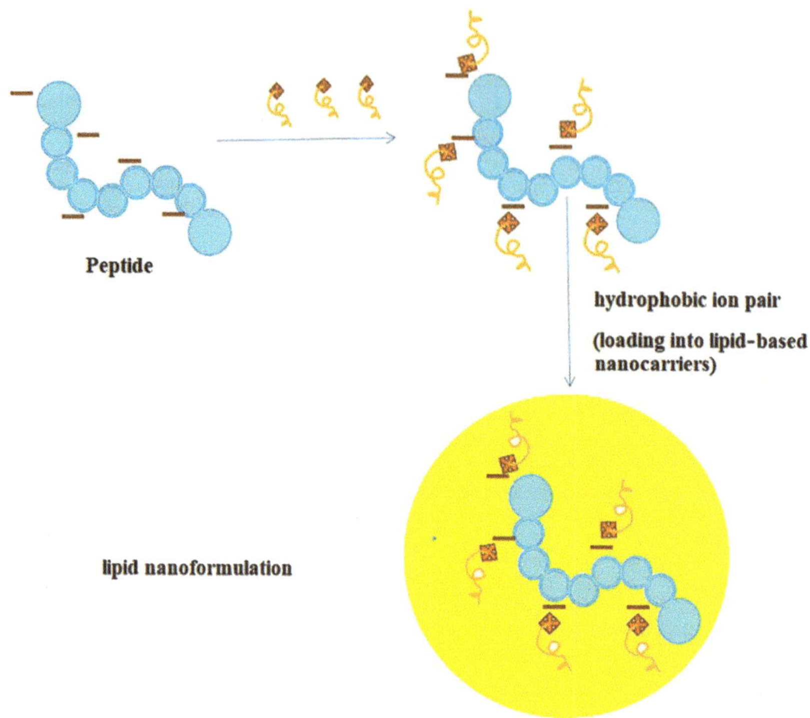

Figure 4.19 Formation of lipid based nanocarriers.

phospholipids, some additives like cholesterol can be added to increase their lipophilic character that will increase the drug action in blood. These liposomes are able to form encapsulated compounds in the presence of water-forming vesicle like structures and improving their solubility. Three types of DD is possible: (1) direct movement to the tumor cells passing through the cellular membrane, (2) structurally modified liposomes with the antibodies functionalized with it act as active carrier and recognize the cancerous cells, and (3) drug can be made to release into the affected area by external stimuli like pH, temperature, and magnetic field, by setting appropriate parameters.

Polymer-based nanocarriers

Chemotherapy is one of the treatment given to the cancerous patients. Drugs like cisplaitn, oxaliplatin, and doxorubicin are administered to the patients at various stages of cancer. These drugs have shown good efficacy but there are certain side effects by the drug when it is given to the patient at various doses frequencies and cycles. To improve the solubility, better distribution of the drug in the affected area, nanocarriers are studied in the present research. One among such is the polymeric nanocarriers; the polymers can be both natural (e.g., cellulose, chitosan) and synthetic polymers (e.g. poly lactic acid, polyamides). These polymeric nanostructured drug carriers enhance the solubility of the drug, cellular uptake, and biocompatibility. Some of the polymeric nanocarriers are micellar, polymeric nanogels, nanocapusules and emulsions, and so on. The advantage of the polymeric nanocarrier is that it can be functionalized or used in combination with other drugs, such as metal inorganic based chemotherapeutic agents, nanostructured drugs, metal nanocompounds, and dendrimers. The increase in the synthesis of biodegradable and water-soluble polymeric nanomaterials, hydrogels that are nontoxic improved the usage of polymeric nanomaterials as DD vehicles (Guo et al., 2021; Haider et al., 2021; Khan et al., 2021).

Polymeric micelles

Polymeric micelles are structures that has both hydrophilic and hydrophobic end. The introduction of drugs in the miceller form enhances the drug solubility that has poor value. For example, quercetin and turmeric are good drugs with pharmaceutical activity against cancer. But the usage of these drugs is limited due to their solubility issue inside the body and low bioavailability. When the polymeric micellar structures like polyactones- and polyhistidine-based polymers are functionalized with the cytotoxic drug, the efficacy of the drug is remarkable (Feczkó, 2021; Shah et al., 2022).

Inorganic nanoparticles for cancer therapy

Inorganic NPs are extensively used as DD carriers, due to their flexibility in synthesis, increased permeability, variable oxidation states that may help in different metabolic activities of the body, stability, and so on. These NPs are tunable to specific applications and can be used in combination therapy with polymeric NPs, carbon nanotubes, lipid nanocarriers, micelles, dendrimers, and so on. The NPs that are used in cancer therapy are Au NPs, Ag NPs, mixed metal oxide nanocarriers, and supramolecular architectures with the gold core, since they are inert and have the ability of surface functionalization, mesoporous silica NPs, metal–organic framework composites, and magnetic NPs. The special features of the inorganic NPs are

1. Surface to volume ratio
2. Improved porosity
3. Significant encapsulation efficiency
4. Flexible oxidation states
5. Good pharmacokinetics
6. Stable
7. Magnetic property
8. Combination therapy (hybrid nanocarriers).

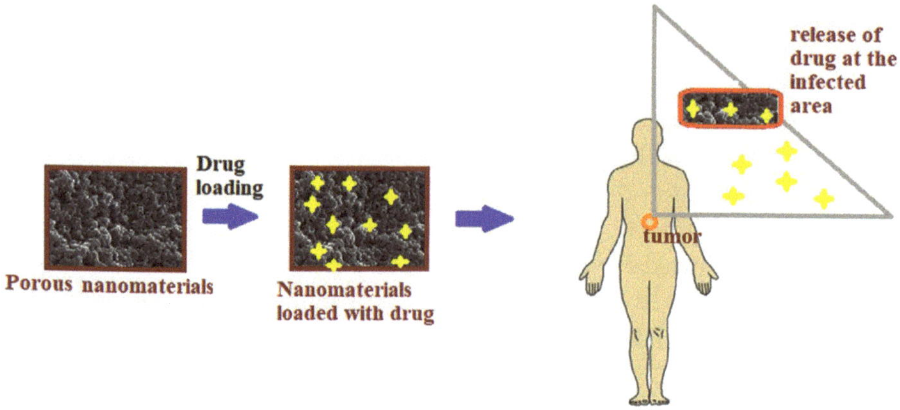

Figure 4.20 Porous inorganic nanomaterials.

Porous inorganic nanomaterials

Clay-type architectures were used as nanodrug carriers for anticancer drugs due to their porous texture and advantageous delivery profiles. Due to their excellent porosity, they have good encapsulation efficiency and can act as an inorganic host for the guest drug (Voicu et al., 2021).

Some of the nanostructured silicon materials, engineered materials with porous architectures are also used as drug carrier (Jung et al., 2021) since they are tunable for their sustained drug release at the appropriate time and better loading capacity. Due to their properties like surface modification according to the cellular mechanism, tunable properties and stablility, they are used as theranostic agents. Sometimes the solubility of the hydrophobic drugs is improved by modifying with these inorganic NPs (Khan et al., 2021) Fig. 4.20.

Combination therapy

Inorganic NPs like Ag NPs, Au NPs, Pt and Pd NPs, magnetic materials, mesoporous silica materials, quantum dots, materials functionalized with inorganic nano and pharmaceutically active metallic NPs are well used as drugs and can be combined with polymeric materials, biopolymer/organic hybrids to improve the biocompatibility, biodegradability, cyclodextrin-coated drugs for improved solubility and enhanced DD. These combined hybrid therapies have unique physical and chemical properties of both the materials and thus became advantageous in the treatment of cancer. For different types of cancer, different combinations will be used. Hydrophobic drugs can be made hydrophilic using combination therapy shown in Fig. 4.21.

Nanotechnology is the emerging area for the DD, especially materials like viral nanocarriers (genetically coded architectures), organic drug carriers, some of which are

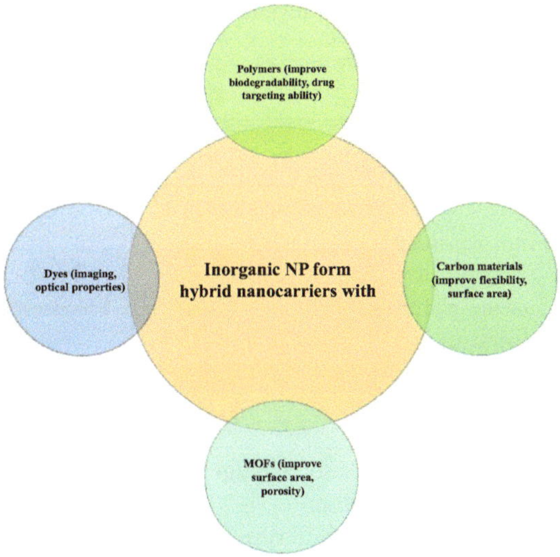

Figure 4.21 Inorganic nanoparticles form hybrid nanocarriers.

peptide drug conjugates, antibody drug conjugates, drug due conjugates, lipid-based hybrid nanocarriers, polymer-based matrixes, micellic drug carriers, and inorganic drug carriers. Combination therapy is another significant part to improve efficacy of any drug. Depending on the type of diseases and their mechanism inside the body, the drug carriers are tailored based on their functionalities.

Conclusion, challenges, and current limitations

Currently, nanomedicines are emerged as a superlative drug for anticancer treatment due to their small size and penetrating power and specific site targeting can be achieved. However, in clinical trials only a few nanocarrier-based cancer therapeutics are successful. Also, there exist a few challenges and limitations in this emerging field. Some of the limitations in various aspects are discussed below.

Barriers in physicochemical studies

The factors that play major role in the assessment of nano pharmaceuticals are physicochemical, pharmacokinetic, and biopharmaceutical characterization (Hua & Wu, 2018). The physicochemical properties of nanocarriers include determination of structure, composition, surface properties, size, porosity, charge, and aggregation behavior Table 4.6. When variation occurs in any of these properties, it is difficult to characterize the nanotechnology-based medicinal products. PD (poly dispersity) plays a vital role in nanocarriers characterization, because even a small change in PD brings a drastic change

Table 4.6 Characterization of physicochemical properties.

Characterization methods	Physiochemical properties	Limitations
TEM	Size distribution, dispersion homogeneity, crystal structure	Expensive, sample preparation, special training and projection limitation
SEM	High resolution, surface morphology, crystal structure	Size and cost, sample must be solid
AFM	Surface potential, magnetic field, friction and surface temperature	Single scan image size, limited magnification
Field flow fractionation	Particle size distribution	Particles in aggregate or agglomerates are not determined
X-ray diffraction	Crystal defects, phase, average grain size and strain	Homogeneous, size limitation, sample must be crystallizable
Dynamic light scattering	Size, stability and scattering of particles	Sedimentation, only applied for suspensions

AFM, Atomic force microscopy; *SEM*, scanning electron microscopy; *TEM*, transmission electron microscopy.

in the properties, such as toxicity and biocompatibility (Shi et al., 2017). Hence, nanomedicine products should be characterized by using many methods. Most of the nanomedicinal drugs has physiological pH, which leads to the aggregation of particles because these nanocarriers interacts with the biological fluids like blood serum. Such type of interactions can alter the functions of nanomedicine compounds. Stability, shelf life, and storage of nanomedicine products are also great challenges. Recently, biodegradable polymers are highly used in these emerging nanomedicine products. When these biodegradable polymers reach the biological fluids, the polymer degrades and interacts with the blood serum, and once again it changes the physiochemical properties, such as size and drug delivering mechanism (Zielińska et al., 2021). Also, the storage of these nanocarriers in aqueous solutions, including buffer can also alter the physiochemical properties of the nanomedicine. Nanomedicine characterization is important to analyze its behavior in human body. Remarkable barriers in development of drug carriers are shown in Figs. 4.22 and 4.23.

Apart from regular criteria for tolerance safety level and usefulness, the required therapeutic characteristics for the anticancer drugs for the administration of the patients might include the following factors:

- Complete knowledge about NPs and their interaction with biological components
- Easy manufacturing procedure
- Should have capacity to react only with target compound without affecting healthier one

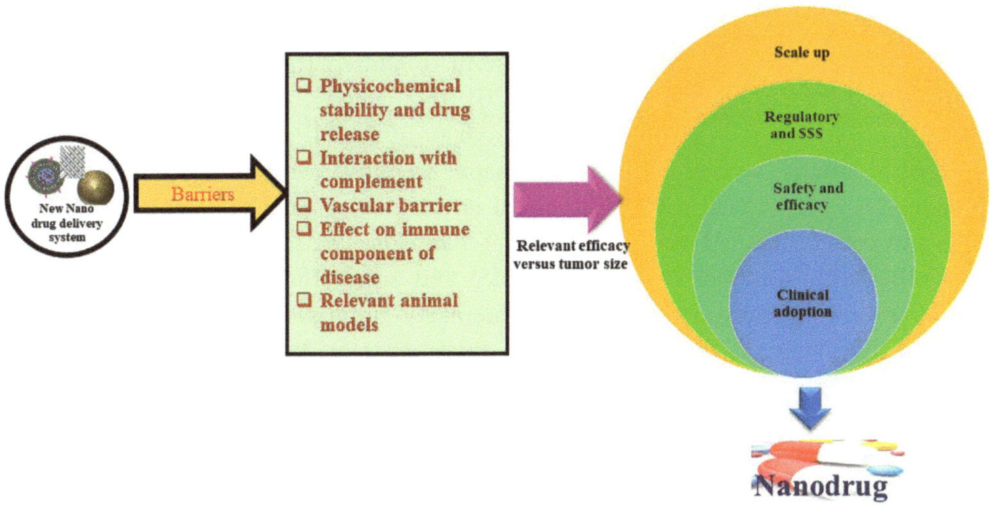

Figure 4.22 Barriers in physico-chemical studies.

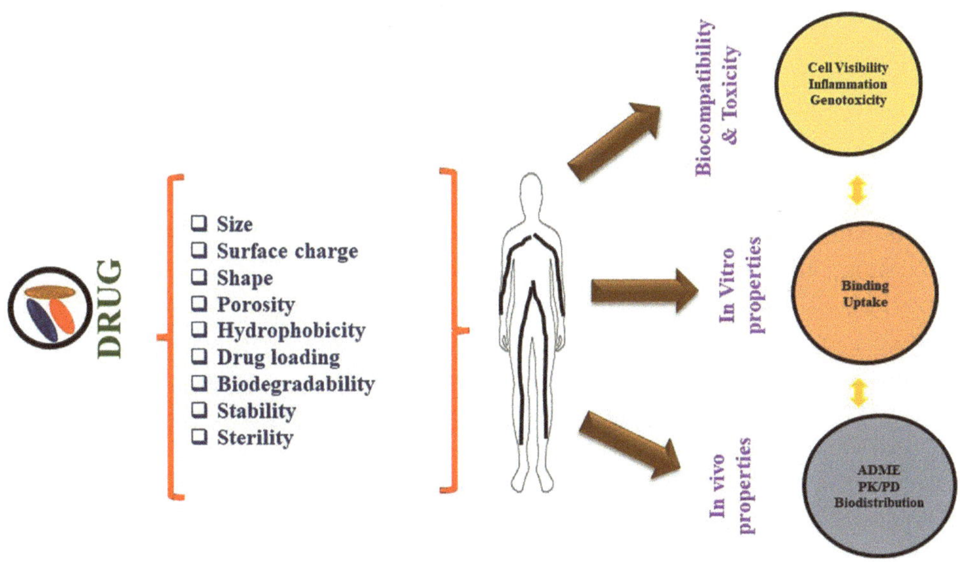

Figure 4.23 Nanomedicine characterization behavior in human body.

- Interaction of various functional groups should be clear and it should not vary during large scale production
- Physical, chemical and pharmacokinetic properties should not be varied
- Should be stable, easy to use, and not produce ill effects.

Safety concern

Due to the general use of NPs, it is important to address the toxicity issues for environment and human health (Abbas et al., 2019). Currently, researchers are attempting to find possible methods to minimize the toxicity of the NPs. The impacts of NPs are relied on solubility, surface morphology, shape, accumulation, size and chemical composition. NPs play a vital role in biological effects due to their interaction with body fluids and cell protein (Abbas et al., 2019). To enhance the stability, the quantum dots are synthesized from cadmium sulfide (CdS) and zinc sulfide (ZnS) as a fluorescent tracer. These quantum dots will deliver potentially cytotoxic cadmium ions (Cd) and zinc ions (Zn), whereas the cytotoxicity of cadmium selenide has been well documented (Accomasso et al., 2018). Cadmium selenide quantum dots will generally have cytocompatibility, with some cell lines. Recently, carbon nanotubes are used instead of NPs. It has been found that a NP around 10-μm size, which has faster circulation in the blood stream will directly affect the vascular system and has a potential risk factor for circulatory disease. Finally, the physiological significance of the concerned drug should be determined by performing an inhalation toxicity study. But still a real test of the effects of inhaled NPs was not implemented, but it costs more than a million dollars for designing and implementation (Oberdörster, 2010). Risk assessments have challenges owing to insufficient data, complication of nanomaterial, evaluation difficulties, and underdeveloped risk analysis frameworks. Only there are few research findings on the toxicology of nanomedicine, which can provide scientific guidance but still the risk analysis should be further assessed, new precautions should be taken to minimize the risk. The risks of all anticancer drugs should be evaluated by its exposure and existing information about the hazards. Exposure risk may be minimized by performing more testing and restructure the drug again.

International standard-regulating bodies have implanted the least measurement types like size, solubility of NPs, which are made as prognosticators to determine the harmfulness of the drugs. For instance, if one person inhales, nanomaterials with size less than 100 nm, will bring pulmonary swelling and oxidative strain (56) and interrupt with functioning of organs due to hydrophobic nature and free radical formation. Meanwhile, uneven sized NPs will create bulky aggregates, which will be deceived in the capillary tube of the lungs and create many side effects to affected patients. Apart from these, it ought to be known that typical toxicology research are mandatory for a product to be commercialized.

Regulatory issues

Several nanomedicinal products for the treatment of cancer have been permitted by the FDA and European health authorities, but the FDAs, EMAs, and other regulatory agencies have not yet implemented specific guidelines for pharmaceutical products, which contains nanomaterials (Foulkes et al., 2020). Recently, FDA released the regulation about "FDA related nanotechnology products" (Fleming et al., 2022). Without proper guidance and regulations, the assessments will be based on individual experience and risk, but this process is long and results in time delay for new arrival of nanocarriers in the field. In addition to clinical test and approval, regulatory bodies should emphasis in the process of world-class technologies, their development and quality. Owing to increase in mortality rate, the clear strategies about this frightening disease is needed very urgently. Unfortunately, the newly developed nanomedicines upsurge the complication of approval process. In general, it is a very difficult task for the regulatory bodies to legalize the requirements for low toxic nanomedicines (Wang et al., 2010).

Scale-up and manufacturing issues

The major issues involved are engineering the novel nanocarrier products for commodity and Current Good Manufacturing Practice in production. Generally, all preclinical and early clinical trials will be done only with a minute quantity of nanomaterial but for large-scale production, there is large possibility for disparities in physical, chemical, and mechanical properties due to the PD nature of nanomaterial. Hence, the manufacturing of nanocarriers for commercial use requires regulation in physicochemical properties, which is possible only with the help of researchers in chemistry and engineering. Setting up a significant condition to attain vital qualities and characteristics for nanocarrier production is difficult. These conditions will include the weight/ratio of polymeric material, solvents, temperature drugs, pressure, pH, and other additives. If the anticancer drug is more reactive toward pH, care should give to these parameters during manufacturing otherwise will create adverse effect (Li et al., 2004). An added problem in the manufacture of nanocarrier drug is environmental protection. Due to nanometer size, these NPs has tendency to mix with air and affect lungs directly. Few NPs have ability to perforate into skin and makes dermic exposure, which is a serious hazard to patients. Owing to this risk, NPs are developed in liquid atmosphere, which have suggestively lesser ecological effect (Nel et al., 2006).

Immunological challenges of nanomedicines

Still, the only toxicities that cannot transfer from preclinical trial to patients is immunotoxicity. This kind of immune response can be provoked by various causes. For example, proteins, polypeptides, amino acids, and nucleic acids in nanocarriers will act as antigens. Reaction between anticancer drug and carcinogenic cells will result in structural changes, which will upsurge immunogenicity. For example, interaction of paclitaxel with albumin (Trynda-Lemiesz, 2004) and reaction of C60 fullerene to

BSA-bovine serum albumin. The manufacturing procedure of NP drugs has more chances for endotoxin pollution, a basis for immune response.

NPs drugs can be antigenic depending on their size, solubility, and surface characteristics. Depending on these physical properties, few NPs get loosened by proteins and identified as foreign particles, results in the stimulation of pathway. NPs have tendency for intensification antigenicity of few antigens and hence behaves as adjuvants. This provides an innovative pathway for the growth of new NP-based vaccines but is harmful to other diseases (Braden et al., 2000).

NPs drugs also linked through few hematologic factors, like hemolysis and thrombogenicity. The hemolysis may immune-mediated or nonimmunogenic over NP—antibody or NP—erythrocyte interaction (Dobrovolskaia, 2015). The cationic charge from amine groups will raise the erythrocyte impairment and hemolytic strength of NPs. Sometimes nanocarrier drugs containing both hydrophobic and hydrophilic groups will perform as surfactants to interrupt erythrocyte membrane (Santos et al., 2020). Hemolysis brought by nanocarrier drugs has numerous side effects, including anemia disorder. Both hemoglobin moiety and cell debris will confer to the NPs, resulting in immune response.

References

Abbas, A. B., Boakye-Yiadom, K. O., Kesse, S., & Farooq, M. A. (2019). *International Journal of Pharmaceutical Sciences and Drug Research*. Available from https://doi.org/10.25004/IJPSDR.2019.110203.

Accomasso, L., Cristallini, C., & Giachino, C. (2018). *Frontiers in Pharmacology*, *9*. Available from https://doi.org/10.3389/fphar.2018.00228.

Alsehli, M. (2020). *Saudi Pharmaceutical Journal*, *28*(3), 255—265. Available from https://doi.org/10.1016/j.jsps.2020.01.004.

Anchordoquy, T. J., Barenholz, Y., Boraschi, D., Chorny, M., Decuzzi, P., Dobrovolskaia, M. A., Farhangrazi, Z. S., Farrell, D., Gabizon, A., Ghandehari, H., Godin, B., La-Beck, N. M., Ljubimova, J., Moghimi, S. M., Pagliaro, L., Park, J. H., Peer, D., Ruoslahti, E., Serkova, N. J., & Simberg, D. (2017). *ACS Nano*, *11*(1), 12—18. Available from https://doi.org/10.1021/acsnano.6b08244.

Aslan, B., Ozpolat, B., Sood, A. K., & Lopez-Berestein, G. (2013). *Journal of Drug Targeting*, *21*(10), 904—913. Available from https://doi.org/10.3109/1061186X.2013.837469.

Bareford, L. M., & Swaan, P. W. (2007). *Advanced Drug Delivery Reviews*, *59*(8), 748—758. Available from https://doi.org/10.1016/j.addr.2007.06.008.

Bayford, R., Rademacher, T., Roitt, I., & Wang, S. X. (2017). *Physiological Measurement*, *38*(8), R183—R203. Available from https://doi.org/10.1088/1361-6579/aa7182.

Bharali, D. J., & Mousa, S. A. (2010). *Pharmacology and Therapeutics*, *128*(2), 324—335. Available from https://doi.org/10.1016/j.pharmthera.2010.07.007.

Bhattacharyya, S., Bhattacharya, R., Curley, S., McNiven, M. A., & Mukherjee, P. (2010). *Proceedings of the National Academy of Sciences of the United States of America*, *107*(33), 14541—14546. Available from https://doi.org/10.1073/pnas.1006507107.

Blanco, E., Kessinger, C. W., Sumer, B. D., & Gao, J. (2009). *Experimental Biology and Medicine*, *234*(2), 123—131. Available from https://doi.org/10.3181/0808-MR-250.

Braden, B. C., Goldbaum, F. A., Chen, B. X., Kirschner, A. N., Wilson, S. R., & Erlanger, B. F. (2000). *Proceedings of the National Academy of Sciences of the United States of America*, *97*(22), 12193—12197. Available from https://doi.org/10.1073/pnas.210396197.

Butcher, N. J., Mortimer, G. M., & Minchin, R. F. (2016). *Nature Nanotechnology*, *11*(4), 310—311. Available from https://doi.org/10.1038/nnano.2016.6.

Cao, W., Li, R., Pei, X., Chai, M., Sun, L., Huang, Y., Wang, J., Barth, S., Yu, F., & He, H. (2022). *Medicine in Drug Discovery*, 100128. Available from https://doi.org/10.1016/j.medidd.2022.100128.

Cho, Y. S., Kim, G. C., Lee, H. M., Kim, B., Kim, H. R., Chung, S. W., Chang, H. W., Ko, Y. G., Lee, Y. S., Kim, S. W., Byun, Y., & Kim, S. Y. (2022). *Journal of Controlled Release*, *344*, 26–38. Available from https://doi.org/10.1016/j.jconrel.2022.02.026.

Choi, P. J., Cooper, E. A., Park, T. I.-H., Denny, W. A., & Jose, J. (2022). *Results in Chemistry*, *4*, 100343. Available from https://doi.org/10.1016/j.rechem.2022.100343.

Decuzzi, P. (2016). *ACS Nano*, *10*(9), 8133–8138. Available from https://doi.org/10.1021/acsnano.6b05536.

Dobrovolskaia, M. A. (2015). *Journal of Controlled Release*, *220*, 571–583. Available from https://doi.org/10.1016/j.jconrel.2015.08.056.

El Hour, M., Moncada-Pazos, A., Blacher, S., Masset, A., Cal, S., Berndt, S., Detilleux, J., Host, L., Obaya, A. J., Maillard, C., Foidart, J. M., Ectors, F., Noel, A., & Lopez-Otin, C. (2010). *Oncogene*, *29*(20), 3025–3032. Available from https://doi.org/10.1038/onc.2010.49.

Farokhzad, O. C., & Langer, R. (2006). *Advanced Drug Delivery Reviews*, *58*(14), 1456–1459. Available from https://doi.org/10.1016/j.addr.2006.09.011.

Feczkó, T. (2021). *Journal of Drug Delivery Science and Technology*, *64*, 102597. Available from https://doi.org/10.1016/j.jddst.2021.102597.

Feng, C., Li, Y., Ferdows, B. E., Patel, D. N., Ouyang, J., Tang, Z., Kong, N., Chen, E., & Tao, W. (2022). *Acta Pharmaceutica Sinica B*. Available from https://doi.org/10.1016/j.apsb.2021.12.021.

Fleige, E., Quadir, M. A., & Haag, R. (2012). *Advanced Drug Delivery Reviews*, *64*(9), 866–884. Available from https://doi.org/10.1016/j.addr.2012.01.020.

Fleming, A., Cursi, L., Behan, J. A., Yan, Y., Xie, Z., Adumeau, L., & Dawson, K. A. (2022). *Bioconjugate Chemistry*, *33*(3), 429–443. Available from https://doi.org/10.1021/acs.bioconjchem.1c00546.

Foulkes, R., Man, E., Thind, J., Yeung, S., Joy, A., & Hoskins, C. (2020). *Biomaterials Science*, *8*(17), 4653–4664. Available from https://doi.org/10.1039/d0bm00558d.

Ganta, S., Devalapally, H., Shahiwala, A., & Amiji, M. (2008). *Journal of Controlled Release*, *126*(3), 187–204. Available from https://doi.org/10.1016/j.jconrel.2007.12.017.

Gao, S., & Hu, M. (2010). *Mini-Reviews in Medicinal Chemistry*, *10*(6), 550–567. Available from https://doi.org/10.2174/138955710791384081.

García-Pinel, B., Porras-Alcalá, C., Ortega-Rodríguez, A., Sarabia, F., Prados, J., Melguizo, C., & López-Romero, J. M. (2019). *Nanomaterials*, *9*(4), 638. Available from https://doi.org/10.3390/nano9040638.

Golden, P. L., Huwyler, J., & Pardridge, W. M. (1998). *Drug Delivery: Journal of Delivery and Targeting of Therapeutic Agents*, *5*(3), 207–212. Available from https://doi.org/10.3109/10717549809052036.

Goldenbogen, B., Brodersen, N., Gramatica, A., Loew, M., Liebscher, J., Herrmann, A., Egger, H., Budde, B., & Arbuzova, A. (2011). *Langmuir: the ACS Journal of Surfaces and Colloids*, *27*(17), 10820–10829. Available from https://doi.org/10.1021/la201160y.

Guo, K., Xiao, N., Liu, Y., Wang, Z., Tóth, J., Gyenis, J., Thakur, V. K., Oyane, A., & Shubhra, Q. T. H. (2021). *Nano Materials Science*. Available from https://doi.org/10.1016/j.nanoms.2021.12.001.

Guo, X., Shi, C., Wang, J., Di, S., & Zhou, S. (2013). *Biomaterials*, *34*(18), 4544–4554. Available from https://doi.org/10.1016/j.biomaterials.2013.02.071.

Haddadzadegan, S., Dorkoosh, F., & Bernkop-Schnürch, A. (2022). *Advanced Drug Delivery Reviews*, *182*, 114097. Available from https://doi.org/10.1016/j.addr.2021.114097.

Haider, M., Zaki, K. Z., El Hamshary, M. R., Hussain, Z., Orive, G., & Ibrahim, H. O. (2021). *Journal of Advanced Research*. Available from https://doi.org/10.1016/j.jare.2021.11.008.

Holme, M. N., Fedotenko, I. A., Abegg, D., Althaus, J., Babel, L., Favarger, F., Reiter, R., Tanasescu, R., Zaffalon, P. L., Ziegler, A., Müller, B., Saxer, T., & Zumbuehl, A. (2012). *Nature Nanotechnology*, *7*(8), 536–543. Available from https://doi.org/10.1038/nnano.2012.84.

Hua, S., & Wu, S. Y. (2018). *Frontiers in Pharmacology*, 9. Available from https://doi.org/10.3389/fphar.2018.01397.

Indermun, S., Govender, M., Kumar, P., Choonara, Y. E., & Pillay, V. (2018). *Stimuli responsive polymeric nanocarriers for drug delivery applications: 1: Types and triggers* (pp. 43–58). Elsevier. Available from https://doi.org/10.1016/B978-0-08-101997-9.00002-3.

Jabir, N. R., Tabrez, S., Ashraf, G. M., Shakil, S., Damanhouri, G. A., & Kamal, M. A. (2012). *International Journal of Nanomedicine*, *7*, 4391–4408. Available from https://doi.org/10.2147/IJN.S33838.

Jhaveri, A., Deshpande, P., & Torchilin, V. (2014). *Journal of Controlled Release*, *190*, 352–370. Available from https://doi.org/10.1016/j.jconrel.2014.05.002.

Johari, B., Kadivar, M., Lak, S., Gholipourmalekabadi, M., Urbanska, A. M., Mozafari, M., Ahmadzadehzarajabad, M., Azarnezhad, A., Afshari, S., Zargan, J., & Kargozar, S. (2016). *International Journal of Artificial Organs*, *39*(10), 524–533. Available from https://doi.org/10.5301/ijao.5000533.

Jung, Y., Huh, Y., & Kim, D. (2021). *Microporous and Mesoporous Materials*, *310*, 110673. Available from https://doi.org/10.1016/j.micromeso.2020.110673.

Kargozar, S., Mozafari, M., Hashemian, S. J., Brouki Milan, P., Hamzehlou, S., Soleimani, M., Joghataei, M. T., Gholipourmalekabadi, M., Korourian, A., Mousavizadeh, K., & Seifalian, A. M. (2018). *Journal of Biomedical Materials Research – Part B Applied Biomaterials*, *106*(1), 61–72. Available from https://doi.org/10.1002/jbm.b.33814.

Karve, S., Werner, M. E., Sukumar, R., Cummings, N. D., Copp, J. A., Wang, E. C., Li, C., Sethi, M., Chen, R. C., Pacold, M. E., & Wang, A. Z. (2012). *Proceedings of the National Academy of Sciences of the United States of America*, *109*(21), 8230–8235. Available from https://doi.org/10.1073/pnas.1120508109.

Khan, M. A., Singh, D., Ahmad, A., & Siddique, H. R. (2021). *European Journal of Pharmaceutical Sciences*, *164*, 105892. Available from https://doi.org/10.1016/j.ejps.2021.105892.

Kono, K. (2001). *Advanced Drug Delivery Reviews*, *53*(3), 307–319. Available from https://doi.org/10.1016/S0169-409X(01)00204-6.

Krutovskikh, V. (2002). *Seminars in Cancer Biology*, *12*(4), 267–276. Available from https://doi.org/10.1016/S1044-579X(02)00013-5.

Li, L., Wartchow, C. A., Danthi, S. N., Shen, Z., Dechene, N., Pease, J., Choi, H. S., Doede, T., Chu, P., Ning, S., Lee, D. Y., Bednarski, M. D., & Knox, S. J. (2004). *International Journal of Radiation Oncology, Biology, Physics*, *58*(4), 1215–1227. Available from https://doi.org/10.1016/j.ijrobp.2003.10.057.

Lu, M., Cohen, M. H., Rieves, D., & Pazdur, R. (2010). *American Journal of Hematology*, *85*(5), 315–319. Available from https://doi.org/10.1002/ajh.21656.

Ma, Y., Nolte, R. J. M., & Cornelissen, J. J. L. M. (2012). *Advanced Drug Delivery Reviews*, *64*(9), 811–825. Available from https://doi.org/10.1016/j.addr.2012.01.005.

Maeda, H., Greish, K., & Fang, J. (2006). *Advances in Polymer Science*, *193*(1), 103–121. Available from https://doi.org/10.1007/12_026.

Malachowski, T., & Hassel, A. (2020). *Engineered Regeneration*, *1*, 35–50. Available from https://doi.org/10.1016/j.engreg.2020.06.001.

Mamot, C., Ritschard, R., Wicki, A., Küng, W., Schuller, J., Herrmann, R., & Rochlitz, C. (2012). *Journal of Drug Targeting*, *20*(5), 422–432. Available from https://doi.org/10.3109/1061186X.2012.680960.

Meers, P. (2001). *Advanced Drug Delivery Reviews*, *53*(3), 265–272. Available from https://doi.org/10.1016/S0169-409X(01)00205-8.

Mi, P. (2020). *Theranostics*, *10*(10), 4557–4588. Available from https://doi.org/10.7150/thno.38069.

Minchinton, A. I., & Tannock, I. F. (2006). *Nature Reviews. Cancer*, *6*(8), 583–592. Available from https://doi.org/10.1038/nrc1893.

Moon, J. J., Suh, H., Li, A. V., Ockenhouse, C. F., Yadava, A., & Irvine, D. J. (2012). *Proceedings of the National Academy of Sciences of the United States of America*, *109*(4), 1080–1085. Available from https://doi.org/10.1073/pnas.1112648109.

Mura, S., Nicolas, J., & Couvreur, P. (2013). *Nature Materials*, *12*(11), 991–1003. Available from https://doi.org/10.1038/nmat3776.

Nel, A., Xia, T., Mädler, L., & Li, N. (2006). *Science (New York, N.Y.)*, *311*(5761), 622–627. Available from https://doi.org/10.1126/science.1114397.

Oberdörster, G. (2010). *Journal of Internal Medicine*, *267*(1), 89–105. Available from https://doi.org/10.1111/j.1365-2796.2009.02187.x.

Prabhakar, U., Maeda, H., K. Jain, R., Sevick-Muraca, E. M., Zamboni, W., Farokhzad, O. C., Barry, S. T., Gabizon, A., Grodzinski, P., & Blakey, D. C. (2013). *Cancer Research*, *73*(8), 2412–2417. Available from https://doi.org/10.1158/0008-5472.CAN-12-4561.

Puri, A., Loomis, K., Smith, B., Lee, J. H., Yavlovich, A., Heldman, E., & Blumenthal, R. (2009). *Critical Reviews in Therapeutic Drug Carrier Systems*, *26*(6), 523–580. Available from https://doi.org/10.1615/CritRevTherDrugCarrierSyst.v26.i6.10.

Rasool, M., Malik, A., Waquar, S., Arooj, M., Zahid, S., Asif, M., Shaheen, S., Hussain, A., Ullah, H., & Gan, S. H. (2022). *Bioengineered*, *13*(1), 759–773. Available from https://doi.org/10.1080/21655979.2021.2012907.

Riley, M. K., & Vermerris, W. (2017). *Nanomaterials*, 7(5). Available from https://doi.org/10.3390/nano7050094.

Samadikuchaksaraei, A. (2001). *Journal of Biomedical Materials Research Part A*, *104*.

Santhosh, P. B., & Ulrih, N. P. (2013). *Cancer Letters*, *336*(1), 8–17. Available from https://doi.org/10.1016/j.canlet.2013.04.032.

Santos, A., Veiga, F., & Figueiras, A. (2020). *Materials*, *13*(1), 65. Available from https://doi.org/10.3390/ma13010065.

Schafer, F. Q., & Buettner, G. R. (2001). *Free Radical Biology and Medicine*, *30*(11), 1191–1212. Available from https://doi.org/10.1016/S0891-5849(01)00480-4.

Shah, S., Famta, P., Raghuvanshi, R. S., Singh, S. B., & Srivastava, S. (2022). *Colloid and Interface Science Communications*, *46*, 100570. Available from https://doi.org/10.1016/j.colcom.2021.100570.

Shang, Q., Su, Y., Leslie, F., Sun, M., & Wang, F. (2022). *Medicine in Drug Discovery*, *14*, 100125. Available from https://doi.org/10.1016/j.medidd.2022.100125.

Shi, J., Kantoff, P. W., Wooster, R., & Farokhzad, O. C. (2017). *Nature Reviews. Cancer*, *17*(1), 20–37. Available from https://doi.org/10.1038/nrc.2016.108.

Shmeeda, H., Amitay, Y., Gorin, J., Tzemach, D., Mak, L., Stern, S. T., Barenholz, Y., & Gabizon, A. (2016). *Journal of Drug Targeting*, *24*(9), 878–889. Available from https://doi.org/10.1080/1061186X.2016.1191081.

Steinmetz, N. F. (2013). *Molecular Pharmaceutics*, *10*(1), 1–2. Available from https://doi.org/10.1021/mp300658j.

Subhan, M. A., Yalamarty, S. S. K., Filipczak, N., Parveen, F., & Torchilin, V. P. (2021). *Journal of Personalized Medicine*, *11*(6). Available from https://doi.org/10.3390/jpm11060571.

Sun, Q., Zhou, Z., Qiu, N., & Shen, Y. (2017). *Advanced Materials*, *29*(14). Available from https://doi.org/10.1002/adma.201606628.

Tam, E. M., Fulton, R. B., Sampson, J. F., Muda, M., Camblin, A., Richards, J., Koshkaryev, A., Tang, J., Kurella, V., Jiao, Y., Xu, L., Zhang, K., Kohli, N., Luus, L., Hutto, E., Kumar, S., Lulo, J., Paragas, V., Wong, C., & Raue, A. (2019). *Science Translational Medicine*, *11*(512). Available from https://doi.org/10.1126/scitranslmed.aax0720.

Trynda-Lemiesz, L. (2004). *Bioorganic and Medicinal Chemistry*, *12*(12), 3269–3275. Available from https://doi.org/10.1016/j.bmc.2004.03.073.

van der Meel, R., Vehmeijer, L. J. C., Kok, R. J., Storm, G., & van Gaal, E. V. B. (2013). *Advanced Drug Delivery Reviews*, *65*(10), 1284–1298. Available from https://doi.org/10.1016/j.addr.2013.08.012.

Voicu, A. I., Gârea, S. A., Ghebaur, A., Nistor, C. L., Sârbu, A., Vasile, E., Mitran, R., & Iovu, H. (2021). *Microporous and Mesoporous Materials*, *328*, 111434. Available from https://doi.org/10.1016/j.micromeso.2021.111434.

Wang, J., Qian, Y., Xu, L., Shao, Y., Zhang, H., Shi, F., Chen, J., Cui, S., Chen, X., Zhu, D., Hu, R., & Chen, Z. (2020). *Materials Science and Engineering: C*, *117*, 111261. Available from https://doi.org/10.1016/j.msec.2020.111261.

Wang, Y., Cheetham, A. G., Angacian, G., Su, H., Xie, L., & Cui, H. (2017). *Advanced Drug Delivery Reviews*, *110–111*, 112–126. Available from https://doi.org/10.1016/j.addr.2016.06.015.

Wang, Y., Zhang, Z., Jain, V., Yi, J., Mueller, S., Sokolov, J., Liu, Z., Levon, K., Rigas, B., & Rafailovich, M. H. (2010). *Sensors and Actuators, B: Chemical*, *146*(1), 381–387. Available from https://doi.org/10.1016/j.snb.2010.02.032.

Wei, M., Gao, Y., Li, X., & Serpe, M. J. (2017). *Polymer Chemistry*, *8*(1), 127–143. Available from https://doi.org/10.1039/c6py01585a.

Wicki, A., Witzigmann, D., Balasubramanian, V., & Huwyler, J. (2015). *Journal of Controlled Release*, *200*, 138–157. Available from https://doi.org/10.1016/j.jconrel.2014.12.030.

Wu, X. Z. (2006). *Medical Hypotheses*, *66*(5), 883–887. Available from https://doi.org/10.1016/j.mehy.2005.11.036.
Xu, L., Xu, S., Xiang, T., Liu, H., Chen, L., Jiang, B., Yao, J., Zhu, H., Hu, R., & Chen, Z. (2022). *Engineered Regeneration*, *3*(1), 92–109. Available from https://doi.org/10.1016/j.engreg.2022.02.004.
Yao, H. P., Zhao, H., Hudson, R., Tong, X. M., & Wang, M. H. (2021). *Drug Discovery Today*, *26*(8), 1857–1874. Available from https://doi.org/10.1016/j.drudis.2021.06.012.
Yao, J., Feng, J., & Chen, J. (2016). *Asian Journal of Pharmaceutical Sciences*, *11*(5), 585–595. Available from https://doi.org/10.1016/j.ajps.2016.06.001.
Zhang, W., Zhai, Z., Huang, S., Mao, Z., Zhang, Y., & Gao, C. (2020). *Giant*, *3*, 100026. Available from https://doi.org/10.1016/j.giant.2020.100026.
Zhu, L., & Torchilin, V. P. (2013). *Integrative Biology (United Kingdom)*, *5*(1), 96–107. Available from https://doi.org/10.1039/c2ib20135f.
Zielińska, A., Szalata, M., Gorczyński, A., Karczewski, J., Eder, P., Severino, P., Cabeda, J. M., Souto, E. B., & Słomski, R. (2021). *Cancers*, *13*(8), 1896. Available from https://doi.org/10.3390/cancers13081896.
Zwicke, G. L., Ali Mansoori, G., & Jeffery, C. J. (2012). *Nano Reviews*, *3*(1), 18496. Available from https://doi.org/10.3402/nano.v3i0.18496.

CHAPTER 5

Role of nanocarriers for inflammation treatment

Akshansh Sharma[1], Ishan Sharma[2], Ankit[3], Sachin Kumar Singh[3], Kamal Dua[4,5], Sadanand Pandey[6] and Deepak Kumar[1]

[1]Department of Pharmaceutical Chemistry, School of Pharmaceutical Sciences, Shoolini University, Solan, Himachal Pradesh, India
[2]Department of Pharmacology, School of Pharmaceutical Sciences, Shoolini University, Solan, Himachal Pradesh, India
[3]School of Pharmaceutical Sciences, Lovely Professional University, Phagwara, Punjab, India
[4]Discipline of Pharmacy, Graduate School of Health, University of Technology Sydney, Ultimo, NSW, Australia
[5]Faculty of Health, Australian Research Centre in Complementary and Integrative Medicine, University of Technology, Sydney, Ultimo, NSW, Australia
[6]Department of Chemistry, College of Natural Sciences, Yeungnam University, Gyeongsan, Gyeongbuk, South Korea

Introduction

According to researchers, the inflammatory response has been discovered to be a critical infective component in several illnesses. In addition to protecting the host from inflammation, the innate immune system also initiates the innate inflammatory response mechanism (Ferrero-Miliani et al., 2007). Inflammation is a biological defense process that may be provoked by different types of factors, including pathogens, reactive oxygen species (ROS), physical agents, and metabolic disturbances. Inflammation is an extremely complicated system, with medical breakthroughs about its molecular mechanisms being made every year (Alamil, 2022). Sepsis, obesity, asthma, cardiovascular and neurodegenerative diseases, tumor, type 2 diabetes, rheumatoid polyarthritis, and bowel and Crohn's diseases (CDs) are now known to be combined by an unregulated inflammatory reaction (Fig. 5.1) (Chovatiya & Medzhitov, 2014).

The use of steroidal or nonsteroidal anti-inflammatory medicines is now a part of the treatment strategy. Additionally, antileukotrienes and proinflammatory cytokine inhibitors are two new therapeutic methods that have recently developed. These remedies provide short half-life; adequate pharmacological action as well as lesser bioavailability and the lack of specificity in biodistribution. Furthermore, patients must be given substantially high doses, which generate off-target adverse effects and have moderate efficacy in treating inflammatory disease symptoms (Tabas & Glass, 2013). Biocompatible nanomedicines with carefully controlled shape, size, and charged surface are now possible (Banerjee et al., 2016; Jindal, 2017; Jo et al., 2015; Agrahari et al., 2019). Several kinds of nanoparticles (NPs) have anti-inflammatory potential, which is being revealed by many discoveries (Browne & Pandit, 2015). Nanotechnology is a burgeoning discipline with potential diagnostical and

Nanotechnology for Drug Delivery and Pharmaceuticals
DOI: https://doi.org/10.1016/B978-0-323-95325-2.00012-2

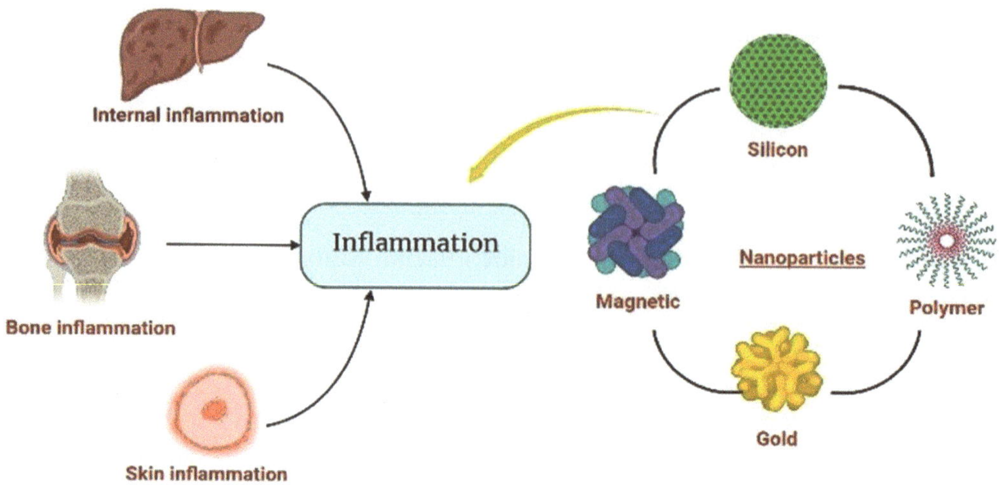

Figure 5.1 Anti-inflammatory activity of different nanoparticles.

therapeutical uses in a variety of medical fields (Langer & Tirrell, 2004; Farokhzad & Langer, 2006; Sharma et al., 2022a). Nanomaterials may be designed and built to demonstrate adaptability to new surroundings and degradation once their goals are fulfilled (Jia et al., 2013; Li et al., 2014a). In healthcare, the utilization of nanosized tools in drug transportation is beneficial. Nanocarriers may be made out of a wide range of materials used to deliver medications in a regulated manner and can identify the region of inflammation and administer a recommended medication if introduced into the human body (Li et al., 2014b). Nanocarriers can be configured to break-down and leave the body after a predetermined amount of time in the form of fecal material or through urine (Albanese et al., 2012). The goal of this chapter is to impart a clearer idea of how nanocarriers might be used in medicine, particularly in the treatment of inflammatory disorders. The applications of nanomaterials as carriers in the identification, prophylaxis, and mitigation of inflammation disorders (Bisht et al., 2021). The advancement of pharmaceutical nanomedicine extends future prospects and the possibilities of drug delivery by assisting in targeted drug therapy, enabling adequate release while maintaining the effective concentration, which further will considerably increase anti-inflammatory agent deposition (Ikoba et al., 2015a).

Overview of inflammatory conditions and treatments

The term "inflammation" is linked to multiple disorders, where anti-inflammatory drugs are proved to be effective in a myriad of conditions (Ma et al., 2017). As athero-sclerosis is the reason behind myocardial infarction which is a fatal disease (Katsuki et al., 2017) and is usually associated with the mechanism where inflammation is triggered by macrophages (Hansson et al., 2006). Researchers discovered that statins have anti-inflammatory properties, and the JUPITER (Justification for the Use of Statins in Prevention: An Intervention Trial Evaluating Rosuvastatin) trial demonstrated that intensive cholesterol lowering therapy can reduce 44% of major cardiovascular events (Takemoto & Liao, 2001). Cancers are one of the causes of mortality worldwide, and inflammation is significantly responsible in tumorigenesis. Tumor growth is aided by the invasion of leukocytes and the release of inflammatory chemokines. Numerous NPs have demonstrated to exhibit tumor-targeted impact, and a drug delivery approach based on nanocarriers boosts the accumulation of drug within the targeted site of action while lowering the drug resistance (Attri et al., 2020; Shukla et al., 2022).Therefore researchers investigated integrated actions against inflammation and tumor development and discovered that they may be employed to treat tumors. Researchers have utilized vesicles or sacs within the membrane of red blood cells (RBC) for efficient encapsulation and delivery of black phosphorus NP quantum dots (BPQDs) (Kumar et al., 2022) with anticancer and anti-inflammatory medicines doxorubicin (DOX) and Kirenol (KIR). RBC@BPQDsDOX/KIR NP platform demonstrated combined actions against inflammation and cancer progression. Moreover, this approach of delivering drugs, which shows integrated effects, is yet to be studied, while the associated biological toxic effects and stability issues require more investigation (Hung et al.). Patient eyesight is jeopardized by ocular problems (Stukenkemper et al., 2015). Many people are affected by diseases like few allergies associated diseases and xerophthalmia where intraocular implants are utilized to treat intraocular defective disorders like uveitis (Multicenter Uveitis Steroid Treatment (MUST) Trial Research Group, 2015) and glaucoma (Hoffman et al., 2002). An inflammatory response is linked to the majority of eye disorders and surgical treatments (Jóhannesson et al., 2020). Ocular medicines have evolved to cure disorders where eye is the specific target. Anti-inflammatory medications can effectively reach structures when encapsulated in nanocarriers. Furthermore, various nanomaterials have varied physicochemical properties, allowing NPs to reach the specific site of action. Chronic inflammatory conditions, including uveitis and age-related macular degeneration, necessitate maintaining a specific therapeutic dose that contributes significantly in therapy. As sometimes biodegradable polymer drug carriers can lead to intraocular inflammation, dexamethasone conjugated with self-arranging block co-polypeptide NPs, which demonstrated long-term cumulative drug release in eyes as well as greater loading capacity. Furthermore, one of the biodegradable nanocarrier is liposome that increases anti-inflammatory drug interaction with the corneal structure, allowing for better ocular absorption of the drug. Anti-inflammatory medications such as ibuprofen, dexamethasone, and other anti-inflammatory medications, when placed within the nanosized moieties, enhanced the efficacy of drug and aided in maintaining a constant concentration in ocular region (Chang et al., 2020). Sepsis is a fatal organ dysfunctioning disorder, which is induced by an uncontrolled response in host which is triggered by infection, and is linked to a high rate of morbidity and death across the world. Sepsis is caused by uncontrolled and unrestrained inflammatory reactions. To demonstrate the integrated effect of microorganism eradication and anti-inflammatory action, antibiotics and anti-inflammatory drugs are employed in clinical therapy. However, there are still drawbacks, like critical side effects, hepatic and renal malfunction, and low absorption. Some of these challenges have been circumvented in recent nanomedicine research. In the mouse model, these nanoscale drug carriers are employed for administering antibiotics within cells. In a septic mouse model, researchers evaluated a codelivery mechanism of anti-inflammatory drugs and antibiotics, which specifically targets microenvironment of infectious agents. Nevertheless, more study is required to completely comprehend the potential of novel drug delivery system (NDDS) (Lim et al., 2021). Inflammation causing disorders have become more prominent than before. Chronic diseases (inflammatory bowel disease (IBD), osteoarthritis, rheumatoid arthritis, skin disorders), and acute disorders, such as acute ischemia inflammation, and acute airway inflammation, trauma, all require prompt and precise therapy. The advancement of nanobased pharmaceuticals has widened the future scope of drug delivery by assisting drug delivery to targeted tissue, enabling release at a more effective concentration range, which will altogether boost anti-inflammatory agent concentration substantially (Wang et al., 2021).

Anti-inflammatory treatment with a nanoparticle-based drug delivery system

Currently, multiple NPs have been analyzed for their anti-inflammatory treatment. For enhanced biocompatibility and targeting abilities, one or more materials are synthesized into nanostructures, with the properties of each material fully used. The development of NPs that regulate the production of anti-inflammatory agents while also phagocytosing markers of inflammatory response or macrophages has enormous potential for the treatment of inflammatory illnesses. Anti-inflammatory nanomedicines have been developed in response to a great deal to focus on developing nanomedicines, which can circumvent the negative effects of traditional medication and possess greater anti-inflammatory action (Dacoba et al., 2017).

Drug delivery system using organic nanoparticles

Majority of carriers are formed of polymer or biomaterial, and organic NPs that are more biocompatible. Natural and artificial polymers are two types of polymers. PLGA [poly(lactic-*co*-glycolic acid)] is a lipophilic synthetic polymer that has shown tremendous promise in medication administration to specific targets. Calcium added to the outer phase of PLGA NPs boosted protein and peptide encapsulation efficacy by 42%

when compared to particles without calcium (Andreadis, 2006). In the case of osteogenic sarcoma, osteoarthrosis, bone cancer metastases, and other bone disorders due to inflammation, PLGA has been employed. PLGA nanospheres to insert doxycycline (DOXY) into a 3D scaffold, which they subsequently tested in vitro.

In an inflammatory model that focuses on cartilage explants, an anti-inflammatory peptide KAFAK [KAFAK was initially loaded into copolymerized 2-acrylamido-2-methylpropane sulfonic acid (AMPS) and *N*-isopropylacrylamide (NIPAM) monomers], which is an inhibitor of mitogen-activated protein kinase-2, was evaluated. The authors observed, however, that due to KAFAK's strong affinity for the NPs' core and the absence of core disintegration, only half of the loaded peptides were released, limiting the therapeutic uses of this approach (Poh et al., 2015).

IBD is a set of persistent gastrointestinal disorders that includes ulcerative colitis (UC) and CD. Oral decoy oligonucleotide (ODN) was proven to be useful in UC mice models (Tahara et al., 2011; Yazeji et al., 2017). This work created an oral medication delivery system by combining chitosan (CS)-modified PLGA nanospheres with NF-kB decoy ODN. ODN stability was enhanced using decoy ODN-loaded CS-PLGA NS, while bloody feces and diarrhea were decreased. Decoy ODN-loaded CSPLGA NS has the potential to be a successful UC treatment method, according to the findings. Rheumatoid arthritis is another frequent chronic inflammatory illness that affects many persons. Low dosages of methotrexate (MTX) and antirheumatic medication that modify disease are used to treat this illness (DMARD). Lutetium-177 (177Lu) was reported to reduce synovial tissue inflammation by Trujillo-Nolasco et al. (2019). Furthermore, 1,4,7,10-tetraazacyclododecane-1,4,7,10-tetraacetic acid (DOTA) was employed as a 177Lu agent, which was produced by combining hyaluronic acid (HA) with 177Lu-DOTA and encapsulating the compound with PLGA and MTX. 177Lu-DOTA-HA-PLGA (MTX) showed promise as an antirheumatic delivery system of drug; however, further animal studies are required to authenticate the findings.

Exosomes are involved in the pathophysiology of a variety of inflammatory disorders, including infections and autoimmune illnesses. Exosomes generated from pathogen-infected mammalian cells, for example, have a wide range of inflammatory properties. Exosomes from mycobacterium disease macrophages transport mycobacteria-derived antigens and stimulate proinflammatory immune responses in vitro in vivo studies, while inhibiting macrophage activation by INF-γ (Bhatnagar et al., 2007; Singh et al., 2014). Similarly, exosomes released by macrophages infected with *Mycobacterium smegmatis* or *Mycobacterium avium* exhibit a higher surface expression of Hsp70 that stimulates the NF-B pathway, resulting in high levels of TNF-α. Exosomes with high quantities of Hsp70 can activate NKκB cells and cause macrophages to produce TNF- α, resulting in a proinflammatory response (Gastpar et al., 2005). In a rat model of autoimmune myocarditis, PEGylated liposomes loaded with the immune system suppressant FK506 were found to reduce the production of cytokines like interferon and tumor necrosis factor, as well as inflammation and fibrosis of the myocardium, after systemic injection. Another immunosuppressive medication, cyclosporine-A, was similarly encapsulated using liposomal nanoformulations. In a rat model, for example, iv treatment of liposomal-cyclosporine-A reduced brain ischemia and reperfusion damage, such as neuroinflammation, by decreasing inflammatory responses such as MPO activity and TNF level (Lee et al., 2011a). Intranasal treatment of a cationic oil-in-water nanoemulsion showed the anti-inflammatory activity of cyclosporine-A in another investigation on neuroinflammation in rats (Singh et al., 2012a). Aside from the nanomedicines mentioned earlier, carriers, such as collagen hydrogel (Lin et al., 2015), gelatine hydrogel (Ratanavaraporn et al., 2012), lactide-*co*-glycoside scaffold (Gower et al., 2014), hyaluronic acid hydrogel (Nakamura et al., 2004), amphiphilic poly-*N*-vinylpyrrolidone (Amph-PVP) (Kuskov et al., 2017), and Emulgel (Gul et al., 2018), have an impact on biocompatibility and anti-inflammatory efficacy and also improve accuracy in drug delivery. These devices used for delivery of drugs come in a variety of shapes that target various tissues. Most of the inflammation is controlled by macrophages, which are responsible for both proinflammatory and anti-inflammatory responses. As a result, several studies concentrate on macrophages. As a result, macrophages are important targets for inflammatory therapy.

Drug delivery systems using inorganic nanoparticles

Drugs inhibiting inflammation and inorganic carriers are frequently used to create inorganic NPs for inflammation treatment. Oxides of nanosized metal particles are much more stable and can be used in a variety of nanomedicine significance as a drug delivery vehicle. Zinc oxide NPs (ZnO NPs) have outstanding biological characteristics because zinc plays an essential role in genetic transmission impulses (Sharma et al., 2022b). These ZnO NPs have been found to be bacteriostatic (Agarwal & Shanmugam, 2020).

ZnO is a potent antibacterial agent. Based on ZnO's antibacterial properties, many NPs have been studied. In one investigation, it was revealed that folic acid–modified PEG-ZnO NPs had an antitumor and anti-inflammatory coeffect in delivery of drug (Vimala & Soundarapandian, 2017).

The QD is a fluorescent semiconductor nanosized particle that has sparked a lot of attention in theranostic research. In addition, new study has found that QD may aid in the administration of medications. Inflammatory disorders are treated with the drugs inhibiting inflammation as NSAIDs. Scientists found a link between celecoxib and QD. The inflamed paw of the mice was clearly targeted by these QD–celecoxib conjugates, which had both an anti-inflammatory and a bioimaging impact (Kalangi et al., 2018).

In an in vitro experiment, researchers used sodium 10-amino-2 methoxyundecanoate (SAM) and N-doped graphene QDs (N-GQDs). Compared to SAM alone, the combination of SAM and N-GQDs enhanced COX-2, iNOS, TNF-a, NF-kß, IL-1a,

IL-1ß, IL-4, and IL-6 downregulation. Because of these alterations, SAM in conjunction with *N*-GQD believed to have inflammation-inhibiting activity (Table 5.1) (Sameer Kumar et al., 2018).

Table 5.1 The importance of drug delivery systems based on organic and inorganic nanosized particle.

Therapeutic agent	Nanocarriers	Disorder	Reference
Organic nanoparticles			
SDF-1α	PLAG	Implant station	Melchels et al. (2010)
Ac2−26	Col IV-targeted PLAG	Atherosclerosis	Fredman et al. (2015)
DOXY	PLAG	Periodontitis and arthritis	Feng et al. (2010)
Teicoplanin	mPEG-PLAG	Osteomyelitis	Peng et al. (2010)
ODN	CS-PLAG	Ulcerative colitis	Tahara et al. (2011)
MTX	Lu-DOTA-HA-PLAG	Rheumatic arthritic	Trujillo-Nolasco et al. (2019)
Curcumin	Exosome	Septic shock	Sun et al. (2010)
Dex	FPC-Exosome	Rheumatic arthritis	Yan et al. (2020)
NA	TGF-β1-Exosome	Colitis	Cai et al. (2012)
NA	G-MDSC Exosome	Colitis	Lin et al. (2015)
qu	M2 Exosome	Atherosclerosis	Wu et al. (2020)
IL-10	Liposome	Obesity	Toita et al. (2016)
PIO	Liposome	Atherosclerosis	Wu et al. (2020)
Dex/Mino	Liposome-PEEK	Orthopedic/dental implant	Xu et al. (2019)
Inorganic nanoparticles			
Monocyte	As@GNC	Osteomyelitis	Shi et al. (2020)
Celecoxib	QD	Local edema	Kalangi et al. (2018)
SAM	N-GQD	NA	Sameer Kumar et al. (2018)
Diclofenac sodium	CNT	Arthritic pain	Spizzirri et al. (2013)
Ketoprofen	PEO/PETA-MWCNT	NA	Im et al. (2010)

Ac2−26, Amino acids 2−26; *Col IV*, collagen IV; *CS*, chitosan; *DOXY*, doxycycline; *Dex*, dexamethasone; *Dex/Mino*, dexamethasone plus minocycline; *FPC*, folic acid (FA)-polyethylene glycol (PEG)-cholesterol (Chol); *G-MDSC*, granulocytic myeloid-derived suppressor cells; *HAL*, hexyl 5-aminolevulinate hydrochloride; *177Lu-DOTA-HA-PLGA*, Lutetium-177−1,4,7,10-Tetraazacyclododecane-1,4,7,10-tetraacetic acid-hyaluronic acid-poly (lactic-*co*-glycolic acid); *IL-10*, Interleukin-10; *mPEG*, poly(ethylene glycol) monomethyl ether; *NA*, not available; *ODN*, oral decoy oligonucleotide; *PLGA*, poly(lactic-*co*-glycolic acid); *PIO*, pioglitazone; *SDF-1a*, stromal cell-derived factor-1a; *sol−gel*, solution to hydrogel. *As@GNC*, aspirin-containing gold nanocage; *CNT*, carbon nanotube; *NA*, not applicable; *PEO/PETA-MWCNT*, poly-ethylene oxide/Pentaerythritol triacrylatemulti-walled carbon nanotubes; *QD*, quantum dot; *SAM*, sodium 10-amino-2-methoxyundecanoate.

When circulating through the circulation, spherical gold NPs coated with the surface modification cetyltrimethylammonium bromide (CTAB) were shown to be nontoxic. Human cells absorb CTAB-treated nanosized particles with almost negligible toxicity, according to a study using transmission electron microscopy. Because of their negative charge, citric-acid-capped gold nanosized particles have a strong opposing reactivity, making surface modification easier. The use of gold NPs for medication administration has been promoted because of its reduced size, minimal cytotoxicity, and lower generation of proinflammatory cytokines (Patra et al., 2010). When mice were given gold NPs intraperitoneally, they accumulated in abdominal adipose tissue. The toxicity of gold NPs was low, and there was little change in inflammatory cytokines in mice's adipose tissue (Chen et al., 2013).

Treatment of inflammatory diseases using nanoparticles

Nanotechnology is a science that could be used to cure inflammatory disorders. Specific forms of inflammatory disorders are bone, skin, and internal inflammation.

Bone inflammation

The management of bone inflammation is progressing successfully because of the advancements made in nanotechnology. Metallic NPs provide a good surface for osteoblasts to bind to bone. Such metallic nanosized particles allow bone forming cells (osteoblasts) to proliferate during a certain period of time, allowing for more effective osteoregeneration (Tran & Webster, 2009). The nanocomposite materials must induce certain proteins to enhance bone regeneration throughout the osteogenesis process. Hydroxyapatite, a nanoscale ceramic element of bone, has shown to have immense promise in terms of enhancing osteoblast productivity (Zhang & Webster, 2009). Nanocomposites have also been shown to increase osteoblast development when used in combination with carbon nanotubes. By eliminating competition from different cells, such as fibroblasts, carbon nanotubes with a diameter of around 60 nm can help in achieving osseointegration (Zhang & Webster, 2009). Heparin, an anti-inflammatory and anticoagulant agent, helps to increase osteoblast and osteogenesis activity by generating anti-inflammatory activity on the surface of titanium (Kim et al., 2011). Titanium (Ti) is one of the most popular nanomaterials in orthopedics due to its corrosion resistance and biocompatibility. Titanium NPs can avoid direct contact between bones during surgical implantation, minimizing the implant materials from triggering inflammation (Carmody et al., 2002). Bone disorders and infectious diseases are commonly treated with magnetic NPs. Magnetic nanosized particles produce a magnetic field that help in the treatment of infections and bone ailments. Few researchers demonstrated gamma-Fe_2O_3. Within a few days, Pareta and colleagues found that gamma-Fe_2O_3 magnetic nanosized particles significantly boosted the density of osteoblasts (Pareta et al., 2008). The use of calcium phosphate as a coating for magnetic NPs can help cure multiple bone disorders (Gu et al., 2013). Anti-inflammatory medicines can also be transferred to bone via poly(amidoamine) (PAMAM) dendrimers. PAMAM dendrimers have primary amino group coupling ability, biocompatibility, and homogeneity (Thomas et al., 2011). Joint inflammation can be treated with superparamagnetic iron oxide NPs integrated with PLGA particles. These particles have demonstrated effectiveness in the treatment of joint disorders as they do not trigger reaction due to inflammation in the joints (Gu et al., 2013).

Internal inflammation

Nanotechnology has been researched for controlled medication release to target and prevent inflammation of interior organs (Du et al., 2014; Liu et al., 2014). A peptide component, for example, was engineered to incorporate with a nanosized particle to promote more cell contact and improve cell signaling pathway and protein production (Webber et al., 2010). During the time peptide NP remains in the body, as it exhibited the ability to specifically target inflammatory cells, while also maintaining therapeutic concentration in a timely manner. Internal inflammation induced by NPs is prevented as peptide nanosized particles do not aggregate overtime in the systemic circulation (Webber et al., 2010). Considering the point that NPs can generate internal inflammation when targeting cells of host, hence particle size and surface coatings are important factors in minimizing this situation. The particle sizes should be between 120 and 200 nm (Higaki, 2009) to minimize particle aggregation and entrapment while targeting the inflamed region. PLA/PLGA NPs with PEG grafts have been demonstrated to have no immunological reactions and considerably reduced interaction with the mononuclear phagocyte system (Higaki, 2009). The association of NPs with proinflammatory cytokines has been researched. Because of the capacity to interact with and control proinflammatory cytokines, mesoporous silica nanosized particles were able to suppress inflammation processes in the cells (Lee et al., 2011b). Rampazzo et al. discovered that modifying polyethylene glycol-amino can increase the absorption of the particles of silica by healthy or cancerous cells, which can be utilized to monitor particle mobility in the organ or cell. According to Singh et al., nanotechnology possesses potential functionality in controlling neuroinflammation, which might be beneficial in the management of multiple sclerosis. Nanosized particles transport medicine to the affected area of the brain, reducing neuroinflammation and slowing disease continuation (Singh et al., 2012b).

Skin inflammation

Nanotechnology has overcome obstacles to treat skin illnesses (Li et al., 2014c; Xin et al., 2014). Nanomaterials are engineered to ensure therapeutic delivery with other therapeutics overtime (Cevc & Vierl, 2010; Wang et al., 2007). As one of the treatments for skin infections, nitric oxide filled the chambers of nanosized particles and was distributed over a controlled period of time. In the case of dermal infections, nitric oxide–conjugated NPs were favored to injection needles (Englander & Friedman, 2010). UV (ultraviolet) radiation is another well-known trigger to skin irritation. The stratum corneum protects the body from UV rays. Sunscreens are a wonderful example of how individuals employ NPs to protect themselves from UV radiation. Sunscreen NPs made of zinc oxide (ZnO) and titanium dioxide (TiO2) are the most popular. ZnO and TiO_2 nanosized particles absorb damaging UVA and UVB rays and reflect both as heat and visible light back into the environment. By absorbing, reflecting, and scattering, ZnO and TiO_2 prevent UV photons from accessing live skin cells (Popov et al., 2010; Kim et al., 2012). A wound repair phenomenon happens once the protective layers of body are damaged. According to the scientists, iron oxide NPs are effective delivery tools for thrombin (Ziv-Polat et al., 2010). Thrombin, a protein that affects inflammatory cells, fibroblasts, and endothelial cells directly, is believed to have a function in tissue healing by activating initial cellular activities (Carney et al., 1992). Thrombin was protected from antithrombin and activated protein C by iron oxide particles. Antibiotics might be administered reliably using NPs to treat skin irritation and wounds. Because of the controlled release capabilities of NPs, antibiotics might be administered in lesser doses, minimizing the chance of antibiotic resistance. Skin inflammation is promoted and caused by a number of different disorders. Psoriasis, for instance, is a persistent inflammatory condition affecting the skin and joints. Psoriasis causes skin regeneration to be many times quicker than normal. Many anti-inflammatory medications, including ketoprofen and spantide II, have the ability to alleviate skin irritation when used together (Kolenyak dos Santos et al., 2013). Both anti-inflammatory medicines and NPs are aided by NPs for permeability through the dermal protective barriers (Shah et al., 2012a, 2012b). To treat skin irritation, diclofenac-conjugated phospholipid nanovesicles were synthesized, which increased drug concentration on the skin while limiting penetration under the skin (Caddeo et al., 2013).

Clinical trials

Nanocarriers for inflammatory disease have successfully passed preclinical testing. And since then, they have been employed in clinical investigations to improve the penetration of active compounds into the skin (Fig. 5.2). Unlike other non-lipid nanocarriers (LNC) formulation, tocopheryl acetate encapsulated within LNC enhanced skin hydration (Moddaresi et al., 2009). For a comparable investigation, Verdu et al. compiled test results from 103 participants. Nanocrystalline silver dressings were used on 77 of the subjects (median age = 80, 41.6% men). These individuals had various ulcers, such as traumatic or surgical, pressure ulcers, and lower extremity ulcers. Overall, 96.1% of the clinical indications in the diseased tissue went entirely after 42.5 days of healing ($P < .001$), whereas 27.3% of the damage healed. Overall, 92.9% of

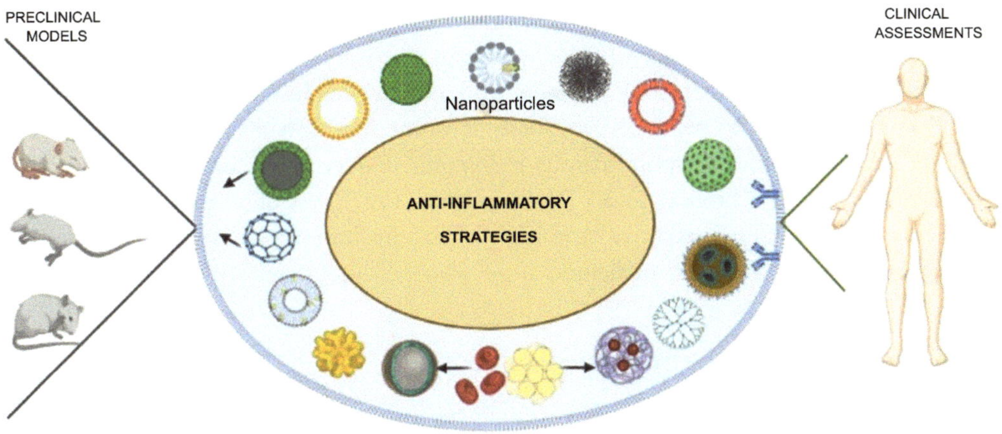

Figure 5.2 Strategies in clinical studies to increase the penetration of active substances.

the patients who were not entirely cured showed substantial enhancement ($P < .05$). All of these analyses support the use of silver NP dressings for improving numerous skin ulcers. Regulating infections and inflammatory disorders initiates with recognizing and characterizing the pathogen. As a result, low-cost, quick, and sensitive diagnostic tests are required. The idea of applying nanotechnology for the diagnosis of diseases is intriguing. Researchers created a particulate probe that linked recombinant *Treponema pallidum* antigens (r-Tp) to gold magnetic NPs coated with acrylic acid. Anti-Tp antibody levels were measured in 1020 serum specimens collected from three hospitals. In most clinical situations (>97%), the probe is precise and reliable, suggesting that nanocomposites are a suitable candidate for syphilis screening (Yang et al., 2013). The flavonoid quercetin conjugated with colloidal silica particles enhances stratum corneum penetration more than quercetin conjugated within lipid NPs (Scalia et al., 2012). Colloidal silica particles notably aid medication permeation into the deeper horny layer strips, implying that silica NPs are a superior alternative for skin disorders, including inflammation and infections. In patients with chronic venous leg ulcers who had been treated by a multilayer bandage, nanocrystalline silver dressings lowered wound neutrophilic inflammation and bacteria. Despite a marginal spike, after healing with silver dressings, serum silver levels remained within the permissible limits (Sibbald et al., 2007). Gingivitis can be caused by pathogenic flora. Unimag, a steady solution of magnetic NPs, can boost bacterial sensitivity to magnetic treatments (Ikoba et al., 2015b).

Ultimately, effective clinical trials have shown that nanotechnology might be used to treat and identify infections and inflammatory disorders in humans. Nanotechnology will inevitably impact the medical business due to its high performance and responsiveness. The existing nanotechnology market is continuously increasing and has a promising future. Nanotechnology items, such as medicines for infectious and inflammatory diseases, are expected to have higher sales in the coming time. StarPharma, for example, utilizes

VivaGel technology to produce anti-HIV and anti-HSV dendrimers (Mazzola, 2003). The FDA has authorized Megace ES belonging to the Par Company, which is an appetizer. It can be used to keep HIV patients from losing weight. SkyePharma is applying DepoFoam technology to produce cytarabine liposome injection that has been authorized by the FDA for treating lympohomatous meningitis. Government investment on nanotechnology R&D has climbed to $3.7 billion since 1997. A vast number of nanodrugs will be included in the market as funding for nanotechnology expands, and this will ensure a bright future for nanomedicines.

Future prospects and conclusions

Cellular and molecular discoveries have enhanced our understanding of the inflammatory response in recent years, leading to the identification of various targets for biological treatments to treat illnesses due to inflammation. Despite encouraging progress in establishing such therapies the extensive distribution of inflammatory signal transduction in a variety of cell types and tissues causes significant off-target undesirable effects as well as systemic toxicity. Current medicines still have clinical challenges to surmount because of poor bioavailability and restricted half-lives, which necessitates frequent and expensive high doses that cause significant adverse effects. Chronic inflammation can often lead to systemic illnesses, whereas acute inflammation can quickly escalate into a severe condition that can be fatal. This has encouraged academic study into nanocarrier design in order to increase anti-inflammatory drug delivery. Nanomedicine has evolved into a multidisciplinary topic that emphasizes the physicochemical and biological elements of NPs in recent years. Anti-inflammatory therapy has made extensive use of nanotechnology. The benefits of diverse materials, whether organic NPs or inorganic NPs, provide different technologies to boost therapeutic results while decreasing side effects. The majority of NP-based medication delivery technologies are listed above. Some NPs are still in the research stage, while other organic NPs have already been utilized in clinical trials. Biocompatible, biodegradable, nontoxic, and regulated drug release are all requirements for the postulated NP-based drug delivery systems. As a result, carriers and facilitators are important components in establishing an effective medication delivery system. Apart from increasing the action and bioavailability of the carrier or support, there will be additional pharmacological choices in the future. QDs offer powerful targeting and bioimaging properties, and their size variability allows them to modulate by inorganic materials, peptides, and antibodies for precise, aimed inflammatory treatment (particularly immune-related inflammation). QDs have been shown to be useful not only in anti-inflammatory therapy, as well as in real-time localization and imaging, which can improve treatment efficiency. Even though NPs have several advantages in terms of administration of drugs, there are still a few issues to work out before they can be used in clinical trials. Exosomes are secretions of tissues that are used as vehicles with high biocompatibility and targeting ability; varied sizes of exosomes may be obtained; exosome purification is unique, so enhancing exosome uniformity is the key to better using their features. Liposomes have been utilized in clinical trials to transport pharmaceuticals; most drug toxicities are decreased when they are encapsulated along liposomes; despite that it is not the optimal carrier for hydrophilic drugs. In terms of metal carriers, ZnO NPs and GNP are unstable, which limits their use. CNTs are intriguing vehicles with excellent biocompatibility, but their targeting potential requires improvement. A deeper knowledge of disorders due inflammatory and the use of NPs for specific diseases would increase the therapeutic impact and minimize pharmacological adverse effects significantly.

Acknowledgment

Prof. Deepak Kumar is thankful to Vice-Chancellor, Shoolini University, Solan, Himachal Pradesh 173229, India for providing support for this work.

References

Agarwal, H., & Shanmugam, V. (2020). A review on anti-inflammatory activity of green synthesized zinc oxide nanoparticle: Mechanism-based approach. *Bioorganic Chemistry*, *94*, 103423. Available from https://doi.org/10.1016/j.bioorg.2019.103423.

Agrahari, V., Burnouf, P. A., Burnouf, T., & Agrahari, V. (2019). Nanoformulation properties, characterization, and behavior in complex biological matrices: Challenges and opportunities for brain-targeted drug delivery applications and enhanced translational potential. *Advanced Drug Delivery Reviews*, *148*, 146–180. Available from https://doi.org/10.1016/j.addr.2019.02.008.

Alamil, J. M. R., et al. (2022). Rediscovering the therapeutic potential of agarwood in the management of chronic inflammatory diseases. *Molecules*, *27*(9), 3038. Available from https://doi.org/10.3390/molecules27093038.

Albanese, A., Tang, P. S., & Chan, W. C. (2012). The effect of nanoparticle size, shape, and surface chemistry on biological systems. *Annual Review of Biomedical Engineering*, *14*, 1–6. Available from https://doi.org/10.1146/annurev-bioeng-071811-150124.

Andreadis, S. T. (2006). Gene-modified tissue-engineered skin: The next generation of skin substitutes. *Tissue Engineering II*, 241–274. Available from https://doi.org/10.1007/10_023.

Attri, A., Thakur, D., Kaur, T., Sensale, S., Peng, Z., Kumar, D., & Singh, R. P. (2020). Nanoparticles incorporating a fluorescence turn-on reporter for real-time drug release monitoring, a chemoenhancer and a stealth agent: Poseidon's trident against cancer? *Molecular Pharmaceutics*, *18*(1), 124–147. Available from https://doi.org/10.1021/acs.molpharmaceut.0c00730.

Banerjee, A., Qi, J., Gogoi, R., Wong, J., & Mitragotri, S. (2016). Role of nanoparticle size, shape and surface chemistry in oral drug delivery. *Journal of Controlled Release*, *238*, 176–185. Available from https://doi.org/10.1016/j.jconrel.2016.07.051.

Bhatnagar, S., Shinagawa, K., Castellino, F. J., & Schorey, J. S. (2007). Exosomes released from macrophages infected with intracellular pathogens stimulate a proinflammatory response in vitro and in vivo. *Blood, The Journal of the American Society of Hematology*, *110*(9), 3234–3244. Available from https://doi.org/10.1182/blood-2007-03-079152.

Bisht, D., Rashid, M., Arya, R. K., Kumar, D., Chaudhary, S. K., Rana, V. S., & Sethiya, N. K. (2021). Revisiting liquorice (*Glycyrrhiza glabra* L.) as anti-inflammatory, antivirals and immunomodulators: Potential pharmacological applications with mechanistic insight. *Phytomedicine Plus*, 100206. Available from https://doi.org/10.1016/j.phyplu.2021.100206.

Caddeo, C., Sales, O. D., Valenti, D., Saurí, A. R., Fadda, A. M., & Manconi, M. (2013). Inhibition of skin inflammation in mice by diclofenac in vesicular carriers: Liposomes, ethosomes and PEVs. *International Journal of Pharmaceutics*, *443*(1–2), 128–136. Available from https://doi.org/10.1016/j.ijpharm.2012.12.041.

Cai, Z., Zhang, W., Yang, F., Yu, L., Yu, Z., Pan, J., Wang, L., Cao, X., & Wang, J. (2012). Immunosuppressive exosomes from TGF-β1 gene-modified dendritic cells attenuate Th17-mediated inflammatory autoimmune disease by inducing regulatory T cells. *Cell Research*, *22*(3), 607–610. Available from https://doi.org/10.1038/cr.2011.196.

Carmody, E. E., Schwarz, E. M., Puzas, J. E., Rosier, R. N., & O'Keefe, R. J. (2002). Viral interleukin-10 gene inhibition of inflammation, osteoclastogenesis, and bone resorption in response to titanium particles. *Arthritis & Rheumatism*, *46*(5), 1298–1308. Available from https://doi.org/10.1002/art.10227.

Carney, D. H., Mann, R., Redin, W. R., Pernia, S. D., Berry, D., Heggers, J. P., Hayward, P. G., Robson, M. C., Christie, J., Annable, C., Fenton, J. W., II, & Glenn, K. C. (1992). Enhancement of incisional wound healing and neovascularization in normal rats by thrombin and synthetic thrombin receptor-activating peptides. *The Journal of Clinical Investigation*, *89*, 1469. Available from https://doi.org/10.1172/JCI115737.

Cevc, G., & Vierl, U. (2010). Nanotechnology and the transdermal route: A state of the art review and critical appraisal. *Journal of Controlled Release*, *141*(3), 277–299. Available from https://doi.org/10.1016/j.jconrel.2009.10.016.

Chang, M. C., Kuo, Y. J., Hung, K. H., Peng, C. L., Chen, K. Y., & Yeh, L. K. (2020). Liposomal dexamethasone–moxifloxacin nanoparticle combinations with collagen/gelatin/alginate hydrogel for corneal infection treatment and wound healing. *Biomedical Materials*, *15*(5), 055022.

Chen, H., Dorrigan, A., Saad, S., Hare, D. J., Cortie, M. B., & Valenzuela, S. M. (2013). In vivo study of spherical gold nanoparticles: Inflammatory effects and distribution in mice. *PLoS One*, *8*(2), e58208. Available from https://doi.org/10.1371/journal.pone.0058208.

Chovatiya, R., & Medzhitov, R. (2014). Stress, inflammation, and defense of homeostasis. *Molecular Cell*, *54*(2), 281–288. Available from https://doi.org/10.1016/j.molcel.2014.03.030.

Dacoba, T. G., Olivera, A., Torres, D., Crecente-Campo, J., & Alonso, M. J. (2017). *Modulating the immune system through nanotechnology*, *Seminars in immunology* (34, pp. 78–102). Academic Press. Available from https://doi.org/10.1016/j.smim.2017.09.007.

Du, D., Chang, N., Sun, S., Li, M., Yu, H., Liu, M., Liu, X., Wang, G., Li, H., Liu, X., & Geng, S. (2014). The role of glucose transporters in the distribution of p-aminophenyl-α-D-mannopyranoside modified liposomes within mice brain. *Journal of Controlled Release*, *182*, 99–110. Available from https://doi.org/10.1016/j.jconrel.2014.03.006.

Englander, L., & Friedman, A. (2010). *Clinical and Aesthetic Dermatology*, *3*, 45–50.

Feng, K., Sun, H., Bradley, M. A., Dupler, E. J., Giannobile, W. V., & Ma, P. X. (2010). Novel antibacterial nanofibrous PLLA scaffolds. *Journal of Controlled Release*, *146*(3), 363–369. Available from https://doi.org/10.1016/j.jconrel.2010.05.035.

Ferrero-Miliani, L., Nielsen, O. H., Andersen, P. S., & Girardin, S. (2007). Chronic inflammation: Importance of NOD2 and NALP3 in interleukin-1β generation. *Clinical & Experimental Immunology*, *147*(2), 227–235. Available from https://doi.org/10.1111/j.1365-2249.2006.03261.x.

Fredman, G., Kamaly, N., Spolitu, S., Milton, J., Ghorpade, D., Chiasson, R., Kuriakose, G., Perretti, M., Farokhzad, O., & Tabas, I. (2015). Targeted nanoparticles containing the proresolving peptide Ac2-26 protect against advanced atherosclerosis in hypercholesterolemic mice. *Science Translational Medicine*, 7(275), 275ra20. Available from https://doi.org/10.1126/scitranslmed.aaa1065, -.

Gastpar, R., Gehrmann, M., Bausero, M. A., Asea, A., Gross, C., Schroeder, J. A., & Multhoff, G. (2005). Heat shock protein 70 surface-positive tumor exosomes stimulate migratory and cytolytic activity of natural killer cells. *Cancer Research*, *65*(12), 5238–5247. Available from https://doi.org/10.1158/0008-5472.CAN-04-3804.

Gower, R. M., Boehler, R. M., Azarin, S. M., Ricci, C. F., Leonard, J. N., & Shea, L. D. (2014). Modulation of leukocyte infiltration and phenotype in microporous tissue engineering scaffolds via vector induced IL-10 expression. *Biomaterials*, *35*(6), 2024–2031. Available from https://doi.org/10.1016/j.biomaterials.2013.11.036.

Gu, W., Wu, C., Chen, J., & Xiao, Y. (2013). Nanotechnology in the targeted drug delivery for bone diseases and bone regeneration. *International Journal of Nanomedicine*, *8*, 2305.

Gul, R., Ahmed, N., Ullah, N., Khan, M. I., Elaissari, A., & Rehman, A. (2018). Biodegradable ingredient-based emulgel loaded with ketoprofen nanoparticles. *AAPS PharmSciTech*, *19*(4), 1869–1881. Available from https://doi.org/10.1208/s12249-018-0997-0.

Hansson, G. K., Robertson, A. K., & Söderberg-Nauclér, C. (2006). Inflammation and atherosclerosis. *Annual Review of Pathology: Mechanisms of Disease*, *1*, 297–329. Available from https://doi.org/10.1146/annurev.pathol.1.110304.100100.

Higaki, M. (2009). Recent development of nanomedicine for the treatment of inflammatory diseases. *Inflammation and Regeneration*, *29*(2), 112–117. Available from https://doi.org/10.2492/inflammregen.29.112.

Hoffman, K. B., Feldman, R. M., Budenz, D. L., Gedde, S. J., Abou Chacra, G., & Schiffman, J. C. (2002). Combined cataract extraction and Baerveldt glaucoma drainage implant: Indications and outcomes. *Ophthalmology*, *109*(10), 1916–1920. Available from https://doi.org/10.1016/S0161-6420(02)01185-5.

Ikoba, U., Peng, H., Li, H., Miller, C., Yu, C., & Wang, Q. (2015a). Nanocarriers in therapy of infectious and inflammatory diseases. *Nanoscale*, 7(10), 4291–4305. Available from https://doi.org/10.1039/C4NR07682F.

Ikoba, U., Peng, H., Li, H., Miller, C., Yu, C., & Wang, Q. (2015b). Nanocarriers in therapy of infectious and inflammatory diseases. *Nanoscale*, 7(10), 4291–4305. Available from https://doi.org/10.1039/C4NR07682F.

Im, J. S., Bai, B. C., & Lee, Y. S. (2010). The effect of carbon nanotubes on drug delivery in an electro-sensitive transdermal drug delivery system. *Biomaterials*, *31*(6), 1414–1419. Available from https://doi.org/10.1016/j.biomaterials.2009.11.004.

Jia, F., Liu, X., Li, L., Mallapragada, S., Narasimhan, B., & Wang, Q. (2013). Multifunctional nanoparticles for targeted delivery of immune activating and cancer therapeutic agents. *Journal of Controlled Release*, *172*(3), 1020–1034. Available from https://doi.org/10.1016/j.jconrel.2013.10.012.

Jindal, A. B. (2017). The effect of particle shape on cellular interaction and drug delivery applications of micro-and nanoparticles. *International Journal of Pharmaceutics*, *532*(1), 450–465. Available from https://doi.org/10.1016/j.ijpharm.2017.09.028.

Jo, D. H., Kim, J. H., Lee, T. G., & Kim, J. H. (2015). Size, surface charge, and shape determine therapeutic effects of nanoparticles on brain and retinal diseases. *Nanomedicine: Nanotechnology, Biology and Medicine*, *11*(7), 1603–1611. Available from https://doi.org/10.1016/j.nano.2015.04.015.

Jóhannesson, G., Gottfredsdóttir, M. S., Ásgrimsdóttir, G. M., Loftsson, T., & Stefánsson, E. (2020). Can postoperative dexamethasone nanoparticle eye drops replace mitomycin C in trabeculectomy. *Acta Ophthalmologica*, *98*(6), 607–612. Available from https://doi.org/10.1111/aos.14370.

Kalangi, S. K., Swarnakar, N. K., Sathyavathi, R., Narayana Rao, D., Jain, S., & Reddanna, P. (2018). Synthesis, characterization, and biodistribution of quantum dot-celecoxib conjugate in mouse paw edema model. *Oxidative Medicine and Cellular Longevity*, 2018. Available from https://doi.org/10.1155/2018/3090517.

Katsuki, S., Matoba, T., Koga, J. I., Nakano, K., & Egashira, K. (2017). Anti-inflammatory nanomedicine for cardiovascular disease. *Frontiers in Cardiovascular Medicine*, *4*, 87. Available from https://doi.org/10.3389/fcvm.2017.00087.

Kim, S. E., Song, S. H., Yun, Y. P., Choi, B. J., Kwon, I. K., Bae, M. S., Moon, H. J., & Kwon, Y. D. (2011). The effect of immobilization of heparin and bone morphogenic protein-2 (BMP-2) to titanium surfaces on inflammation and osteoblast function. *Biomaterials*, *32*(2), 366–373. Available from https://doi.org/10.1016/j.biomaterials.2010.09.008.

Kim, S. Y., Jeong, S. H., Lee, E. Y., Park, Y. H., Bae, H. C., Jang, Y. S., Maeng, E. S., Kim, M. K., & Son, S. W. (2012). *Toxicology and Environmental Health Sciences*, *3*, 258–261.

Kolenyak dos Santos, F., Helena Oyafuso, M., Priscila Kiill, C., Palmira Daflon-Gremiao, M., & Chorilli, M. (2013). Nanotechnology-based drug delivery systems for treatment of hyperproliferative skin diseases—A review. *Current Nanoscience*, *9*(1), 159–167.

Kumar, A., Singh, K. R., Ghate, M. D., Lalhlenmawia, H., Kumar, D., & Singh, J. (2022). Bioinspired quantum dots for cancer therapy: A mini-review. *Materials Letters*, 131742. Available from https://doi.org/10.1016/j.matlet.2022.131742.

Kuskov, A. N., Kulikov, P. P., Goryachaya, A. V., Tzatzarakis, M. N., Docea, A. O., Velonia, K., Shtilman, M. I., & Tsatsakis, A. M. (2017). Amphiphilic poly-*N*-vinylpyrrolidone nanoparticles as carriers for non-steroidal, anti-inflammatory drugs: In vitro cytotoxicity and in vivo acute toxicity study. *Nanomedicine: Nanotechnology, Biology and Medicine, 13*(3), 1021–1030. Available from https://doi.org/10.1016/j.nano.2016.11.006.

Langer, R., & Tirrell, D. A. (2004). Designing materials for biology and medicine. *Nature, 428*(6982), 487–492. Available from https://doi.org/10.1038/nature02388.

Lee, S., Yun, H. S., & Kim, S. H. (2011a). The comparative effects of mesoporous silica nanoparticles and colloidal silica on inflammation and apoptosis. *Biomaterials, 32*(35), 9434–9443. Available from https://doi.org/10.1016/j.biomaterials.2011.08.042.

Lee, S., Yun, H. S., & Kim, S. H. (2011b). The comparative effects of mesoporous silica nanoparticles and colloidal silica on inflammation and apoptosis. *Biomaterials, 32*(35), 9434–9443. Available from https://doi.org/10.1016/j.biomaterials.2011.08.042.

Li, M., Deng, H., Peng, H., & Wang, Q. (2014a). Functional nanoparticles in targeting glioma diagnosis and therapies. *Journal of Nanoscience and Nanotechnology, 14*(1), 415–432. Available from https://doi.org/10.1166/jnn.2014.8757.

Li, M. H., Yu, H., Wang, T. F., Chang, N. D., Zhang, J. Q., Du, D., Liu, M. F., Sun, S. L., Wang, R., Tao, H. Q., & Geng, S. L. (2014b). Tamoxifen embedded in lipid bilayer improves the oncotarget of liposomal daunorubicin in vivo. *Journal of Materials Chemistry B, 2*(12), 1619–1625. Available from https://doi.org/10.1039/C3TB21423K.

Li, W., Li, X., Wang, Q., Pan, Y., Wang, T., Wang, H., Song, R., & Deng, H. (2014c). Antibacterial activity of nanofibrous mats coated with lysozyme-layered silicate composites via electrospraying. *Carbohydrate Polymers, 99*, 218–225. Available from https://doi.org/10.1016/j.carbpol.2013.07.055.

Lim, J., Lee, Y. Y., Choy, Y. B., Park, W., & Park, C. G. (2021). Sepsis diagnosis and treatment using nanomaterials. *Biomedical Engineering Letters, 11*(3), 197–210. Available from https://doi.org/10.1007/s13534-021-00200-0.

Lin, X., Zhao, N., Yan, P., Hu, H., & Xu, F. J. (2015). The shape and size effects of polycation functionalized silica nanoparticles on gene transfection. *Acta Biomaterialia, 11*, 381–392. Available from https://doi.org/10.1016/j.actbio.2014.09.004.

Liu, M., Li, M., Sun, S., Li, B., Du, D., Sun, J., Cao, F., Li, H., Jia, F., Wang, T., & Chang, N. (2014). The use of antibody modified liposomes loaded with AMO-1 to deliver oligonucleotides to ischemic myocardium for arrhythmia therapy. *Biomaterials, 35*(11), 3697–3707. Available from https://doi.org/10.1016/j.biomaterials.2013.12.099.

Ma, L., Manaenko, A., Ou, Y. B., Shao, A. W., Yang, S. X., & Zhang, J. H. (2017). Bosutinib attenuates inflammation via inhibiting salt-inducible kinases in experimental model of intracerebral hemorrhage on mice. *Stroke; A Journal of Cerebral Circulation, 48*(11), 3108–3116. Available from https://doi.org/10.1161/STROKEAHA.117.017681.

Mazzola, L. (2003). *Nature Biotechnology, 21*, 1137–1143. Available from https://doi.org/10.1016/j.copbio.2003.10.007.

Melchels, F. P., Feijen, J., & Grijpma, D. W. (2010). A review on stereolithography and its applications in biomedical engineering. *Biomaterials, 31*(24), 6121–6130. Available from https://doi.org/10.1016/j.biomaterials.2010.04.050.

Moddaresi, M., Tamburic, S., Williams, S., Jones, S. A., Zhao, Y., & Brown, M. B. (2009). Effects of lipid nanocarriers on the performance of topical vehicles in vivo. *Journal of Cosmetic Dermatology, 8*(2), 136–143. Available from https://doi.org/10.1111/j.1473-2165.2009.00440.x.

Multicenter Uveitis Steroid Treatment (MUST) Trial Research Group. (2015). Benefits of systemic anti-inflammatory therapy vs fluocinolone acetonide intraocular implant for intermediate uveitis, posterior uveitis, and panuveitis: Fifty-four–month results of the Multicenter Uveitis Steroid Treatment (MUST) trial and follow-up study. *Ophthalmology, 122*(10), 1967–1975. Available from https://doi.org/10.1016/j.ophtha.2015.06.042.

Nakamura, K., Yokohama, S., Yoneda, M., Okamoto, S., Tamaki, Y., Ito, T., Okada, M., Aso, K., & Makino, I. (2004). High, but not low, molecular weight hyaluronan prevents T-cell-mediated liver injury by reducing proinflammatory cytokines in mice. *Journal of Gastroenterology*, *39*(4), 346–354. Available from https://doi.org/10.1007/s00535-003-1301-x.

Farokhzad, O. C., & Langer, R. (2006). *Advanced Drug Delivery Reviews*, *58*, 1456–1459. Available from https://doi.org/10.1016/j.addr.2006.09.011.

Pareta, R. A., Taylor, E., & Webster, T. J. (2008). Increased osteoblast density in the presence of novel calcium phosphate coated magnetic nanoparticles. *Nanotechnology*, *19*(26), 265101.

Patra, C. R., Bhattacharya, R., Mukhopadhyay, D., & Mukherjee, P. (2010). Fabrication of gold nanoparticles for targeted therapy in pancreatic cancer. *Advanced Drug Delivery Reviews*, *62*(3), 346–361. Available from https://doi.org/10.1016/j.addr.2009.11.007.

Peng, K. T., Chen, C. F., Chu, I. M., Li, Y. M., Hsu, W. H., Hsu, R. W., & Chang, P. J. (2010). Treatment of osteomyelitis with teicoplanin-encapsulated biodegradable thermosensitive hydrogel nanoparticles. *Biomaterials*, *31*(19), 5227–5236. Available from https://doi.org/10.1016/j.biomaterials.2010.03.027.

Poh, S., Lin, J. B., & Panitch, A. (2015). Release of anti-inflammatory peptides from thermosensitive nanoparticles with degradable cross-links suppresses pro-inflammatory cytokine production. *Biomacromolecules*, *16*(4), 1191–1200. Available from https://doi.org/10.1021/bm501849p.

Popov, A. P., Zvyagin, A. V., Lademann, J., Roberts, M. S., Sanchez, W., Priezzhev, A. V., & Myllylä, R. (2010). Designing inorganic light-protective skin nanotechnology products. *Journal of Biomedical Nanotechnology*, *6*(5), 432–451. Available from https://doi.org/10.1166/jbn.2010.1144.

Ratanavaraporn, J., Furuya, H., & Tabata, Y. (2012). Local suppression of pro-inflammatory cytokines and the effects in BMP-2-induced bone regeneration. *Biomaterials*, *33*(1), 304–316. Available from https://doi.org/10.1016/j.biomaterials.2011.09.050.

Browne, S., & Pandit, A. (2015). Biomaterial-mediated modification of the local inflammatory environment. *Frontiers in Bioengineering and Biotechnology*, *3*, 67. Available from https://doi.org/10.3389/fbioe.2015.00067.

Sameer Kumar, R., Shakambari, G., Ashokkumar, B., Nelson, D. J., John, S. A., & Varalakshmi, P. (2018). Nitrogen-doped graphene quantum dot-combined sodium 10-amino-2-methoxyundecanoate: Studies of proinflammatory gene expression and live cell imaging. *ACS Omega*, *3*(9), 11982–11992. Available from https://doi.org/10.1021/acsomega.8b02085.

Scalia, S., Franceschinis, E., Bertelli, B., & Iannuccelli, V. (2012). *Skin Pharmacology and Physiology*, *2*, 57–67. Available from https://doi.org/10.1021/ac400517e.

Shah, P. P., Desai, P. R., Patel, A. R., & Singh, M. S. (2012b). Skin permeating nanogel for the cutaneous co-delivery of two anti-inflammatory drugs. *Biomaterials*, *33*(5), 1607–1617.

Shah, P. P., Desai, P. R., & Singh, M. (2012a). Effect of oleic acid modified polymeric bilayered nanoparticles on percutaneous delivery of spantide II and ketoprofen. *Journal of Controlled Release*, *158*(2), 336–345.

Sharma, A., Dulta, K., Nagraik, R., Dua, K., Singh, S. K., Chellappan, D. K., Kumar, D., & Shin, D. S. (2022a). Potentialities of aptasensors in cancer diagnosis. *Materials Letters*, *308*, 131240. Available from https://doi.org/10.1016/j.matlet.2021.131240.

Sharma, A., Nagraik, R., Venkidasamy, B., Khan, A., Dulta, K., Chauhan, P. K., Kumar, D., & Shin, D. S. (2022b). In-vitro antidiabetic, antioxidant, antimicrobial and cytotoxic activity of *Murraya koenigii* leaf extract Intercedes ZnO nanoparticles. *Luminescence: The Journal of Biological and Chemical Luminescence*. Available from https://doi.org/10.1002/bio.4244.

Shi, M., Zhang, P., Zhao, Q., Shen, K., Qiu, Y., Xiao, Y., Yuan, Q., & Zhang, Y. (2020). Dual functional monocytes modulate bactericidal and anti-inflammation process for severe osteomyelitis treatment. *Small (Weinheim an der Bergstrasse, Germany)*, *16*(4), 1905185. Available from https://doi.org/10.1002/smll.201905185.

Shukla, M. K., Dubey, A., Pandey, S., Singh, S. K., Gupta, G., Prasher, P., Chellappan, D. K., Oliver, B. G., Kumar, D., & Dua, K. (2022). Managing apoptosis in lung diseases using nano-assisted drug delivery system. *Current Pharmaceutical Design*. Available from https://doi.org/10.2174/1381612828666220413103831.

Sibbald, R. G., Contreras-Ruiz, J., Coutts, P., Fierheller, M., Rothman, A., & Woo, K. (2007). Bacteriology, inflammation, and healing: A study of nanocrystalline silver dressings in chronic venous leg ulcers. *Advances in Skin & Wound Care*, *20*(10), 549–558.

Singh, A. V., Khare, M., Gade, W. N., & Zamboni, P. (2012a). Theranostic implications of nanotechnology in multiple sclerosis: A future perspective. *Autoimmune Diseases*, 2012. Available from https://doi.org/10.1155/2012/160830.

Singh, A. V., Khare, M., Gade, W. N., & Zamboni, P. (2012b). Theranostic implications of nanotechnology in multiple sclerosis: A future perspective. *Autoimmune Diseases*, 2012. Available from https://doi.org/10.1155/2012/160830.

Singh, P. P., LeMaire, C., Tan, J. C., Zeng, E., & Schorey, J. S. (2014). Exosomes released from *M. tuberculosis* infected cells can suppress IFN-γ mediated activation of naïve macrophages. *PLoS One*, *6*(4), e18564. Available from https://doi.org/10.1371/journal.pone.0018564.

Spizzirri, U. G., et al. (2013). Spherical gelatin/CNTs hybrid microgels as electro-responsive drug delivery systems. *International Journal of Pharmaceutics*, *448*, 115–122. Available from https://doi.org/10.1016/j.ijpharm.2013.03.013.

Stukenkemper, T., Dose, A., Caballo Gonzalez, M., Groenen, A. J., Hehir, S., Andrés-Guerrero, V., Herrero Vanrell, R., & Cameron, N. R. (2015). Block copolypeptide nanoparticles for the delivery of ocular therapeutics. *Macromolecular Bioscience*, *15*(1), 138–145. Available from https://doi.org/10.1002/mabi.201400471.

Sun, D., Zhuang, X., Xiang, X., Liu, Y., Zhang, S., Liu, C., Barnes, S., Grizzle, W., Miller, D., & Zhang, H. G. (2010). A novel nanoparticle drug delivery system: The anti-inflammatory activity of curcumin is enhanced when encapsulated in exosomes. *Molecular Therapy*, *18*(9), 1606–1614. Available from https://doi.org/10.1038/mt.2010.105.

Thomas, T. P., Goonewardena, S. N., Majoros, I. J., Kotlyar, A., Cao, Z., Leroueil, P. R., & Baker, J. R., Jr. (2011). *Arthritis and Rheumatism*, *63*, 2671–2680. Available from https://doi.org/10.1002/art.30459.

Tabas, I., & Glass, C. K. (2013). Anti-inflammatory therapy in chronic disease: Challenges and opportunities. *Science (New York, N.Y.)*, *339*(6116), 166–172. Available from https://doi.org/10.1126/science.1230720.

Tahara, K., Samura, S., Tsuji, K., Yamamoto, H., Tsukada, Y., Bando, Y., Tsujimoto, H., Morishita, R., & Kawashima, Y. (2011). Oral nuclear factor-κB decoy oligonucleotides delivery system with chitosan modified poly (D,L-lactide-co-glycolide) nanospheres for inflammatory bowel disease. *Biomaterials*, *32*(3), 870–878. Available from https://doi.org/10.1016/j.biomaterials.2010.09.034.

Takemoto, M., & Liao, J. K. (2001). Pleiotropic effects of 3-hydroxy-3-methylglutaryl coenzyme a reductase inhibitors. *Arteriosclerosis, Thrombosis, and Vascular Biology*, *21*(11), 1712–1719. Available from https://doi.org/10.1161/hq1101.098486.

Toita, R., Kawano, T., Murata, M., & Kang, J. H. (2016). Anti-obesity and anti-inflammatory effects of macrophage-targeted interleukin-10-conjugated liposomes in obese mice. *Biomaterials*, *110*, 81–88. Available from https://doi.org/10.1002/ange.201913700.

Tran, N., & Webster, T. J. (2009). *WIREs Nanomedicine Nanobiotechnology*, *1*, 336–351. Available from https://doi.org/10.1002/wnan.23.

Trujillo-Nolasco, R. M., Morales-Avila, E., Ocampo-Garcia, B. E., Ferro-Flores, G., Gibbens-Bandala, B. V., Escudero-Castellanos, A., & Isaac-Olive, K. (2019). Preparation and in vitro evaluation of radiolabeled HA-PLGA nanoparticles as novel MTX delivery system for local treatment of rheumatoid arthritis. *Materials Science and Engineering: C*, *103*, 109766. Available from https://doi.org/10.1016/j.msec.2019.109766.

Vimala, K., & Soundarapandian, K. (2017). Erbitux conjugated zinc oxide nanoparticles to enhance antitumor efficiency via targeted drug delivery system for breast cancer therapy. *Annals of Oncology*, *28*, x41. Available from https://doi.org/10.1093/annonc/mdx658.008.

Wang, H., Zhou, Y., Sun, Q., Zhou, C., Hu, S., Lenahan, C., Xu, W., Deng, Y., Li, G., & Tao, S. (2021). Update on nanoparticle-based drug delivery system for anti-inflammatory treatment. *Frontiers in Bioengineering and Biotechnology*, *9*, 106. Available from https://doi.org/10.3389/fbioe.2021.630352.

Wang, Q., Zhang, N., Hu, X., Yang, J., & Du, Y. (2007). Alginate/polyethylene glycol blend fibers and their properties for drug controlled release. *Journal of Biomedical Materials Research. Part A*, *82*(1), 122–128. Available from https://doi.org/10.1002/jbm.a.31075.

Webber, M. J., Kessler, J. A., & Stupp, S. I. (2010). Emerging peptide nanomedicine to regenerate tissues and organs. *Journal of Internal Medicine*, *267*(1), 71–88. Available from https://doi.org/10.1111/j.1365-2796.2009.02184.x.

Wu, G., Zhang, J., Zhao, Q., Zhuang, W., Ding, J., Zhang, C., Gao, H., Pang, D. W., Pu, K., & Xie, H. Y. (2020). Molecularly engineered macrophage-derived exosomes with inflammation tropism and intrinsic heme biosynthesis for atherosclerosis treatment. *Angewandte Chemie*, *132*(10), 4097–4103. Available from https://doi.org/10.1002/ange.201913700.

Xin, S., Li, X., Wang, Q., Huang, R., Xu, X., Lei, Z., & Deng, H. (2014). *Journal of Biomedical Nanotechnology*, *10*, 803–810. Available from https://doi.org/10.1166/jbn.2014.1748.

Xu, X., Li, Y., Wang, L., Li, Y., Pan, J., Fu, X., Luo, Z., Sui, Y., Zhang, S., Wang, L., & Ni, Y. (2019). Triple-functional polyetheretherketone surface with enhanced bacteriostasis and anti-inflammatory and osseointegrative properties for implant application. *Biomaterials*, *212*, 98–114. Available from https://doi.org/10.1016/j.biomaterials.2019.05.014.

Yan, F., Zhong, Z., Wang, Y., Feng, Y., Mei, Z., Li, H., Chen, X., Cai, L., & Li, C. (2020). Exosome-based biomimetic nanoparticles targeted to inflamed joints for enhanced treatment of rheumatoid arthritis. *Journal of Nanobiotechnology*, *18*(1), 1–5. Available from https://doi.org/10.1186/s12951-020-00675-6.

Yang, D., Ma, J., Zhang, Q., Li, N., Yang, J., Raju, P. A., Peng, M., Luo, Y., Hui, W., Chen, C., & Cui, Y. (2013). Polyelectrolyte-coated gold magnetic nanoparticles for immunoassay development: Toward point of care diagnostics for syphilis screening. *Analytical Chemistry*, *85*(14), 6688–6695. Available from https://doi.org/10.1021/ac400517e.

Yazeji, T., Moulari, B., Beduneau, A., Stein, V., Dietrich, D., Pellequer, Y., & Lamprecht, A. (2017). Nanoparticle-based delivery enhances anti-inflammatory effect of low molecular weight heparin in experimental ulcerative colitis. *Drug Delivery*, *24*(1), 811–817. Available from https://doi.org/10.1080/10717544.2017.1324530.

Zhang, L., & Webster, T. J. (2009). Nanotechnology and nanomaterials: Promises for improved tissue regeneration. *Nano Today*, *4*, 66–80. Available from https://doi.org/10.1016/j.nantod.2008.10.014.

Ziv-Polat, O., Topaz, M., Brosh, T., & Margel, S. (2010). Enhancement of incisional wound healing by thrombin conjugated iron oxide nanoparticles. *Biomaterials*, *31*(4), 741–747. Available from https://doi.org/10.1016/j.biomaterials.2009.09.093.

Further reading

Chellappan, D. K., et al. (2022). Exploring the role of antibiotics and steroids in managing respiratory diseases. *Journal of Biochemical and Molecular Toxicology*, *36*(10), e23174. Available from https://doi.org/10.1002/jbt.23174, In this issue.

Tocco, I., Zavan, B., Bassetto, F., & Vindigni, V. (2012). Nanotechnology-based therapies for skin wound regeneration. *Journal of Nanomaterials*, *2012*. Available from https://doi.org/10.1155/2012/714134.

CHAPTER 6

Nanodiagnostics and nanomedicines for neurodegenerative disorders

Kunjbihari Sulakhiya[1], Anglina Kisku[1], Rishi Paliwal[2], Deepak K Gupta[3], Yashraj Yadav[4], Ajay Pal[5] and Suneel Kumar[6]

[1]NeuroPharmacology Research Laboratory (NPRL), Department of Pharmacy, Indira Gandhi National Tribal University, Amarkantak, Madhya Pradesh, India
[2]Nanomedicine and Bioengineering Research Laboratory (NBRL), Department of Pharmacy, Indira Gandhi National Tribal University, Amarkantak, Madhya Pradesh, India
[3]Department of Pharmacy, Indira Gandhi National Tribal University, Amarkantak, Madhya Pradesh, India
[4]Department of Pharmacology, Acropolis Institute of Pharmaceutical Education and Research, Indore, Madhya Pradesh, India
[5]School of Medicine, Temple University, Philadelphia, PA, United States
[6]Department of Biomedical Engineering, Rutgers, The State University of New Jersey, Piscataway, NJ, United States

Introduction

Neurodegenerative diseases (NDs) are a diverse collection of illnesses marked by the progressive deterioration of the central nervous system (CNS) or peripheral nervous system (PNS) structure and function. The most common neurodegenerative disorders include Parkinson's, Alzheimer's, amyotrophic lateral sclerosis (ALS), Huntington's, multiple sclerosis (MS), ataxia, and other diseases. These are characterized by the loss of neurons and unwanted protein accumulation or intracellular form of protein aggregation. The phrase "ND" refers to a group of illnesses that predominantly damage the brain's neurons, jeopardizing human health. Because the senior population has grown in recent years, these age-related diseases are becoming more frequent (Gitler et al., 2017). The brain is a very sophisticated organ with a massive network of connections that enable us to do remarkable feats. The brain is made up of billions of cells known as nerve cells that are the essential cells of the brain. These nerve cells, also known as neurons, play a significant role in the optimal functioning of the human. These neurons communicate so humans can talk, think, move, learn, memorize, and do everything else required to perform daily work. Because of the brain's intricacy, even little miscommunications between cells can create problems (Bargmann & Newsome, 2014).

Brain cells are interconnected; thus miscommunications in one region can affect other brain functions, which may cause brain disease. Although the brain can be affected by various diseases and disorders, the most complex is known as NDs. Neurons die, and the brain shrinks due to this sickness (JP Shonkoff, 2000). Neurons die as a result of neurodegenerative disorders. The phrase neurodegeneration is made up of two words: neuro, which means brain, and degenerative, which means to

Nanotechnology for Drug Delivery and Pharmaceuticals
DOI: https://doi.org/10.1016/B978-0-323-95325-2.00023-7

breakdown or die. Miscommunications between brain cells cause neurodegenerative illnesses, which are a prime examples. These illnesses can affect a person's ability to walk, speak, remember, think, and much more. The etiology of many neurodegenerative conditions is unknown due to the complexity of these diseases. There are a variety of well-known neurodegenerative disorders that start in various parts of the brain (Berman & Bayati, 2018). Different Western medical pieces of literature have documented the existence of NDs beginning in the early 19th century. Later, numerous studies have been reported on the histopathological examination of the senile brain. During colonial India in the 17th and 18th centuries, neurological and NDs were diagnosed with symptoms, considered psychiatric disorders, and treated accordingly (Basu, 2017).

An essential characteristic of NDs includes a gradual damage of neurons in the brain and peripheral organs and protein depositions with altered physicochemical properties. At the molecular level, proteins are utilized to classify neurodegenerative disorders and have significance in the pathogenesis of NDs. The most prevalent proteins associated with the etiology of neurological illnesses are amyloid, tau, prion, synuclein, TAR-DNA-binding protein 43 kDa, and sarcoma protein (Wells et al., 2019). Proteins expressed by genes connected to trinucleotide repeat illnesses, neuroserpin, ferritin, and familial cerebral amyloidosis are examples of hereditary ailments. Clinical symptoms are influenced by the participation of various functional systems and do not always imply a molecular pathologic basis. Seeding of pathogenic proteins and hierarchical involvement of anatomic regions are typical in neurodegenerative disorders. It is not uncommon for NDs to overlap and for different conditions to coexist. Although substantial research is undertaken to achieve this goal, only a subset of the neuropathologic categories of neurodegenerative illnesses has been converted into in vivo detectable biomarkers (Erkkinen et al., 2018).

A lack of a clear understanding of causes and diverse pathophysiological mechanisms leads to difficulty developing effective and safe treatment. Currently available medicines only provide symptomatic management without removing the root cause of the diseases; thus only a temporary halt of the disease progression is achieved. Clinically used drugs target the neuroinflammation, oxidative stress, acetylcholine level, NMDA (*N*-methyl-D-aspartate) receptor, and misfolding proteins involved in the disease progression. No proper cure is available for the treatment of NDs; therefore accurate diagnosis is essential for developing safe and effective treatment for NDs (Duraes et al., 2018).

Nanotechnology has advanced rapidly in recent decades, with significant potential benefits for CNS disease diagnosis and treatment. It uses nanomaterials to deliver the medicines to targets through the blood–brain barrier (BBB). These nanoengineered materials or instruments interact with the biological systems at the cellular and molecular level to alter the physiology of the human body through several mechanisms, such as stimulation, inhibition, and interaction, with targets while minimizing the adverse effects (Cui et al., 2021). Thus nanotechnology has great significance in diagnosing and treating various NDs, including PD, Alzheimer's disease (AD), ALS, Huntington's disease (HD), MS, and Friedreich ataxia (FA). In this book chapter, we are discussing the common pathophysiology- and nanotechnology-based diagnostic and therapeutic agents that could be helpful in the treatment and management of various NDs.

Etiopathogenesis and pharmacology of neurodegenerative disorders

NDs are the prevalent illnesses defined by the progressive damage of the neurons of CNS and PNS, as well as the accumulation of proteins with altered physicochemical characteristics. Because of their growing medical and societal relevance, neurodegenerative disorders are a significant focus of research and clinical study. Because of their incidence, expense, complicated biochemistry and pathology, and the absence of mechanism-based therapies, NDs pose some of the most challenging problems for fundamental research and clinical medicine (Dugger & Dickson, 2017). Clinical manifestations are determined by the involvement of various functional systems and may not always reflect a molecular pathologic basis. It is common for neurodegenerative illnesses to overlap and for different conditions to coexist. Only a portion of the neuropathologic categories of neurodegenerative disorders has been translated into in vivo detectable biomarkers, although much research is underway to attain this objective (Kovacs, 2017).

Alzheimer's disease

It is the most common form of dementia accounting for 60%–70% of all cases. Dementia is caused by various diseases and disorders that directly or indirectly damage the brain. According to WHO, dementia is a syndrome in which memory, reasoning, behaviors, and the capacity to do daily tasks deteriorate. Globally, more than 55 million people have dementia, with 10 million new cases diagnosed yearly. According to the dementia in India 2020 report, this equates to one in every 27 persons, which may rise to 7.6 million by 2030 (Divya, 2020). According to AD facts and figures for 2020, the number of AD patients (65 years and older) in America could rise dramatically from 5.8 million to 13.8 million by 2050 (Hampel et al., 2021). Glutamate excitotoxicity is one of the leading causes of neurodegeneration in ADs. The interaction of Aβ aggregates with glutamatergic neurotransmission could be a critical factor in the Aβ-induced alteration of excitatory synaptic transmission and plasticity linked to cognitive impairment (Fig. 6.1). NMDA and, to some extent, AMPA (α-amino-3-hydroxy-5-methyl-4-isoxazole proprionic acid) NMDA and, to a lesser extent, AMPA receptors in the brain can be dysregulated by a species (Hampel et al., 2021). Although the

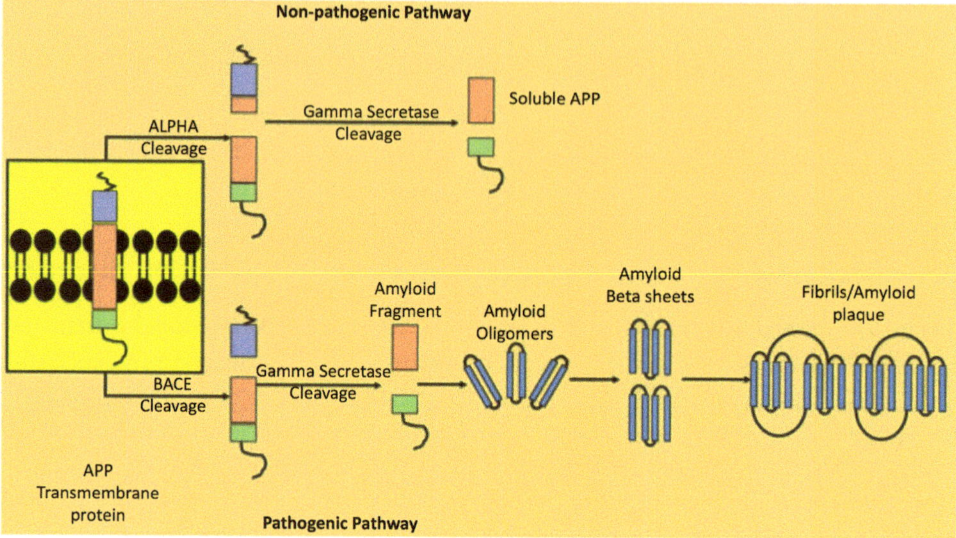

Figure 6.1 The amyloid cascade hypothesis. Amyloid cascade hypothesis involves two pathway namely pathogenic and nonpathogenic. Pathogenic pathway results in formation of amyloid plague through series of cleavage of BACE. Nonpathogenic pathway results in the generation of soluble APP by the ALPHA cleavage (alpha-site APP-cleaving enzyme). Formation of amyloid plague has significant role in the AD pathogenesis through the neuronal damage (Behl et al., 2020). *AD*, Alzheimer's disease; *APP*, amyloid precursor protein; *BACE*, beta-site APP-cleaving enzyme. *Adopted from Behl, T., et al. (2020). Exploring the potential of therapeutic agents targeted towards mitigating the events associated with amyloid-β cascade in Alzheimer's disease. International Journal of Molecular Sciences, 21(20), 7443.*

fundamental etiology of ADs is unknown, many factors are believed to have a role in its progression, including aberrant proteins, oxidative stress, accumulation of excessive metal ions, and decreased acetylcholine (Ach) levels in the brain (Bozdag Pehlivan, 2013). Drugs approved for treating ADs have limited and short-term symptomatic effects in the dementia stage. These drugs have neurochemical systems as drug targets causing cognitive failure and behavioral disturbances (Bozdag Pehlivan, 2013).

Parkinson's disease

Similarly, PD is also the most common occurring NDs in elder people having an age of >65 years. According to Global Burden of Disease Research, the prevalence of PD has increased twofold in the last two decades (from 2.5 million in 1990 to 6.1 million patients in 2016) (Dorsey et al., 2018). According to estimates from 2016, India has roughly 0.58 million individuals living with PD, with a significant increase in prevalence rate in the coming years. The majority of cases of PD are due to sporadic causes,

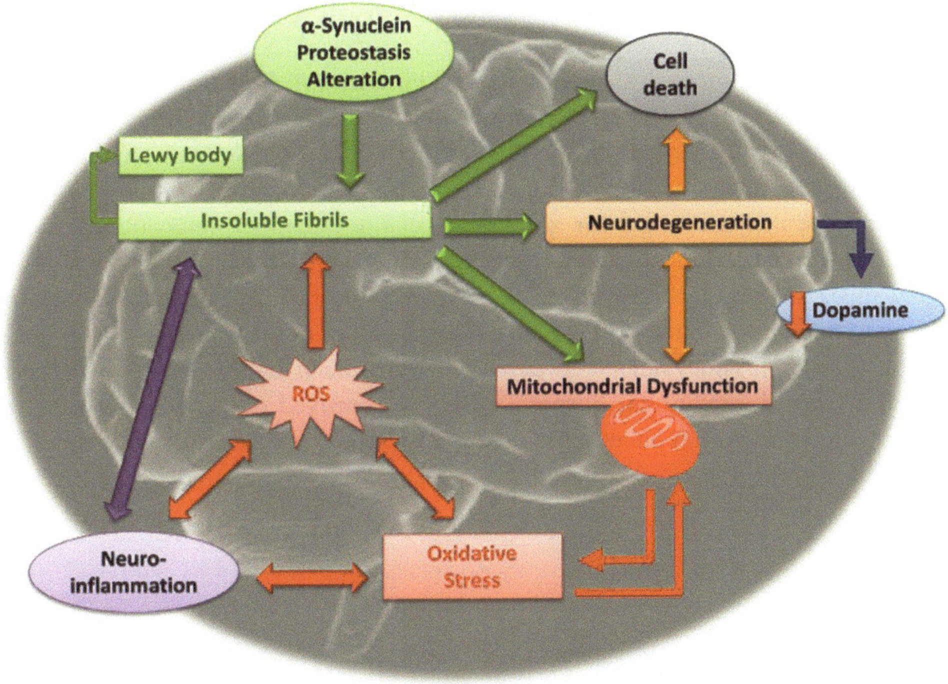

Figure 6.2 Interaction between the major molecular mechanisms involved in the pathogenesis of PD. There are various mechanisms such as oxidative stress, neuroinflammation, mitochondrial dysfunction involve in the PD pathogenesis. Together, these causes formation of insoluble fibrils, lewy body, and α-synuclein which leads to cell death, neurodegeneration, and decrease in dopamine level in the brain (Ciulla et al., 2019). *PD*, Parkinson's disease. *Adopted from Ciulla, M., et al. (2019). Role of dietary supplements in the management of Parkinson's disease. Biomolecules, 9(7), 271.*

while only 5%–10% of patients are monogenic (Rajan et al., 2020). Progressive loss of dopaminergic neurons in the substantia nigra and the creation of Lewy bodies in the surviving neurons are the pathological features of PD (Fig. 6.2). The most common treatment for motor complaints is levodopa (Pan et al., 2021). However, symptoms of PD increase with time as the disease develops, and problems linked with long-term levodopa medication begin to emerge (Lafuente et al., 2019).

Amyotrophic lateral sclerosis

The most prevalent condition affecting motor neurons is ALS, which also occurs in older people, with a peak incidence at 70 years of age, affecting 4.5 million people (Park et al., 2022). About 90%–95% of ALS cases are periodic, whereas only 5%–10% are hereditary. ALS patients have average endurance of 2–4 years after onset, and death occurs due to respiratory failure. It is highly prevalent in Europe and North

America compared to Asia and Latin America (Brown et al., 2021). The corticomotoneuronal is believed to be the primary cell implicated in ALS. As a result of antegrade impacts, the spinal motoneuron is damaged. This concept does not rule out most of the current hypotheses about ALS etiology, but it does focus attention on one cell type, the cortical motor neuron (Eisen et al., 1992). ALS is a deadly neurodegenerative illness of the human motor system caused by an unknown cause. Developments have inspired interest in the area of our knowledge of the glutamate neurotransmitter system and the identification of causative genes connected to the onset of familial ALS. Survival in ALS is now acknowledged to rely on many factors, including clinical presentation (phenotype), rate of disease development, and the presence of a genetic mutation (Fig. 6.3). Issues related to clinical heterogeneity have been found (Kiernan et al., 2011). For the treatment purpose, FDA has approved only two drugs: Riluzole and edaravone. Riluzole reduces glutamate excitotoxicity, whereas edaravone exhibits a free radical scavenging effect (Wang et al., 2020). When compared to standard therapy alone, intravenous (IV) edaravone may not give a clinically significant benefit (Witzel et al., 2022).

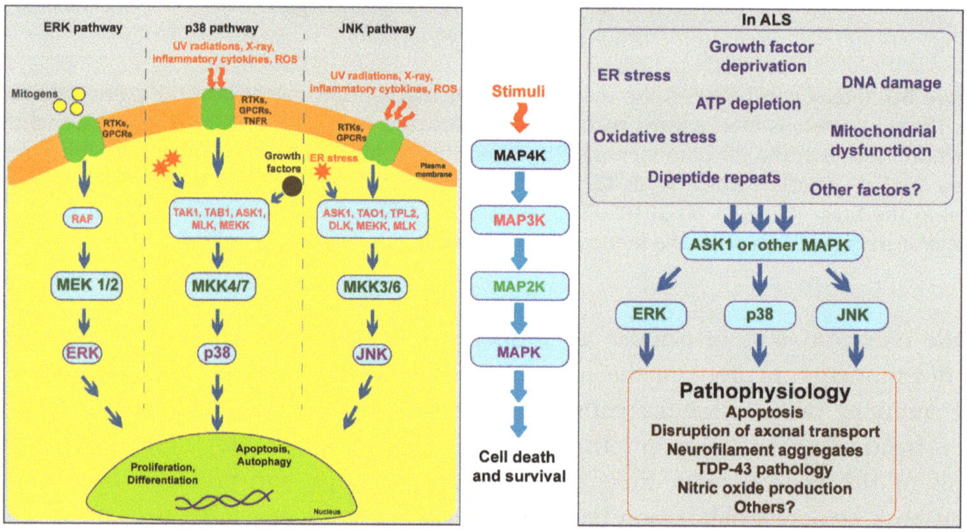

Figure 6.3 Overview of MAPK pathway showing the interaction of multiple MAPK members under normal physiological conditions and in ALS pathogenesis. Figure shows that there are several causative factors which are involved in the pathophysiology of ALS. These factors include endopplasmic reticulum (ER) stress, adenosine triphosphate (ATP) depletion, DNA damage, Oxidative stress, mitochondrial dysfunction which stimulate the MAPK pathway resulting in the activation of ERK, p38 and JNK pathway. Further, these downstream pathways causing cell death through apoptosis, neurofilament aggregates, nitric oxide production, axonal transport disruption (Sahana & Zhang, 2021). *ALS*, Amyotrophic lateral sclerosis; *MAPK*, mitogen-activated protein kinase. *Adopted form Sahana, T. G., & Zhang, K. (2021). Mitogen-activated protein kinase pathway in amyotrophic lateral sclerosis. Biomedicines, 9(8), 969.*

Friedreich ataxia

FA is a rare hereditary illness affecting the neurological system and causes mobility difficulties. It generally starts in childhood and progresses to ataxia or a loss of muscular coordination. Nerve fibers in the spinal cord and peripheral nerves deteriorate and thinner in FA. The cerebellum, the brain region that controls balance and movement, degenerates somewhat (Fig. 6.4). Awkward, unstable motions and decreased sensory capabilities are the outcomes of this injury. FA is the most prevalent form of genetic ataxia in the United States, affecting roughly one person in every 50,000 (La Pean et al., 2008). An aberrant FXN gene is found in around one in every 90 European–Americans (Delatycki et al., 2000). The condition does not affect one's ability to think or reason (cognitive functions). FA is caused by a mutation in the FXN gene, which carries the genetic coding for the frataxin protein (Fig. 6.5). The illness affects people who inherit two faulty copies of the gene, one from each parent.

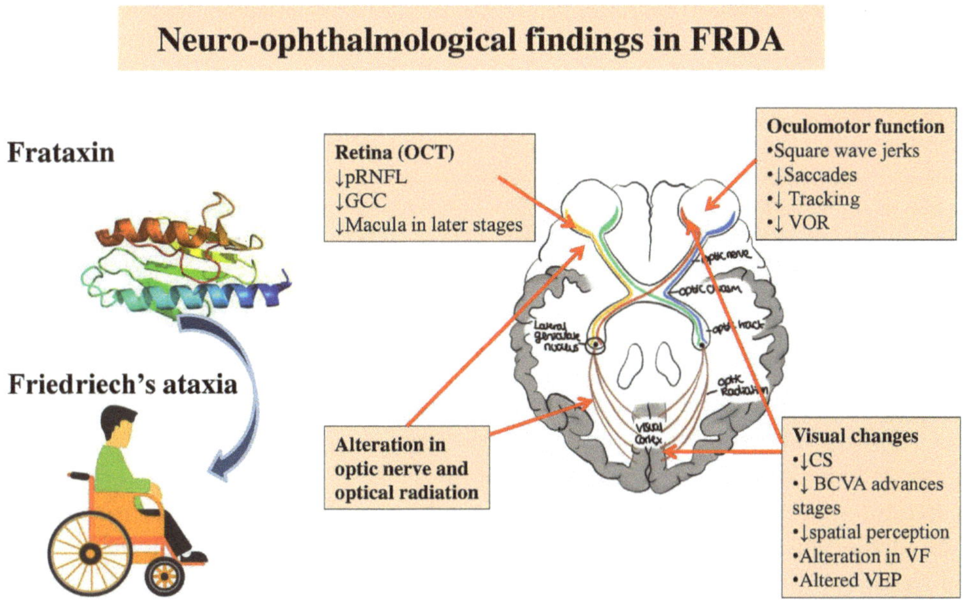

Figure 6.4 ***Neuro-ophthalmological findings in FRDA.*** Several neuro-ophthalmological findings are reported in the FRDA which are affecting the retina, optic nerve, oculomotor function, and vision. Frataxin protein involve in the pathogenesis of FRDA through ophthalmological changes by altering optic nerve, vision, retinal, and oculomotor function by decreasing various molecular factors including GCC, CS, BCVA, VOR, etc. *BCVA*, Best-corrected visual acuity; *CS*, contrast sensitivity; *FRDA*, Friedreich's ataxia; *GCC*, ganglion cell complex; *OCT*, optical coherence tomography; *pRNFL*, peripapillary retinal nerve fiber layer; *VEP*, visual evoked potential.; *VF*, visual field; *VOR*, vestibulo-ocular reflexes.

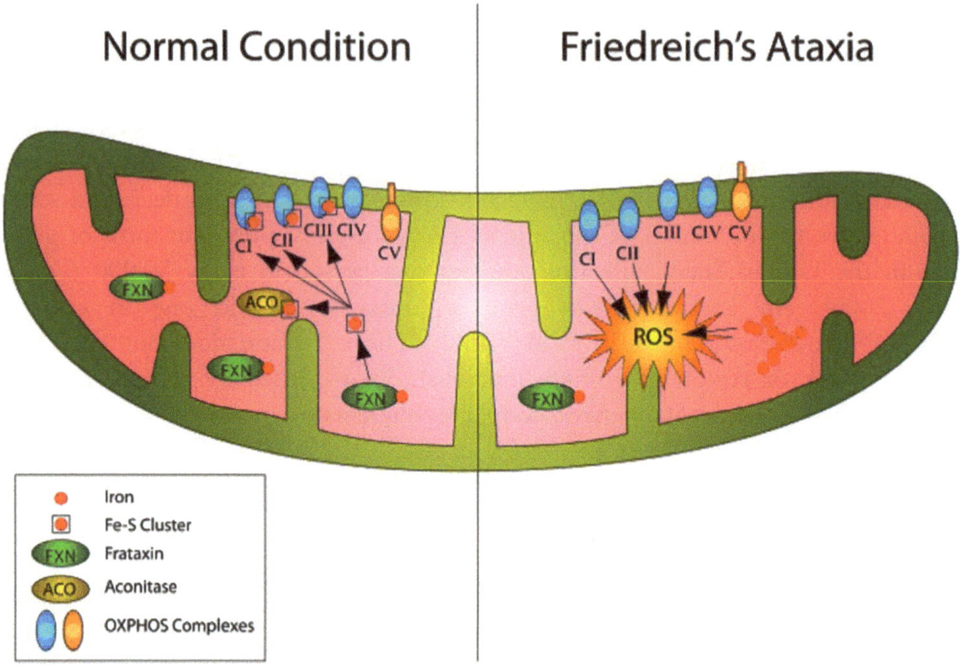

Figure 6.5 Overview of the deregulations associated with Friedreich's ataxia caused by a lack of frataxin expression. Reduced frataxin levels result in increased ROS buildup, oxidative stress, Fe–S protein dysfunction, and mitochondrion iron accumulation (La Rosa et al., 2020). *ROS*, Reactive oxygen species. *Adopted from La Rosa, P., Bertini, E. S., & Piemonte, F. (2020). The NRF2 signaling network defines clinical biomarkers and therapeutic opportunity in Friedreich's ataxia. International Journal of Molecular Sciences, 21(3), 916.*

Although a carrier will not acquire the disease, they may pass on the gene mutation to their offspring. The condition can be passed down to both male and female children. FA can reduce life expectancy; however, some persons with less severe symptoms of FA live into their sixties or beyond. Nikolaus Friedreich, a German doctor who first reported the illness in the 1860s, is the name of the ailment (La Pean et al., 2008). The treatment of a person with FA requires a multispecialty team approach. Physical therapy might help you keep your arms and legs working longer. Swallowing and speaking problems should be constantly monitored. Hearing aids can help those with hearing loss (38). There is currently no effective therapy for this condition. A genetic method can be utilized to slow down FA. Genetic counseling and gene therapy might be part of the strategy. According to genetic counseling, a child has a 25% FA if both parents are carriers. Amniocentesis, for example, can be performed to discover persons who are carriers. It is also possible to make a preimplantation FA diagnosis. DNA banking is required in gene therapy. It is beneficial to research FA to treat this condition. Gene therapy is a technique for repairing a patient's damaged cells. Gene shipping vehicles include viral vectors, such as HSV-1 amplicon and lentivirus vectors. Both are capable of restoring frataxin to its natural state (Nelwan, 2017).

Huntington's disease

HD is rare hereditary autosomal governing NDs characterized by involuntary choreatic movements with cognitive and behavioral disturbances. One defective gene on chromosome 4, one of the 23 human chromosomes that make up an individual's entire genetic code, is the sole cause of HD, a degenerative brain disease. It is commonly occurring between the ages of 30–50 years. Patients die due to pneumonia and suicide. The rate of prevalence is 2.7 per 100,000 worldwide (Ajitkumar & De Jesus, 2021). George Huntington, M.D., the physician who initially characterized the disease in the late 1800s, is named for him. The faulty gene codes for a protein called huntingtin. Although it goes by the name "huntingtin," this protein's typical function is uncertain since its inaccurate version is the cause of HD, according to experts. Defective huntingtin protein causes aberrant involuntary movements of arms, legs, head, face, and upper torso, a significant loss of thinking and reasoning abilities, such as memory, focus, judgment, and the capacity to plan and organize, among other things, as well as irritability, sadness, and other mood disorders (Walker, 2007) (Fig. 6.6). HD symptoms often emerge between 30 and 50, although they can present as early as 2 years or as late as 80 years (Huntington's Disease). The focus of treatment is on symptom management that consists of the following therapies as first-line strategies:

Irritability: Experts believe that an atypical antipsychotic medication is the best treatment for extreme anger and threatening conduct. Experts recommend starting with a selective serotonin reuptake inhibitor (SSRI), a kind of antidepressant, for less acute and nonthreatening agitation.

Chorea (involuntary movements): Some doctors think starting with an atypical antipsychotic medication like olanzapine is the best way to go. Others begin with tetrabenazine (TBZ), a drug newly authorized by the FDA for HD. Experts also prescribe SSRIs as a routine therapy for obsessive–compulsive thoughts and behaviors (Mestre et al., 2009).

Multiple sclerosis

MS is chronic and debilitating NDs characterized by fatigue, loss of balance and coordination, vision problems, tremors, and slurred speech. Globally, it affects 35.9 per 100,000 people (2.8 million). In the United States, about 1 million people are living with MS. The median age of diagnosis is 32 years. Females are having higher

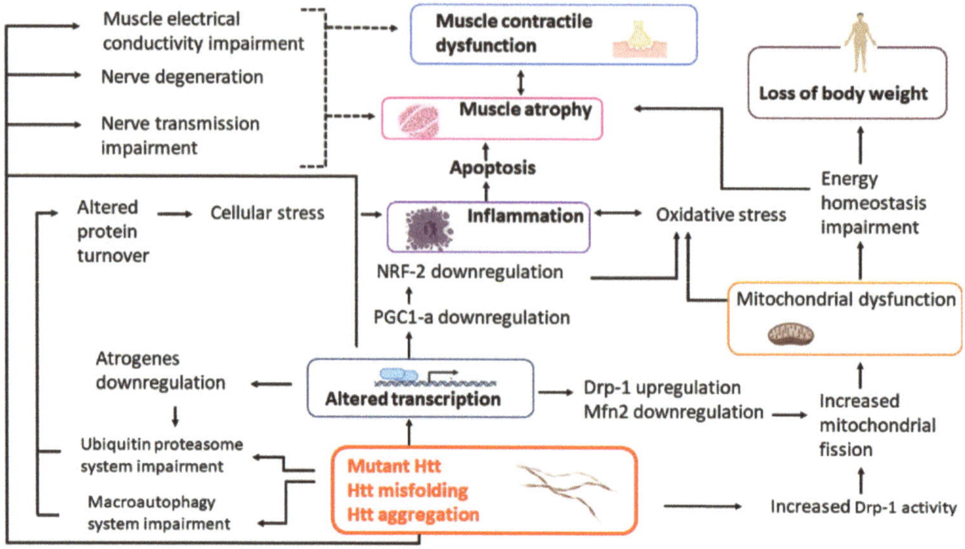

Figure 6.6 The main causes of muscle wasting and atrophy in HD, as well as their linkages, are represented in the scheme. Putative relationships are represented by dotted lines (Bozzi & Sciandra, 2020). *HD*, Huntington's disease; *Htt*, huntingtin. *Created with BioRender.com Bozzi, M., & Sciandra, F. (2020). Molecular mechanisms underlying muscle wasting in Huntington's disease. International Journal of Molecular Sciences, 21(21), 8314.*

incidence rate than males (Walton et al., 2020). MS symptoms and indications vary considerably from person to person and during the disease, depending on where the damaged nerve fibers are located (Poser et al., 1983).

Movement is typically hampered by symptoms such as (Fig. 6.7):

1. Certain neck motions, particularly bending the neck forward, cause electric shock feelings (Lhermitte sign).
2. Numbness or weakness in one or more limbs, commonly on one side of the body at a time or in the trunk and legs.
3. Tremors, a loss of coordination, or a shaky stride are all symptoms of PD.
4. Long-term double vision
5. Wholly or partially lost vision, generally in one eye at a time, and often accompanied by pain while moving the eyes.
6. Vision is blurry.

Other neurodegenerative disorders

Lewy body disease

The name Lewy body disease (LBD) was coined to characterize a condition that was previously divided into three categories (A, B, and C) based on the location of

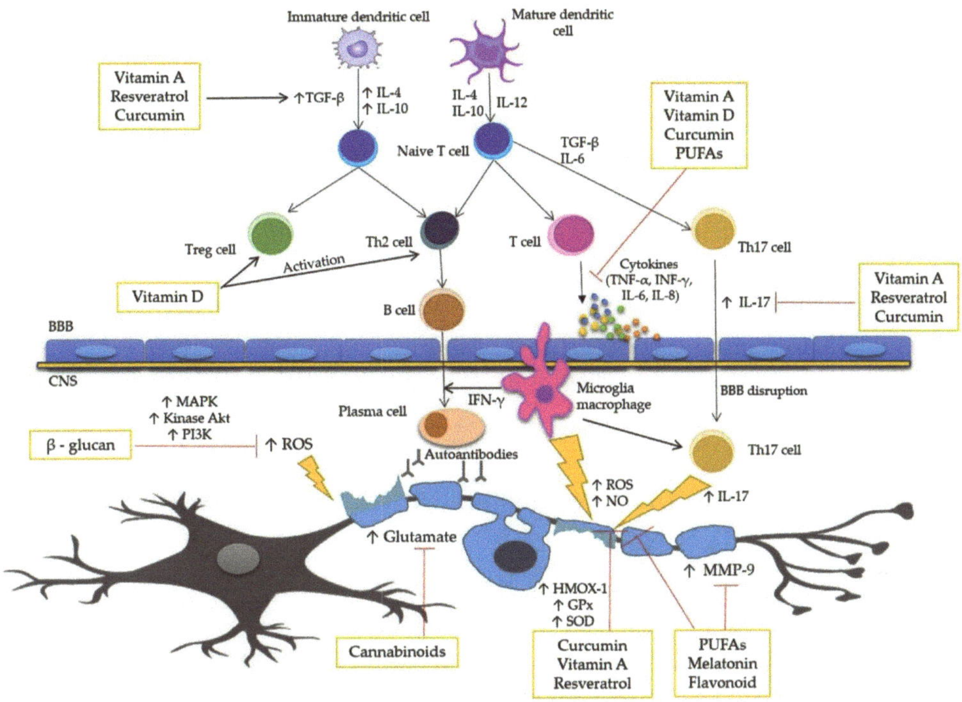

Figure 6.7 MS pathophysiology and possible bioactive chemical action location. Oxidative stress, which increases inflammation and, as a result, damages the myelin sheath and leads to neuronal death, is one of the key elements in the pathophysiology of MS. Many inflammatory and oxidative stress mediators, including cytokines like IL-1, IL-6, IL-17, TNF- and INF-, are released during the course of MS. Numerous immune system cells, particularly macrophages, B-cells, and T cells, as well as enhanced BBB permeability all contribute to the demyelination process (BBB). The probable action site of the bioactive antioxidant molecules is shown in this picture (Miller et al., 2019). *BBB*, Blood–brain barrier; *MS*, multiple sclerosis. *Adopted from Miller, E. D., et al. (2019). A review of various antioxidant compounds and their potential utility as complementary therapy in multiple sclerosis. Nutrients, 11(7), 1528.*

lewy body (LB) throughout the CNS. The clinical signs of 'dementia–Parkinson's syndrome" are seen in Group A (a diffuse form of LBD). The most striking pathologic characteristic is the extensive development of many Lewy bodies in the cerebral cortex and basal ganglia in addition to the brainstem and diencephalon (as in group C), which is exacerbated by variable degrees of senility. Group B is the bridging type between groups A and C. Idiopathic PD is equivalent to Group C (brain stem form of LBD). In this illness, the neuropathologic basis of progressive dementia is also explored. LBD is a clinicopathologic entity, with the diffuse variety of the illness presenting mostly as primary progressive dementia (Kosaka et al., 1984). For individuals >65 years, LB dementia is the second most frequent kind of degenerative dementia. LBD signs and symptoms can include visual hallucinations, poor regulation of body functions (autonomic nervous system), sleep difficulties, movement disorders, cognitive problems, fluctuating attention, apathy, and depression. Some health problems make you more likely to develop the disease (Kovacs, 2019). Almost all major neurodegenerative illnesses contain protein abnormalities with amyloid features; however, only a minority of these conditions have significant extracellular protein aggregates, which are the distinguishing hallmark of non-neural amyloidoses. Amyloid plaques can be detected in the brain parenchyma, and amyloid angiopathy can be discovered in the walls of blood vessels. Amyloid plaques come in a variety of shapes and sizes and are classified as diffuse ("primitive") plaques, dense-cored ("burnt-out") plaques, "classical" plaques, and cotton plaques (Dugger & Dickson, 2017).

Nanodiagnostics and manomedicines for neurodegenerative diseases

Nanotechnology's dramatic intervention in the last few decades has opened up enormous opportunities for developing novel ocular delivery methods that are both safe and effective. Several nanoparticles (NP)-based drug delivery methods (polymeric, lipid, and inorganic NPs) have been studied to diagnose and treat NDs in the modern period (Sarkar & Dyawanapelly, 2021). Engineered nanomaterials, which have diameters of 1−100 nm, are promising biomedical tools with the potential to tackle pharmacokinetic as well as pharmacodynamic issues, thanks to their physicochemical properties and the capacity to multifunctionalize them, allowing them to have multiple functions at once, including the ability to pass the BBB (Re et al., 2012). Maintaining drug stability in their active form before reaching the site of pathology and creating compounds targeted toward surface receptors and associated pathways of interest are two further challenges in identifying CNS therapies (Zhao et al., 2020). Numerous nanomedicines used as diagnostic and therapeutic agents for NDs are summarized below (Table 6.1).

Nanomedicines for Alzheimer's disease

More treatments for neurodegenerative illnesses will emerge as nanotechnologies become more widely used in biomedical applications. For AD and PD, nanomedicines can provide novel therapeutic options for conditions, such as neuroinflammation and misfolded proteins, therapeutic impact monitoring, and, most importantly, brain medication delivery (Soursou et al., 2015). Nanomaterial formulations have been demonstrated to reduce oxidative stress and inflammation and overcome barriers in passage through the BBB. However, the precise method for transport over the BBB varies and has not yet been fully explained (Li et al., 2015). Although the pathophysiology of CNS illnesses is now well understood, early diagnosis and

Table 6.1 Nanodiagnostics and nanomedicines employed for neurodegenerative disorders.

Neurodegenerative disorders	Type of nanodiagnostics and nanomedicines	Remarks	Application	References
AD	Au nanorods	• Inhibits Aβ aggregation under near infrared (NIR) irradiation	The concept combines two well-known Aβ inhibitors, polyoxometalates and Aβ15−20 (Aβ-targeted peptide inhibitor), with the unusually high NIR absorption ability of AuNRs	Li et al. (2017)
	Au nanoparticles	• Au nanoparticle attenuates Aβ-induced neuroinflammation and neuroapoptosis • ↓levels of Aβ, BACE-1, the microgliosis, astrocytosis, and RAGE expression	Anthocyanin-loaded PEG-AuNPs are a unique way to prevent age-related neurodegenerative disorders	Kim et al. (2017)
	CeO_2 or ceria nanoparticles or nanoceria	• ↓Endogenous peroxynitrite and protected against Aβ-induced mitochondrial fragmentation and neuronal cell death • Protects neurons against Aβ-mediated cytotoxicity	Nanoceria may help to prevent neurodegeneration	Cimini et al. (2012), Dowding et al. (2014)
	Chitosan nanoparticles	• ↑IgG against Aβ42 in serum and a ↓ titer of IgG against Aβ42 in the brain after the last immunization	Peptide vaccines for AD	Songjiang and Lixiang (2009)

(*Continued*)

Table 6.1 (Continued)

Neurodegenerative disorders	Type of nanodiagnostics and nanomedicines	Remarks	Application	References
	Exosomes	• $\downarrow$ the total Aβ1−42 levels • $\downarrow$ BACE1 mRNA levels	In wild-type mice, the robust mRNA (60%) and protein (62%) knockdown of BACE1, a therapeutic target in AD, indicated the therapeutic potential of exosome-mediated siRNA delivery	Alvarez-Erviti et al. (2011)
	Fluorescent quantum dots	• Achieved gene silencing efficiency of almost 51%	A unique way of siRNA distribution into nerve cells that may be used to monitor siRNA delivery	Li et al. (2012)
	Liposomes	• Inhibits Aβ1−42 aggregation • Inhibits Aβ42 aggregation in solution • Destabilization of Aβ42 aggregates was • observed in solution • Insoluble and soluble Aβ1−40 was $\downarrow$ by 33% and 32%, respectively; Insoluble and soluble Aβ1−42 was $\downarrow$ by 26% and 11%, respectively • Strongly $\downarrow$ the levels of soluble Aβ species with MW up to 90 kDa, 70.5% • $\downarrow$ number and total area of brain Aβ plaques by 34% • long-term recognition • memory recovered in Novel-object recognition test • Withdrawn Aβ peptides and $\uparrow$ plasma Aβ levels	• Integrity tests in the presence of serum proteins showed that these painted nanoliposomes satisfy the criteria for in vivo usage • Modified ApoE-derived peptide (mApoE-PA-LIP) is a valuable nanodevice that can pass the BBB both in vitro and in vivo • Bifunctionalized liposomes, which improve peptide removal across the BBB and peripheral clearance, destabilize Brain A aggregates	Airoldi et al. (2014), Bana et al. (2014), Mancini et al. (2017)

	Lipoprotein-based nanoparticles	• ↑microglial and astroglial degeneration of Aβ • Attenuated microgliosis • ↓Amyloid plaques in both the cortices and hippocampi • Attenuates impairment of neuronal integrity and neuron loss • ↑spatial learning and memory on the measures of Morris water maze performance	Nanostructures having a high affinity for Aβ could be used as new nanoplatforms for AD therapy	Song et al. (2014)
	Nanolipidic particles	• ↑neuronal α-secretase enhancing ability *in vitro* up to 91%	It has a far higher oral bioavailability in vivo than free (−)-epigallocatechin-3-gallate (EGCG)	Smith et al. (2010)
	PLA nanoparticles	In the radial arm maze test, there was a tendency toward higher working memory. ↑cue memory in the test conducted under fear Two forms of fibrils, fAβ (1−40) and fAβ (1−42), had more significant destabilizing effects	In Tg2576 mice, a new nanocurcumin formulation produced very stable nanoparticles with positive therapeutic benefits	Baysal et al. (2013), Cheng et al. (2013)
	PLGA nanoparticle's	↑ immune responses and serum IgG levels ↓memory impairment more effectively and ↓ brain inflammation	• Immunotherapy with A (1−15) loaded PLGA microparticles could be a promising strategy for developing a safe vaccine in the future • Nanospheres that have been developed reduce brain inflammation, resulting in a reduction in β-amyloid plaques	Puras et al. (2011), Sanchez-Lopez et al. (2017)

(*Continued*)

Table 6.1 (Continued)

Neurodegenerative disorders	Type of nanodiagnostics and nanomedicines	Remarks	Application	References
	Polystyrene nanoparticles	Significantly protected cells from Aβ-associated cytotoxicity	Nano-N2PY, or other nanoparticles conjugated to metal chelators, could be a promising new treatment for AD	Liu et al. (2009)
	POM@P nanoparticles	POM@P nanoparticles rescued Aβ-induced cytotoxicity	Flexible organic–inorganic hybrid systems may facilitate the creation of new multifunctional materials for AD treatment	Li et al. (2013)
	WS_2 nanosheets	Inhibited Aβ aggregation and dissociated preformed Aβ aggregates • Rescued Aβ40-induced cytotoxicity	The high NIR absorption property of WS_2 allows amyloid aggregates to be dissolved when exposed to NIR light	Li et al. (2015)
	VP025	Significantly inhibited caspase-3 activation in hippocampalTissues • Significantly attenuated the Aβ-induced depression in LTP	It attenuates the age-related decline in spatial learning and long-term potentiation by attenuating the simultaneous activation of sphingomyelinase and caspase three due to its capacity to diminish age-related oxidative changes	Miller et al. (2009)

PD	CeO_2 or ceria nanoparticles or nanoceria	• Protected against the MPTP-induced decline in striatal dopamine	Disease-modifying therapy to treat PD	Dillon et al. (2011)
	C(60)(OH)(24)	• Protected cells from oxidative damage • Prevent mitochondrial dysfunction, including improvement of MMP and complex I and II activities • ↑total GSH levels, also prevented the total GSH loss and ↑[GSSG]/[GSHt] ratio significantly. And $C_{60}(OH)_{24}$ pretreatment attenuates the ↑[GSSG]/[GSHt] ratio	A direct and indirect antioxidant inducer, C(60)(OH)(24), is a protective antioxidant for the mitochondria	Cai et al. (2008)
	Dendrigraft poly-L-lysines	• ↓caspase-3 activity in brains • ↑locomotor activity in open field test • Rescued TH-positive neurons ↓levels of TNF-α and NO	*Caspase-3* shRNA, Brain-targeted nanoparticles with rabies virus glycoprotein peptide modifications (synergistic therapeutic effects)	Liu et al. (2013)
	Fe_3O_4 nanoparticles	• ↑locomotor activity • ↓the mRNA levels of α-synuclein and enhanced TH mRNA levels • ↑TH expression and ↓ α-synuclein Expression	NGF shRNA for -syn-carrying multifunctional superparamagnetic nanoparticles may facilitate effective repair in a PD model	Niu et al. (2017)

(*Continued*)

Table 6.1 (Continued)

Neurodegenerative disorders	Type of nanodiagnostics and nanomedicines	Remarks	Application	References
	Lactoferrinmodified nanoparticles	• ↓ROS levels • Protected against rotenone-induced neurotoxicity • Suppressed the expression of α-synuclein	Curcumin-loaded lactoferrin nanoparticles combined with dopaminergic neurotoxicity could be a potential medication delivery approach	Bollimpelli et al. (2016)
	Nanocomposites	Delay of climbing ability lost ↓lipid peroxidation	Alginate-curcumin nanocomposite was effective in delaying the climbing handicap of PD model flies	Siddique et al. (2013)
	PAMAM dendrimer	• ↑locomotor activity in rats • Rescued dopaminergic neurons • 6-OHDA-induced PD rats • ↓apomorphine-induced rotation and improved locomotor activity • ↓dopaminergic neuronal loss	*GDNF* gene	Huang et al. (2009, 2010)
	PBCA nanoparticles	• overturned the scopolamine-induced amnesia • ↑locomotor activity	NGF	Kurakhmaeva et al. (2009)
	PLGA nanoparticles	• considerably heightened placing task scores • Restored the motor function in the foot-fault asymmetry test • ↓amphetamine-induced rotations • No changes in mitochondrial damage or ultrastructure	L-Dopamine Dopamine	Gambaryan et al. (2014)

	Polyanhydride nanoparticles	• ↓oxidative stress-induced mitochondrial dysfunction	Apocynin	Brenza et al. (2017)
	Resveratrol nanoemulsion	• ↑levels of GSH and SOD	Vitamin E and resveratrol	Pangeni et al. (2014)
	VP025	• ↓amphetamine-induced rotation rates • ↓spontaneous locomotor activity • Restored the dopamine for 6 weeks • notably secure striatal dopamine • rescue ipsilateral nigral dopaminergic neurons • ↓ipsilateral microglial activation • ↓p38 activation, which can mediate apoptotic cell death	VP025 shows protective effects on the 6-OHDA-lesioned nigrostriatal pathway, suggesting that it could be used to treat PD	Crotty et al. (2008), Fitzgerald et al. (2008)
Amyotrophic lateral sclerosis	Au-particles coated with SOD1 MAEHP	Quick diagnosis ↑BBB penetration	Delay ALS disease progression	Liu et al. (2006), Marcuzzo et al. (2019)
	Riluzole-carbon nanoparticles	Glutamate inhibitor	Delivered to pathogenic areas precisely	Mukherjee et al. (2020)
	BP-nanosheets	Capture excess Cu^{2+} Pass across the BBB under near-infrared laser irradiation	BBB's inherent photothermal effect	Chen et al. (2018)
	CeO_2 NPs	↓Oxidative stress	Improved the strength and lifespan of SOD1G93A mice	Bordoni et al. (2020)
	(INVITE)-loaded-curcumin micelles	Accurate drug targeting via mesenchymal stromatal cells (MSCs) innate	Enhance the therapeutic effect of MSCs	Yavarpour-Bali et al. (2019)

(*Continued*)

Table 6.1 (Continued)

Neurodegenerative disorders	Type of nanodiagnostics and nanomedicines	Remarks	Application	References
Friedreich ataxia	Nanosurf FlexAFM 5 microscope	Monitor cellular fluctuations	*Nanodiagnostic*	Vannocci et al. (2019)
	Magnetic nanoparticles	↑frataxin protein	Radiation therapy, Orthopedic implants	Swasti and DK (2017)
HD	Se−NPs	↑Huntingtin protein aggregation	HD therapy	Mukherjee et al. (2020), Cong et al. (2019)
	Cur-SLN	↓mitochondrial malfunction, oxidative stress, and inflammation ↑locomotor activity	Potential therapeutic impact on 3-NP-induced HD model	Yavarpour-Bali et al. (2019)
	Mn_3O_4 nanozymes			González et al. (2021)
Multiple sclerosis	PNC	↑FOXP3 level ↓GFAP, ↓Iba1 ↑BDNF, ↑NGF	Prevent inflammation in the CNS	Yavarpour-Bali et al. (2019)
	Quantum dot complexed with MMP-9-Si RNA, MMP-1-loadedPLGA pMHC-coated iron oxide nanoparticles ITE- and MOG-loaded gold NPs Mannosylated liposomes carrying myelin basic protein (MBP) fragments Epigallocatechin gallate- and a-lipoic acid loaded gold NPs	Nanoparticles MMP9 expression in brain, microvascular endothelial cells, leukocyte inhibition Inhibition of MMP-9 and inflammation Dendritic cell-induced T-reg cell differentiation Nullified MBP antibodies showing EAE abrogation Strong antioxidant activity		Ojha and Kumar (2018)

	CeO NPs	Strong antioxidant activity		
	Fullerene (C60) suspension	Strong antioxidant activity		
	Nano-encapsulated *Helicobacter pylori*	Hypothesized for future MS therapy		
	Tempamine-loaded PEGylated liposomes	Inhibit EAE in mice		
	Trimethyl chitosan-loaded IFN-b microparticles	Sustained drug release		
	Fullerenol (polyhydroxylated C60)	Substantial neuroprotection antagonizing glutamate receptors		
	NAC loaded Polyamidoamine dendrimers	Suppress neuroinflammation and increase motor function in cerebral palsy		
Other NDs	Poloxamer 188 (PX) coated PLGA-nanoparticles	↑BBB transport	Neuroprotective effect	Wang et al. (2020)
	CS−ALG−STPP NPs	↓Stage and period of GTCS	Antiepileptogenic	Yavarpour-Bali et al. (2019)

AD, Alzheimer's disease; *Au*, gold; *BP*, black phosphorus; *BBB*, blood−brain barrier; *BDNF*, brain derived neurotrophic factor; *CeO2 NPs*, cerium oxide NPs; *Cur-SLN*, curcumin solid lipid nanoparticle; *CS−ALG−STPP NPs*, chitosan−alginate−sodium tripolyphosphate nanoparticles; *GSH*, glutathione; *LTP*, long-term potentiation; *MBP*, myelin binding proetin; *MPTP*, 1-methyl-4-phenyl-1,2,3,6-tetrahydropyridine; *NGF*, nerve growth factor; *MSC*, mesenchyma stromatal cell; *PEG*, poly(ethylene glycol); *PLA*, poly-lactic acid; *PLGA*, poly(lactic-*co*-glycolic acid); *GTCS*, generalized tonic-clonic seizures; *HD*, Huntington's disease; *INVITE*, insulin-D-alpha-tocopherol succinate micelles; *MAEHP*, 2-methyl-*N*-(2-aminoethyl)-3-hydroxyl-4-pyridinone); *NIR*, near infrared; *NMDA*, *N*-methyl-D-aspartic acid receptor; *PD*, Parkinson's disease; *PNC*, polymerized nano-curcumin; *PLGA*: poly(lactic-*co*-glycolic acid); *PX-18*, 2-*N*,*N*-bis(oleoyloxyethyl) amino-1-ethanesulfonic acid; *Se−NPs*, selenium nanoparticle; *SOD*, superoxide dismutase.

therapy are still not apparent, and medicines directly only target symptoms. Additionally, although several innovative medications have been discovered (such as proteins, peptides, siRNAs, and synthetic compounds), most of them may not succeed due to unsatisfactory drug pharmacokinetics, generalized targeting, and maybe worsened side effects (Zhang et al., 2018). Nanotechnology, however, has made great strides in recent years and may offer significant potential benefits for detecting and treating CNS diseases (Zhang et al., 2018). The diagnostic value of the CSF biomarkers tau protein, Aβ42 (a 42-amino-acid variation of beta-amyloid), and amyloid precursor protein is crucial. One possible biomarker for Alzheimer's is amyloid beta-derived diffusible ligands (ADDL). The link between CSF ADDL levels and disease status could lead to more accurate AD diagnosis and treatment. It is accomplished by combining ADDL-specific monoclonal antibodies with bio barcode amplification, a protein detection technique based on ultrasensitive NPs (Singh et al., 2008). Metal chelators are one of the agents having the capacity to inhibit and reverse Aβ aggregation. Chelation therapy's disadvantages include the inability to overcome the BBB, limited absorption, and severe side effects. Because of the specific properties outlined above, nanotechnology-based drug delivery systems (NBDDS) are effective instruments for overcoming these drawbacks (Bozdag Pehlivan, 2013).

Nanomedicines for Parkinson's disease

The nano-enabled scaffold device (NESD) for targeted dopamine (DA) delivery was created to alleviate the adverse side effects of traditional PD therapy. NBDDS offer more options for targeted Levodopa distribution, an isomer of dihydroxyphenylalanine, a dopamine metabolic precursor. Multifunctional NBDDS have been described for PD imaging and treatment purposes. Extremely fluorescent core/shell CdSe/CdS quantum rods have been created and made water-soluble and highly biocompatible by intercalating an amphiphilic polymer and conjugating diamino PEG molecules (Bozdag Pehlivan, 2013).

Nanomaterials are a rapidly expanding field in ND treatment, with the potential to alter therapeutic agent delivery and create a whole new class of therapeutics for canonically complex illnesses.

Nanomedicine for amyotrophic lateral sclerosis

ALS is a significant motor neuron disease progression to neurodegenerative disorders. Pathology is neuroprotected by carboxy fullerenes nanotubes with SOD, including Riluzole, a glutamate inhibitor, which can be delivered more precisely to pathogenic areas using carbon NPs with high carrying capacity (Mukherjee et al., 2020). Gold particles coated with SOD1 can be coupled with SOD1 aggregate to provide a colorimetric detection method for quick diagnosis

(Marcuzzo et al., 2019). To promote BBB penetration, Liu et al. (2006) designed NPs to be functionalized with PS80, and an iron chelator was used to conjugate the NPs platform (e.g., 2-methyl-*N*-(2-aminoethyl)-3-hydroxyl-4-pyridinone) (MAEHP). Despite biological benefits, it has certain limitations, for example, low solubility, easy degradation by rapid enzymatic degradation, "off-target" effect, immune system clearance, unfavorable pharmacokinetic properties, and overcoming these challenges nanotechnologies have been provided the better drug delivery opportunities. Some of the nanomedicines have been approved by FDA, such as Genexol-PM, Abraxane, and Kadcyla. With the help of a nanocarrier, subsequent transport across the BBB became efficient and avoided extensive systemic distribution. In several neurodegenerative illnesses, iron chelators (e.g., Deferiprone, Clioquinol, Apocynin) have shown therapeutic effectiveness in managing transition-metal dyshomeostasis (Wang et al., 2020). Due to the BBB's inherent photothermal activity, black phosphorus (BP) nanosheets were demonstrated to be able to cross the BBB under near-infrared laser irradiation while also trapping extra Cu^{2+} to shield neuronal cells from transition-metal-induced neurotoxicity (Chen et al., 2018). The high amount of oxidative stress is one of the critical features of ALS. As a result, oxidative stress targets the therapy with cerium oxide NPs (CeO_2 NPs), which have regenerative antioxidant characteristics. CeO_2 NPs improved the strength and lifespan of SOD1G93A mice, according to DeCoteau and colleagues (Bordoni et al., 2020). Curcumin has shown potential as an antioxidant in treating various NDs (Zhou et al., 2011). Insulin-D-alpha-tocopherol succinate micelles (INVITE)-loaded-curcumin micelles were employed to enhance the therapeutic efficacy of MSCs. It ensures accurate drug targeting via MSCs' innate ability to reach injured tissues while protecting the integrated drug from premature release and avoiding toxic effects on MSCs (Yavarpour-Bali et al., 2019). The novel medication delivery mechanism outlined above has been offered as an ultimate approach for treating neurodegenerative illnesses like ALS.

Nanomedicine for Friedreich ataxia

Gait and limb ataxia, lower limb flexia, and dysarthria are all symptoms of FA (FRDA), an uncommon pediatric condition. Synthetic transcription factors (e.g., Syn-TEF1) are developing as strategies that can increase prospects for gene-level therapeutic intervention is needed to treat this condition. Gene therapy and targeting the genetic region is another promising approach for improving symptoms caused by low FXN expression. Adults and children with FRDA are enrolled in Phase II research to assess the safety, pharmacodynamics, and efficacy of omaveloxolone. These therapy methods for FRDA are thoroughly reviewed in several recent papers, such as histone deacetylase inhibitors (HDACi), resveratrol, NRF2 inducers, interferon (IF) gamma, erythropoietin mimetics, cell therapy, frataxin protein replacement, frataxin protein stabilization cytokine therapy, Crestor, EPI-743, epicatechin, CAT-4001, Methylprednisolone, TAK-831 (Zhang et al., 2019). A nanodiagnostic Nanosurf FlexAFM 5 microscope is used to keep track of cellular changes related to metabolism (Vannocci et al., 2019). In place of frataxin protein, magnetic NPs in the body take up iron particles and drive them toward sulfur using an external magnetic field to produce iron—sulfur clusters (Swasti & DK, 2017).

Nanomedicine for Huntington's disease

HD is a catastrophic ND marked by quiet motor, cognitive, and behavioral abnormalities. The only medicine approved by the Food and Drug Administration (FDA) for symptomatic treatment of HD is TBZ (Kang et al., 2018). However, rosmarinic-acid-loaded SLNs are given intranasally to treat HD's behavioral dysfunctions and oxidative stress (Bhatt et al., 2015; Lamptey et al., 2022). Chitosan/siRNA complexes create NPs with a size of 200 nm, which is suitable for in vivo administration. The release of structurally intact siRNA from NPs, which is required for nanocarrier-mediated RNA gene silencing, has formerly been reported (Sava et al., 2020). Cong et al. (2019) beautifully demonstrated neuronal protection and behavioral dysfunction treatment in a *Caenorhabditis elegans* model of HD via Se NPs-mediated reduced huntingtin protein aggregation. Since low or insufficient levels of Se are a hallmark of most NDs, including HD, this formulation holds promise as a significant lead for HD therapy in the future (Mukherjee et al., 2020; Cong et al., 2019). Cur-SLN is a potential method for reducing mitochondrial deficits in the 3-NP-induced HD model. It could also benefit other neurodegenerative illnesses involving mitochondrial malfunction, oxidative stress, and inflammation (Yavarpour-Bali et al., 2019). Mn_3O_4 nanozymes help people with physical, cognitive, and behavioral problems (González et al., 2021).

Nanomedicine for multiple sclerosis

MS is a neurodegenerative illness caused by a chronic inflammatory autoimmune disease of the CNS. In curcumin-loaded NP-receiving rats, glial activation markers, such as GFAP (an astrocyte marker) and Iba1 (a microglia/macrophage marker), were considerably reduced. In comparison to free curcumin, there was a decrease in immune cell infiltration and a reduction in the extent of demyelination areas (Yavarpour-Bali et al., 2019). MMP9 expression in the brain, microvascular endothelial cells, and leukocyte inhibition is reduced by quantum dots complexed with MMP-9-Si RNA and MMP-1-loaded PLGA NPs. pMHC-coated iron oxide

NPs aid the inhibition of MMP-9 and inflammation. ITE- and MOG-loaded gold NPs result in dendritic cell-induced T-reg cell differentiation. MBP antibodies that reveal EAE abrogation are nullified by mannosylated liposomes that carry MBP fragments. Gold NPs loaded with epigallocatechin gallate and a-lipoic acid CeO NPs are powerful antioxidants. A potent antioxidant is a fullerene (C60) suspension. Future MS therapy could use nano-encapsulated *Helicobacter pylori*. A tempamine-loaded PEGylated liposome significantly reduces EAE in mice. Trimethyl chitosan-loaded IFN-b microparticles give sustained drug release. Antagonizing glutamate receptors, fullerenol (polyhydroxylated C60) provides substantial neuroprotection. NAC-loaded polyamidoamine dendrimers reduce neuroinflammation and boost muscle activity in cerebral palsy patients (Ojha & Kumar, 2018).

Nanomedicine for other neurodegenerative diseases

Poloxamer 188 (PX) was used to coat poly(lactic-*co*-glycolic acid) (PLGA) NPs so they could pass through the BBB while carrying BDNF (NP-BDNF-PX), according to Igor and coworkers. In mice with traumatic brain injury (TBI) an extensively high amount of BDNF was observed in the brain after IV administration compared to control, and the neuroprotective effect was also significantly improved (Wang et al., 2020). Hashemian et al. found that encapsulating curcumin on chitosan—alginate—sodium tripolyphosphate NPs (CS—ALG—STPP NPs) has an antiepileptogenic impact, reducing the stage and duration of generalized tonic—clonic seizures (Yavarpour-Bali et al., 2019).

Translational nanodiagnostics and nanomedicine-based products for neurodegenerative diseases

Approved nanotechnology products for neurodegenerative diseases

NDs, as described above, represent a broad spectrum of catastrophic disorders that worsen overtime and are linked to the loss or decline of neurons in particular parts of the CNS. The restricted availability of medication molecules across the BBB poses a significant problem for treating these disorders. Furthermore, drug delivery methods based on nanotechnology have a lot of promise for managing and treating these illnesses. The use of nano-based drug delivery systems for the treatment of NDs will be covered in this section. Scientists now have bright prospects for the study and treatment of NDs thanks to the present uses of nanotechnology in biomedicine and in the disciplines of nanomedicine and neuroscience. When surface modified with specific nanoengineered materials, drugs can be delivered while maintaining drug release, increasing bioavailability, and protecting components from degradation. These characteristics of nanomaterials put them at the forefront of potential future diagnostic and therapeutic applications for NDs (Bozdag Pehlivan, 2013; Zhang et al., 2018; Kassem et al., 2020; Nikalje, 2015). The parenterally administered NPs—unique possible colloidal carrier systems and matrix-like components made from polymers or lipids—are given intravenously. This approach manipulates bioengineered materials with functional groups on the nanoscale scale (1−100 nm), which can interact molecularly with biological systems (Kassem et al., 2020; Pansare, 2015). Therapeutically approved peptides and proteins can be found in the FDA's THPdb database, which was built using information from 985 publications and 70 patents. The THPdb database contains information on 380 drug derivatives and 239 therapeutic peptides and proteins that the US FDA has authorized (Usmani et al., 2017).

With improvements in NDs' cell biology, pathology, and neurophysiology, as well as the upcoming smart NPs design that can cross the BBB and target the desired site in the CNS, NP-based approaches focused on neuroprotective and neuroregenerative techniques in NDs can significantly benefit. Several NPs have been studied during the past 10 years to improve the bioavailability and therapeutic effectiveness of medications that target NDs (Alam et al., 2014).

Under clinical trials and patents, products for neurodegenerative diseases

Only a few clinical trials using therapeutic antibodies and secretase inhibitors for AD have been completed, and the majority have been stopped (Pardridge, 2020). It is interesting to note that since 2003, there have not been any new AD drugs developed globally (Sun & Benet, 2020). A recent search of the NIH library revealed only two research relevant to NP delivery, which provided further evidence. The first is scheduled to begin in 2023, entitled "Safety, tolerability and efficacy assessment of intranasal NPs of APH-1105, a new alpha-secretase modulator for mild to moderate cognitive impairment related to Alzheimer's disease" (Annovis Bio Inc., 2021). Gold nanocrystals were used in this investigation. Updates on the current research are awaited, even though gold nanocrystals have recently been approved to treat MS (Marisa Wexler, 2021). Positive outcomes will only encourage the use of NPs in future studies. As a potential treatment for MS, PD, and ALS, Clene is currently developing CNM-Au8 using gold nanocrystals. The therapy aims to remove the harmful byproducts of cellular metabolism while promoting the chemical reactions cells need to produce energy. It is anticipated to contribute to neuronal protection and the production of myelin, the fatty sheath around neuronal axons that the immune system attacks in MS (Table 6.2).

Table 6.2 Application of nanomaterial and nanoparticles in neurodegenerative studies.

Nanomaterials/ nanoparticles	Size (nm)	Diseases	Therapeutic effects/application	References
Gold	1–150	ADPD	Inhibition of Aβ-42 aggregation increases the expression of BDNF to boost neuronal survival and prevent the development of amyloid fibrils. Inhibition of PC12 cells and substantia nigra striatum dopaminergic neuronal apoptosis	Asil et al. (2020), Hou et al. (2020), Hu et al. (2018), Jagaran and Singh (2021)
Silver	1–100	ADPD	Up-regulation of hydrogen sulfide (H_2S) and Ag2S reduces neurotoxicityAnti-cholinesterase and antioxidant activity as a plant-based anti-AD drugAlter gene and protein expression of Aβ deposition	Asil et al. (2020), Jagaran and Singh (2021), Gonzalez-Carter et al. (2017), Youssif et al. (2019)
Selenium		PD	Decrease in amyloid plaques in AD lesions	Jagaran and Singh (2021), Huo et al. (2019)
Magnetic @NMs	1–500	AD	Target and identify amyloid plaques in AD, control the homeostasis of metals in the brain, and administer a hefty dose of the medication to achieve high local concentration and prevent toxicity.	(Asil et al., 2020; Jagaran & Singh, 2021)
Polymeric NMs	1–1000	ADPD	Improve oral bioavailability, raise brain absorption, and boost drug bioactivity by crossing the BBB and enhancing the viability of brain cells	Asil et al. (2020), Jagaran and Singh (2021)
Graphene	1–100	ADPD	Bolster neural cell survival and aid in neural regeneration	
Fullerene	0.4–1.6	ADPD	Antioxidant activity against the cytotoxicity of oxidative stress induces neural stem cell proliferation and rescues the function of the injured CNS	
Carbon nanotubes	1–100	ADPD	Improve network connectivity, synapse formation, neuronal activity, and the functional regeneration of neurons following brain trauma	

AD, Alzheimer's disease; *BBB*, blood–brain barrier; *BDNF*, brain derived neurotrophic factor; *CNS*, central nervous system; *NM*, nanomaterials; *PD*, Parkinson's disease.

Conclusion

Nanotechnology is widely applied in nanomedicines and neuroscience for the early diagnosis and management of NDs, including AD, PD, ALS, HD, and MS. When surface-modified with different molecules, nanoengineered materials can deliver numerous agents, improve bioavailability, sustain medication release, and shield compounds from degradation. These characteristics of nanomaterials put them in the vanguard of potential future diagnostic and therapeutic applications for NDs. Even with a better understanding of the pathophysiology of NDs, the early diagnosis and treatment are not well clear. Further, various therapeutic options are available for managing NDs; however, unfavorable pharmacokinetic profiles, nonselective targeting, and undesirable side effects limit their use. Nanomedicines are the novel therapeutic options for neuroinflammation and misfolded proteins NDs to deliver the specific medicines at specific brain sites. Nanomaterial formulations have been demonstrated to reduce oxidative stress and inflammation and overcome barriers through the BBB. However, the precise method for transport over the BBB varies and has not yet been fully explained (BBB). With improvements in NDs' cell biology, pathology, and neurophysiology, as well as the upcoming smart NPs design that can cross the BBB and target the desired site in the CNS, NP-based approaches focused on neuroprotective and neuroregenerative techniques in NDs can significantly benefit. Several NPs have been researched during the past 10 years to improve the bioavailability and therapeutic effectiveness of medications that target NDs. Plant-based nanomedicines are developing for their better efficacy and safety. Several nanotechnological-based diagnostic and therapeutic products are being developed for the early diagnosis and management of NDs.

References

Airoldi, C., et al. (2014). Nanoliposomes presenting on surface a cis-glycofused benzopyran compound display binding affinity and aggregation inhibition ability towards Amyloid β-42 peptide. *European Journal of Medicinal Chemistry*, *85*, 43–50.

Ajitkumar, A., & De Jesus, O. (2021). *Huntington disease. StatPearls [Internet]*. StatPearls Publishing.

Alam, Q., et al. (2014). A nanotechnological approach to the management of Alzheimer's disease and type 2 diabetes. *CNS & Neurological Disorders-Drug Targets (Formerly Current Drug Targets-CNS & Neurological Disorders)*, *13*(3), 478–486.

Alvarez-Erviti, L., et al. (2011). Delivery of siRNA to the mouse brain by systemic injection of targeted exosomes. *Nature Biotechnology*, *29*(4), 341–345.

Annovis Bio Inc. (2021). *A multicenter, randomized, double-blind, placebo-controlled, dose-finding study to evaluate the safety, tolerability, pharmacokinetic and pharmacodynamic effects of Posiphen® in subjects with early Alzheimer's disease (AD) or Early Parkinson's Disease (PD)*, clinicaltrials.gov.

Asil, S. M., et al. (2020). Nanomaterial based drug delivery systems for the treatment of neurodegenerative diseases. *Biomaterials Science*, *8*(15), 4109–4128.

Bana, L., et al. (2014). Liposomes bi-functionalized with phosphatidic acid and an ApoE-derived peptide affect Aβ aggregation features and cross the blood-brain-barrier: Implications for therapy of Alzheimer disease. *Nanomedicine: Nanotechnology, Biology and Medicine*, *10*(7), 1583–1590.

Bargmann, C. I., & Newsome, W. T. (2014). The brain research through advancing innovative neurotechnologies (BRAIN) initiative and neurology. *JAMA Neurology*, *71*(6), 675–676.
Basu, S. (2017). History of neurodegenerative diseases and its impact on the aged population in India: An assessment. *Indian Journal of History of Science*, *52*, 106–115.
Baysal, I., et al. (2013). Interaction of selegiline-loaded PLGA-b-PEG nanoparticles with beta-amyloid fibrils. *Journal of Neural Transmission*, *120*(6), 903–910.
Behl, T., et al. (2020). Exploring the potential of therapeutic agents targeted towards mitigating the events associated with amyloid-β cascade in Alzheimer's disease. *International Journal of Molecular Sciences*, *21*(20), 7443.
Berman, T., & Bayati, A. (2018). What are neurodegenerative diseases and how do they affect the brain? *Frontiers for Young Minds*, *6*.
Bhatt, R., et al. (2015). Development, characterization and nasal delivery of rosmarinic acid-loaded solid lipid nanoparticles for the effective management of Huntington's disease. *Drug Delivery*, *22*(7), 931–939.
Bollimpelli, V. S., et al. (2016). Neuroprotective effect of curcumin-loaded lactoferrin nanoparticles against rotenone-induced neurotoxicity. *Neurochemistry International*, *95*, 37–45.
Bordoni, M., et al. (2020). Biomaterials in neurodegenerative disorders: A promising therapeutic approach. *International Journal of Molecular Sciences*, *21*(9), 3243.
Bozdag Pehlivan, S. (2013). Nanotechnology-based drug delivery systems for targeting, imaging and diagnosis of neurodegenerative diseases. *Pharmaceutical Research*, *30*(10), 2499–2511.
Bozzi, M., & Sciandra, F. (2020). Molecular mechanisms underlying muscle wasting in Huntington's disease. *International Journal of Molecular Sciences*, *21*(21), 8314.
Brenza, T. M., et al. (2017). Neuronal protection against oxidative insult by polyanhydride nanoparticle-based mitochondria-targeted antioxidant therapy. *Nanomedicine: Nanotechnology, Biology and Medicine*, *13*(3), 809–820.
Brown, C. A., et al. (2021). Estimated prevalence and incidence of amyotrophic lateral sclerosis and SOD1 and C9orf72 genetic variants. *Neuroepidemiology*, *55*(5), 342–353.
Cai, X., et al. (2008). *Polyhydroxylated fullerene derivative C60 (OH) 24 prevents mitochondrial dysfunction and oxidative damage in an* MPP^+*-induced cellular model of Parkinson's disease. Journal of Neuroscience Research*, *86*(16), 3622–3634.
Chen, W., et al. (2018). Black phosphorus nanosheets as a neuroprotective nanomedicine for neurodegenerative disorder therapy. *Advanced Materials*, *30*(3), 1703458.
Cheng, K. K., et al. (2013). Highly stabilized curcumin nanoparticles tested in an in vitro blood-brain barrier model and in Alzheimer's disease Tg2576 mice. *The AAPS Journal*, *15*(2), 324–336.
Cimini, A., et al. (2012). Antibody-conjugated PEGylated cerium oxide nanoparticles for specific targeting of Aβ aggregates modulate neuronal survival pathways. *Acta Biomaterialia*, *8*(6), 2056–2067.
Ciulla, M., et al. (2019). Role of dietary supplements in the management of Parkinson's disease. *Biomolecules*, *9*(7), 271.
Cong, W., et al. (2019). Selenium nanoparticles as an efficient nanomedicine for the therapy of Huntington's disease. *ACS Applied Materials & Interfaces*, *11*(38), 34725–34735.
Crotty, S., et al. (2008). Neuroprotective effects of novel phosphatidylglycerol-based phospholipids in the 6-hydroxydopamine model of Parkinson's disease. *European Journal of Neuroscience*, *27*(2), 294–300.
Cui, W., et al. (2021). Application of nanomaterials in neurodegenerative diseases. *Current Stem Cell Research & Therapy*, *16*(1), 83–94.
Delatycki, M. B., Williamson, R., & Forrest, S. M. (2000). Friedreich ataxia: An overview. *Journal of Medical Genetics*, *37*(1), 1–8.
Dillon, C., et al. (2011). Cerium oxide nanoparticles protect against MPTP-induced dopaminergic neurodegeneration in a mouse model for Parkinson's disease. *Nanotechnology*, *3*, 451–454.
Divya, G. (2020). *Just a fraction of an estimated 5 million Indians with dementia and Alzheimer's are diagnosed. Do we need a new policy to ensure their well-being?* The Hindu.
Dorsey, E. R., et al. (2018). Global, regional, and national burden of Parkinson's disease, 1990–2016: A systematic analysis for the Global Burden of Disease Study 2016. *The Lancet Neurology*, *17*(11), 939–953.

Dowding, J. M., et al. (2014). Cerium oxide nanoparticles protect against Aβ-induced mitochondrial fragmentation and neuronal cell death. *Cell Death & Differentiation*, *21*(10), 1622–1632.
Dugger, B. N., & Dickson, D. W. (2017). Pathology of neurodegenerative diseases. *Cold Spring Harbor Perspectives in Biology*, *9*(7), a028035.
Duraes, F., Pinto, M., & Sousa, E. (2018). Old drugs as new treatments for neurodegenerative diseases. *Pharmaceuticals*, *11*(2), 44.
Eisen, A., Kim, S., & Pant, B. (1992). Amyotrophic lateral sclerosis (ALS): A phylogenetic disease of the corticomotoneuron? *Muscle & Nerve*, *15*(2), 219–224.
Erkkinen, M. G., Kim, M.-O., & Geschwind, M. D. (2018). Clinical neurology and epidemiology of the major neurodegenerative diseases. *Cold Spring Harbor Perspectives in Biology*, *10*(4), a033118.
Fitzgerald, P., et al. (2008). Treatment with phosphotidylglycerol-based nanoparticles prevents motor deficits induced by proteasome inhibition: Implications for Parkinson's disease. *Behavioural Brain Research*, *195*(2), 271–274.
Gambaryan, P. Y., et al. (2014). Increasing the efficiency of Parkinson's disease treatment using a poly (lactic-co-glycolic acid)(PLGA) based L-DOPA delivery system. *Experimental Neurobiology*, *23*(3), 246.
Gitler, A. D., Dhillon, P., & Shorter, J. (2017). Neurodegenerative disease: Models, mechanisms, and a new hope. *Disease Models & Mechanisms*, *10*(5), 499–502.
González, L. F., Bevilacqua, L. E., & Naves, R. (2021). Nanotechnology-based drug delivery strategies to repair the mitochondrial function in neuroinflammatory and neurodegenerative diseases. *Pharmaceutics*, *13*(12), 2055.
Gonzalez-Carter, D. A., et al. (2017). *Silver nanoparticles reduce brain inflammation and related neurotoxicity through induction of H_2S-synthesizing enzymes. Scientific Reports*, 7(1), 1–14.
Hampel, H., et al. (2021). The amyloid-β pathway in Alzheimer's disease. *Molecular Psychiatry*, 1–23.
Hou, K., et al. (2020). Chiral gold nanoparticles enantioselectively rescue memory deficits in a mouse model of Alzheimer's disease. *Nature Communications*, *11*(1), 1–11.
Hu, K., et al. (2018). Neuroprotective effect of gold nanoparticles composites in Parkinson's disease model. *Nanomedicine: Nanotechnology, Biology and Medicine*, *14*(4), 1123–1136.
Huang, R., et al. (2010). Gene therapy using lactoferrin-modified nanoparticles in a rotenone-induced chronic Parkinson model. *Journal of the Neurological Sciences*, *290*(1–2), 123–130.
Huang, R., et al. (2009). Neuroprotection in a 6-hydroxydopamine-lesioned Parkinson model using lactoferrin-modified nanoparticles. *The Journal of Gene Medicine: A Cross-Disciplinary Journal for Research on the Science of Gene Transfer and its Clinical Applications*, *11*(9), 754–763.
Huntington's Disease, Alzheimer's & Association. https://www.alz.org/alzheimers-dementia/what-is-dementia/types-of-dementia/huntington-s-disease/ accessed on July 16, 2022.
Huo, X., et al. (2019). A novel synthesis of selenium nanoparticles encapsulated PLGA nanospheres with curcumin molecules for the inhibition of amyloid β aggregation in Alzheimer's disease. *Journal of Photochemistry and Photobiology B: Biology*, *190*, 98–102.
Jagaran, K., & Singh, M. (2021). Nanomedicine for neurodegenerative disorders: Focus on Alzheimer's and Parkinson's diseases. *International Journal of Molecular Sciences*, *22*(16), 9082.
JP Shonkoff, D. P. (2000). *National Research Council (US) and Institute of Medicine (US) Committee on Integrating the Science of Early Childhood Development. From Neurons to Neighborhoods: The Science of Early Childhood Development.* Washington, DC: National Academies Press (US).
Kang, Y. J., Cutler, E. G., & Cho, H. (2018). Therapeutic nanoplatforms and delivery strategies for neurological disorders. *Nano Convergence*, *5*(1), 1–15.
Kassem, L. M., Ibrahim, N. A., & Farhana, S. A. (2020). Nanoparticle therapy is a promising approach in the management and prevention of many diseases: Does it help in curing Alzheimer's disease? *Journal of Nanotechnology, 2020*.
Kiernan, M. C., et al. (2011). Amyotrophic lateral sclerosis. *The Lancet*, *377*(9769), 942–955.
Kim, M. J., et al. (2017). Enhanced neuroprotection of anthocyanin-loaded PEG-gold nanoparticles against Aβ1–42-induced neuroinflammation and neurodegeneration via the NF-KB/JNK/GSK3β signaling pathway. *Nanomedicine: Nanotechnology, Biology and Medicine*, *13*(8), 2533–2544.
Kosaka, K., et al. (1984). Diffuse type of Lewy body disease: Progressive dementia with abundant cortical Lewy bodies and senile changes of varying degree—A new disease? *Clinical Neuropathology*, *3*(5), 185–192.

Kovacs, G. G. (2017). *Concepts and classification of neurodegenerative diseases. Handbook of clinical neurology* (pp. 301–307). Elsevier.

Kovacs, G. G. (2019). Molecular pathology of neurodegenerative diseases: Principles and practice. *Journal of Clinical Pathology*, *72*(11), 725–735.

Kurakhmaeva, K. B., et al. (2009). Brain targeting of nerve growth factor using poly (butyl cyanoacrylate) nanoparticles. *Journal of Drug Targeting*, *17*(8), 564–574.

La Pean, A., et al. (2008). Predictors of progression in patients with Friedreich ataxia. *Movement Sisorders: Official Journal of the Movement Disorder Society*, *23*(14), 2026–2032.

La Rosa, P., Bertini, E. S., & Piemonte, F. (2020). The NRF2 signaling network defines clinical biomarkers and therapeutic opportunity in Friedreich's ataxia. *International Journal of Molecular Sciences*, *21*(3), 916.

Lafuente, J. V., Requejo, C., & Ugedo, L. (2019). Nanodelivery of therapeutic agents in Parkinson's disease. *Progress in Brain Research*, *245*, 263–279.

Lamptey, R. N. L., et al. (2022). A review of the common neurodegenerative disorders: Current therapeutic approaches and the potential role of nanotherapeutics. *International Journal of Molecular Sciences*, *23*(3), 1851.

Li, M., et al. (2015). Chemically exfoliated WS2 nanosheets efficiently inhibit amyloid β-peptide aggregation and can be used for photothermal treatment of Alzheimer's disease. *Nano Research*, *8*(10), 3216–3227.

Li, M., et al. (2013). Self-assembled peptide-polyoxometalate hybrid nanospheres: Two in one enhances targeted inhibition of amyloid β-peptide aggregation associated with Alzheimer's disease. *Small (Weinheim an der Bergstrasse, Germany)*, *9*(20), 3455–3461.

Li, M., et al. (2017). Using multifunctional peptide conjugated Au nanorods for monitoring β-amyloid aggregation and chemo-photothermal treatment of Alzheimer's disease. *Theranostics*, 7(12), 2996.

Li, S., et al. (2012). Delivery of quantum dot-siRNA nanoplexes in SK-N-SH cells for BACE1 gene silencing and intracellular imaging. *Molecular Therapy-Nucleic Acids*, *1*, e20.

Liu, G., et al. (2006). Nanoparticle iron chelators: A new therapeutic approach in Alzheimer disease and other neurologic disorders associated with trace metal imbalance. *Neuroscience Letters*, *406*(3), 189–193.

Liu, G., et al. (2009). Nanoparticle-chelator conjugates as inhibitors of amyloid-β aggregation and neurotoxicity: A novel therapeutic approach for Alzheimer disease. *Neuroscience Letters*, *455*(3), 187–190.

Liu, Y., et al. (2013). Targeting caspase-3 as dual therapeutic benefits by RNAi facilitating brain-targeted nanoparticles in a rat model of Parkinson's disease. *PLoS One*, *8*(5), e62905.

Mancini, S., et al. (2017). Multifunctional liposomes delay phenotype progression and prevent memory impairment in a presymptomatic stage mouse model of Alzheimer disease. *Journal of Controlled Release*, *258*, 121–129.

Marcuzzo, S., et al. (2019). FM19G11-loaded gold nanoparticles enhance the proliferation and self-renewal of ependymal stem progenitor cells derived from ALS mice. *Cells*, *8*(3), 279.

Mestre, T., et al. (2009). Therapeutic interventions for symptomatic treatment in Huntington's disease. *Cochrane Database of Systematic Reviews* (3).

Miller, A.-M., et al. (2009). The deficit in long-term potentiation induced by chronic administration of amyloid-β is attenuated by treatment of rats with a novel phospholipid-based drug formulation, VP025. *Experimental Gerontology*, *44*(4), 300–304.

Miller, E. D., et al. (2019). A review of various antioxidant compounds and their potential utility as complementary therapy in multiple sclerosis. *Nutrients*, *11*(7), 1528.

Mukherjee, S., et al. (2020). Recent advancements of nanomedicine in neurodegenerative disorders theranostics. *Advanced Functional Materials*, *30*(35), 2003054.

Marisa Wexler, M.S. (2021). *Clene awaits US patent covering gold nanocrystals' use in treating MS.*

Nelwan, M. (2017). Friedreich ataxia: Treatment with genetic approach. *Journal of Advances in Biology & Biotechnology*, *14*(4), 1–12.

Nikalje, A. P. (2015). Nanotechnology and its applications in medicine. *Medicinal Chemistry (Shariqah (United Arab Emirates))*, *5*(2), 081–089.

Niu, S., et al. (2017). Inhibition by multifunctional magnetic nanoparticles loaded with alpha-synuclein RNAi plasmid in a Parkinson's disease model. *Theranostics*, 7(2), 344.

Ojha, S., & Kumar, B. (2018). A review on nanotechnology-based innovations in diagnosis and treatment of multiple sclerosis. *Journal of Cellular Immunotherapy*, *4*(2), 56–64.
Pan, L., et al. (2021). Tau in the pathophysiology of Parkinson's disease. *Journal of Molecular Neuroscience*, *71*(11), 2179–2191.
Pangeni, R., et al. (2014). Vitamin E loaded resveratrol nanoemulsion for brain targeting for the treatment of Parkinson's disease by reducing oxidative stress. *Nanotechnology*, *25*(48), 485102.
Pansare, V. J. (2015). *Fundamental and applied studies in nanoparticle biomedical imaging, stabilization, and processing*. Princeton University.
Pardridge, W. M. (2020). Treatment of Alzheimer's disease and blood-brain barrier drug delivery. *Pharmaceuticals*, *13*(11), 394.
Park, J., Kim, J.-E., & Song, T.-J. (2022). The global burden of motor neuron disease: An analysis of the 2019 Global Burden of Disease Study. *Frontiers in Neurology*, *13*.
Poser, C. M., et al. (1983). New diagnostic criteria for multiple sclerosis: Guidelines for research protocols. *Annals of Neurology: Official Journal of the American Neurological Association and the Child Neurology Society*, *13*(3), 227–231.
Puras, G., et al. (2011). Encapsulation of Aβ-15 in PLGA microparticles enhances serum antibody response in mice immunized by subcutaneous and intranasal routes. *European Journal of Pharmaceutical Sciences*, *44*(3), 200–206.
Rajan, R., et al. (2020). Genetic architecture of Parkinson's disease in the Indian population: Harnessing genetic diversity to address critical gaps in Parkinson's disease research. *Frontiers in Neurology*, *11*, 524.
Re, F., Gregori, M., & Masserini, M. (2012). Nanotechnology for neurodegenerative disorders. *Maturitas*, *73*(1), 45–51.
Sahana, T. G., & Zhang, K. (2021). Mitogen-activated protein kinase pathway in amyotrophic lateral sclerosis. *Biomedicines*, *9*(8), 969.
Sanchez-Lopez, E., et al. (2017). New potential strategies for Alzheimer's disease prevention: Pegylated biodegradable dexibuprofen nanospheres administration to APPswe/PS1dE9. *Nanomedicine: Nanotechnology, Biology and Medicine*, *13*(3), 1171–1182.
Sarkar, A., & Dyawanapelly, S. (2021). Nano diagnostics and nanotherapeutics for age-related macular degeneration. *Journal of Controlled Release*, *329*, 1262–1282.
Sava, V., et al. (2020). Enriched chitosan nanoparticles loaded with siRNA are effective in lowering Huntington's disease gene expression following intranasal administration. *Nanomedicine: Nanotechnology, Biology and Medicine*, *24*, 102119.
Siddique, Y. H., et al. (2013). Synthesis of alginate-curcumin nanocomposite and its protective role in transgenic Drosophila model of Parkinson's disease. *International Scholarly Research Notices*, 2013.
Singh, S., Singh, M., & Gambhir, I. S. (2008). Nanotechnology for Alzheimer's disease detection. *Digest Journal of Nanomaterials and Biostructures*, *3*(2), 75–79.
Smith, A., et al. (2010). Nanolipidic particles improve the bioavailability and β-secretase inducing ability of epigallocatechin-3-gallate (EGCG) for the treatment of Alzheimer's disease. *International Journal of Pharmaceutics*, *389*(1–2), 207–212.
Song, Q., et al. (2014). Lipoprotein-based nanoparticles rescue the memory loss of mice with Alzheimer's disease by accelerating the clearance of amyloid-beta. *ACS Nano*, *8*(3), 2345–2359.
Songjiang, Z., & Lixiang, W. (2009). Amyloid-beta associated with chitosan nano-carrier has favorable immunogenicity and permeates the BBB. *AAPS PharmSciTech*, *10*(3), 900–905.
Soursou, G., et al. (2015). Applications of nanotechnology in diagnostics and therapeutics of Alzheimer's and Parkinson's disease. *Current Drug Metabolism*, *16*(8), 705–712.
Sun, A., & Benet, L. Z. (2020). Late-stage failures of monoclonal antibody drugs: A retrospective case study analysis. *Pharmacology*, *105*(3–4), 145–163.
Swasti, W., & DK, W. (2017). Magnetic nanoparticle/magnetic fluid approach to control neuromuscular degeneration in Friedreich's ataxia. *International Journal of Nanotechnology and Applications*, *11*(3), 277–283.
Usmani, S. S., et al. (2017). THPdb: Database of FDA-approved peptide and protein therapeutics. *PLoS One*, *12*(7), e0181748.
Vannocci, T., et al. (2019). A new tool to determine the cellular metabolic landscape: Nanotechnology to the study of Friedreich's ataxia. *Scientific Reports*, *9*(1), 1–9.

Walker, F. O. (2007). Huntington's disease. *The Lancet*, *369*(9557), 218–228.
Walton, C., et al. (2020). Rising prevalence of multiple sclerosis worldwide: Insights from the Atlas of MS. *Multiple Sclerosis Journal*, *26*(14), 1816–1821.
Wang, G. Y., et al. (2020). Advances in nanotechnology-based strategies for the treatments of amyotrophic lateral sclerosis. *Materials Today Bio*, *6*, 100055.
Wells, C., et al. (2019). Prionoid proteins in the pathogenesis of neurodegenerative diseases. *Frontiers in Molecular Neuroscience*, *12*, 271.
Witzel, S., et al. (2022). Safety and effectiveness of long-term intravenous administration of edaravone for treatment of patients with amyotrophic lateral sclerosis. *JAMA Neurology*.
Yavarpour-Bali, H., Ghasemi-Kasman, M., & Pirzadeh, M. (2019). Curcumin-loaded nanoparticles: A novel therapeutic strategy in treatment of central nervous system disorders. *International Journal of Nanomedicine*, *14*, 4449.
Youssif, K. A., et al. (2019). Anti-Alzheimer potential, metabolomic profiling and molecular docking of green synthesized silver nanoparticles of Lampranthus coccineus and Malephora lutea aqueous extracts. *PLoS One*, *14*(11), e0223781.
Zhang, S., Napierala, M., & Napierala, J. S. (2019). Therapeutic prospects for Friedreich's ataxia. *Trends in Pharmacological Sciences*, *40*(4), 229–233.
Zhang, W., et al. (2018). Application of nanodiagnostics and nanotherapy to CNS diseases. *Nanomedicine: Nanotechnology, Biology, and Medicine*, *13*(18), 2341–2371.
Zhao, N., et al. (2020). Microglia-targeting nanotherapeutics for neurodegenerative diseases. *APL Bioengineering*, *4*(3), 030902.
Zhou, H., Beevers, C. S., & Huang, S. (2011). The targets of curcumin. *Current Drug Targets*, *12*(3), 332–347.

CHAPTER 7

Potentialities of nanomedicine and nanocarriers for infectious disease treatment

Jhansi Lakshmi Parimi[1,2], Soumi Sadhu[3], Sayan Mukherjee[2], Swati Bhati[3], Padmavati Manchikanti[1] and Santanu Dhara[2]

[1]Plant Metabolic Pathway Laboratory, Rajiv Gandhi School of Intellectual Property Law (RGSOIPL), Biomaterial and Tissue Engineering Laboratory (BMTE), Indian Institute of Technology Kharagpur, Kharagpur, West Bengal, India
[2]Biomaterial and Tissue Engineering Laboratory (BMTE), Indian Institute of Technology Kharagpur, Kharagpur, West Bengal, India
[3]Department of Life Sciences, School of Basic Sciences and Research, Sharda University, Greater Noida, Uttar Pradesh, India

Introduction

The expressions "infection" and "disease" are not the same and are the most demanding needs for the new technological interventions. Infectious agents are classified into five types: bacteria, viruses, fungus, protozoa, helminths, and prions. These pathogens enter host systems through direct contact, inhalation, or ingestion. Phenomenal invasive mechanisms of infective pathogens and the tissue functional impairment and associated symptomatic diseases are growing day by day (Ranjita, 2013). The need for controlling the spread of highly virulent and contagious agents is the current pressing need for health-care professionals, researchers, and regulatory bodies. The advent of nanotechnology came as a gist of hope for this purpose.

Different types of infectious diseases

Infectious diseases are mainly classified by the way they will spread across. In general, they spread by direct contact or through the air. These infections will be location specific in most cases like intestinal, blood, skin, respiratory and urogenital. They may occur by the attack of bacteria, viruses, parasites, fungi, and helminths (Marcato & Durán, 2008; Sousa et al., 2020). Table 7.1 is the clear gist of various organisms and their potential infections caused along with the conventional and modern therapeutic treatment strategies. All of these infections will be cleared off with long-term treatment strategies, for example, AIDS.

Nanotechnology for Drug Delivery and Pharmaceuticals
DOI: https://doi.org/10.1016/B978-0-323-95325-2.00022-5

Table 7.1 A brief list of most prevalent infectious diseases and their conventional and nano-based treatment choices.

Type of infection	Name of the agent	Conventional treatment	Nanoapproach	Remarks	References
Bacterial					
Tuberculosis	*Mycobacterium tuberculosis*	Isoniazid (INH) Rifampin, Pyrazinamide, and Ethambutol	Rifampin SLN's Isoniazid liposomes	Emulsion solvent diffusion technique	
Pneumonia	*Streptococcus pneumonia*	Azithromycin (adult) Erythromycin and Amoxicillin (children)	Liposomal antibiotic delivery system	Pressurized metered-dose inhalers	Chono et al. (2008)
Gonorrhea	*Neisseria gonorrhoeae*	Ceftriaxone or ceftriaxone (IM)	5-Mercapto-2-nitrobenzoic acid-coated silver nanoclusters	Significant improvement in activity	
Tetanus	*Clostridium tetani*	Penicillin or metronidazole	PLGA NP modified with tetanus toxoid and MUC1 lipopeptide (a TLR ligand)	Enhanced T-cell response	
Diptheria	*Coryne bacterium diphtheriae*	Penicillin or erythromycin and toxoid for immunization	Polymeric nanoparticles elicited vaccine (diphtheria toxoid)	Serum IgG antibody response significantly higher than free diphtheria toxoid	
Meningitis	*Neisseria meningitides, S. pneumoniae*, and *Haemophilus influenzae*	Broad-spectrum cephalosporin (cefotaxime or ceftriaxone)	CG3R6-TAT antimicrobial peptide micellar nanoparticle	Antibacterial activity against *Cryptococcus neoformans*	

Viral					
AIDS	Human immune deficiency virus	ART	Albumin-based nanoparticles loaded with zidovudine, polyhexyl cyano acrylate-based nanoparticles (PHCA nanoparticles) loaded with zidovudine and zalcitabine	Shows enhanced drug uptake by macrophage	
Influenza	Influenza viruses	Oseltamivir, zanamivir, and peramivir	Oseltamivir loaded SeNPs and Diphyllin and Bafilomycin, vacuolar ATPase inhibitors, loaded into PEG-functionalized PLGA nanoparticles	Lower cytotoxicity but twofold and fivefold higher antiviral activity	
Hepatitis	HBV	Entecavir, tenofovir, lamivudine, adefovir, and telbivudine	Nanosphere synthesized by cross linking CS with genipin and subsequently reacting the product with glycidyl trimethyl-ammonium chloride	Shown their cytopathic effects in LLC-MK2 and LR7 cell	
Poliomyelitis	Poliovirus	Oral polio vaccine for prevention	CeO_2 NPs	Shown antiviral activity	
Measels, mumps, rubella	Morbillivirus, paramyxovirus, and rubella virus	(MMR) vaccine for prevention, and the analgesic drug for the treatment	Low MW CS formulated with measles antigen was entrapped and subsequently coated with sodium alginate	Oral vaccine delivery	

(*Continued*)

Table 7.1 (Continued)

Type of infection	Name of the agent	Conventional treatment	Nanoapproach	Remarks	References
Fungal					
Candidiasis	*Candida* sp.	Fluconazole	Curcumin-hydroxypropyl-β-cyclodextrin (CUR:HPβCD)@Ag (cAgNP)-loaded bacterial cellulose hydrogel	Effective antimicrobial activity ($P < .001$) against *Candida auris*	
Athletic foot	Dermatophytes	Oral antifungal medications such as ITZ, fluconazole, or prescription strength terbinafine	Miconazole loaded NLCs	Better penetration	
Nail fungus	*Trichophyton rubrum*	Terbinafine and ITZ	ITZ stacked PLGA nanoparticle	ITZ release demonstrated a rupture followed by a slow discharge release by 75% above 5 days	
Histoplasmosis	*Histoplasma capsulatum*	ITZ	NP-based strategy for vaccination	Calnexin induces expansion of antigen-specific CD4 + T cells that confer immunity	
Jock itch	Dermatophytes	Clotrimazole, miconazole, tolnaftate, or terbinafine	Azole antifungal polyvinyl pyrrolidone coated silver nanoparticles	Carries azole antifungal, such as fluconazole orvoriconazole	

Protozoa					
Amebiasis	*Entamoeba histolytica*	Antiamoebic drug such as metronidazole, and antibiotics such as paromomycin			
Malaria	*Plasmodium* sp.	Atovaquone–proguanil, quinine sulfate with doxycycline, and primaquine phosphate	Nanoparticles like liposomes, SLNs, NLCs, metallic nanoparticles, nano-emulsions mediated drug delivery	Shown promising results	
Trichomoniasis	*Trichomonas vaginalis*	Metronidazole, Tinidazole	Nano-liposomal metronidazole	Showing IC50 value of 15.90 μg/mL (6 h)	
Toxoplasmosis	*Toxoplasma gondii*	Combination of drugs such as pyrimethamine and sulfadiazine along with folinic acid	Spiramycin/propolis-loaded CS /alginate nanoparticles	The highest significant parasite percent reduction of (>96%) in the liver, spleen, and brain	

ART, Antiretroviral therapy; *CS*, chitosan; *HBV*, Hepatitis B virus; *ITZ*, Itraconazole; *NLCs*, nanostructure lipid carriers; *PEG*, poly ethylene glycol; *PLGA*, polylactic-*co*-glycolic acid; *SeNPs*, selenium nanoparticles; *SLNs*, solid lipid nanoparticles; *MMR*, measles, mumps, rubella.

Conventional versus modern approaches

The conventional approach to treating infectious diseases so far unfortunately uses large doses of medication to achieve the intended therapeutic benefit. The main problem posed by them includes poor solubility of the active ingredients or poor bioavailability of the medications recommended to eradicate or treat them. Advancements in the technology at the level of miniaturization in terms of size and dose have come as a gist of home for all those first-class medications used for the treatment of infectious diseases (Patra et al., 2018). The dose reduction and solubility issues have become the reality and serve the deliverables to mankind in the form of nanomaterials like lipid-based vesicles, polymeric carrier systems, and crystals, as shown in Fig. 7.1. They not only helped in the reduction of doses but also reduced the side effects brought about by the high dosage regimen and thereby helped in the reduction of the cost involved with it (Bell et al., 2013).

The alarming rate at which contagious infections and drug-resistant microorganisms are spreading is cause for concern. Leading to an increased understanding of microscopic pathogenesis and a broad number of antibiotic medications, microbial infection-related morbidity and death remain high. The increased usage of antibiotics for human, animal, and plant health and wellness, as well as the advent of antibiotic-resistant pathogenic bacteria strains, is an unpleasant consequence. As more than just an outcome, new strategies and antimicrobial medications were undoubtedly required to treat infections (Kirtane et al., 2021). The emergence of resistance is an uncomplicated mechanism that is frequently overlooked. Antimicrobials are chemicals that effectively eliminate the activity, growth, or development of bacteria by inhibiting either formation molecules as well as tampering with the building of cell walls. The

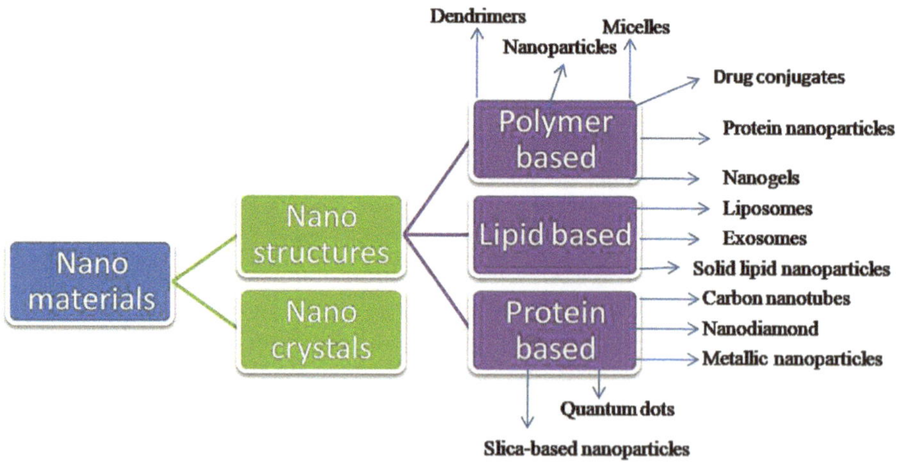

Figure 7.1 Classes of nanomaterials along with the subtypes.

prevalence of multidrug resistance of microorganisms that cause outbreaks within health center care units is expanding, and the consequent microorganisms have evolved impervious to more conventional medications. As a result, there are nearly no medications that could be exploited against these strains, which have a low-permeability outer membrane barrier and an array of effective multidrug efflux pumps paired with a plethora of unique resistance mechanisms (Yang et al., 2019; Yeh et al., 2020). In this regard, a rational fabrication approach to nanocarrier-based antibiotic delivery may tackle the problem of cell permeability.

Nanotechnology approaches against microbial resistance

The significant developments brought about by nanomedicine approaches started gaining importance in the pharmaceutical development industry to prevent the untoward effects associated with them. The target-specific delivery and carrying capacity of the nanomaterials to target specific conditions and their associated targets are the best performers and doable alternatives (Cano et al., 2020). These carrier systems work by enhancing the bioavailability of the loaded molecules by protecting them with the associated factors of absorption, distribution, metabolism, and elimination kinetics. A detailed list has been given in Table 7.1. The recent developments involving the nanomaterial surface properties modification to specifically target biofilms, including the use of Zinc (Raghupathi et al., 2011), gold (Mohammed Fayaz et al., 2011), and silver (Su et al., 2011), are not only limited to infections but also useful for the implant surfaces coating that is intended to be used in biological tissues and surfaces to protect them from microbial attack.

Nanotechnology potential in drug delivery

Improving the therapeutic effectiveness as a viable medication delivery by conquering the antibiotic resistance of bacteria, increased long-term effectiveness (Alt et al., 2004) and enhanced solubility facilitate therapeutic bioavailability by making them amenable from both lipophilic and hydrophilic surroundings, reduced toxicity, and controlled release that reduces the costs associated with them (Huang et al., 2011).

Nanocarrier-mediated treatment strategies

The role of nanomaterials in eradicating infectious diseases is a multifaceted upcoming area showing great potential interns of its benefits associated with them. Nanoparticles possess the capacity to improve the efficacy of antiinfective drugs with fewer or reduced side effects associated with their counterparts (Chen et al., 2010; Huang et al., 2011) as shown in Fig. 7.2. The prime advantage associated with these carrier systems

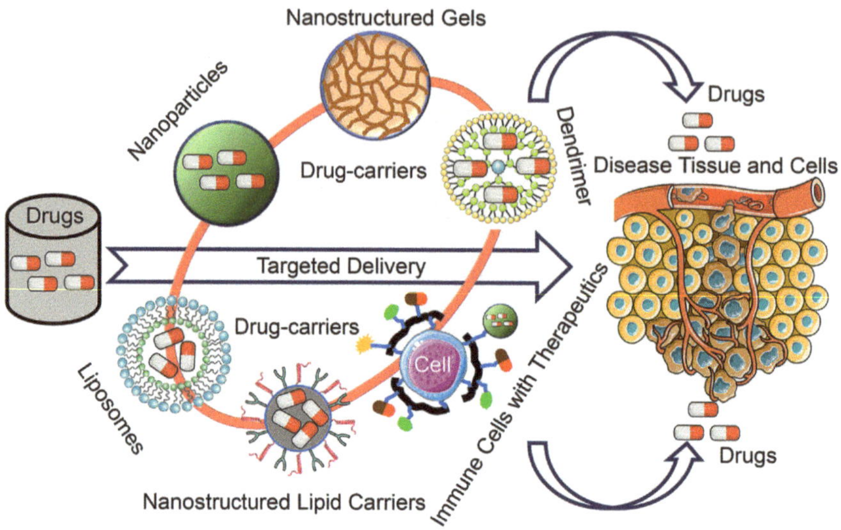

Figure 7.2 Different nanocarrier-based systems for localized and targeted delivery of drugs and other therapeutics. *From Majumder, J., Taratula, O., & Minko, T. (2019). Nanocarrier-based systems for targeted and site-specific therapeutic delivery. Advanced Drug Delivery Reviews, 144, 57–77. https://doi.org/10.1016/j.addr.2019.07.010. Copyright received.*

is dose reductions and dosage frequency, improved efficacy, and reduction of their limitations. Research efforts are underway to bring these initiatives into the light to help in the mitigation of the problems associated with conventional delivery agents.

Sustained systemic delivery

The management of several infectious diseases demands long-term treatment, which in turn poses a huge load on the physical and economic status of the patients (Bangia et al., 2019; Liu et al., 2019), for example, HIV, and TB. Long-term high dosage regimens often result in discrepancies in patient compliance, which in turn affects the treatment goals. To avoid these problems, the development of controlled delivery systems is in development that helps in the distribution of dosage to the need of the patient, that is time-dependent and dose-dependent release systems (Zhou et al., 2021). They are broadly categorized as follows:

1. Delivery systems use carrier systems the control drug release of the loaded drugs (polymers and lipids) (Liu et al., 2016), and
2. Delivery systems that are based on the slow dissolution of poorly soluble drugs (Pradeepa et al., 2016).

A substantial number of research attempts have focused on polymer-based drug delivery systems; vesicular sustained drug delivery techniques were evolved, such as transferases, niosomes, liposomes, and ethosomes, governed by the pharmaceutical features (Eleraky et al., 2020) as depicted in Fig. 7.2. For example, MiKasomes, a liposomal formulation developed by NeXstar Pharmaceuticals for the drug, amikacin. Combating dermatological infections, ethosomes act as a carrier in delivering antibacterial, antifungal, and antiviral drugs (Raveendran et al., 2017). In these ethosomal-based delivery techniques the permeability of drugs has been enhanced for dermatological application. The principal component of the ethosomal carrier is ethanol, interacting with the lipid molecules to amplify the fluidity of the stratum—corneum layer of skin, which ultimately improves the intracellular permeability (Akhtar & Pathak, 2012). Dextenza is an insert release system composed of dexamethasone, having sustained the release capability of up to one month after being delivered in the eye. Mydriasert and Lacrisert, like topical ocular inserts, have several benefits, like the perpetual release, and extended interaction time for possessing the mucoadhesive character of polymers (Mirzaeei & Barfar, 2021).

Targeted medication delivery through receptors (active) and stimuli

The in vivo pharmacokinetic translation of the improved permeability, sustained release, and ligand (receptor) recalling remains doubtful in the case of nanocarriers. Due to the variable chemical nature of ligands, inconsistent ligand-receptor interaction, and controlled release of targeted drug nanocarriers consequences will occur. For overcoming these shortcomings, drug delivery becomes more feasible through miming natural ligand interactions and designing stimuli-responsive carrier systems that identify their microenvironment by recognizing specific ligands and reacting enthusiastically. It requires the chemical modification of biocompatible materials undergoing hydrolytic cleavage, specific protonation, or supramolecular conformational change in response to the desired physical or chemical stimulus as shown clearly in Fig. 7.3

Predominantly in the last decade, a group of researchers had explored stimuli-responsive techniques for drug delivery application, concerning their design and approach as nanocarriers. Cellular pH can trigger the release of targeted drugs through late endosomes or stimulate the escape of nanocarriers into the cytoplasm from lysosomal vesicles. The physical stimuli imposed in extracellular environments can also trigger the drug release, such as pharmacologically active molecules that can be targeted to an infected region and can be magnetically released by using iron oxide—based nanoparticles (Bringas et al., 2012). Heat, light, or ultrasound-sensitive nanoparticles also can initiate triggered drug release. In the case of antimicrobial drug delivery, enzyme receptiveness was explored. For instance, one study has revealed the ligand-stimulated release of antibiotics like vancomycin, achieved by the nanocarrier designed with lipase-sensitive nanogels (Xiong et al., 2012), pointedly showing bactericidal activity against the growth of *Staphylococcus aureus* as well as killing the

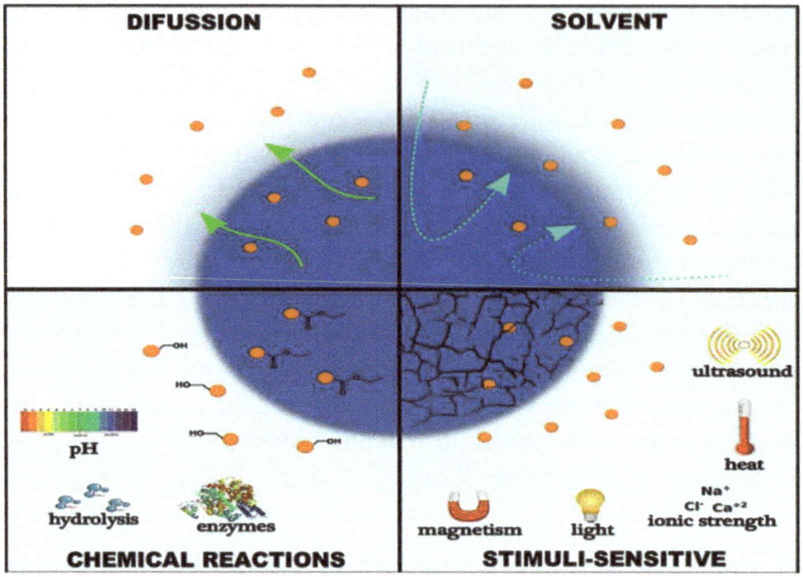

Figure 7.3 An assortment of mechanisms for controlled release of drugs using different types of nanocarriers. *Modified with permission from Patra, J. K., Das, G., Fraceto, L. F., Campos, E. V. R., Rodriguez-Torres, M. del P., Acosta-Torres, L. S., Diaz-Torres, L. A., Grillo, R., Swamy, M. K., Sharma, S., Habtemariam, S., & Shin, H.-S. (2018). Journal of Nanobiotechnology, 16(1). https://doi.org/10.1186/s12951-018-0392-8. Copyright received.*

intracellular bacteria. Nanocarriers encircled with carbohydrate backbone moieties can capture the uptake mechanism and enhance the drug delivery to tissue-resident macrophages as in triggered shipping of ciprofloxacin-loaded mannose-functionalized liposomes administered as a spray to the lung of rats, and drug introduction in macrophages (Chono et al., 2008). Infectious diseases lead to the overexpression of mannose receptors on immune cells (i.e., antigen-presenting dendritic cells and macrophages). Therefore, designing them with mannosylated nanocarrier is one of the widely investigated attempts focusing on these receptors (Kaur et al., 2008).

Local delivery

Because infections frequently enter and persist on epithelial surfaces, localized medication delivery to these surfaces offers tremendous potential. Local distribution to the site of infection, as opposed to systemic treatment, is expected to increase on-target (and reduce off-target) medication exposure. Of course, its application to systemic illnesses is restricted. Several advantages of employing nanoformulation for local therapeutics have been revealed in preclinical research, mostly in rats. Medications encapsulated in nanocarriers provide drugs for longer periods, lowering dose frequency

(Kaur et al., 2008). Nanocarriers can be programed to release medications in response to particular triggers and to manage drug exposure overtime. Nanocarriers may boost therapeutic absorption and effectiveness against intracellular infections in cells as shown in Fig. 7.2. Finally, encapsulating labile medicines in nanocarriers may provide protection (such as nucleic acids).

The lung is another crucial organ that can be directly infected through microbial invasions. Lung-targeted drug delivery systems provide incredible prospects to amend pharmacokinetics both systemically and locally using novel drug delivery techniques for the large surface area of the alveolar region (Kurmi et al., 2010).

Transport of nanocarriers across the human skin is a challenging job, for its limited penetrable barrier for utmost penetrants (Moser et al., 2001). Campbell et al. suggested accumulating those drug carriers in stratum−corneal layers of skin (Lalloz et al., 2018) will provide a drug reservoir for sustained targeted release of the drug molecules into the skin layers. Nanocarrier-mediated skin delivery systems can be composed of liposomes, micelles, polymeric nanoparticles, and surfactant-based nanoformulations.

Strategies used to treat infectious diseases

Cell-based evaluation of antibacterial nanoparticles

Nanoparticles are the best modalities to attack microorganisms. The multifaceted applications of different nanomaterials react with the microbial cells and surfaces through various mechanisms as depicted in Fig. 7.1. A detailed discussion of these strategies and their evading mechanisms has been detailed in the following sections and the examples along with interventional approaches have been mentioned in Table 7.2.

Antibacterial nanoparticles against planktonic bacteria

Pradeepa et al.'s research attempt to use bacterial *exo*-polysaccharide as a stabilizing agent to make Gold (Au) nanoparticles for treating multidrug-resistant bacteria is a step forward in this category (Escárcega-González et al., 2018). The antibiotics fluoroquinolones were put into Au nanoparticles with lowered MIC and MBC on drug-resistant gram-positive and negative bacteria (Grace & Pandian, 2007). Antibacterial nanoparticles are frequently made with chitosan using daptomycin encapsulated in nanocarriers for MRSA (Silva et al., 2015).

A report regarding pH-sensitive chitosan/PMLA nanoparticles loaded with amoxicillin *Helicobacter pylori* eradication showed multifold benefits compared to conventional treatment modality (Arif et al., 2018). To achieve mucoadhesive and anticoagulant characteristics, this nanosystem was coupled with cysteine. PEGylated lysozyme was used to make antimicrobial protein-based nanoparticles owing to their

Table 7.2 Diverse types of biomimetic nanoparticles and their usefulness.

Type of biomimetic nanoparticles	Applications	References
Virus-based nanoparticles		
Virosomes	Vaccination, drug/gene delivery	Liu et al. (2019); Mohammadzadeh et al. (2017)
Virus-like particles	Vaccines, drug delivery	
Self-assembling nanoparticles	Vaccines	
Fully synthetic nanoparticles	Drug delivery, gene therapy	
Nanoparticles derived from bacteria or fungi		
Nanoparticles derived from components of the bacterial/fungal membrane	Targeted drug delivery	Tang et al. (2018), Yang et al. (2019)
Outer membrane vesicles	Biomimetic therapies, targeted drug delivery	
Nanoparticles coated with bacterial membrane	Antibacterial nanotherapies, vaccines	
Nanoparticles mimicking mammalian cells		
Cell membrane-coated nanoparticles	Bio detoxification, drug/gene delivery, vaccines	Chen et al. (2018)
Nanoparticles decorated with functional biomolecules	Targeted drug/gene delivery	Robbins et al. (2010), Molinaro et al. (2018)
Shedding microvesicles	Targeted drug delivery	
Exosomes	Nanotherapies, targeted drug/gene delivery	
Other biomimetic nanoparticles		
High-density lipoproteins	Biomimetic nanotherapies, drug delivery, biodetoxification	

inherent natural anti-infective nature (Ibrahim et al., 2002). Nanoparticle's adhesive contact with the bacterial surface resulted in a sustained release and protracted attack on the cell wall layer (Praditya et al., 2019). Lipophilic antibiotics are well entrapped by lipid-based nanoparticles. To create lipid—polymer hybrid nanosystems, the polymers can be integrated into lipid nanoparticles as demonstrated by Dave et al. (2017) using soya lecithin and polylactic acid to create norfloxacin-loaded hybrid nanoparticles. Dendritic MSNs are preferred as delivery agents for proteins and DNA, because of their center—radial pore design, large pore channel, and accessible pore volume (Du & Qiao, 2015). Dendritic MSNs were supplied with lysozyme, an antibacterial enzyme that damages bacterial walls. When compared to free lysozyme, the MIC of lysozyme-loaded nanocarriers against *Escherichia coli* was lower (500 vs. 2500 g/mL). MSNs were able to maintain a total suppression of *E. coli* growth for 5 days. The biomembrane-coated nanoparticles can be used to administer antibiotics on demand.

Antibacterial nanoparticles against biofilm bacteria

Targeting bacterial biofilms with nanoparticles is a novel method. Diffusive permeation can be seen in the spread of nanoparticles through the biofilm layer. Nanoparticles can be transported into porous media because of their small size (Botequim et al., 2012). Nanoparticles are thought to diffuse into the biofilm through water-filled pores (Aljuffali et al., 2015). Some antibacterial substances cannot penetrate the biofilm because it is exceedingly nonwetting (Sun et al., 2012). The free antibiotic stopped planktonic bacteria from growing without allowing them to enter the biofilm.

Chitosan with a positive charge, which shows an affinity for polymers and DNA in biofilms, can be used to make antibiofilm nanoparticles (Tan et al., 2018). Biocompatible magnetic nanoparticles for biofilm elimination were made with chitosan, PEG, and Fe_3O_4 (Wang et al., 2018). The antibiotic Gentamicin was chosen to be put into the magnetic nanocarriers. Chitosan and PEG were protonated in an acidic environment to help them interact with the bacterial membrane. The nanoparticles were able to penetrate deep into the mature *S. aureus* biofilm.

Antibacterial nanoparticles against intracellular bacteria

In recent years, two biopolymer nanoparticles have been employed to treat intracellular bacteria (Smitha et al., 2015). They created chitin nanoparticles that transport rifampicin to neutrophils, eliminating intracellular infections. Rifampicin was released continuously from the nanoparticles for 72 h. The immune cells that serve as a host for *M*ycobacterium *tuberculosis* are known as macrophages. For intra-macrophage *M. tuberculosis* eradication, rifampicin and levofloxacin were combined with cyclodextrin and conjugated to curdlan-based nanoparticles (Yunus Basha et al., 2019) *Agrobacterium* and *Rhizobium* produce *curdlan*, which is a linear glucan. Macrophages that express the dectin-1 receptor identify it (Ganbold & Baigude, 2018). The internalization of nanoparticles by macrophages was 1.8 times higher than that of fibroblast cells, demonstrating that curdlan in nanoparticles is advantageous for macrophage uptake, and within 4 h, the nanocarriers killed >95% of intra-macrophage bacteria.

Animal-based evaluation of antibacterial nanoparticles

Skin and subcutaneous region infection

Nanoparticle delivery to the skin can be employed in a variety of ways, including topical, subcutaneous, and intravenous treatments. The surface of Au nanoparticles was coated with chitosan and 2-mercapto-1-methylimidazole, permitting multivalent interaction with bacterial membranes (Lu et al., 2018). The nanoparticles were cross-linked with gelatin to create a wound dressing to treat skin infections. The nanoparticles were used to treat an *MRSA*-infected wound on a rabbit's back.

Based on polydopamine-coated Au nanorods, chemo-photothermal therapy against subcutaneous infection was created, with an appearance comparable to normal skin. This platform became positively charged in the acidic environment of the bacterium-formed abscess, allowing bacteria to congregate in the infection site, as demonstrated by fluorescence imaging. This nanosystem was given to mice intravenously to heal a subcutaneous abscess using near-infrared (NIR) irradiation. The hyperthermal activity of NIR resulted in increased Ag release and *MRSA* mortality for abscess ablation and wound healing acceleration (Wallock-Richards et al., 2014). Poly-caprolactone (PCL) was used to incorporate carvacrol into polymeric nanocarriers, which were subsequently combined with hydrogel for topical distribution (Mir et al., 2019). Carvacrol is a monoterpene that has antibacterial properties against a wide spectrum of bacteria (Nostro & Papalia, 2012). In the presence of bacterial lipase the nanoparticles were enzyme-sensitive, releasing carvacrol. To eradicate *MRSA*, Hsu et al. (2017) created chloramphenicol-loaded lipid-based nanocarriers for follicular distribution. For the production of flexible vesicles, deoxycholic acid or dimyristoyl phosphatidylcholine was combined into liposomes with the goal of facile extrusion into follicles. The simultaneous integration of SME and oxacillin in NLCs for synergistic bactericidal activity against *MRSA* is another example of lipid-based nanoparticles (Alalaiwe et al., 2018). Yang et al. (2018) created gentamicin-loaded MSNs with a lipid bilayer coating on the surface. The *S. aureus*-targeting peptide ubiquicidin was added to the bilayer shell of MSNs. Bacterial toxins could weaken the lipid bilayer, allowing gentamicin to be released quickly.

Pulmonary infection

The respiratory tract is the more vulnerable site for the entry of microbes, causing lung disorders. Nano-formulations will be in use for the inclusion into the formulations meant to treat them, majorly administered through intravenous or intrathecal injections (Kang et al., 2019). Encapsulation of tigecycline in Ga2O3:Cr3 + nanoparticles linked with intercellular adhesion molecule 1 (ICAM) has been evaluated in the infection model of tigecycline-resistant *Klebsiella pneumoniae* (TRKP) in the lungs via the intratracheal route. In another study (Deacon et al., 2015), Tobramycin-loaded chitosan/alginate nanoparticles functionalized with DNase studies to evaluate the capacity to decrease mucus viscoelasticity via DNA cleavage. This model is used for the evaluation of DNase-enhanced nanoparticles boosted nanoparticle penetration in cystic fibrosis patients' sputum. Hsu et al. (2017) nanocomposite made off with vancomycin, ciprofloxacin micelles along with PCL, showed commendable performance of penetration enhancement through the *Pseudomonas aeruginosa* with hardly any colonies present in the course of study.

Gastrointestinal infections

To treat gastrointestinal (GI) tract infection, antimicrobial nanoparticles can be used orally. The antibiotics are protected from a breakdown in GI fluids by the nanocarriers. Some nanoparticles have a bioadhesive property that allows them to stay longer in the GI system for better oral bioavailability (Zhao et al., 2019). Oral MSNs are attractive candidates for protecting medicines against enzymolysis in the GI tract (Ping et al., 2016) antimicrobial peptide defensin-loaded MSNs and metronidazole−montmorillonite and cationic PEI nanocomposites for the treatment of *H. pylori* infection in the GI tract (Angsantikul et al., 2018) causes bacterial membrane lysis, allowing more antibiotics to enter the cytoplasm. These nanocarriers were successfully used to neutralize the effects of *H. pylori* from the GI tract, resulting in fewer stomach ulcers and inflammation. The membrane of a gastric epithelial cell was coated onto poly(lactic-*co*-glycolic acid) (PLGA) nanoparticles to make biomimetic nanocarriers containing clarithromycin as the model antibiotic for targeting the *H. pylori* infection site (Huttunen & Aittoniemi, 2011).

The other infection sites

Systemic, bone, and vaginal infections were all treated using antibacterial nanoparticles. Bacteremia, followed by sepsis, can result from a systemic bacterial infection. Rai et al. (2016) used a high-density conjugated antimicrobial peptide on the surface of Ag nanoparticles to eradicate *MRSA*. In comparison to the nonconjugated group the peptide-conjugated nanoparticles reduced *MRSA* levels in circulation. Bone infection was also treated using metallic nanoparticles. To remove *S. aureus* bone invasion in mice (Qadri et al., 2017) produced Ag−Cu nanoparticles. Magnetic Fe_3O_4 nanoparticles were also used to treat osteomyelitis by inducing heat to destroy biofilms (Fang et al., 2017). The combination of vancomycin and heat had a higher bone volume (24%) than the infection control group (18%). At very low concentrations, ZnO nanoparticles were found to have antibacterial action (Król et al., 2017). ZnO nanoparticles were integrated into a PVA hydrogel for vaginal administration to treat vaginitis (Bai et al., 2015).

Virus-based nanoparticles

Virion proteins interact with cell surface components to efficiently bind to host cells. Viruses have also evolved a variety of ways of evading the immune system of their hosts. As a result, many methods for creating biomimetic nanoparticles have been developed, utilizing virus-specific properties.

The first strategy involves incorporating virus-derived proteins into unilamellar liposomes, and virosomes (Almeida et al., 1975; Kaneda, 2000). In general, influenza virus envelope glycoproteins, such as hemagglutinin and neuraminidase, are reconstituted with liposomes to prepare virosomes for vaccination or therapeutic delivery (Daemen et al., 2005). Other enveloped viruses that can be utilized to make virosomes include the hemagglutinating virus of Japan, respiratory syncytial virus, and vesicular stomatitis virus (Lederhofer et al., 2018; Mohammadzadeh et al., 2017).

To circumvent the drawbacks of virus like particles (VLPs') innate tropism, multiple chemical functionalization strategies for conjugating diverse types for targeted delivery (Smith et al., 2013). VLPs are originally generated for vaccination because their antigenicity is comparable to that of their primary viruses.

Nanoparticles derived from fungal pathogens

Diverse components of the fungal cell membrane are being in use for nanoparticle preparation to incorporate natural features or to achieve targeted treatment (Baker et al., 2007; Pizarro-Cerdá & Cossart, 2006). *Cryptococcus neoformans*-targeted drug delivery system (Tang et al., 2018). Fungal strains from *Fusarium* species are used for the production of metallic nanoparticles, like silver nanoparticles through extracellular reduction (Ahmad et al., 2003; Bansal et al., 2004; Birla et al., 2013; Dias et al., 2002). A brief list of extracellular vesicles used for the infection management has been listed in Table 7.2.

Nanoparticles mimicking mammalian cells

Diverse methodologies for engineering nanoparticles to mimic mammalian cells have recently been produced (Chen et al., 2018; Chu et al., 2018; Zhang et al., 2018). They possess the capacity to target the cells with biodegradable polymers having the capacity to deliver them in a controlled fashion, for example, PLGA (Fang et al., 2018; Hu et al., 2011). Different coating and coextrusion approaches are used to prepare membrane vesicles and so on.

Microfluidic devices can also be used to conceal nanoparticles in biological membranes (Molinaro et al., 2018; Rao et al., 2017). Proteins derived from leukocyte plasma membranes were combined with lipid nanoparticles to create leukocytes capable of encapsulating medications of varied solubilities and delivering carrier molecules to the inflamed endothelium in a site-specific manner. Functional compounds have been added to nanoparticles to gain specific biological properties. To induce leukocyte-like tenacious adherence, nanoparticles coated with ligands that mediate two leukocyte adhesion pathways, for example, were utilized (Robbins et al., 2010). Self-peptides generated from a human membrane protein CD47, on the other hand, can significantly delay macrophage-mediated clearance when applied intravenously (Rodriguez et al., 2013).

Exosomes and microvesicles are two forms of CDVs that are generated by nearly every cell type in both normal and pathological situations. Because CDVs are key mediators for intercellular communications and the horizontal transfer of membrane/cargo molecules, they are being used as intelligent drug delivery carriers, taking advantage of their abilities to escape immune clearance, recognize target cells, and overcome biological barriers, either in their natural state or after genetic or chemical modification (Ha et al., 2016; Vader et al., 2016).

Conclusion and perspectives

Infectious diseases are for the most part important drivers of global mortality and morbidity. The new formulation strategies adopted for the existing and new drugs by nanostrategies are showing promising potential to overcome the challenges associated with the prevalent bacterial, viral, and parasitic infections, such as improvement in bioavailability, toxicity reduction, and subtherapeutic drug accumulation at the infection sites. These carriers are not only useful for the delivery of drugs but also proved to be effective and efficient carriers for vaccine delivery strategies too.

Nanomedicine's potential to aid in improving treatment or controlling modalities of infectious diseases paves the way for the future of this technology. Succinct no. of research efforts listed and explained in this chapter enlighten the potential therapeutic advantages and prospective applications for the global population. The design of carriers to equivocate mechanisms of microbial drug resistance by controlling them intracellularly and by improving cellular uptake of drugs, and surface functionalization with molecules that possess the capability to penetrate through the biofilm matrix. Coencapsulation of drug combinations is underway to synergize the potential of the free-drug combinations.

Acknowledgments

The authors wish to thank the Department of Science and Technology (DST) for the WoS-B research fellowship—DST/WOS-B/2017/477-HFN (Dr. Jhansi Lakshmi Parimi) and Sayan Mukherjee to IIT Kharagpur, Department of Life Sciences, School of Basic Sciences and Research, Sharda University (Dr. Soumi Sadhu and Ms. Swati Bhati) for the generous support of the studies which contributed to this chapter.

References

Ahmad, A., Mukherjee, P., Senapati, S., Mandal, D., Khan, M. I., Kumar, R., & Sastry, M. (2003). Extracellular biosynthesis of silver nanoparticles using the fungus *Fusarium oxysporum*. *Colloids and Surfaces B: Biointerfaces*, *28*(4), 313–318. Available from https://doi.org/10.1016/S0927-7765(02)00174-1.

Akhtar, N., & Pathak, K. (2012). Preclinical and clinical aspects of antimicrobial drugs delivered through ethosomal vesicles. *Anti-Infective Agents*, *10*(1), 15–25. Available from https://doi.org/10.2174/2211362611201010015.

Alalaiwe, A., Wang, P. W., Lu, P. L., Chen, Y. P., Fang, J. Y., & Yang, S. C. (2018). Human kinetoplastid protozoan infections: Where are we going next? *Frontiers in Microbiology*, *9*. Available from https://doi.org/10.3389/fimmu.2018.01493.

Aljuffali, I., Huang, C.-H., & Fang, J.-Y. (2015). Nanomedical strategies for targeting skin microbiomes. *Current Drug Metabolism*, *16*(4), 255–271. Available from https://doi.org/10.2174/1389200216666150812124923.

Almeida, J. D., Edwards, D. C., Brand, C. M., & Heath, T. D. (1975). Formation of virosomes from influenza subunits and liposomes. *The Lancet*, *306*(7941), 899–901. Available from https://doi.org/10.1016/S0140-6736(75)92130-3.

Alt, V., Bechert, T., Steinrücke, P., Wagener, M., Seidel, P., Dingeldein, E., Domann, E., & Schnettler, R. (2004). *Biomaterials*, *25*(18), 4383–4391. Available from https://doi.org/10.1016/j.biomaterials.2003.10.078.

Angsantikul, P., Thamphiwatana, S., Zhang, Q., Spiekermann, K., Zhuang, J., Fang, R. H., Gao, W., Obonyo, M., & Zhang, L. (2018). *Advanced Therapeutics*, *1*(2), 1800016. Available from https://doi.org/10.1002/adtp.201800016.

Arif, M., Dong, Q. J., Raja, M. A., Zeenat, S., Chi, Z., & Liu, C. G. (2018). *Materials Science and Engineering C*, *83*, 17–24. Available from https://doi.org/10.1016/j.msec.2017.08.038.

Bai, X., Li, L., Liu, H., Tan, L., Liu, T., & Meng, X. (2015). *ACS Applied Materials and Interfaces*, 7(2), 1308–1317. Available from https://doi.org/10.1021/am507532p.

Baker, L. G., Specht, C. A., Donlin, M. J., & Lodge, J. K. (2007). *Eukaryotic Cell*, *6*(5), 855–867. Available from https://doi.org/10.1128/EC.00399-06.

Bangia, R., Sharma, G., Dogra, S., & Katare, O. P. (2019). *Expert Opinion on Drug Delivery*, *16*(4), 377–396. Available from https://doi.org/10.1080/17425247.2019.1593962.

Bansal, V., Rautaray, D., Ahmad, A., & Sastry, M. (2004). *Journal of Materials Chemistry*, *14*(22), 3303–3305. Available from https://doi.org/10.1039/b407904c.

Bell, I. R., Schwartz, G. E., Boyer, N. N., Koithan, M., & Brooks, A. J. (2013). *European Journal of Integrative Medicine*, *5*(2), 126–140. Available from https://doi.org/10.1016/j.eujim.2012.11.002.

Birla, S. S., Gaikwad, S. C., Gade, A. K., & Rai, M. K. (2013). *The Scientific World Journal*, *2013*. Available from https://doi.org/10.1155/2013/796018.

Botequim, D., Maia, J., Lino, M. M. F., Lopes, L. M. F., Simões, P. N., Ilharco, L. M., & Ferreira, L. (2012). *Langmuir: the ACS Journal of Surfaces and Colloids*, *28*(20), 7646–7656. Available from https://doi.org/10.1021/la300948n.

Bringas, E., Köysüren, Ö., Quach, D. V., Mahmoudi, M., Aznar, E., Roehling, J. D., Marcos, M. D., Martínez-Máñez, R., & Stroeve, P. (2012). *Chemical Communications*, *48*(45), 5647–5649. Available from https://doi.org/10.1039/c2cc31563g.

Cano, A., Ettcheto, M., Espina, M., López-Machado, A., Cajal, Y., Rabanal, F., Sánchez-López, E., Camins, A., García, M. L., & Souto, E. B. (2020). *Journal of Nanobiotechnology*, *18*(1). Available from https://doi.org/10.1186/s12951-020-00714-2.

Chen, M., Xie, S., Wei, J., Song, X., Ding, Z., & Li, X. (2018). *ACS Applied Materials and Interfaces*, *10*(43), 36814–36823. Available from https://doi.org/10.1021/acsami.8b16092.

Chen, W. Y., Lin, J. Y., Chen, W. J., Luo, L., Wei-Guang Diau, E., & Chen, Y. C. (2010). *Nanomedicine: Nanotechnology, Biology, and Medicine*, *5*(5), 755–764. Available from https://doi.org/10.2217/nnm.10.43.

Chono, S., Tanino, T., Seki, T., & Morimoto, K. (2008). Efficient drug targeting to rat alveolar macrophages by pulmonary administration of ciprofloxacin incorporated into mannosylated liposomes for treatment of respiratory intracellular parasitic infections. *Journal of Controlled Release*, *127*(1), 50–58. Available from https://doi.org/10.1016/j.jconrel.2007.12.011.

Chu, D., Dong, X., Shi, X., Zhang, C., & Wang, Z. (2018). *Advanced Materials, 30*(22), 1706245. Available from https://doi.org/10.1002/adma.201706245.

Daemen, T., Demare, A., Bungener, L., Dejonge, J., Huckriede, A., & Wilschut, J. (2005). *Advanced Drug Delivery Reviews, 57*(3), 451–463. Available from https://doi.org/10.1016/j.addr.2004.09.005.

Dave, V., Yadav, R. B., Kushwaha, K., Yadav, S., Sharma, S., & Agrawal, U. (2017). *Bioactive Materials, 2*(4), 269–280. Available from https://doi.org/10.1016/j.bioactmat.2017.07.002.

Deacon, J., Abdelghany, S. M., Quinn, D. J., Schmid, D., Megaw, J., Donnelly, R. F., Jones, D. S., Kissenpfennig, A., Elborn, J. S., Gilmore, B. F., Taggart, C. C., & Scott, C. J. (2015). *Journal of Controlled Release, 198*, 55–61. Available from https://doi.org/10.1016/j.jconrel.2014.11.022.

Dias, M. A., Lacerda, I. C. A., Pimentel, P. F., de Castro, H. F., & Rosa, C. A. (2002). *Letters in Applied Microbiology, 34*(1), 46–50. Available from https://doi.org/10.1046/j.1472-765x.2002.01040.x.

Du, X., & Qiao, S. Z. (2015). *Small (Weinheim an der Bergstrasse, Germany), 11*(4), 392–413. Available from https://doi.org/10.1002/smll.201401201.

Eleraky, N. E., Allam, A., Hassan, S. B., & Omar, M. M. (2020). *Pharmaceutics, 12*(2). Available from https://doi.org/10.3390/pharmaceutics12020142.

Escárcega-González, C. E., Garza-Cervantes, J. A., Vázquez-Rodríguez, A., & Morones-Ramírez, J. R. (2018). *International Journal of Polymer Science, 2018*. Available from https://doi.org/10.1155/2018/7045852.

Fang, C. H., Tsai, P. I., Huang, S. W., Sun, J. S., Chang, J. Z. C., Shen, H. H., Chen, S. Y., Lin, F. H., Hsu, L. T., & Chen, Y. C. (2017). *BMC Infectious Diseases, 17*(1). Available from https://doi.org/10.1186/s12879-017-2621-4.

Fang, R. H., Kroll, A. V., Gao, W., & Zhang, L. (2018). *Advanced Materials, 30*(23). Available from https://doi.org/10.1002/adma.201706759.

Ganbold, T., & Baigude, H. (2018). *ACS Applied Materials and Interfaces, 10*(17), 14463–14474. Available from https://doi.org/10.1021/acsami.8b02073.

Grace, A. N., & Pandian, K. (2007). *Journal of Bionanoscience, 1*(2), 96–105. Available from https://doi.org/10.1166/jbns.2007.018.

Ha, D., Yang, N., & Nadithe, V. (2016). *Acta Pharmaceutica Sinica B, 6*(4), 287–296. Available from https://doi.org/10.1016/j.apsb.2016.02.001.

Hsu, C. Y., Yang, S. C., Sung, C. T., Weng, Y. H., & Fang, J. Y. (2017). *International Journal of Nanomedicine, 12*, 8227–8238. Available from https://doi.org/10.2147/IJN.S147226.

Hu, C. M. J., Zhang, L., Aryal, S., Cheung, C., Fang, R. H., & Zhang, L. (2011). *Proceedings of the National Academy of Sciences of the United States of America, 108*(27), 10980–10985. Available from https://doi.org/10.1073/pnas.1106634108.

Huang, L., Dai, T., Xuan, Y., Tegos, G. P., & Hamblin, M. R. (2011). *Antimicrobial Agents and Chemotherapy, 55*(7), 3432–3438. Available from https://doi.org/10.1128/AAC.01803-10.

Huttunen, R., & Aittoniemi, J. (2011). *Journal of Infection, 63*(6), 407–419. Available from https://doi.org/10.1016/j.jinf.2011.08.004.

Ibrahim, H. R., Aoki, T., & Pellegrini, A. (2002). *Current Pharmaceutical Design, 8*(9), 671–693. Available from https://doi.org/10.2174/1381612023395349.

Kaneda, Y. (2000). *Advanced Drug Delivery Reviews, 43*(2–3), 197–205. Available from https://doi.org/10.1016/S0169-409X(00)00069-7.

Kang, X. Q., Shu, G. F., Jiang, S. P., Xu, X. L., Qi, J., Jin, F. Y., Liu, D., Xiao, Y. H., Lu, X. Y., & Du, Y. Z. (2019). *Theranostics, 9*(10), 2739–2753. Available from https://doi.org/10.7150/thno.33452.

Kaur, A., Jain, S., & Tiwary, A. K. (2008). Mannan-coated gelatin nanoparticles for sustained and targeted delivery of didanosine: In vitro and in vivo evaluation. *Acta Pharmaceutica, 58*(1), 61–74. Available from https://doi.org/10.2478/v10007-007-0045-1.

Kirtane, A. R., Verma, M., Karandikar, P., Furin, J., Langer, R., & Traverso, G. (2021). *Nature Nanotechnology, 16*(4), 369–384. Available from https://doi.org/10.1038/s41565-021-00866-8.

Król, A., Pomastowski, P., Rafińska, K., Railean-Plugaru, V., & Buszewski, B. (2017). *Advances in Colloid and Interface Science, 249*, 37–52. Available from https://doi.org/10.1016/j.cis.2017.07.033.

Kurmi, B. D., Kayat, J., Gajbhiye, V., Tekade, R. K., & Jain, N. K. (2010). *Expert Opinion on Drug Delivery, 7*(7), 781–794. Available from https://doi.org/10.1517/17425247.2010.492212.

Lalloz, A., Bolzinger, M. A., Faivre, J., Latreille, P. L., Garcia Ac, A., Rakotovao, C., Rabanel, J. M., Hildgen, P., Banquy, X., & Briançon, S. (2018). *International Journal of Pharmaceutics*, *553*(1–2), 120–131. Available from https://doi.org/10.1016/j.ijpharm.2018.09.046.

Lederhofer, J., van Lent, J., Bhoelan, F., Karneva, Z., de Haan, A., Wilschut, J. C., & Stegmann, T. (2018). *Pharmaceutical Research*, *35*(9). Available from https://doi.org/10.1007/s11095-018-2453-y.

Liu, J., Dai, S., Wang, M., Hu, Z., Wang, H., & Deng, F. (2016). *Virologica Sinica*, *31*(4), 279–287. Available from https://doi.org/10.1007/s12250-016-3756-y.

Liu, Y., Shi, L., Su, L., Van der Mei, H. C., Jutte, P. C., Ren, Y., & Busscher, H. J. (2019). *Chemical Society Reviews*, *48*(2), 428–446. Available from https://doi.org/10.1039/c7cs00807d.

Lu, B., Ye, H., Shang, S., Xiong, Q., Yu, K., Li, Q., Xiao, Y., Dai, F., & Lan, G. (2018). *Nanotechnology*, *29*(42), 425603. Available from https://doi.org/10.1088/1361-6528/aad7a7.

Marcato, P. D., & Durán, N. (2008). *Journal of Nanoscience and Nanotechnology*, *8*(5), 2216–2229. Available from https://doi.org/10.1166/jnn.2008.274.

Mir, M., Ahmed, N., Permana, A. D., Rodgers, A. M., Donnelly, R. F., & Rehman, A. U. (2019). *Pharmaceutics*, *11*(11). Available from https://doi.org/10.3390/pharmaceutics11110606.

Mirzaeei, S., & Barfar, D. (2021). *Advanced Pharmaceutical Bulletin*. Available from https://doi.org/10.34172/apb.2022.056.

Mohammadzadeh, Y., Gholami, S., Rasouli, N., Sarrafzadeh, S., Seyed Tabib, N. S., Samiee Aref, M. H., Abdoli, A., Biglari, P., Fotouhi, F., Farahmand, B., Tavassoti Kheiri, M., & Jamali, A. (2017). *Journal of Liposome Research*, *27*(2), 83–89. Available from https://doi.org/10.3109/08982104.2016.1144205.

Mohammed Fayaz, A., Girilal, M., Mahdy, S. A., Somsundar, S. S., Venkatesan, R., & Kalaichelvan, P. T. (2011). *Process Biochemistry*, *46*(3), 636–641. Available from https://doi.org/10.1016/j.procbio.2010.11.001.

Molinaro, R., Evangelopoulos, M., Hoffman, J. R., Corbo, C., Taraballi, F., Martinez, J. O., Hartman, K. A., Cosco, D., Costa, G., Romeo, I., Sherman, M., Paolino, D., Alcaro, S., & Tasciotti, E. (2018). *Advanced Materials*, *30*(15). Available from https://doi.org/10.1002/adma.201702749.

Moser, K., Kriwet, K., Naik, A., Kalia, Y. N., & Guy, R. H. (2001). *European Journal of Pharmaceutics and Biopharmaceutics*, *52*(2), 103–112. Available from https://doi.org/10.1016/S0939-6411(01)00166-7.

Nostro, A., & Papalia, T. (2012). *Recent Patents on Anti-Infective Drug Discovery*, 7(1), 28–35. Available from https://doi.org/10.2174/157489112799829684.

Patra, J. K., Das, G., Fraceto, L. F., Campos, E. V. R., Rodriguez-Torres, M., del, P., Acosta-Torres, L. S., Diaz-Torres, L. A., Grillo, R., Swamy, M. K., Sharma, S., Habtemariam, S., & Shin, H.-S. (2018). *Journal of Nanobiotechnology*, *16*(1). Available from https://doi.org/10.1186/s12951-018-0392-8.

Ping, Y., Hu, X., Yao, Q., Hu, Q., Amini, S., Miserez, A., & Tang, G. (2016). *Nanoscale*, *8*(36), 16486–16498. Available from https://doi.org/10.1039/c6nr05551f.

Pizarro-Cerdá, J., & Cossart, P. (2006). Bacterial adhesion and entry into host cells. *Cell*, *124*(4), 715–727. Available from https://doi.org/10.1016/j.cell.2006.02.012.

Pradeepa., Vidya, S. M., Mutalik, S., Udaya Bhat, K., Huilgol, P., & Avadhani, K. (2016). *Life Sciences*, *153*, 171–179. Available from https://doi.org/10.1016/j.lfs.2016.04.022.

Praditya, D., Kirchhoff, L., Brüning, J., Rachmawati, H., Steinmann, J., & Steinmann, E. (2019). *Frontiers in Microbiology*, *10*(MAY). Available from https://doi.org/10.3389/fmicb.2019.00912.

Qadri, S., Haik, Y., Mensah-Brown, E., Bashir, G., Fernandez-Cabezudo, M. J., & al-Ramadi, B. K. (2017). *Nanomedicine: Nanotechnology, Biology, and Medicine*, *13*(7), 2241–2250. Available from https://doi.org/10.1016/j.nano.2017.05.013.

Raghupathi, K. R., Koodali, R. T., & Manna, A. C. (2011). *Langmuir: The ACS Journal of Surfaces and Colloids*, *27*(7), 4020–4028. Available from https://doi.org/10.1021/la104825u.

Rai, A., Pinto, S., Velho, T. R., Ferreira, A. F., Moita, C., Trivedi, U., Evangelista, M., Comune, M., Rumbaugh, K. P., Simões, P. N., Moita, L., & Ferreira, L. (2016). *Biomaterials*, *85*, 99–110. Available from https://doi.org/10.1016/j.biomaterials.2016.01.051.

Ranjita, S. (2013). *Journal of Pharmaceutical Investigation*, *43*(1), 1–26. Available from https://doi.org/10.1007/s40005-013-0051-x.

Rao, L., Cai, B., Bu, L. L., Liao, Q. Q., Guo, S. S., Zhao, X. Z., Dong, W. F., & Liu, W. (2017). *ACS Nano*, *11*(4), 3496–3505. Available from https://doi.org/10.1021/acsnano.7b00133.

Raveendran, S., Rochani, A. K., Maekawa, T., & Kumar, D. S. (2017). *Materials*, *10*(8). Available from https://doi.org/10.3390/ma10080929.

Robbins, G. P., Saunders, R. L., Haun, J. B., Rawson, J., Therien, M. J., & Hammer, D. A. (2010). *Langmuir: The ACS Journal of Surfaces and Colloids*, *26*(17), 14089−14096. Available from https://doi.org/10.1021/la1017032.

Rodriguez, P. L., Harada, T., Christian, D. A., Pantano, D. A., Tsai, R. K., & Discher, D. E. (2013). *Science (New York, N.Y.)*, *339*(6122), 971−975. Available from https://doi.org/10.1126/science.1229568.

Silva, N. C., Silva, S., Sarmento, B., & Pintado, M. (2015). *Drug Delivery*, *22*(7), 885−893. Available from https://doi.org/10.3109/10717544.2013.858195.

Smith, M. T., Hawes, A. K., & Bundy, B. C. (2013). *Current Opinion in Biotechnology*, *24*(4), 620−626. Available from https://doi.org/10.1016/j.copbio.2013.01.011.

Smitha, K. T., Nisha, N., Maya, S., Biswas, R., & Jayakumar, R. (2015). *International Journal of Biological Macromolecules*, *74*, 36−43. Available from https://doi.org/10.1016/j.ijbiomac.2014.11.006.

Sousa, F., Ferreira, D., Reis, S., & Costa, P. (2020). *Pharmaceuticals*, *13*(9), 248. Available from https://doi.org/10.3390/ph13090248.

Su, H. L., Lin, S. H., Wei, J. C., Pao, I. C., Chiao, S. H., Huang, C. C., & Lin, J. J. (2011). *PLoS One*, *6*.

Sun, L. M., Zhang, C. L., & Li, P. (2012). *Journal of Agricultural and Food Chemistry*, *60*(24), 6150−6156. Available from https://doi.org/10.1021/jf3010405.

Tan, Y., Ma, S., Leonhard, M., Moser, D., Haselmann, G. M., Wang, J., Eder, D., & Schneider-Stickler, B. (2018). *Carbohydrate Polymers*, *200*, 35−42. Available from https://doi.org/10.1016/j.carbpol.2018.07.072.

Tang, Y., Wu, S., Lin, J., Cheng, L., Zhou, J., Xie, J., Huang, K., Wang, X., Yu, Y., Chen, Z., Liao, G., & Li, C. (2018). *Nano Letters*, *18*(10), 6207−6213. Available from https://doi.org/10.1021/acs.nanolett.8b02229.

Vader, P., Mol, E. A., Pasterkamp, G., & Schiffelers, R. M. (2016). Extracellular vesicles for drug delivery. *Advanced Drug Delivery Reviews*, *106*, 148−156. Available from https://doi.org/10.1016/j.addr.2016.02.006.

Wallock-Richards, D., Doherty, C. J., Doherty, L., Clarke, D. J., Place, M., Govan, J. R. W., & Campopiano, D. J. (2014). *PLoS One*, *9*(12). Available from https://doi.org/10.1371/journal.pone.0112726.

Wang, X., Thompson, C. D., Weidenmaier, C., & Lee, J. C. (2018). *Nature Communications*, *9*(1). Available from https://doi.org/10.1038/s41467-018-03847-z.

Xiong, M. H., Bao, Y., Yang, X. Z., Wang, Y. C., Sun, B., & Wang, J. (2012). *Journal of the American Chemical Society*, *134*(9), 4355−4362. Available from https://doi.org/10.1021/ja211279u.

Yang, G., Chen, S., & Zhang, J. (2019). *Frontiers in Pharmacology*, *10*. Available from https://doi.org/10.3389/fphar.2019.00751.

Yang, S., Han, X., Yang, Y., Qiao, H., Yu, Z., Liu, Y., Wang, J., & Tang, T. (2018). *ACS Applied Materials and Interfaces*, *10*(17), 14299−14311. Available from https://doi.org/10.1021/acsami.7b15678.

Yeh, Y. C., Huang, T. H., Yang, S. C., Chen, C. C., & Fang, J. Y. (2020). *Frontiers in Chemistry*, *8*. Available from https://doi.org/10.3389/fchem.2020.00286.

Yunus Basha, R., T.S., S. K., & Doble, M. (2019). *Carbohydrate Polymers*, *218*, 53−62. Available from https://doi.org/10.1016/j.carbpol.2019.04.056.

Zhang, Q., Dehaini, D., Zhang, Y., Zhou, J., Chen, X., Zhang, L., Fang, R. H., Gao, W., & Zhang, L. (2018). *Nature Nanotechnology*, *13*(12), 1182−1190. Available from https://doi.org/10.1038/s41565-018-0254-4.

Zhao, G., Chen, Y., He, Y., Chen, F., Gong, Y., Chen, S., Xu, Y., Su, Y., Wang, C., & Wang, J. (2019). *Biomaterials Science*, 7(6), 2440−2451. Available from https://doi.org/10.1039/c9bm00003h.

Zhou, J., Krishnan, N., Jiang, Y., Fang, R. H., & Zhang, L. (2021). *Nano Today*, *36*. Available from https://doi.org/10.1016/j.nantod.2020.101031.

CHAPTER 8

Recent plant-based nanomedicine and nanocarrier for cancer treatment

Monu Kumar Shukla[1], Anik Kumar Das[2], Anshuman Gaurav[3], Dheeraj Bisht[4], Anita Singh[4] and Deepak Kumar[1]
[1]Department of Pharmaceutical Chemistry, School of Pharmaceutical Sciences, Shoolini University, Solan, Himachal Pradesh, India
[2]Department of Pharmacology, School of Pharmaceutical Sciences, Shoolini University, Solan, Himachal Pradesh, India
[3]School of Pharmaceutical Sciences, Shoolini University, Solan, Himachal Pradesh, India
[4]Department of Pharmaceutical Sciences, Sir J.C. Bose Technical Campus Bhimtal, Kumaun University, Nanital, Uttarakhand, India

Introduction

Cancer is affecting millions of individuals every year in the world. It is defined by the uncontrolled proliferation and spread of aberrant cells to other organs, encroaching on numerous other bodily components (Cooper & Hausman, 2007; Ramos et al., 2017). Males are generally affected by lung, prostate, colorectal, stomach, and liver cancers, while breast, colorectal, cervix, lung, and thyroid cancers are the most common cancers in women. Among the various forms, liver, lung, breast, colorectal, and stomach, cancer accounts for 4 million annual cases. Despite 9.6 million people die each year, cancer is the second most leading cause of mortality (Sung et al., 2021).

With the progress of techniques from traditional procedures, nanotechnology has been expanded its reach into biomedical applications. Nanotechnology in the field of medicine has influenced since the early 1990s (Bayda et al., 2020; Capek, 2006; Patra et al., 2018; Prasad et al., 2018). This is referred to as "technology transfer," and is crucial in health research and medicine (Harris & Tanner, 2000). Nanotechnology is characterized as particles in the "nanometre" range, which is also referred to as nanoscale or nanoparticles (NPs) (Khan et al., 2019; Lalley et al., 2014). In the realm of nanomedicine, new advancements in biological science research have been focused on NPs via protein and nucleic acids to establish a detailed analysis of drug delivery (Shukla et al., 2022).

Several formulated anticancer drugs used as delivery systems possessing various noteworthy restrictions, such as lesser hydrophilicity, unsuitable to oral formulation, shorter half-life, and severe adverse effects (Cho et al., 2008; Sandha et al., 2020). These limitations highlight the requirements for developing different novel drug delivery systems, which should be effective and safe for various types of cancers

Nanotechnology for Drug Delivery and Pharmaceuticals
DOI: https://doi.org/10.1016/B978-0-323-95325-2.00011-0

(Taylor et al., 1997). Similar work had been reported by Granja et al. and colleagues, which developed combination therapy to deliver phytochemicals with blockers of P-glycoprotein for treating multidrug resistance in various cancer cell lines. Tumor microenvironment also plays important role in the obstacle of cancer treatment and other conditions such as multidrug resistance (Granja et al., 2016).

On the other hand, nanomaterials help as a combination therapy for the delivery of many synthetic, semisynthetic and plant-based anticancer drugs required for the diagnosis and treatment of cancers. These nanomaterials with plant-based anticancer drugs could be modified into single systems for multiple effects via increasing the therapeutic effects, improvement in the tumor accumulation, and conjugation with different targeting moieties (Gulia et al., 2022; Maeda, 2010; Thanki et al., 2013). They are also useful in the diagnosis of cancers, delivering drugs in solid tumors and in targeting cancer therapy (Kumar et al., 2022). Meanwhile, various nanocarriers with modified drugs and drug delivery systems have been developed nowadays in the treatment of various types of cancers with better clinical results (Aliosmanoglu & Basaran, 2012; Khan & Gurav, 2018; Mansoori et al., 2007; Schluep et al., 2009). This book chapter includes literature regarding the advancement in the plant-based nanocarrier systems with different approaches in the diagnosis and treatment of cancer.

Advancement in plant-based nanocarrier systems for cancer treatment

Nanotechnology is a new era based on the behavior and structural properties of nanomaterials that range in nano-to-micro sizes (Ferrari, 2005). By surpassing conventional procedures, nanomedicine has recently revealed a significant potential for cancer cures (Duncan, 2003; Nie et al., 2007). The goal is to improve therapeutic efficacy by developing nanomedicine that is low in toxicity and provide a novel and efficacious treatment in cancer (Chandratre & Dash, 2015; Nie et al., 2007). Recently, various multifunctional systems have been developed to improve the cancer diagnosis and treatment. These systems will be useful for delivering drugs in different targeted cancers. Nowadays, the most difficult task for scientists is to detect the treatment response, which should be depicted in many ways to understand how the medicine is hitting specific targets in the tumor (Nie et al., 2007; Patra et al., 2018). Green nanomaterials derived from plants in combination with inorganic materials, such as silver (Ag), gold (Au), zinc (Zn), and copper (Co), have been reported to suppress the growth of malignant cell lines (16). These phytofabricated metallic NPs are also reported for anticancer activity carrying active compounds found in plants such as curcumin, quercetin, epigallocatechin-3-gallate (EGCG) etc. (Andleeb et al., 2021; Nie et al., 2007; Wei et al., 2019). Berberine (an isoquinoline alkaloid) is an active chemical constituent, which has been reported for anticancer activity and derived primarily from the bark, roots, rhizomes, and stem of *Hydrastis canadensis*, *Berberis vulgaris*, *Coptis chinensis*, and *Phellodendron amurense*. The nanocarrier strategy has provided an improved delivery opportunity for berberine for antimetastatic and antitumor efficacies (Javed Iqbal et al., 2021). Similar to apigenin (found in chamomile tea, parsley, and celery), artemisinin is a sesquiterpene lactone extracted from the herb *Artemisia annua* (a traditional Chinese medicinal), and honokiol is a major compound isolated from the herb *Magnolia officinalis/grandiflora* (a Chinese medicinal herb) (Jeetah et al., 2014). Drug penetration over biological barricades is followed by precise accumulation in tumor tissues, resulting in improved anticancer efficacy with minimal off-target consequences. The use of passive and active NPs to target drugs is a common practice (Chi et al., 2020; Khan et al., 2018). Nanocarriers containing anticancer drugs are passively targeted in tissues, utilizing pathophysiological aspects of tumor vasculature. The geometry of tumor vessels deteriorates, and lymphatic drainage is disturbed, resulting in a greater penetration and retention impact (Sledge & Miller, 2003; Teicher, 2000). The size of nanocarriers and the damaged tumor vasculature further enhance passive anticancer drug targeting (Basile et al., 2012). The lymphatic system in tumor tissues is compromised, resulting in higher interstitial pressure in the core than in the periphery. This enables nanocarriers to penetrate into the interstitial region and retain there for longer periods of time, which result in greater anticancer action in tumors (Haley & Frenkel, 2008). Specific tumor-associated receptors or antigens have been identified via an attachment of targeting moiety on the NPs' surfaces. Through the receptor-mediated endocytosis process, these targeting ligands can trigger release of the drug from nanomaterials inside target cells (Yu et al., 2012). Internalization of drugs into tumors by receptor targeting is a great way to improve chemotherapy (Gabizon, 2001). Targeting moieties identified as overexpressed receptors in cancer cells allow for extremely selective drug localization in tumors (Adams et al., 2001; Gosk et al., 2008). Consequently, nanocarriers are also responsible to change the tumor microenvironment via releasing the drugs from nanocarriers inside the tumor vicinity due to stimuli, such as pH, redox potential, hyperthermia, and specific enzymes in the tumor microenvironment. As a result, there is a higher concentration of drugs in the tumor microenvironment, which causes considerably better treatment (Chi et al., 2020; Khan et al., 2018) (Fig. 8.1).

Different plant-based nanocarrier systems for the treatment of cancer

Plant-based NPs have been a hotspot of study due to the expanding uses of NPs in cancer therapy and management (Gulia et al., 2022). The traditional techniques of producing nanodelivery system frequently necessitate the use of strong chemical reduction agents, which are expensive, complicated, and can yield extremely harmful products (Gulia et al., 2022). As a result, more cost-effective and ecologically friendly alternatives are unquestionably required to reduce the danger of pollution (Varma, 2012). In this section, we summarize several plants-based nanodelivery systems that are currently being employed for anticancer therapies (Fig. 8.2).

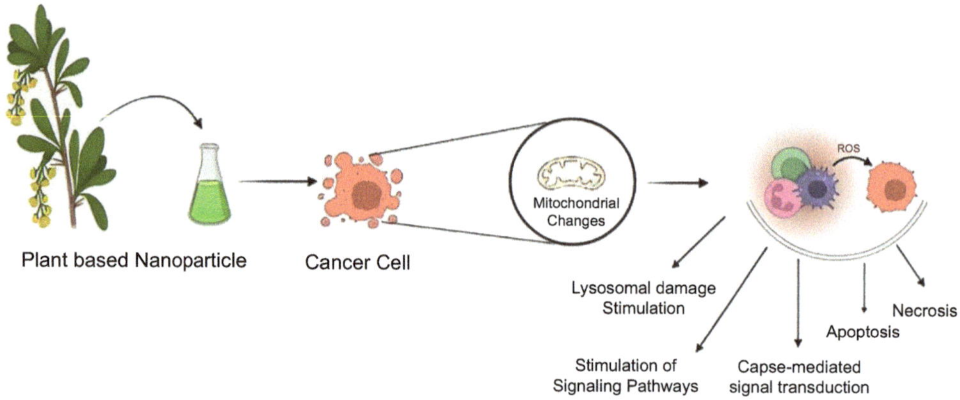

Figure 8.1 Illustration of plant-based nanoparticles for the treatment of cancer via targeting malignant cells.

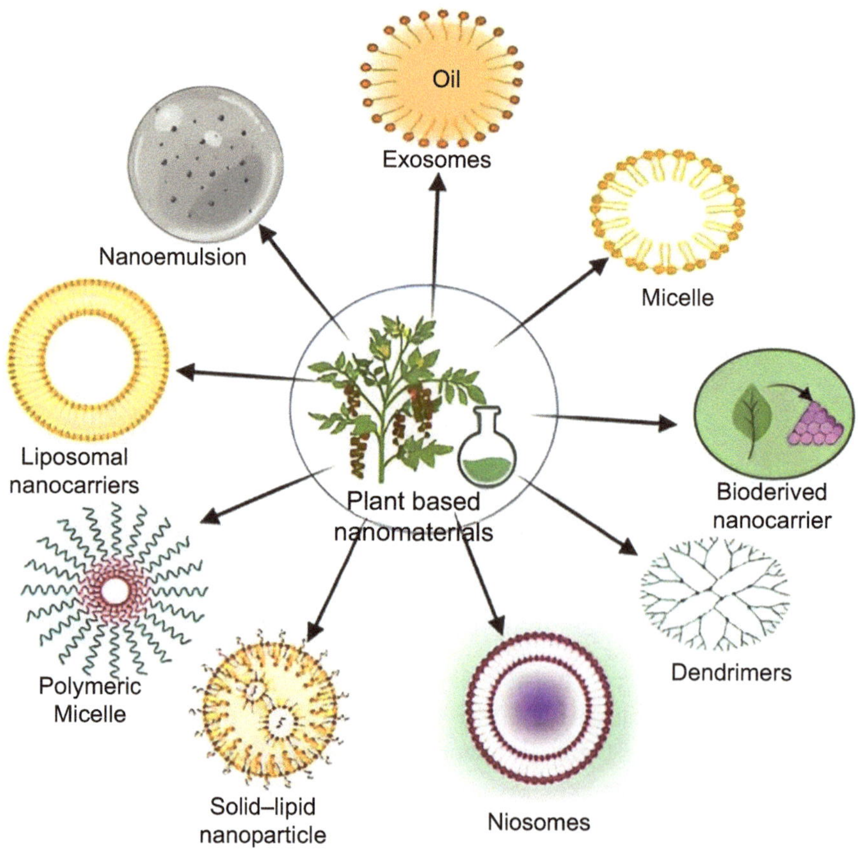

Figure 8.2 Schematic representation of available various types of plant-based nanoformulations.

Liposomal nanocarriers

Nanocarriers based on lipids have made great progress in cancer treatment. There are different lipid-based formulations available, which include liposomal nanocarriers, nanostructured lipid carriers, and solid lipid NPs (SLNs). Liposomal systems are spherical in shape, which is generally composed of lipid bilayer with a hollow core carrying anticancer drugs to deliver into tumors and cancer cell lines (Buse & El-Aneed, 2010; Emilian Leucuta, 2010). These bilayer structures are generally made up of natural phospholipids, cholesterol, and other chemicals, which made suitable transporters for various drugs with varying solubilities (Stone et al., 2016).

SLNs are NPs with colloidal carrier systems that are generally made of lipids, such as polymeric NPs, liposomes, and nanoemulsions, which combine the benefits of colloidal equivalents (Wissing et al., 2004). SLNs are the most popular methods used for increasing the oral bioavailability of water-soluble drugs. SLNs of second generation (a nanostructured lipid carriers) are a mixture of diverse lipids with specified liquid lipid content (Fang et al., 2012). These lipid carriers have been found to have a lower likelihood of drug leakage and gelation, as well as the ability to lengthen drug half-lives and improve the EPR effect, all of which improve the therapeutic efficacy of antitumor drugs (Yang et al., 2014).

Using the reverse phase process, Neda et al. generated drug-encapsulated liposomes by mixing various concentrations of phosphatidylcholine, artemisinin, and cholesterol, then evaporating them. PEGylated artemisinin-containing liposomes were also explored. With nanoformulation sizes of 500 and 455 nm, PEG—artemisinin—liposomes and artemisinin—liposomes entrapped 92% and 96% of artemisinin, respectively. These nanoformulations had lesser IC_{50} values as compared to pure artemisinin in cytotoxicity experiments on MCF-7 cells, PEGylated NPs were more effective due to the permeability of the PEG, which helped in the release (Neda et al., 2013).

Micelles

Micelles are amphiphilic surfactant lipid molecules that form spherical vesicles in water (Husseini & Pitt, 2008). It has hydrophilic heads on the surface and hydrophobic tails on the inside, allowing hydrophobic drugs to be protected from the outside environment. These are also useful for very less water-soluble drugs to improve their bioavailability (Palazzolo et al., 2018). The plant-based micelles are reported as MPEG—PCL-based micelles with curcumin and doxorubicin, which had 0.4% encapsulation efficiency on drug release. Pure drugs were likewise released at the same time and over a long period of time. CUR-DOX MPEG-PCL micelles showed stronger anticancer effects when compared to pure drugs that suppressed LL/2 lung cancer cell lines in biological experiment (Gao et al., 2013).

Polymeric micelles

Polymeric micelles (PMs) are self-assembled core–shell complexes with a lypophilic core and a lypophobic shell that form in selected solvents (Gothwal et al., 2016; Li et al., 2015). For increased solubility, Zhai and colleagues created pluronic P123- and solutol HS15-based apigenin-loaded PMs. PMs created employing a thin-film dispersion approach with 16.9 nm of diameter and a 96.36% entrapment efficacy. The apigenin released from the micelles was 84% after 36 h, which indicates the release pattern from the PMs. In a cytotoxicity study for HepG2 and MCF-7, higher inhibitions were reported in apigenin-loaded PMs as compared to pure drug. This happened due to the solubility of apigenin and the micelles absorption by the cell lines (Zhai et al., 2013). As carriers of hydrophobic anticancer drugs, PMs have been reported suitable for different parameters, such as high retention time, enhanced drug permeability, good drug encapsulation, better penetration ability, and as carriers for hydrophobic anticancer drugs (Cabral et al., 2011).

Dendrimers

Dendrimers are symmetric spherical shaped branched polymers having a diameter of 1–10 nm, which are produced chemically (Abbasi et al., 2014). They are generally made up of synthetic and natural polymers (i.e., sugar, amino acids, and nucleotides). Generally, drugs are entrapped in the core of dendrimer via electrostatic interactions, hydrogen bonds, or hydrophobic interactions. Lypophilic and lypophobic anticancer drugs could be linked covalently with the dendrimer surfaces. Depending on the linkers used, different parameters of drugs, such as solubility, effective concentration at target site, and release rate is regulated after attachment with various groups present on dendrimers (Sharma et al., 2017). Sharma and colleagues reported polyamidoamine (PAMAM)-based gallic acid dendrimers with the method related to Tomalia's divergent growth, which was further tested on MCF-7. The drug loading of these dendrimers has increased because of large surface utility and adaptability. In terms of IC_{50} values, gallic acid–loaded PAMAM dendrimers outperformed free gallic acid that demonstrated a promising nanoplatform for increased cytotoxicity in MCF-7 cell lines. Dendritic polymers could be easily functionalized due to unique qualities, such as minimal immunogenicity, water solubility, antigenicity, and high stability, which made them a viable drug delivery platform. Despite their promising features, dendrimers used in polymer therapeutics have a drawback like multistep synthesis due to which production costs always increased (Sharma et al., 2011).

Niosomes

Niosomes are nonlecithin carriers with more stability as compared to liposomes. They are nonionic surfactant-based vesicle systems featuring benefits, including biocompatibility, biodegradability, and the ability to encapsulate both hydrophilic and hydrophobic drugs (Marianecci et al., 2014). They were designed to circumvent liposome limits, particularly those related to phospholipid oxidation. Niosomes also offer reduced production costs, bilayer fluidity, longer shelf life, and microviscosity, which may be controlled easily (Pereira et al., 2016). Pereira et al. reported that the PHLIP-coated niosomes are more stable and smaller than the pHLIP-coated liposomes having pH-dependent cellular uptake with excellent tumor targeting. As a result, niosome contains hydrophilic and/or lipophilic drugs that could be entering the cells efficiently via pH-dependent mechanism. The plant-based noisome are also reported for the delivery of thymoquinone (TQ) that is found in *Carum carvi* L. seeds. Two distinct formulations comprising TQ and Carum (Nio/TQ and Nio/Carum, respectively) were also loaded inside the niosomes. Percent of entrapment efficiency of Carum- and TQ-loaded niosomes were about 86.25% ± 1.85 and 92.32% ± 2.32, respectively. In comparison to free TQ, both loaded formulations delivered a regulated release. MTT assays revealed that loaded niosomes have higher anticancer activity than free drugs against the MCF-7 cancer cell lines, and flow cytometric analyses validated these findings (Barani et al., 2019).

Nanoemulsions

On other hand the nanoemulsions are generally composed of four different compositions, such as water, oil, emulsifier, and coemulsifier in the proper proportions, with particles size from 10 to 100 nm in diameter (Jaiswal et al., 2015). These nanoemulsions have carried distinct properties, such as biodegradability, simplicity of manufacture, and regulated drug release, that could be extensively explored as drug carriers for hydrophobic chemotherapeutics (Gorain et al., 2020). Furthermore, nanoemulsions increase the drug solubility as well as prevent the drug inactivation in the gastrointestinal system, but also, allowing pharmaceuticals to be efficiently dispersed and absorbed, and hence improving drug bioavailability (Chime et al., 2014). Nanoemulsions are reported for holding strong biocompatibility due to the presence of safe grade excipients that enhance the entrapment efficiency of the hydrophobic components as well as better physicochemical stability and bioavailability with efficient efficacy and safety (Choudhury et al., 2017). Pine essential oil (*Pinus koraiensis*)-based nanoemulsions have been reported for anticancer activity against MGC-803 tumor-carrying nude mice (Zhang et al., 2020).

Bioderived nanocarriers

Bioderived nanocarriers play an important role in the delivery of anticancer drugs due to their high biocompatibility, stability, and biodegradability (Kumar et al., 2022; Nishimura et al., 2014). Nanocarriers made from synthetic polymers can include different compositions of surfactants and solvents, which might restrict their efficacy and generate toxicological problems (Kumar et al., 2022).

Protein-based nanocarriers are generally formulated with the help of animal-based protein (i.e., albumin, collagen, and gelatin), or plant-based protein (i.e., ferritin) has been lately studied for delivering the drugs (Kumar et al., 2022; Tarhini et al., 2017). Protein-based nanocarriers provide a number of benefits in terms of drug delivery, including biodegradability, ease of surface modification, lack of immunological reactions, and low toxicity. Since 1972, scientists have been researching the use of albumin-based NPs in biomedicine (Verma et al., 2018). Abraxane is a marketed product, prepared of albumin-bound paclitaxel nanocarriers, which are conjugated with anticancer drugs for the treatment of different cancers approved by the US Food and Drug Administration (FDA) (Ma & Mumper, 2013). On the other hand, the hollow protein nanocage of apoferritin (APO) undergoes assembly and disassembly of process after the removal of iron core with high applicability for the preparation of bioderived nanocarriers for cancer therapy (Dostalova et al., 2017).

Exosomes

Exosomes are nanosized extracellular vesicles found in different bodily fluids and are generally released from various types of cells and tissues (Syn et al., 2017). They also have a hydrophobic core and may store water-soluble drugs that make them a promising vehicle to deliver plant-based and other natural drugs. Exosomes have a natural targeting potential, which are stable and have a high capacity to cross biological barriers. Besides these properties, they are also less immunogenic as compared to other nanocarriers (Conlan et al., 2017; Srinivasan et al., 2016). Exosomes may contain a large number of bioactive compounds by nature. If the cargo of exosomes needs to be changed, it is very tough to load the extra drugs in the exosomes, since the damaged exosomes lacking exosomal signals might trigger unwanted immune responses (Johnsen et al., 2014). Zhang et al. prepared folic acid—based ginger-derived nanovectors (GDNVs) that behave like exosomes produced from edible ginger with higher biocompatibility rather than cationic liposomes. These NPs showed efficient properties for cancer targeting/therapeutics delivery (Zhang et al., 2016). The functions and structures of exosomes will be better understood in the therapeutic setting of exosome treatment (Luan et al., 2017).

Solid lipid nanoparticles

For several drugs, solid lipid NPs (SLNPs) have broad applicability for delivering anticancer drugs as a nanocarrier system. These particles are made up of lipids and range in size from 50 to 1000 nm. They are stable at both room and body temperatures. Lipid acids, mono-, di-, or triglycerides, glyceride mixes, or waxes stabilized with biocompatible surfactants are among the lipids utilized to make SLNPs. Meanwhile, SLNPs have different properties, such as physical stability, protection of drugs from degradation, controlled release, and ease of preparation over other drug delivery systems. The manufacture of SLNPs is quite inexpensive and might be performed on a large scale. SLNPs have far less storage and drug leakage issues than liposomes (Ekambaram et al., 2012). Xu et al. used the thin film hydration method to make silibinin-containing TPGS and phosphatidylcholine SLNPs, which were tested against MDA-MB-231 cancer cell lines. The results showed that SLNPs had nearly double the cellular absorption of free silibinin. Same results in cell viability, invasion, and migration experiments backed up these claims. They discovered that suppressing the invasive and migratory properties of MDA-MB-231 cells at 20 mg/mL of SLNPs via downregulating of the MMP-9 and Snail pathways (Kumar et al., 2021; Xu et al., 2013).

Plant-based compounds used in cancer therapy

Various researches on polyphenols, triterpenoids, flavonoids, alkaloids, and their derivatives have revealed a possible cancer-fighting mechanism that could target particular areas individually or in combination with different active chemicals and can be used for novel drug delivery system (Le Marchand, 2002; Sharma et al., 2022; Yadav et al., 2021). In order to promote the unique application in medical field, nanotechnology plays an important role in the creation of nanobased materials for different application including biomedical (Honary et al., 2015; Verma et al., 2019).

Table 8.1 shows a list of different medicinal plants and their phytochemicals together with their anticancer properties. Several researchers have been reported the effectiveness of medicinal plants and their extracts against cancer. Plants containing different phytoconstituents have revealed a potential mechanism against cancer either alone or in combination (Le Marchand, 2002; Regassa et al., 2022).

Nanotechnology plays critical role in the development of NPs in order to advance the novel application in the field of medicine (Honary et al., 2015; Verma et al., 2019). In Table 8.2, various compounds discovered in medicinal plants and their phytochemicals are reported which can cause cytotoxicity in a variety of malignant cells and can be used for nanodrug delivery system.

Future prospects and barriers of nanomaterials for cancer therapy

Nanomedicine involves several types of NPs as possible diagnostic and treatment tools for cancer (Rao et al., 2016; von Roemeling et al., 2017). Photosynthesized NPs have a promising future due to their environmental friendliness, low cost, and good biocompatibility (Ovais et al., 2018). In the near future, plant-based metallic NPs are expected to have potential cancer treatment agents, either alone or in conjunction

Table 8.1 List of various medicinal plants and their phytochemicals with different anticancer activity.

S. no.	Plants	Phytochemicals	Anticancer activity	Reference
1.	*Aloe vera*	Aloin	Inhibition of different human neuroectodermal tumors	Pecere et al. (2000)
2.	*Apium graveolens*	Polyacetylenes	Leukemia cell lines	Zidorn et al. (2005)
3.	*Alisma orientale*	Triterpenes	MDA-MB-231, MCF-7 and HepG2, cell lines	Xu et al. (2015)
4.	*Aristolochia cucurbitifolia*	Isoquinoline alkaloids and their derivatives	Human liver cancer cells	Wu et al. (2004)
5.	*Aristolochia manshuriensis*	Isoquinoline alkaloids and derivatives	Bone cancer	Wu et al. (2004)
6.	*Atractylodes macrocephala*	Sesquiterpenes	Lung carcinoma cells	Wu et al. (2004)
7.	*Withania somnifera*	Alkaloids	Dalton ascitic lymphoma	Christina et al. (2004)
8.	*Winchia calophylla*	Indole alkaloids	A-549 and P-388 tumor cell lines	Gan et al. (2006)
9.	*Petroselinum crispum*	Polyacetylenes	Leukemia cell lines	Zidorn et al. (2005)
10.	*Nauclea orientalis*	Isoquinoline alkaloids and derivatives	Lung cancer	Sichaem et al. (2010)
11.	*Juglans mandshurica*	Quinones	Lung cancer	Li et al. (2007)

Table 8.2 List of plant-based anticancer compounds and their anticancer activity.

S. no.	Compound	Source	Anticancer activities	References
1.	Colchicine	*Colchium autumnale*	Multiple solid tumors via inhibition of matrix metalloproteases)	Wei et al. (2019)
2.	Combretastatin	*Combretum caffrum*	Human breast cancer Combretum	Dark et al. (1997)
3.	Vinorelbine	Periwinkle plant (*Vinca species*)	Breast cancer	Canobbio et al. (1991)
4.	Vindesine	*Catharanthus roseus*	Lymphomas; breast and lung cancers; Kaposi's sarcoma, Leukemias; advanced testicular cancer	Cragg and Newman (2005)
5.	Resveratrol	Berries and grapes, peanut seeds, polygonum roots	Colorectal tumor SW480 cells and hepatoblastoma HepG2	Latruffe et al. (2002)
6.	Podophyllotoxin	*Podophyllum peltatum*	Testicular and bronchial cancers	Issell (1982)
7.	Paclitaxel	*Taxus brevifolia*	Ovarian cancer and Breast cancer	Cragg and Newman (2005)
8.	Larotaxel	*Taxus baccata*	Bladder cancer, pancreatic cancer, breast cancer	Risinger et al. (2009)
9.	Docetaxol	*Taxus species*	Ovarian cancer, Breast cancer	Cragg and Newman (2005)
10.	Isoliquiritigenin	*Glycyrrhiza uralensis*	A549 lung cancer cell line	Jung et al. (2014)
11.	Cabazitaxel	*T. baccata*	Prostate cancer	De Bono et al. (2010)
12.	2S-abyssinone II Verubulin	*Broussonetia papyrifera*	Glioblastoma; brain tumors	Maiti et al. (2007), Chamberlain et al. (2014), Mahal et al. (2014)
13.	Vinflunine	*C. roseus* (L.) G. Don (Apocynaceae)	Breast and lung cancers; testicular cancer; Kaposi's sarcoma	Cragg and Newman (2005)
14.	Vincristine	*C. roseus G. Don.*	cytotoxicity, depolymerisation of tubulin	Cragg and Newman (2005)

with anticancer drugs approved by FDA. More researches are needed to identify the precise role of phytochemicals in metallic NP formation, stability, and therapeutic potential. Biological components, such as aptamers, antibodies, peptides, and different small molecules can also be bonded to the surface of these metallic NPs to target a specific receptor in cancer cell lines (Hauert & Bhatia, 2014). These NPs can also be conjugated with anticancer drugs and delivered to their intended targets. Furthermore, the heat treatment of these biogenic metallic NPs could pave the path for new cancer nanomedicines. After the NPs reached to their target sites, external energy sources such as optics or magnetism can damage them, allowing the NPs to heat in vivo in a localized area and caused death in cancer cells (Panchapakesan & Wickstrom, 2007). Overall, creating functionalized NPs in conjunction with different biological and computational approaches is the next frontier. Regardless of the fact that nanocarriers have set the path for a breakthrough in cancer nanotherapy, and there are indeed significant challenges ahead. Before applicability of plant-based NPs in clinical trials for cancer diagnosis and treatment, more study is needed to confirm their biocompatibility and biodegradability, as well as their absorption, retention, clearance, dose, and delivery method (Ovais et al., 2016; Yadav et al., 2021). NPs diffuse incorrectly throughout diseased tissues due to biophysical impediments such as increased osmotic pressures within malignant cells. As a result, various approaches to circumventing biophysical barriers have been proposed, such as surface modifiers. Furthermore, the interactions of plant-derived NPs with proteins, such as tubulin and ubiquitin, should be explored further, formation of protein-based NPs may unanticipated in vivo effects and biological functions (Neda et al., 2013; Ovais et al., 2016). Clinical studies on the toxicity of plant-based NPs are lacking; thus future study should focus on identifying the harmfull effects associated with their use before putting the procedure through clinical trials.

Conclusion

More than 65% of anticancer drugs have come from natural sources in the last 25 years. Chemical synthesis (partial or complete) has been critical in supplying large quantities of naturally derived chemicals as well as developing new analogs. Many chemical compounds have very low bioavailability and solubility; nanotechnology allows for increased drug bioavailability, circulation time, and multiple drugs loading, which lead to the improvement of efficacy and lower toxicity. Plant-based NPs are currently being utilized to treat and diagnose cancer in a laboratory setting. Several researches have been undertaken in recent years due to the biocompatibility and efficacy of these plant-based NPs as cancer therapeutic agents. Flavonoids, phenolic compounds, alkaloids, flavanols, terpenes, steroids, and a variety of other secondary metabolites found in plants have been demonstrated to kill malignant cells. As a result, more research is needed to determine if secondary metabolites found in plant extracts have a good or detrimental impact on the anticancer efficacy of these NPs. Despite the challenges, we believe phytochemical-based nanocarriers will soon become a contender in cancer nanomedicine.

Acknowledgment

Authors (Monu Kumar Shukla, Anik Kumar Das, Anshuman Gaurav, and Deepak Kumar) are grateful to Vice Chancellor, Shoolini University for providing the necessary support for carrying out this work.

References

Abbasi, E., Aval, S. F., Akbarzadeh, A., Milani, M., Nasrabadi, H. T., Joo, S. W., Hanifehpour, Y., Nejati-Koshki, K., & Pashaei-Asl, R. (2014). Dendrimers: Synthesis, applications, and properties. *Nanoscale Research Letters*, *9*(1), 247. Available from https://doi.org/10.1186/1556-276X-9-247.

Adams, G. P., Schier, R., McCall, A. M., Simmons, H. H., Horak, E. M., Alpaugh, R. K., Marks, J. D., & Weiner, L. M. (2001). High affinity restricts the localization and tumor penetration of single-chain fv antibody molecules. *Cancer Research*, *61*(12), 4750–4755. Available from https://doi.org/10.1155/2020/9184284.

Aliosmanoglu, A., & Basaran, I. (2012). Nanotechnology in cancer treatment. *Journal of Nanomedicine and Biotherapeutic Discovery*, *2*, 1–3. Available from https://doi.org/10.4172/2155-983X.1000107.

Andleeb, A., Andleeb, A., Asghar, S., Zaman, G., Tariq, M., Mehmood, A., Nadeem, M., Hano, C., Lorenzo, J. M., & Abbasi, B. H. (2021). A systematic review of biosynthesized metallic nanoparticles as a promising anti-cancer-strategy. *Cancers*, *13*(11), 2818. Available from https://doi.org/10.3390/cancers13112818.

Barani, M., Mirzaei, M., Torkzadeh-Mahani, M., & Adeli-Sardou, M. (2019). Evaluation of carum-loaded niosomes on breast cancer cells: Physicochemical properties, in vitro cytotoxicity, flow cytometric, DNA fragmentation and cell migration assay. *Scientific Reports*, *9*(1). Available from https://doi.org/10.1038/s41598-019-43755-w.

Basile, L., Pignatello, R., & Passirani, C. (2012). Active targeting strategies for anticancer drug nanocarriers. *Current Drug Delivery*, *9*(3), 255–268. Available from https://doi.org/10.2174/156720112800389089.

Bayda, S., Adeel, M., Tuccinardi, T., Cordani, M., & Rizzolio, F. (2020). The history of nanoscience and nanotechnology: From chemical-physical applications to nanomedicine. *Molecules (Basel, Switzerland)*, *25*(1), 1–15. Available from https://doi.org/10.3390/molecules25010112.

Buse, J., & El-Aneed, A. (2010). Properties, engineering and applications of lipid-based nanoparticle drug-delivery systems: Current research and advances. *Nanomedicine (London, England)*, *5*(8), 1237–1260. Available from https://doi.org/10.2217/nnm.10.107.

Cabral, H., Matsumoto, Y., Mizuno, K., Chen, Q., Murakami, M., Kimura, M., Terada, Y., Kano, M. R., Miyazono, K., Uesaka, M., Nishiyama, N., & Kataoka, K. (2011). Accumulation of sub-100 nm polymeric micelles in poorly permeable tumours depends on size. *Nature Nanotechnology*, *6*(12), 815–823. Available from https://doi.org/10.1038/nnano.2011.166.

Canobbio, L., Boccardo, F., Guarneri, D., Calabria, C., Decensi, A., Curotto, A., Martorana, G., & Giuliani, L. (1991). Phase II study of navelbine in advanced renal cell carcinoma. *European Journal of Cancer and Clinical Oncology*, *27*(6), 804–805. Available from https://pubmed.ncbi.nlm.nih.gov/2711204/.

Capek, I. (2006). Nanotechnology and nanomaterials. *Nanocomposite structures and dispersions: Science and Nanotechnology: Fundamental Principles and Colloidal Particles (Studies in Interface Science)*, *1*, 1–69. Available from. Available from http://www.amazon.co.uk/Nanocomposite-structures-dispersions-Nanotechnology.

Chamberlain, M. C., Grimm, S., Phuphanich, S., Recht, L., Zhu, J. Z., Kim, L., Rosenfeld, S., & Fadul, C. E. (2014). A phase 2 trial of verubulin for recurrent glioblastoma: A prospective study by the

Brain Tumor Investigational Consortium (BTIC). *Journal of Neuro-oncology, 118*(2), 335–343. Available from https://doi.org/10.1007/s11060-014-1437-y.

Chandratre, S. S., & Dash, A. K. (2015). Multifunctional nanoparticles for prostate cancer therapy. *AAPS PharmSciTech, 16*(1), 98–107. Available from https://doi.org/10.1208/s12249-014-0202-z.

Chi, X., Liu, K., Luo, X., Yin, Z., Lin, H., & Gao, J. (2020). Recent advances of nanomedicines for liver cancer therapy. *Journal of Materials Chemistry B., 8*(17), 3747–3771. Available from https://doi.org/10.1039/C9TB02871D.

Chime, S. A., Kenechukwu, F. C., & Attama, A. A. (2014). Nanoemulsions—Advances in formulation, characterization and applications in drug delivery. *Application of Nanotechnology in Drug Delivery, 25*(3), 77–126. Available from https://doi.org/10.5772/58673.

Cho, K., Wang, X. U., Nie, S., & Shin, D. M. (2008). Therapeutic nanoparticles for drug delivery in cancer. *Clinical Cancer Research, 14*(5), 1310–1316. Available from https://doi.org/10.4236/ajps.2015.619300.

Choudhury, H., Gorain, B., Chatterjee, B., K Mandal, U., Sengupta, P., & K Tekade, R. (2017). Pharmacokinetic and pharmacodynamic features of nanoemulsion following oral, intravenous, topical and nasal route. *Current Pharmaceutical Design, 23*(17), 2504–2531. Available from https://doi.org/10.2174/1381612822666161201143600, 1.

Christina, A. J., Joseph, D. G., Packialakshmi, M., Kothai, R., Robert, S. J., Chidambaranathan, N., & Ramasamy, M. (2004). Anticarcinogenic activity of *Withania somnifera* Dunal against Dalton's ascitic lymphoma. *Journal of Ethnopharmacology, 93*(2–3), 359–361. Available from https://doi.org/10.1016/j.jep.2004.04.004, 1.

Conlan, R. S., Pisano, S., Oliveira, M. I., Ferrari, M., & Pinto, I. M. (2017). Exosomes as reconfigurable therapeutic systems. *Trends in Molecular Medicine, 23*(7), 636–650. Available from https://doi.org/10.1016/j.molmed.2017.05.003, 1.

Cooper, G. M., & Hausman, R. E. (2007). The development and causes of cancer. *The Cell: A Molecular Approach*, 743. Available from. Available from http://www.ncbi.nlm.nih.gov/books/NBK9963.

Cragg, G. M., & Newman, D. J. (2005). Plants as a source of anti-cancer agents. *Journal of Ethnopharmacology, 100*(1–2), 72–79. Available from https://doi.org/10.1016/j.jep.2005.05.011.

Dark, G. G., Hill, S. A., Prise, V. E., Tozer, G. M., Pettit, G. R., & Chaplin, D. J. (1997). Combretastatin A-4, an agent that displays potent and selective toxicity toward tumor vasculature. *Cancer Research, 57*(10), 1829–1834, 15. Available from http://www.ncbi.nlm.nih.gov/pubmed/9157969.

De Bono, J. S., Oudard, S., Ozguroglu, M., Hansen, S., Machiels, J. P., Kocak, I., Gravis, G., Bodrogi, I., Mackenzie, M. J., Shen, L., & Roessner, M. (2010). Prednisone plus cabazitaxel or mitoxantrone for metastatic castration-resistant prostate cancer progressing after docetaxel treatment: A randomised open-label trial. *The Lancet, 376*(9747), 1147–1154. Available from https://doi.org/10.1016/S0140-6736(10)61389-X, 2.

Dostalova, S., Vasickova, K., Hynek, D., Krizkova, S., Richtera, L., Vaculovicova, M., Eckschlager, T., Stiborova, M., Heger, Z., & Adam, V. (2017). Apoferritin as an ubiquitous nanocarrier with excellent shelf life. *International Journal of Nanomedicine, 12*, 2265. Available from https://doi.org/10.2147/IJN.S130267.

Duncan, R. (2003). The dawning era of polymer therapeutics. *Nature Reviews. Drug Discovery, 2*(5), 347–360. Available from https://doi.org/10.1038/nrd1088.

Ekambaram, P., Sathali, A. H., & Priyanka, K. (2012). Solid lipid nanoparticles: A review. *Scientific Reviews and Chemical Communications., 2*(1). Available from https://www.tsijournals.com/articles/solid-lipid-nanoparticles-a-review.pdf.

Emilian Leucuta, S. (2010). Nanotechnology for delivery of drugs and biomedical applications. *Current Clinical Pharmacology, 5*(4), 257–280. Available from https://doi.org/10.2174/157488410793352003.

Fang, C.-L., Al-Suwayeh, A., Fang, S., & Nanostructured, J.-Y. (2012). Lipid carriers (NLCs) for drug delivery and targeting. *Recent Patents on Nanotechnology*, 7(1), 41–55. Available from https://doi.org/10.2174/187221051130701 0041.

Ferrari, M. (2005). Cancer nanotechnology: Opportunities and challenges. *Nature Reviews. Cancer, 5*(3), 161–171. Available from https://doi.org/10.1038/nrc1566.

Gabizon, A. A. (2001). Pegylated liposomal doxorubicin: Metamorphosis of an old drug into a new form of chemotherapy. *Cancer Investigation*, *19*(4), 424–436. Available from https://doi.org/10.1081/cnv-100103136.

Gan, L. S., Yang, S. P., Wu, Y., Ding, J., & Yue, J. M. (2006). Terpenoid indole alkaloids from *Winchia calophylla*. *Journal of Natural Products*, *69*(1), 18–22. Available from https://doi.org/10.1021/np0502701, 27.

Gao, X., Luo, W., Li, Z., Qian, L., Shi, F., & Liu, M. (2013). Codelivery of curcumin and doxorubicin by MPEG-PCL results in improved efficacy of systemically administered chemotherapy in mice with lung cancer. *International Journal of Nanomedicine*, *8*, 3521. Available from https://doi.org/10.2147/IJN.S45250.

Gorain, B., Choudhury, H., Nair, A. B., Dubey, S. K., & Kesharwani, P. (2020). Theranostic application of nanoemulsions in chemotherapy. *Drug Discovery Today*, *25*(7), 1174–1188. Available from https://doi.org/10.1016/j.drudis.2020.04.013, 1.

Gosk, S., Moos, T., Gottstein, C., & Bendas, G. (2008). VCAM-1 directed immunoliposomes selectively target tumor vasculature in vivo. *Biochimica et Biophysica Acta*, *1778*(4), 854–863. Available from https://doi.org/10.1016/j.bbamem.2007.12.021.

Gothwal, A., Khan, I., & Gupta, U. (2016). Polymeric micelles: Recent advancements in the delivery of anticancer drugs. *Pharmaceutical Research*, *33*(1), 18–39. Available from https://doi.org/10.1007/s11095-015-1784-1.

Granja, A., Pinheiro, M., & Reis, S. (2016). Epigallocatechin gallate nanodelivery systems for cancer therapy. *Nutrients.*, *8*(5), 307. Available from https://doi.org/10.3390/nu8050307.

Gulia, K., James, A., Pandey, S., Dev, K., Kumar, D., & Sourirajan, A. (2022). Bio-inspired smart nanoparticles in enhanced cancer theranostics and targeted drug delivery. *Journal of Functional Biomaterials*, *13*(4), 207. Available from https://doi.org/10.3390/jfb13040207.

Haley, B., & Frenkel, E. (2008). Nanoparticles for drug delivery in cancer treatment. *Urologic Oncology*, *26*(1), 57–64. Available from https://doi.org/10.1016/j.urolonc.2007.03.015.

Harris, E., & Tanner, M. (2000). Health technology transfer. *British Medical Journal*, *321*(7264), 817–820. Available from https://doi.org/10.1136/bmj.321.7264.817.

Hauert, S., & Bhatia, S. N. (2014). Mechanisms of cooperation in cancer nanomedicine: Towards systems nanotechnology. *Trends in Biotechnology*, *32*(9), 448–455. Available from https://doi.org/10.1016/j.tibtech.2014.06.010, 1.

Honary, S., Barabadi, H., Ebrahimi, P., Naghibi, F., & Alizadeh, A. (2015). Development and optimization of biometal nanoparticles by using mathematical methodology: A microbial approach. *Journal of Nano Research*, *30*, 106–115. Available from https://doi.org/10.4028/http://www.scientific.net/JNanoR.30.106.

Husseini, G. A., & Pitt, W. G. (2008). Micelles and nanoparticles for ultrasonic drug and gene delivery. *Advanced Drug Delivery Reviews*, *60*(10), 1137–1152. Available from https://doi.org/10.1016/j.addr.2008.03.008, 2008.

Issell, B. F. (1982). The podophyllotoxin derivatives VP16-213 and VM26. *Cancer Chemotherapy and Pharmacology*, 7(2), 73–80. Available from https://doi.org/10.1007/BF00254525.

Jaiswal, M., Dudhe, R., & Sharma, P. K. (2015). Nano emulsion: An advanced mode of drug delivery system. *3 Biotech*, *5*(2), 123–127. Available from https://doi.org/10.1007/s13205-014-0214-0.

Javed Iqbal, M., Quispe, C., Javed, Z., Sadia, H., Qadri, Q. R., Raza, S., Salehi, B., Cruz-Martins, N., Abdulwanis Mohamed, Z., Sani Jaafaru, M., Abdull Razis, A. F., & Sharifi-Rad, J. (2021). Nanotechnology-based strategies for berberine delivery system in cancer treatment: Pulling strings to keep berberine in power. *Frontiers in Molecular Biosciences*, *2021*(7), 1–12. Available from https://doi.org/10.3389/fmolb.2020.624494.

Jeetah, R., Bhaw-Luximon, A., & Jhurry, D. (2014). Nanopharmaceutics: Phytochemical-based controlled or sustained drug-delivery systems for cancer treatment. *Journal of Biomedical Nanotechnology*, *10*(9), 1810–1840. Available from https://doi.org/10.1166/jbn.2014.1884.

Johnsen, K. B., Gudbergsson, J. M., Skov, M. N., Pilgaard, L., Moos, T., & Duroux, M. (2014). A comprehensive overview of exosomes as drug delivery vehicles—Endogenous nanocarriers for targeted cancer therapy. *Biochimica et Biophysica Acta (BBA)-Reviews on Cancer*, *1846*(1), 75–87. Available from https://doi.org/10.1016/j.bbcan.2014.04.005, 1.

Jung, S. K., Lee, M. H., Kim, J. E., Singh, P., Lee, S. Y., Jeong, C. H., Lim, T. G., Chen, H., Chi, Y. I., Kundu, J. K., & Lee, N. H. (2014). Isoliquiritigenin induces apoptosis and inhibits xenograft tumor growth of human lung cancer cells by targeting both wild type and L858R/T790M mutant EGFR. *Journal of Biological Chemistry, 289*(52), 35839–35848. Available from https://doi.org/10.1074/jbc.M114.585513, 26.

Khan, I., Saeed, K., & Khan, I. (2019). Nanoparticles: Properties, applications and toxicities. *Arabian Journal of Chemistry [Internet], 12*(7), 908–931. Available from https://doi.org/10.1016/j.arabjc.2017.05.011. Available from.

Khan, T., & Gurav, P. (2018). Phytonanotechnology: Enhancing delivery of plant based anti-cancer drugs. *Frontiers in Pharmacology, 8*, 1002. Available from https://doi.org/10.3389/fphar.2017.01002, Feb 9.

Khan, S., Imran, M., Butt, T. T., Ali Shah, S. W., Sohail, M., Malik, A., Das, S., Thu, H. E., Adam, A., & Hussain, Z. (2018). Curcumin based nanomedicines as efficient nanoplatform for treatment of cancer: New developments in reversing cancer drug resistance, rapid internalization, and improved anticancer efficacy. *Trends in Food Science & Technology, 80*, 8–22. Available from https://doi.org/10.1016/j.tifs.2018.07.026.

Kumar, A., Singh, K. R., Ghate, M. D., Lalhlenmawia, H., Kumar, D., & Singh, J. (2022). Bioinspired quantum dots for cancer therapy: A mini-review. *Materials Letters, 19*, 131742. Available from https://doi.org/10.1016/j.matlet.2022.131742.

Kumar, A., Sharipov, M., Turaev, A., Azizov, S., Azizov, I., Edwin, M., Abbas, R., et al. (2022). Polymer-based hybrid nanoarchitectures for cancer therapy applications. *Polymers, 14*(15), 3027. Available from https://doi.org/10.3390/polym14153027.

Kumar, S., Sharma, A. K., Lalhlenmawia, H., & Kumar, D. (2021). *Natural compounds targeting major signaling pathways in lung cancer. Targeting Cellular Signalling Pathways in Lung Diseases* (pp. 821–846). Available from https://link.springer.com/chapter/10.1007/978-981-33-6827-9_37.

Kumar, A., Singh, K. R. B., Ghate, M. D., Lalhlenmawia, H., Kumar, D., & Singh, J. (2022). Bioinspired quantum dots for cancer therapy: A mini-review. *Materials Letters, 313*, 131742. Available from https://doi.org/10.1016/j.matlet.2022.131742.

Lalley, J., Dionysiou, D. D., Varma, R. S., Shankara, S., Yang, D. J., & Nadagouda, M. N. (2014). Silver-based antibacterial surfaces for drinking water disinfection—An overview. *Current Opinion in Chemical Engineering, 1*(3), 25–29. Available from https://d1wqtxts1xzle7.cloudfront.net/43443955.

Latruffe, N., Delmas, D., Jannin, B., Malki, M. C., Passilly-Degrace, P., & Berlot, J. P. (2002). Molecular analysis on the chemopreventive properties of resveratrol, a plant polyphenol microcomponent. *International Journal of Molecular Medicine, 10*(6), 755–760. Available from https://doi.org/10.3892/ijmm.10.6.755.

Le Marchand, L. (2002). Cancer preventive effects of flavonoids—A review. *Biomedicine & Pharmacotherapy, 56*(6), 296–301. Available from https://doi.org/10.1016/S0753-3322(02)00186-5.

Li, Z. B., Wang, J. Y., Jiang, B., Zhang, X. L., An, L. J., & Bao, Y. M. (2007). Benzobijuglone, a novel cytotoxic compound from *Juglans mandshurica*, induced apoptosis in HeLa cervical cancer cells. *Phytomedicine: International Journal of Phytotherapy and Phytopharmacology, 14*(12), 846–852. Available from https://doi.org/10.1016/j.phymed.2007.09.004, 4.

Li, W., Huang, L., Ying, X., Jian, Y., Hong, Y., Hu, F., & Du, Y. (2015). Antitumor drug delivery modulated by a polymeric micelle with an upper critical solution temperature. *Angewandte Chemie International Edition, 54*(10), 3126–3131. Available from https://doi.org/10.1002/anie.201411524.

Luan, X., Sansanaphongpricha, K., Myers, I., Chen, H., Yuan, H., & Sun, D. (2017). Engineering exosomes as refined biological nanoplatforms for drug delivery. *Acta Pharmacologica Sinica, 38*(6), 754–763. Available from https://doi.org/10.1038/aps.2017.12.

Ma, P., & Mumper, R. J. (2013). Paclitaxel nano-delivery systems: A comprehensive review. *Journal of Nanomedicine & Nanotechnology, 4*(2), 1000164. Available from https://doi.org/10.4172/2157-7439.1000164, 18.

Maeda, H. (2010). Tumor-selective delivery of macromolecular drugs via the EPR effect: Background and future prospects. *Bioconjugate Chemistry, 21*(5), 797–802. Available from https://doi.org/10.1021/bc100070g.

Mahal, K., Resch, M., Ficner, R., Schobert, R., Biersack, B., & Mueller, T. (2014). Effects of the tumor-vasculature-disrupting agent verubulin and two heteroaryl analogues on cancer cells, endothelial cells, and blood vessels. *ChemMedChem*, *9*(4), 847–854. Available from https://doi.org/10.1002/cmdc.201300531.

Maiti, A., Cuendet, M., Croy, V. L., Endringer, D. C., Pezzuto, J. M., & Cushman, M. (2007). Synthesis and biological evaluation of (±)-abyssinone II and its analogues as aromatase inhibitors for chemoprevention of breast cancer. *Journal of Medicinal Chemistry*, *50*(12), 2799–2806. Available from https://doi.org/10.1021/jm070109i, 14.

Mansoori, G. A., Mohazzabi, P., McCormack, P., & Jabbari, S. (2007). Nanotechnology in cancer prevention, detection and treatment: Bright future lies ahead. *World Review of Science, Technology and Sustainable Development*, *4*(2-3), 226–257. Available from https://doi.org/10.1504/WRSTSD.2007.013584.

Marianecci, C., Di Marzio, L., Rinaldi, F., Celia, C., Paolino, D., Alhaique, F., Esposito, S., & Carafa, M. (2014). Niosomes from 80s to present: The state of the art. *Advances in Colloid and Interface Science*, *1*(205), 187–206. Available from https://doi.org/10.1016/j.cis.2013.11.018.

Neda, D., Dariush, N., Mohsen, C., Hassan, E. S., Mohammadreza, M. S., Ali, F., & Akbarzadeh, A. (2013). Effect of artemisinin liposome and artemisinin liposome polyethyleneglycol on MCF-7 cell line. *International Journal of Life Sciences Biotechnology and Pharma Research*, *2*, 349–355. Available from http://doi = 10.1.1.300.9719&rep = rep1&type = pdf.

Nie, S., Xing, Y., Kim, G. J., & Simons, J. W. (2007). Nanotechnology applications in cancer. *Annual Review of Biomedical Engineering*, *9*(1), 257–288. Available from https://doi.org/10.1146/annurev.bioeng.9.060906.152025.

Nishimura, Y., Ishii, J., Ogino, C., & Kondo, A. (2014). Genetic engineering of bio-nanoparticles for drug delivery: A review. *Journal of Biomedical Nanotechnology*, *10*(9), 2063–2085. Available from https://doi.org/10.1166/jbn.2014.1951, 1.

Ovais, M., Khalil, A. T., Islam, N. U., Ahmad, I., Ayaz, M., Saravanan, M., Shinwari, Z. K., & Mukherjee, S. (2018). Role of plant phytochemicals and microbial enzymes in biosynthesis of metallic nanoparticles. *Applied Microbiology and Biotechnology*, *102*(16), 6799–6814. Available from https://doi.org/10.1007/s00253-018-9146-7.

Ovais, M., Khalil, A. T., Raza, A., Khan, M. A., Ahmad, I., Islam, N. U., Saravanan, M., Ubaid, M. F., Ali, M., & Shinwari, Z. K. (2016). Green synthesis of silver nanoparticles via plant extracts: Beginning a new era in cancer theranostics. *Nanomedicine: Nanotechnology, Biology, and Medicine*, *12*(23), 3157–3177. Available from https://doi.org/10.2217/nnm-2016-0279.

Palazzolo, S., Bayda, S., Hadla, M., Caligiuri, I., Corona, G., Toffoli, G., & Rizzolio, F. (2018). The clinical translation of organic nanomaterials for cancer therapy: A focus on polymeric nanoparticles, micelles, liposomes and exosomes. *Current Medicinal Chemistry*, *25*(34), 4224–4268. Available from https://doi.org/10.2174/0929867324666170830113755.

Panchapakesan, B., & Wickstrom, E. (2007). Nanotechnology for sensing, imaging, and treating cancer. *Surgical Oncology Clinics of North America*, *16*(2), 293–305. Available from https://doi.org/10.1016/j.soc.2007.03.002, 1.

Patra, J. K., Das, G., Fraceto, L. F., Campos, E. V., Rodriguez-Torres, M. D., Acosta-Torres, L. S., Diaz-Torres, L. A., Grillo, R., Swamy, M. K., Sharma, S., & Habtemariam, S. (2018). Nano based drug delivery systems: Recent developments and future prospects. *Journal of Nanobiotechnology*, *16*(1), 1–33. Available from https://doi.org/10.1186/s12951-018-0392-8.

Pecere, T., Gazzola, M. V., Mucignat, C., Parolin, C., Dalla Vecchia, F., Cavaggioni, A., Basso, G., Diaspro, A., Salvato, B., Carli, M., & Palu, G. (2000). Aloe-emodin is a new type of anticancer agent with selective activity against neuroectodermal tumors. *Cancer Research*, *60*(11), 2800–2804, 1. Available from http://www.ncbi.nlm.nih.gov/pubmed/10850417.

Pereira, M. C., Pianella, M., Wei, D., Moshnikova, A., Marianecci, C., Carafa, M., Andreev, O. A., & Reshetnyak, Y. K. (2016). pH-sensitive pHLIP® coated niosomes. *Molecular Membrane Biology*, *33*(3-5), 51–63. Available from https://doi.org/10.1080/09687688.2017.1342969, 3.

Prasad, M., Lambe, U. P., Brar, B., Shah, I., J M., Ranjan, K., et al. (2018). Nanotherapeutics: An insight into healthcare and multi-dimensional applications in medical sector of the modern world. *Biomedicine & Pharmacotherapy = Biomedecine & Pharmacotherapie*, *97*, 1521–1537. Available from https://doi.org/10.1016/j.biopha.2017.11.026.

Ramos, A. P., Cruz, M. A. E., Tovani, C. B., & Ciancaglini, P. (2017). Biomedical applications of nanotechnology. *Biophysical Reviews*, *9*(2), 79–89. Available from https://doi.org/10.1007/s12551-016-0246-2. Available from.

Rao, P. V., Nallappan, D., Madhavi, K., Rahman, S., Jun Wei, L., & Gan, S. H. (2016). Phytochemicals and biogenic metallic nanoparticles as anticancer agents. *Oxidative Medicine and Cellular Longevity*, *2016*. Available from https://doi.org/10.1155/2016/3685671, Jan 1.

Regassa, H., Sourirajan, A., Kumar, V., Sadanand, P., Kumar, D., & Dev, K. (2022). A review of medicinal plants of the himalayas with anti-proliferative activity for the treatment of various Cancers. *Cancers*, *14* (16), 3898. Available from https://doi.org/10.3390/cancers14163898.

Risinger, A. L., Giles, F. J., & Mooberry, S. L. (2009). Microtubule dynamics as a target in oncology. *Cancer Treatment Reviews*, *35*(3), 255–261. Available from https://doi.org/10.1016/j.ctrv.2008.11.001, 1.

Sandha, K. K., Shukla, M. K., & Gupta, P. N. (2020). Recent advances in strategies for extracellular matrix degradation and synthesis inhibition for improved therapy of solid tumors. *Current Pharmaceutical Design*, *26*(42), 5456–5467. Available from https://doi.org/10.2174/1381612826666200728141601.

Schluep, T., Hwang, J., Hildebrandt, I. J., Czernin, J., Choi, C. H., Alabi, C. A., Mack, B. C., & Davis, M. E. (2009). Pharmacokinetics and tumor dynamics of the nanoparticle IT-101 from PET imaging and tumor histological measurements. *Proceedings of the National Academy of Sciences*, *106*(27), 11394–11399. Available from https://doi.org/10.1073/pnas.090548710620.

Sharma, A., Gautam, S. P., & Gupta, A. K. (2011). Surface modified dendrimers: Synthesis and characterization for cancer targeted drug delivery. *Bioorganic & Medicinal Chemistry*, *19*(11), 3341–3346. Available from https://doi.org/10.1016/j.bmc.2011.04.046, 1.

Sharma, A., Nagraik, R., Venkidasamy, B., Khan, A., Dulta, K., Chauhan, P. K., Kumar, D., & Shin, D. S. (2022). In-vitro antidiabetic, antioxidant, antimicrobial and cytotoxic activity of *Murraya koenigii* leaf extract Intercedes ZnO nanoparticles. *Luminescence: The Journal of Biological and Chemical Luminescence*. Available from https://doi.org/10.1002/bio.4244, Apr 1.

Sharma, A. K., Gothwal, A., Kesharwani, P., Alsaab, H., Iyer, A. K., & Gupta, U. (2017). Dendrimer nanoarchitectures for cancer diagnosis and anticancer drug delivery. *Drug Discovery Today*, *22*(2), 314–326. Available from https://doi.org/10.1016/j.drudis.2016.09.013, 1.

Shukla, M. K., Dubey, A., Pandey, S., Singh, S. K., Gupta, G., Prasher, P., Chellappan, D. K., Oliver, B. G., Kumar, D., & Dua, K. (2022). Managing apoptosis in lung diseases using nano-assisted drug delivery system. *Current Pharmaceutical Design*, *13*. Available from https://pubmed.ncbi.nlm.nih.gov/35422206/.

Sichaem, J., Surapinit, S., Siripong, P., Khumkratok, S., Jong-aramruang, J., & Tip-pyang, S. (2010). Two new cytotoxic isomeric indole alkaloids from the roots of *Nauclea orientalis*. *Fitoterapia*, *81*(7), 830–833. Available from https://doi.org/10.1016/j.fitote.2010.05.004, 1.

Sledge, G. W., & Miller, K. D. (2003). Exploiting the hallmarks of cancer: The future conquest of breast cancer. *European Journal of Cancer (Oxford, England: 1990)*, *39*(12), 1668–1675. Available from https://doi.org/10.1016/s0959-8049(03)00273-9.

Srinivasan, S., Vannberg, F. O., & Dixon, J. B. (2016). Lymphatic transport of exosomes as a rapid route of information dissemination to the lymph node. *Scientific Reports*, *6*(1), 1–4. Available from https://doi.org/10.1038/srep24436, 18.

Stone, N. R. H., Bicanic, T., Salim, R., & Hope, W. (2016). Liposomal amphotericin B (AmBisome (®)): A review of the pharmacokinetics, pharmacodynamics, clinical experience and future directions. *Drugs*, *76*(4), 485–500. Available from https://doi.org/10.1007/s40265-016-0538-7.

Sung, H., Ferlay, J., Siegel, R. L., Laversanne, M., Soerjomataram, I., Jemal, A., et al. (2021). Global cancer statistics 2020: GLOBOCAN estimates of incidence and mortality worldwide for 36 cancers in 185 countries. *CA: A Cancer Journal for Clinicians*, *71*(3), 209–249. Available from https://acsjournals.onlinelibrary.wiley.com/doi/pdf/10.3322/caac.21660.

Syn, N. L., Wang, L., Chow, E. K., Lim, C. T., & Goh, B. C. (2017). Exosomes in cancer nanomedicine and immunotherapy: Prospects and challenges. *Trends in Biotechnology*, *35*(7), 665–676. Available from https://doi.org/10.1016/j.tibtech.2017.03.004, 1.

Tarhini, M., Greige-Gerges, H., & Elaissari, A. (2017). Protein-based nanoparticles: From preparation to encapsulation of active molecules. *International Journal of Pharmaceutics*, *522*(1-2), 172–197. Available from https://doi.org/10.1016/j.ijpharm.2017.01.067.

Taylor, C. W., Dalton, W. S., Mosley, K., Dorr, R. T., & Salmon, S. E. (1997). Combination chemotherapy with cyclophosphamide, vincristine, adriamycin, and dexamethasone (CVAD) plus oral quinine and verapamil in patients with advanced breast cancer. *Breast Cancer Research and Treatment*, *42*(1), 7–14. Available from https://doi.org/10.1023/A:1005716214718.

Teicher, B. A. (2000). Molecular targets and cancer therapeutics: Discovery, development and clinical validation. *Drug Resistance Updates*, *3*(2), 67–73. Available from https://doi.org/10.1054/drup.2000.0123.

Thanki, K., Gangwal, R. P., Sangamwar, A. T., & Jain, S. (2013). Oral delivery of anticancer drugs: Challenges and opportunities. *Journal of Controlled Release*, *170*(1), 15–40. Available from https://doi.org/10.1016/j.jconrel.2013.04.020.

Varma, R. S. (2012). Greener approach to nanomaterials and their sustainable applications. *Current Opinion in Chemical Engineering*, *1*(2), 123–128. Available from https://doi.org/10.1016/j.coche.2011.12.002.

Verma, D., Gulati, N., Kaul, S., Mukherjee, S., & Nagaich, U. (2018). Protein based nanostructures for drug delivery. *Journal of Pharmaceutics*, *2018*. Available from https://doi.org/10.1155/2018/9285854.

Verma, S. K., Das, A. K., Gantait, S., Kumar, V., & Gurel, E. (2019). Applications of carbon nanomaterials in the plant system: A perspective view on the pros and cons. *Science of the Total Environment*, *1*(667), 485–499. Available from https://doi.org/10.1016/j.scitotenv.2019.02.409.

von Roemeling, C., Jiang, W., Chan, C. K., Weissman, I. L., & Kim, B. Y. (2017). Breaking down the barriers to precision cancer nanomedicine. *Trends in Biotechnology*, *35*(2), 159–171. Available from https://doi.org/10.1016/j.tibtech.2016.07.006, 1.

Wei, Q.-Y., He, K.-M., Chen, J.-L., Xu, Y.-M., & Lau, A. T. Y. (2019). Phytofabrication of nanoparticles as novel drugs for anticancer applications. *Molecules (Basel, Switzerland)*, *24*(23), 4246. Available from https://doi.org/10.3390/molecules24234246.

Wissing, S., Kayser, O., & Müller, R. (2004). Solid lipid nanoparticles for parenteral drug delivery. *Advanced Drug Delivery Reviews*, *56*(9), 1257–1272. Available from https://doi.org/10.1016/j.addr.2003.12.002.

Wu, T. S., Damu, A. G., Su, C. R., & Kuo, P. C. (2004). Terpenoids of *Aristolochia* and their biological activities. *Natural Product Reports*, *21*(5), 594–624. Available from https://doi.org/10.1039/b401950d.

Xu, P., Yin, Q., Shen, J., Chen, L., Yu, H., Zhang, Z., & Li, Y. (2013). Synergistic inhibition of breast cancer metastasis by silibinin-loaded lipid nanoparticles containing TPGS. *International Journal of Pharmaceutics*, *454*(1), 21–30. Available from https://doi.org/10.1016/j.ijpharm.2013.06.053, 15.

Xu, W., Li, T., Qiu, J. F., Wu, S. S., Huang, M. Q., Lin, L. G., Zhang, Q. W., Chen, X. P., & Lu, J. J. (2015). Anti-proliferative activities of terpenoids isolated from *Alisma orientalis* and their structure-activity relationships. *Anti-Cancer Agents in Medicinal Chemistry (Formerly Current Medicinal Chemistry-Anti-Cancer Agents)*, *15*(2), 228–235. Available from https://doi.org/10.2174/1871520614666140601213514, 1.

Yadav, R., Das, J., Lalhlenmawia, H., Tonk, R. K., Singh, L., & Kumar, D. (2021). Targeting cancer using phytoconstituents-based drug delivery. *Advanced Drug Delivery Systems in the Management of Cancer*, *1*, 499–508. Available from https://doi.org/10.1016/B978-0-323-85503-7.00033-X.

Yang, Y., Corona, A., Schubert, B., Reeder, R., & Henson, M. A. (2014). The effect of oil type on the aggregation stability of nanostructured lipid carriers. *Journal of Colloid and Interface Science*, *418*, 261–272. Available from https://doi.org/10.1016/j.jcis.2013.12.024.

Yu, M. K., Park, J., & Jon, S. (2012). Targeting strategies for multifunctional nanoparticles in cancer imaging and therapy. *Theranostics*, *2*(1), 3–44. Available from https://doi.org/10.7150/thno.3463.

Zhai, Y., Guo, S., Liu, C., Yang, C., Dou, J., Li, L., & Zhai, G. (2013). Preparation and in vitro evaluation of apigenin-loaded polymeric micelles. *Colloids and Surfaces A: Physicochemical and Engineering Aspects*, *429*, 24–30. Available from https://doi.org/10.1016/j.colsurfa.2013.03.051.

Zhang, M., Xiao, B., Wang, H., Han, M. K., Zhang, Z., Viennois, E., Xu, C., & Merlin, D. (2016). Edible ginger-derived nano-lipids loaded with doxorubicin as a novel drug-delivery approach for colon cancer therapy. *Molecular Therapy*, *24*(10), 1783–1796. Available from https://doi.org/10.1038/mt.2016.159, 1.

Zhang, Y., Xin, C., Cheng, C., & Wang, Z. (2020). Antitumor activity of nanoemulsion based on essential oil of *Pinus koraiensis* pinecones in MGC-803 tumor-bearing nude mice. *Arabian Journal of Chemistry*, *13*(11), 8226–8238. Available from https://doi.org/10.1016/j.arabjc.2020.09.058, 1.

Zidorn, C., Jöhrer, K., Ganzera, M., Schubert, B., Sigmund, E. M., Mader, J., Greil, R., Ellmerer, E. P., & Stuppner, H. (2005). Polyacetylenes from the Apiaceae vegetables carrot, celery, fennel, parsley, and parsnip and their cytotoxic activities. *Journal of Agricultural and Food Chemistry*, *53*(7), 2518–2523. Available from https://doi.org/10.1021/jf048041s, 6.

CHAPTER 9

Utility of nanomedicine and nanocarriers for noninfectious disease treatment

Jaya Tuteja[1], Aparna Vyas[2] and Arpit Sand[1]
[1]Department of Chemistry, Manav Rachna University, Faridabad, India
[2]Department of Mathematics, Manav Rachna University, Faridabad, India

Introduction

It is known as the technology to control the size of the material at nanoscale ranging from 1 to 100 nanometers, where these particles show unexceptionally features of high activity, large surface areas, and can be applied to various novel applications to achieve high efficacy. Nanotechnology requires the knowledge of nanoscale science, basic concepts of chemistry, physics, and biology along with the expertise of engineering and technology. It encompasses of nanoscale imaging, modulating the matter at nanoscale length. It has been seen that gas, liquids, and solids show extraordinary behavior or unexemplary physical, chemical, and biological properties at nano size compared to their bulk size. Magnetic and conducting properties of materials can be easily altered while working at small scale. Unusual raise in chemical reactivity of materials can be seen due to high surface area of nanoparticles (NPs). In short, nanotechnology is a field, which is rapidly growing these days and showing revolutionary impacts on our health issues for various diseases with the help of nanomedicines and nanocarriers (Godin et al., 2020; McGrady et al., 2010). The combination of nanotechnology and medicine is called nanomedicine. The nanomedicines come with the advantage of integrated development in the field of molecular and cellular biology, genetics, and proteomics at nano level. It has been known from decades that the inner working of our body system that includes glucose, cell wall, DNA, antibodies, enzymes, hemoglobin, and so on exists in nano dimension range. It can be said that due to nanometric scale of biological mechanism, they allow nanomedicine to potentially cross all the barriers and reach to the delivery site without any hindrance and enact with DNA in blood/within organs, tissues, or cells. The usual medication is exposed to entire body, which leads to unwanted side effects and reduces the amount of medicine where it actually needed. With the support of nanotechnology, we can solve this concern, as nanomedicines require less medication and reach directly to the

Nanotechnology for Drug Delivery and Pharmaceuticals
DOI: https://doi.org/10.1016/B978-0-323-95325-2.00014-6

site of action with high efficiency. As a simple example, we can consider the application of nanomedicine in cancer treatment, the existing chemotherapy treatment for cancer seems like spraying the entire crop with large amount of poison to kill few unwanted weeds rather than to spread on the specific area. Along with this the added advantages of using nanotherapies, nanomedicines, and nanotechnology are the improved efficiency, reduced medicine amount, low toxicity, and improved quality of life. Although nanotechnology has found its place in almost all diseases, here, in this chapter, we will be majorly focusing on application of nanotechnology in noninfectious diseases.

Chemistry and mechanism of action for nanomedicine and nanocarriers for noninfectious disease treatment

It is known now from years that nanomedicine has come into role owing to its site specificity. The nanocarrier helps to administrate the drug to particular site to minimize the side effect that can be produced by off-targeted interaction of drug molecule with body. Nanosystems makes hydrophobic drug feasible to reach to the site of delivery in high concentration. It is being suggested from the literature that when NPs enter into body or in the bloodstream, it started for protein binding on the surface of NPs. The NPs tagged with protein then further be treated by liver and kidney by filtration. Further modification for enhancing the efficacy can be done by modulating the surface of NPs with carbohydrates, acetyl group, proteins, and so on, which resulted into alterations of time in drug release

Nanotechnology in central nervous system diseases

Since two decades, nanomedicines have arrived as a novel and revolutionary techniques to solve much of our medical concerns specifically for cancer treatment and other infectious diseases (van der Meel et al., 2019). The term nano includes everything that comes under the range of 1–100 nm, which includes nanocarriers, nanodrugs, nanovaccines, and so on (Soares et al., 2018). The advantage of using nanomedicines in treatment of central nervous system (CNS) disease is its extremely small size that makes them suitable to cross the blood–brain barrier (BBB) and make them feasible to reach the targeted site. The BBB is a microvasculature structure with unique properties, which protects the CNS from various toxins and pathogens. The structure of BBB is made up of various endothelial cells that are tightly packed with specific adherences junctions resulting into restrictions of various toxins and pathogens to reach to the CNS. The disadvantage of being such restricted barrier is that it does not allow the treatment of CNS disorders to reach to the CNS except passage of only allow few small size nonpolar and hydrophobic agents (Faouzi & GaëlleRoullin, 2021; Pardridge, 2005).

The BBB allows few essential molecules, such as water, and oxygen, to reach to brain but restricts conventional anticancer drugs to reach to BBB. Nanotechnology has proved its excellence in this respect and served a primary tool to overcome this issue. These nanotherapies/nanomedicines or nanocarriers are designed in such a way that they can cross the BBB easily and reaches to the targeted site. The advantages these nano world offers are their tridimensional shapes, suitable dimensions, versatile character due to low surface area (De Jong et al., 2008), and, most importantly, the surface modifications that can be done by tuning the surface charges, by attaching it various ligands, stabilizers, and so on (Ceña & Játiva, 2018). These nanotherapies in a combination of nanotechnology are applied to such type of rare diseases which are caused by genetic disorders (Commissioner, 2020).

CNS is turning to be a disease that is affecting much of the Americans specially children which causes a rare pathology disease (Jones & Townsend, 2017); these neurological disorder not only impacts on the spinal cord and brain activities but also on all the nerves by attacking the CNS. The root cause of such neurological disorders is generally lifestyle, environment, genetic mutations, and so on. Everyone is aware about the nuclear bomb incident on Japan's Nagasaki and Hiroshima, still few percent of population is facing challenges due to genetic mutations. It is hard to reverse the mutations once it is done. These disorders can exhibit any or more of the symptoms, including paralysis, memory loss, poor coordination, and loss of consciousness, congenital abnormalities, malnutrition, and sometimes these symptoms results into life threatening for some patients. Fig. 9.1 depicts the utility of nanocarriers as drug delivery agents for CNS disease treatment.

The most important thing to treat any of the disease is its diagnosis, until unless the disease is diagnosed properly treatment cannot play much role. Unfortunately, the diagnosis of neurological disorders is very difficult, because the diagnosis demands the collection of some tissue samples and it is not possible to collect tissues from brain except during the postmortem. As a new technology, various imaging techniques have appeared to resolve this concern, but high-radiation exposure and extremely expensive cost and low availability made these methods not so friendly to satisfy every patient's need (Jones & Townsend, 2017).

Here we are talking about the application of nanomedicines for such type of diseases, but again a question arises how we can judge the toxicity and efficiency of these drugs, as the relevant model for such rare disease is difficult to be found. Thus strong in vivo studies and preclinical trials are required for a thorough study of medicines impact on integrity of BBB (Gribkoff & Kaczmarek, 2017). It has been seen from the literature that the use of cationic NPs produces neurotoxicity by disrupting the endothial cells of BBB, which indicates the much required assessment of BBB integrity while applying with nanotechnology/nanomedicines for CNS diseases (Lockman et al., 2004). Considering all the abovementioned things, another hurdle arises in the

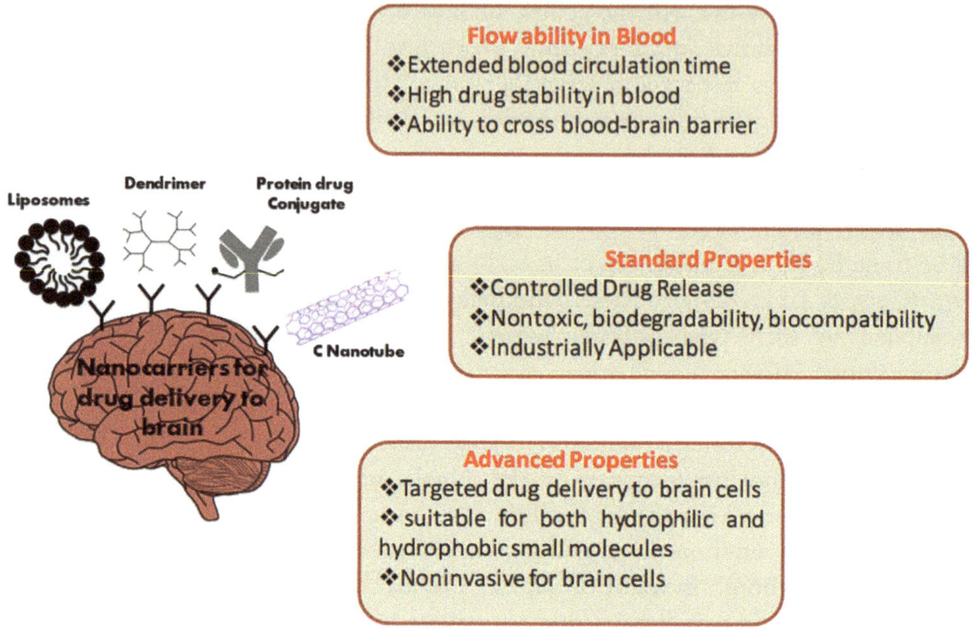

Figure 9.1 Utility of nanocarriers for drug delivery in central nervous system diseases.

therapy of BBB after the treatment of CNS disease, which seems difficult owing to the blocking of large molecules by BBB. In this respect, nanotechnology plays an important role and helps to make the macromolecule drugs cross the BBB with the support of various nanovectors and nanocarriers. Referring to various literatures through PubMed and other sources has indicated the small number of publications for nanotheraputic treatment of rare CNS diseases. Big pharmaceutical companies and other brands do show much interest in development and clinical trials of nanotherapy/nanomedicines owing to relatively small number of patients with this disease and the cost applied to this R and D work seems quite high. However, few developed nanotherapies are listed here in Table 9.1.

After looking for various nanotherapies discovered and their various advantages and disadvantages, let us have brief discussion on the modes or strategies to cross the BBB. Another major hurdle in treatment of CNS disease is the perfect selection of route of administration of drugs to bypass the BBB.

Parenteral administration

The parenteral administration of drug means the intravenous route, performed by injection or by insertion. So far intravenous drug administration is considered best route for human body in general. But considering the other side, the drug administered via parenteral route for CNS treatment should be of higher ability to pass

Table 9.1 Few examples of nanotherapies developed in literature.

Nanocarriers	Primary material	Advantages	Disadvantages	Reference
Liposomes	Phospholipids	High adaptability for hydrophilic and hydrophobic drugs; protection of drugs, high diffusion through BBB	Can cause neurotoxicity, low stability	Zylberberg and Matosevic (2016)
Micelles	Surfactants	Produces no toxicity, highly stable, control drug release capacity	Only lipophilic drugs can be loaded, poor loading capacity	Talelli et al. (2015)
Dendrimers	Organic dendrimers	Efficient for both hydrophobic and hydrophilic drugs, good stability and efficient targeted delivery	Concerns of toxicity and clearance, high accumulation in organs	Zeng et al. (2016)
Solid lipid nanoparticles	Solid lipids	Highly compatible and biodegradable without producing neurotoxicity, efficient diffusion through BBB	Low drug efficiency for hydrophilic drugs	Duan et al. (2020)
Polymeric nanoparticles	Natural/synthetic polymers	Biodegradable, biocompatible, controlled and efficient drug release, drug protection, targeted delivery	High neurotoxicity	Leite et al. (2019)
Carbon nanoparticles	Carbon quantum dots, nanotubes, etc.	High surface functionalities, good electrical and mechanical properties	High toxicity, low biodegradability	Kafa et al. (2016)
Metal nanoparticles	Au, ZnO, Ag, SPIONs	good electrical, optical, and mechanical properties	High neurotoxicity	Paul and Sharma, (2010)

BBB, Blood–brain barrier.

through the BBB. As shown in Table 9.1 too, many of these nanotherapies that are capable of bypassing the BBB imposes high amount of neurotoxicity too. As a solution to this problem, we can think of administrating the drug via intracerebral infusion. The intracerebral infusion route is well known to achieve targeted site delivery where injections are administrated locally generally by opting surgical route (Griffith et al., 2020).

Intranasal drug delivery

It means the drug delivery through the nose to brain, its direct and interesting route of drug administration; it also does allow crossing the BBB. There are two different regions for the drug administration: the respiratory and olfactory areas. This route has been examined by various researchers with successful results for numerous neuroinflammation diseases (Giunchedi et al., 2020).

Intracarotid infusion

It involves the transfusion of drugs through carotid artery; the same artery carries the blood from heart to brain (Joshi et al., 2008). Drug delivery through this route comes with the advantage of high local concentration of drug in short span of time thus very good for targeted delivery. The only disadvantage with this delivery method is that it is not studied much so far for the treatment of CNS diseases; still few examples can be seen in the literature (Joshi et al., 2007).

Transmucosal drug delivery

It is also one of the targeted drug delivery routes where drug is administrated using heterotropic mucosal graft for quick uptake of a drug in systematic circulation by avoiding metabolism route (Abhang et al., 2014). The same method could also be used for the drugs to be administrated via vaginal, nasal, and oral routes for gels, tablets, and others.

Nanotherapies for central nervous system disease

Niemann–Pick type C disease is a rare type of genetic disorder where body shows inability to metabolize cholesterol or transport fatty substances within cells (National Organization for Rare Disorder, 2017), which results in the accumulation of fats in other parts of body, such as brain, lever, kidney, lungs, and spleen. This leads to disfunctioning of body might be resulting in to life-threatening complications (Griffin et al., 2004). Till this date, no drug has been approved for the complete cure of Niemann–Pick type C disease. Few nanotherapies-based drugs have been developed these days, which are responding good, among which one is 2-hydroxypropyl-β-cyclodextrin, commercially known as VTS-270 manufactured by Mallinckrodt Pharmaceuticals (Farmer et al., 2019).

Spinocerebellar ataxia

It is one type of neurological disorder characterized by abnormality in some part of brain, which is responsible for controlled movement, and sometimes it affects spinal cord. Spinocerebellar ataxia (SCA) includes both genetic and nongenetic diseases (Klockgether et al., 2019). The symptoms include less understanding, low balance, slurred speech ability; sometimes serious illnesses might lead to early death too. So far no definite drug has been developed to treat SCA; few drugs have been used to improve the quality of life for those suffering from this disease. For instance, a biomimic peptide of 15 amino acid sequence covalently linked to an amphiphillic peptide self-assembled in to NPs can be used to improve quality life in SCA (Webber et al., 2011).

From overall discussion regarding CNS disease can come to a conclusion that the nanotherapies not only have improved the treatment but also help to diagnose the disease at early stages. It helped to better understand about the disease and its consequences. However, the treatment and diagnosis process is still developing and facing new challenges with the demand in advancements. There are many drugs that have been developed and cannot be used due to various hindrances like not able to cross the BBB, no site-targeting delivery. In this regard, nanocarriers show great versatility and thus are of utmost importance in the CNS diseases.

Nanotechnology in diabetes

Diabetes or in layman language "sugar" is a disease that is noninfectious but has influenced a major population of all countries especially in United States and India. Diabetes is generally caused by person's lifestyle, and other root cause can be hereditary or genetic. It is difficult to believe that it is the fifth major reason of death in most of the developing and developed countries (Veiseh et al., 2015). The main cause of diabetes is the deficiency in insulin production either not at all or very low production of insulin resulting into higher glucose production. The excessive glucose production if not controlled converted into high blood sugar that might lead to complex complications. If sugar shoots tremendous high may be due to just after meal consumption or any side effects of medicine, it can cause serious effect on kidney, eye sight, heart failure, and so on (Landon et al., 2009). Diabetes is a disease which cannot be cured completely; only way to stay healthy is the control monitoring of blood sugar and keep a track on its rising schedule and taking medicines to regulate blood, sugar, doing physical exercises, taking proper diet to control blood sugar (García-Pérez et al., 2013).

Insulin is a peptide consisting of 51 amino acids comprising in 2 chains, one contain 21 amino acids and other consists of 30 amino acids connected via disulfide bonds. Considering the old conceptual oral treatment of sugar generally glycogen like peptide receptor are used (Meier, 2012). The oral treatment generally includes supplying insulin in the replacement of insulin at earliest in closest area or targeted site. Here comes the role of nanotherapy; for instance, various nanoparticles of liposomes, lipids, or micelles can be used as nanocarriers for targeted site delivery. Among these, liposomoes are of great interest as they are made up of phospholipids and are nontoxic, biocompatible and biodegradable in nature (Akbarzadeh et al., 2013). They are very efficient for both lipophilic and hydrophilic drug loading with high targeted site delivery; researchers have noticed the application of liposomes for high efficient insulin trapping with minimum leaking (Allison, 2007). More advanced nanocarrier is niosome: They are synthetically designed nanosized microscopic vesicles, composed of nonionic surfactants impregnated with cholesterol (Ag Seleci et al., 2016). They are suitable carriers for a variety of drugs due to the presence of lipophillic, amphillic, and hydrophilic moieties in it (Ning et al., 2005). Literature study has indicated the improved efficacy in reducing blood sugar level for metformin-loaded niosomes over metformin (Hasan et al., 2013).

As recent advancement biodegradable patches has been of much interest for diabetes management, as an example insulin-loaded poly(vinyl alcohol)-sodium alginate composite has been prepared by electrospinning method (Sharma et al., 2013). It was observed that the patch shows much more efficacy than traditional medicines with almost 100% drug release and significant decrease in blood sugar level.

Nanotechnology in respiratory diseases

Respiratory diseases are the one which can show mild to severe symptoms. The lungs are most affected organ in such type of diseases; asthma, and obstructive pulmonary diseases are the one which is going to be discussed here. These come under the category of noninfectious diseases. It has been in today's world that nanomedicines have already found its existence for various types of chronic diseases treatment. Here too we will discuss how the use of nanomedicines and nanotechnology has improved the efficacy in the treatment of respiratory diseases. For such treatment, drugs are generally inhaled or transported through general route to lungs, as preferable one inhalation route is chosen over oral administration owing to its direct reach to lungs with minimum side effects, minimum resistance to drug, and high therapeutic dose.

We have already seen the application of nanosized liposomes and polymeric NPs in diabetes management. For respiratory disease treatment too, polymeric NPs as drug carrier are preferred owing to high compatibility and biodegradability (Bailey & Berkland, 2009). The capability of holding or entrapping the drug efficiently for controlled and targeted drug release in response to required pH, temperature conditions makes polymeric NPs as suitable nanocarrier for respiratory diseases (Liechty et al., 2010). Surface functionalization for chemical conjugation with DNA, peptide, sugar molecules is the added advantages for efficient targeted drug delivery with these polymeric NPs (Beck-Broichsitter et al., 2012).

Asthma

It is a disease that causes breathing concerns and is known as a very common chronic disease. The asthma patient is generally seen with the common characteristics of shortness of breath, coughing, sneezing, not being comfortable with any kind of pollution or smog, not being able to stand for long duration, and so on. Corticosteroids and bronchodilators are the conventional therapeutic treatments which show tremendous decrease in the symptoms of the disease but comes with the disadvantage of long-term side effects of lungs, which might lead to chronic lung infections, affect immunity, and much more (Barnes, 2012). Considering these long-term side effects, nanomedicines play advantageous role by overcoming various barriers produced by physiological factors, for instance, airway mucus, where endothelium makes a significant wall and dug to be administrated has to cross the wall to reach the targeted site (Schneider et al., 2017). Let us consider a very common example of COVID-19; everyone knows that severe symptoms of the second wave were issues in breathing and high infection in lungs, for which steroids were generally administrated for treatment. If we compare the free or steroid bounded with NPs, we will see steroids with NPs have more sustained therapeutic effects to cross the airway mucus. Salbutamol, which is a steroid when administrated with salbutamol, embedded with NPs has been observed to provide sustained relief in patient conditions due to the high dosing ability of drug at lungs. Other suitable nanocarriers are telodendrimers, a class of dendrimers that are suitable for asthmatic patients treatment as they show high drug loadability with a steady release of the same with the added advantage of crossing ll physiological barrier (Jackson et al., 2004). Dexamethasone drugs loaded on telodendrimer have been reported to improve lung infection effectively if compared to giving dexamethasone alone (Kenyon et al., 2013). Apart from those mentioned above, various types of lipids, polymer-type NPs as nanocarriers, have been employed in literature to improve the efficacy of drug (Di Gioia et al., 2015). The most recent literature in this area has been seen using DNA NPs for lung infection with the ability to pass the lung airways (Mastorakos et al., 2015).

Chronic obstructive pulmonary disease

In this disease generally, airway is blocked, which causes difficulty in breathing commonly known as COPD. Chronic coughing and airways blockage damages the lungs to a significant level that is almost difficult to repair. The traditional medicines available in the market for inhaling can sometimes reduce the symptoms but cannot repair or cure the damage already taken place to lungs (Vogelmeier et al., 2017). Prednisolone and theophylline are the drugs generally employed to lower the symptoms of COPD, as they face challenges in crossing the airways they are used along with the application of various nanocarriers. In today's world, multifunctional polymeric vesicles are of great interest to researchers, which are generally composed of PEGs and PLGA that show the ability to cross the barrier (Vij, 2011). Additionally, an activator, generally dimethyl fumarate, is also employed toward lower airways to reduce inflammation in lungs (Muralidharan et al., 2016). Recent studies have also shown quite a good impact of using metallic NPs of Au and TiO_2 as nanocarriers for COPD treatment (Geiser et al., 2013; Roulet et al., 2012). Here it is worth mentioning that along with the treatment of COPD, its early diagnosis also plays crucial role. If COPD is detected in early stages before producing much impact on lungs that would really help to recover the patient soon, if diagnosis is delayed the COPD can show chronic symptoms. The occurrence of COVID-19, unfortunately, made us possible to understand how lung infection and breathing concerns can cause much disaster in human life. We can see the efficient application of nanotechnology in COPD diagnosis as well. It has been seen that noninvasive magnetic resonance imaging with superparamagnetic iron oxide NPs shows high efficiency in early diagnosis.

Nanomaterials in treatment of autoimmune diseases

Autoimmune diseases are the ones that are developed owing to the disruption of the immune system or in other terms resulted due to the disorders of our immune system. The treatment methodologies so far available in the market for autoimmune diseases are lacking the site specificity, they act on whole body instead of the selective part, they possess antiinflammatory properties, or, we can say that they are immunosuppressive drugs that produce much negative effects if compared to their positive outcomes, such as these drugs produce the disadvantage of impairing immune systems against cancer and other chronic diseases. From numerous researches, it has been seen that after years of development still we are unable to develop a drug that can suppress specific autoimmune organ/tissue without impacting normal immune functionality. It still remains a challenge to overcome all these drawbacks and develop a successful drug.

Nanocarriers for targeted therapy in cancer treatment

Overall in the treatment of any disease targeted delivery is the prime concern to avoid side effects of the particular in other parts of the body, to improve the efficacy of drug. The successful targeted delivery can be achieved by ligand–acceptor linking in close proximity, which is generally <0.5 mm and possible in nanoscale (Zensi et al., 2009). The ligand−acceptor linkage can be further enhanced by the functionalization of NPs with peptides, proteins, carbohydrates, and other small molecules. These biodegradable nanocarriers are of utmost importance owing to their application in cancer treatment, which may include biodegradable polymers, liposomes, and lipids majorly used due to high compatibility too. The important parameters for targeted delivery are generally controlled release of drug and highly stable NPs for longer retention in blood circulation (Guan et al., 2007). 2D nanocarriers like layered double hydroxide are of much interest for drug loading to treat against cancer disease. The advantages of high surface area and versatile functionalization, anion exchange capability makes them useful as potential candidate for cancer treatment drugs. As an example, raloxifine hydrochloride, which is a known anticancer drug, can be administrated upon loading with various layered double hydroxides of aluminum and magnesium (Senapati et al., 2018). Polymeric NPs, which are suitable for both small molecules as well as larger molecules like proteins and peptides, can be further optimized for successful targeted delivery of cancer-related drugs (Perez et al., 2001). They are becoming of keen interest due to the controlled time-dependent release of drug via diffusion and swelling on polymeric NPs. An innovative approach for developing copolyemric NPs along with polymeric NPs actually helps to regulate the drug retention for longer time and allows time-dependent release.

It is interesting to know that various liposomes, be it natural or synthetic, loaded with anticancer drug has been already approved by FDA to be administrated to patients for treatment (Torchilin, 2005). For example, doxorubicin with PEGylated liposomes, curcumin loaded with PEGylated hybrid liposomes, curcumin and paclitaxel combination loaded on hybrid polymeric NPs (Ogawara et al., 2009; Ruttala & Ko, 2015). Micelles owing to their architectural design represent a promising delivery nanocarrier for cancer chemotherapy as drug is encapsulated by physical, chemical, and electrostatic interactions (Park et al., 2008). The combination of drugs, such as paclitaxel and cisplatin, for ovarian and breast cancer treatment has been seen to provide targeted drug delivery when administrated with drug loaded on amphiphilic copolymer block (Wan et al., 2019). Fig. 9.2 compiles the conventional versus modern approach for cancer treatment.

The application of nanomaterials in vaccine design including COVID-19 vaccines

No one of us is unaware of the disastrous effects of the outburst of COVID-19 virus, and we are still struggling for the particular medicine for the treatment of COVID-19. During the major outburst, doctors prescribed the existing chloroquine, ribavirin, ritonavir, darunavir, camostat, and so on; these drugs were somehow capable of

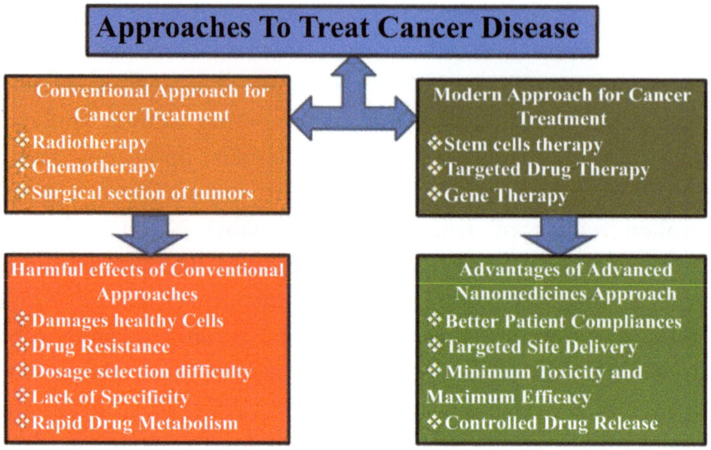

Figure 9.2 Compiles the conventional versus modern approached for cancer treatment.

minimizing the effect of COVID-19 but were not able to treat the infection. Those drugs also failed in solubility, reaching to targeted site thus demands for a modern drug that can resolve all the related concerns. Literature survey informed us that various nanocarriers have been used to deliver the therapeutic drug at targeted site that includes polymeric and inorganic carriers.

Here, nanotherapy does his work in delivering drug molecules to the infected cell by binding the virus' epitopes with ligand-conjugated NPs, which resulted in to the failure of viruses' entry in cells and virus can be neutralized without infecting cells.

Conclusion and prospects

Nanotechnology and its advancement are expected to show tremendous results with rapid and strong developments. Various scientists in this area have predicted that it is going to show revolutionary advantage in medicine field. It can be said that we are currently in the era of first or second generation of nanomaterials and nanocarriers as drug delivery agents. These nanomedicines have found their place in diagnostics, treatment, monitoring, regulations, and much more. It has been seen from the research reports that therapeutics, which are nanomaterials based, show great potential in treatment of diabetes, cancer, tumors, infections, neurodegenerative diseases, and so on (Ibanez et al., 2015; Liu et al., 2015; Lv et al., 2014). Along with the physical and chemical properties of nanomaterials the shape and size of the same also influences its therapeutic performance (Fischer & Chan, 2007).

However, still various challenges exist in this area; after much development, there exists a potential risk of cytotoxicity with nanomaterials. Several reports can be noticed on the toxicity of nanomaterials owing to the absorbance of these nanomaterials on biological membrane via electrostatic interactions and can cause damage to cells by protein denaturingration, cell damage, DNA damage, and so on (Zhang & Karn, 2005). For instance, under the treatment of CNS diseases, it is evident that they can cross the BBB to reach to diseased site, but simultaneously they can cause other several nervous diseases (Service, 2004). Another example to quote is the application of carbon nanotubes (CNT) generally employed as nanocarrier owing to its various advantages comes with the disadvantage of impacting cardiovascular systems. They can also cause cell apoptosis, disruption in cell cycle (Manna et al., 2005). It is also seen that these CNT can impact on lung and our immune system too (Renwick et al., 2004).

Thus it would not be wrong to say that the long-term toxicity of these usable nanocarriers is still unclear and should be studied intensively. Undoubtedly, the properties of these nanocarriers are indispensable for treating chronic disease; only thing to focus is the cytotoxicity produced by them and to calculate the positive and negative impacts before proceeding for the treatment.

Acknowledgment

The authors would like to thank Prof. Kunj Behari from University of Allahabad, Allahabad for helpful discussions and insightful suggestions.

References

Abhang, P., Momin, M., Inamdar, M., & Kar, S. (2014). Transmucosal drug delivery—An overview. *Drug Delivery Letters*, *4*, 26–37. Available from https://www.ingentaconnect.com/content/ben/ddl/2014/00000004/00000001/art00005.

Ag Seleci, D., Seleci, M., Walter, J.-G., Stahl, F., & Scheper, T. (2016). Niosomes as nanoparticular drug carriers: Fundamentals and recent applications. *Journal of Nanomaterials*, 7372306. Available from https://www.hindawi.com/journals/jnm/2016/7372306/.

Akbarzadeh, A., et al. (2013). Liposome: Classification preparation and applications. *Nanoscale Research Letters*, *8*, 102. Available from https://nanoscalereslett.springeropen.com/articles/10.1186/1556-276X-8-102.

Allison, S. D. (2007). Liposomal drug delivery. *Journal of Infusion Nursing: The Official Publication of the Infusion Nurses Society*, *30*, 89–95. Available from https://doi.org/10.1097/01.nan.0000264712.26219.67.

Bailey, M. M., & Berkland, C. J. (2009). Nanoparticle formulations in pulmonary drug delivery. *Medicinal Research Reviews*, *29*, 196–212. Available from https://doi.org/10.1002/med.20140.

Barnes, P. J. (2012). Severe asthma: Advances in current management and future therapy. *The Journal of Allergy and Clinical Immunology*, *129*, 48–59. Available from https://doi.org/10.1016/j.jaci.2011.11.006.

Beck-Broichsitter, M., Merkel, O. M., & Kissel, T. (2012). Controlled pulmonary drug and gene delivery using polymeric nano-carriers. *Journal of Controlled Release*, *161*, 214–224. Available from https://doi.org/10.1016/j.jconrel.2011.12.004.

Ceña, V., & Játiva, P. (2018). Nanoparticle crossing of blood–brain barrier: A road to new therapeutic approaches to central nervous system diseases. *Nanomedicine*, *13*, 1513–1516. Available from https://doi.org/10.2217/nnm-2018-0139.

Commissioner O. Of the rare diseases at FDA. (2020). Available online: https://www.fda.gov/patients/rare-diseases-fda (accessed 10.09.20).

De Jong, W. H., Hagens, W. I., Krystek, P., Burger, M. C., Sips, A. J. A. M., & Geertsma, R. E. (2008). Particle size-dependent organ distribution of gold nanoparticles after intravenous administration. *Biomaterials*, *29*, 1912–1919. Available from https://doi.org/10.1016/j.biomaterials.2007.12.037.

Di Gioia, S., et al. (2015). Nanocomplexes for gene therapy of respiratory diseases: Targeting and overcoming the mucus barrier. *Pulmonary Pharmacology & Therapeutics*, *34*, 8–24. Available from https://doi.org/10.1016/j.pupt.2015.07.003.

Duan, Y., Dhar, A., Patel, C., Khimani, M., Neogi, S., Sharma, P., Siva Kumar, N., & Vekariya, R. L. (2020). A brief review on solid lipid nanoparticles: Part and parcel of contemporary drug delivery systems. *RSC Advances*, *10*, 26777–26791. Available from https://doi.org/10.1039/D0RA03491F.

Faouzi, A., & GaëlleRoullin, V. (2021). Think big start small: How nanomedicine could alleviate the burden of rare CNS diseases. *Pharmaceuticals*, *14*, 109. Available from https://doi.org/10.3390%2Fph14020109.

Farmer, C. A., Thurm, A., Farhat, N., Bianconi, S., Keener, L. A., & Porter, F. D. (2019). Long-term neuropsychological outcomes from an open-label phase I/IIa trial of 2-hydroxypropyl-β-cyclodextrins (VTS-270) in Niemann-Pick disease type C1. *CNS Drugs*, *33*, 677–683. Available from https://doi.org/10.1007/s40263-019-00642-2.

Fischer, H. C., & Chan, W. C. (2007). Nanotoxicity: The growing need for in vivo study. *Current Opinion in Biotechnology*, *18*(6), 565–571. Available from https://doi.org/10.1016/j.copbio.2007.11.008.

García-Pérez, L.-E., Álvarez, M., Dilla, T., Gil-Guillén, V., & Orozco-Beltrán, D. (2013). Adherence to therapies in patients with type 2 diabetes. *Diabetes Therapy*, *4*, 175–194. Available from https://link.springer.com/article/10.1007/s13300-013-0034-y.

Geiser, M., et al. (2013). Cellular uptake and localization of inhaled gold nanoparticles in lungs of mice with chronic obstructive pulmonary disease. *Particle and Fibre Toxicology*, *10*, 19.

Giunchedi, P., Gavini, E., & Bonferoni, M. C. (2020). Nose-to-brain delivery. *Pharmaceutics*, *12*, 138.

Godin, B., Sakamoto, J. H., Serda, R. E., et al. (2010). Emerging applications of nanomedicine for the diagnosis and treatment of cardiovascular diseases. *Trends in Pharmacological Sciences*, *31*(5), 199–205. Available from https://doi.org/10.1016/j.tips.2010.01.003.

Gribkoff, V. K., & Kaczmarek, L. K. (2017). The need for new approaches in CNS drug discovery: Why drugs have failed and what can be done to improve outcomes. *Neuropharmacology*, *120*, 11–19. Available from https://doi.org/10.1016/j.neuropharm.2016.03.021.

Griffin, L. D., Gong, W., Verot, L., & Mellon, S. H. (2004). Niemann–Pick type C disease involves disrupted neurosteroidogenesis and responds to allopregnanolone. *Nature Medicine*, *10*, 704–711. Available from https://www.nature.com/articles/nm1073.

Griffith, J. I., Rathi, S., Zhang, W., Zhang, W., Drewes, L. R., Sarkaria, J. N., & Elmquist, W. F. (2020). Addressing BBB heterogeneity: A new paradigm for drug delivery to brain tumors. *Pharmaceutics*, *12*, 1205.

Guan, J., He, H., Yu, B., & Lee, L. J. (2007). *Polymeric nanoparticles and nanopore membranes for controlled drug and gene delivery. Biomedical Nanostructures* (pp. 115–137). Hoboken, NJ: Wiley-Interscience. Available from http://doi.org/10.1002/9780470185834.ch6.

Hasan, A. A., Madkor, H., & Wageh, S. (2013). Formulation and evaluation of metformin hydrochloride-loaded niosomes as controlled release drug delivery system. *Drug Delivery*, *20*, 120–126. Available from https://www.tandfonline.com/doi/abs/10.3109/10717544.2013.779332.

Ibanez, I. L., Notcovich, C., Catalano, P. N., Bellino, M. G., & Duran, H. (2015). The redox-active nanomaterial toolbox for cancer therapy. *Cancer Letters*, *359*(1), 9–19. Available from https://doi.org/10.1016/j.canlet.2015.01.013.

Jackson, J. K., Zhang, X., Llewellen, S., Hunter, W. L., & Burt, H. M. (2004). The characterization of novel polymeric paste formulations for intratumoral delivery. *International Journal of Pharmaceutics*, *270*, 185–198. Available from https://doi.org/10.1016/j.ijpharm.2003.10.010.

Jones, T., & Townsend, D. (2017). History and future technical innovation in positron emission tomography. *Journal of Medical Imaging*, *4*, 011013. Available from https://doi.org/10.1117/1.JMI.4.1.011013.

Joshi, S., Emala, C. W., & Pile-Spellman, J. (2007). Intra-arterial drug delivery: A concise review. *Journal of Neurosurgical Anesthesiology*, *19*, 111–119. Available from https://doi.org/10.3171/jns.1994.81.5.0752.

Joshi, S., Meyers, P. M., & Ornstein, E. (2008). Intracarotid delivery of drugs. *Anesthesiology*, *109*, 543–564. Available from https://doi.org/10.1097/aln.0b013e318182c81b.

Kafa, H., Wang, J. T.-W., Rubio, N., Klippstein, R., Costa, P. M., Hassan, H. A. F. M., Sosabowski, J. K., Bansal, S. S., Preston, J. E., Abbott, N. J., et al. (2016). Translocation of LRP1 targeted carbon nanotubes of different diameters across the blood–brain barrier in vitro and in vivo. *Journal of Controlled Release: Official Journal of the Controlled Release Society*, *225*, 217–229. Available from https://doi.org/10.1016/j.jconrel.2016.01.031.

Kenyon, N. J., et al. (2013). Self-assembling nanoparticles containing dexamethasone as a novel therapy in allergic airways inflammation. *PLoS One*, *8*, e77730. Available from https://doi.org/10.1371/journal.pone.0077730.

Klockgether, T., Mariotti, C., & Paulson, H. L. (2019). Spinocerebellar ataxia. *Nature Reviews Disease Primers*, *5*, 24. Available from https://www.nature.com/articles/s41572-019-0074-3.

Landon, M. B., et al. (2009). A multicenter randomized trial of treatment for mild gestational diabetes. *The New England Journal of Medicine*, *361*, 1339–1348. Available from https://doi.org/10.1002/(sici)1096-9136(199807)15:7%3C539::aid-dia668%3E3.0.co;2-s.

Leite, P. E. C., Pereira, M. R., Harris, G., Pamies, D., dos Santos, L. M. G., Granjeiro, J. M., Hogberg, H. T., Hartung, T., & Smirnova, L. (2019). Suitability of 3D human brain spheroid models to distinguish toxic effects of gold and poly-lactic acid nanoparticles to assess biocompatibility for brain drug delivery. *Particle and Fibre Toxicology*, *16*, 22. Available from https://doi.org/10.1186/s12989-019-0307-3.

Liechty, W. B., Kryscio, D. R., Slaughter, B. V., & Peppas, N. A. (2010). Polymers for drug delivery systems. *Annual Review of Chemical and Biomolecular Engineering*, *1*, 149–173. Available from https://www.annualreviews.org/doi/abs/10.1146/annurev-chembioeng-073009-100847.

Liu, L., Lv, H. Y., Teng, Z. Y., Wang, C. Y., & Wang, G. X. (2015). Glucose sensors based on core–shell magnetic nanomaterials and their application in diabetes management: A review. *Current Pharmaceutical Design*, *21*(37), 5359–5368.

Lockman, P. R., Koziara, J. M., Mumper, R. J., & Allen, D. D. (2004). Nanoparticle surface charges alter blood–brain barrier integrity and permeability. *Journal of Drug Targeting*, *12*, 635–641. Available from https://doi.org/10.1080/10611860400015936.

Lv, X. N., Wang, P., Bai, R., et al. (2014). Inhibitory effect of silver nanomaterials on transmissible virus-induced host cell infections. *Biomaterials*, *35*(13), 4195–4203.

Manna, S. K., Sarkar, S., Barr, J., et al. (2005). Single-walled carbon nanotube induces oxidative stress and activates nuclear transcription factor-κB in human keratinocytes. *Nano Letters*, *5*(9), 1676–1684. Available from https://doi.org/10.1021/nl0507966.

Mastorakos, P., et al. (2015). Highly compacted biodegradable DNA nanoparticles capable of overcoming the mucus barrier for inhaled lung gene therapy. *Proceedings of the National Academy of Sciences of the United States of America*, *112*, 8720–8725. Available from https://doi.org/10.1073/pnas.1502281112.

McGrady, E., Conger, S., Blanke, S., & Landry, B. J. (2010). Emerging technologies in healthcare: Navigating risks evaluating rewards. *Journal of Healthcare Management*, *55*(5), 353–364. Available from https://pubmed.ncbi.nlm.nih.gov/21077584/.

Meier, J. J. (2012). GLP-1 receptor agonists for individualized treatment of type 2 diabetes mellitus. *Nature Reviews Endocrinology.*, *8*, 728. Available from https://www.nature.com/articles/nrendo.2012.140.

Muralidharan, P., Hayes, D., Black, S. M., & Mansour, H. M. (2016). Microparticulate/nanoparticulate powders of a novel Nrf2 activator and an aerosol performance enhancer for pulmonary delivery targeting the lung Nrf2/Keap-1 pathway. *Molecular Systems Design & Engineering*, *1*, 48–65. Available from https://doi.org/10.1039/C5ME00004A.

National Organization for Rare Disorder, NORD (2017). Niemann Pick disease type C. Available online: https://rarediseases.org/rare-diseases/niemann-pick-disease-type-c.

Ning, M., Guo, Y., Pan, H., Yu, H., & Gu, Z. (2005). Niosomes with sorbitan monoester as a carrier for vaginal delivery of insulin: Studies in rats. *Drug Delivery*, *12*, 399–407. Available from https://doi.org/10.1080/10717540590968891.

Ogawara, K.-i, Un, K., Tanaka, K.-i, Higaki, K., & Kimura, T. (2009). In vivo anti-tumor effect of PEG liposomal doxorubicin (DOX) in DOX-resistant tumor-bearing mice: Involvement of cytotoxic effect on vascular endothelial cells. *Journal of Controlled Release: Official Journal of the Controlled Release Society*, *133*, 4–10. Available from https://doi.org/10.1016/j.jconrel.2008.09.008.

Pardridge, W. M. (2005). The blood–brain barrier: Bottleneck in brain drug development. *NeuroRx: The Journal of the American Society for Experimental Neuro Therapeutics*, *2*, 3–14.

Park, J. H., et al. (2008). Polymeric nanomedicine for cancer therapy. *Progress in Polymer Science*, 33113–33137. Available from https://doi.org/10.1016/j.progpolymsci.2007.09.003.

Paul, W., & Sharma, C. P. (2010). *Inorganic nanoparticles for targeted drug delivery. Biointegration of Medical Implant Materials* (pp. 204–235). Amsterdam, The Netherlands: Elsevier ISBN 978-1-84569-509-5. Available from https://doi.org/10.1016/B978-0-08-102680-9.00013-5.

Perez, C., et al. (2001). Poly (lactic acid)-poly (ethylene glycol) nanoparticles as new carriers for the delivery of plasmid DNA. *Journal of Controlled Release: Official Journal of the Controlled Release Society*, *75*, 211–224. Available from https://doi.org/10.1016/s0168-3659(01)00397-2.

Renwick, L. C., Brown, D., Clouter, A., & Donaldson, K. (2004). Increased inflammation and altered macrophage chemotactic responses caused by two ultrafine particle types. *Occupational and Environmental Medicine*, *61*(5), 442–447. Available from https://doi.org/10.1136/oem.2003.008227.

Roulet, A., et al. (2012). Intratracheally administered titanium dioxide or carbon black nanoparticles do not aggravate elastase-induced pulmonary emphysema in rats. *BMC Pulmonary Medicine*, *12*, 38. Available from https://bmcpulmmed.biomedcentral.com/articles/10.1186/1471-2466-12-38.

Ruttala, H. B., & Ko, Y. T. (2015). Liposomal co-delivery of curcumin and albumin/paclitaxel nanoparticle for enhanced synergistic antitumor efficacy. *Colloids and Surfaces B: Biointerfaces*, *128*, 419–426. Available from https://doi.org/10.1016/j.colsurfb.2015.02.040.

Schneider, C. S., et al. (2017). Nanoparticles that do not adhere to mucus provide uniform and long-lasting drug delivery to airways following inhalation. *Science Advances*, *3*, e1601556. Available from https://doi.org/10.1126/sciadv.1601556.

Senapati, S., et al. (2018). Engineered cellular uptake and controlled drug delivery using two dimensional nanoparticle and polymer for cancer treatment. *Molecular Pharmaceutics*, *15*, 679–694. Available from https://doi.org/10.1021/acs.molpharmaceut.7b01119.

Service, R. F. (2004). Nanotechnology grows up. *Science (New York, N.Y.)*, *304*(5678), 1732–1734. Available from https://doi.org/10.1126/science.304.5678.1732.

Sharma, A., et al. (2013). Electrospun composite nanofiber-based transmucosal patch for anti-diabetic drug delivery. *Journal of Materials Chemistry B*, *1*, 3410–3418. Available from https://doi.org/10.1039/C3TB20487A.

Soares, S., Sousa, J., Pais, A., & Vitorino, C. (2018). Nanomedicine: Principles properties and regulatory issues. *Frontiers in Chemistry*, *6*, 360. Available from https://doi.org/10.3389/fchem.2018.00360.

Talelli, M., Barz, M., Rijcken, C. J. F., Kiessling, F., HenninkW, E., & Lammers, T. (2015). Core-crosslinked polymeric micelles: Principles preparation biomedical applications and clinical translation. *Nano Today*, *10*, 93–117. Available from https://doi.org/10.1016/j.nantod.2015.01.005.

Torchilin, V. P. (2005). Recent advances with liposomes as pharmaceutical carriers. *Nature Reviews Drug Discovery*, *4*, 145. Available from https://www.nature.com/articles/nrd1632.

van der Meel, R., Sulheim, E., Shi, Y., Kiessling, F., Mulder, W. J. M., & Lammers, T. (2019). Smart cancer nanomedicine. *Nature Nanotechnology*, *14*, 1007–1017. Available from https://doi.org/10.1038/s41565-019-0567-y.

Veiseh, O., Tang, B. C., Whitehead, K. A., Anderson, D. G., & Langer, R. (2015). Managing diabetes with nanomedicine: Challenges and opportunities. *Nature Reviews. Drug Discovery*, *14*, 45. Available from https://www.nature.com/articles/nrd4477.

Vij, N. (2011). Nano-based theranostics for chronic obstructive lung diseases: Challenges and therapeutic potential. *Expert Opinion on Drug Delivery*, *8*, 1105–1109. Available from https://doi.org/10.1517/17425247.2011.597381.

Vogelmeier, C. F., et al. (2017). Global strategy for the diagnosis management and prevention of chronic obstructive lung disease 2017 report. GOLD executive summary. *American Journal of Respiratory and Critical Care Medicine*, *195*, 557–582. Available from https://doi.org/10.1164/rccm.201701-0218pp.

Wan, X., et al. (2019). Co-delivery of paclitaxel and cisplatin in poly(2-oxazoline) polymeric micelles: Implications for drug loading release pharmacokinetics and outcome of ovarian and breast cancer treatments. *Biomaterials*, *192*, 1–14. Available from https://doi.org/10.1016/j.biomaterials.2018.10.032.

Webber, M. J., Tongers, J., Newcomb, C. J., Marquardt, K.-T., Bauersachs, J., Losordo, D. W., & Stupp, S. I. (2011). Supramolecular nanostructures that mimic VEGF as a strategy for ischemic tissue repair. *Proceedings of the National Academy of Sciences of the United States of America*, *108*, 13438–13443.

Zeng, Y., Kurokawa, Y., Zeng, Q., Win-Shwe, T.-T., Nansai, H., Zhang, Z., & Sone, H. (2016). Effects of polyamidoamine dendrimers on a 3-D neurosphere system using human neural progenitor cells. *Toxicological Sciences: An Official Journal of the Society of Toxicology*, *152*, 128–144. Available from https://doi.org/10.1093/toxsci/kfw068.

Zensi, A., et al. (2009). Albumin nanoparticles targeted with Apo E enter the CNS by transcytosis and are delivered to neurones. *Journal of Controlled Release*, *137*, 78–86. Available from https://doi.org/10.1016/j.jconrel.2009.03.002.

Zhang, W. X., & Karn, B. (2005). Nanoscale environmental science and technology: Challenges and opportunities. *Environmental Science & Technology*, *39*(5), 94A–95A. Available from https://pubs.acs.org/doi/pdf/10.1021/es053197%2B.

Zylberberg, C., & Matosevic, S. (2016). Pharmaceutical liposomal drug delivery: A review of new delivery systems and a look at the regulatory landscape. *Drug Delivery*, *23*, 3319–3329. Available from https://doi.org/10.1080/10717544.2016.1177136.

CHAPTER 10

Passive and active targeted drug delivery strategies

Gunjan Nagpure[1], Kshitij RB Singh[2], Jay Singh[2] and Ravindra Pratap Singh[1]
[1]Department of Biotechnology, Faculty of Science, Indira Gandhi National Tribal University, Amarkantak, Madhya Pradesh, India
[2]Department of Chemistry, Institute of Science, Banaras Hindu University, Varanasi, Uttar Pradesh, India

Introduction

A targeted drug delivery system is known to transport drugs to targeted cells, organs selectively, and tissues via varieties of drug carrier that is usually fabricated to improve the therapeutic as well as pharmacological properties of conventional drugs and to overcome specific toxic effects of conventional drug delivery, such as drug degradation, lack of selectivity, limited solubility, and increased bioavailability. Moreover, it also permits targeting drugs transport to specific cells, reduces poor biodistribution and typical tissue damage, and controls drug release carrier to decrease toxicity and harmful side effects (Smith et al., 2015). With the features of being biodegradable and non-toxic, it shows its promising efficiency in enhancing the permeability, improving drug concentration, and drug retention in the lesion site (Zhan et al., 2017). Moreover, organic and inorganic, including metals, polymers, micelles, dendrimers, and liposomes, are often used in fabricating the target-specific drug delivery system. However, ideal nanodrug delivery system with potential characteristics is being selected for the treatment on the basis of the biophysical and biochemical properties of the targeted drugs (Watkins et al., 2015).

During the last decade, in the market, some formulations have already been developed; there is still no availability of a suitable universal platform for all kinds of drug delivery. As a result, recent nanotechnologies possess possible boundaries.

1. Usually, poor drug loading is $<5\%$, which demonstrates the weight percentage of the transported drug contrasted with nanocarrier composition. As a result, the amount of carrier material that is administered is too high, which leads to adverse side effects, or either administered drug quantity is not adequate to attain the effective pharmacological concentration in the body.
2. There is difficulty in fabricating an efficient nano delivery system associated with high biodegradability, immunogenicity, and aggregation on needed cells or tissues. This could be attributed to targeted nanoparticles (NPs) and physiochemical

Nanotechnology for Drug Delivery and Pharmaceuticals
DOI: https://doi.org/10.1016/B978-0-323-95325-2.00021-3

features. To overcome these critical issues, it is essential to fabricate NPs along with the size, composition, shape, functionalization, and surface charge required to overcome emerging concerns (Patra et al., 2018).

This concise book chapter attempts to highlight an overview of passive and active targeted drug delivery strategies to empower efficient NPs to be targeted to appropriate bindings, specifically tumors. Herein, this chapter also elaborates some of the physiochemical properties of nanocarriers (molecular weight, size, and surface charge) in drug delivery system.

Passive targeted drug delivery

Passive targeting is present naturally in the body. Hormones, neurotransmitters, and growth factors have natural tendency to target receptors at their sites of action, Moreover, well-accepted evidence shows that the blood vessel's endothelium becomes more porous under a definite hypoxia state and inflammation than in the active state. At the time of the hypoxia stage, developing tumors recruit new vessels as well as it is reliant on blood supply for their maturation and development. Further, during this stage, there is an expansion in cellular hypoxia-inducible transcription factor, thereby stimulating growth factors like platelet-derived growth factor, tumor necrosis factor-α, and the vascular endothelial growth factor (VEGF), which gives rise to new blood vessels, and this process is called angiogenesis (Folkman, 1995). These newly formed blood vessels are enlarged with an irregular basement membrane and with interendothelial junctions (Jain & Stylianopoulos, 2010) consisting of 200–2000-nm range capillary pore size and have uneven capillary bed (Hobbs et al., 1998). This displays the enhanced permeation of the enhanced permeation and retention (EPR) effect. Further, as in tumors with significant gaps, there is the presence of leaky vasculature in the case of inflamed tissues, in inflammatory rheumatoid arthritis (RA), inflammatory bowel disease (IBD), and in tumor tissue, which makes it possible to target passively the administered nanocarriers of relevant size to discharge into the targeted tissue. RA is the most prevalent inflammatory disease featured by progressive cartilage and bone destruction that results in shortened lifespan, enhanced mortality rates, and severe functional limitations (Pham, 2011). IBD is featured by chronic inflammation in the intestine, which comprises Crohn's disease and ulcerative colitis, with high risks of cancerization and painful clinical manifestations. Abdominal pain, twofold higher risk of fatal colorectal cancer, rectal bleeding, fever, severe diarrhea, anemia, and weight loss are symptoms of patients suffering from IBD relative to healthy populations (Baumgart & Sandborn, 2007; Pohl et al., 2000). Within the tumor interstitium, the lymphatic vessels are jeopardized in tumor tissues, causes poor or ineffective drainage of fluid. This displays the improved retention feature of the EPR effect. Further, this phenomenon of passive accumulation is referred to as targeting and retention or extravasation together, reported as the EPR effect (Fig. 10.1) (MAEDA et al., 1979; Matsumura et al., 1987; Matsumura & Maeda, 1986; Yu et al., 2016). When macromolecules, NPs, or drugs with molecular size 40 kDa conjugate are intravenously injected in the conditions mentioned earlier and through large fenestrations, they get discharged into the tumor interstitium.

Furthermore, owing to the EPR via the passive targeting, several nanocarriers and macromolecules have appeared to accumulate in infarct tissues and tumors (Abra et al., 2002; Jain, 1999; Torchilin, 2011; Torchilin et al., 1992). The schematic illustration of this approach along with active targeting is depicted in Fig. 10.2 (Attia et al., 2019). Moreover, the absence of normal lymphatic drainage in tumors is devoted to NP retention. Thus this novel characteristic is not relevant to small molecule drugs, which

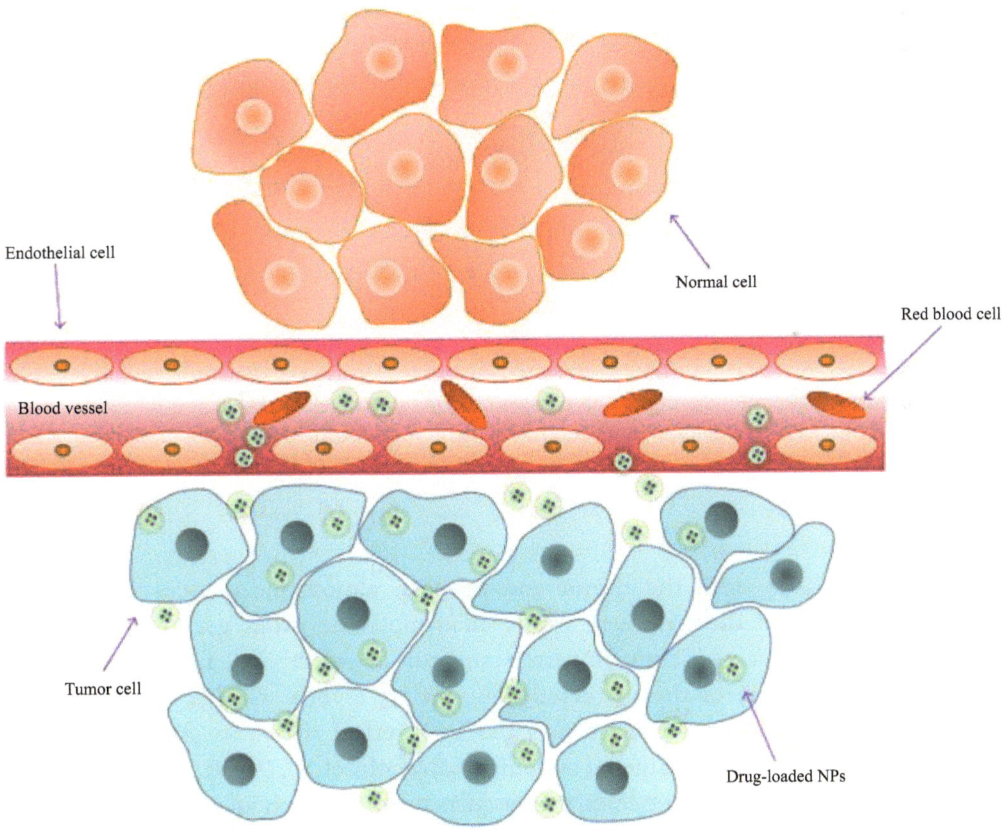

Figure 10.1 This figure represents EPR effect. *EPR*, Enhanced permeation and retention. *From Yu, X., Trase, I., Ren, M., Duval, K., Guo, X. & Chen, Z. (2016). Journal of Nanomaterials, 2016, 1–15 [distributed under attribution 4.0 international (CC BY 4.0)]*

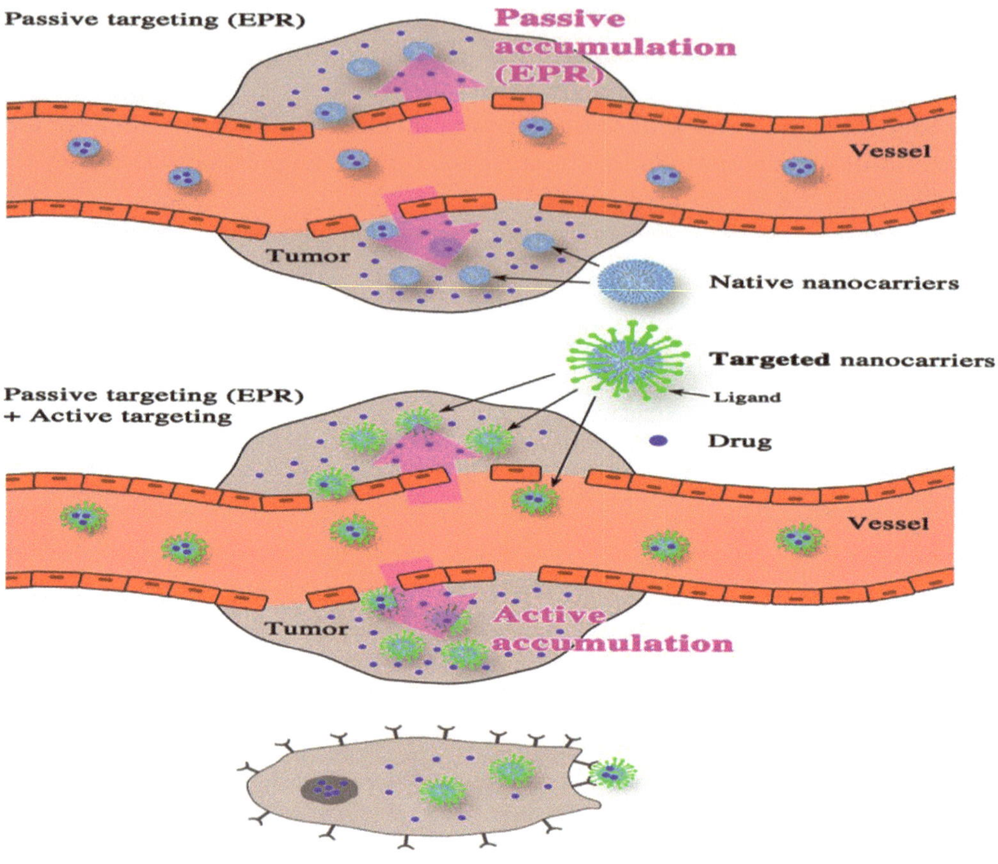

Figure 10.2 The schematic illustration of passive targeting (EPR) and the active targeting into a tumor. *EPR*, Enhanced permeation and retention. *Reproduced with permission from Attia, M. F., Anton, N., Wallyn, J., Omran, Z., & Vandamme, T. F. (2019). Journal of Pharmacy and Pharmacology, 71(8), 1185–1198.*

quickly get washout from the tumor and have an almost short circulation period. Further, in nanosized drug carriers, when small-molecule drugs get encapsulated, it increases their pharmacokinetics, imparts some tumor selectivity, and decreases side effects. Recently, some of the marketed nanocarriers involve Caelyx and Doxil that are intensely utilized in dispensaries, and the EPR effect shows its good standard in designing the passive tumor-targeted systems (Kobayashi et al., 2014). The EPR effect is highly dependent on the degree of perivascular tumor growth and the density of the stromal response, intratumor pressure, and the degree of angiogenesis and lymphangiogenesis (Arap et al., 1998). However, to achieve vascular normalization, it is feasible to regulate the EPR effect mechanically and chemically, owning to an increased nanocarrier accumulation. Moreover, in chemical EPR enhancers, the molecules, such as nitric oxide, bradykinin (kinin), prostaglandins, peroxynitrite, VEGF/vascular permeability factor, and other cytokines, induce vascular normalization or hypertension, which temporarily could enhance tumor perfusion. Further, to increase nanosystems and modulate tumors vasculature, other approaches utilizes radiation, ultrasound, photoimmunotherapy, or hyperthermia methods, but these methods possess several limitations that require urgent attention from the researcher (Fang et al., 2011; Huynh & Zheng, 2015; Kobayashi et al., 2014; Maeda, 2001).

Physiochemical properties of nanocarriers

According to strategy toxicity profiles, pharmacokinetics and biodistribution gets influenced by the nanocarrier's physicochemical properties. Further, it has been investigated that the size of the particles, surface charge, and longevity affect the pathway and the efficacy of cellular uptake for quantum dots, liposomes, gold NPs, silica NPs, and polymers by affecting their interaction with cells and the adhesion of the particles (Chithrani et al., 2006; Chono et al., 2007; Foged et al., 2005; Lee et al., 1993; Lu et al., 2009; Osaki et al., 2004; Yin Win & Feng, 2005).

Further, to discharge via the neo vasculature leaky pores, the carriers must acquire an appropriate size and diffusion through the tumor interstitium. Thus the size is crucial for the permeation and retention effect in the tumors and is, thus, bounded by the vessel aperture of tumor (200−800 nm) (Chono et al., 2007; Torchilin, 2011). Hence, for effective EPR-mediated drug delivery, it is necessary to control the size of the nanocarrier. Dreher et al. (2006) reported macromolecules with sizes from 2−3 nm and smaller weights of 3−10 kDa, which extravasates quickly compared to 70- and 2,000-kDa molecules with 7- and 25-nm diameters, respectively. According to reports, it has been investigated that for the nanocarriers with particles from size 10 to 500 nm, the EPR effect serves as the most effective approach. It has been reported that, in such cases, molecules with smaller particle size and weight would diffuse out from the tumor interstitium. Hence, in various nanocarrier systems, such as micelles, liposomes, immunoglobulins, DNA polyplexes, and polymer-drug conjugates, approximately up to size 700−800 kDa, the EPR effect was distinguished (Fang et al., 2011; MAEDA et al., 1979; Seymour et al., 1995).

In addition to molecular weight and size, the surface charge also significantly influences the EPR effect (Alexis et al., 2008; Baselga, 2006; Bertrand & Leroux, 2012). Within large tumors, nanocarrier's surface charge affects the cellular association and the penetration effect. Maeda et al. reported that the presence of sulfate groups and carboxylate sugars, on the luminal surface, offer the blood vessels negative charge (Maeda et al., 2009). On the other hand, nanocarriers containing a positive charge can get discharged from the circulation (Chonn et al., 1991; He et al.,

2010; Levchenko et al., 2002; Nishida et al., 1991; Salvador-Morales et al., 2009; Scherphof & Kamps, 2001; Xiao et al., 2011). Whereas depending on the overall charge, nanocarriers exhibit variable effects carrying a negative charge on surface (Arvizo et al., 2011; Gabizon & Papahadjopoulos, 1988; Peer & Margalit, 2004; Roux et al., 2003; Yamamoto et al., 2001). Hence, studies investigate the surface of the nanocarriers carrying a net positive charge that aids the synergy with the blood vessels of tumor, which in turn inhibits their passage back to the systemic circulation. In addition, after the process of endocytosis, the nanocarriers could depart from the endosomes and invade into the cytoplasm of the cell with endosomal membranes via disorderly cationic lipid interaction (Ding & Ma, 2013; Hafez et al., 2001; Hu-Lieskovan et al., 2005). However, PEGylation is reported as a clinically accepted device that regulates the surface properties of the NPs and produces a "secrecy" drug delivery carrier. Moreover, binding of target ligand on the surface is feasible by the utilization of certain chemicals, which increases the intracellular uptake of the drug (Noble et al., 2014).

Active targeted drug delivery

The active targeting strategy provides better control of the accurate drug. It shows its promising applications in delivering genes, drugs, and theragnostics to the target location by evading normal tissues and increasing the healing efficacy by minimum complexity. Moreover, compared to passively targeted nanosystems, active targeting exhibits its potential capability to enhance the amount of drug delivered to the target cell. As a result, drugs accumulate in the tumor region, and efficiency of drug increases by the active targeting strategy. However, this is accomplished by grafting the ligands on the nanocarriers' surface, and ligands bind to the receptors, which is further manifested by angiogenic endothelial cells or cancer cells. This strategy will improve the active targeting of drug-loaded NPs and further increases the effects of passive targeting to make the NPs more specific toward the target site. However, this approach will enhance the drug penetration and ameliorate the nanocarriers' empathy for the surface of cancer cells (Attia et al., 2019).

Moreover, in 1980 the first confirmation of this aspect was put forward with the antibodies insertion in the surface of liposomes accompanied by various other types of ligands, such as nucleic acids, aptamers, and peptides, which facilitate their uptake by specific cancerous or effected cells (Kamaly et al., 2012; Leserman et al., 1980; Wang et al., 2014). Moreover, among good targets, nicotinic acetylcholine or transferrin receptors (Tfr) can be cited as an agent that permits the drug to reach the brain tumor's environment that concerns to vascular targeting of endothelial cells. Further, for demonstrating biomedical imaging/drug delivery application, glioma was targeted with transferrin ligands grafted on micelles (Zhang et al., 2012), superparamagnetic iron oxide NPs (SPIONPs), dendrimers (He et al., 2011; Li et al., 2012), and solid lipid NPs (Jain et al., 2013). Moreover, from the reported literature, it is evident that nicotinic acetylcholine grafted by micelles can reach glioblastoma and central nervous system via targeting (Zhan et al., 2011, 2012, 2010).

Further, the parallel overexpression of molecules and proteins on the cancer cell's surface around or in the tumor interstitium, also called receptors, represents an anchor for attachment to, or interaction with the ligands that are functionalized on the nanocarrier's surface. The two most accepted approaches of targeted drug delivery have been reported: the classic receptor-mediated targeting, where the NP is designed with ligands that bind specific receptors of interest, and the engineering of stimuli-sensitive nanosystems that will respond to the disease microenvironment or tumor and the alternation in the pathological area in a way that would trigger the drug release (Cheng et al., 2012; Koshkaryev et al., 2013; Peer et al., 2007; Shi et al., 2011). Recently, the siRNA-encapsulated double-targeted photolabile-caged cell-penetrating peptide (PcCPP/NGR) liposomes were studied in vivo and in vitro to demonstrate promising efficiency in silencing the c-myc gene. PcCPP/NGR liposomes displayed endosomal escape and enhanced uptake in the HT1080 cell line. As a result, PcCPP/NGR liposomes preferably accumulate in tumor and detain its growth through interference of RNA (McNeeley et al., 2009). Consequent clinical translation and preclinical trials were performed for targeting docetaxel encapsulated with polymeric micelles (BIND-014) (Hrkach et al., 2012).

Moreover, along with active targeting, the micelles get combined with passive targeting via EPR provided by a prostate-specific membrane antigen substrate analog inhibitor and by peptide derivative *S,S*-2-[3-[5-amino-1-carboxypentyl]-ureido]-pentanoic acid (ACUPA) (Attia et al., 2019). Furthermore, one of the highly studied clinically targeted agents and preclinical trials are performed for antibodies and their fragments. Reynolds et al. investigated that HER2-targeted liposomal doxorubicin evolved to provide a clinical advantage by increasing the therapeutic potential of HER2-based therapies and compressing the cardiotoxicity noted with anthracyclines that are recently accessible for HER2-overexpressing cancers (Reynolds et al., 2012). Moreover, another alternative of antibodies and peptides is vitamins and sugars, a small natural molecule that does not induce any complexities or toxicity but gets quickly metabolized. Moreover, the crucial example of a small targeting molecule is glycosylated solid lipid NPs encapsulated with doxorubicin that exhibits in vivo similar biodistribution and enhanced cellular uptake compared to nontargeted.

Conclusion

Targeted drug delivery strategies emerged as the most relevant approach in past decades due to potential clinical applications in the pharmaceutical industry. This chapter focused on the advantages of promising nanocarriers and the EPR effect in designing the passive targeted strategy and the mode of active targeting strategy that shows benefits in real-time targeting and control and release of drug at the targeted site of action. Multiple vital benefits of passive and active systems have been discussed in this chapter that would motivate readers to study the potential role of targeted drug delivery strategy in the pharmaceutical industry.

References

Abra, R. M., Bankert, R. B., Chen, F., Egilmez, N. K., Huang, K., Saville, R., … Yokota, S. J. (2002). *Journal of Liposome Research*, *12*(1–2), 1–3. Available from https://doi.org/10.1081/LPR-120004770.

Alexis, F., Pridgen, E., Molnar, L. K., & Farokhzad, O. C. (2008). *Molecular Pharmaceutics*, *5*(4), 505–515. Available from https://doi.org/10.1021/mp800051m.

Arap, W., Pasqualini, R., & Ruoslahti, E. (1998). *Science (New York, N.Y.)*, *279*(5349), 377–380. Available from https://doi.org/10.1126/science.279.5349.377.

Arvizo, R. R., Miranda, O. R., Moyano, D. F., Walden, C. A., Giri, K., Bhattacharya, R., … Mukherjee, P. (2011). *PLoS One*, *6*(9). Available from https://doi.org/10.1371/journal.pone.0024374.

Attia, M. F., Anton, N., Wallyn, J., Omran, Z., & Vandamme, T. F. (2019). *Journal of Pharmacy and Pharmacology*, *71*(8), 1185–1198. Available from https://doi.org/10.1111/jphp.13098.

Baselga, J. (2006). *Science (New York, N.Y.)*, *312*(5777), 1175–1178. Available from https://doi.org/10.1126/science.1125951.

Baumgart, D. C., & Sandborn, W. J. (2007). *Lancet*, *369*(9573), 1641–1657. Available from https://doi.org/10.1016/S0140-6736(07)60751-X.

Bertrand, N., & Leroux, J. C. (2012). *Journal of Controlled Release*, *161*(2), 152–163. Available from https://doi.org/10.1016/j.jconrel.2011.09.098.

Cheng, Z., Al Zaki, A., Hui, J. Z., Muzykantov, V. R., & Tsourkas, A. (2012). *Science (New York, N.Y.)*, *338*(6109), 903–910. Available from https://doi.org/10.1126/science.1226338.

Chithrani, B. D., Ghazani, A. A., & Chan, W. C. W. (2006). *Nano Letters*, *6*(4), 662–668. Available from https://doi.org/10.1021/nl052396o.

Chonn, A., Cullis, P. R., & Devine, D. V. (1991). *Journal of Immunology*, *146*(12), 4234–4241.

Chono, S., Tanino, T., Seki, T., & Morimoto, K. (2007). *Journal of Pharmacy and Pharmacology*, *59*(1), 75–80. Available from https://doi.org/10.1211/jpp.59.1.0010.

Ding, H. M., & Ma, Y. Q. (2013). *Scientific Reports*, *3*. Available from https://doi.org/10.1038/srep02804.

Dreher, M. R., Liu, W., Michelich, C. R., Dewhirst, M. W., Yuan, F., & Chilkoti, A. (2006). *Journal of the National Cancer Institute*, *98*(5), 335–344. Available from https://doi.org/10.1093/jnci/djj070.

Fang, J., Nakamura, H., & Maeda, H. (2011). *Advanced Drug Delivery Reviews*, *63*(3), 136–151. Available from https://doi.org/10.1016/j.addr.2010.04.009.

Foged, C., Brodin, B., Frokjaer, S., & Sundblad, A. (2005). *International Journal of Pharmaceutics*, *298*(2), 315–322. Available from https://doi.org/10.1016/j.ijpharm.2005.03.035.

Folkman, J. (1995). *Nature Medicine*, *1*(1), 27–30. Available from https://doi.org/10.1038/nm0195-27.

Gabizon, A., & Papahadjopoulos, D. (1988). *Proceedings of the National Academy of Sciences of the United States of America*, *85*(18), 6949–6953. Available from https://doi.org/10.1073/pnas.85.18.6949.

Hafez, I. M., Maurer, N., & Cullis, P. R. (2001). *Gene Therapy*, *8*(15), 1188–1196. Available from https://doi.org/10.1038/sj.gt.3301506.

He, C., Hu, Y., Yin, L., Tang, C., & Yin, C. (2010). *Biomaterials*, *31*(13), 3657–3666. Available from https://doi.org/10.1016/j.biomaterials.2010.01.065.

He, H., Li, Y., Jia, X. R., Du, J., Ying, X., Lu, W. L., … Wei, Y. (2011). *Biomaterials*, *32*(2), 478–487. Available from https://doi.org/10.1016/j.biomaterials.2010.09.002.

Hobbs, S. K., Monsky, W. L., Yuan, F., Roberts, W. G., Griffith, L., Torchilin, V. P., & Jain, R. K. (1998). *Proceedings of the National Academy of Sciences of the United States of America*, *95*(8), 4607–4612. Available from https://doi.org/10.1073/pnas.95.8.4607.

Hrkach, J., Von Hoff, D., Ali, M. M., Andrianova, E., Auer, J., Campbell, T., ... Zale, S. (2012). *Science Translational Medicine*, *4*(128). Available from https://doi.org/10.1126/scitranslmed.3003651.

Hu-Lieskovan, S., Heidel, J. D., Bartlett, D. W., Davis, M. E., & Triche, T. J. (2005). *Cancer Research*, *65* (19), 8984–8992. Available from https://doi.org/10.1158/0008-5472.CAN-05-0565.

Huynh, E., & Zheng, G. (2015). *Nanomedicine: Nanotechnology, Biology, and Medicine*, *10*(13), 1993–1995. Available from https://doi.org/10.2217/nnm.15.86.

Jain, A., Singhai, P., Gurnany, E., Updhayay, S., & Mody, N. (2013). *Journal of Nanoparticle Research*, *15* (3). Available from https://doi.org/10.1007/s11051-013-1518-4.

Jain, R. K. (1999). *Annual Review of Biomedical Engineering*, *1*, 241–263. Available from https://doi.org/10.1146/annurev.bioeng.1.1.241.

Jain, R. K., & Stylianopoulos, T. (2010). *Nature Reviews Clinical Oncology*, *7*(11), 653–664. Available from https://doi.org/10.1038/nrclinonc.2010.139.

Kamaly, N., Xiao, Z., Valencia, P. M., Radovic-Moreno, A. F., & Farokhzad, O. C. (2012). *Chemical Society Reviews*, *41*(7), 2971–3010. Available from https://doi.org/10.1039/c2cs15344k.

Kobayashi, H., Watanabe, R., & Choyke, P. L. (2014). *Theranostics*, *4*(1), 81–89. Available from https://doi.org/10.7150/thno.7193.

Koshkaryev, A., Sawant, R., Deshpande, M., & Torchilin, V. (2013). *Advanced Drug Delivery Reviews*, *65* (1), 24–35. Available from https://doi.org/10.1016/j.addr.2012.08.009.

Lee, K. D., Nir, S., & Papahadjopoulos, D. (1993). *Biochemistry*, *32*(3), 889–899. Available from https://doi.org/10.1021/bi00054a021.

Leserman, L. D., Barbet, J., Kourilsky, F., & Weinstein, J. N. (1980). *Nature*, *288*(5791), 602–604. Available from https://doi.org/10.1038/288602a0.

Levchenko, T. S., Rammohan, R., Lukyanov, A. N., Whiteman, K. R., & Torchilin, V. P. (2002). *International Journal of Pharmaceutics*, *240*(1–2), 95–102. Available from https://doi.org/10.1016/S0378-5173(02)00129-1.

Li, Y., He, H., Jia, X., Lu, W. L., Lou, J., & Wei, Y. (2012). *Biomaterials*, *33*(15), 3899–3908. Available from https://doi.org/10.1016/j.biomaterials.2012.02.004.

Lu, F., Wu, S. H., Hung, Y., & Mou, C. Y. (2009). *Small (Weinheim an der Bergstrasse, Germany)*, *5*(12), 1408–1413. Available from https://doi.org/10.1002/smll.200900005.

Maeda, H. (2001). *Advances in Enzyme Regulation*, *41*(1), 189–207. Available from https://doi.org/10.1016/S0065-2571(00)00013-3.

Maeda, H., Bharate, G. Y., & Daruwalla, J. (2009). *European Journal of Pharmaceutics and Biopharmaceutics*, *71*(3), 409–419. Available from https://doi.org/10.1016/j.ejpb.2008.11.010.

MAEDA, H., TAKESHITA, J., & KANAMARU, R. (1979). *International Journal of Peptide and Protein Research*, *14*(2), 81–87. Available from https://doi.org/10.1111/j.1399-3011.1979.tb01730.x.

Matsumura, Y., & Maeda, H. (1986). *Cancer Research*, *46*(8), 6387–6392.

Matsumura, Y., Oda, T., & Maeda, H. (1987). *Japanese Journal of Cancer and Chemotherapy*, *14*(3), 821–829.

McNeeley, K. M., Karathanasis, E., Annapragada, A. V., & Bellamkonda, R. V. (2009). *Biomaterials*, *30* (23–24), 3986–3995. Available from https://doi.org/10.1016/j.biomaterials.2009.04.012.

Nishida, K., Mihara, K., Takino, T., Nakane, S., Takakura, Y., Hashida, M., & Sezaki, H. (1991). *Pharmaceutical Research: An Official Journal of the American Association of Pharmaceutical Scientists*, *8*(4), 437–444. Available from https://doi.org/10.1023/A:1015886708598.

Noble, G. T., Stefanick, J. F., Ashley, J. D., Kiziltepe, T., & Bilgicer, B. (2014). *Trends in Biotechnology*, *32*(1), 32–45. Available from https://doi.org/10.1016/j.tibtech.2013.09.007.

Osaki, F., Kanamori, T., Sando, S., Sera, T., & Aoyama, Y. (2004). *Journal of the American Chemical Society*, *126*(21), 6520–6521. Available from https://doi.org/10.1021/ja048792a.

Patra, J. K., Das, G., Fraceto, L. F., Campos, E. V. R., Rodriguez-Torres, M., del, P., ... Shin, H.-S. (2018). *Journal of Nanobiotechnology*, *16*(1). Available from https://doi.org/10.1186/s12951-018-0392-8.

Peer, D., & Margalit, R. (2004). *Neoplasia (New York, N.Y.)*, *6*(4), 343–353. Available from https://doi.org/10.1593/neo.03460.

Peer, D., Karp, J. M., Hong, S., Farokhzad, O. C., Margalit, R., & Langer, R. (2007). *Nature Nanotechnology*, *2*(12), 751–760. Available from https://doi.org/10.1038/nnano.2007.387.

Pham, C. T. N. (2011). *WIREs Nanomedicine and Nanobiotechnology*, *3*(6), 607–619. Available from https://doi.org/10.1002/wnan.157.

Pohl, C., Hombach, A., & Kruis, W. (2000). *Hepato-Gastroenterology*, *47*(31), 57–70.

Reynolds, J. G., Geretti, E., Hendriks, B. S., Lee, H., Leonard, S. C., Klinz, S. G., ... Wickham, T. J. (2012). *Toxicology and Applied Pharmacology*, *262*(1), 1–10. Available from https://doi.org/10.1016/j.taap.2012.04.008.

Roux, E., Lafleur, M., Lataste, E., Moreau, P., & Leroux, J. C. (2003). *Biomacromolecules*, *4*(2), 240–248. Available from https://doi.org/10.1021/bm025651x.

Salvador-Morales, C., Zhang, L., Langer, R., & Farokhzad, O. C. (2009). *Biomaterials*, *30*(12), 2231–2240. Available from https://doi.org/10.1016/j.biomaterials.2009.01.005.

Scherphof, G. L., & Kamps, J. A. A. M. (2001). *Progress in Lipid Research*, *40*(3), 149–166. Available from https://doi.org/10.1016/S0163-7827(00)00020-5.

Seymour, L. W., Miyamoto, Y., Maeda, H., Brereton, M., Strohalm, J., Ulbrich, K., & Duncan, R. (1995). *European Journal of Cancer*, *31*(5), 766–770. Available from https://doi.org/10.1016/0959-8049(94)00514-6.

Shi, J., Xiao, Z., Kamaly, N., & Farokhzad, O. C. (2011). *Accounts of Chemical Research*, *44*(10), 1123–1134. Available from https://doi.org/10.1021/ar200054n.

Smith, B. E., Roder, P. B., Zhou, X., & Pauzauskie, P. J. (2015). *Nanoscale*, *7*(16), 7115–7126. Available from https://doi.org/10.1039/c4nr06164k.

Torchilin, V. (2011). *Advanced Drug Delivery Reviews*, *63*(3), 131–135. Available from https://doi.org/10.1016/j.addr.2010.03.011.

Torchilin, V. P., Klibanov, A. L., Huang, L., O'Donnell, S., Nossiff, N. D., & Khaw, B. A. (1992). *FASEB Journal*, *6*(9), 2716–2719. Available from https://doi.org/10.1096/fasebj.6.9.1612296.

Wang, X., Li, S., Shi, Y., Chuan, X., Li, J., Zhong, T., ... Zhang, Q. (2014). *Journal of Controlled Release*, *193*, 139–153. Available from https://doi.org/10.1016/j.jconrel.2014.05.028.

Watkins, R., Wu, L., Zhang, C., Davis, R. M., & Xu, B. (2015). *International Journal of Nanomedicine*, *10*, 6055–6074. Available from https://doi.org/10.2147/IJN.S92162.

Xiao, K., Li, Y., Luo, J., Lee, J. S., Xiao, W., Gonik, A. M., ... Lam, K. S. (2011). *Biomaterials*, *32*(13), 3435–3446. Available from https://doi.org/10.1016/j.biomaterials.2011.01.021.

Yamamoto, Y., Nagasaki, Y., Kato, Y., Sugiyama, Y., & Kataoka, K. (2001). *Journal of Controlled Release*, *77*(1–2), 27–38. Available from https://doi.org/10.1016/S0168-3659(01)00451-5.

Yin Win, K., & Feng, S. S. (2005). *Biomaterials*, *26*(15), 2713–2722. Available from https://doi.org/10.1016/j.biomaterials.2004.07.050.

Yu, X., Trase, I., Ren, M., Duval, K., Guo, X., & Chen, Z. (2016). *Journal of Nanomaterials*, *2016*, 1–15. Available from https://doi.org/10.1155/2016/1087250.

Zhan, C., Li, B., Hu, L., Wei, X., Feng, L., Fu, W., & Lu, W. (2011). *Angewandte Chemie – International Edition*, *50*(24), 5482–5485. Available from https://doi.org/10.1002/anie.201100875.

Zhan, C., Wei, X., Qian, J., Feng, L., Zhu, J., & Lu, W. (2012). *Journal of Controlled Release*, *160*(3), 630–636. Available from https://doi.org/10.1016/j.jconrel.2012.02.022.

Zhan, C., Yan, Z., Xie, C., & Lu, W. (2010). *Molecular Pharmaceutics*, *7*(6), 1940–1947. Available from https://doi.org/10.1021/mp100238j.

Zhan, J., Ting, X. L., & Zhu, J. (2017). *IOP conference series: materials science and engineering* (207). Institute of Physics Publishing 1. Available from https://doi.org/10.1088/1757-899X/207/1/012017.

Zhang, P., Hu, L., Yin, Q., Feng, L., & Li, Y. (2012). *Molecular Pharmaceutics*, *9*(6), 1590–1598. Available from https://doi.org/10.1021/mp200600t.

CHAPTER 11

Utility of various drug delivery systems and their advantages and disadvantages

Hareem Fatima[1], Shazia Shukrullah[1], Humaira Hussain[2], Hira Aslam[1] and Muhammad Yasin Naz[1]
[1]Department of Physics, University of Agriculture Faisalabad, Faisalabad, Pakistan
[2]Department of Chemistry, University of Okara, Okara, Pakistan

Introduction

Nanotechnology in drug delivery

Nanotechnology seems to be more widely utilized in medicine in recent decades, with implications in diagnostics, therapy, and cancer attacking that are both convenient and quite successful. Numerous benefits of nanotechnology-based therapeutic transport platforms in cancer therapy have been evidenced, including excellent pharmacokinetics, specific aiming of cancerous cells, lesser drug resistance, and lower toxicity (Bayda et al., 2018; Belgamwar et al., 2021). The dimension and properties of nanostructures utilized in medication distribution mechanisms are typically developed or selected depending on the pathophysiological mechanisms of malignancies. Nanostructures in anticancer treatment physically attack malignant sites via the transport action of nanocarriers and the locating function of the targeted chemical upon absorption. They then provide the medicines to cancerous tissues in essence to destroy them. Conventional chemotherapeutic medicines and nucleotides are among the medicines found on the interior of the nanotransporters, suggesting that they might be used for both chemotherapeutic and genetic manipulation (Chen et al., 2015). Furthermore, for certain weakly hydrophilic medicines, nanoparticles provide a substrate for encapsulation and delivery throughout bloodstream (Chan et al., 2009; Keck & Muller, 2006). Nanoparticles (NPs) may enhance the half-life of medicines and promote their concentration within malignant cells because of particle's length and surface features, as well as their role of increasing penetration and persistence (Kalyane et al., 2019; Shi et al., 2017). Simultaneously, the aiming mechanism shields healthy tissues against chemical cytotoxic effects, reducing the undesirable consequences of tumor treatment. In comparison to unbound doxorubicin, doxorubicin-coated liposomal nanocarriers decreased cardiotoxicity (Cortes & Saura, 2010; Gradishar et al., 2005). NP-based medicines have been used in cancer immunotherapeutic as well as elimination therapy, in

Nanotechnology for Drug Delivery and Pharmaceuticals
DOI: https://doi.org/10.1016/B978-0-323-95325-2.00015-8

contrast to chemotherapeutics and genetic manipulation, according to many investigations (Riley & Day, 2017). The nanocarriers-based medication distribution method is thought to improve immunology and counteract the unfavorable milieu seen in tumors (Wang et al., 2021).

Targets for drug delivery

Developing novel as well as revolutionary cancer therapies is a significant challenge all around the globe (Rahib et al., 2021). A growing quantity of nanocarrier-based therapeutic medicines has indeed been marketed or initiated preclinical trials in past few years. The curative effectiveness of certain tumorous cells has significantly improved as the variety of techniques for treating tumors has increased, as has the idea of personalized therapy. Chemotherapy is a well-known as well as frequently utilized form of cancer treatments. Chemotherapy kills rapidly developing cells without discrimination, comprising both normal and tumor ones, which has severe adverse consequences, such as bone marrow depletion, loss of hair, gastric and cardio problems (Zhang et al., 2021). As a result, a significant part of melanoma studies in recent years has focused on creating medicines that more precisely attack cancerous tissues rather than healthy ones. Even though specific targeting treatment has achieved significant success in terms of accuracy of treatment, there are indeed numerous inevitable negative effects, and emergence of resistance has long remained a concern. Unfortunately, ranked as the second largest cause of mortality, yet several carcinoma treatments are ineffective. As a result, a growing number of research studies are looking for targeted tumor treatment and medication resistance solutions (Table 11.1).

Advantages of nanoparticles

Fig. 11.1 summarizes the benefits of nanocarriers (Jacob et al., 2021; Wang et al., 2014). An additional benefit of nanostructures in medication administration is that

Table 11.1 The attributes of an exquisite nanotransporter.

Terms of production	Qualities of encapsulation	Discharge profile of drug
Less complicated	Sustainable	Balanced and manageable
Easily expandable on large scale	Zero premature payload discharge or leaking	Selectively directed
Overall inexpensive	Nonpoisonous	Triggered by external signals like temperature, light, and pH
Experimentally verified	Biocompatible	
Minimal variation between batches	Environment friendly	

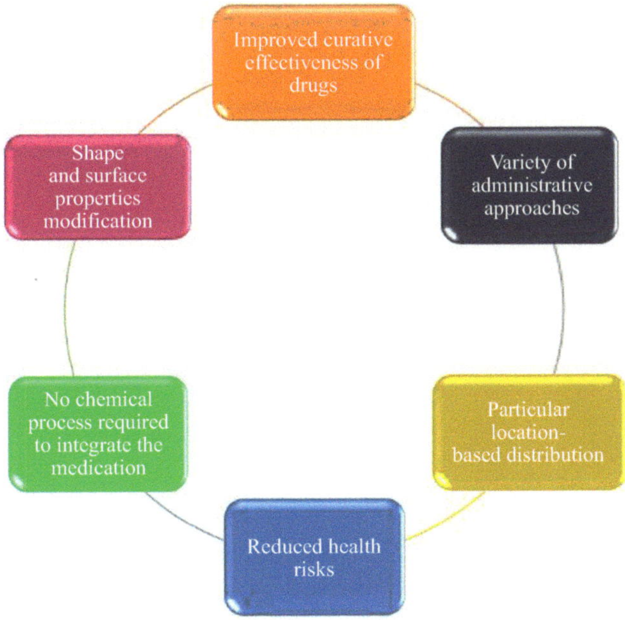

Figure 11.1 Various distinct benefits of utilization of nanocarriers

they are simple to expand on a large scale. The ability to integrate medicines within organisms without causing a reaction mechanism is essential for maintaining pharmacological functionality. Furthermore, the platforms may be used in a variety of ways, including parenteral, ophthalmic, intravenous, and rectal administration.

Drug release from nanoparticles

Medications in nanostructures embedded using polymeric materials are discharged via the polymer-based membrane, dispersion or erosion processes. Because this bilayer serves as an obstacle to release of drug, the medication's diffusibility and solubility in it are critical variables in the discharge mechanism. The release of drug and polymeric degradability are two key elements in creating an effective nanostructured structure. The quantity of therapeutic distribution is affected by a number of variables, some of which are illustrated in Fig. 11.2. As a result, the release mechanism is governed by the dissolution, dispersion, and biological decomposition of matrix components (Estabragh et al., 2021; Kumar et al., 2021).

One of the three main physicochemical pathways for drug delivery from nanotransporter to cell locations is as follows:

- The polymeric nanomaterials are hydrated, producing swelling and eventual release of drug through dispersion.

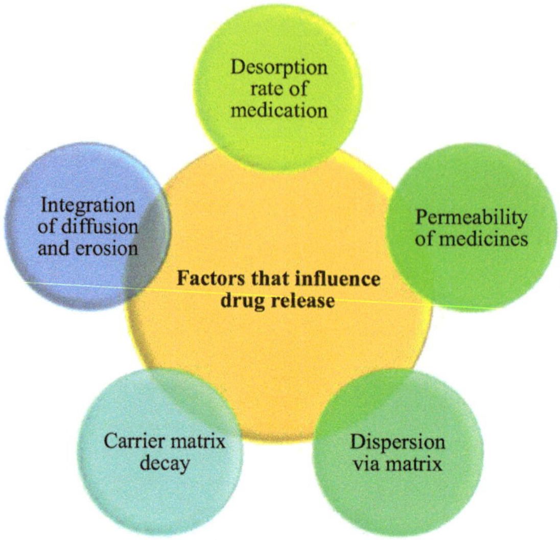

Figure 11.2 Factors that affect the release of a medication.

- Polymer breakage, splitting, or decomposition caused by an enzyme, enabling the encapsulated medication from the internal structure to be freed.
- Desorption of the medication from the swelled nanostructures after separation from the polymer (Operti et al., 2021).

Nanoparticles as therapeutic administration platforms

The dimensions, geometries, and physicochemical characteristics of nanocarriers employed in medicinal therapy are typically particular because these three factors have a significant impact upon the effectiveness of nanodrug distribution and, therefore, regulate treatment effectiveness (Bahrami et al., 2017). Nanomaterials with a length of 1–100 nm are often used in anticancer treatment because they may transport medicines efficiently and have an increased penetration and persistence (EPR) impact. Finer particulates (under 10–12 nm) may readily drain from typical capillaries and be cleansed through kidneys (Asgeirsson et al., 2007), whereas NPs bigger than 100 nm are more likely to get eliminated through circulatory flow by phagocytes. Furthermore, NPs' surface properties may affect their half-life and bioavailability. For example, particles encapsulated with water-soluble compounds like polyethylene glycol reduce opsonization and hence prevent immune system release (Perry et al., 2012). As a result, nanostructures are often changed to acquire hydrophilicity that extends the duration in the movement of medicines and improves their diffusion and deposition in malignancies (Ju et al., 2014; Sykes et al., 2014). The different properties of nanomaterials influence their curative efficacy in tumor treatment when used together.

Figure 11.3 Nanocarriers of various kinds employed in cancer treatment.

Fig. 11.3 depicts several kinds of nanostructures for treatment of cancer, and the following section will discuss their individual benefits in anticancer therapy.

Organic nanocarriers

Organic nanomaterials have been investigated for years and include a diverse range of components. Liposomes, the very initial nanoscale medication authorized for medical use (Zylberberg & Matosevic, 2016), are made up of an exterior lipid membrane and a center that contains mostly a hydrophilic or a hydrophobic medication. Liposomes may imitate the physiological properties (such as movement and flexibility) of human tissue by altering the lipid network composition that could assist accomplish the goal of more efficient medical drug administration (Johnsen et al., 2014; Sercombe et al., 2015). Liposomes have progressed over numerous stages of evolution thanks to years of study. Liposomes are a suitable framework for an in situ administration of chemotherapeutic medicines like paclitaxel and doxorubicin, amongst several additional cytotoxic compounds, along with nucleotides in cancer treatment. Liposomes are frequently being used in the treatment of various types of cancers, for example, prostate and breast cancer (Huang et al., 2020; Tang et al., 2020; Yari et al., 2019). When contrasted to untreated paclitaxel, several paclitaxel-liposomes were proven to have better anticancer effectiveness and enhanced biodistribution (Jiang et al., 2020b). Liposomal-DOX has been used to minimize cardiotoxicity and has similar effectiveness in the treatment of breast tumors (Andreopoulou et al., 2007).

Additionally, liposome-based nanostructures have provided a medication combining possibility, which may improve curative efficacy and even overcome multidrug resistance (Salzano et al., 2015; Yin et al., 2017). Liposomal oriented medicines are now being used in preclinical trials for melanoma therapy in greater numbers. One kind of particles is polymer-based nanomaterials, which have particular geometric configurations for targeted therapy that are produced by various monomers (Naz et al., 2019). The cross-linking of lactic acid and glycolic acid results in polylactic-*co*-glycolic acid, a ubiquitous polymer-based compound. PLGA is extensively utilized as a drug transportation vehicle due to its improved biodegradability and biocompatibility, along with the EPR phenomenon (Danhier et al., 2012; Makimoto et al., 2021). Furthermore, dendrimers are a kind of polymeric material that has been used in therapeutic applications. These are biodegradable and adaptable polysaccharides that have a three-dimensional tree-like structure (Rajani et al., 2020; Shyma & Sheri, 2020). Along the membrane, their numerous functional units improve the capacity to pack and distribute medicinal substances. Polymeric micelles, which are made up of amphiphilic biopolymer and are distinguished by polymeric self-accumulation into nanoclusters, are another type of polymeric nano transporters that have been studied extensively. The water-insoluble center allows hydrophobic antitumor medicines to be consumed and supplied easily, whereas the water-soluble section improves stability, decreasing medicine absorption by the reticuloendothelial pathway and extending drug dissolution rate (Yang et al., 2020; Yao et al., 2020).

Inorganic nanocarriers

Inorganic nanocarriers offer a greater coverage area per volumetric proportion than organic nanomaterials. They feature a versatile surface coupling composition that can be readily changed, as well as a simple production process, but this typically comes at the cost of biodegradability and biocompatibility (Wang et al., 2016). Silicon-based particulates, magnetic nanostructures, quantum dots, carbon-based nanotubes, and gold nanoparticles are among the inorganic nanocarriers that have been investigated. Gold nanostructures are by far the extensively researched inorganic nanomaterials, and heterogeneous composite complexes depending on the gold nucleus are a potential option for drug administration. The gold nucleus is totally nonpoisonous and stable, and surface-modified gold nanoparticulates are said to improve chemical deposition and reverse treatment susceptibility in malignancies. Gold nanomaterials are also believed to have a role in multimodal tumor therapies, such as genetic engineering, hyperthermia treatments, and vaccinations (Cheng et al., 2013; Conde et al., 2015; Thambiraj et al., 2018). Carbon nanostructures are a kind of hollow cylindrical structure which, owing to its distinctive chemical, mechanical, and biological characteristics, have proven to have a lot of promise in the medicine distribution area. As a consequence, antitumor medicines, such as methotrexate, paclitaxel, and doxorubicin, have been delivered through CNTs to treat a range of malignancies. Nevertheless, when CNTs are subjected to near-infrared wavelengths, they generate thermal energy, which may be used in treating cancer via photothermal therapy (Mangla et al., 2020; Rastogi et al., 2014). Solid NPs that are ideal for medication administration are known as mesoporous silica nanoscale transporters (Li et al., 2019; Wu et al., 2011). The high intrinsic porous capacity allows them to encompass the most chemotherapeutic medicines possible, while the supramolecular constituents serve as a covering, enabling drugs to be captured and released. Silica NPs are amongst the finest transporters for therapeutic transportation because of their superior pharmacokinetics and therapeutic effectiveness, along with their excellent durability (Safarzadeh Kozani et al., 2021; Tieu et al., 2019; Zhang et al., 2019a). Furthermore, spongy silica-based nanostructures have exhibited substantial promise in chemoprevention, since their immunoadjuvant characteristics constitute antigenic cross delivery and lymphocyte division. Metal- and oxide-based NPs are often found in magnetic NPs (MNPs) utilized for medication transport. MNPs are often layered with biological compounds, such as fatty acids and polysaccharides, to enhance their durability and bioavailability. They have demonstrated great effectiveness in anticancer therapy using medication and genetic treatment (Mandriota et al., 2019; Rahman et al., 2021; Roacho-Perez et al., 2018). Additionally, utilizing magnetic nanomaterials to induce the heat elimination of lesions, magnetic heating may be used as an effective oncology therapy (Gorbet & Ranjan, 2020; Raouf et al., 2020).

Hybrid nanocarriers

Even though both inorganic and organic nanocarriers have benefits and drawbacks, integrating these compounds in a singular hybrid therapeutic agent gives the multipurpose transporter superior physiological characteristics, which may improve therapeutic effectiveness and decrease resistance to antibiotics (Tariq & Bokhari, 2020). In the therapy of pancreatic carcinoma, breast malignancy, and aggressive prostatic melanoma, polymer-lipid hybridized nanocomposties that contain an interior polymeric center and a lipid based exterior have been reported to be a viable pharmaceutical administration platform (Chen et al., 2020; Lin et al., 2019; Mandal et al., 2013; Persano et al., 2021). This kind of hybridized particles offer superior bioavailability of fatty acids with the mechanical stability of polymeric nanostructures, allowing it to encapsulate simultaneously hydrophobic and hydrophilic medicines for a more effective curative impact (Dave et al., 2019; Tahir et al., 2017). Nevertheless, cancerous individuals may efficiently incorporate this network, avoiding rapid elimination by the reticuloendothelial mechanism (Gao et al., 2014; Yang et al., 2013). A typical technique of particle's development is to combine inorganic as well as organic mixed NPs. A liposome—silica mixture nanomaterial, for instance, is made up of a silicon dioxide center and a lipid membrane that has been produced and proven to be effective in transporting medicines to eradicate breast and prostate carcinomas cells (Ramani et al., 2017). In a mice framework of pancreatic malignancy, the lipid-silica nanostructure was also shown to provide a foundation for the combinatorial administration of paclitaxel and gemcitabine. Researchers assembled permeable silicon particles and large liposomes upon a microfluidic chip to develop an innovative nano-in-micro framework, and combinational distribution of produced nucleic nanostructured materials and medicines in this framework had been found to substantially increase cellular damage of DOX-resistant breast carcinoma cell lines. Moreover, CNTs as well as the chitin-based composite particle utilized to transmit methotrexate to pulmonary carcinoma tissues have been exhibited to enhance antitumor effect while decreasing toxicities in healthy individuals (Liu et al., 2016; Sheikhpour et al., 2020). Additionally, metallic heterostructures (including Mn and Au) and PLGA combination nanomaterials have the capability to combine specific pharmaceutical distribution with hyperthermia, potentially enhancing cancer cell destruction. A further approach for particle development is to combine biological material with synthetic ones. Nanoscience for covering cell membranes, for instance, is gaining greater interest. By encapsulating nanostructures with organically produced cellular membrane, this technique attempts to impart physiological properties on them instantly, enhancing the strength and security of traditional nanocarriers (Raza et al., 2021). Cell walls, originating from leukocytes, cancerous cells, platelets, red blood cells and even microbes, are among the coating materials. Researchers have discovered that encasing mesoporous silicon substances with a purified cellular membrane from leukocytes can help to stop the nanotransporter from being cleared by phagocytes, and the attributes of this blended material permit the medicine to stay in bloodstream for longer time, resulting in improved cancer accumulation. Correspondingly, tumor cell surface-caped nanoporous silica particles have been used in certain research to enhance the durability and homing potential of nanovehicles (Parodi et al., 2013). Furthermore, the creation of double-surface-coated nanostructures may improve nanocarrier functionality even further. (Ai et al., 2021; Jiang et al., 2019; Wu et al., 2019) (Table 11.2).

Comparison of Various Nanocarrier Systems

.

Classification on the basis of administration routes

A large number of papers are examined, and the findings are divided into different categories, as indicated in Fig. 11.4, based on the pathways of medicine administration: transdermal, parenteral, oral, ocular and pulmonary.

Table 11.2 Overview of the benefits and drawbacks of medication delivering nanosystems.

Nanotransporter type	Strengths	Weakness
Organic substances	lipophobic or Lipophilic payload can be incorporated Solubilization is determined by periphery cluster modification, which allows load distribution to be guided	The amount of external aromatic rings is linked to cytotoxicity Cationic dendrimers associate to cytotoxic effects
Hybrid materials	Scalability of manufacturing is practical Biomaterial Fabrication is quite low-cost feasible to transport hydrophilic drugs Increases the dissolving of hydrophobic payload in water	Drug is evacuated prematurely Entrapment efficacy is poor Inadequate weight carrying capability
Inorganic compounds	Payload is released in a regulated manner Pore depth is adjustable and consistent steady design	Possible cellular damage by moieties non-biocompatible non-biodegradable

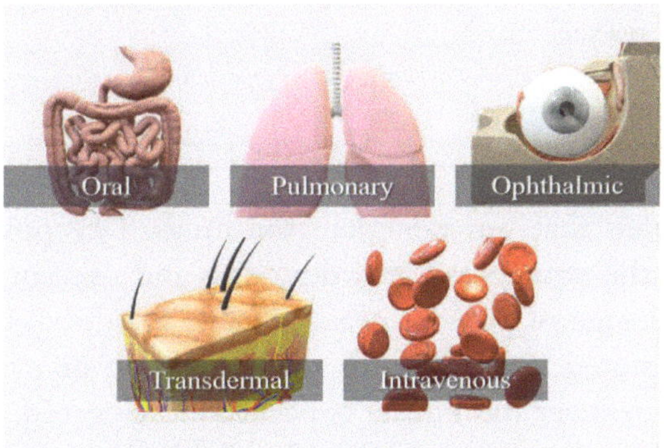

Figure 11.4 Different administration routes for drug delivery systems.

Pulmonary drug delivery systems

Until recently, pulmonary administration has mainly been utilized to treat lung diseases. The inherent capacity of the lungs to transport substances into the circulatory system has increasingly been used to carry medicines to the blood circulating. This technique offers a painless replacement to traumatic infusions, with a quick start of reaction and high absorption. There are three types of breathing gadgets: loose powdered inhalers, nebulizers, and pressurized metered-dose inhalers (MDIs). MDIs include medicines in the form of a fluid or a dispersion of tiny particulates maintained at elevated pressures in a liquid propellant. A meter device releases the medicine via an aperture. Nebulizers, at the other side, do not need propellants and may produce huge

Table 11.3 Advantages and limitations of pulmonary drug delivery systems.

Advantages	Limitations
Biopharma characteristics are improved	Insufficient statistics on consumer safety are published
Drug discharge that lasts a long time	Matrix breakdown in certain formulations causes an alteration in medication dissolution rate
Establishing a large concentration in a certain area	The hazardous consequences of bursting discharge of medicine out of such nanocarriers are questionable
Increasing the biocompatibility of a drug.	Medication elimination in macrophages
Drug stays in the lungs for a longer period of time	Due to their tiny sizes, these should really be encapsulated in microcapsules for thorough pulmonary administration
Packaging chemotherapy medicines into nanovehicles has the ability to cure lung carcinoma	In nebulization, nanocarriers clump together and coagulate
Genetic transfer is a possibility	Upon nebulization, there is a waste of laden medication
Preventing negative medication side effects	
Encapsulation efficiency is excellent	
Ensures minimal toxic effects	
Patient compliance is being improved	

amounts of tiny droplets that can penetrate the lungs. Dry powder is a system that transmits medicine to the airways as a powdery dust and necessitates certain process to ensure that a precise dosage of powder gets accessible for the individual to ingest. The medication is usually stored in a tablet for physical filling or even in a unique shape within the inhaler. Whenever the inhaler is packed or triggered, the person places the device in one's mouth and pulls a long breath, allowing the medication to be delivered (Dua et al., 2017; Paranjpe & Muller-Goymann, 2014; Patil & Sarasija, 2012; Patra et al., 2018; Thakur et al., 2020) (Table 11.3).

Oral drug delivery systems

Because of its apparent benefits of simplicity of distribution, better consumer satisfaction, and comfort, the oral path is among the foremost often utilized methods of medication management. There is hardly any command over release profile from instant releasing dose methods, resulting in continuously fluctuating, unexpected, plasma levels. A customized releasing dosage form is one in which the drug transportation features of timescale and position are selected to achieve curative or economic goals not available with traditional dose formats. Two kinds of modified releasing administration

Table 11.4 Advantages and limitations of oral drug delivery systems.

Advantages	Limitations
The start of effect is quicker, and the period of activity is prolonged	Gel formation upon dispersion
Drugs are released in a regulated and managed manner	There is a plenty of water in colloidal formations
Keeping an unwanted plasma spike at bay	Throughout retention, drugs are ejected
Orally administration offers minimal variation	Water-soluble medicines have a restricted load bearing ability
The medication is protected against internal intestinal metabolism	Rapid transitions from one state to another
Liver level filtration is being reduced	While storing, particulate diameter increases
Increasing the biodistribution of a drug when taken orally	

formulations are elongated releasing and delayed releasing. Elongated dose formulations are designed to keep the medication accessible for a long time once it is been consumed. When contrasted to the medication given in a traditional dose format, it leads to the decrease in dosing frequency. These medicines generally offer a number of advantages, notably improved efficacy in the management of severe diseases, fewer adverse consequences, increased accessibility, and more patient satisfaction owing to a simpler dosage regimen. Sustained-release and controlled-release are terms that are frequently used simultaneously. To manage or modify medication delivery from an active ingredient, a variety of artistic choices are accessible. Matrix, reservoir, capillary networks, and ion swap compounds make up the most of oral dose forms (Fonseca-Santos et al., 2015; Homayun et al., 2019; Kalepu et al., 2013; Maroni et al., 2005; Pandey & Khuller, 2004; Xu et al., 2020) (Table 11.4).

Intravenous drug delivery systems

The creation of novel treatment nanostructures is anticipated to be accelerated as a result of genetic analysis, putting a greater demand on the manufacturing of pharmaceutical distribution methods. The immense size, delicate structure, limited biologic life span, and restricted capacity to penetrate cell walls are all characteristics of this family of medicines. These characteristics, as well as the modes of delivery of bioactive molecules, may restrict their practical use to specific pathological conditions that justify the cost and discomfort of repeated infusion. Numerous bio-disposable polymer-based parenteral deposit compositions, such as microparticles and implantation, are becoming commercially accessible to enhance the effectiveness and extend the action of protein and peptide medicines (Ak et al., 2021; Ezrahi et al., 2019; Raj & Raveendran, 2019; Rizwanullah et al., 2020).

Installations may be medically placed within the body, with medication distribution occurring at a regulated pace over a period of up to 1 year. Another alternative is to utilize bio-disposable implantation, which may be inserted with a wide diameter cannula and provide the benefit of only requiring one operation (such implants need not to be eliminated).

Traditionally, a framework is manufactured into a readily injection form for delivery at the appropriate target location in injecting modified release pharmaceutical formulations. A firm, gel, or fluid dose formulation could be used. As an injecting reservoir administration method for comparatively tiny medicines, proteins, and peptides, granular dosing schedules including disintegrating microparticles made of poly (lactic-*co*-glycolic acid) have indeed been utilized. Injection gels often include a mediator to breakdown the matrix along with curative ingredient, and when injected, they create an "implant-like" deposit (Ahmad et al., 2020; Jiang et al., 2020a; Kwatra et al., 2012; Sakpakdeejaroen et al., 2021; Talevi & Quiroga, 2018) (Table 11.5).

Table 11.5 Advantages and limitations of intravenous drug delivery systems.

Advantages	Limitations
Antitumor medicines that are very irritating may be administered since they get diluted by the blood	If a medication is given too quickly, it could cause hemolysis and certain severe complications
A consistent plasma concentration of the medication may be sustained via i.v. administration	Because there is a significant risk of bacterial impurities on this pathway, specific sterile techniques are required
When the medication has a brief period of effect and the reaction can be monitored accurately, drug dosage escalation is feasible	It is not feasible to self-medicate
Drugs may be administered in a consistent manner	Phlebitis may be caused by regional inflammation
It is possible to deliver a high amount of infusion	Toxicity may have serious consequences, particularly when organs like the brain, heart, and lungs are engaged
Because the vein's innermost layer is vulnerable, irritant and nonisotonic liquids may be given intravenously	Intravenous administration of certain medicines may result in organ damage, inflammation, and skin peeling
The compound enters the bloodstream quickly and has complete accessibility to the whole body, resulting in fast activity, making this pathway most effective in critical circumstances	Once infused, the medication's activity cannot be stopped
Completely biocompatible	

Transdermal drug delivery systems

Over the past few years, systematic medication administration by transdermal method has piqued people's attention. Transdermal drug carriers transfer medicines into the blood stream at a preset pace via the epidermis, bypassing gut and hepatic breakdown. As a result, the quantity of bioactive component needed for transdermal administration may be much lower than it does with oral administration. Low medication effectiveness, due to inadequate skin permeation or diffusion of medicines by the most common compositions, is one of the main constraints for treating these illnesses. The main epidermal barrier, the innermost layer, must be overcome by switching the penetrating route from transcellular to paracellular or follicular. Skin permeability has been improved using nanostructures, such as solid-lipid NPs and nanostructured lipid carriers (NLCs). These may be made in a single-step method that produces medicine-holding solid lipid nanoparticles (SLNs) and/or NLCs. Bioavailability and biocompatibility, regulated and prolonged medicine dissolution profiles, intimate interaction and high epidermis adherence, skin moisture, and layer creation to enhance epidermal penetration are all benefits of nanocarriers for transdermal therapeutic administration. For about 1–7 days, Transdermal distribution maintains serum concentrations and enhance response rates (Campos et al., 2020; Lohan et al., 2015; Manca et al., 2021; Tessema et al., 2020; Wang & Tang, 2021) (Table 11.6).

Ophthalmic drug delivery systems

Ophthalmic transportation of drugs has recently gotten a lot of interest since it requires fewer recurrent dosage than that of eye drops, allows constant medicine supply, and extends the period of therapeutic activity by improving corneal penetration. Contact lenses, ocular insertions, high viscosity fluids, and hydrogel distribution techniques are

Table 11.6 Advantages and limitations of transdermal drug delivery systems.

Advantages	Disadvantages
Exceptional stability throughout preservation	There is a limitation of a well-controlled medication release system
It is possible to reach particular follicles	Wastage of a large quantity of the medication
Minimize systematic accumulation and harmful impacts	Drug distribution via the skin is restricted
Medication absorption is higher	
Development method is simple and repeatable	
Deposition and development of a layer that aids in moisture retention	
Bio-disposable and nontoxic	
Improved skin absorption and/or permeability	

all examples of ophthalmic administration platforms. Due to various unique anatomical and physiological characteristics of the eyes, ophthalmic medication transport has numerous restrictions and remains difficult. The eyes are indeed a complicated yet clever organ with a number of obstacles that must be surmounted in terms of reaching particular eye tissues. To circumvent such obstacles and increase ophthalmic region biocompatibility, innovative pharmaceutical transportation methods of nanostructures were explored. One of the most frequent methods of medication administration to the anterior region of the ocular is topical administration. This method of injection has numerous benefits and is also the preferred method for treating peripheral ophthalmic disorders. Organic NPs (i.e., liposomal) employed as ocular transport devices may cross the blood–ocular boundary, allowing for prolonged and regulated release profile, as well as protecting medicines from certain enzymes and extending drug accumulation and habitation duration in the eyes. Optic disorders affecting the posterior portion of the ocular are notoriously tricky to cure. The posterior portion of the eyes may be targeted in a variety of methods (Abdelbary et al., 2016; Abdelbary et al., 2017; Attama et al., 2008; Leonardi et al., 2014; Onugwu et al., 2021; Youshia et al., 2012) (Table 11.7).

Table 11.7 Advantages and limitations of ocular drug delivery systems.

Advantages	Disadvantages
Keeping medication contents in the retina, vitreous and aqueous humor at a safe level	Other than biocompatibility, grain size, polarity, length of exposure, and dosing frequency all have a role in ocular toxicity
Superb bioavailability and durability	The effects of nanostructures on retinal receptors have yet to be fully investigated
Keeps eye toxins at bay	For such treatments, no long-term clinical investigations had been conducted lately, as well as the majority of previous research included almost in vitro evaluations
Improve the accessibility and dispersion of ophthalmic drugs	Medication stacking capability is limited
Precorneal medication persistence duration is being improved	Rapid discharged at the beginning
Boosting of medication absorption in the cornea	
Discharge that is both steady and regulated	
Pharmacological characteristics that are acceptable	
Ocular permeability is significant	
Entrapment efficacy is improved	

Parental drug delivery systems

Drug-carrying nanocarriers could be administered through i.v. infusion, intramuscular injection, subcutaneous injections, and straight into targeted regions. Drug distribution by nanocarriers might take place through erosion (like metabolic breakdown) or dispersion, which can result in long-term release of drug. Current studies have shown the capacity of nanocarriers to incorporate peptides and proteins. Throughout this case, solid nanostructures are hardly a good transport because of their low encapsulation efficiency, but nanofluids are a good substitute. Proteins and peptides may be preserved against severe external circumstances using this technique (Ajorlou & Khosroushahi, 2017; Gaucher et al., 2010; Kharkar et al., 2020; Liu et al., 2011; Qureshi et al., 2017; Singh et al., 2020) (Table 11.8).

Hazards of nanomedicines

Nanomedicine offers a wide range of uses and advantages; however, it yet is not really a perfect treatment. As the dimension spectrum shrinks, the quantity of interface atoms increases, consequently interparticular tension and adhesion issues grow more prominent. Additionally, due to the tiny length of the nanostructures, these might also exhibit a significant elimination pace from the organism, preventing their utility in diagnostics or medication administration (Zhang et al., 2019b). Trapping by the

Table 11.8 Advantages and limitations of parental drug delivery systems.

Advantages	Disadvantages
Increasing the permeability of drugs	Introduction of cytotoxic agents along with drugs
Cytotoxic activity is reduced	Systematic elimination through reticuloendothelial network
Longer duration for the medication to circulate	Hydrophilic medicines have a limited chemical loading
Adjuvants for vaccines have a lot of promise	There are not enough large-scale clinical trials
There are not many adverse hazards	Cellular breakdown can occur from drug's bursting discharge
The removal rate is much less, and the distribution volume is less	
Increase in medication bloodstream concentrations by 3–5 times	
Release profile that is both regulated and long-lasting	
Physically stable for an extended time	
Easily practically expandable	

mononuclear macrophage mechanism is advantageous for NP liver delivery. However, if such nanomaterials were intended for therapeutic activity in different areas of the system, this feature might be a concern. These particulates are recognized by the host's immune mechanism, which leads to phagocytosis and eventual elimination from the organism. Because of the greater surface coverage, the chemical responsiveness of such particles doubled, raising questions about how they respond during various circumstances and if they may penetrate cellular barriers and invade cells. In contrast, NPs' enhanced chemical reaction generates reactive oxygen species, which might induce oxidative tension, swelling, and disruption to DNA, proteins and surfaces, leading to toxic effects. The fact that NPs have little or zero shared attributes apart from their sizes is a significant disadvantage of nanoscience. As a result, every particle should be assessed separately. Furthermore, alterations in size and shape may result in a variety of mechanical and molecular reactions: a material that seems harmless at 100 nm could turn hazardous at 1 nm, and likewise.

Further disadvantage is that these entities are very dependent on their environment. They have the potential to dissolve or agglomerate, producing morphological alterations and toxicities. Molecular structure, surface characteristics, surface texture, absorption, and the existence of NP's functionality ligands are all variables which might affect safety (Simonazzi et al., 2018). Within the organism, unpredictable reactions among these NPs may occur, resulting in unanticipated responses. They may also act independently inside the system, entering capillaries, moving through the site of injection toward various body regions, crossing cell walls, and inadvertently entering the blood–brain barrier (Moura et al., 2019). As per research, nanocarriers may build up in the tissues of a variety of organisms. Furthermore, it is impossible to anticipate if individuals will be capable of eliminating these nanomaterials or if they would keep collecting in the organism. Bio-disposable nanomaterials are often eliminated, while nonbiodegradable particles may aggregate in the tissues to harm them (Meng, 2013; Zeb et al., 2020).

Future tendencies for nanocarriers in drug distribution

In the past several years, many new approaches have been created for medical therapy. The most of commercialized NPs developments in healthcare have been oriented toward medication transport. The utilization of nanotech to create nanosystems for medication delivery is generating great optimism and excitement in the study of therapeutics. Specialists engaged in this area have been looking for the mixture of the perfect nanotransporter and ideal nanodrug to create the transportation network. This may significantly decrease medication quantity and increase its permeability, which further contributes toward the client eating a lesser amount, providing the equivalent effect. Administering the medication in the right location in biological bodies improves regional concentration of drug at the target region and minimizes or prevents the adverse impacts. Nanostructures may be attached to a receptor, like being an antigen, to promote a specific treatment strategy. Bare viruses' capsids have similarly been utilized to carry medicines as a novel pharmaceutical approach. Consequently, nanocarrier technologies may change the entire drug treatment approach, putting them into a leadership stance in the nearest future. As it is now, the potential of this developing area appears to be limitless. Nevertheless, the corporate industry and government authorities should properly overcome the enormous technical and economic barriers first so that true potential of nanoscience can be completely utilized. In particular, concerns linked to the toxicology of nanomaterials compositions must not be overlooked. Entire testing techniques must be developed to assess long- and short-term safety assessments of nanometric pharmaceutical administration devices. Nanoscience in biomedicine is anticipated to generate breakthroughs and serve a significant part, not just in delivery of drugs and genetic manipulation but as well as in bioimaging, diagnostics, and biosensing, altering the face of biotechnology and pharmaceutical sectors in the coming years.

Conclusion

As mentioned in the above section, medicines may be granted to a client via several delivering methods, including intraveneous, pulmonary, transdermal, and oral pathway. With the decoding of the genetic code, biotech firms are quickly creating a significant amount of protein and peptide-based medicines, and it is anticipated that within the coming couple of years, these groups will represent a substantial basis of the modern pharmaceuticals. These biotechnologies create pharmaceutical administration difficulties since these are typically big compounds that breakdown quickly in the circulating blood. Furthermore, NPs have a poor capacity to penetrate cellular components and usually cannot be administered orally. The potential of alternative administration routes will be determined by the medication, illness condition, and intended location of activity. A few locations are easily reachable, including buccal, vaginal, and nasal, whereas most are quite difficult to approach, best analogy can be the parts of brain. Genetic engineering is also going to be among the greatest interesting emerging areas as biotech firms get engaged in medication transportation. Currently, aside from the study on the capabilities described in this chapter, customized dosage has evolved among the major emphasis sectors. A recent study provided a really excellent summary of liquid and solid medication dose forms utilized in customized therapy.

Emerging developments in the area of nanofabrication have brought up the potential of creating a different generation of programed medication administration devices. A similar gadget is microchip-driven dosing mechanism. Chip comprises an electrochemical impenetrable surface that divides the succession of storage comprising the constituent(s) to be discharged. Depending on electrolytic processes, the barrier dissolves and the medication(s) are subsequently dispersed or liberated through the repository. Their tiny scale and possibility for combination with microelectronics paired with capacity to retain and distribute medication(s) on command represents an exciting universe of opportunities in therapeutics.

In summation the industry for medication conveyance devices has evolved significantly and will keep expanding at an amazing pace. Today's medicine carrier innovations allow the integration of bioactive compounds into novel targeted transport, therefore, offering many clinical and economic benefits. A significant amount of businesses are engaged in the construction of innovative pharmaceutical carriers, which is evidenced by an increasing amount of commodities on the industry as well as the quantity of licenses issued in the recent times. Tomorrow's medicines will certainly be extremely demanding in regards of the creation of conveyance methods, and biopharmaceutical experts must be prepared for a tough job in future.

References

Abdelbary, A. A., Abd-Elsalam, W. H., & Al-Mahallawi, A. M. (2016). Fabrication of novel ultradeformable bilosomes for enhanced ocular delivery of terconazole: In vitro characterization, ex vivo permeation and in vivo safety assessment. *International Journal of Pharmaceutics*, *513*(1–2), 688–696.

Abdelbary, A., Salem, H. F., Khallaf, R. A., & Ali, A. M. (2017). Mucoadhesive niosomal in situ gel for ocular tissue targeting: In vitro and in vivo evaluation of lomefloxacin hydrochloride. *Pharmaceutical Development and Technology*, *22*(3), 409–417.

Ahmad, A., Ansari, M. M., Kumar, A., Vyawahare, A., Mishra, R. K., Jayamurugan, G., Raza, S. S., & Khan, R. (2020). Comparative acute intravenous toxicity study of triple polymer-layered magnetic nanoparticles with bare magnetic nanoparticles in Swiss albino mice. *Nanotoxicology*, *14*(10), 1362–1380.

Ai, X., Wang, S., Duan, Y., Zhang, Q., Chen, M. S., Gao, W., & Zhang, L. (2021). Emerging approaches to functionalizing cell membrane-coated nanoparticles. *Biochemistry*, *60*(13), 941–955.

Ajorlou, E., & Khosroushahi, A. Y. (2017). Trends on polymer-and lipid-based nanostructures for parenteral drug delivery to tumors. *Cancer Chemotherapy and Pharmacology*, *79*(2), 251–265.

Ak, G., Bozkaya, U. F., Yilmaz, H., Sari Turgut, O., Bilgin, I., Tomruk, C., Uyanikgil, Y., & Hamarat Sanlier, S. (2021). An intravenous application of magnetic nanoparticles for osteomyelitis treatment: An efficient alternative. *International Journal of Pharmaceutics*, *592*, 119999.

Andreopoulou, E., Gaiotti, D., Kim, E., Downey, A., Mirchandani, D., Hamilton, A., Jacobs, A., Curtin, J., & Muggia, F. (2007). Pegylated liposomal doxorubicin HCL (PLD; Caelyx/Doxil): Experience with long-term maintenance in responding patients with recurrent epithelial ovarian cancer. *Annals of Oncology: Official Journal of the European Society for Medical Oncology/ESMO*, *18*(4), 716–721.

Asgeirsson, D., Venturoli, D., Fries, E., Rippe, B., & Rippe, C. (2007). Glomerular sieving of three neutral polysaccharides, polyethylene oxide and bikunin in rat. Effects of molecular size and conformation. *Acta Physiologica (Oxford, England)*, *191*(3), 237–246.

Attama, A. A., Reichl, S., & Müller-Goymann, C. C. (2008). Diclofenac sodium delivery to the eye: In vitro evaluation of novel solid lipid nanoparticle formulation using human cornea construct. *International Journal of Pharmaceutics*, *355*(1–2), 307–313.

Bahrami, B., Hojjat-Farsangi, M., Mohammadi, H., Anvari, E., Ghalamfarsa, G., Yousefi, M., & Jadidi-Niaragh, F. (2017). Nanoparticles and targeted drug delivery in cancer therapy. *Immunology Letters*, *190*, 64–83.

Bayda, S., Hadla, M., Palazzolo, S., Riello, P., Corona, G., Toffoli, G., & Rizzolio, F. (2018). Inorganic nanoparticles for cancer therapy: a transition from lab to clinic. *Current Medicinal Chemistry*, *25*(34), 4269–4303.

Belgamwar, V. S., Mishra, S. S., Bhoyar, V. T., & Banode, K. B. (2021). Nanopharmaceuticals: An approach for effective management of breast cancer. *Nanopharmaceutical Advanced Delivery Systems*. Available from https://doi.org/10.1002/9781119711698.ch15, In press.

Campos, P. M., Praca, F. G., Mussi, S. V., Figueiredo, S. A., Fantini, M. C. A., Fonseca, M. J. V., Torchilin, V. P., & Bentley, M. (2020). Liquid crystalline nanodispersion functionalized with cell-penetrating peptides improves skin penetration and anti-inflammatory effect of lipoic acid after in vivo skin exposure to UVB radiation. *Drug Delivery and Translational Research*, *10*(6), 1810−1828.

Chan, J. M., Zhang, L., Yuet, K. P., Liao, G., Rhee, J.-W., Langer, R., & Farokhzad, O. C. (2009). PLGA−lecithin−PEG core−shell nanoparticles for controlled drug delivery. *Biomaterials*, *30*(8), 1627−1634.

Chen, Y., Deng, Y., Zhu, C., & Xiang, C. (2020). Anti prostate cancer therapy: Aptamer-functionalized, curcumin and cabazitaxel co-delivered, tumor targeted lipid-polymer hybrid nanoparticles. *Biomedicine & Pharmacotherapy*, *127*, 110181.

Chen, Y., Gao, D. Y., & Huang, L. (2015). In vivo delivery of miRNAs for cancer therapy: Challenges and strategies. *Advanced Drug Delivery Reviews*, *81*, 128−141.

Cheng, J., Gu, Y. J., Cheng, S. H., & Wong, W. T. (2013). Surface functionalized gold nanoparticles for drug delivery. *Journal of Biomedical Nanotechnology*, *9*(8), 1362−1369.

Conde, J., Ambrosone, A., Hernandez, Y., Tian, F., Mccully, M., Berry, C. C., Baptista, P. V., Tortiglione, C., & Jesus, M. (2015). 15 years on siRNA delivery: Beyond the state-of-the-art on inorganic nanoparticles for RNAi therapeutics. *Nano Today*, *10*(4), 421−450.

Cortes, J., & Saura, C. (2010). Nanoparticle albumin-bound (nab™)-paclitaxel: Improving efficacy and tolerability by targeted drug delivery in metastatic breast cancer. *European Journal of Cancer Supplements*, *8*(1), 1−10.

Danhier, F., Ansorena, E., Silva, J. M., Coco, R., Le Breton, A., & Preat, V. (2012). PLGA-based nanoparticles: An overview of biomedical applications. *Journal of Controlled Release: Official Journal of the Controlled Release Society*, *161*(2), 505−522.

Dave, V., Tak, K., Sohgaura, A., Gupta, A., Sadhu, V., & Reddy, K. R. (2019). Lipid-polymer hybrid nanoparticles: Synthesis strategies and biomedical applications. *Journal of Microbiological Methods*, *160*, 130−142.

Dua, K., Bebawy, M., Awasthi, R., Tekade, R. K., Tekade, M., Gupta, G., De Jesus Andreoli Pinto, T., & Hansbro, P. M. (2017). Application of chitosan and its derivatives in nanocarrier based pulmonary drug delivery systems. *Pharmaceutical Nanotechnology*, *5*(4), 243−249.

Estabragh, M. a R., Bami, M. S., Ohadi, M., Banat, I. M., & Dehghannoudeh, G. (2021). Carrier-based systems as strategies for oral delivery of therapeutic peptides and proteins: A mini-review. *International Journal of Peptide Research and Therapeutics*, *27*(2), 1589−1596.

Ezrahi, S., Aserin, A., & Garti, N. (2019). Basic principles of drug delivery systems—The case of paclitaxel. *Advances in Colloid and Interface Science*, *263*, 95−130.

Fonseca-Santos, B., Gremião, M. P. D., & Chorilli, M. (2015). Nanotechnology-based drug delivery systems for the treatment of Alzheimer's disease. *International Journal of Nanomedicine*, *10*, 4981.

Gao, L. Y., Liu, X. Y., Chen, C. J., Wang, J. C., Feng, Q., Yu, M. Z., Ma, X. F., Pei, X. W., Niu, Y. J., Qiu, C., Pang, W. H., & Zhang, Q. (2014). Core-shell type lipid/rPAA-Chol polymer hybrid nanoparticles for in vivo siRNA delivery. *Biomaterials*, *35*(6), 2066−2078.

Gaucher, G., Marchessault, R. H., & Leroux, J. C. (2010). Polyester-based micelles and nanoparticles for the parenteral delivery of taxanes. *Journal of Controlled Release: Official Journal of the Controlled Release Society*, *143*(1), 2−12.

Gorbet, M. J., & Ranjan, A. (2020). Cancer immunotherapy with immunoadjuvants, nanoparticles, and checkpoint inhibitors: Recent progress and challenges in treatment and tracking response to immunotherapy. *Pharmacology & Therapeutics*, *207*, 107456.

Gradishar, W. J., Tjulandin, S., Davidson, N., Shaw, H., Desai, N., Bhar, P., Hawkins, M., & O'shaughnessy, J. (2005). Phase III trial of nanoparticle albumin-bound paclitaxel compared with polyethylated castor oil−based paclitaxel in women with breast cancer. *Journal of Clinical Oncology*, *23* (31), 7794−7803.

Homayun, B., Lin, X., & Choi, H. J. (2019). Challenges and recent progress in oral drug delivery systems for biopharmaceuticals. *Pharmaceutics*, *11*(3), 129.

Huang, M., Pu, Y., Peng, Y., Fu, Q., Guo, L., Wu, Y., & Zheng, Y. (2020). Biotin and glucose dual-targeting, ligand-modified liposomes promote breast tumor-specific drug delivery. *Bioorganic & Medicinal Chemistry Letters*, *30*(12), 127151.

Jacob, E. M., Borah, A., Pillai, S. C., & Kumar, D. S. (2021). Garcinol encapsulated Ph-sensitive biodegradable nanoparticles: A novel therapeutic strategy for the treatment of inflammatory bowel disease. *Polymers (Basel)*, *13*(6), 862.

Jiang, Q., Liu, Y., Guo, R., Yao, X., Sung, S., Pang, Z., & Yang, W. (2019). Erythrocyte-cancer hybrid membrane-camouflaged melanin nanoparticles for enhancing photothermal therapy efficacy in tumors. *Biomaterials*, *192*, 292−308.

Jiang, W., Chen, J., Gong, C., Wang, Y., Gao, Y., & Yuan, Y. (2020a). Intravenous delivery of enzalutamide based on high drug loading multifunctional graphene oxide nanoparticles for castration-resistant prostate cancer therapy. *Journal of Nanobiotechnology*, *18*(1), 50.

Jiang, Y., Zhou, Y., Zhang, C. Y., & Fang, T. (2020b). Co-delivery of paclitaxel and doxorubicin by pH-responsive prodrug micelles for cancer therapy. *International Journal of Nanomedicine*, *15*, 3319−3331.

Johnsen, K. B., Gudbergsson, J. M., Skov, M. N., Pilgaard, L., Moos, T., & Duroux, M. (2014). A comprehensive overview of exosomes as drug delivery vehicles—Endogenous nanocarriers for targeted cancer therapy. *Biochimica et Biophysica Acta (BBA)-Reviews on Cancer*, *1846*(1), 75−87.

Ju, C., Mo, R., Xue, J., Zhang, L., Zhao, Z., Xue, L., Ping, Q., & Zhang, C. (2014). Sequential intra-intercellular nanoparticle delivery system for deep tumor penetration. *Angewandte Chemie (International (Ed.) in English)*, *53*(24), 6253−6258.

Kalepu, S., Manthina, M., & Padavala, V. (2013). Oral lipid-based drug delivery systems—An overview. *Acta Pharmaceutica Sinica B*, *3*(6), 361−372.

Kalyane, D., Raval, N., Maheshwari, R., Tambe, V., Kalia, K., & Tekade, R. K. (2019). Employment of enhanced permeability and retention effect (EPR): Nanoparticle-based precision tools for targeting of therapeutic and diagnostic agent in cancer. *Materials Science & Engineering C: Materials for Biological Applications*, *98*, 1252−1276.

Keck, C. M., & Muller, R. H. (2006). Drug nanocrystals of poorly soluble drugs produced by high pressure homogenisation. *European Journal of Pharmaceutics and Biopharmaceutics: Official Journal of Arbeitsgemeinschaft fur Pharmazeutische Verfahrenstechnik e.V*, *62*(1), 3−16.

Kharkar, P. B., Talkar, S. S., & Patravale, V. B. (2020). An industrially viable technique for fabrication of docetaxel NLCs for oncotherapy. *International Journal of Pharmaceutics*, *577*, 119082.

Kumar, R., Jha, K., & Barman, D. (2021). Nanotechnology in oral cancer prevention and therapeutics: A literature review. *Indian Journal of Medical and Paediatric Oncology*, *42*(02), 146−152.

Kwatra, S., Taneja, G., & Nasa, N. (2012). Alternative routes of drug administration-transdermal, pulmonary & parenteral. *Indo Global Journal of Pharmaceutical Sciences*, *2*(4), 409−426.

Leonardi, A., Bucolo, C., Romano, G. L., Platania, C. B., Drago, F., Puglisi, G., & Pignatello, R. (2014). Influence of different surfactants on the technological properties and in vivo ocular tolerability of lipid nanoparticles. *International Journal of Pharmaceutics*, *470*(1−2), 133−140.

Li, Z., Zhang, Y., & Feng, N. (2019). Mesoporous silica nanoparticles: Synthesis, classification, drug loading, pharmacokinetics, biocompatibility, and application in drug delivery. *Expert Opinion on Drug Delivery*, *16*(3), 219−237.

Lin, C., Hu, Z., Yuan, G., Su, H., Zeng, Y., Guo, Z., Zhong, F., Jiang, K., & He, S. (2019). HIF1α-siRNA and gemcitabine combination-based GE-11 peptide antibody-targeted nanomedicine for enhanced therapeutic efficacy in pancreatic cancers. *Journal of Drug Targeting*, *27*(7), 797−805.

Liu, D., Liu, Z., Wang, L., Zhang, C., & Zhang, N. (2011). Nanostructured lipid carriers as novel carrier for parenteral delivery of docetaxel. *Colloids and Surfaces B: Biointerfaces*, *85*(2), 262−269.

Liu, X., Situ, A., Kang, Y., Villabroza, K. R., Liao, Y., Chang, C. H., Donahue, T., Nel, A. E., & Meng, H. (2016). Irinotecan delivery by lipid-coated mesoporous silica nanoparticles shows improved efficacy and safety over liposomes for pancreatic cancer. *ACS Nano*, *10*(2), 2702−2715.

Lohan, S. B., Bauersachs, S., Ahlberg, S., Baisaeng, N., Keck, C. M., Muller, R. H., Witte, E., Wolk, K., Hackbarth, S., Roder, B., Lademann, J., & Meinke, M. C. (2015). Ultra-small lipid nanoparticles promote the penetration of coenzyme Q10 in skin cells and counteract oxidative stress. *European Journal of Pharmaceutics and Biopharmaceutics: Official Journal of Arbeitsgemeinschaft fur Pharmazeutische Verfahrenstechnik e.V*, *89*, 201–207.

Makimoto, A., Fang, J., & Maeda, H. (2021). Development of a selective tumor-targeted drug delivery system: Hydroxypropyl-acrylamide polymer-conjugated pirarubicin (P-THP) for pediatric solid tumors. *Cancers (Basel)*, *13*(15), 3698.

Manca, M. L., Manconi, M., Meloni, M. C., Marongiu, F., Allaw, M., Usach, I., Peris, J. E., Escribano-Ferrer, E., Tuberoso, C. I. G., & Gutierrez, G. (2021). Nanotechnology for natural medicine: Formulation of neem oil loaded phospholipid vesicles modified with argan oil as a strategy to protect the skin from oxidative stress and promote wound healing. *Antioxidants*, *10*(5), 670.

Mandal, B., Bhattacharjee, H., Mittal, N., Sah, H., Balabathula, P., Thoma, L. A., & Wood, G. C. (2013). Core–shell-type lipid–polymer hybrid nanoparticles as a drug delivery platform. *Nanomedicine: Nanotechnology, Biology and Medicine*, *9*(4), 474–491.

Mandriota, G., Di Corato, R., Benedetti, M., De Castro, F., Fanizzi, F. P., & Rinaldi, R. (2019). Design and application of cisplatin-loaded magnetic nanoparticle clusters for smart chemotherapy. *ACS Applied Materials & Interfaces*, *11*(2), 1864–1875.

Mangla, B., Javed, S., Kohli, K., Ahsan, A., & Ahsan, W. (2020). Reassessment of therapeutic applications of carbon nanotubes: A majestic and futuristic drug carrier. *Critical Reviews in Therapeutic Drug Carrier Systems*, *37*(4), 331–373.

Maroni, A., Zema, L., Cerea, M., & Sangalli, M. E. (2005). Oral pulsatile drug delivery systems. *Expert Opinion on Drug Delivery*, *2*(5), 855–871.

Meng, J. (2013). *Nanostructures with biocompatible and biodegradable characteristics. Nanopharmaceutics: The Potential Application of Nanomaterials* (pp. 571–589). World Scientific.

Moura, R. P., Martins, C., Pinto, S., Sousa, F., & Sarmento, B. (2019). Blood-brain barrier receptors and transporters: An insight on their function and how to exploit them through nanotechnology. *Expert Opinion on Drug Delivery*, *16*(3), 271–285.

Naz, S., Wang, M., Han, Y., Hu, B., Teng, L., Zhou, J., Zhang, H., & Chen, J. (2019). Enzyme-responsive mesoporous silica nanoparticles for tumor cells and mitochondria multistage-targeted drug delivery. *International Journal of Nanomedicine*, *14*, 2533–2542.

Onugwu, A. L., Agbo, C. P., Nwagwu, C. S., Uzondu, S. E., Echezona, A. C., Nwabueze Ogbonna, J. D., Kenechukwu, F. C., Umeyor, C. E., Uronnachi, E. M., Akpa, P. A., Momoh, M. A., Nnamani, P. O., Muller-Goymann, C. C., & Attama, A. A. (2021). Development of lipid-based microsuspensions for improved ophthalmic delivery of gentamicin sulphate. *Therapeutic Delivery*, *12*(9), 671–683.

Operti, M. C., Bernhardt, A., Grimm, S., Engel, A., Figdor, C. G., & Tagit, O. (2021). PLGA-based nanomedicines manufacturing: Technologies overview and challenges in industrial scale-up. *International Journal of Pharmaceutics*, *605*, 120807.

Pandey, R., & Khuller, G. K. (2004). Polymer based drug delivery systems for mycobacterial infections. *Current Drug Delivery*, *1*(3), 195–201.

Paranjpe, M., & Muller-Goymann, C. C. (2014). Nanoparticle-mediated pulmonary drug delivery: A review. *International Journal of Molecular Sciences*, *15*(4), 5852–5873.

Parodi, A., Quattrocchi, N., Van De Ven, A. L., Chiappini, C., Evangelopoulos, M., Martinez, J. O., Brown, B. S., Khaled, S. Z., Yazdi, I. K., Enzo, M. V., Isenhart, L., Ferrari, M., & Tasciotti, E. (2013). Synthetic nanoparticles functionalized with biomimetic leukocyte membranes possess cell-like functions. *Nature Nanotechnology*, *8*(1), 61–68.

Patil, J. S., & Sarasija, S. (2012). Pulmonary drug delivery strategies: A concise, systematic review. *Lung India*, *29*(1), 44–49.

Patra, J. K., Das, G., Fraceto, L. F., Campos, E. V. R., Rodriguez-Torres, M. D. P., Acosta-Torres, L. S., Diaz-Torres, L. A., Grillo, R., Swamy, M. K., Sharma, S., Habtemariam, S., & Shin, H. S. (2018). Nano based drug delivery systems: Recent developments and future prospects. *Journal of Nanbiotechnology*, *16*(1), 71.

Perry, J. L., Reuter, K. G., Kai, M. P., Herlihy, K. P., Jones, S. W., Luft, J. C., Napier, M., Bear, J. E., & Desimone, J. M. (2012). PEGylated PRINT nanoparticles: The impact of PEG density on protein binding, macrophage association, biodistribution, and pharmacokinetics. *Nano Letters*, *12*(10), 5304–5310.

Persano, F., Gigli, G., & Leporatti, S. (2021). Lipid-polymer hybrid nanoparticles in cancer therapy: Current overview and future directions. *Nano Express*, *2*, 1–15.

Qureshi, O. S., Kim, H. S., Zeb, A., Choi, J. S., Kim, H. S., Kwon, J. E., Kim, M. S., Kang, J. H., Ryou, C., Park, J. S., & Kim, J. K. (2017). Sustained release docetaxel-incorporated lipid nanoparticles with improved pharmacokinetics for oral and parenteral administration. *Journal of Microencapsulation*, *34*(3), 250–261.

Rahib, L., Wehner, M. R., Matrisian, L. M., & Nead, K. T. (2021). Estimated projection of US cancer incidence and death to 2040. *JAMA Network Open*, *4*(4), e214708.

Rahman, S., Kumar, V., Kumar, A., Abdullah, T. S., Rather, I. A., & Jan, A. T. (2021). Molecular perspective of nanoparticle mediated therapeutic targeting in breast cancer: An Odyssey of endoplasmic reticulum unfolded protein response (UPR(ER)) and beyond. *Biomedicines*, *9*(6), 635.

Raj, G. M., & Raveendran, R. (2019). *Introduction to basics of pharmacology and toxicology: Volume 1: General and molecular pharmacology: Principles of drug action*. Springer Nature.

Rajani, C., Borisa, P., Karanwad, T., Borade, Y., Patel, V., Rajpoot, K., & Tekade, R. K. (2020). *Cancer-targeted chemotherapy: emerging role of the folate anchored dendrimer as drug delivery nanocarrier. Pharmaceutical applications of dendrimers* (pp. 151–198). Elsevier.

Ramani, M., Nguyen, T. D. T., Aryal, S., Ghosh, K. C., & Delong, R. K. (2017). Elucidating the RNA nano–bio interface: Mechanisms of anticancer poly I: C RNA and zinc oxide nanoparticle interaction. *The Journal of Physical Chemistry C*, *121*(29), 15702–15710.

Raouf, I., Khalid, S., Khan, A., Lee, J., Kim, H. S., & Kim, M. H. (2020). A review on numerical modeling for magnetic nanoparticle hyperthermia: Progress and challenges. *Journal of Thermal Biology*, *91*, 102644.

Rastogi, V., Yadav, P., Bhattacharya, S. S., Mishra, A. K., Verma, N., Verma, A., & Pandit, J. K. (2014). Carbon nanotubes: An emerging drug carrier for targeting cancer cells. *Journal of Drug Delivery*, *2014*, 670815.

Raza, F., Zafar, H., Zhang, S., Kamal, Z., Su, J., Yuan, W. E., & Mingfeng, Q. (2021). Recent advances in cell membrane-derived biomimetic nanotechnology for cancer immunotherapy. *Advanced Healthcare Materials*, *10*(6), e2002081.

Riley, R. S., & Day, E. S. (2017). Gold nanoparticle-mediated photothermal therapy: Applications and opportunities for multimodal cancer treatment. *Wiley Interdisciplinary Reviews: Nanomedicine and Nanobiotechnology*, *9*(4), e1449.

Rizwanullah, M., Ahmad, J., Amin, S., Mishra, A., Ain, M. R., & Rahman, M. (2020). Polymer-lipid hybrid systems: Scope of intravenous-to-oral switch in cancer chemotherapy. *Current Nanomedicine (Formerly: Recent Patents on Nanomedicine)*, *10*(2), 164–177.

Roacho-Perez, J. A., Gallardo-Blanco, H. L., Sanchez-Dominguez, M., Garcia-Casillas, P. E., Chapa-Gonzalez, C., & Sanchez-Dominguez, C. N. (2018). Nanoparticles for death-induced gene therapy in cancer. *Molecular Medicine Reports*, *17*(1), 1413–1420.

Safarzadeh Kozani, P., Safarzadeh Kozani, P., & Rahbarizadeh, F. (2021). Chemotherapeutic, toxin, and therapeutic protein delivery via nucleolin aptamer-functionalized nanoplatforms for targeted cancer therapy. *Trends in Medical Sciences*, *1*(1), e113773.

Sakpakdeejaroen, I., Somani, S., Laskar, P., Mullin, M., & Dufès, C. (2021). Regression of melanoma following intravenous injection of plumbagin entrapped in transferrin-conjugated, lipid–polymer hybrid nanoparticles. *International Journal of Nanomedicine*, *16*, 2615.

Salzano, G., Navarro, G., Trivedi, M. S., De Rosa, G., & Torchilin, V. P. (2015). Multifunctional polymeric micelles co-loaded with anti-survivin siRNA and paclitaxel overcome drug resistance in an animal model of ovarian cancer. *Molecular Cancer Therapeutics*, *14*(4), 1075–1084.

Sercombe, L., Veerati, T., Moheimani, F., Wu, S. Y., Sood, A. K., & Hua, S. (2015). Advances and challenges of liposome assisted drug delivery. *Frontiers in Pharmacology*, *6*, 286.

Sheikhpour, M., Naghinejad, M., Kasaeian, A., Lohrasbi, A., Shahraeini, S. S., & Zomorodbakhsh, S. (2020). The applications of carbon nanotubes in the diagnosis and treatment of lung cancer: A critical review. *International Journal of Nanomedicine*, *15*, 7063–7078.

Shi, J., Kantoff, P. W., Wooster, R., & Farokhzad, O. C. (2017). Cancer nanomedicine: Progress, challenges and opportunities. *Nature Reviews. Cancer*, *17*(1), 20–37.

Shyma, M., & Sheri, P. (2020). Dendrimers—A emerging tool for drug delivery. *Journal of Pharmaceutical Sciences and Research*, *12*(10), 1309–1314.

Simonazzi, A., Cid, A. G., Villegas, M., Romero, A. I., Palma, S. D., & Bermúdez, J. M. (2018). *Nanotechnology applications in drug controlled release. Drug targeting and stimuli sensitive drug delivery systems* (pp. 81–116). Elsevier.

Singh, A., Thakur, S., Singh, H., Singh, H., Kaur, S., Kaur, S., Dudi, R., Mondhe, D. M., & Jain, S. K. (2020). Novel vitamin E TPGS based docetaxel nanovesicle formulation for its safe and effective parenteral delivery: Toxicological, pharmacokinetic and pharmacodynamic evaluation. *Journal of Liposome Research*, *31*(4), 365–380.

Sykes, E. A., Chen, J., Zheng, G., & Chan, W. C. (2014). Investigating the impact of nanoparticle size on active and passive tumor targeting efficiency. *ACS Nano*, *8*(6), 5696–5706.

Tahir, N., Madni, A., Balasubramanian, V., Rehman, M., Correia, A., Kashif, P. M., Makila, E., Salonen, J., & Santos, H. A. (2017). Development and optimization of methotrexate-loaded lipid-polymer hybrid nanoparticles for controlled drug delivery applications. *International Journal of Pharmaceutics*, *533*(1), 156–168.

Talevi, A., & Quiroga, P. A. (2018). *ADME processes in pharmaceutical sciences*. Springer.

Tang, B., Peng, Y., Yue, Q., Pu, Y., Li, R., Zhao, Y., Hai, L., Guo, L., & Wu, Y. (2020). Design, preparation and evaluation of different branched biotin modified liposomes for targeting breast cancer. *European Journal of Medicinal Chemistry*, *193*, 112204.

Tariq, H., & Bokhari, S. a I. (2020). Surface-functionalised hybrid nanoparticles for targeted treatment of cancer. *IET Nanobiotechnology/IET*, *14*(7), 537–547.

Tessema, E. N., Bosse, K., Wohlrab, J., Mrestani, Y., & Neubert, R. H. H. (2020). Investigation of ex vivoskin penetration of coenzyme Q10 from microemulsions and hydrophilic vream. *Skin Pharmacology and Physiology*, *33*(6), 293–299.

Thakur, A. K., Chellappan, D. K., Dua, K., Mehta, M., Satija, S., & Singh, I. (2020). Patented therapeutic drug delivery strategies for targeting pulmonary diseases. *Expert Opinion on Therapeutic Patents*, *30*(5), 375–387.

Thambiraj, S., Hema, S., & Shankaran, D. R. (2018). Functionalized gold nanoparticles for drug delivery applications. *Materials Today: Proceedings*, *5*(8), 16763–16773.

Tieu, T., Alba, M., Elnathan, R., Cifuentes-Rius, A., & Voelcker, N. H. (2019). Advances in porous silicon–based nanomaterials for diagnostic and therapeutic applications. *Advanced Therapeutics*, *2*(1), 1800095.

Wang, B., Yang, Q., Wang, Y., & Li, Z. (2014). The toolbox of designing nanoparticles for tumors. *Mini Reviews in Medicinal Chemistry*, *14*(9), 707–716.

Wang, F., Li, C., Cheng, J., & Yuan, Z. (2016). Recent advances on inorganic nanoparticle-based cancer therapeutic agents. *International Journal of Environmental Research and Public Health*, *13*(12), 1182.

Wang, S., Sun, Z., & Hou, Y. (2021). Engineering nanoparticles toward the modulation of emerging cancer immunotherapy. *Advanced Healthcare Materials*, *10*(5), e2000845.

Wang, Z., & Tang, M. (2021). Research progress on toxicity, function, and mechanism of metal oxide nanoparticles on vascular endothelial cells. *Journal of Applied Toxicology*, *41*(5), 683–700.

Wu, M., Le, W., Mei, T., Wang, Y., Chen, B., Liu, Z., & Xue, C. (2019). Cell membrane camouflaged nanoparticles: A new biomimetic platform for cancer photothermal therapy. *International Journal of Nanomedicine*, *14*, 4431–4448.

Wu, S.-H., Hung, Y., & Mou, C.-Y. (2011). Mesoporous silica nanoparticles as nanocarriers. *Chemical Communications*, *47*(36), 9972–9985.

Xu, Y., Shrestha, N., Préat, V., & Beloqui, A. (2020). Overcoming the intestinal barrier: A look into targeting approaches for improved oral drug delivery systems. *Journal of Controlled Release*, *322*, 486–508.

Yang, H., Khan, A. R., Liu, M., Fu, M., Ji, J., Chi, L., & Zhai, G. (2020). Stimuli-responsive polymeric micelles for the delivery of paclitaxel. *Journal of Drug Delivery Science and Technology*, *56*, 101523.

Yang, Z., Luo, X., Zhang, X., Liu, J., & Jiang, Q. (2013). Targeted delivery of 10-hydroxycamptothecin to human breast cancers by cyclic RGD-modified lipid—polymer hybrid nanoparticles. *Biomedical Materials*, *8*(2), 025012.

Yao, Y., Zhou, Y., Liu, L., Xu, Y., Chen, Q., Wang, Y., Wu, S., Deng, Y., Zhang, J., & Shao, A. (2020). Nanoparticle-based drug delivery in cancer therapy and its role in overcoming drug resistance. *Frontiers in Molecular Biosciences*, 7, 193.

Yari, H., Nkepang, G., & Awasthi, V. (2019). Surface modification of liposomes by a lipopolymer targeting prostate specific membrane antigen for theranostic delivery in prostate cancer. *Materials (Basel)*, *12*(5), 756.

Yin, X., Chi, Y., Guo, C., Feng, S., Liu, J., Sun, K., & Wu, Z. (2017). Chitooligosaccharides modified reduction-sensitive liposomes: enhanced cytoplasmic drug delivery and osteosarcomas-tumor inhibition in animal models. *Pharmaceutical Research*, *34*(10), 2172—2184.

Youshia, J., Kamel, A. O., El Shamy, A., & Mansour, S. (2012). Design of cationic nanostructured heterolipid matrices for ocular delivery of methazolamide. *International Journal of Nanomedicine*, 7, 2483—2496.

Zeb, A., Rana, I., Choi, H. I., Lee, C. H., Baek, S. W., Lim, C. W., Khan, N., Arif, S. T., Sahar, N. U., Alvi, A. M., Shah, F. A., Din, F. U., Bae, O. N., Park, J. S., & Kim, J. K. (2020). Potential and applications of nanocarriers for efficient delivery of biopharmaceuticals. *Pharmaceutics*, *12*(12), 1184.

Zhang, D. X., Esser, L., Vasani, R. B., Thissen, H., & Voelcker, N. H. (2019a). Porous silicon nanomaterials: Recent advances in surface engineering for controlled drug-delivery applications. *Nanomedicine (Lond)*, *14*(24), 3213—3230.

Zhang, Y., Li, M., Gao, X., Chen, Y., & Liu, T. (2019b). Nanotechnology in cancer diagnosis: Progress, challenges and opportunities. *Journal of Hematology & Oncology*, *12*(1), 137.

Zhang, Y., Yu, M., Jing, Y., Cheng, J., Zhang, C., Cheng, L., Lu, H., Cai, M.-C., Wu, J., & Wang, W. (2021). Baseline immunity and impact of chemotherapy on immune microenvironment in cervical cancer. *British Journal of Cancer*, *124*(2), 414—424.

Zylberberg, C., & Matosevic, S. (2016). Pharmaceutical liposomal drug delivery: A review of new delivery systems and a look at the regulatory landscape. *Drug Delivery*, *23*(9), 3319—3329.

CHAPTER 12

Clinical applications and future clinical trials of the drug delivery system

Kemal Çetin[1,2], Koray Şarkaya[3] and Adil Denizli[4]
[1]Department of Biomedical Engineering, Necmettin Erbakan University, Konya, Turkey
[2]Science and Technology Research and Application Center (BITAM), Necmettin Erbakan University, Konya, Turkey
[3]Department of Chemistry, Pamukkale University, Denizli, Turkey
[4]Department of Chemistry, Hacettepe University, Ankara, Turkey

Introduction

Drug efficacy tends to decrease due to various factors, such as drug side effects during treatment, inability to reach the targeted area at the desired concentration, rapid excretion from the bloodstream, and low solubility. In addition, it is well known that antineoplastic agents used in cancer treatment can damage healthy cells as well as tumor cells (Roy et al., 2003). As a consequence, there is indeed a growing interest in drug delivery systems (DDSs) utilized for the decrement of the harmful aspects of drugs even while maintaining their bioavailability (Pérez-Herrero & Fernández-Medarde, 2015). DDSs are systems responsible for the delivery of a therapeutic agent to the targeted site in the body at a predetermined period of time, prevent the physiological metabolization of the drug without being affected by the environment in the body, and increase the drug's effectiveness (Siegel & Rathbone, 2012). Over the years, scientists in the biomedical and pharmaceutical fields have focused on intelligent DDSs. The main goals of DDSs are to improve therapeutic effects, reduce toxicity, and decrease the frequency of drug intake. As well as the synthesis of a new active substance, it is important to develop systems that will ensure that the active substance is delivered to the target area under optimal conditions (Yavuz et al., 2018). DDSs can be regarded as systems capable of fulfilling these expectations. In other words, DDSs are expected to have features, such as ease of use, noninteraction of the active substance in a way that would disrupt its structure, low cytotoxicity, being biocompatible and biodegradable, being easily produced, and having a long shelf life (Pavlukhina & Sukhishvili, 2011).

Controlled drug release systems have been developed to provide higher safety and effectiveness of drug administration while reducing side effects. The primary objective of controlled release systems is to provide the desired blood concentration as soon as possible by delivering the active substance to the desired tissue or organ and to

Nanotechnology for Drug Delivery and Pharmaceuticals
DOI: https://doi.org/10.1016/B978-0-323-95325-2.00020-1

maintain this concentration within the stipulated time period (Qiu & Park, 2001). After the drug has been administrated, the active substance level in the blood should remain stable within the plasma range (therapeutic window) to keep its effectiveness and not to cause toxicity. Classically, the drug is taken orally in the form of tablets or capsules at periodic intervals, or it could be given directly into the bloodstream via injection. For these methods, a fluctuating profile occurs between the minimum effective and minimum toxic concentration levels, and after each fluctuation, a high dose of medication should be taken again. In the therapeutic window range for drug release systems, drugs can be released over an extended period of time (Çetin & Denizli, 2015). DDSs can be broadly classified based on dosage formulations into nanoparticles, polymeric microcapsules, micelles, liposomes, microspheres, microcryogels, hydrogels, and so on (Çetin & Denizli, 2022; Özbaş et al., 2021; Yavuz et al., 2018). Proteins, peptides, oligonucleotides, inorganic materials, antibodies, and vaccines, as well as gene-based drugs, all are instances of pharmaceutical compounds (Vargason et al., 2021). DDSs could be designed in different forms, taking into administration routes and features of an active compound. Besides the traditional approaches, such as oral, parenteral, injectable, transdermal, inhalation, implant, suppository, rectal, ocular, ophthalmic, and otic dosage forms, new DDSs like targeted administration and drug-device combinations have been gaining popularity in drug development systems (Wen et al., 2015). These progressions pave the way for numerous clinical trials in a variety of fields, along with the delivery of antibiotic, anticancer, and antifungal drugs, and also gene drugs, analgesics, and anti-inflammatory drugs. On the other hand, there is a lot more interest to use DDSs to deliver novel drugs designed for proteomics or genomics, and also their applications in targeted therapeutics (Allen & Cullis, 2004). General stages from fabrication to be a commercial product for DDSs are shown in Fig. 12.1. Thus this chapter deals with current trends and future trials of clinical applications of DDSs as well as their in vitro and in vivo performances, and preclinical assessment.

Clinical applications

Oral drug delivery systems

Oral drug delivery appears to be the most popular route of drug delivery owing to factors, such as ease, patient-related factors, convenience of large-scale manufacturing, and cost-effectiveness (Alqahtani et al., 2021). More than half of the drug molecule products that have been validated in the market so far are used orally (Prasad et al., 2017). Furthermore, it is estimated that current oral formulations for human use account for approximately 90% of the global market share (Prasad et al., 2017). Despite the fact that some active chemical and enzymatic obstacles, as well as low permeability of intestinal epithelium in the gastrointestinal (GI) tract, could reduce the effectiveness of this carrier,

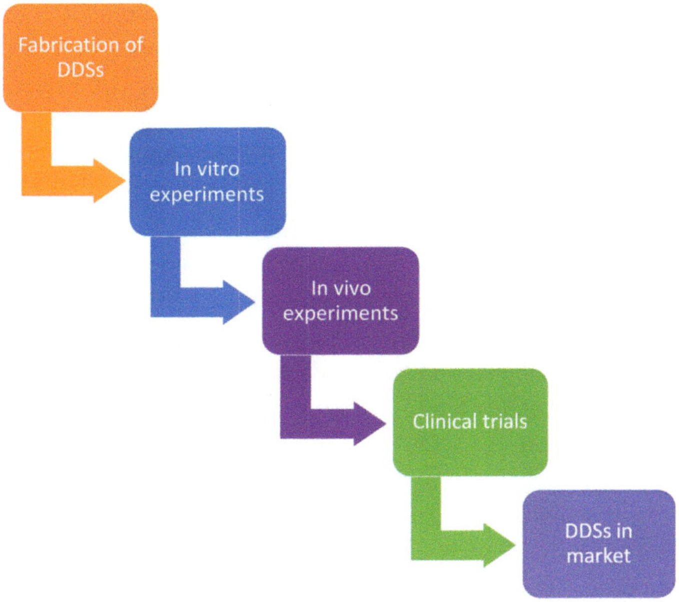

Figure 12.1 General steps of DDSs from fabrication to be commercial products in the market. *DDSs*, Drug delivery systems.

oral delivery system is painless, patient-friendly, comfortable for self-medication, especially for chronic therapy, cost-effective, more aseptic, pliable dosage form design, and viable for outpatients (Choonara et al., 2014; Park et al., 2011).

GI tract is a system that is responsible for digestion and includes the long tubular structure between the mouth and the anus, as well as many organs associated with these structures (Kagan & Hoffman, 2008). It is known that oral DDS appears to be the most likely route of delivery of a therapeutic agent in the GI tract, and it could be utilized for both systemic delivery and local digestive disease treatment (Ensign et al., 2012). In addition, oral medications can be directed to specific sites of the GI system for localized treatment of diseases, including infections, inflammations, colorectal and gastric cancers, other intestinal diseases, gastroesophageal reflux disorders, and gastric–duodenal ulcers (Alqahtani et al., 2021; Hua, 2020).

Despite the advantages of oral administration, difficulties may arise due to changes in absorption of molecules, such as proteins, peptides, or oligonucleotide-based therapeutics caused by interactions with membrane permeability, gastric contents/secretion, intestinal transit, rapid enzymatic degradation, and poor digestion (Marques et al., 2011). Biotechnology advancements have accelerated the cost-effective, large-scale production of therapeutics, such as proteins, vaccines, and hormones, helping to make them easily accessible for therapeutic applications in medical practices and clinical studies (Park et al., 2011). Furthermore, therapeutic proteins and peptides-based pharmaceuticals are gaining popularity as biotechnology advances provide them to be used in the treatment of a variety of diseases (Chin et al., 2012). In spite of the emergence of a new generation of biotechnology-based therapeutics (proteins, peptides, etc.) that can play a decisive role in achieving effective treatment, biologic drugs have low oral bioavailability due to GI barriers and are, therefore, not suitable for direct oral administration (Brown et al., 2020). Efforts to solve problems related to GI tract rely on a deeper comprehension of GI tract physiology both in normal and diseased states (Hua, 2020).

Nano-drug carriers can be used effectively to overcome multiple barriers originating through GI tract since DDS is nano in size and the active substance is entrapped in the carrier system (Wang et al., 2020). Nanoparticles protect the encapsulated active substance from chemical or enzymatic degradation, keeping it in the systemic circulation for a longer period of time and tracking the active compounds' release profile (Date et al., 2016; Severino et al., 2012; Tang et al., 2009). The nanoparticulate formulation development approach is thought to be particularly beneficial for some drugs, the oral bioavailability of which remains poor due to poor solubility (Naeem et al., 2020). Because of the high specific surface area of nanoparticles, it has been suggested in the literature that some drugs with solubility issues can be improved by encapsulating them in a nanocarrier system with dimensions reduced to nanoscales (Chan & Kwok, 2011; Gao et al., 2014; Liu et al., 2010; Merisko-Liversidge & Liversidge, 2011). As a result, effectiveness of the treatment could be higher, the lower dose amount is provided and prospective side effects could be significantly lowered, and medication adherence can continue to get better (Grama et al., 2011; Homayun et al., 2019; Liu et al., 2013). According to the traditional diagnosis, Glucagon-like peptide-1 receptor agonists can be used in the treatment of type 2 diabetes if given by injection (Buckley et al., 2018). Buckley et al. examined the potential to increase drug absorption by coformulating *N*-[8-(2-hydroxybenzoyl)amino]caprylate with semaglutide, a glucagon-type peptide 1 analog. According to in vivo studies, including both animal and human trials, the transient increase in absorption provided by *N*-[8-(2-hydroxybenzoyl)amino]caprylate coformulation may help the development of effective oral peptide-based therapies has been noted (Buckley et al., 2018).

Clinical treatments for cancer, one of the world's most frequent diseases, remain insufficient despite breakthroughs in chemotherapy (Ünal et al., 2015). Most anticancer drugs have traditionally been administered via intravenous injection (Liu et al., 1997; O'neill & Twelves, 2002). On the other hand, oral anticancer drugs have been more popular in recent years owing to their sufficient reliability and patients' choice for oral therapy. Oral options are typically selected if they are at least as suitable as intravenous alternatives in terms of conformity, tolerability, practicality, and potency (Stuurman et al., 2013). The most significant difficulty is the low oral bioavailability of many anticancer drugs, including paclitaxel, camptothecin, docetaxel, and doxorubicin which prevents them from being administered orally (Thanki et al., 2013). Formulation approaches based on anticancer drug encapsulation in the nanoparticulate system; these drugs may become more useful for oral administration (Agüeros et al., 2009; Arima et al., 2001; Ercan et al., 2018; Grosse et al., 1997; Oostendorp et al., 2009; Upadhyay et al., 2006).

Oral administration of protein and peptide structures is also possible. Till previously, injections were widely accepted as the favored method of delivering therapeutic proteins and peptides (Shaji & Patole, 2008). Insulin is currently one of the most frequently studied subjects because diabetes is a chronic disease that may necessitate multiple injections per day (Wong et al., 2016). On the other hand, due to convenient administration conditions, such as painlessness and self-medication, insulin delivery via oral administration could be a preferred method over injection (Fonte et al., 2015). Individual patients' responses can be used to adjust the frequency of insulin dosing based on efficacy and toxicity (Plapied et al., 2011). Furthermore, because it makes a first pass to the liver before entering the systemic bloodstream, the oral route resembles the endogenous pathway of insulin once delivered (Pérez-Herrero & Fernández-Medarde, 2015). For this aim, designing a nanoparticle system to deliver insulin provides a solution to the GI barriers encountered with oral insulin delivery (Li et al., 2008; Suri et al., 2007). Moreover, insulin release and absorption in the gut can be regulated by nanoparticles (Ahmad et al., 2011; Elçioğlu & Sezer, 2014). One of the most often utilized nanoparticle systems is polymeric nanoparticles generated from natural or synthetic polymers (Kumari et al., 2010). Promising approaches are those that are stable, biocompatible, and flexible. Besides these, polymeric-based nanoparticles are the most suitable nanocarriers for oral insulin delivery since they are sensitive to environmental conditions like temperature and light, and their pharmacokinetic features are consistent. The development of an orally given insulin formulation has been reported in several studies in recent decades (Cetin et al., 2012; Chen et al., 2013; Lin et al., 2007; Lopes et al., 2014; Sonaje et al., 2010; Sonia & Sharma, 2012).

Despite various difficulties, controlled release formulations of a number of pharmaceutical moieties have been developed with success. Clinical trials are being conducted on some oral controlled/sustained DDSs. In a clinical trial to test IntelliCap CR capsules' in vivo drug release ability, 12 normal healthy volunteers were given IntelliCap CR capsules filled with metoprolol as the BCS 1 model drug (BCS: Biopharmaceutical Classification System) and cross-designed to release the drug with various release profiles (Söderlind et al., 2015). As a reference, an oral metoprolol solution is provided. Standard bioavailability variables were also studied. For these applications, it was revealed that the expected release profiles and in vivo release were in agreement. The IntelliCap CR capsules, which were programmed to deliver two different and equal medication pulses, only delivered roughly half of the second dose, while the first pulse was delivered as expected. As a consequence, the IntelliCap technology was observed to be well suited for producing timely and reliable pharmacokinetic data for sustained-release profiles for in vivo studies (Söderlind et al., 2015).

Geetha et al. (2015) used calcium carbonate, sodium alginate, and hydroxypropylmethylcellulose to prepare multiunit-induced gastric floating beads for localized and extended-release of sesamol for the treatment of stomach malignancies. Multiunit gastro-retaining floating beads (10 mg/kg) performed better compared with pure sesamol and were equivalent to methotrexate (2 mg/kg) in preclinical studies. As a result, the majority of natural phytochemicals or antioxidants have been shown to be effective as a pretreatment (Geetha et al., 2015). Kim et al. (2015) developed an oxycodone once-daily controlled-release tablet that corresponded to the simulated release profiles studied in both in vivo and in vitro experiments. Drug's pharmacokinetics were evaluated in humans and compared to those of the commercial product to investigate if the once-a-day controlled-release tablet would be a good alternative with a lower dose frequency and less variation in their plasma drug levels. The results of this study show that oxycodone once-a-day controlled-release tablets have the ability to increase patient satisfaction, tolerability, and effectiveness (Kim et al., 2015).

In another study, using a rabbit model, Szkutnik-Fiedler et al. (2017) sought to find out the effect of venlafaxine administration, both chronic and single, on the pharmacokinetics of tramadol. In this study, animals were given 75 mg of venlafaxine (an extended-release capsule) and 100 mg of tramadol (a slow-release pill) each orally and classified into four groups according to different frequencies of drug intake at different day periods. According to the findings, it was determined that among these groups, those who were treated with venlafaxine for 7 and 14 days had a faster tramadol elimination than the control group who received a single dose of tramadol alone (Szkutnik-Fiedler et al., 2017). Alam et al. (2015) designed and studied mucoadhesive elementary osmotic pump tablets containing trimetazidine hydrochloride to examine the ideal regulated release and enhance oral drug absorption. To that end, the prepared tablets were applied to numerous quality-control tests as well as in vitro drug release. It is also understood that a texture analyzer evaluation of mucoadhesion properties revealed that the designed osmotic systems had good mucoadhesion potential. In addition, compared to the commercial formulation (Vastarel MR), in vivo pharmacokinetic tests in rabbits demonstrated a 3.01-fold improvement in oral bioavailability. These investigations successfully proved the bioavailability augmentation capability of mucoadhesive elementary osmotic pumps as prospective pharmacological systems for various pharmaceuticals (Alam et al., 2015).

Tran et al. (2013) studied on the dissolution behavior and in vivo bioavailability as well as the controlled release profile in healthy human volunteers to overcome the disadvantages of isradipine, which has a short half-life, is poorly soluble in water, has poor bioavailability, and low dissolution rate. Ribeiro et al. (2007) used hydroxypropylmethylcellulose matrix tablets containing multicomponent complex forms of vinpocetine, cyclodextrin, and tartaric acid to maintain blood levels of vinpocetine for a prolonged period. Performances of these formulations based on both in vitro and in vivo were compared to those of a vinpocetine instant release dose form (Ribeiro et al., 2007). These findings indicate that both controlled release strategies and multicomponent complexation significantly improved the oral bioavailability of vinpocetine. Hayashi et al. (2007) aimed to compare of theophylline's features in vitro and in vivo with the two once-daily sustained-release preparations. They compared cluster tablets to traditional gel matrix tablets in dissolving and pharmacokinetic testing in vivo experiments. According to results, the tablet with a novel approach in this study had much reduced the intersubject variance of theophylline plasma levels than the traditional matrix tablets (Hayashi et al., 2007). Rajinikanth et al. (2007) produced a unique intragastric floating-in-situ gelling device for the delivery of amoxicillin for the treatment of peptic ulcer. The prepared gelling system has been shown to create hard gels in the stomach microenvironment and to eliminate *Helicobacter pylori* from the GI tract more successfully compared to amoxicillin suspension due to the longer GI residency length (Rajinikanth et al., 2007).

To overcome metformin's poor solubility, Hu et al. (2006) used centrifugal granulation to manufacture metformin hydrochloride sustained-release pellets. Surface modification approaches, Eudragit types and ratios, and the relationship between in vitro release and in vivo absorption have all been studied extensively. The experiments demonstrated that talc alteration prevented drug dumping, which helped to control drug release. According to the findings, a sustained-release effect and increased relative bioavailability were achieved by limiting metformin hydrochloride distribution to the small intestine with differentially coated pellets (Hu et al., 2006).

Transdermal patches

Oral and hypodermic injections (parenteral administration) routes are among the most common methods for the route of administration of pharmaceutical compounds to the body (Mazzitelli et al., 2013). However, the use of these methods can be limited due to some disadvantages. For example, some pharmaceutical drugs are taken into the body by the parenteral route rather than the oral route, as stomach acids reduce the effect of pharmaceutical components due to GI enzymes (Berti & Lipsky, 1995). Since parenteral drug administration is an invasive method and usually needs to be performed under the supervision of a specialist health-care personnel, it may not be possible to administer it continuously (Berti & Lipsky, 1995). Transdermal drug administration is an intriguing alternative to DDSs based on oral or parenteral routes (Römgens et al., 2015; Schoellhammer et al., 2014). For example, the transdermal route versus the oral DDS eliminates both the GI tract and the first-pass side effect (Prausnitz & Langer, 2008). Furthermore, the transdermal route is painless for patients and self-administered;, also it is cost-effective, and it can provide drug release up to about a week, as well as increase patient compliance so these factors are considered advantageous properties of transdermal routes over parenteral routes (Prausnitz & Langer, 2008). The great advantage of this route is undoubtedly that it offers a practical way for patients who cannot take oral medication (Moffatt et al., 2021). The fact that patient compliance problems encountered in oral administration are mostly seen in children and the elderly has made transdermal patches important in the fields of pediatrics and geriatrics (Marwah et al., 2014). It can be preferred as an immediate drug administration method for patients who have lost consciousness (Marwah et al., 2014). Moreover, transdermal DDSs are easy to apply, and drug administration can be stopped at any time after patch removal (Singh et al., 2014).

The skin has been used for cosmetic and medical purposes throughout the history of mankind. Transdermal patches are controlled-release DDSs that deliver the drug through the skin (Dhiman et al., 2011). Thanks to the transdermal patches-type materials, the transdermal DDSs adhere to the upper part of the skin, and after the therapeutic agent is performed directly to the skin, the active substance is delivered to the circulation by penetrating the skin (Pastore et al., 2015). Many drugs that can be formulated by transdermal DDSs can be injected into the bloodstream through the skin. The skin, the part of the body that occupies the most space in terms of mass (Pastore et al., 2015), prevents the loss of excess water and other body components while keeping body temperature stable, and it is an ideal application to examine both the systemic and local release of biologically active substances (Prausnitz et al., 2012). The most significant property for the function of the skin acts as a barrier to help protect the body from various factors (Proksch et al., 2008). Because other tissues, such as the permeable epithelium of the GI tract and the lung, are the primary entry routes, the skin allows very little entry (Prausnitz et al., 2012). Ultraviolet radiation, chemicals (cosmetics), allergens, and microorganisms are among some of the factors from which skin protects the body (Benson, 2012). On the other hand, stratum corneum (SC), the outermost layer of the skin, limits the uptake of small lipophilic molecules into the skin, so it may cause limitations in the applications of transdermal DDSs (Parhi et al., 2015). For example, although effective results are obtained with the application of some compounds, such as nicotine and steroids, through the skin, SC limits the passage of many active substances (Iannone et al., 2019; Petersen et al., 2011). Therefore there is a need for methods to provide a safe increment in the permeability of SC for transdermal delivery of ionic or larger molecules. Chemical enhancers help in drug penetration by altering the SC's highly organized lipid structure through physicochemical interactions, reacting with intercellular protein, or accelerating drug permeation into the SC (Marwah et al., 2014). Alcohols, amides, ketones, ether alcohols, fatty acids, glycols, sulphoxides, terpenes, pyrrolidones, and surfactants can act as chemical penetration enhancers, allowing therapeutics to pass through the skin barrier and improve skin permeability (Lane, 2013).

Prodrug administration is one of the methods that can increase permeability for transdermal drug administration (Kiptoo et al., 2009). Accordingly, among the active substances belonging to the same pharmacological group, those with superior properties may be preferred for transdermal transfer. If there is no active substance with superior properties on the skin, a prodrug can be applied (N'Da, 2014). An increment in the moisture of the skin is provided by hydration has been reported by most researchers in the literature as its penetration enhancing properties in the delivery of therapeutic agents through the skin (Tan et al., 2010).

Lipophilic active ingredients have a higher priority of transdermal penetration than hydrophilic active ingredients (Williams & Barry, 2012). Liposomes are artificial vesicles of various sizes, charges, and lipid compositions composed of synthetic or natural phospholipids, which resemble cell-type membrane structures in a bilayer and aqueous structure (Akbarzadeh et al., 2013). Also, these features help to penetrate the skin by trapping the active ingredients in the hydrophilic center (Tran, 2013). They can be considered ideal drug nanocarriers in clinical applications because they contain hydrophobic and hydrophilic parts together, then highly biocompatible, and are less toxic (Bozzuto & Molinari, 2015). Drug loading into liposomes can be managed to accomplish passively during liposome forming or through the dehydration—rehydration vesicles method after liposome forming (Antimisiaris, 2010). Depending on the intended use and target organ, liposomes can be prepared as emulsions, suspensions, aerosols, gels, creams, or dry powders (Laouini et al., 2012). Different liposome formulations have been developed for finding more effective alternative methods for the treatment of cancer, mainly chemotherapeutics (Muthu & Feng, 2013). The main ones of these formulations can be summarized as follows: polyethylene glycol (PEG)-coated liposomal doxorubicin, non-PEG-coated liposomal doxorubicin, liposomal daunorubicin, liposome-encapsulated platinum compounds, immunoliposomes (antibody-mediated transport), cisplatin, annamycin, amphotericin B, daunorubicin, verteporfin, cytarabine, nystatin, tretinoin, inactivated hepatitis A virus (strain RG-SB), and morphine sulfate (Chowdhary et al., 2003; D'Acremont et al., 2006; Herzog et al., 2009; Hoarau et al., 2004; Hofheinz et al., 2005; Immordino et al., 2006; Meunier et al., 1991; Stathopoulos et al., 2012; Tomkinson et al., 2003; Usonis et al., 2003). Liposome delivery of hepatitis A and flu vaccines has also been approved and is still in use. Peptides derived from virus coats have been utilized in these formulations since they were seen to be more helpful in enhancing the inflammatory reaction (Wallis et al., 2019). Although liposomes have advantages such as serving increment in the therapeutic efficacy while decrement in the toxicity of the drug they contain, active targeting to the relevant organ/tissue, biocompatibility, they also have disadvantages, such as low solubility, drug overflow, and oxidation of phospholipids (Ueki et al., 2015). These disadvantages are ameliorated in part by lipid modifications and the adding of different substances to the lipid content. The lipid content of liposomes is an important factor in their in vivo stability and interaction. PEG is a polyether diol compound, and it has a myriad of benefits, along with biological properties, high solubility in aqueous or organic solvents, and low immunogenicity (Immordino et al., 2006). PEG-modified liposomes are useful because increased blood circulation leads to the formation of a barrier protection hydrated layer on top of the liposomes, protecting them from phagocytic cells (Gabizon, 2001). When we look at the biotechnological applications of liposomes, we find that lipid-DNA complexes known as lipoplexes can successfully compete with viral gene transfection systems (Schwendener, 2007).

Although the skin serves as a natural physical barrier to particle penetration, the size of diseased skin and hair follicles offers application potential for the delivery of nano-/microparticular systems. According to studies, particles larger than 10 nm in diameter cannot pass through the SC and the living epidermis layer but it is possible to pass through the hair root openings (Yang et al., 2013). Nanovesicles, such as liposomes, not only increase skin permeability but also effects drug solubility and drug delivery across the skin (Pegoraro et al., 2012). As a result of using nano/microparticle vesicles in combination with methods such as iontophoresis, it can act as a physical penetration enhancer within the scope of biomedicine approaches (Higaki et al., 2006; Pagneux et al., 2020; Shehata et al., 2020; Xu et al., 2017; Zou et al., 2021).

Although the delivery of hydrophilic biological macromolecules, for example, proteins, can be inhibited by hydrophobic SC, it is found in the literature that peptides can be applied as penetration enhancers to overcome this situation (Carrigan & Imperiali, 2005; Futaki et al., 2001; Lemeshko, 2010; Ookubo et al., 2014; Pham et al., 2004). In a prior study, Tahara et al. (2010) used the solid-in-oil (S/O) nanodispersion method for delivery and immunization of protein under the skin. They used protein transduction domains (PTDs) to increase the permeability of proteins in an S/O nanodispersion. When employed in this fashion, with an S/O nanodispersion supplemented with arginine-rich peptides, PTDs have been demonstrated to be one of the most extensively used chemical enhancers for transcutaneous protein transport (Tahara et al., 2012). PTDs were employed to transport protein to the skin in a previous investigation, and cyclosporine A (CsA) and R7 conjugation were also used (Rothbard et al., 2000). Although it is systemically effective, as is CsA, it is ineffective topically due to poor skin penetration. To address this issue, R7-CsA was created by converting a heptamer arginine to CsA via a pH-sensitive linker. Unlike unmodified CsA, which was unable to penetrate the skin, R7-CsA was efficiently delivered to cells in mouse and human skin. R7-CsA inhibited cutaneous inflammation whilst also attaining dermal T lymphocytes. To improve the ability of poorly absorbed medications to pass tissue barriers, this study devised a new topical method for the treatment of inflammatory skin conditions (Rothbard et al., 2000).

Microneedling (MN) is a method that stimulates mechanical modification in the SC layer and provides the formation of micron-sized channels or pores of the skin (Kim et al., 2012). MN systems are made up of an array of needles ranging in length up to 100 μm and in a few microns diameter, enabling micron-sized channels through the skin without discomfort, it allows large biological macromolecules to penetrate into the subcutaneous tissues, then reach the bloodstream (Lim et al., 2018). There has been an increased interest in the manufacture and use of improved MNs for study in drug delivery research (Prausnitz, 2004). The application principle of MNs is as follows: depending on needle length, MNs selectively tear the SC and outer layer of the living epidermis. Thus in topical application, microchannels allow drug substances to pass through the SC, which is the main level barrier of transdermal transmission (Jain et al., 2016). Stimulated microchannels close on their own in a short period of time, allowing the epidermal barrier to remain intact (Sachdeva & Banga, 2011). The advantage of this technique is that it facilitates the passage of the upper parts of the skin, and because the MNs do not touch the papillary dermis layer where the nerve endings are located, drug release with this method is minimally invasive and painless (Cheung & Das, 2016). They are fabricated from a wide range of materials, including silicon, metal, ceramic, silica glass, carbohydrate, and polymers, and are produced using micro-based processing and manufacturing technologies (Waghule et al., 2019). Besides that, different kinds of MNs, such as hollow MNs, solid MNs, dissolving MNs, coated MNs, as well as hydrogel-forming MNs, can be assembled (Sabri et al., 2020).

MNs are being utilized in different administrations, including transdermal, ocular, and intracellular administration. However, the most prevalent application for MNs is still transdermal, notably for vaccine administration (Kim et al., 2012). According to in vitro studies, it has been determined that solid MNs increase the permeability of both nanoparticle and biological macromolecules, through the skin (Prausnitz & Langer, 2008). MNs were first used as a painless substitute for hypodermic injections. As a direct consequence, systems based on MNs are currently being evaluated in clinical trials for the delivery of insulin, oligonucleotide, parathyroid hormone, and influenza vaccine (Clementoni et al., 2010; Dardano et al., 2016; Prausnitz et al., 2009). In vivo studies have shown that oligonucleotide delivery, insulin-induced blood glucose reduction, and immune response induction from protein and DNA vaccines via MNs are possible (Deng et al., 2016; Prausnitz & Langer, 2008).

MNs have been safely and effectively used for the treatment of skin-related diseases including cancer (Nagarkar et al., 2020). In a study on female subjects, MNs containing water-soluble and biocompatible polymers like hyaluronic acid, carboxymethylcellulose, and polyvinylpyrrolidone penetrated the skin with 90% of skin penetration, and drug release was studied (Shim et al., 2018). It has been reported that after 8 weeks of applying drug-loaded MNs to the wrinkles around the eyes (crow's feet) of female subjects, a statistically significant disappearance of the wrinkles was observed after about 4 weeks (Shim et al., 2018). After epidermal application, Kim et al. reported in situ amphiphilic triblock copolymer-based dissolving MNs that produce nanomicelles upon dissolution. MNs containing tumor model antigen (ovalbumin, OVA) and resiquimod (R848) were applied to the skin of EG7-OVA tumor-bearing mice and increased anticancer activity (Kim et al., 2018). Naguib et al. (2014) introduced MN technology into the therapy that could improve the clinical efficacy of topical 5-fluorouracil (5-Fu) against malignancies including basal cell carcinoma. 5-Aminolevulinic acid (5-Ala)-coated MNs were produced by Jain and colleagues for photodynamic treatment of skin malignancies (Jain et al., 2016). Finally, while very low dose—coated 5-Ala-MNs inhibited tumor growth by 57%, a topical cream containing only 5-Ala was unable to control tumor volume and increased tumor growth (Jain et al., 2016). Uddin et al. (2020) developed a unique 3D-printed polymeric MN array for better cisplatin administration to A-431 epidermoid skin tumors in cancer treatment. According to an optical coherence tomography analysis, 3D-printed MNs have an excellent piercing capacity of up to 80% penetration depth. As a result, Franz cell diffusion studies demonstrated 80%—90% cisplatin release within a week, while in vivo testing with Balb/c nude mice revealed adequate antineoplastic agent permeabilization with high tumor regression and anticancer efficacy (Uddin et al., 2020). Hao et al. (2020) developed a near-infrared light-responsive monomethoxy-poly(ethylene glycol)-poly(caprolactone) nanoparticle that is loaded with 5-Fu and indocyanine green loaded, and they combined it with a hyaluronic acid dissolvable MN system to treat skin cancer, along with melanoma and human epidermoid cancer. The findings suggested that this MN system could be used to effectively treat skin cancer (Hao et al., 2020). Song et al. (2020) prepared MN systems sensitive to near-infrared radiation as a minimally invasive and effective treatment of superficial skin tumors. The synergistic effect of two-stage detachable MN phototherapy and chemotherapy in the treatment of skin cancer was evaluated. A self-degradable MN system with hyaluronic acid and dextran nanoparticles, along with anti-PD-1 administration, was also employed to treat cancer (Wang et al., 2016). This administration method could be performed with other immunomodulators to provide combination therapy, which can boost antitumor activity, according to the researchers (Wang et al., 2016).

The functionality of the use of transdermal patches to prevent nausea has been also examined (Aktar et al., 2014). Release of doxylamine as an active ingredient was investigated in vivo and in vitro (Venter et al., 2001). During in vitro experiments, it was discovered that the wounded skin was subjected to necrosis. It was speculated that this would increase the drug's permeability. It was assumed that after approximately 4.5 h, cell necrosis occurs, the barrier function of the SC decreases, and drug permeability increases (Venter et al., 2001). A comparison was made concerning the type of membrane to be used in Alzheimer's disease study, and it is concluded that synthetic membranes can be used as a substitute for both animal and human skin (Simon et al., 2016).

A study which is about controlled release of the transdermal patch containing the active ingredient donepezil was reported (Galipoğlu et al., 2014). The effects of different concentrations of DL-limonene, which was chosen as a penetration enhancer, were researched. The optimum concentration of DL-limonene was determined to produce the highest flux. Also, the study concluded that the alternative delivery approach in Alzheimer's disease treatment for donepezil is appropriate for use in a transdermal patch (Galipoğlu et al., 2014).

Transdermal drug release is considered an alternative route to commercial hypertension products. For example, the controlled release studies with nifedipine have revealed that gels containing sodium alginate or pectin are suitable materials in the production of nifedipine-loaded transdermal films. The addition of propylene glycol improves the flexibility and mechanical strength of the films. Moreover, an increase in bioadhesiveness was also demonstrated (Bektas et al., 2014). A transdermal patch containing the active ingredients isosorbide dinitrate and bisoprolol was also developed, and its in vitro/in vivo studies were also investigated (Zhao et al., 2007). The patch containing isosorbide dinitrate and bisoprolol in a 3:2 (mg/mg) ratio had a better antihypertensive effect than bisoprolol alone (Zhao et al., 2007).

Transdermal patches have become commonly used for cosmetic, topical, and transdermal drug delivery (Pastore et al., 2015). Nicotine patches were the first transdermal therapeutic system in medicine to provide controlled nicotine release for the cessation of smoking. It also led to the recognition of transdermal patches through the use of nicotine patches (Foulds et al., 1992). In today's market, there are numerous transdermal therapeutic systems containing various active substances. Transdermal patches containing nicotine, opioid derivatives, sex hormones, scopolamine, and nitroglycerin are the most commonly used (Pastore et al., 2015; Prausnitz & Langer, 2008).

Although transdermal DDSs have some advantages over traditional routes, there are some limitations when using this route. For example, because chronic conditions, such as hypertension, angina, and diabetes, necessitate long-term drug therapy, it is more suitable for chronic conditions rather than acute conditions (Reddy et al., 2014). Some patients may experience skin irritation near the application site (Williams & Barry, 2012). Cutaneous metabolism can have an impact on the system's therapeutic performance (Zhang et al., 2009). Furthermore, ionic drugs are unsuitable for transdermal therapy (Dhote et al., 2012).

Pulmonary drug delivery systems

The pulmonary route is a method of delivering drugs through the lungs. The medication is administered via oral inhalation or nasal spray in this manner. Thanks to their large surface areas and constant contact with air, the lungs might well be preferred as a drug transport route (Djupesland, 2013). Delivery of drugs through the lungs is a noninvasive technique performed to treat inflammatory diseases, such as cystic fibrosis, asthma, and chronic obstructive pulmonary disease (Velino et al., 2019). Inhalable dry powders have been done to develop antituberculosis drugs to the lungs in aerosol form for tuberculosis treatment (Pham et al., 2015). These powders, which are made of antituberculosis drug-loaded particles, are in a form that can be delivered directly to the lungs (Pham et al., 2015). The lungs make up about 6% of the body mass (Hastedt et al., 2016). The lungs of mammals consist of bronchi, bronchioles, and alveoli, and it is responsible organs for respiration. The large surface area of the lungs is a significant factor for warm-blooded animals that need high amounts of oxygen. Factors, such as the size of the surface area of the alveoli and the thickness of the blood–gas barrier, affect the surface area capacity of the lungs (Bachofen & Schürch, 2001).

In addition to providing respiration, the lungs have a high potential to be used to deliver drugs throughout the body. Due to its advantages, such as large surface area, rapid incorporation of drugs into the systemic circulation, administration of the drug in low doses and not requiring surgery, reduced drug barrier effect, the local application against various lung diseases, and low-level catabolic enzymatic activities, drug transport from the lungs can be favored against oral or injectable treatment methods (Hastedt et al., 2016; Patton & Byron, 2007). For example, because once compared to conventional routes of administration such as the orally ingested, a lower dose of a drug can be applied via the pulmonary route for the local treatment of airborne diseases with rapid efficacy by directly reaching the lung epithelium (Douafer et al., 2020). Besides that, drug metabolism in the lung is gradual due to low intra- and extracellular enzyme activity (Shanker et al., 2010). Even chemicals with a low absorption capacity can be relatively well absorbed through pulmonary administration (Gessler et al., 2011). Because the drug is applied directly to the target, the dosage of the administered drug can be reduced, lowering the possibility of side effects. Drug delivery to other parts of the body can also be accomplished by targeting the alveolar region via the lungs. Drugs that reach the alveolar region, which is surrounded by blood vessels and epithelial cells, can be absorbed into the alveolar wall's thin epithelial cells and, thus, enter the systemic circulation quickly (Patton & Byron, 2007; Patton et al., 2004). The first-pass effect, which also occurs before the drug enters the systemic circulation and causes a decrease in dosage, is passivated, allowing for rapid intervention (Jaganathan & Godin, 2012; Kovalainen et al., 2015). Pulmonary route is also appropriate for the delivery of protein- or peptide-based therapeutic compounds, which cannot be administered orally due to enzymatic degradation and low intestinal absorption and, therefore, must be administered parenterally into the body (Hamman et al., 2005). Due to its ability to treat the majority of both local and systemic diseases, pulmonary drug delivery has gotten a lot of interest in recent years. Pulmonary administration may be preferred for not only the local treatment but also for systemic drug administration (Yang et al., 2008).

The mucus layer covering the respiratory tract is the first defense mechanism which drugs to be used for drug transport from the lungs or DDSs come into contact with the body (Smola et al., 2008). This layer serves as a physical and biological barrier against pathogens and other potentially harmful substances that enter the respiratory tract. The mucus layer's ciliated structure holds respirable materials and ensures their removal (Taherali et al., 2018). Although the mucus layer aids the immune system, it is resistant to the effects of drugs administered to the body for therapeutic purposes. Furthermore, one of the greatest challenges in ensuring effective transport of therapeutic agents from the lungs is that the drug carriers cannot easily penetrate the mucus layer. Hence, the desired amount of the therapeutic agent is not delivered to the target, and the treatment is rendered ineffective (Sosnik et al., 2014). In the case of lung diseases, for example, cystic fibrosis or asthma, the mucus layer thickens with increasing viscosity and becomes an impermeable barrier (Lai et al., 2009). Furthermore, the composition of the mucus layer changes due to various factors, such as smoking and air pollution, and the effectiveness of the barrier function provided to the lungs is compromised. The permeability of the epithelial tissue increases as a result of the aforementioned factors, the respiratory tract is blocked due to excessive mucus secretion, and pulmonary function is impaired as a result of bacterial infection and inflammation in the lungs (Kampa & Castanas, 2008). Consequently, the agents used to treat the disease are ineffective, and such diseases can lead to death. The ability of drug carriers to penetrate the mucus layer is primarily determined by the size of the carriers used and how they interact with the mucus. These two parameters are the most important constraints influencing carrier penetration behavior and must be optimized to achieve penetration (Maghsoudnia et al., 2020). Systemic drug delivery through the lungs and effective drug absorption through the respiratory tract necessitate at least temporary mucus layer disruption (Hussain et al., 2004).

For drug delivery through the lungs to be efficient, a suitable drug formulation with physicochemical properties is required. Aside from colloidal DDSs, such as micellar solutions, vesicles, and liquid crystal dispersions, nanomaterials consisting of small particles with diameters ranging from 10 to 400 nm are the most commonly used as DDSs (Müller-Goymann, 2004). The goal of developing these formulations is to have optimal drug loading and release properties, as well as systems with biocompatibility. The drug is introduced into the system's structure, and even if the drug is amphiphilic, molecular interactions may cause it to change (Adams et al., 2003). Furthermore, various methods to increase the penetration of nanoparticles used to transport drugs through the mucus layer have been studied in the literature (Wu et al., 2018). The corona formed around the particles after they enter the lower airway tracts, which is specific to the surface properties of the particles, may affect their interaction with the cells (He et al., 2019). Therefore, while building a DDS capable of penetrating the lung mucus layer, the surface qualities of particles or other drug carriers are crucial, and particle—mucus interactions must be thoroughly explored. It is discussed in the literature that there are different parameters for particles to penetrate through the mucus layer (Lieleg et al., 2010).

For drug delivery via aerosols through the lungs, a variety of carriers, including liposomes and polymeric particles, are employed. Solid lipid nanoparticles and lipid nanocarriers, on the other hand, have received interest in recent years as polymeric systems with appropriate physicochemical features to enhance the efficiency of drug transport via the lungs (Weber et al., 2014). For pulmonary drug delivery applications, lipid nanoparticles have favorable circumstances. It is predicted that lipids in their structure will be well sustained in the respiratory tract if biodegradable and nontoxic lipids are preferred (Iqbal et al., 2012). They can also encapsulate other therapeutic compounds in the polymer matrix or be administered in aerosols due to their adjustable size (Üner & Yener, 2007). Furthermore, because of the convenience in which their surfaces can be modified, they can be adsorbed on mucosal surfaces or penetrate more quickly. The long-term and continuous drug release characteristics ensure that the therapeutic effect is more efficient and sustainable, enabling for longer dose intake intervals and better drug feedback by the patient (Patlolla et al., 2010). In general, antibiotics are administered intravenously or orally to treat infectious diseases. However, it has been stated in the literature that because the respiratory tract can be directly contacted against lung infections, antibiotic inhalation as a topical application may be possible (Traini & Young, 2009). Inhalable antibiotics have long been used to treat and prolong the recovery of patients with cystic fibrosis who have respiratory tract infections (Ryan et al., 2011). Because of the success of aerosol antibiotics in the treatment of cystic fibrosis, similar treatment for other chronic airborne infectious diseases is being considered (Quon et al., 2014). There are some studies for lipid nanoparticles as pulmonary delivery systems for antibiotics. The presence of levofloxacin-loaded nano lipid carriers caused a decrement in the formation of a bacterial biofilm, emphasizing the nanodevice's importance as a different treatment way for cystic fibrosis (Islan et al., 2016). Moreover, numerous drugs (including proteins and genes) have been used with solid lipid nanoparticles, including clotrimazole (Souto et al., 2004), celecoxib (Patlolla et al., 2010), cyclosporine-A (Essaghraoui et al., 2019), dexamethasone (Wang et al., 2014), diazepam (Abdelbary & Fahmy, 2009), insulin (Liu et al., 2008), interferon-alpha (Li et al., 2010), and siRNA (Zhang et al., 2020). Because of their limited residence duration in the lungs, the medications in today's inhalation formulations for chronic lung disorders should be given at least twice a day, highlighting the importance of lipid nanocarriers in the future (Pensado et al., 2014).

Implantable systems

As technology progresses, it has become growingly important to design dosage forms as controlled release systems, especially in implant form, in applications requiring long-term local or systemic effects or treatment. There are various benefits of designing DDSs as an implant. For instance, it prevents the loss of active substances undergoing the first-pass effect from the liver and also reduces side effects (Stevenson et al., 2000). Furthermore, implant systems could eradicate the disadvantages of being affected by the GI system and being kept there for a limited time encountered to oral administration (Stevenson et al., 2000). The primary downside of the oral administration of a drug is the long and complex delivery time through the GI tract. If the drug cannot be taken orally, a parenteral route of administration is an alternative. Many proteins/peptides and other drugs that really are sensitive to GI tract adverse conditions are administered intravenously (Muheem et al., 2016). The timeframe of action of the drug for most therapeutically active substances is short in intravenous administering drugs, requiring frequent injections. Injectable controlled-release dose forms will not become more commercially desirable than alternative delivery methods unless and until they provide the requisite efficacy and safety namely. Most drugs' percutaneous absorption is limited in the case of topical application due to the physiological properties of the drugs and the presence of a highly impermeable SC (Suhonen et al., 1999). It has initiated to be tried as a route of administration during the development of implant systems, notably for active substances that cannot be administered orally and have a very wide therapeutic range. To prevent cases where the active substance could not reach the affected area due to the structure of the active substance molecule and biological factors, it is aimed to apply the drug directly to the affected area or its surroundings (Kumar & Kumar, 2001). This type of treatment was previously attempted utilizing conventional dosage forms (suppository, eye drops, inhalation aerosols, etc.) but due to concerns, such as blood level volatility and side effects, it was necessary to develop dosage forms for controlled drug release. Silicones were first used in 1964 to adjust the amount of drug release, and in the 1990s, two different implant systems, one made of silicone and the other of lactide/glycolide copolymer, were introduced to the market for use in humans (Okumu & Cleland, 2002).

Implantable controlled DDSs provide a new alternative for situations in which oral or intravenous drug administration is restricted. For example, implantable devices can be intended to keep the concentration of a therapeutic agent within between the minimum effective and minimum toxic levels for controlled, sustained therapeutic release over long periods, lowering the risk of patient noncompliance caused in oral therapy (Bertelmann & Schulze, 2015; Bolash et al., 2015). Once the device is incorporated into the affected tissue, a higher local therapeutic agent concentration can be achieved, reducing adverse systemic side effects and also the difficulties and pain associated with parenteral therapy (Pons-Faudoa et al., 2019). Besides that, if the active form of the drug ingredients can only be given intravenously, implant systems may be favored for one-time administration, considering the doses which must be repeated (Danckwerts & Fassihi, 2008). Through the use of implantable drug delivery devices, in particular, has the capability to minimize treatment follow-up clinic visits as well as health-care provider obedience. As a result, implantable drug delivery technologies place a premium on site-specificity and addressing medication nonadherence, altering the clinical landscape for chronic disease therapies like cardiovascular disease, diabetes, hypertension, and respiratory disorders (Alfaqawi et al., 2017; Ali et al., 2016; Almeida et al., 2015; Baert et al., 2008; Barnwal et al., 2017; Bourge et al., 2016; Carle et al., 2014).

On the other hand, there are a few drawbacks. For instance, implant materials should not be toxic. However, degradable implants, in specific, may produce harmful by-products (Song & Song, 2007). Furthermore, putting and attempting to remove nonbiodegradable implants necessitate a minor surgical procedure. Implants also could be painful or inconvenient. Drug leaking or uncontrolled drug release may happen in implants (Rauck et al., 2003). Finally, the cost of implants is high due to the materials and production methods utilized (Bhola et al., 2008; Gargallo-Albiol et al., 2019).

Biomaterials come to the forefront in the choice of materials to use as implant materials during the technological advancement process. According to the studies, cell proliferation is much higher on biomaterial-containing surfaces than on nonbiomaterial-containing surfaces (Bansal et al., 2011; Kunrath et al., 2020; Ordikhani et al., 2015; Ratner, 2002; Silva et al., 2010; Tamargo et al., 1993; Zhou et al., 1998). Success of an implant is significantly dependent on the surface properties of the implant material. After an implant material is placed in the body, all cell reactions occurring on its surface have been associated with the physicochemical and biological compatibility of the surface properties of the implant (Olivares-Navarrete et al., 2015). Chitosan, gelatin, polylactic acid, polyglycolic acid, and polylactic-*co*-glycolic acid are significant examples that are widely in use in human tissue and cells engineering studies for controlled biomolecule release in vivo (Chung et al., 2016; Kutlu et al., 2014; Song et al., 2013). Antibacterial properties, as well as synergistic properties for the repair and regeneration of damaged tissues, must be included in next-generation implant materials (Knobben et al., 2006; Phuengkham et al., 2014). The possibility of a contamination problem in the surgical units in which the implants are placed in the body, have a great impact on the success of orthopedic implants (Pye et al., 2009; Yazici et al., 2016). A probable bacterial infection may result in biofilm formation on the implant surfaces, weak interactions between the tissue and the implant, and the implant may need to be reupholstered surgical intervention (Liu et al., 2015; Uçkay et al., 2013). According to the literature, controlled release from biomaterials can inhibit such infections (Çetin et al., 2021; Feng et al., 2016; Gimeno et al., 2015).

Recently, the development of implantable systems for delivery of therapeutic agents to bone has gained importance in the treatment of bone pathologies. Long-term systemic drug treatments are commonly used to treat osteomyelitis, osteoporosis, bone cancers, and osteoporosis. Aside from bone-implantable systems; however, localized drug delivery has some advantages over conventional drug therapy in which it produces effective drug concentrations in diseased and/or infected bone areas while limiting various systemic side effects. Various implantable devices designed as DDSs for the treatment of bone disorders were reported in the literature (Bose & Tarafder, 2012; Caplin & García, 2019; Peter et al., 2005; Ray et al., 2019; Trajkovski et al., 2012). While cells are widely in use in experimental bone regeneration strategies, technological obstacles prevent these therapies from becoming transliterated (Newman & Benoit, 2016). Put another way, utilizing controlled drug delivery to mimic the spatiotemporal sequence of endogenous variables may also provide excellent tissue regeneration perspectives (Newman & Benoit, 2016; Newman et al., 2018).

Future clinical trials

Drug delivery is an interdisciplinary field in which chemists, biologists, materials scientists, biomedical engineers, and pharmacists work together to develop relevant concepts and transform them into clinical practice (Sen Gupta, 2016). A variety of controlled-release nanomaterials will be more and more used for DDSs in the future as materials science, pharmaceutical science, and biomedical science advance (Liu et al., 2016). Materials and technologies that react with the body at subcellular (i.e. molecule) scales with a high degree of specificity are used in nanotechnology applications in medicine and physiology (Sahoo et al., 2007). The application of nanotechnology in medicine has the potential to significantly affect human health care with advancing medical science and disease treatment (Sahoo et al., 2007). Although DDSs have been shown to have great effectivity in diagnosis and treatment, potential drug availability needs to be investigated before DDSs are implemented in clinics (Rudzińska et al., 2021). That is, from a material functionality point of view, most controlled DDSs work well in vitro but are not as stable in more complex in vivo environments. Moreover, the challenge of integrating programmability, targetability, and environmental responsiveness is still another challenge (Zhang et al., 2013). Thus consistent results will be a major challenge for researchers to develop primarily preclinical research of advanced DDSs, from translational production to clinical trial success (Ragelle et al., 2017). Many clinical studies concentrate on biomaterials and formulation investigations, which appear to be in their early stages of biomedical use (Bisso & Leroux, 2020). Animal studies and transdisciplinary research will provide valuable data for possible pharmacological therapy and diagnostic tests but they will take a lot of time and money (Patra et al., 2018). The future of a smarter and multicentric approach to nanomedicine and controlled DDSs appears bright, given the growing global trend toward the hunt for more precise medications and diagnostics.

In terms of future prospects, new and breakthrough concepts are urgently needed, such as nanoparticles that may efficiently carry nucleic acids into cells (Liu et al., 2017). While nanoparticles are a safer alternative to virus particles for gene transfer, they are nonetheless ineffective. In this context, the development of techniques based on biomimetics that attempts to evolve things already formed by nature is expected to lead to great advances in gene transfer via nanoparticles in the next years (Couvreur, 2013). The requirement for transported DNA to escape lysosomal confinement and permeate via nuclear pores, in particular, has not yet been thoroughly investigated (Couvreur, 2013). In addition, advances in immunology and the human genome will illuminate the types of targeting molecules that can achieve site-specific drug release (Ye et al., 2019). In parallel with nanotechnological developments, it will allow the construction of very small robots that can mix with the bloodstream and perform chemical and physical functions (Luo et al., 2018). Overall, understanding the mechanisms of transmission from different inputs of the body, such as the intestine, lung, and skin biologically and physicochemically will allow the development of new drug release strategies.

Conclusion

Recently, drug delivery methods have been extensively explored and designed to provide an improvement in the release of various therapeutic agents. In the clinical perspective, ideal DDSs should have the ability to transport the active compounds to the targeted area and release it within the therapeutic window, while also being biocompatible and biodegradable within the desired time. Novel DDSs have presented several advantages, including local delivery, lower adverse effects, and increased patient tolerance. In addition, these new systems for the treatment of many common diseases, such as diabetes, cancer, Parkinson's, Alzheimer's, and cardiovascular diseases show great promise for the future. These applications related to the industry have seen significant growth in recent decades, fueled by an increase in the number of researchers, research funding, venture capital, and start-ups. These instances show that medication delivery methods have a significant therapeutic and commercial influence. As a result of these advances, new technologies, such as micro/nanoparticles, transdermal patches, inhalers, drug reservoir implants, liposomes, or vehicles have emerged. While increased research activity is a clear sign of the progress of the field, the clinical and commercial transformation of early-stage research concepts is vital to the future expansion and relevance of the field.

References

Abdelbary, G., & Fahmy, R. H. (2009). Diazepam-loaded solid lipid nanoparticles: Design and characterization. *AAPS PharmSciTech*, *10*(1), 211–219. Available from https://doi.org/10.1208/s12249-009-9197-2.

Adams, M. L., Lavasanifar, A., & Kwon, G. S. (2003). Amphiphilic block copolymers for drug delivery. *Journal of Pharmaceutical Sciences*, *92*(7), 1343–1355. Available from https://doi.org/10.1002/jps.10397.

Agüeros, M., Ruiz-Gatón, L., Vauthier, C., Bouchemal, K., Espuelas, S., Ponchel, G., & Irache, J. M. (2009). Combined hydroxypropyl-β-cyclodextrin and poly(anhydride) nanoparticles improve the oral permeability of paclitaxel. *European Journal of Pharmaceutical Sciences*, *38*(4), 405–413. Available from https://doi.org/10.1016/j.ejps.2009.09.010.

Ahmad, A., Othman, I., Zaini, A., & Chowdhury, E. H. (2011). Oral nano-insulin therapy: Current progress on nanoparticle-based devices for intestinal epithelium-targeted insulin delivery. *Journal of Nanomedicine & Nanotechnology*, *s4*(01), 1–10. Available from https://doi.org/10.4172/2157-7439.S4-007.

Akbarzadeh, A., Rezaei-Sadabady, R., Davaran, S., Joo, S. W., Zarghami, N., Hanifehpour, Y., Samiei, M., Kouhi, M., & Nejati-Koshki, K. (2013). Liposome: Classification, preparation, and applications. *Nanoscale Research Letters*, *8*(1), 102. Available from https://doi.org/10.1186/1556-276X-8-102.

Aktar, B., Erdal, M. S., Sagirli, O., Güngör, S., & Özsoy, Y. (2014). Optimization of biopolymer based transdermal films of metoclopramide as an alternative delivery approach. *Polymers*, *6*(5), 1350–1365. Available from https://doi.org/10.3390/polym6051350.

Alam, N., Beg, S., Rizwan, M., Ahmad, A., Ahmad, F. J., Ali, A., & Aqil, M. (2015). Mucoadhesive elementary osmotic pump tablets of trimetazidine for controlled drug delivery and reduced variability in oral bioavailability. *Drug Development and Industrial Pharmacy*, *41*(4), 692–702. Available from https://doi.org/10.3109/03639045.2014.900076.

Alfaqawi, F., Lip, P. L., Elsherbiny, S., Chavan, R., Mitra, A., & Mushtaq, B. (2017). Report of 12-months efficacy and safety of intravitreal fluocinolone acetonide implant for the treatment of chronic diabetic macular oedema: A real-world result in the United Kingdom. *Eye (Basingstoke)*, *31*(4), 650–656. Available from https://doi.org/10.1038/eye.2016.301.

Ali, M., Akin, A., Bahamondes, L., Brache, V., Habib, N., Landoulsi, S., & Hubacher, D. (2016). Extended use up to 5 years of the etonogestrel-releasing subdermal contraceptive implant: Comparison to levonorgestrel-releasing subdermal implant. *Human Reproduction*, *31*(11), 2491–2498. Available from https://doi.org/10.1093/humrep/dew222.

Allen, T. M., & Cullis, P. R. (2004). Drug delivery systems: Entering the mainstream. *Science (New York, N.Y.)*, *303*(5665), 1818–1822. Available from https://doi.org/10.1126/science.1095833.

Almeida, D. R. P., Chin, E. K., Mears, K., Russell, S. R., & Mahajan, V. B. (2015). Spontaneous dislocation of a fluocinolone acetonide implant (retisert) into the anterior chamber and its successful extraction in sympathetic ophthalmia. *Retinal Cases and Brief Reports*, *9*(2), 142–144. Available from https://doi.org/10.1097/ICB.0000000000000119.

Alqahtani, M. S., Kazi, M., Alsenaidy, M. A., & Ahmad, M. Z. (2021). Advances in oral drug delivery. *Frontiers in Pharmacology*, *12*, 618411. Available from https://doi.org/10.3389/fphar.2021.618411.

Antimisiaris, S. G. (2010). Preparation of DRV liposomes. *Methods in Molecular Biology (Clifton, N.J.)*, *605*, 51–75. Available from https://doi.org/10.1007/978-1-60327-360-2_3.

Arima, H., Yunomae, K., Hirayama, F., & Uekama, K. (2001). Contribution of P-glycoprotein to the enhancing effects of dimethyl-β-cyclodextrin on oral bioavailability of tacrolimus. *Journal of Pharmacology and Experimental Therapeutics*, *297*(2), 547–555.

Bachofen, H., & Schürch, S. (2001). Alveolar surface forces and lung architecture. *Comparative Biochemistry and Physiology Part A: Molecular and Integrative Physiology*, *129*(1), 183–193. Available from https://doi.org/10.1016/S1095-6433(01)00315-4.

Baert, L., Schueller, L., Tardy, Y., Macbride, D., Klooster, G. v t, Borghys, H., Clessens, E., Van Den Mooter, G., Van Gyseghem, E., Van Remoortere, P., Wigerinck, P., & Rosier, J. (2008). Development of an implantable infusion pump for sustained anti-HIV drug administration. *International Journal of Pharmaceutics*, *355*(1–2), 38–44. Available from https://doi.org/10.1016/j.ijpharm.2008.01.029.

Bansal, S. S., Goel, M., Aqil, F., Vadhanam, M. V., & Gupta, R. C. (2011). Advanced drug delivery systems of curcumin for cancer chemoprevention. *Cancer Prevention Research*, *4*(8), 1158–1171. Available from https://doi.org/10.1158/1940-6207.CAPR-10-0006.

Barnwal, P., Das, S., Mondal, S., Ramasamy, A., Maiti, T., & Saha, A. (2017). Probuphine® (buprenorphine implant): A promising candidate in opioid dependence. *Therapeutic Advances in Psychopharmacology*, 7(3), 119–134. Available from https://doi.org/10.1177/2045125316681984.

Bektas, A., Cevher, E., Güngör, S., & Özsoy, Y. (2014). Design and evaluation of polysaccharide-based transdermal films for the controlled delivery of nifedipine. *Chemical and Pharmaceutical Bulletin*, *62*(2), 144–152. Available from https://doi.org/10.1248/cpb.c13-00579.

Benson, H. A. E. (2012). *Skin structure, function, and permeation. Transdermal and Topical Drug Delivery: Principles and Practice* (pp. 1–22). John Wiley and Sons. Available from https://doi.org/10.1002/9781118140505.ch1.

Bertelmann, T., & Schulze, S. (2015). Long-term follow-up of patient with diabetic macular edema receiving fluocinolone acetonide intravitreal implant. *Ophthalmology and Therapy*, *4*(1), 51–58. Available from https://doi.org/10.1007/s40123-015-0028-0.

Berti, J. J., & Lipsky, J. J. (1995). Transcutaneous drug delivery: A practical review. *Mayo Clinic Proceedings*, *70*(6), 581–586. Available from https://doi.org/10.4065/70.6.581.

Bhola, M., Neely, A. L., & Kolhatkar, S. (2008). Immediate implant placement: Clinical decisions, advantages, and disadvantages. *Journal of Prosthodontics*, *17*(7), 576–581. Available from https://doi.org/10.1111/j.1532-849x.2008.00359.x.

Bisso, S., & Leroux, J. C. (2020). Nanopharmaceuticals: A focus on their clinical translatability. *International Journal of Pharmaceutics*, *578*. Available from https://doi.org/10.1016/j.ijpharm.2020.119098.

Bolash, R., Udeh, B., Saweris, Y., Guirguis, M., Dalton, J. E., Makarova, N., & Mekhail, N. (2015). Longevity and cost of implantable intrathecal drug delivery systems for chronic pain management: A retrospective analysis of 365 patients. *Neuromodulation*, *18*(2), 150–155. Available from https://doi.org/10.1111/ner.12235.

Bose, S., & Tarafder, S. (2012). Calcium phosphate ceramic systems in growth factor and drug delivery for bone tissue engineering: A review. *Acta Biomaterialia*, *8*(4), 1401–1421. Available from https://doi.org/10.1016/j.actbio.2011.11.017.

Bourge, R. C., Waxman, A. B., Gomberg-Maitland, M., Shapiro, S. M., Tarver, J. H., Zwicke, D. L., Feldman, J. P., Chakinala, M. M., Frantz, R. P., Torres, F., Cerkvenik, J., Morris, M., Thalin, M., Peterson, L., & Rubin, L. J. (2016). Treprostinil administered to treat pulmonary arterial hypertension using a fully implantable programmable intravascular delivery system: Results of the delivery for PAH trial. *Chest*, *150*(1), 27–34. Available from https://doi.org/10.1016/j.chest.2015.11.005.

Bozzuto, G., & Molinari, A. (2015). Liposomes as nanomedical devices. *International Journal of Nanomedicine*, *10*, 975–999. Available from https://doi.org/10.2147/IJN.S68861.

Brown, T. D., Whitehead, K. A., & Mitragotri, S. (2020). Materials for oral delivery of proteins and peptides. *Nature Reviews Materials*, *5*(2), 127–148. Available from https://doi.org/10.1038/s41578-019-0156-6.

Buckley, S. T., Bækdal, T. A., Vegge, A., Maarbjerg, S. J., Pyke, C., Ahnfelt-Rønne, J., Madsen, K. G., Schéele, S. G., Alanentalo, T., Kirk, R. K., Pedersen, B. L., Skyggebjerg, R. B., Benie, A. J., Strauss, H. M., Wahlund, P. O., Bjerregaard, S., Farkas, E., Fekete, C., Søndergaard, F. L., & Knudsen, L. B. (2018). Transcellular stomach absorption of a derivatized glucagon-like peptide-1 receptor agonist. *Science Translational Medicine*, *10*(468). Available from https://doi.org/10.1126/scitranslmed.aar7047.

Caplin, J. D., & García, A. J. (2019). Implantable antimicrobial biomaterials for local drug delivery in bone infection models. *Acta Biomaterialia*, *93*, 2–11. Available from https://doi.org/10.1016/j.actbio.2019.01.015.

Carle, M. V., Chu, T. G., & Boyer, D. S. (2014). Fluocinolone acetonide (Iluvien) extended-release intravitreal implant for diabetic macular edema. *Expert Review of Ophthalmology*, *9*(2), 81–88. Available from https://doi.org/10.1586/17469899.2014.902310.

Carrigan, C. N., & Imperiali, B. (2005). The engineering of membrane-permeable peptides. *Analytical Biochemistry*, *341*(2), 290–298. Available from https://doi.org/10.1016/j.ab.2005.03.026.

Çetin, K., & Denizli, A. (2015). 5-Fluorouracil delivery from metal-ion mediated molecularly imprinted cryogel discs. *Colloids and Surfaces B: Biointerfaces*, *126*, 401–406. Available from https://doi.org/10.1016/j.colsurfb.2014.12.038.

Çetin, K., & Denizli, A. (2022). Polyethylenimine-functionalized microcryogels for controlled release of diclofenac sodium. *Reactive and Functional Polymers*, *170*, 105125. Available from https://doi.org/10.1016/j.reactfunctpolym.2021.105125.

Çetin, K., Aslıyüce, S., Idil, N., & Denizli, A. (2021). Preparation of lysozyme loaded gelatin microcryogels and investigation of their antibacterial properties. *Journal of Biomaterials Science, Polymer Edition*, *32* (2), 189–204. Available from https://doi.org/10.1080/09205063.2020.1825303.

Cetin, M., Aktas, M. S., Vural, I., & Ozturk, M. (2012). Salmon calcitonin-loaded Eudragit® and Eudragit®-PLGA nanoparticles: In vitro and in vivo evaluation. *Journal of Microencapsulation*, *29*(2), 156–166. Available from https://doi.org/10.3109/02652048.2011.635426.

Chan, H. K., & Kwok, P. C. L. (2011). Production methods for nanodrug particles using the bottom-up approach. *Advanced Drug Delivery Reviews*, *63*(6), 406–416. Available from https://doi.org/10.1016/j.addr.2011.03.011.

Chen, M. C., Mi, F. L., Liao, Z. X., Hsiao, C. W., Sonaje, K., Chung, M. F., Hsu, L. W., & Sung, H. W. (2013). Recent advances in chitosan-based nanoparticles for oral delivery of macromolecules. *Advanced Drug Delivery Reviews*, *65*(6), 865–879. Available from https://doi.org/10.1016/j.addr.2012.10.010.

Cheung, K., & Das, D. B. (2016). Microneedles for drug delivery: Trends and progress. *Drug Delivery*, *23* (7), 2338–2354. Available from https://doi.org/10.3109/10717544.2014.986309.

Chin, J., Foyez Mahmud, K. A., Kim, S. E., Park, K., & Byun, Y. (2012). Insight of current technologies for oral delivery of proteins and peptides. *Drug Discovery Today: Technologies*, *9*(2), e105–e112. Available from https://doi.org/10.1016/j.ddtec.2012.04.005.

Choonara, B. F., Choonara, Y. E., Kumar, P., Bijukumar, D., du Toit, L. C., & Pillay, V. (2014). A review of advanced oral drug delivery technologies facilitating the protection and absorption of protein and peptide molecules. *Biotechnology Advances*, *32*(7), 1269–1282. Available from https://doi.org/10.1016/j.biotechadv.2014.07.006.

Chowdhary, R. K., Shariff, I., & Dolphin, D. (2003). Drug release characteristics of lipid based benzoporphyrin derivative. *Journal of Pharmacy and Pharmaceutical Sciences*, *6*(1), 13–19. Available from http://www.ualberta.ca/~csps/JPPS6(1)/D.Dolphin/visudyne.pdf.

Chung, T. W., Chou, T. H., & Wu, K. Y. (2016). Gelatin/PLGA hydrogel films and their delivery of hydrophobic drugs. *Journal of the Taiwan Institute of Chemical Engineers*, *60*, 8–14. Available from https://doi.org/10.1016/j.jtice.2015.10.006.

Clementoni, M. T., B-Roscher, M., & Munavalli, G. S. (2010). Photodynamic photorejuvenation of the face with a combination of microneedling, red light, and broadband pulsed light. *Lasers in Surgery and Medicine*, *42*(2), 150–159. Available from https://doi.org/10.1002/lsm.20905.

Couvreur, P. (2013). Nanoparticles in drug delivery: Past, present and future. *Advanced Drug Delivery Reviews*, *65*(1), 21–23. Available from https://doi.org/10.1016/j.addr.2012.04.010.

D'Acremont, V., Herzog, C., & Genton, B. (2006). Immunogenicity and safety of a virosomal hepatitis A vaccine (Epaxal®) in the elderly. *Journal of Travel Medicine*, *13*(2), 78–83. Available from https://doi.org/10.1111/j.1708-8305.2006.00001.x.

Danckwerts, M., & Fassihi, A. (2008). Implantable controlled release drug delivery systems: A review. *Drug Development and Industrial Pharmacy*, *17*(11), 1465–1502. Available from https://doi.org/10.3109/03639049109026629.

Dardano, P., Caliò, A., Politi, J., Rea, I., Rendina, I., & de Stefano, L. (2016). Optically monitored drug delivery patch based on porous silicon and polymer microneedles. *Biomedical Optics Express*, *7*(5), 1645–1655. Available from https://doi.org/10.1364/BOE.7.001645.

Date, A. A., Hanes, J., & Ensign, L. M. (2016). Nanoparticles for oral delivery: Design, evaluation and state-of-the-art. *Journal of Controlled Release*, *240*, 504–526. Available from https://doi.org/10.1016/j.jconrel.2016.06.016.

Deng, Y., Chen, J., Zhao, Y., Yan, X., Zhang, L., Choy, K., Hu, J., Sant, H. J., Gale, B. K., & Tang, T. (2016). Transdermal delivery of siRNA through microneedle array. *Scientific Reports*, *6*. Available from https://doi.org/10.1038/srep21422.

Dhiman, S., Singh, T. G., & Rehni, A. K. (2011). Transdermal patches: A recent approach to new drug delivery system. *International Journal of Pharmacy and Pharmaceutical Sciences*, *3*(5), 26–34. Available from http://www.ijppsjournal.com/Vol3Suppl5/2695.pdf.

Dhote, V., Bhatnagar, P., Mishra, P. K., Mahajan, S. C., & Mishra, D. K. (2012). Iontophoresis: A potential emergence of a transdermal drug delivery system. *Scientia Pharmaceutica*, *80*(1), 1–28. Available from https://doi.org/10.3797/scipharm.1108-20.

Djupesland, P. G. (2013). Nasal drug delivery devices: Characteristics and performance in a clinical perspective—A review. *Drug Delivery and Translational Research*, *3*(1), 42–62. Available from https://doi.org/10.1007/s13346-012-0108-9.

Douafer, H., Andrieu, V., & Brunel, J. M. (2020). Scope and limitations on aerosol drug delivery for the treatment of infectious respiratory diseases. *Journal of Controlled Release*, *325*, 276–292. Available from https://doi.org/10.1016/j.jconrel.2020.07.002.

Elçioğlu, H. K., & Sezer, A. D. (2014). Nanoparticle insulin drug delivery—Applications and new aspects. In A. D. Sezer (Ed.), *Application of nanotechnology in drug delivery* (pp. 237–256). InTech. Available from https://doi.org/10.5772/58538.

Ensign, L. M., Cone, R., & Hanes, J. (2012). Oral drug delivery with polymeric nanoparticles: The gastrointestinal mucus barriers. *Advanced Drug Delivery Reviews*, *64*(6), 557–570. Available from https://doi.org/10.1016/j.addr.2011.12.009.

Ercan, A., Çelebier, M., Varan, G., Öncül, S., Nenni, M., Kaplan, O., & Bilensoy, E. (2018). Global omics strategies to investigate the effect of cyclodextrin nanoparticles on MCF-7 breast cancer cells. *European Journal of Pharmaceutical Sciences*, *123*, 377–386. Available from https://doi.org/10.1016/j.ejps.2018.07.060.

Essaghraoui, A., Belfkira, A., Hamdaoui, B., Nunes, C., Lima, S. A. C., & Reis, S. (2019). Improved dermal delivery of cyclosporine a loaded in solid lipid nanoparticles. *Nanomaterials*, *9*(9), 1204. Available from https://doi.org/10.3390/nano9091204.

Feng, W., Geng, Z., Li, Z., Cui, Z., Zhu, S., Liang, Y., Liu, Y., Wang, R., & Yang, X. (2016). Controlled release behaviour and antibacterial effects of antibiotic-loaded titania nanotubes. *Materials Science and Engineering C*, *62*, 105–112. Available from https://doi.org/10.1016/j.msec.2016.01.046.

Fonte, P., Araújo, F., Silva, C., Pereira, C., Reis, S., Santos, H. A., & Sarmento, B. (2015). Polymer-based nanoparticles for oral insulin delivery: Revisited approaches. *Biotechnology Advances*, *33*(6), 1342–1354. Available from https://doi.org/10.1016/j.biotechadv.2015.02.010.

Foulds, J., Stapleton, J., Feyerabend, C., Vesey, C., Jarvis, M., & Russell, M. A. H. (1992). Effect of transdermal nicotine patches on cigarette smoking: A double blind crossover study. *Psychopharmacology*, *106*(3), 421–427. Available from https://doi.org/10.1007/BF02245429.

Futaki, S., Ohashi, W., Suzuki, T., Niwa, M., Tanaka, S., Ueda, K., Harashima, H., & Sugiura, Y. (2001). Stearylated arginine-rich peptides: A new class of transfection systems. *Bioconjugate Chemistry*, *12*(6), 1005–1011. Available from https://doi.org/10.1021/bc015508l.

Gabizon, A. A. (2001). Stealth liposomes and tumor targeting: One step further in the quest for the magic bullet. *Clinical Cancer Research*, 7(2), 223–225.

Galipoğlu, M., Erdal, M. S., & Güngör, S. (2014). Biopolymer-based transdermal films of donepezil as an alternative delivery approach in Alzheimer's disease treatment. *AAPS PharmSciTech*, *16*(2), 284–292. Available from https://doi.org/10.1208/s12249-014-0224-6.

Gao, H., Wang, Y., Chen, C., Chen, J., Wei, Y., Cao, S., & Jiang, X. (2014). Incorporation of lapatinib into core-shell nanoparticles improves both the solubility and anti-glioma effects of the drug. *International Journal of Pharmaceutics*, *461*(1–2), 478–488. Available from https://doi.org/10.1016/j.ijpharm.2013.12.016.

Gargallo-Albiol, J., Barootchi, S., Salomó-Coll, O., & Wang, H. (2019). Advantages and disadvantages of implant navigation surgery. A systematic review. *Annals of Anatomy – Anatomischer Anzeiger*, *225*, 1–10. Available from https://doi.org/10.1016/j.aanat.2019.04.005.

Geetha, T., Deol, P. K., & Kaur, I. P. (2015). Role of sesamol-loaded floating beads in gastric cancers: A pharmacokinetic and biochemical evidence. *Journal of Microencapsulation*, *32*(5), 478–487. Available from https://doi.org/10.3109/02652048.2015.1057248.

Gessler, T., Beck-Broichsitter, M., Schmehl, T., & Seeger, W. (2011). Evaluating the controlled release properties of inhaled nanoparticles using isolated, perfused, and ventilated lung models. *Journal of Nanomaterials*, *2011*. Available from https://doi.org/10.1155/2011/163791.

Gimeno, M., Pinczowski, P., Pérez, M., Giorello, A., Martínez, M. Á., Santamaría, J., Arruebo, M., & Luján, L. (2015). A controlled antibiotic release system to prevent orthopedic-implant associated infections: An in vitro study. *European Journal of Pharmaceutics and Biopharmaceutics*, *96*, 264–271. Available from https://doi.org/10.1016/j.ejpb.2015.08.007.

Grama, C. N., Ankola, D. D., & Kumar, M. N. V. R. (2011). Poly(lactide-*co*-glycolide) nanoparticles for peroral delivery of bioactives. *Current Opinion in Colloid and Interface Science*, *16*(3), 238–245. Available from https://doi.org/10.1016/j.cocis.2010.11.005.

Grosse, P. Y., Bressolle, F., & Pinguet, F. (1997). Methyl-β-cyclodextrin in HL-60 parental and multidrug-resistant cancer cell lines: Effect on the cytotoxic activity and intracellular accumulation of doxorubicin. *Cancer Chemotherapy and Pharmacology*, *40*(6), 489–494. Available from https://doi.org/10.1007/s002800050692.

Hamman, J. H., Enslin, G. M., & Kotzé, A. F. (2005). Oral delivery of peptide drugs: Barriers and developments. *BioDrugs: Clinical Immunotherapeutics, Biopharmaceuticals and Gene Therapy*, *19*(3), 165–177. Available from https://doi.org/10.2165/00063030-200519030-00003.

Hao, Y., Chen, Y. W., He, X. L., Yang, F., Han, R. X., Yang, C. L., Li, W., & Qian, Z. Y. (2020). Near-infrared responsive 5-fluorouracil and indocyanine green loaded MPEG-PCL nanoparticle integrated with dissolvable microneedle for skin cancer therapy. *Bioactive Materials*, *5*(3), 542–552. Available from https://doi.org/10.1016/j.bioactmat.2020.04.002.

Hastedt, J. E., Bäckman, P., Clark, A. R., Doub, W., Hickey, A., Hochhaus, G., Kuehl, P. J., Lehr, C.-M., Mauser, P., McConville, J., Niven, R., Sakagimi, M., & Weers, J. G. (2016). Scope and relevance of a pulmonary biopharmaceutical classification system AAPS/FDA/USP workshop March 16-17th, 2015 in Baltimore, MD. *AAPS Open*, *2*(1). Available from https://doi.org/10.1186/s41120-015-0002-x.

Hayashi, T., Kanbe, H., Okada, M., Kawase, I., Ikeda, Y., Onuki, Y., Kaneko, T., & Sonobe, T. (2007). In vitro and in vivo sustained-release characteristics of theophylline matrix tablets and novel cluster tablets. *International Journal of Pharmaceutics*, *341*(1–2), 105–113. Available from https://doi.org/10.1016/j.ijpharm.2007.03.048.

He, Y., Liang, Y., Han, R., Lu, W. L., Mak, J. C. W., & Zheng, Y. (2019). Rational particle design to overcome pulmonary barriers for obstructive lung diseases therapy. *Journal of Controlled Release*, *314*, 48–61. Available from https://doi.org/10.1016/j.jconrel.2019.10.035.

Herzog, C., Hartmann, K., Künzi, V., Kürsteiner, O., Mischler, R., Lazar, H., & Glück, R. (2009). Eleven years of Inflexal® V-a virosomal adjuvanted influenza vaccine. *Vaccine*, *27*(33), 4381–4387. Available from https://doi.org/10.1016/j.vaccine.2009.05.029.

Higaki, M., Kameyama, M., Udagawa, M., Ueno, Y., Yamaguchi, Y., Igarashi, R., Ishihara, T., & Mizushima, Y. (2006). Transdermal delivery of $CaCO_3$ -nanoparticles containing insulin. *Diabetes Technology & Therapeutics*, *8*(3), 369–374. Available from https://doi.org/10.1089/dia.2006.8.369.

Hoarau, D., Delmas, P., David, S., Roux, E., & Leroux, J. C. (2004). Novel long-circulating lipid nanocapsules. *Pharmaceutical Research*, *21*(10), 1783–1789. Available from https://doi.org/10.1023/B:PHAM.0000045229.87844.21.

Hofheinz, R. D., Gnad-Vogt, S. U., Beyer, U., & Hochhaus, A. (2005). Liposomal encapsulated anti-cancer drugs. *Anti-Cancer Drugs*, *16*(7), 691–707. Available from https://doi.org/10.1097/01.cad.0000167902.53039.5a.

Homayun, B., Lin, X., & Choi, H. J. (2019). Challenges and recent progress in oral drug delivery systems for biopharmaceuticals. *Pharmaceutics*, *11*(3), 129. Available from https://doi.org/10.3390/pharmaceutics11030129.

Hu, L. D., Liu, Y., Tang, X., & Zhang, Q. (2006). Preparation and in vitro/in vivo evaluation of sustained-release metformin hydrochloride pellets. *European Journal of Pharmaceutics and Biopharmaceutics*, *64*(2), 185–192. Available from https://doi.org/10.1016/j.ejpb.2006.04.004.

Hua, S. (2020). Advances in oral drug delivery for regional targeting in the gastrointestinal tract – Influence of physiological, pathophysiological and pharmaceutical factors. *Frontiers in Pharmacology*, *11*, 524. Available from https://doi.org/10.3389/fphar.2020.00524.

Hussain, A., Arnold, J. J., Khan, M. A., & Ahsan, F. (2004). Absorption enhancers in pulmonary protein delivery. *Journal of Controlled Release*, *94*(1), 15–24. Available from https://doi.org/10.1016/j.jconrel.2003.10.001.

Iannone, M., Palermo, A., de la Torre, X., Romanelli, F., Sansone, A., Sansone, M., Lenzi, A., & Botrè, F. (2019). Effects of transdermal administration of testosterone gel on the urinary steroid profile in hypogonadal men: Implications in antidoping analysis. *Steroids*, *152*, 108491. Available from https://doi.org/10.1016/j.steroids.2019.108491.

Immordino, M. L., Dosio, F., & Cattel, L. (2006). Stealth liposomes: Review of the basic science, rationale, and clinical applications, existing and potential. *International Journal of Nanomedicine*, *1*(3), 297–315. Available from http://www.dovepress.com/getfile.php?fileID = 2667.

Iqbal, M. A., Md, S., Sahni, J. K., Baboota, S., Dang, S., & Ali, J. (2012). Nanostructured lipid carriers system: Recent advances in drug delivery. *Journal of Drug Targeting*, *20*(10), 813–830. Available from https://doi.org/10.3109/1061186x.2012.716845.

Islan, G. A., Tornello, P. C., Abraham, G. A., Duran, N., & Castro, G. R. (2016). Smart lipid nanoparticles containing levofloxacin and DNase for lung delivery. Design and characterization. *Colloids and Surfaces B: Biointerfaces*, *143*, 168–176. Available from https://doi.org/10.1016/j.colsurfb.2016.03.040.

Jaganathan, H., & Godin, B. (2012). Biocompatibility assessment of Si-based nano- and micro-particles. *Advanced Drug Delivery Reviews*, *64*(15), 1800–1819. Available from https://doi.org/10.1016/j.addr.2012.05.008.

Jain, A. K., Lee, C. H., & Gill, H. S. (2016). 5-Aminolevulinic acid coated microneedles for photodynamic therapy of skin tumors. *Journal of Controlled Release*, *239*, 72–81. Available from https://doi.org/10.1016/j.jconrel.2016.08.015.

Kagan, L., & Hoffman, A. (2008). Systems for region selective drug delivery in the gastrointestinal tract: Biopharmaceutical considerations. *Expert Opinion on Drug Delivery*, *5*(6), 681–692. Available from https://doi.org/10.1517/17425247.5.6.681.

Kampa, M., & Castanas, E. (2008). Human health effects of air pollution. *Environmental Pollution*, *151*(2), 362–367. Available from https://doi.org/10.1016/j.envpol.2007.06.012.

Kim, J. Y., Lee, S. H., Park, C. W., Rhee, Y. S., Kim, D. W., Park, J., Lee, M., Seo, J. W., & Park, E. S. (2015). Design and in vivo evaluation of oxycodone once-a-day controlled-release tablets. *Drug Design, Development and Therapy*, *9*, 695–706. Available from https://doi.org/10.2147/DDDT.S77356.

Kim, N. W., Kim, S. Y., Lee, J. E., Yin, Y., Lee, J. H., Lim, S. Y., Kim, E. S., Duong, H. T. T., Kim, H. K., Kim, S., Kim, J. E., Lee, D. S., Kim, J., Lee, M. S., Lim, Y. T., & Jeong, J. H. (2018). Enhanced cancer vaccination by in situ nanomicelle-generating dissolving microneedles. *ACS Nano*, *12*(10), 9702–9713. Available from https://doi.org/10.1021/acsnano.8b04146.

Kim, Y. C., Park, J. H., & Prausnitz, M. R. (2012). Microneedles for drug and vaccine delivery. *Advanced Drug Delivery Reviews*, *64*(14), 1547–1568. Available from https://doi.org/10.1016/j.addr.2012.04.005.

Kiptoo, P. K., Paudel, K. S., Hammell, D. C., Pinninti, R. R., Chen, J., Crooks, P. A., & Stinchcomb, A. L. (2009). Transdermal delivery of bupropion and its active metabolite, hydroxybupropion: A prodrug strategy as an alternative approach. *Journal of Pharmaceutical Sciences*, *98*(2), 583–594. Available from https://doi.org/10.1002/jps.21463.

Knobben, B. A. S., van Horn, J. R., van der Mei, H. C., & Busscher, H. J. (2006). Evaluation of measures to decrease intra-operative bacterial contamination in orthopaedic implant surgery. *Journal of Hospital Infection*, *62*(2), 174–180. Available from https://doi.org/10.1016/j.jhin.2005.08.007.

Kovalainen, M., Mönkäre, J., Riikonen, J., Pesonen, U., Vlasova, M., Salonen, J., Lehto, V. P., Järvinen, K., & Herzig, K. H. (2015). Novel delivery systems for improving the clinical use of peptides. *Pharmacological Reviews*, *67*(3), 541–546. Available from https://doi.org/10.1124/pr.113.008367.

Kumar, M. N. V. R., & Kumar, N. (2001). Polymeric controlled drug-delivery systems: Perspective issues and opportunities. *Drug Development and Industrial Pharmacy*, *27*(1), 1–30. Available from https://doi.org/10.1081/DDC-100000124.

Kumari, A., Yadav, S. K., & Yadav, S. C. (2010). Biodegradable polymeric nanoparticles based drug delivery systems. *Colloids and Surfaces B: Biointerfaces*, *75*(1), 1–18. Available from https://doi.org/10.1016/j.colsurfb.2009.09.001.

Kunrath, M. F., Diz, F. M., Magini, R., & Galárraga-Vinueza, M. E. (2020). Nanointeraction: The profound influence of nanostructured and nano-drug delivery biomedical implant surfaces on cell behavior. *Advances in Colloid and Interface Science*, *284*, 102265. Available from https://doi.org/10.1016/j.cis.2020.102265.

Kutlu, C., Çakmak, A. S., & Gumusderelioglu, M. (2014). Double-effective chitosan scaffold-PLGA nanoparticle system for brain tumour therapy: In vitro study. *Journal of Microencapsulation*, *31*(7), 700–707. Available from https://doi.org/10.3109/02652048.2014.913727.

Lai, S. K., Wang, Y. Y., Wirtz, D., & Hanes, J. (2009). Micro- and macrorheology of mucus. *Advanced Drug Delivery Reviews*, *61*(2), 86–100. Available from https://doi.org/10.1016/j.addr.2008.09.012.
Lane, M. E. (2013). Skin penetration enhancers. *International Journal of Pharmaceutics*, *447*(1–2), 12–21. Available from https://doi.org/10.1016/j.ijpharm.2013.02.040.
Laouini, A., Jaafar-Maalej, C., Limayem-Blouza, I., Sfar, S., Charcosset, C., & Fessi, H. (2012). Preparation, characterization and applications of liposomes: State of the art. *Journal of Colloid Science and Biotechnology*, *1*(2), 147–168. Available from https://doi.org/10.1166/jcsb.2012.1020.
Lemeshko, V. V. (2010). Potential-dependent membrane permeabilization and mitochondrial aggregation caused by anticancer polyarginine-KLA peptides. *Archives of Biochemistry and Biophysics*, *493*(2), 213–220. Available from https://doi.org/10.1016/j.abb.2009.11.004.
Li, P., Dai, Y. N., Zhang, J. P., Wang, A. Q., & Wei, Q. (2008). Chitosan-alginate nanoparticles as a novel drug delivery system for nifedipine. *International Journal of Biomedical Science*, *4*(3), 221–228. Available from http://www.ijbs.org/User/ContentFullText.aspx?VolumeNO = 4&StartPage = 221&Type = pdf.
Li, S., Zhao, B., Wang, F., Wang, M., Xie, S., Wang, S., Han, C., Zhu, L., & Zhou, W. (2010). Yak interferon-alpha loaded solid lipid nanoparticles for controlled release. *Research in Veterinary Science*, *88*(1), 148–153. Available from https://doi.org/10.1016/j.rvsc.2009.06.010.
Lieleg, O., Vladescu, I., & Ribbeck, K. (2010). Characterization of particle translocation through mucin hydrogels. *Biophysical Journal*, *98*(9), 1782–1789. Available from https://doi.org/10.1016/j.bpj.2010.01.012.
Lim, D. J., Vines, J. B., Park, H., & Lee, S. H. (2018). Microneedles: A versatile strategy for transdermal delivery of biological molecules. *International Journal of Biological Macromolecules*, *110*, 30–38. Available from https://doi.org/10.1016/j.ijbiomac.2017.12.027.
Lin, Y. H., Mi, F. L., Chen, C. T., Chang, W. C., Peng, S. F., Liang, H. F., & Sung, H. W. (2007). Preparation and characterization of nanoparticles shelled with chitosan for oral insulin delivery. *Biomacromolecules*, *8*(1), 146–152. Available from https://doi.org/10.1021/bm0607776.
Liu, D., Yang, F., Xiong, F., & Gu, N. (2016). The smart drug delivery system and its clinical potential. *Theranostics*, *6*(9), 1306–1323. Available from https://doi.org/10.7150/thno.14858.
Liu, G., Franssen, E., Fitch, M. I., & Warner, E. (1997). Patient preferences for oral vs intravenous palliative chemotherapy. *Journal of Clinical Oncology*, *15*(1), 110–115. Available from https://doi.org/10.1200/JCO.1997.15.1.110.
Liu, H., Zhao, Y., Zhao, D., Gong, T., Wu, Y., Han, H., Xu, T., Peschel, A., Han, S., & Qu, D. (2015). Antibacterial and anti-biofilm activities of thiazolidione derivatives against clinical staphylococcus strains. *Emerging Microbes and Infections*, *4*(1), e1. Available from https://doi.org/10.1038/emi.2015.1.
Liu, J., Gong, T., Fu, H., Wang, C., Wang, X., Chen, Q., Zhang, Q., He, Q., & Zhang, Z. (2008). Solid lipid nanoparticles for pulmonary delivery of insulin. *International Journal of Pharmaceutics*, *356*(1–2), 333–344. Available from https://doi.org/10.1016/j.ijpharm.2008.01.008.
Liu, X., Liu, C., Zhang, W., Xie, C., Wei, G., & Lu, W. (2013). Oligoarginine-modified biodegradable nanoparticles improve the intestinal absorption of insulin. *International Journal of Pharmaceutics*, *448*(1), 159–167. Available from https://doi.org/10.1016/j.ijpharm.2013.03.033.
Liu, Y., Sun, C., Hao, Y., Jiang, T., Zheng, L., & Wang, S. (2010). Mechanism of dissolution enhancement and bioavailability of poorly water soluble celecoxib by preparing stable amorphous nanoparticles. *Journal of Pharmacy and Pharmaceutical Sciences*, *13*(4), 589–606. Available from https://doi.org/10.18433/j3530j.
Liu, Y., Xu, C. F., Iqbal, S., Yang, X. Z., & Wang, J. (2017). Responsive nanocarriers as an emerging platform for cascaded delivery of nucleic acids to cancer. *Advanced Drug Delivery Reviews*, *115*, 98–114. Available from https://doi.org/10.1016/j.addr.2017.03.004.
Lopes, M. A., Abrahim, B. A., Seiça, R., Veiga, F., Rodrigues, C. R., & Ribeiro, A. J. (2014). Intestinal uptake of insulin nanoparticles: Facts or myths? *Current Pharmaceutical Biotechnology*, *15*(7), 629–638. Available from https://doi.org/10.2174/1389201015666140915151319.
Luo, M., Feng, Y., Wang, T., & Guan, J. (2018). Micro-/nanorobots at work in active drug delivery. *Advanced Functional Materials*, *28*(25), 1706100. Available from https://doi.org/10.1002/adfm.201706100.
Maghsoudnia, N., Eftekhari, R. B., Sohi, A. N., Zamzami, A., & Dorkoosh, F. A. (2020). Application of nano-based systems for drug delivery and targeting: A review. *Journal of Nanoparticle Research*, *22*(8), 245. Available from https://doi.org/10.1007/s11051-020-04959-8.

Marques, M. R. C., Loebenberg, R., & Almukainzi, M. (2011). Simulated biological fluids with possible application in dissolution testing. *Dissolution Technologies, 18*(3), 15–28. Available from https://doi.org/10.14227/DT180311P15.

Marwah, H., Garg, T., Goyal, A. K., & Rath, G. (2014). Permeation enhancer strategies in transdermal drug delivery. *Drug Delivery, 23*(2), 564–578. Available from https://doi.org/10.3109/10717544.2014.935532.

Mazzitelli, S., Pagano, C., Giusepponi, D., Nastruzzi, C., & Perioli, L. (2013). Hydrogel blends with adjustable properties as patches for transdermal delivery. *International Journal of Pharmaceutics, 454*(1), 47–57. Available from https://doi.org/10.1016/j.ijpharm.2013.06.081.

Merisko-Liversidge, E., & Liversidge, G. G. (2011). Nanosizing for oral and parenteral drug delivery: A perspective on formulating poorly-water soluble compounds using wet media milling technology. *Advanced Drug Delivery Reviews, 63*(6), 427–440. Available from https://doi.org/10.1016/j.addr.2010.12.007.

Meunier, F., Prentice, H. G., & Ringden, O. (1991). Liposomal amphotericin B (AmBisome): Safety data from a phase II/III clinical trial. *Journal of Antimicrobial Chemotherapy, 28*, 83–91. Available from https://doi.org/10.1093/jac/28.suppl_b.83.

Moffatt, K., Quinn, C., McCague, P. J., & Donnelly, R. F. (2021). Exploration into the opinions of patients with HIV, healthcare professionals and the lay public of the use of microneedles in clinical practice: Highlighting the translational potential for their role in HIV infection. *Drug Delivery and Translational Research, 11*(3), 1199–1217. Available from https://doi.org/10.1007/s13346-020-00848-8.

Muheem, A., Shakeel, F., Jahangir, M. A., Anwar, M., Mallick, N., Jain, G. K., Warsi, M. H., & Ahmad, F. J. (2016). A review on the strategies for oral delivery of proteins and peptides and their clinical perspectives. *Saudi Pharmaceutical Journal, 24*(4), 413–428. Available from https://doi.org/10.1016/j.jsps.2014.06.004.

Müller-Goymann, C. C. (2004). Physicochemical characterization of colloidal drug delivery systems such as reverse micelles, vesicles, liquid crystals and nanoparticles for topical administration. *European Journal of Pharmaceutics and Biopharmaceutics, 58*(2), 343–356. Available from https://doi.org/10.1016/j.ejpb.2004.03.028.

Muthu, M. S., & Feng, S. S. (2013). Theranostic liposomes for cancer diagnosis and treatment: Current development and pre-clinical success. *Expert Opinion on Drug Delivery, 10*(2), 151–155. Available from https://doi.org/10.1517/17425247.2013.729576.

N'Da, D. D. (2014). Prodrug strategies for enhancing the percutaneous absorption of drugs. *Molecules (Basel, Switzerland), 19*(12), 20780–20807. Available from https://doi.org/10.3390/molecules191220780.

Naeem, M., Awan, U. A., Subhan, F., Cao, J., Hlaing, S. P., Lee, J., Im, E., Jung, Y., & Yoo, J. W. (2020). Advances in colon-targeted nano-drug delivery systems: Challenges and solutions. *Archives of Pharmacal Research, 43*(1), 153–169. Available from https://doi.org/10.1007/s12272-020-01219-0.

Nagarkar, R., Singh, M., Nguyen, H. X., & Jonnalagadda, S. (2020). A review of recent advances in microneedle technology for transdermal drug delivery. *Journal of Drug Delivery Science and Technology, 59*, 101923. Available from https://doi.org/10.1016/j.jddst.2020.101923.

Naguib, Y. W., Kumar, A., & Cui, Z. (2014). The effect of microneedles on the skin permeability and antitumor activity of topical 5-fluorouracil. *Acta Pharmaceutica Sinica B, 4*(1), 94–99. Available from https://doi.org/10.1016/j.apsb.2013.12.013.

Newman, M. R., & Benoit, D. S. W. (2016). Local and targeted drug delivery for bone regeneration. *Current Opinion in Biotechnology, 40*, 125–132. Available from https://doi.org/10.1016/j.copbio.2016.02.029.

Newman, M. R., Russell, S. G., Schmitt, C. S., Marozas, I. A., Sheu, T. J., Puzas, J. E., & Benoit, D. S. W. (2018). Multivalent presentation of peptide targeting groups alters polymer biodistribution to target tissues. *Biomacromolecules, 19*(1), 71–84. Available from https://doi.org/10.1021/acs.biomac.7b01193.

O'neill, V. J., & Twelves, C. J. (2002). Oral cancer treatment: Developments in chemotherapy and beyond. *British Journal of Cancer, 87*(9), 933–937. Available from https://doi.org/10.1038/sj.bjc.6600591.

Okumu, F. W., & Cleland, J. L. (2002). Implants and injectables. In M. J. Rathbone, J. Hadgraft, & M. S. Roberts (Eds.), *Modified-release drug delivery technology* (pp. 657–662). CRC Press. Available from https://doi.org/10.1201/9780203910337-55.

Olivares-Navarrete, R., Hyzy, S. L., Slosar, P. J., Schneider, J. M., Schwartz, Z., & Boyan, B. D. (2015). Implant materials generate different peri-implant inflammatory factors: Poly-ether-ether-ketone promotes fibrosis and microtextured titanium promotes osteogenic factors. *Spine (Philadelphia, Pa.: 1986)*, *40*(6), 399–404. Available from https://doi.org/10.1097/BRS.0000000000000778.

Ookubo, N., Michiue, H., Kitamatsu, M., Kamamura, M., Nishiki, T. i, Ohmori, I., & Matsui, H. (2014). The transdermal inhibition of melanogenesis by a cell-membrane-permeable peptide delivery system based on poly-arginine. *Biomaterials*, *35*(15), 4508–4516. Available from https://doi.org/10.1016/j.biomaterials.2014.01.052.

Oostendorp, R. L., Huitema, A., Rosing, H., Jansen, R. S., ter Heine, R., Keessen, M., Beijnen, J. H., & Schellens, J. H. M. (2009). Coadministration of ritonavir strongly enhances the apparent oral bioavailability of docetaxel in patients with solid tumors. *Clinical Cancer Research*, *15*(12), 4228–4233. Available from https://doi.org/10.1158/1078-0432.CCR-08-2944.

Ordikhani, F., Dehghani, M., & Simchi, A. (2015). Antibiotic-loaded chitosan–laponite films for local drug delivery by titanium implants: Cell proliferation and drug release studies. *Journal of Materials Science: Materials in Medicine*, *26*(12), 1–12. Available from https://doi.org/10.1007/S10856-015-5606-0/FIGURES/5.

Özbaş, Z., Özkahraman, B., Bayrak, G., Kılıç Süloğlu, A., Perçin, I., Boran, F., & Tamahkar, E. (2021). Poly(vinyl alcohol)/(hyaluronic acid-*g*-kappa-carrageenan) hydrogel as antibiotic-releasing wound dressing. *Chemical Papers*, *75*(12), 6591–6600. Available from https://doi.org/10.1007/s11696-021-01824-3.

Pagneux, Q., Ye, R., Chengnan, L., Barras, A., Hennuyer, N., Staels, B., Caina, D., Osses, J. I. A., Abderrahmani, A., Plaisance, V., Pawlowski, V., Boukherroub, R., Melinte, S., & Szunerits, S. (2020). Electrothermal patches driving the transdermal delivery of insulin. *Nanoscale Horizons*, *5*(4), 663–670. Available from https://doi.org/10.1039/c9nh00576e.

Parhi, R., Suresh, P., & Patnaik, S. (2015). Physical means of stratum corneum barrier manipulation to enhance transdermal drug delivery. *Current Drug Delivery*, *12*(2), 122–138. Available from https://doi.org/10.2174/1567201811666140515145329.

Park, K., Kwon, I. C., & Park, K. (2011). Oral protein delivery: Current status and future prospect. *Reactive and Functional Polymers*, *71*(3), 280–287. Available from https://doi.org/10.1016/j.reactfunctpolym.2010.10.002.

Pastore, M. N., Kalia, Y. N., Horstmann, M., & Roberts, M. S. (2015). Transdermal patches: History, development and pharmacology. *British Journal of Pharmacology*, *172*(9), 2179–2209. Available from https://doi.org/10.1111/bph.13059.

Patlolla, R. R., Chougule, M., Patel, A. R., Jackson, T., Tata, P. N. V., & Singh, M. (2010). Formulation, characterization and pulmonary deposition of nebulized celecoxib encapsulated nanostructured lipid carriers. *Journal of Controlled Release*, *144*(2), 233–241. Available from https://doi.org/10.1016/j.jconrel.2010.02.006.

Patra, J. K., Das, G., Fraceto, L. F., Campos, E. V. R., Rodriguez-Torres, M., del, P., Acosta-Torres, L. S., Diaz-Torres, L. A., Grillo, R., Swamy, M. K., Sharma, S., Habtemariam, S., & Shin, H.-S. (2018). Nano based drug delivery systems: Recent developments and future prospects. *Journal of Nanobiotechnology*, *16*(1). Available from https://doi.org/10.1186/s12951-018-0392-8.

Patton, J. S., & Byron, P. R. (2007). Inhaling medicines: Delivering drugs to the body through the lungs. *Nature Reviews Drug Discovery*, *6*(1), 67–74. Available from https://doi.org/10.1038/nrd2153.

Patton, J. S., Fishburn, C. S., & Weers, J. G. (2004). The lungs as a portal of entry for systemic drug delivery. *Proceedings of the American Thoracic Society*, *1*(4), 338–344. Available from https://doi.org/10.1513/pats.200409-049TA.

Pavlukhina, S., & Sukhishvili, S. (2011). Polymer assemblies for controlled delivery of bioactive molecules from surfaces. *Advanced Drug Delivery Reviews*, *63*(9), 822–836. Available from https://doi.org/10.1016/j.addr.2011.03.017.

Pegoraro, C., MacNeil, S., & Battaglia, G. (2012). Transdermal drug delivery: From micro to nano. *Nanoscale*, *4*(6), 1881–1894. Available from https://doi.org/10.1039/c2nr11606e.

Pensado, A., Seijo, B., & Sanchez, A. (2014). Current strategies for DNA therapy based on lipid nanocarriers. *Expert Opinion on Drug Delivery*, *11*(11), 1721–1731. Available from https://doi.org/10.1517/17425247.2014.935337.

Pérez-Herrero, E., & Fernández-Medarde, A. (2015). Advanced targeted therapies in cancer: Drug nanocarriers, the future of chemotherapy. *European Journal of Pharmaceutics and Biopharmaceutics*, *93*, 52–79. Available from https://doi.org/10.1016/j.ejpb.2015.03.018.

Peter, B., Pioletti, D. P., Laïb, S., Bujoli, B., Pilet, P., Janvier, P., Guicheux, J., Zambelli, P. Y., Bouler, J. M., & Gauthier, O. (2005). Calcium phosphate drug delivery system: Influence of local zoledronate release on bone implant osteointegration. *Bone*, *36*(1), 52–60. Available from https://doi.org/10.1016/j.bone.2004.10.004.

Petersen, K. K., Rousing, M. L., Jensen, C., Arendt-Nielsen, L., & Gazerani, P. (2011). Effect of local controlled heat on transdermal delivery of nicotine. *International Journal of Physiology, Pathophysiology and Pharmacology*, *3*(3), 236–242. Available from http://www.ijppp.org/files/IJPPP1109001.pdf.

Pham, D. D., Fattal, E., & Tsapis, N. (2015). Pulmonary drug delivery systems for tuberculosis treatment. *International Journal of Pharmaceutics*, *478*(2), 517–529. Available from https://doi.org/10.1016/j.ijpharm.2014.12.009.

Pham, W., Kircher, M. F., Weissleder, R., & Tung, C.-H. (2004). Enhancing membrane permeability by fatty acylation of oligoarginine peptides. *Chembiochem: A European Journal of Chemical Biology*, *5*(8), 1148–1151. Available from https://doi.org/10.1002/cbic.200400063.

Phuengkham, H., Teeranachaideekul, V., Chulasiri, M., & Nasongkla, N. (2014). Preparation and optimization of chlorophene-loaded nanospheres as controlled release antimicrobial delivery systems. *Pharmaceutical Development and Technology*, *21*(1), 8–13. Available from https://doi.org/10.3109/10837450.2014.959180.

Plapied, L., Duhem, N., des Rieux, A., & Préat, V. (2011). Fate of polymeric nanocarriers for oral drug delivery. *Current Opinion in Colloid and Interface Science*, *16*(3), 228–237. Available from https://doi.org/10.1016/j.cocis.2010.12.005.

Pons-Faudoa, F. P., Ballerini, A., Sakamoto, J., & Grattoni, A. (2019). Advanced implantable drug delivery technologies: Transforming the clinical landscape of therapeutics for chronic diseases. *Biomedical Microdevices*, *21*(2), 47. Available from https://doi.org/10.1007/s10544-019-0389-6.

Prasad, V., De Jesús, K., & Mailankody, S. (2017). The high price of anticancer drugs: Origins, implications, barriers, solutions. *Nature Reviews Clinical Oncology*, *14*(6), 381–390. Available from https://doi.org/10.1038/nrclinonc.2017.31.

Prausnitz, M. R. (2004). Microneedles for transdermal drug delivery. *Advanced Drug Delivery Reviews*, *56*(5), 581–587. Available from https://doi.org/10.1016/j.addr.2003.10.023.

Prausnitz, M. R., & Langer, R. (2008). Transdermal drug delivery. *Nature Biotechnology*, *26*(11), 1261–1268. Available from https://doi.org/10.1038/nbt.1504.

Prausnitz, M. R., Elias, P. M., Franz, T. J., Schmuth, M., Tsai, J. C., Menon, G. K., Holleran, W. M., & Feingold, K. R. (2012). Skin barrier and transdermal drug delivery. In J. L. Bolognia, J. J. Jorizzo, J. V. Schaffer, J. P. Callen, L. Cerroni, W. R. Heymann, G. J. Hruza, A. J. Mancini, J. McGrath, J. W. Patterson, & T. Schwarz (Eds.), *Dermatology* (3rd (ed.), pp. 2065–2073). Elsevier.

Prausnitz, M. R., Mikszta, J. A., Cormier, M., & Andrianov, A. K. (2009). Microneedle-based vaccines. *Current Topics in Microbiology and Immunology*, *333*(1), 369–393. Available from https://doi.org/10.1007/978-3-540-92165-3_18.

Proksch, E., Brandner, J. M., & Jensen, J. M. (2008). The skin: An indispensable barrier. *Experimental Dermatology*, *17*(12), 1063–1072. Available from https://doi.org/10.1111/j.1600-0625.2008.00786.x.

Pye, A. D., Lockhart, D. E. A., Dawson, M. P., Murray, C. A., & Smith, A. J. (2009). A review of dental implants and infection. *Journal of Hospital Infection*, *72*(2), 104–110. Available from https://doi.org/10.1016/j.jhin.2009.02.010.

Qiu, Y., & Park, K. (2001). Environment-sensitive hydrogels for drug delivery. *Advanced Drug Delivery Reviews*, *53*(3), 321–339. Available from https://doi.org/10.1016/S0169-409X(01)00203-4.

Quon, B. S., Goss, C. H., & Ramsey, B. W. (2014). Inhaled antibiotics for lower airway infections. *Annals of the American Thoracic Society*, *11*(3), 425–434. Available from https://doi.org/10.1513/AnnalsATS.201311-395FR.

Ragelle, H., Danhier, F., Préat, V., Langer, R., & Anderson, D. G. (2017). Nanoparticle-based drug delivery systems: A commercial and regulatory outlook as the field matures. *Expert Opinion on Drug Delivery*, *14*(7), 851–864. Available from https://doi.org/10.1080/17425247.2016.1244187.

Rajinikanth, P. S., Balasubramaniam, J., & Mishra, B. (2007). Development and evaluation of a novel floating in situ gelling system of amoxicillin for eradication of *Helicobacter pylori*. *International Journal of Pharmaceutics*, *335*(1–2), 114–122. Available from https://doi.org/10.1016/j.ijpharm.2006.11.008.

Ratner, B. D. (2002). Reducing capsular thickness and enhancing angiogenesis around implant drug release systems. *Journal of Controlled Release*, *78*(1–3), 211–218. Available from https://doi.org/10.1016/S0168-3659(01)00502-8.

Rauck, R. L., Cherry, D., Boyer, M. F., Kosek, P., Dunn, J., & Alo, K. (2003). Long-term intrathecal opioid therapy with a patient-activated, implanted delivery system for the treatment of refractory cancer pain. *Journal of Pain*, *4*(8), 441–447. Available from https://doi.org/10.1067/S1526-5900(03)00730-2.

Ray, P., Hasnain, M. S., Koley, A., & Nayak, A. K. (2019). *Bone-implantable devices for drug delivery applications. Bioelectronics and medical devices: From materials to devices – Fabrication, applications and reliability* (pp. 355–392). Elsevier. Available from https://doi.org/10.1016/B978-0-08-102420-1.00021-2.

Reddy, Y. K., Reddy, D. M., & Kumar, M. A. (2014). Transdermal drug delivery system: A review. *Indian Journal of Research in Pharmacy and Biotechnology*. *Online*, *2*, 1094–1103.

Ribeiro, L. S. S., Falcão, A. C., Patrício, J. A. B., Ferreira, D. C., & Veiga, F. J. B. (2007). Cyclodextrin multicomponent complexation and controlled release delivery strategies to optimize the oral bioavailability of vinpocetine. *Journal of Pharmaceutical Sciences*, *96*(8), 2018–2028. Available from https://doi.org/10.1002/jps.20294.

Römgens, A. M., Bader, D. L., Bouwstra, J. A., Baaijens, F. P. T., & Oomens, C. W. J. (2015). Diffusion profile of macromolecules within and between human skin layers for (trans)dermal drug delivery. *Journal of the Mechanical Behavior of Biomedical Materials*, *50*, 215–222. Available from https://doi.org/10.1016/j.jmbbm.2015.06.019.

Rothbard, J. B., Garlington, S., Lin, Q., Kirschberg, T., Kreider, E., McGrane, P. L., Wender, P. A., & Khavari, P. A. (2000). Conjugation of arginine oligomers to cyclosporin A facilitates topical delivery and inhibition of inflammation. *Nature Medicine*, *6*(11), 1253–1257. Available from https://doi.org/10.1038/81359.

Roy, I., Ohulchanskyy, T. Y., Pudavar, H. E., Bergey, E. J., Oseroff, A. R., Morgan, J., Dougherty, T. J., & Prasad, P. N. (2003). Ceramic-based nanoparticles entrapping water-insoluble photosensitizing anticancer drugs: A novel drug–carrier system for photodynamic therapy. *Journal of the American Chemical Society*, *125*(26), 7860–7865. Available from https://doi.org/10.1021/ja0343095.

Rudzińska, M., Daglioglu, C., Savvateeva, L. V., Kaci, F. N., Antoine, R., & Zamyatnin, A. A. (2021). Current status and perspectives of protease inhibitors and their combination with nanosized drug delivery systems for targeted cancer therapy. *Drug Design, Development and Therapy*, *15*, 9–20. Available from https://doi.org/10.2147/DDDT.S285852.

Ryan, G., Singh, M., & Dwan, K. (2011). Inhaled antibiotics for long-term therapy in cystic fibrosis. *Cochrane Database of Systematic Reviews*, *3*. Available from https://doi.org/10.1002/14651858.cd001021.pub2.

Sabri, A. H., Kim, Y., Marlow, M., Scurr, D. J., Segal, J., Banga, A. K., Kagan, L., & Lee, J. B. (2020). Intradermal and transdermal drug delivery using microneedles – Fabrication, performance evaluation and application to lymphatic delivery. *Advanced Drug Delivery Reviews*, *153*, 195–215. Available from https://doi.org/10.1016/j.addr.2019.10.004.

Sachdeva, V., & Banga, A. K. (2011). Microneedles and their applications. *Recent Patents on Drug Delivery & Formulation*, *5*(2), 95–132. Available from https://doi.org/10.2174/187221111795471445.

Sahoo, S. K., Parveen, S., & Panda, J. J. (2007). The present and future of nanotechnology in human health care. *Nanomedicine: Nanotechnology, Biology, and Medicine*, *3*(1), 20–31. Available from https://doi.org/10.1016/j.nano.2006.11.008.

Schoellhammer, C. M., Blankschtein, D., & Langer, R. (2014). Skin permeabilization for transdermal drug delivery: Recent advances and future prospects. *Expert Opinion on Drug Delivery*, *11*(3), 393–407. Available from https://doi.org/10.1517/17425247.2014.875528.

Schwendener, R. A. (2007). Liposomes in biology and medicine. *Advances in Experimental Medicine and Biology*, *620*, 117–128. Available from https://doi.org/10.1007/978-0-387-76713-0_9.

Sen Gupta, A. (2016). Role of particle size, shape, and stiffness in design of intravascular drug delivery systems: Insights from computations, experiments, and nature. *Wiley Interdisciplinary Reviews: Nanomedicine and Nanobiotechnology*, *8*(2), 255−270. Available from https://doi.org/10.1002/wnan.1362.

Severino, P., Andreani, T., Macedo, A. S., Fangueiro, J. F., Santana, M. H. A., Silva, A. M., & Souto, E. B. (2012). Current state-of-art and new trends on lipid nanoparticles (SLN and NLC) for oral drug delivery. *Journal of Drug Delivery*, *2012*, 1−10. Available from https://doi.org/10.1155/2012/750891.

Shaji, J., & Patole, V. (2008). Protein and peptide drug delivery: Oral approaches. *Indian Journal of Pharmaceutical Sciences*, *70*(3), 269. Available from https://doi.org/10.4103/0250-474X.42967.

Shanker, M., Willcutts, D., Roth, J. A., & Ramesh, R. (2010). Drug resistance in lung cancer. *Lung Cancer: Targets and Therapy*, *1*, 23−36. Available from http://www.dovepress.com/getfile.php?fileID = 6320.

Shehata, T. M., Nair, A. B., Al-Dhubiab, B. E., Shah, J., Jacob, S., Alhaider, I. A., Attimarad, M., Elsewedy, H. S., & Ibrahim, M. M. (2020). Vesicular emulgel based system for transdermal delivery of insulin: Factorial design and in vivo evaluation. *Applied Sciences*, *10*(15), 5341. Available from https://doi.org/10.3390/app10155341.

Shim, W. S., Hwang, Y. M., Park, S. G., Lee, C. K., & Kang, N. G. (2018). Role of polyvinylpyrrolidone in dissolving microneedle for efficient transdermal drug delivery: In vitro and clinical studies. *Bulletin of the Korean Chemical Society*, *39*(6), 789−793. Available from https://doi.org/10.1002/bkcs.11476.

Siegel, R. A., & Rathbone, M. J. (2012). *Overview of controlled release mechanisms. Fundamentals and applications of controlled release drug delivery* (pp. 19−43). US: Springer. Available from https://doi.org/10.1007/978-1-4614-0881-9_2.

Silva, G. R. D., Fialho, S. L., Siqueira, R. C., Jorge, R., & Cunha Júnior, A. D. S. (2010). Implants as drug delivery devices for the treatment of eye diseases. *Article Brazilian Journal of Pharmaceutical Sciences*, *46*, 585−595.

Simon, A., Amaro, M. I., Healy, A. M., Cabral, L. M., & de Sousa, V. P. (2016). Comparative evaluation of rivastigmine permeation from a transdermal system in the Franz cell using synthetic membranes and pig ear skin with in vivo-in vitro correlation. *International Journal of Pharmaceutics*, *512*(1), 234−241. Available from https://doi.org/10.1016/j.ijpharm.2016.08.052.

Singh, O., Garg, T., Rath, G., & Goyal, A. K. (2014). Microbicides for the treatment of sexually transmitted HIV infections. *Journal of Pharmaceutics*, *2014*, 1−18. Available from https://doi.org/10.1155/2014/352425.

Smola, M., Vandamme, T., & Sokolowski, A. (2008). Nanocarriers as pulmonary drug delivery systems to treat and to diagnose respiratory and non respiratory diseases. *International Journal of Nanomedicine*, *3* (1), 1−19.

Söderlind, E., Abrahamsson, B., Erlandsson, F., Wanke, C., Iordanov, V., & Von Corswant, C. (2015). Validation of the IntelliCap® system as a tool to evaluate extended release profiles in human GI tract using metoprolol as model drug. *Journal of Controlled Release*, *217*, 300−307. Available from https://doi.org/10.1016/j.jconrel.2015.09.024.

Sonaje, K., Lin, K. J., Wey, S. P., Lin, C. K., Yeh, T. H., Nguyen, H. N., Hsu, C. W., Yen, T. C., Juang, J. H., & Sung, H. W. (2010). Biodistribution, pharmacodynamics and pharmacokinetics of insulin analogues in a rat model: Oral delivery using pH-responsive nanoparticles vs. subcutaneous injection. *Biomaterials*, *31*(26), 6849−6858. Available from https://doi.org/10.1016/j.biomaterials.2010.05.042.

Song, G., & Song, S. (2007). A possible biodegradable magnesium implant material. *Advanced Engineering Materials*, *9*(4), 298−302. Available from https://doi.org/10.1002/adem.200600252.

Song, Gao, Jiang, G., Liu, T., Zhang, X., Zeng, Z., Wang, R., Li, P., & Yang, Y. (2020). Separable microneedles for synergistic chemo-photothermal therapy against superficial skin tumors. *ACS Biomaterials Science & Engineering*, *6*(7), 4116−4125. Available from https://doi.org/10.1021/acsbiomaterials.0c00793.

Song, K., Liu, Y., MacEdo, H. M., Jiang, L., Li, C., Mei, G., & Liu, T. (2013). Fabrication and evaluation of a sustained-release chitosan-based scaffold embedded with PLGA microspheres. *Materials Science and Engineering C*, *33*(3), 1506−1513. Available from https://doi.org/10.1016/j.msec.2012.12.054.

Sonia, T. A., & Sharma, C. P. (2012). An overview of natural polymers for oral insulin delivery. *Drug Discovery Today*, *17*(13–14), 784–792. Available from https://doi.org/10.1016/j.drudis.2012.03.019.

Sosnik, A., Das Neves, J., & Sarmento, B. (2014). Mucoadhesive polymers in the design of nano-drug delivery systems for administration by non-parenteral routes: A review. *Progress in Polymer Science*, *39* (12), 2030–2075. Available from https://doi.org/10.1016/j.progpolymsci.2014.07.010.

Souto, E. B., Wissing, S. A., Barbosa, C. M., & Müller, R. H. (2004). Development of a controlled release formulation based on SLN and NLC for topical clotrimazole delivery. *International Journal of Pharmaceutics*, *278*(1), 71–77. Available from https://doi.org/10.1016/j.ijpharm.2004.02.032.

Stathopoulos, G. P., & Boulikas, T. (2012). Lipoplatin formulation review article. *Journal of Drug Delivery*, *2012*, 1–10. Available from https://doi.org/10.1155/2012/581363.

Stevenson, C. L., Theeuwes, F., & Wright, J. C. (2000). Osmotic implantable delivery systems. In D. L. Wise (Ed.), *Handbook of pharmaceutical controlled release technology* (pp. 225–253). Marcel Dekker Inc. Available from https://doi.org/10.1201/9781482289985.

Stuurman, F. E., Nuijen, B., Beijnen, J. H., & Schellens, J. H. M. (2013). Oral anticancer drugs: Mechanisms of low bioavailability and strategies for improvement. *Clinical Pharmacokinetics*, *52*(6), 399–414. Available from https://doi.org/10.1007/s40262-013-0040-2.

Suhonen, T. M., A. Bouwstra, J., & Urtti, A. (1999). Chemical enhancement of percutaneous absorption in relation to stratum corneum structural alterations. *Journal of Controlled Release*, *59*(2), 149–161. Available from https://doi.org/10.1016/S0168-3659(98)00187-4.

Suri, S. S., Fenniri, H., & Singh, B. (2007). Nanotechnology-based drug delivery systems. *Journal of Occupational Medicine and Toxicology*, *2*(1). Available from https://doi.org/10.1186/1745-6673-2-16.

Szkutnik-Fiedler, D., Grabowski, T., Balcerkiewicz, M., Michalak, M., Pilipczuk, I., Wyrowski, è., Urjasz, H., & Grześkowiak, E. (2017). The influence of a single and chronic administration of venlafaxine on tramadol pharmacokinetics in a rabbit model. *Pharmacological Reports*, *69*(3), 555–559. Available from https://doi.org/10.1016/j.pharep.2017.01.027.

Tahara, Y., Honda, S., Kamiya, N., & Goto, M. (2012). Transdermal delivery of insulin using a solid-in-oil nanodispersion enhanced by arginine-rich peptides. *MedChemComm*, *3*(12), 1496. Available from https://doi.org/10.1039/c2md20059g.

Tahara, Y., Namatsu, K., Kamiya, N., Hagimori, M., Kamiya, S., Arakawa, M., & Goto, M. (2010). Transcutaneous immunization by a solid-in-oil nanodispersion. *Chemical Communications*, *46*(48), 9200–9202. Available from https://doi.org/10.1039/c0cc03600e.

Taherali, F., Varum, F., & Basit, A. W. (2018). A slippery slope: On the origin, role and physiology of mucus. *Advanced Drug Delivery Reviews*, *124*, 16–33. Available from https://doi.org/10.1016/j.addr.2017.10.014.

Tamargo, R. J., Myseros, J. S., Epstein, J. I., Yang, M. B., Chasin, M., & Brem, H. (1993). Interstitial chemotherapy of the 9L gliosarcoma: Controlled release polymers for drug delivery in the brain. *Cancer Research*, *53*(2), 329–333.

Tan, G., Xu, P., Lawson, L. B., He, J., Freytag, L. C., Clements, J. D., & John, V. T. (2010). Hydration effects on skin microstructure as probed by high-resolution cryo-scanning electron microscopy and mechanistic implications to enhanced transcutaneous delivery of biomacromolecules. *Journal of Pharmaceutical Sciences*, *99*(2), 730–740. Available from https://doi.org/10.1002/jps.21863.

Tang, B. C., Dawson, M., Lai, S. K., Wang, Y.-Y., Suk, J. S., Yang, M., Zeitlin, P., Boyle, M. P., Fu, J., & Hanes, J. (2009). Biodegradable polymer nanoparticles that rapidly penetrate the human mucus barrier. *Proceedings of the National Academy of Sciences*, *106*(46), 19268–19273. Available from https://doi.org/10.1073/pnas.0905998106.

Thanki, K., Gangwal, R. P., Sangamwar, A. T., & Jain, S. (2013). Oral delivery of anticancer drugs: Challenges and opportunities. *Journal of Controlled Release*, *170*(1), 15–40. Available from https://doi.org/10.1016/j.jconrel.2013.04.020.

Tomkinson, B., Bendele, R., Giles, F. J., Brown, E., Gray, A., Hart, K., LeRay, J. D., Meyer, D., Pelanne, M., & Emerson, D. L. (2003). OSI-211, a novel liposomal topoisomerase I inhibitor, is active in SCID mouse models of human AML and ALL. *Leukemia Research*, *27*(11), 1039–1050. Available from https://doi.org/10.1016/S0145-2126(03)00092-4.

Traini, D., & Young, P. M. (2009). Delivery of antibiotics to the respiratory tract: An update. *Expert Opinion on Drug Delivery*, *6*(9), 897–905. Available from https://doi.org/10.1517/17425240903110710.

Trajkovski, B., Petersen, A., Strube, P., Mehta, M., & Duda, G. N. (2012). Intra-operatively customized implant coating strategies for local and controlled drug delivery to bone. *Advanced Drug Delivery Reviews*, *64*(12), 1142–1151. Available from https://doi.org/10.1016/j.addr.2012.05.016.

Tran, P. H. L., Tran, T. T. D., Piao, Z. Z., Van Vo, T., Park, J. B., Lim, J., Oh, K. T., Rhee, Y. S., & Lee, B. J. (2013). Physical properties and in vivo bioavailability in human volunteers of isradipine using controlled release matrix tablet containing self-emulsifying solid dispersion. *International Journal of Pharmaceutics*, *450*(1–2), 79–86. Available from https://doi.org/10.1016/j.ijpharm.2013.04.022.

Tran, T.-N. T. (2013). Cutaneous drug delivery: An update. *Journal of Investigative Dermatology Symposium Proceedings*, *16*(1), S67–S69. Available from https://doi.org/10.1038/jidsymp.2013.28.

Uçkay, I., Hoffmeyer, P., Lew, D., & Pittet, D. (2013). Prevention of surgical site infections in orthopaedic surgery and bone trauma: State-of-the-art update. *Journal of Hospital Infection*, *84*(1), 5–12. Available from https://doi.org/10.1016/j.jhin.2012.12.014.

Uddin, M. J., Scoutaris, N., Economidou, S. N., Giraud, C., Chowdhry, B. Z., Donnelly, R. F., & Douroumis, D. (2020). 3D printed microneedles for anticancer therapy of skin tumours. *Materials Science and Engineering: C*, *107*, 110248. Available from https://doi.org/10.1016/j.msec.2019.110248.

Ueki, A., Un, K., Mino, Y., Yoshida, M., Kawakami, S., Ando, H., Ishida, H., Yamashita, F., Hashida, M., & Kiso, M. (2015). Synthesis and evaluation of glyco-coated liposomes as drug carriers for active targeting in drug delivery systems. *Carbohydrate Research*, *405*, 78–86. Available from https://doi.org/10.1016/j.carres.2014.06.028.

Ünal, H., Öztürk, N., & Bilensoy, E. (2015). Formulation development, stability and anticancer efficacy of core-shell cyclodextrin nanocapsules for oral chemotherapy with camptothecin. *Beilstein Journal of Organic Chemistry*, *11*, 204–212. Available from https://doi.org/10.3762/bjoc.11.22.

Üner, M., & Yener, G. (2007). Importance of solid lipid nanoparticles (SLN) in various administration routes and future perspective. *International Journal of Nanomedicine*, *2*(3), 289–300.

Upadhyay, A. K., Singh, S., Chhipa, R. R., Vijayakumar, M. V., Ajay, A. K., & Bhat, M. K. (2006). Methyl-β-cyclodextrin enhances the susceptibility of human breast cancer cells to carboplatin and 5-fluorouracil: Involvement of Akt, NF-κB and Bcl-2. *Toxicology and Applied Pharmacology*, *216*(2), 177–185. Available from https://doi.org/10.1016/j.taap.2006.05.009.

Usonis, V., Bakasénas, V., Valentelis, R., Katiliene, G., Vidzeniene, D., & Herzog, C. (2003). Antibody titres after primary and booster vaccination of infants and young children with a virosomal hepatitis A vaccine (Epaxal®). *Vaccine*, *21*(31), 4588–4592. Available from https://doi.org/10.1016/S0264-410X(03)00509-7.

Vargason, A. M., Anselmo, A. C., & Mitragotri, S. (2021). The evolution of commercial drug delivery technologies. *Nature Biomedical Engineering*, *5*(9), 951–967. Available from https://doi.org/10.1038/s41551-021-00698-w.

Velino, C., Carella, F., Adamiano, A., Sanguinetti, M., Vitali, A., Catalucci, D., Bugli, F., & Iafisco, M. (2019). Nanomedicine approaches for the pulmonary treatment of cystic fibrosis. *Frontiers in Bioengineering and Biotechnology*, *17*, 406. Available from https://doi.org/10.3389/fbioe.2019.00406.

Venter, J. P., Muller, D. G., Du Plessis, J., & Goosen, C. (2001). A comparative study of an in situ adapted diffusion cell and an in vitro Franz diffusion cell method for transdermal absorption of doxylamine. *European Journal of Pharmaceutical Sciences*, *13*(2), 169–177. Available from https://doi.org/10.1016/S0928-0987(01)00110-5.

Waghule, T., Singhvi, G., Dubey, S. K., Pandey, M. M., Gupta, G., Singh, M., & Dua, K. (2019). Microneedles: A smart approach and increasing potential for transdermal drug delivery system. *Biomedicine and Pharmacotherapy*, *109*, 1249–1258. Available from https://doi.org/10.1016/j.biopha.2018.10.078.

Wallis, J., Shenton, D. P., & Carlisle, R. C. (2019). Novel approaches for the design, delivery and administration of vaccine technologies. *Clinical and Experimental Immunology*, *196*(2), 189–204. Available from https://doi.org/10.1111/cei.13287.

Wang, C., Ye, Y., Hochu, G. M., Sadeghifar, H., & Gu, Z. (2016). Enhanced cancer immunotherapy by microneedle patch-assisted delivery of anti-PD1 antibody. *Nano Letters*, *16*(4), 2334−2340. Available from https://doi.org/10.1021/acs.nanolett.5b05030.

Wang, W., Zhou, F., Ge, L., Liu, X., & Kong, F. (2014). A promising targeted gene delivery system: Folate-modified dexamethasone-conjugated solid lipid nanoparticles. *Pharmaceutical Biology*, *52*(8), 1039−1044. Available from https://doi.org/10.3109/13880209.2013.876655.

Wang, W., Yan, X., Li, Q., Chen, Z., Wang, Z., & Hu, H. (2020). Adapted nano-carriers for gastrointestinal defense components: Surface strategies and challenges. *Nanomedicine: Nanotechnology, Biology and Medicine*, *29*, 102277. Available from https://doi.org/10.1016/j.nano.2020.102277.

Weber, S., Zimmer, A., & Pardeike, J. (2014). Solid lipid nanoparticles (SLN) and nanostructured lipid carriers (NLC) for pulmonary application: A review of the state of the art. *European Journal of Pharmaceutics and Biopharmaceutics*, *86*(1), 7−22. Available from https://doi.org/10.1016/j.ejpb.2013.08.013.

Wen, H., Jung, H., & Li, X. (2015). Drug delivery approaches in addressing clinical pharmacology-related issues: Opportunities and challenges. *AAPS Journal*, *17*(6), 1327−1340. Available from https://doi.org/10.1208/s12248-015-9814-9.

Williams, A. C., & Barry, B. W. (2012). Penetration enhancers. *Advanced Drug Delivery Reviews*, *64*, 128−137. Available from https://doi.org/10.1016/j.addr.2012.09.032.

Wong, C. Y., Martinez, J., & Dass, C. R. (2016). Oral delivery of insulin for treatment of diabetes: Status quo, challenges and opportunities. *Journal of Pharmacy and Pharmacology*, *68*, 1093−1108. Available from https://doi.org/10.1111/jphp.12607.

Wu, L., Shan, W., Zhang, Z., & Huang, Y. (2018). Engineering nanomaterials to overcome the mucosal barrier by modulating surface properties. *Advanced Drug Delivery Reviews*, *124*, 150−163. Available from https://doi.org/10.1016/j.addr.2017.10.001.

Xu, B., Jiang, G., Yu, W., Liu, D., Zhang, Y., Zhou, J., Sun, S., & Liu, Y. (2017). H_2O_2-responsive mesoporous silica nanoparticles integrated with microneedle patches for the glucose-monitored transdermal delivery of insulin. *Journal of Materials Chemistry B*, *5*(41), 8200−8208. Available from https://doi.org/10.1039/c7tb02082a.

Yang, W., Peters, J. I., & Williams, R. O. (2008). Inhaled nanoparticles—A current review. *International Journal of Pharmaceutics*, *356*(1−2), 239−247. Available from https://doi.org/10.1016/j.ijpharm.2008.02.011.

Yang, Y., Bugno, J., & Hong, S. (2013). Nanoscale polymeric penetration enhancers in topical drug delivery. *Polymer Chemistry*, *4*(9), 2651−2657. Available from https://doi.org/10.1039/c3py00049d.

Yavuz, H., Çetin, K., Akgönüllü, S., Battal, D., & Denizli, A. (2018). Therapeutic protein and drug imprinted nanostructures as controlled delivery tools. In A. M. Grumezescu (Ed.), *Design and development of new nanocarriers* (pp. 439−473). William Andrew Publishing. Available from https://doi.org/10.1016/b978-0-12-813627-0.00012-0.

Yazici, H., O'Neill, M. B., Kacar, T., Wilson, B. R., Oren, E. E., Sarikaya, M., & Tamerler, C. (2016). Engineered chimeric peptides as antimicrobial surface coating agents toward infection-free implants. *ACS Applied Materials & Interfaces*, *8*(8), 5070−5081. Available from https://doi.org/10.1021/acsami.5b03697.

Ye, H., Zhou, Y., Liu, X., Chen, Y., Duan, S., Zhu, R., Liu, Y., & Yin, L. (2019). Recent advances on reactive oxygen species-responsive delivery and diagnosis system. *Biomacromolecules*, *20*(7), 2441−2463. Available from https://doi.org/10.1021/acs.biomac.9b00628.

Zhang, H., Leal, J., Soto, M. R., Smyth, H. D. C., & Ghosh, D. (2020). Aerosolizable lipid nanoparticles for pulmonary delivery of mRNA through design of experiments. *Pharmaceutics*, *12*(11), 1042. Available from https://doi.org/10.3390/pharmaceutics12111042.

Zhang, Q., Grice, J., Wang, G., & Roberts, M. (2009). Cutaneous metabolism in transdermal drug delivery. *Current Drug Metabolism*, *10*(3), 227−235. Available from https://doi.org/10.2174/138920009787846350.

Zhang, Y., Chan, H. F., & Leong, K. W. (2013). Advanced materials and processing for drug delivery: The past and the future. *Advanced Drug Delivery Reviews*, *65*(1), 104−120. Available from https://doi.org/10.1016/j.addr.2012.10.003.

Zhao, J. H., Fu, J. H., Wang, S. M., Su, C. H., Shan, Y., Kong, S. J., Wang, Y., Lu, W. L., Zhang, H., Zhang, S., Li, L., Zhang, E. H., Wang, L., Pei, Q. L., Wang, J. C., Zhang, X., & Zhang, Q. (2007). A novel transdermal patch incorporating isosorbide dinitrate with bisoprolol: In vitro and in vivo characterization. *International Journal of Pharmaceutics*, *337*(1–2), 88–101. Available from https://doi.org/10.1016/j.ijpharm.2006.12.030.

Zhou, T., Lewis, H., Foster, R. E., & Schwendeman, S. P. (1998). Development of a multiple-drug delivery implant for intraocular management of proliferative vitreoretinopathy. *Journal of Controlled Release*, *55*(2–3), 281–295. Available from https://doi.org/10.1016/S0168-3659(98)00061-3.

Zou, J.-J., Le, J.-Q., Zhang, B.-C., Yang, M.-Y., Jiang, J.-L., Lin, J.-F., Wu, P.-Y., Li, C., Chen, L., & Shao, J.-W. (2021). Accelerating transdermal delivery of insulin by ginsenoside nanoparticles with unique permeability. *International Journal of Pharmaceutics*, *605*, 120784. Available from https://doi.org/10.1016/j.ijpharm.2021.120784.

CHAPTER 13

Advantages of nanodrug targeting than conventional dosage system

Fulden Ulucan-Karnak[1] and Cansu İlke Kuru[2,3]
[1]Ege University, Institute of Health Sciences, Medical Biochemistry Department, Izmir, Turkey
[2]Graduate School of Natural and Applied Sciences, Department of Biotechnology, Ege University, Izmir, Turkey
[3]Buca Municipality Science and Art Center, Izmir, Turkey

Introduction

Drug targeting is the delivery of a drug to specified physiological areas, cells, tissues, or organs where the drug's pharmacological effects are needed. When a potential drug is injected into the bloodstream, it distributes uniformly throughout the body, and drug distribution at places other than the therapeutic sites can result in hazardous side effects. A higher therapeutic index can be provided by increasing distribution to therapeutic sites and improved drug action at the undesired locations can be achieved by decreasing delivery to unwanted sites (Yokoyama, 2005). Targeted drug delivery technologies and bloodstream therapies are currently unrelated to artificial organs, and targeted drug delivery is rarely considered a component of biomaterial sciences. The need for nanosized carriers for effective medication targeting is well known. The blood vessels are physically clogged when carrier systems with a higher diameter capillary system are injected into the circulation. Drug targeting, on the other hand, is done with carrier systems with a diameter of 200 nm or less, whereas capillary blood capillaries have a diameter of about 5 μm (Zhou et al., 2018). Carrier systems with a diameter greater than 400 nm are valued to be easily and quickly caught by reticuloendothelial systems. Consequently, such massive carrier systems are unable to circulate in the bloodstream for long enough to efficiently deliver therapeutic doses to therapeutic targets. Drug carriers with diameters ranging between 10 and 200 nm are utilized in drug targeting through the bloodstream, resulting in a substantial volume of delivery to the target areas due to long-term circulation in the blood (Matoba et al., 2017).

Nanosized drug delivery systems (NDDSs) are a type of nanomaterial that can improve drug stability and water solubility, increase cycle duration, boost target cell or tissue absorption rate, and limit enzyme degradation, all while improving medication safety and effectiveness (Quan et al., 2015). Inhalation, oral administration, and intravenous injection are all techniques for delivering NDDSs, and all of them have a better bioavailability (Deng et al., 2020). Furthermore, as the use of nanomaterials grows, so

Nanotechnology for Drug Delivery and Pharmaceuticals
DOI: https://doi.org/10.1016/B978-0-323-95325-2.00003-1

does the risk of exposure to nanomaterials in clinical settings. Consequently, nanomaterials will have additional opportunities to interact with different biological components, potentially affecting human health (Matoba et al., 2017). Thus this chapter aims to explain nanoDDSs, their advantages and limitations, and their future in therapy.

Administration of drugs

The chemical and physical structure of the drugs determines the administration route of the drugs, and administration routes determine their pharmacokinetics of them, as well. The drug administration routes are commonly categorized as enteral and parenteral. Oral and rectal are two enteral routes (into the gastrointestinal tract). Parenteral routes involve sublingual (under the tongue) and injection that might change depending on the site of administration, such as into a vein (intravenous), into a muscle (intramuscular), or beneath the skin (subcutaneous) (subcutaneous). There are many other parenteral routes such as topical that is applied to a body surface, such as the skin, nose, or eyes, pulmonary that is applied to the lungs, and intraosseous that is applied to the bone marrow (Fig. 13.1) (Sheila, 2017).

The intended route and the amount of administration, the characteristics and properties of the intended absorption site, and the potential effect of the drug on this site should be over the site of administration must be considered when designing a drug dosage formulations (Ruiz & Scioli Montoto, 2018). As compared with the conventional systems, drug release systems also have their own route of administrations. This route is known as the

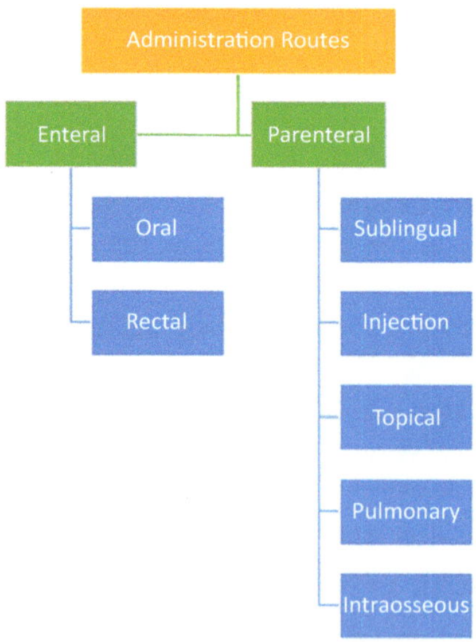

Figure 13.1 Administration routes of drugs.

pathway of the drug into the intended tissue or organ (Reza Rezaie et al., 2018). The drug is intended to cross the cell membrane for reaching the systemic circulation system. This can be possible either carrier-mediated membrane transporters or passive diffusion. There are many parameters that can affect the adsorption mechanism, such as drug-specific factors (solubility, pH, pK_a, ionization, and bioavailability), physicochemical variables (the particle size and their surface areas, the rate of disintegration, and the nature of the dose form), and patient-related factors (age, stomach-emptying time, intestinal transit time, illness state, absorption site blood flow, and presystemic metabolism) (Alagga & Gupta, 2021). Safety, efficacy, patient preference, dose, pharmacoeconomics, and time are the main principles for choosing the right administration route of the drugs. Safety and efficacy must be considered in order to avoid complications, such as anaphylaxis and septical shocks. Patient preference and pharmacoeconomics should be considered if the safety and efficacy parameters of the two routes are nearly identical (Zhou et al., n.d.; Kim & Jesus, 2021).

Conventional dosage systems

Conventional DDS (capsules, tablets, ointments syrups, etc.) are the traditional methods of drug administration. They have either disadvantages or advantages (Table 13.1) (Coelho et al., 2010).In conventional dosage systems the main challenge can be drug metabolism limitation. Drug metabolism can also affect plasma concentrations and relatively drug–drug interactions (Susa & Preuss, 2021; Wen et al., 2015). In pharmacokinetics, it is known that the drug is metabolized very fast after a single dose, and the drug level in the biological system increased quickly and exponentially decreased (Fig. 13.2A) (Dhillon & Gill, 2006). The quick profile and fluctuations in the drug levels cannot help to provide the best therapeutic effect. Minimum effective concentration (MEC) should be provided; therefore multiple doses could be applied (Price & Patel, 2021). But this can be also caused to toxic concentrations and poor patient compliance (Fig. 13.2B). Or, it is possible to take a single dose higher than the required dose, but it also results in adverse effects (Fig. 13.2C) (Adepu & Ramakrishna, 2021).

Table 13.1 Disadvantages and advantages of conventional drug delivery system.

Advantages	Disadvantages
Safe and low cost	Poor absorption and bioavailability
Noninvasive	No target specificity
Accurate and flexible	Low excretion and metabolism
Higher shelf-life	Repeated dosing
Accommodate patient variation	Poor patient compliance

Source: Derived from Coelho, J. F., Ferreira, P. C., Alves, P., Cordeiro, R., Fonseca, A. C., Góis, J. R., & Gil, M. H. (2010). Drug delivery systems: Advanced technologies potentially applicable in personalized treatments. *EPMA Journal, 1*(1), 164–209. https://doi.org/10.1007/s13167-010-0001-x.

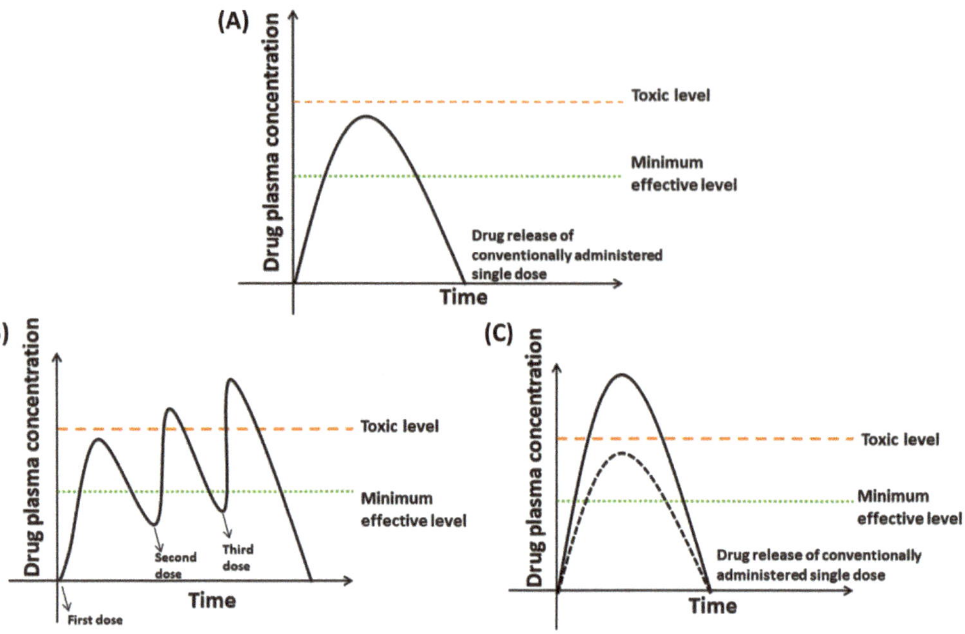

Figure 13.2 Drug levels after being administered into (A) a single conventional dose, (B) multiple doses, and (C) an increased single dose. *Reproduced with permission from Adepu, S. & Ramakrishna. (2021).* Molecules, 26 *[distributed under attribution 4.0 International (CC BY 4.0)]*

It is necessary to develop novel systems to overcome conventional dosage systems' challenges. For this purpose, drug carrier systems are great candidates for controlling the drug release rate and absorption to provide therapeutic effects for an intended duration. The drug concentration should provide in the range between the minimal effective concentration (MEC) and the minimum toxic concentration to achieve this effect. Even DDSs provide the intended drug concentration; they are not guaranteed to deliver the drug to the targeted site. Therefore, target-specific DDSs must be developed for controlling the biodistribution of the drug (Maiti & Sen, 2017). Target-specific drug carrier system development includes surface modification in order to provide passive (enhanced permeability and retention effect) or active targeting. Targeted DDSs are mainly important and advantageous systems ineffective cancer therapies due to the specificity between healthy cells and tumor cells (Din et al., 2017).

Drug delivery systems

Despite the primary goal of drug studies being to develop new molecules to treat different diseases the long duration of these investigations, the high cost, and the always expected ending yield have initiated alternative searches in this field. The purpose of these searches is to improve the life quality and the treatment of the patient (Makurvet, 2021). The goal in DDSs is to provide long-term release by providing a high and stable drug level on the most appropriate site of the body with a therapeutic dose (Tiwari et al., 2012). To extend the action of an active drug agent on the body, some chemical measures can be performed. To delay absorption the applications can be changed, such as making a poorly soluble salt or prodrug of the material, using enzyme inhibitors to prevent biotransformation, or changing the chemical structure of the substance. The most reliable and safest way to prolong the impact is to make modifications in the form of medicinal dosages, and numerous strategies are utilized for this goal (Hajnal et al., 2016). The purpose of a controlled system is to deliver the correct medicine to the correct location at the correct time and concentration. Controlled drug delivery is a constantly changing technique based on the premise that limiting the amount and pace of medication release, as well as using lower doses, may result in a better benefit (Raval et al., 2010). As can be seen, the delivery of the drug over long periods at the optimum amount and steady state is desired in the controlled drug release, while the drug level fluctuates between the maximum and minimum values in conventional release systems or injectable systems (Heng, 2018).

Smart drug delivery systems

Direct targeting of natural or synthetic targeting molecules, as well as targeting medications with high-order interactions with the target, is becoming more popular by the day. The targeted transfer of biotechnology and gene therapies or diagnostic products to tissues, organs, and cells in a specific location of the body is one key reason for this (Yu et al., 2012). This selective targeting enables the safe use of physiologically active chemical substances that are hazardous at high dosages, with fewer undesired side effects and the best therapeutic response possible. Smart drug delivery methods have been created in recent years that are appropriate for the structure of the drug, the place of action, and even the duration of action. In these DDSs, different nanosystems, such as smart polymers, porous nanostructures, graphene, and quantum dots (GQDs) based, are used. These smart drug carrier systems have been utilized extensively in medicine for transporting anticancer, antiparasitic, and antiinflammatory drugs. In this context, they may be given to the body by oral, transdermal, and ocular routes (Patra et al., 2018).

Polymers

Smart or stimuli-responsive polymers are defined as polymers that can respond to an external chemical or physical stimulation. Smart polymers were originally employed to control biologically active cargos released more than half a century ago, and they have since played a key role in nanomedicine (Liu et al., 2016). Because of their surface and bulk qualities, polymers are widely used in medication delivery. They are used in medicinal formulations as well as DDSs. These DDSs could be implanted to administer controlled doses of medication. Because of their optimal drug loading and releasing properties, polymers utilized in colloidal drug carrier systems, which are made up of tiny particles, have a significant advantage in DDSs (Srivastava et al., 2016). During the preparation of these systems the selection of polymeric material that allows us to control the active substance output is very important. The active substances placed in the polymer structured system are implanted to reach specific organs or tissues. In this way, the side effects and the effective therapeutic dose are reduced (Zhang et al., 2008).

Based on soluble nanopolymers, Hu et al. offered a proteomic approach for finding in vitro and ingrown cells pharmaceutical targets. Dendrimers are soluble nanopolymers with a high branching structure that makes them desirable as drug carriers and contrast agents for imaging. They are known for their high solubility, structural homogeneity, regulated surface functions, low cytotoxicity, and cell penetration ability. They chose the 4.0 generation (G4) poly(amidoamine) (PAMAM) dendrimer, which has 64 amine groups and 4.5-nm diameter. Its size is comparable to many folded proteins, but it still has sufficient numbers of reactive groups for the conjugation process. The methotrexate (MTX), an antifolate and antimetabolite agent utilized to treat cancer and autoimmune illnesses by inhibiting folic acid metabolism, was conjugated to the dendrimer for proof-of-principle tests (Hu et al., 2011).

Plasmonic photothermal treatment (PPTT) is a cancer-ablation technique that photon energy is converted into heat by several radiative and non-radiative events. Silver NPs (Ag NPS) and other plasmonic NPs exhibit strong optical absorbance properties. Furthermore, carbon nanotubes (CNTs) with strong cell penetration and thermal conductivity ability may boost Ag-NPs' efficiency for PPTT. The use of silver to decorate multiwalled CNTs has been used to improve their thermal conductivity in the study of Behnam et al. (2018). These particles' (CNT/Ag NPs) capacity was investigated experimentally in order to reduce melanoma tumor size following PTT. Then, the PTT of these two nanomaterials was compared. Melanoma tumors were produced in inbred mice by injecting the B16/F10 cell line. The tumors were injected with various NPs, which were subsequently irradiated with a laser diode at a predetermined time. According to tumor size monitoring, CNTs and silver combinations increased the optical absorption of CNT and tumor-killing in the PPTT technique. CNT/Ag NPs have the potential to be a powerful agent in the PPTT approach for treating solid tumors (Behnam et al., 2018). Polymers have a lot of advantages when it comes to drug delivery. This leads to better medication delivery and pharmacokinetics, as well as a better understanding of all safety aspects. There is still a need to produce nano-level therapies with newly developed qualities that use polymeric materials to address unmet medical requirements and allow personalized medicine to be practiced. Currently, the key goals in this field are to enable and promote additional research activities aimed at developing convertible and competitive products. With an interdisciplinary and open-minded approach, rapid and successful translation of developing polymeric drug delivery methods can be realized in the future (Bennet & Kim, 2014; Srivastava et al., 2016).

Porous nanostructures

Nanomaterials are gaining favor among scientists for application in the treatment of diseases, particularly malignancies. Mesoporous silica nanoparticles (NPs) (MSNs), for example, have great properties that make them ideal nanocarriers for storing, delivering, and preserving drug molecules until they reach their target. Different types of targeting ligands can be added to MSNs' outermost surfaces to deliver drugs to tumor tissues more efficiently. In order to prevent cargo trapped in mesopores from being released prematurely, stimuli-responsive nano gates can be used to block pore openings (Martínez-Carmona et al., 2015; Saadat et al., 2019). MSNPs (mesoporous silica NPs) are biomedical NPs that can be implemented into a range of applications. Researchers created a novel multifunctional nanodevice that includes a zwitterionic 2-methacryloyloxyethyl phosphorylcholine attachment on polyethyleneimine (PEI) surface to minimize unspecific protein attachment. In this study, the device was employed to transport two separate cargos at the same time: daunorubicin and siRNA. Anti-TWIST siRNA is important for regulating TWIST knockdown and sensitizing cells to chemotherapeutics such as daunorubicin, which is used to treat ovarian cancer. This study is the first time anti-TWITS-siRNA/daunorubicin codelivered silencing has been achieved with negligible fouling adsorption. The explained multifunctional technique could be used to treat ovarian cancer, which is currently incurable (Sanchez-Salcedo et al., 2018).

Surface-modified DDSs with a negative charge have a higher tendency to concentrate in tumor tissues, making them promising for in vivo applications. For boosting nucleolin-positive cell uptake, Zhang et al. (2017) developed NPs based on PEI, MTX, and DNA aptamer AS1411. Because NR interacts with AS1411 and MTX interacts with the folate receptor, these NPs enter the cells via receptor-mediated endocytosis. The nanosystem performed well for the combined therapy after loading sorafenib, with a 35.6% inhibition rate (Zhang et al., 2017). Porous nanostructures play a very important role especially in drug targeting and controlled release. It is easier to administer a medicine to a particular spot if it is enclosed within the cavity of a hollow NP. It is worth noting that researchers are focusing to work with nontoxic porous NPs with high biodegradability for medication delivery, as it makes disposal usage and easy storage. The development stages of this kind of simple technology with porous materials that have extraordinarily high drug loading capacities remain the most difficult task (Esquivel-Castro et al., 2019).

Graphene–quantum dots

GQDs are based on a single layer of 2D-graphene fragments, and they have great potential carbon-based nanomaterials with enormous biological potential in the future. According to recent research on GQDs, they are less poisonous and hydrophobic than graphene and have a sustained bright fluorescence. Their inherent fluorescence has gotten a lot of attention in anticancer research since it could help track human cells in vitro (Ghazy et al., 2021). Similar to graphene and GO, the addition of extra active groups on the GQD surface allows for multimodal conjugation, making them excellent carriers for cancer cell treatment and surveillance. Furthermore, due to their unique structural properties, GQD has been shown to boost the chemotherapeutic efficacy of anticancer drugs that are ineffective due to drug resistance (Iannazzo et al., 2017). The work by Iannazzo et al. describes a GQD-based DDS for the targeted administration of doxorubicin (DOX) to the cancer cells that are biocompatible and cell traceable. GQD was linked to the biotin (BTN) tumor targeting module, which can quickly identify biotin receptors that are overexpressed on cancer cells and loaded with DOX. In biological experiments on A549 cells the synthetic carrier was determined to be exceedingly safe (GQD and GQD–BTN). Cell uptake was found higher and delayed following treatment compared to the targeting module BTN (GQD–DOX) treatment or with the free drug alone, which had a significant impact on the cytotoxicity of GQD–BTN–DOX-treated cancer cells (Iannazzo et al., 2017).

In the Vatanparast and Shariatinia's study, using density-functional theory computations, the interaction of 5-fluorouracil (FU) drug with undoped/doped GQDs was investigated. The results exhibited which doping GQDs with AlN and AlP increased GQDs tendency to adsorb FU drugs substantially. As a result of the findings, AlN- and AlP-doped GQDs could be employed as possible carriers for FU medication delivery (Vatanparast & Shariatinia, 2018). GQDs have great capabilities of transporting not only anticancer medications in several DDRS modes but also genes, peptides, and other non-anticancer pharmaceuticals as nanocarriers. However, several hurdles must be overcome before they may be used in biomedicine and clinical practice. Despite the tremendous improvement in GQD biocompatibility, more research on their long-term toxicity and how GQDs affect the immune, reproductive, and neurological systems in various animal models are required. Although DDRS research for GQDs is still in its early phases, future research is projected to be able to successfully address present challenges with GQD implementation by proposing more safer and easier synthesis methods for efficient and mass production of DDRS (Zhao et al., 2020).

Therapeutic proteins delivery

Recent biotech advances have enabled the successful delivery of therapeutic proteins to treat life-threatening diseases. These improvements have boosted therapeutic proteins' importance in the pharmaceutical business, yet therapeutic transport to the targeted region remains a substantial barrier to achieving desired therapeutic effects. Stability in vitro and in vivo, immunogenicity, and shorter half-lives are three pharmacological issues that restrict the safety and efficacy of protein therapeutics (Pisal et al., 2010). The majority of therapeutic proteins are normally given orally, which has a number of drawbacks, including enzymatic breakdown, low solubility, and nonlinear pharmacokinetics. Therapeutic proteins have also been administered by intranasal, pulmonary, mucosal, intra-vaginal, and transdermal routes in addition to this method (Rehman et al., 2016). Novel pharmaceutical modifications being researched to solve these issues involve covalent attachment of poly(ethylene glycol), polysialic acid, or glycolic acid, as well as the creation of new formulations. Such approaches could lead to the development of next-generation protein therapies (Bolhassani et al., 2017; Pisal et al., 2010). Several therapeutic delivery channels have been developed and tested for efficient transport of therapeutic proteins to the desired location with minimal side effects to protect therapeutic proteins from enzymatic degradation (Rehman et al., 2016).

Yu et al. presented a novel technique for building de novo activatable protein NPs (APNPs) for therapeutic peptides targeted delivery. They have the ability to circulate for a long time in the bloodstream and can be developed to target specific disorders. APNPs have been found to aid in NR2B9c delivery, a neuroprotective peptide that has roles after cell entry, and melittin, a cytolytic peptide that destroys the lipid bilayer, for stroke and cancer treatment, respectively. Because of their great properties, ease of creation, and low cost, APNPs have a lot of potential as a versatile platform for the regulated delivery of therapeutic peptides (Yu et al., 2018). In Huang et al.'s study, they created a CD44-targeted intracellular delivery of therapeutic proteins based on hyaluronic acid nanogel (HA-NG). In both CD44-negative U87 cancer cells and CD44-positive 4T1 and MDA-MB-231 cells, 80-nm HA-NG showed significantly greater cellular uptake than its 150-nm equivalents. The facile and regulated manufacturing of small, bioresponsive, and endosome-disrupting, HA-NG holds considerable promise for targeted protein treatment (Huang et al., 2019). Pharmaceutical scientists have significant challenges in delivering therapeutic proteins to their target sites, which limits their utility. Other noninvasive methods for sufficient delivery of therapeutic proteins are also being studied that the protein or peptide must remain active and reach its target site without degradation. Pharmaceutical researchers are always working to create and develop new generalizable therapeutic delivery techniques and nanomaterials for delivering proteinous medicines to their target sites efficiently and without causing cytotoxicity. Such therapeutic protein delivery systems will aid in the fight against life-threatening diseases and will transform medical therapy (Rehman et al., 2016).

Advantages of the drug delivery systems

Traditional DDSs have been turned into smart DDSs that respond to stimuli thanks to incredible advances in biomedical nanotechnology over the last few decades. Well-defined nanoplatforms can improve targeting efficacy while minimizing payload side effects/toxicities by reacting to particular internal or external triggers, both of which are key factors in boosting patient compliance (Liu et al., 2016). The advantages of controlled delivery systems over traditional drug forms include: lowering the dose of medication given to the patient, extending the dosing interval, ensuring that the drug remains in the desired time and therapeutic dose, providing treatment at a low dose, eliminating side effects and harmful effects, ensuring that the drug substance delivers the treatment to the desired target region, and preventing the disintegration of drugs with short in vivo half-lives (Adepu & Ramakrishna, 2021). Smart DDSs are a common component of multiparticulate drug carriers, and they provide therapeutic and technological benefits (Lengyel et al., 2019).

Drug delivery systems evolution to micro/nanorobots

The drug delivery approach was started with the liposomes in 1965 and over the 50 years, it was continued with polymeric systems, dendrimers, modified versions of polymeric systems, biologic molecule-based drug carriers, and so on (Fig. 13.3). Drug carrier systems have become more advanced and complex structure due to the used

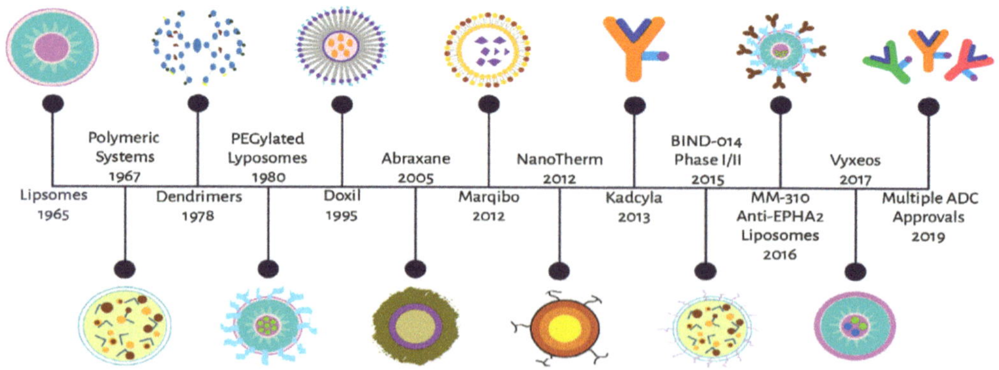

Figure 13.3 Historical overview of the development of drug carriers. *Reproduced with permission from Piscatelli, J. A., Ban, J., Lucas, A. T. & Zamboni, W. C. (2021).* Pharmaceutics, 13*(1), 1–28 [distributed under attribution 4.0 International (CC BY 4.0)]*

drug's ADME (absorption, distribution, metabolism, and elimination) characteristics (Li et al., 2017; Piscatelli et al., 2021).

After the 2000s, microrobot term was showed up in biomedical applications with programmable machines for the mobility, sensing, and operation of predefined tasks (Erkoc et al., 2019). With their great in vitro and preclinical outcomes, micro- and nanosized robots are increasingly being researched for individualized and precision therapeutic diagnosis, medication delivery, and surgery (Agrahari et al., 2020). In recent years, there are some novel strategies on DDSs that are called micro/nanorobots. This type of invention can be implemented in surgical operation, targeted drug delivery, and disease diagnosis with the aid of its autonomous movement properties. Exogenous (magnetic fields, light, acoustic fields, electric fields, etc.) or endogenous powers (magnetic fields, light, acoustic fields, electric fields, etc.) were used to power micro/nanorobots (chemical reaction energy) (Hu et al., 2020).

Micro/nanorobots' performance and implementations in biological systems could be mainly affected by the chosen propulsion mechanisms. Propulsion mechanisms can be external (magnetic, ultrasound, light, electrical, etc.) or self-propulsion (catalysis-based or biological). All power sources and propulsion alternative have their own advantages and limitations. Designing a micro/nanorobot includes the optimization of propulsion mechanism, power source, and implementation in vivo or in vitro. Therefore it should be chosen according to the intended use of the targeted drug delivery (Luo et al., 2018; Ricotti et al., 2015). Important issues, advantages, and challenges with the micro/nanorobots development were summarized in the review of Singh et al.; they stated that the key points of the development stages include mainly chosen of actuation, material and control types, and these parameters affect biodegradability, biocompatibility, reproduction, and the stability of the developed systems (Singh et al., 2019).

Micro/nanorobots are commonly chosen for delivering the drug to the intended site with the aid of their capability, propulsion, cargo, and penetration abilities. These innovative approaches improve the therapeutic effects of the medicine while reducing the drug's systemic negative effects. It is a must to explain that micro/nanorobots have different propulsion mechanisms as driving power according to the other DDS (Wang et al., 2020). Micro/nanomotor-combined DDSs are great candidates to overcome current drug carrier systems with the aid of their propulsion mechanisms with providing less toxicity, higher drug loading capacity, increased tissue penetration, and active delivery in vivo (Srivastava et al., 2019).

Conclusion

Drug discovery and delivery strategies are always the most important field in biochemistry- and medicine-related investigations. Some challenges, advantages, and novel solutions have been explained and discussed in this chapter in order to emphasize the current status. As it is known, nanomaterials are commonly referred to as drug carrier systems with their great properties as modifiability, biodegradability, and biocompatibility. But their toxicities should be more detailed investigated (Prabhakar & Banerjee, 2020).

Although drug carrier systems have many advantages, they have also faced many challenges. For example, scale-up procedures could be high cost, and complex processes and safety concerns are still not enlighted (Lu et al., 2016). It should be thoroughly examined whether new drug delivery techniques with high clinical efficacy, cheap cost, patient friendliness, and nontoxicity are produced. The biosafety of these systems has yet to be thoroughly examined in both healthy and diseased individuals. In addition, any in vitro process that has been conducted to confirm their safety has been finished (Hussain et al., 2019). A wide range of smart DDSs has been proven in the academic sector for a number of fascinating systems. These nanoplatforms, on the other hand, lack a well-defined manufacturing technique, toxicity assessment experience, and a clear link between preclinical and clinical trials, making regulatory and ethical approval extremely difficult. As a result, such advanced stimulus-sensitive nano-DDSs are not currently licensed for clinical use (Liu et al., 2016).

Future of nanomedicine and drug delivery systems

Even the publications and patents are increasing day by day in the nanomedicine field; nanotherapeutic delivery systems have various challenges during clinical translation as biological challenges, safety, scale-up, cost, and regulations (Zhang et al., 2020). These safety- and ethical-related issues also affect the translation of these technologies into the clinic (Jain, 2015). Also after the COVID-19 outbreak, nanomedicine would be evolved and reshaped for providing effective, faster, and economical diagnosis and treatment strategies (Al-Ahmady & Ali-Boucetta, 2020).

It is a very increasing rate of demand to develop novel DDSs for long-term delivery for different times, localized and targeted delivery in order to enhance patient compliance, drug efficiency and minimize the side effects. Also, it is very important to translate these novel systems into clinical applications (Bae & Park, 2020). Approaches for overcoming low bioavailability and drug solubility enable commercializing the developed systems. There are many examples of commercialized DDSs but they are still not sufficient numbers. In the current days of pandemic situation, two COVID-19 vaccines (mRNA-1273, developed by Moderna, and BNT162b2, by Pfizer in collaboration with BioNTech) drug delivery devices based on lipid NPs have been approved for emergency use in the United States (Vargason et al., 2021). Drug delivery technologies took part in OECD International Futures Project on "The Bioeconomy to 2030: Designing a Policy Agenda" as future health technologies (Tait et al., 2007).

The global market for DDSs is predicted to increase at a compound annual growth rate (CAGR) of 6.1% from $231.0 billion in 2020 to $310.0 billion in 2025 (Global Markets & Technologies for Advanced Drug Delivery Systems, 2021).

As pharmaceutical science, materials science, and biomedical science developments, different controlled releasing nanomaterials will be utilized for smart DDSs in the future. Researchers will face a tremendous hurdle in translating improved preclinical research of advanced DDSs into reproducible manufacturing that leads to clinical trial success. However, it is important to remember that the ultimate goal of all our efforts is to help patients. Future research on smart DDSs for controlled drug delivery should focus on clinical translation, allowing for the deployment of more stimulus-sensitive nanomedicine in clinical settings (Liu et al., 2016).

References

Adepu, S., & Ramakrishna. (2021). Controlled drug delivery systems: Current status and future directions. *Molecules (Basel, Switzerland), 26*.

Agrahari, V., Agrahari, V., Chou, M. L., Chew, C. H., Noll, J., & Burnouf, T. (2020). Intelligent micro-/nanorobots as drug and cell carrier devices for biomedical therapeutic advancement: Promising development opportunities and translational challenges. *Biomaterials, 260*. Available from https://doi.org/10.1016/j.biomaterials.2020.120163.

Alagga, A.A., Gupta, V. Drug Absorption. [Updated 2022 Jun 23]. In: StatPearls [Internet]. Treasure Island (FL): StatPearls Publishing; 2022 Jan. Available from: https://www.ncbi.nlm.nih.gov/books/NBK557405/.

Al-Ahmady, Z., & Ali-Boucetta. (2020). Nanotoxicology future could be reshaped post-COVID-19 Pandemic. *Frontiers in Nanotechnology Nanomedicine*.

Bae, Y. H., & Park, K. (2020). Advanced drug delivery 2020 and beyond: Perspectives on the future. *Advanced Drug Delivery Reviews, 158*, 4–16. Available from https://doi.org/10.1016/j.addr.2020.06.018.

Behnam, M. A., Emami, F., Sobhani, Z., Koohi-Hosseinabadi, O., Dehghanian, A. R., Zebarjad, S. M., Moghim, M. H., & Oryan, A. (2018). Novel combination of silver nanoparticles and carbon nanotubes for plasmonic photo thermal therapy in melanoma cancer model. *Advanced Pharmaceutical Bulletin, 8*(1), 49–55. Available from https://doi.org/10.15171/apb.2018.006.

Bennet, D., & Kim, S. (2014). *Polymer nanoparticles for smart drug delivery*. InTech. Available from https://doi.org/10.5772/58422.

Bolhassani, A., Jafarzade, B. S., & Mardani, G. (2017). In vitro and in vivo delivery of therapeutic proteins using cell penetrating peptides. *Peptides, 87*, 50–63. Available from https://doi.org/10.1016/j.peptides.2016.11.011.

Coelho, J. F., Ferreira, P. C., Alves, P., Cordeiro, R., Fonseca, A. C., Góis, J. R., & Gil, M. H. (2010). Drug delivery systems: Advanced technologies potentially applicable in personalized treatments. *EPMA Journal, 1*(1), 164–209. Available from https://doi.org/10.1007/s13167-010-0001-x.

Deng, Y., Zhang, X., Shen, H., He, Q., Wu, Z., Liao, W., & Yuan, M. (2020). Application of the nano-drug delivery system in treatment of cardiovascular diseases. *Frontiers in Bioengineering and Biotechnology*, 7. Available from https://doi.org/10.3389/fbioe.2019.00489.

Dhillon, S., & Gill, K. (2006). Basic pharmacokinetics, In *Clinical Pharmacokinetics*, 1–44.

Din, F. U., Aman, W., Ullah, I., Qureshi, O. S., Mustapha, O., Shafique, S., & Zeb, A. (2017). Effective use of nanocarriers as drug delivery systems for the treatment of selected tumors. *International Journal of Nanomedicine, 12*, 7291–7309. Available from https://doi.org/10.2147/IJN.S146315.

Erkoc, P., Yasa, I. C., Ceylan, H., Yasa, O., Alapan, Y., & Sitti, M. (2019). Mobile microrobots for active therapeutic delivery. *Advanced Therapeutics, 2*(1), 1800064. Available from https://doi.org/10.1002/adtp.201800064.

Esquivel-Castro, T. A., Ibarra-Alonso, M. C., Oliva, J., & Martínez-Luévanos, A. (2019). Porous aerogel and core/shell nanoparticles for controlled drug delivery: A review. *Materials Science and Engineering C, 96*, 915–940. Available from https://doi.org/10.1016/j.msec.2018.11.067.

Ghazy, E., Kumar, A., Barani, M., Kaur, I., Rahdar, A., & Behl, T. (2021). Scrutinizing the therapeutic and diagnostic potential of nanotechnology in thyroid cancer: Edifying drug targeting by nano-oncotherapeutics. *Journal of Drug Delivery Science and Technology, 61*, 102221. Available from https://doi.org/10.1016/j.jddst.2020.102221.

Global Markets and Technologies for Advanced Drug Delivery Systems. (2021). https://www.bccresearch.com/market-research/pharmaceuticals/advanced-drug-delivery-administration.html

Hajnal, K., Gabriel, H., Aura, R., Erzsébet, V., & Blanka, S. S. (2016). Prodrug strategy in drug development. *Acta Medica Marisiensis, 62*(3), 356–362. Available from https://doi.org/10.1515/amma-2016-0032.

Heng, P. W. S. (2018). Controlled release drug delivery systems. *Pharmaceutical Development and Technology, 23*(9), 833. Available from https://doi.org/10.1080/10837450.2018.1534376.

Hu, L., Iliuk, A., Galan, J., Hans, M., & Tao, W. A. (2011). Identification of drug targets in vitro and in living cells by soluble-nanopolymer-based proteomics. *Angewandte Chemie - International Edition, 50*(18), 4133–4136. Available from https://doi.org/10.1002/anie.201006459.

Hu, M., Ge, X., Chen, X., Mao, W., Qian, X., Yuan, W.-E., & Micro. (2020). Nanorobot: A promising targeted drug delivery system. *Pharmaceutics, 12*(7).

Huang, K., He, Y., Zhu, Z., Guo, J., Wang, G., Deng, C., & Zhong, Z. (2019). Small, traceable, endosome-disrupting, and bioresponsive click nanogels fabricated via microfluidics for CD44-targeted cytoplasmic delivery of therapeutic proteins. *ACS Applied Materials and Interfaces, 11*(25), 22171–22180. Available from https://doi.org/10.1021/acsami.9b05827.

Hussain, A., Singh, S., Das, S. S., Anjireddy, K., Karpagam, S., & Shakeel, F. (2019). Nanomedicines as drug delivery carriers of anti-tubercular drugs: From pathogenesis to infection control. *Current Drug Delivery, 16*(5), 400–429. Available from https://doi.org/10.2174/1567201816666190201144815.

Iannazzo, D., Pistone, A., Salamò, M., Galvagno, S., Romeo, R., Giofré, S. V., Branca, C., Visalli, G., & Di Pietro, A. (2017). Graphene quantum dots for cancer targeted drug delivery. *International Journal of Pharmaceutics, 518*(1–2), 185–192. Available from https://doi.org/10.1016/j.ijpharm.2016.12.060.

Jain, K. K. (2015). Future of nanomedicine: Impact on healthcare and society. *Nanomedicine: Nanotechnology, Biology, and Medicine, 10*(21), 3199–3202. Available from https://doi.org/10.2217/nnm.15.153.

Kim, J., & Jesus, D. (2021). Medication routes of administration. *StatPearls*.

Lengyel, K.-S., Antal., Laki, A., & Antal. (2019). Microparticles, microspheres, and microcapsules for advanced drug delivery. *Scientia Pharmaceutica, 87*(3).

Li, Z., Tan, S., Li, S., Shen, Q., & Wang, K. (2017). Cancer drug delivery in the nano era: An overview and perspectives (Review). *Oncology Reports, 38*(2), 611–624. Available from https://doi.org/10.3892/or.2017.5718.

Liu, D., Yang, F., Xiong, F., & Gu, N. (2016). The smart drug delivery system and its clinical potential. *Theranostics, 6*(9), 1306–1323. Available from https://doi.org/10.7150/thno.14858.

Lu, H., Wang, J., Wang, T., Zhong, J., Bao, Y., & Hao, H. (2016). Recent progress on nanostructures for drug delivery applications. *Journal of Nanomaterials, 2016*, 1–12. Available from https://doi.org/10.1155/2016/5762431.

Luo, M., Feng, Y., Wang, T., & Guan, J. (2018). Micro-/nanorobots at work in active drug delivery. *Advanced Functional Materials, 28*(25), 1706100. Available from https://doi.org/10.1002/adfm.201706100.

Maiti, S., & Sen, K. K. (2017). *Drug delivery concepts* Introductory, & Chapter *Advanced Technology for Delivering Therapeutics*. InTech.

Makurvet, F. D. (2021). Biologics vs. small molecules: Drug costs and patient access. *Medicine in Drug Discovery, 9*, 100075. Available from https://doi.org/10.1016/j.medidd.2020.100075.

Martínez-Carmona, M., Colilla, & Vallet-Regí. (2015). *Smart mesoporous nanomaterials for antitumor therapy* (Vol. 5). http:///pmc/articles/PMC5304809/

Matoba, T., Koga, J. i, Nakano, K., Egashira, K., & Tsutsui, H. (2017). Nanoparticle-mediated drug delivery system for atherosclerotic cardiovascular disease. *Journal of Cardiology, 70*(3), 206–211. Available from https://doi.org/10.1016/j.jjcc.2017.03.005.

Patra, J. K., Das, G., Fraceto, L. F., Campos, E. V. R., Rodriguez-Torres, M., del, P., Acosta-Torres, L. S., Diaz-Torres, L. A., Grillo, R., Swamy, M. K., Sharma, S., Habtemariam, S., & Shin, H.-S. (2018). Nano based drug delivery systems: Recent developments and future prospects. *Journal of Nanobiotechnology*, *16*(1). Available from https://doi.org/10.1186/s12951-018-0392-8.

Pisal, D. S., Kosloski, M. P., & Balu-Iyer, S. V. (2010). Delivery of therapeutic proteins. *Journal of Pharmaceutical Sciences*, *99*(6), 2557−2575. Available from https://doi.org/10.1002/jps.22054.

Piscatelli, J. A., Ban, J., Lucas, A. T., & Zamboni, W. C. (2021). Complex factors and challenges that affect the pharmacology, safety and efficacy of nanocarrier drug delivery systems. *Pharmaceutics*, *13*(1), 1−28. Available from https://doi.org/10.3390/pharmaceutics13010114.

Prabhakar, P., & Banerjee, M. (2020). Nanotechnology in drug delivery system: Challenges and opportunities. *Journal of Pharmaceutical Sciences and Research*, *12*, 492.

Price, G., & Patel, D. A. (2021). Drug bioavailability. *StatPearls*.

Quan, X. Q., Kang, L., Yin, X. Z., Jin, Z. H., & Gao, Z. G. (2015). Synthesis of PEGylated hyaluronic acid for loading dichloro(1,2-diaminocyclohexane)platinum(II) (DACHPt) in nanoparticles for cancer treatment. *Chinese Chemical Letters*, *26*(6), 695−699. Available from https://doi.org/10.1016/j.cclet.2015.04.024.

Raval, A., Parikh, J., & Engineer, C. (2010). Mechanism of controlled release kinetics from medical devices. *Brazilian Journal of Chemical Engineering*, *27*(2), 211−225. Available from https://doi.org/10.1590/S0104-66322010000200001.

Rehman, K., Akash, M. S. H., Akhtar, B., Tariq, M., Mahmood, A., & Ibrahim, M. (2016). Delivery of therapeutic proteins: Challenges and strategies. *Current Drug Targets*, *17*(10), 1172−1188. Available from https://doi.org/10.2174/1389450117666151209120139.

Reza Rezaie, H., Esnaashary, M., Aref arjmand, A., & Öchsner, A. (2018). *Classification of drug delivery systems* (pp. 9−25). Springer Science and Business Media LLC. https://doi.org/10.1007/978-981-10-0503-9_2.

Ricotti, L., Cafarelli, A., Iacovacci, V., Vannozzi, L., & Menciassi, A. (2015). Advanced micro-nano-bio systems for future targeted therapies. *Current Nanoscience*, *11*(2), 144−160. Available from https://doi.org/10.2174/1573413710666141114221246.

Ruiz, M. E., & Scioli Montoto, S. (2018). *Routes of drug administration* (pp. 97−133). Springer Science and Business Media LLC. https://doi.org/10.1007/978-3-319−99593-9_6.

Saadat, M., Zahednezhad, F., Zakeri-Milani, P., Heidari, H. R., Shahbazi-Mojarrad, J., & Valizadeh, H. (2019). Drug targeting strategies based on charge dependent uptake of nanoparticles into cancer cells. *Journal of Pharmacy and Pharmaceutical Sciences*, *22*(1), 191−220. Available from https://doi.org/10.18433/jpps30318.

Sanchez-Salcedo, S., Vallet-Regí, M., Shahin, S. A., Glackin, C. A., & Zink, J. I. (2018). Mesoporous core-shell silica nanoparticles with anti-fouling properties for ovarian cancer therapy. *Chemical Engineering Journal*, *340*, 114−124. Available from https://doi.org/10.1016/j.cej.2017.12.116.

Sheila, A. (2017). *Doggrell, introduction, pharmacology, administration, & absorption.*

Singh, A. V., Ansari, M. H. D., Laux, P., & Luch, A. (2019). Micro-nanorobots: Important considerations when developing novel drug delivery platforms. *Expert Opinion on Drug Delivery*, *16*(11), 1259−1275. Available from https://doi.org/10.1080/17425247.2019.1676228.

Srivastava, A., Yadav, T., Sharma, S., Nayak, A., Akanksha Kumari, A., & Mishra, N. (2016). Polymers in drug delivery. *Journal of Biosciences and Medicines*, *04*(01), 69−84. Available from https://doi.org/10.4236/jbm.2016.41009.

Srivastava, S. K., Clergeaud, G., Andresen, T. L., & Boisen, A. (2019). Micromotors for drug delivery in vivo: The road ahead. *Advanced Drug Delivery Reviews*, *138*, 41−55. Available from https://doi.org/10.1016/j.addr.2018.09.005.

Susa, S., & Preuss, C. V. (2021). Drug metabolism. *StatPearls*.

Tait, J., Bruce, A., & Chataway. (2007). Health biotechnology to 2030. *Futures*, *33*(0), 7−8.

Tiwari, G., Tiwari, R., Bannerjee, S., Bhati, L., Pandey, S., Pandey, P., & Sriwastawa, B. (2012). Drug delivery systems: An updated review. *International Journal of Pharmaceutical Investigation*, *2*(1), 2. Available from https://doi.org/10.4103/2230-973x.96920.

Vargason, A. M., Anselmo, A. C., & Mitragotri, S. (2021). The evolution of commercial drug delivery technologies. *Nature Biomedical Engineering*, *5*(9), 951−967. Available from https://doi.org/10.1038/s41551-021-00698-w.

Vatanparast, M., & Shariatinia, Z. (2018). AlN and AlP doped graphene quantum dots as novel drug delivery systems for 5-fluorouracil drug: Theoretical studies. *Journal of Fluorine Chemistry*, *211*, 81–93. Available from https://doi.org/10.1016/j.jfluchem.2018.04.003.

Wang, J., Dong, R., Wu, H., Cai, Y., & Ren, B. (2020). A review on artificial micro/nanomotors for cancer-targeted delivery, diagnosis, and therapy. *Nano-Micro Letters*, *12*(1). Available from https://doi.org/10.1007/s40820-019-0350-5.

Wen, H., Jung, H., & Li, X. (2015). Drug delivery approaches in addressing clinical pharmacology-related issues: Opportunities and challenges. *AAPS Journal*, *17*(6), 1327–1340. Available from https://doi.org/10.1208/s12248-015-9814-9.

Yokoyama, M. (2005). Drug targeting with nano-sized carrier systems. *Journal of Artificial Organs*, *8*(2), 77–84. Available from https://doi.org/10.1007/s10047-005-0285-0.

Yu, M. K., Park, J., & Jon, S. (2012). Targeting strategies for multifunctional nanoparticles in cancer imaging and therapy. *Theranostics*, *2*(1), 3–44. Available from https://doi.org/10.7150/thno.3463.

Yu, X., Gou, X., Wu, P., Han, L., Tian, D., Du, F., Chen, Z., Liu, F., Deng, G., Chen, A. T., Ma, C., Liu, J., Hashmi, S. M., Guo, X., Wang, X., Zhao, H., Liu, X., Zhu, X., Sheth, K., & Zhou, J. (2018). Activatable protein nanoparticles for targeted delivery of therapeutic peptides. *Advanced Materials*, *30*(7), 1705383. Available from https://doi.org/10.1002/adma.201705383.

Zhang, C., Yan, L., Wang, X., Zhu, S., Chen, C., Gu, Z., & Zhao, Y. (2020). Progress, challenges, and future of nanomedicine. *Nano Today*, *35*, 101008. Available from https://doi.org/10.1016/j.nantod.2020.101008.

Zhang, F., Correia, A., Mäkilä, E., Li, W., Salonen, J., Hirvonen, J. J., Zhang, H., & Santos, H. A. (2017). Receptor-mediated surface charge inversion platform based on porous silicon nanoparticles for efficient cancer cell recognition and combination therapy. *ACS Applied Materials and Interfaces*, *9*(11), 10034–10046. Available from https://doi.org/10.1021/acsami.7b02196.

Zhang, L., Gu, F. X., Chan, J. M., Wang, A. Z., Langer, R. S., & Farokhzad, O. C. (2008). Nanoparticles in medicine: Therapeutic applications and developments. *Clinical Pharmacology and Therapeutics*, *83*(5), 761–769. Available from https://doi.org/10.1038/sj.clpt.6100400.

Zhao, C., Song, X., Liu, Y., Fu, Y., Ye, L., Wang, N., Wang, F., Li, L., Mohammadniaei, M., Zhang, M., Zhang, Q., & Liu, J. (2020). Synthesis of graphene quantum dots and their applications in drug delivery. *Journal of Nanobiotechnology*, *18*(1). Available from https://doi.org/10.1186/s12951-020-00698-z.

Zhou, Q., Zhu, J.J., Chen, Xu, M., & Wang, H., et al. (n.d.). The optimal choice of medication administration route regarding intravenous, intramuscular, and subcutaneous injection. *Patient Prefer Adherence*.

Zhou, X., Hao, Y., Yuan, L., Pradhan, S., Shrestha, K., Pradhan, O., Liu, H., & Li, W. (2018). Nanoformulations for transdermal drug delivery: A review. *Chinese Chemical Letters*, *29*(12), 1713–1724. Available from https://doi.org/10.1016/j.cclet.2018.10.037.

CHAPTER 14

Risk assessment of various nanomaterials: health safety perspective

Najla Bentrad[1] and Houcine Touati[2]
[1]Faculty of Biological Sciences, Department of Biology and Physiology of Organisms, University of Sciences and Technology Houari Boumediene, Bab Ezzouar, Algeria
[2]Institute of Chemistry of Environments and Materials, National School of Engineers of Poitiers (ENSI), University of Poitiers—UMR CNRS 7285, Poitiers Cedex 9, France

Introduction

Nanoparticles (NPs) and nanotechnologies are a quickly expanding field of study, which exist at the intersection of the atomic and material scales, have very specific structural characteristics. These NPs, unlike traditional materials, have properties that vary according to their sizes. Optical, electrical, catalytic, thermal, magnetic, mechanical, and biological properties are the most common properties of NPs. When they are very thin, both classical and quantum mechanics phenomena affected them. In the past, artisans used NPs to lend their pottery a lustrous finish. This method, which was used in the Middle Ages and in recent time, was based on the use of metallic salts (most notably copper and silver) that, when combined and then exposed to a reducing atmosphere, migrated to the surface of the pottery, eventually being reduced to their metallic fundamental state and forming copper and silver NPs, which were the source of the shiny effect (Padovani et al., 2003; Pradell et al., 2008). The NPs have remarkable mechanical properties as they range from the superplasticity observed in nanocrystalline copper materials to the superplasticity observed in materials made from carbon nanotubes (Lu et al., 2000) to 10-fold resistances like the matrices reinforcement made from carbon nanotubes (Qi, Teo, et al., 2003; Qi, Vermesh, et al., 2003). Multiwall carbon nanotubes have a strength that is comparable to diamond.

NPs are generated from natural occurrence (storms, volcano eruptions, etc.), unintended sources (wood fires, automotive exhaust, braking, etc.), and manufacturing sources all produce NPs (NPs manufactured intentionally by humans). The current state of understanding about the effects of nanometric particles in emissions poses questions about NPs' health consequences. Indeed, several factors lead one to believe that these ultrafine emission particles have unique toxic properties. According to a recent study, there are currently few details that directly investigate the toxicity of

Nanotechnology for Drug Delivery and Pharmaceuticals
DOI: https://doi.org/10.1016/B978-0-323-95325-2.00007-9

engineered NPs (Ostiguy et al., 2006). The electrical properties of NPs are also special. For example, the carbon nanotubes are added to composite matrices such as Al_2O_3 to make them more effective (Wang, Wang, et al., 2004; Zhan et al., 2002, 2003), which increases the material's conductivity by an extensive amount. Chemical NPs (mostly composed of polymers), metallic NPs such as gold or silver NPs, metal oxides (such as Fe_2O_3, TiO_2), and composites may all be distinguished (e.g., quantum dots Cd–Se–Zn). Their numerous properties make them perfect targets for catalysis because they are used and empty energy levels are similar (quantum confinement) (Kamat, 2002).

A wide variety of industries use them for various purposes related to construction and textile industries (Vigneshwaran et al., 2006). The CeO_2 NPs can effectively alter oxidation states, functioning as oxygen and free radical traps. Also, some metal oxide NPs may absorb UV light. NPs of ZnO and TiO_2 are often used in cosmetics (sun creams) because they have strong UV protection while remaining translucent (because the NPs have dimensions lower than the wavelengths of the visible light 400–700 nm). Additional clinical research studies are required to determine the hazards of nanoparticles in humans and animal beings. Nonetheless, deleterious effects have been determined, especially in animals, even though different toxicological factors and the variety of nanomaterials that have been tested. For example, a study of the major review papers on NP toxicity reveals that the following are the most important considerations in assessing the toxicological effects of NPs: concerning exposure and duration of exposure. Nonetheless, deleterious effects have been determined, especially in animals, although these are still fragmentary in terms of the different toxicological factors and the variety of nanomaterials that have been tested. The following factors are the most relevant in evaluating the toxicological effects of NPs, according to the report on NP toxicity: factors affecting exposure and duration; factors affecting the exposed organism: human susceptibility, particle contact with biological materials, particle evolution once within the organism; factors affecting NPs, physicochemical properties (Fig. 14.1). To quantify and predict the impact of different physicochemical properties of NPs as well as their toxicological effects and health hazards risk is critical. Other properties or damage of the body's defense mechanisms (Dhawan & Sharma, 2010; Lanone & Boczkowski, 2006; Lin et al., 2012; Nel et al., 2006; Oberdörster et al., 2005, 2007) are described in this book chapter As a limited number of studies are available, knowledge of the function of physicochemical characteristics of engineered NPs in their toxic effects is still in progress. These findings reveal that, in addition to evidence on the determinants of the toxicological effects of ultrafine particles in air quality, the following parameters impact the toxicological effects of manufactured NPs. NPs are distinguished by their nanometric dimension, which endows them with novel biological capabilities. At least two traits stand out: an increase in surface reactivity as the fraction of atoms present on their surface increases, and an

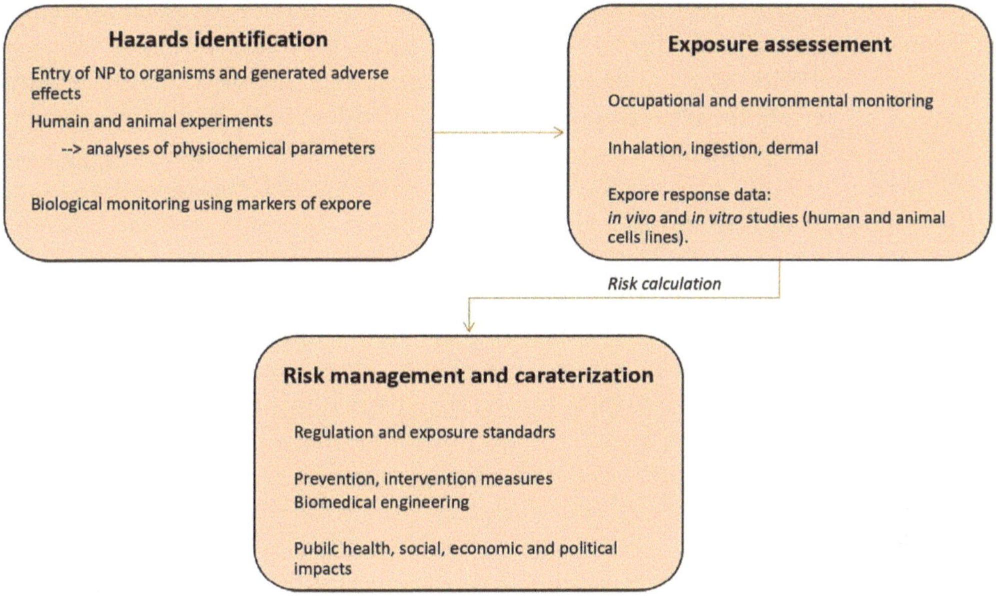

Figure 14.1 Overview of some analysis techniques and steps involved in NPs risk assessments. *NPs*, Nanoparticles.

increase in NP availability at the cell and organ levels. The capacity of NPs to infiltrate cells more successfully than micrometer-sized particles supports their utility in delivering therapeutic medicines into cells (Moghimi et al., 2005). When NPs are exposed through the respiratory (nasal cavity, tracheobronchial tree, deep lung, or gastrointestinal paths), the size of the NPs determines where they are deposited. Because of their nanometric sizes, these particles may penetrate the bloodstream after passing through both respiratory and gastrointestinal defense systems, allowing them to be dispersed across the body.

Since chemical reactions take place at the particle surface (Amato, 1989), the reactivity of NPs of the same structure but larger sizes will be higher. In rats and mice, for example, intratracheal instillation of TiO_2 particles with a diameter of 20 nm causes a greater inflammatory response (Oberdörster et al., 2000). The number of neutrophils fits the same dose—response curve for many particles as the TiO_2 dose is calculated in terms of the total surface area administered, which is a significant departure from the typical situation in which toxicity is proportional to substance mass. Other related findings in other experiments are searching at the toxicological effects of inhaled stable micro- and NPs (Brown et al., 2001; Donaldson et al., 2002). These results demonstrate that the greater specific surface area, greater access to the interstitium, and sustained accumulation of nanosized particles can explain their more pronounced pulmonary effects as compared to micrometer-sized particles. It showed that the particle surface area is more positively associated with lung injury parameters than particle density, length, or number when biopersistence is measured and consequent dose—responses with particles are of considerably different sizes. However, a comparison of the two particles revealed that they do not enter the interstitium in comparable amounts. For example, the amount of carbon black flowing into the interstitium constituted around 4% of the dosage, whereas TiO_2 was on the order of 50% (Oberdörster et al., 1992). Diffusion of particles in the presence of differential concentration is referred to NPs that do not stay clustered in emission: they disperse quickly and can be detected well away from the source of emission. It is well understood that the spectrum of particles grows quickly to give rise to material transition in a greater diameter range (2—100 nm) known as "accumulation mode."

The resuspension of particles from powder is extremely complex as size, shape, electrostatic charge, and atmospheric humidity are all variables that can affect this process. The proportion of atoms exposed on a particle's surface grows exponentially as the particle size decreases. This chapter aims at summarizing existing information about the toxicological effects of NPs deposited in natural ecosystems and living organisms and their health risk consequences. It is therefore a problem of systematizing current information on the determinants of possible toxicological effects of nanomaterials in the atmosphere, considering existing evidence on ultrafine particles of air pollutants and data on NPs. Then we will look at alternative assessment methods that take advantage of at least one of the physical and molecular properties at function. Finally, we can synthesize information on NP toxicity based on different exposure paths.

Exposure assessment to nanoparticles

The assessment of health risks related to nanomaterials requires the identification, and characterization of associated hazards exposure and some research programs tends to identify and understand population exposure to NPs in a contaminated environment (Grieger et al., 2009; Isigonis et al., 2019). NPs oxidize with a very rapid kinetics and thus cause an explosion. These powdered products are in most cases combustible and can give rise to explosions often called "dust explosions" (Eckhoff, 1993).

Diffusion

The NPs will disperse in a concentration gradient, moving from high to low concentration regions. The particles suspended in the air form an aerosol; because of their nanometric sizes, ultrafine aerosols behave substantially differently from micrometric aerosols (Maynard & Kuempel, 2005).

These aerosols will disperse over enormous distances and last for relatively extended periods of time in contaminated habitats, thereby exposing a larger number of individuals at uncertain amounts (Seaton et al., 2009). Particles' spatial arrangement approaches that of gases as its size approaches the molecular level and therefore tends to follow the characteristics of gas diffusion, which may deposit in the atmosphere.

Maynard and Baron (2004) characterized that the aerosol concentrations observed in their investigation were quite low, ranging from 0.7 to 53 g/m^3, and many particles were compact, even in the form of clusters of nonbreathable materials. Workplace assessments of suspended fine particles during handling of carbon nanotube powders revealed no significant increase, which suggests that the suspended particles were micron-sized or bigger (Maynard & Baron, 2004).

Exposure paths of the population

There are two forms of nanomaterial exposure for the general public (Nel et al., 2006; Reijnders, 2006).

The direct exposures to nanomaterials coming from personal hygiene items, medicines, food packaging, clothes and fabrics, and medical prosthesis. Indirect exposures come as a result of the wear, degradation, or in tires, inks, fuels, electronic devices, fabrics, or deposited on windows, solar panels, and other surfaces (Nel et al., 2006; Reijnders, 2006). Human inhalation involves a previous understanding of the processes of emission, transport, and accumulation in the environment (US-EPA, 2005).

Dermal deposition

Nanomaterials in cosmetics (especially sunscreens) exposure are most of the time a minority compared to inhalation or ingestion, in the context of nanomaterials (Miyani & Hughes, 2016; Pflücker et al., 2001; Sanches et al., 2020).

Ingestion

Food and water contamination should be investigated. While the use of nanomaterials for soil remediation is considered, transfer into the food chain cannot be ruled out. NPs used as food additives or dentures can also be eaten, although this type of exposure is less common (US-EPA, 2005).

Deposition in respiratory system

The nasopharyngeal, tracheobronchial, and alveolar regions serve as a deposition location for different-sized NPs (US-EPA, 2005).

With more specifically to the alveolar region, the main mechanism of elimination is phagocytosis by macrophages within 6–12 h. Several studies in rats showed that the clearance of NPs by macrophages was significantly lower than that of microparticles, suggesting that NPs either reside in epithelial cells or migrate further upward into the stroma (Marante et al., 2020; Semmler et al., 2004).

Risk characterization of nanoparticles in suspension

Quantitative and qualitative assessment of exposure requires aerosol measurements in the work environment. Aerosol measurements are required for a quantitative assessment of exposure. It has the benefit of avoiding metrological issues and covering all exposures. It would eventually allow researchers to investigate the geographical and temporal patterns of nanomaterial exposure in the overall population (US-EPA, 2005).

The occurrence of transition metals in NPs because of the manufacturing process is a factor that can play a role in the toxicological effects of processed NPs. Indeed, transition metals play a role in reactions that produce reactive sources of oxygen, as well as molecules implicated in the toxicological effects of ultrafine particles in the atmosphere and engineered NPs. This has been shown with iron with ultrafine particles with waste in the atmosphere and carbon nanotubes (Shvedova et al., 2003). The toxicity of various forms of multileaf nanotubes on keratinocytes was linked to the amount of iron used in the production process in the previous case. Similar findings on murine macrophages were recently reported (Kagan et al., 2006).

Different shapes of manufactured NPs are available (spheres, fibers, tubes, rings, and sheets). Long-term exposure to natural or man-made fibers has been linked to an increased risk of pulmonary fibrosis and cancer, according to toxicological reports (Greim et al., 2001). The dosage, duration, and biopersistence of the fibers are all important factors. The fibrous shape of titanium dioxide (TiO_2) is more toxic than the spherical form, according to in vitro experiments on cells in culture. Watanabe et al. (2002) used TiO_2 spheres and fibers (1−2 m in diameter) to expose rat alveolar macrophages to comparable concentrations (Gaffet 2011; Shinji et al., 2005). Cells exposed to TiO_2 in the form of fibers displayed vacuoles and membrane modifications, indicating cellular pain and toxicity, while cells exposed to spherical TiO_2 particles showed no changes. Inhaling these locally made particles was highly harmful to rats, but the consequences might be averted by preexposing them for 5 min every day for 3 days. Allowing the particles to develop for 3.5 min also allowed them to agglomerate, which removed the toxic effect (Carranza et al., 2001).

Nonspecific measure

Mass measurement does not seem to be an effective measure for nanosized particles a priori: in reality, mass measurement methods only apply for particles larger than 0.1 m due to sensitivity concerns. On the supply chain, there are many optical counters to choose from, including those that are cheap. However, the interference range of these instruments is mostly above 0.1 m, that is, for particle sizes at the NP's upper limit.

Measurement of the concentration in numbers

The condensation nucleus meter technology and electrical measurement counts are now available for measuring NP's concentration.

Condensation nuclei counters

Condensation particle counters or CPC, were invented since optical detection is widely established but nonoperational below 100 nm. To render particles smaller than this threshold observable, the approach was to artificially expand them. The particles are immersed in a solution filled with *n*-butanol vapors and are then cooled to allow the vapors to condense on their surface, diffusing them. The most product lines (TSI 3022 or Grimm) have average qualities such as alcohol consumption, counting from 0 to 106 p/cm^3, a reaction time of around 1 s, a low detection limit of about 5 nm, and a high detection limit of about 1 μm.

Metering by electrical measurement

The electrical aerosol detector (EAD) is also directly derived from this analytical method. The charging is carried out upstream by the corona effect, followed by a detection assembly as described before. In-depth feedback would be necessary to give an opinion on this device.

The electrical low-pressure impactor (ELPI) employs two techniques: particle selection by inertia and electrical sensing. It is employed by the ELPI particle counter and enables for size categorization by inertia for particles with cutoff sizes ranging from 7 nm to 10 μm. The EAD is also directly derived from it. Corona effect did upstream the loading, followed by a detection set as described previously. In-depth feedback would be necessary to give an opinion on this device.

Electrical counting

It is feasible to count particles if they are charged and then gathered on a particular support that allows electrical detection through an electrometer. Electrical mobility analysis (SMPS) is mainly used in the laboratory and it is also less efficient to measure the concentration in numbers: on the one hand; it is necessary to provide the density of the aerosol measured; it is preferable to use it for concentrations greater than 1000 or even 10,000 particles/cm^3, which directs it toward situations of medium and high concentration. A counting system follows a differential mobility analyzer (DMA), usually a particle counter. Specific "nano-DMA" geometries allow specialized SMPS in the 3–50-nm range, for example.

Size distribution measurement

The principle of diffusion batteries (DBS) is based on passaging the aerosol through a succession of grids. The smaller the particles are, the more they diffuse and are trapped during passaging a grid. These are divided in three groups:

- DBS;
- electrical impactors;
- electric mobility analyzers.

The DBS has 11 measurement channels that are screened in order. It can detect particles with sizes ranging from 2 to 200 nm (Witschger & Fabries, 2005). The downside of this method is that it takes a long time to react and is less accurate than electric mobility analyzers.

Measurement of the surface

The Nanoparticle Surface Area Monitor (NSAM) works on the same principle as the electrical electrosol aerosol detector (EAD). The aerosols were first positively charged by the corona effect, and the total charge deposited was then quantified using a Faraday cage—electrometer assembly setup. The next critical step is to convert the measured charge into a surface concentration, which is expressed in $\mu m^2/cm^3$ (Witschger & Fabries, 2005).

Specific measure

The main interest of the specific measurement is to evaluate the exposure of people by characterizing accurately environmental NPs allowing an analysis deferred in time particles whether they are of natural or anthropic origin. For this purpose, the existing devices can be classified into three categories:

1. Whether counting or measuring by size "granulometry," these devices provide instantaneous information mostly. However, they do not offer the possibility of distinguishing various origins of NPs from other ultrafine particles. The term "nonspecific measurement" will be used in this first case.
2. This differentiation is provided by a second kind, which will use the phrase "particular measure."
3. There is a third kind that is relatively unique in that it is based on the ability of preliminary marking of the particles, marking permitting then their identification: the phrase "indirect detection by tracing."

Real-time measurement

Work aimed at dynamically coupling sampling and it has carried particle analysis out for several years. A first realization concerned the solution of atmospheric particles with continuous coupling to an analysis by ion chromatography.

A complete work on the adaptation of the laser-induced fluorescence technique (LIBS) in air quality (Hahn & Lunden, 2000) is necessary with an SMPS particle size analyzer (Ostiguy et al., 2006); in this case, it is a procedure of extracting a size range and then analyzing it by LIBS.

Offline: sampling for analysis

The main distinction among the "air," "water," and "soil" concerns for determining its physicochemical characteristics. As far as sampling is concerned, it essentially cited filter sampling. It can be "total": in this case, it is a single filter, ensuring the sampling of all the particles, possibly upstream, which means that the selection concerns the particles lower than 1 μm. It can also be segmented: using a cascade impactor (such as ELPI), media unique to a size class can be produced (7–30 nm). The collecting medium must be adjusted to the future analysis approach: the sample time, and hence the amount of material collected, must also be adjusted: in one example, we will aim to extract the most out of a product, while in another, we will try to keep it as small as possible to minimize particle interference.

Contamination levels, whose low values may rule out some approaches needing extensive testing such as bacterial endotoxin test (BET).

The necessity to sample and quantify the nanoparticulate percentage in water and soil, whereas observation technologies (mostly transmission electron microscopy) enable the first three challenges to be addressed (provided that a granulometric, morphological, and chemical knowledge base of the manufactured NPs sought is available).

Air detection

Airborne particle detection is not a new activity; interest and operations in the field date back to the middle of the 19th century. Aerosol metrology has a long history and has been the focus of several broad synthesis documents (Witschger & Fabries, 2005). Only a subset (NPs) is addressed here, based on a particular human exposure. As a result, the strategies covered in this book chapter are those that have provided real-world operational solutions to date.

Occupational exposure

Two cases must be distinguished regarding occupational exposure: on the one hand, a process whose purpose is not the production of NPs, but whose implementation generates them (Ostiguy et al., 2006; Witschger & Fabries, 2005). The number and diversity of situations are wide; for example, we can cite diesel fumes (general mechanics, parking lots, highway tolls, etc.) or welding fumes (Ostiguy et al., 2006; NF EN 481 (X43–276), 1993), or the case of the extractive industry; the case where the production of NPs is intentional.

Nanotoxicity toward bacteria

Silver NPs are already commonly used for their bactericidal properties. Finally, studies indicate that NPs may be bactericidal against some bacterial types. After numerous exposures to metal nanooxides, for example, 100% mortality was seen in *Escherichia coli* or *Bacillus megaterium* cultures. Endospores of *Bacillus subtilis* appear to be more robust, with a 48% effect after 60 min (Stoimenov et al., 2002). In poor medium, *E. coli* and *B. subtilis* grow at concentrations more than or equal to 0.4 mg/L. In contrast, no influence on growth was detected in rich media. Finally, a 4-mg/L drop in respiratory rate was seen in a slightly aerobic medium (Fortner et al. 2005). As ZnO NPs are also being considered for textile applications (self-cleaning cotton), some tests have been carried out by immersing NP-impregnated fabrics in ultrapure water with bacteria (Brant et al., 2005), or on functionalized thin films for a bactericidal effect (Elahifard et al., 2007; Franklin et al., 2007; Kiwi & Nadtochenko, 2005; Sunada et al., 2003). However, the oxidation state of the NPs plays a major role in their bactericidal power. Only Ag NPs containing the oxidized form are toxic, unlike metallic NPs with no oxidation state (Lok et al., 2007; Pareek et al., 2021; Rtimi et al., 2015). These nonfunctionalized gold nanotubes have no harmful impact on the same bacteria when they are present, but not irradiated. The toxicity of zinc oxide (ZnO) NPs has been investigated in both solid and liquid environments (Adams et al., 2006; Huang et al., 2008; Reddy et al., 2007; Yan et al., 2011) and in liquid media (Reddy et al., 2007; Perelshtein et al., 2008; Brayner et al., 2006; Król et al., 2017), and for ZnO NPs, TiO_2 NPs are studied for their bactericidal effect in different forms in liquid suspension (Joo et al., 2005; Verran et al., 2007; Zhang et al., 2006).

Nanoparticle's size, dissolution, and aggregation impact

In solid media, the toxicity of ZnO NPs at 100 nM is very significant (Huang et al., 2008; Perelshtein et al., 2008); however, Brayner et al. (2006) show that 10−15-nm NPs have a bactericidal effect on *E. coli* at much lower than concentrations of 1.3 mM (Brayner et al., 2006; Król et al., 2017). According to Franklin et al. (2007), there is no influence on the size of the NPs; they observe identical toxicities for 30-nM ZnO NPs as for ZnO microparticles or the ionic form: $ZnCl_2$. Similarly, for Zhang et al. (2006), the concentration of ZnO NPs is more important than their sizes. The Zn^{2+} ions released during the dissolution of the NPs again seem to cause the bactericidal effect. These discrepancies are most likely due to variances in NP composition and the toxicity testing settings, especially as NPs have a tendency to agglomerate (Adams et al., 2006; Verran et al., 2007). Aggregation is prevented and bactericidal action is maintained by adding bovine serum albumin (Lok et al., 2007). Sondi and Salopek-Sondi (2004) also remarked that metallic silver NPs are harmful only when they come into touch with a solid medium, as opposed to a liquid medium when they just noticed a growth delay. Once the NPs are aggregated, they are no longer bactericidal, which allows the other bacteria in the environment to develop normally. Note that extracellular peptides and proteins also cause the precipitation of NPs (Moreau et al., 2007).

Intracellular and extracellular nanoparticles

In the environment, bacteria are sometimes at the origin of the formation of "natural" NPs, intracellular or precipitated on extracellular polysaccharides. It is the result of detoxification, with U, Pb, Cu, Al, Cd NPs detected in the presence of *Bacillus sphaericus* (Pollmann et al., 2006) or biomineralization (an example of silica NPs) in *Shewanella oneidensis* bacteria (Furukawa and O'Reilly, 2007).

The presence of zinc inclusions inside bacteria with a different crystalline composition from that of the NPs is attributed to a probable dissolution of the NPs, then to the internalization and precipitation of Zn^{2+} ions in the bacteria in the presence of ZnO NPs. Indeed, unlike eukaryotic cells whose cell membrane is capable of invagination (endocytosis, phagocytosis), bacterial ion channels are, in most cases, too small to allow the internalization of NPs (Brayner et al., 2006; Huang et al., 2008; Moore, 2006).

The largest ports are those used during the secretion of proteins intended for the outer membrane of the bacteria or to be released into the culture medium. It is therefore likely that they are closed and therefore inaccessible to NPs (Chen et al., 2017; Neal, 2008). Some cases of internalization of NPs (silver 80 nm) have been observed in bacteria treated with antibiotics, which are more permeable to NPs than untreated bacteria (Daoud et al., 2005; Kyriacou et al., 2003; Schraufnagel, 2020; Xu et al., 2004).

Radical oxidizing species

Among the potential effects of nanomaterials, interaction with living organisms is a major question because of the particular properties of NPs, which make them so interesting, However, it might represent a significant danger for humans and the environment. Once in the cell, their catalytic properties could generate radical species (ROS: radical oxygen species) and cause serious alterations in the DNA (which would be an unfortunate side effect of the use of sunscreens). TiO_2 NPs systematically exhibit a bactericidal effect observed with ZnO NPs (Adams et al., 2006), and it is increased by irradiation (Adams et al., 2006; Daoud et al., 2005). Electrostatic forces generally adsorbed NPs on the cell wall. The proximity of the NPs to the cell membrane would then cause toxicity, and ROS are produced during the following reactions.

The ROS produced by the oxidation of NPs (TiO_2 and ZnO in particular) would trigger lipid peroxidation in the bacterial lipopolysaccharide layer. In the presence of TiO_2 NPs, *E. coli*'s exterior and internal membranes are destroyed (Sunada et al., 2003). The latter are less resistant to irradiation in the presence of TiO_2 than the peptidoglycans analyzed by ATR-FTIR (Kiwi & Nadtochenko, 2005).

Indeed, MgO particles supplemented with Cl_2 also appear to cause significant membrane damage (Stoimenov et al., 2002).

Oxidative stress

Finally, the preliminary study indicates that NPs may be bactericidal against specific bacterial strains. After numerous exposures to metal nanooxides, for example, 100% mortality was seen in *E. coli* or *B. megaterium* cultures. Endospores of *B. subtilis* appear to be more robust, with a 48% impact found after 60 min (Stoimenov et al., 2002). In a weak medium, *E. coli* and *B. subtilis* grow at concentrations more than or equal to 0.4 mg/L. In contrast, there was no effect on growth in rich media. Finally, in a mildly aerobic medium, there was a 4-mg/L decrease in respiratory rate. When the generation of oxidants, or reactive forms of oxygen, exceeds the capability of the body's antioxidant mechanisms, an imbalance arises. Oxidative stress can also be caused by a decrease in antioxidant system capacity combined with an increase in oxidant production. Increased concentrations of reactive forms of oxygen of species oxygen lead to an oxidation of lipids, proteins, and nucleic acids. According to Nel et al. (2006), identifying that oxidative stress is vital in the genesis start of the toxic effects of NPs is significant not only from a pathophysiological impact standpoint, but also for creating techniques to screen for their toxicity.

Associated health risks

Lam (2003) used intratracheal instillation to expose mice to single-walled carbon nanotubes at various doses (Muller et al., 2005; Muller et al., 2008; Sharma et al., 2007; Shvedova et al., 2005). Carbon nanotubes implanted in mice cause an immediate lung inflammatory reaction as well as a delayed fibrosis response (Duke et al., 2017; Ostiguy et al., 2006; Shvedova et al., 2005). For example, a significant increase occurs in the lung inflammation parameters when 20 nm of TiO_2 particles is administered (Bakand et al., 2012; Ferin & Oberdörster, 1992; Oberdörster et al., 1994).

Toxicity of nanoparticles by skin contact

Modern sunscreens contain insoluble titanium dioxide or zinc oxide nanoparticles, which are effective filters of UV light. A large number of studies suggest that insoluble NPs do not penetrate into or through human skin (Monteiro-Riviere et al., 2011; Nohynek & Dufour, 2012). Also, iron oxide is a basic component of various formulations, such as lipsticks; however, only particle sizes are greater than 100 nm (Nohynek & Dufour, 2012). Overall, the weight of scientific evidence suggests that insoluble NPs used in sunscreens pose no or negligible risk to human health, but offer significant health benefits, such as protecting human skin from UV-induced skin aging and cancer.

Toxicity of nanoparticles by ingestion

Micrometer-sized particles have been shown to translocate from the intestinal lumen via the epithelium, either via intestinal lymphatic tissue or through intestinal epithelial cells, the enterocytes. This translocation is dependent on the particles' physicochemical qualities (Hoet et al., 2004). Monosheet carbon nanotubes, for example, were disseminated in the majority of organs and tissues in mice, with the exception of the brain, which was provided through gavage (Wang, Padture, et al., 2004). Another ingestion investigation in mice showed that developing enterocytes in the small intestine may collect unconjugated colloidal gold NPs. Nanometric-sized particles are therefore likely to get through the intestine and enter the systemic circulation (Hillyer & Albrecht, 2001). Polyalkylsulfurized fullerene is not hazardous when provided orally, according to an in vivo toxicity investigation of fullerenes (C60) in rats. Toxicity is reported in rats when this chemical is administered intraperitoneally (at 600 mg/kg) or intravenously. Because the kidney is in charge of excretion, it might sustain injury (Chen et al., 1998). Except for the study given previously on the systemic dispersion of single-leaf nanotubes in mice, there is no evidence (Wang, Padture, et al., 2004). Since human exposure to inorganic nanomaterials (selenium NPs) is inevitable, a comprehensive safety assessment of inorganic nanomaterials is required. It is well known that autophagy plays a dual role in cell survival and death. Furthermore, inorganic nanomaterials have been shown to induce disruption of autophagy in cells (Guo et al., 2020).

Ecotoxicity

Animal studies

As for the environment, the uncontrolled release of NPs could have serious consequences (Kreyling et al., 2002; Nemmar et al., 2002; Nikula et al., 2001; Oberdörster et al., 2005; Oberdörster, 2004). Some NPs are even being considered for depollution, trapping halides, such as arsenic and mercury (Dreher, 2003; Du et al., 2013; Elliott & Zhang, 2001; Galvez & Balk, 2017; He et al., 2010). However, it is possible that most NPs do not represent a real danger for humans and the environment, but in the absence of precise toxicological data, the precautionary principle must be applied. The remediation of polluted aquifers demonstrates the durability of iron NPs' sensitivity to chlorinated contaminants for several weeks, as well as their mobility in these aquifers (Zhang, 2003).

Regarding the toxicity of these NPs to wildlife, it should be noted that the data are few and contradictory. After 48 h of exposure to 0.5 mg/L of nC60 (fullerene), no death was seen in the marine creature *Micropterus salmoides*. A research on *Pimephales promelas* exposed to 0.5-mg/L fullerene or 0.2-mg/L carbon nanotubes found no mortality after 48 h. However, only an abstract of an oral communication is provided, which does not specify how the tested solutions were prepared. After 18 h, *P. promelas* subjected to 1 mg/L of nC60 solubilized in THF died completely (Fang et al., 2007). Oberdörster's group (Oberdörster, 2004) also looked into fullerene's chronic toxicity on the aquatic organism *Daphnia magna*. Although no information on the fullerene solubilization procedure is supplied, it is expected that it is the same. Under these circumstances, the LC50 after 48 h is 460 g/L. It was found a delay in the surviving Daphnia at concentrations more than or equal to 500 g/L. Three invertebrates, *D. magna*, *Hyalella azteca*, a marine copepod, and two fish, *P. promelas* and *Oryzias latipes*, were tested with colloidal fullerene (nC60) (Oberdörster, 2004). Bioaccumulation in *Daphnia*, a peak accumulation, is observed after 2 days of exposure to colloidal fullerene, corresponding to about 2 ppm/mg of tissues for an exposure concentration of 30 ppm (Oberdörster, 2004). Indeed, since these studies are preventive, there is currently no database on the quantities of NPs that could be released into the environment. It has carried a few predictive studies out based on the current production of NPs, for example, for TiO_2 or by extrapolating measurements made in the environment for CeO_2 (Cassee et al., 2011; Dale et al., 2017; Park et al., 2008). It is also possible to distinguish between dispersed nanomaterials (cosmetics, detergents, and drugs) and nondispersed (used in surface treatments). Dispersed NPs are potentially much more likely to be found in the environment. The state of their surface coating will be decisive and may, depending on the context, lead to an increase or decrease in toxicity (Kreyling et al., 2002, 2020; Reijnders, 2006).

Human studies

Laboratory-made ultrafine particles exhibit a high deposition on the whole respiratory system in healthy people, and an even greater deposition in asthmatic or chronic lung disease subjects (Brown et al., 2002; Delfino et al., 2005; Peters, Döring, et al., 1997; Peters, Wichmann, et al., 1997; Wyatt et al., 2020). NPs, whether synthesized by the liquid or gaseous route, must change medium at the time of contact with the pulmonary cells (Colvin, 2003). When ROS are produced, mitochondria are damaged, which results in NLRP3 inflammasome activation and cellular inflammation. Early phases of autophagy are brought on by vesicular trafficking blockade, accumulation of nanomaterials in autophagosomes, or suppression of the PI3K/Akt/mTOR pathway

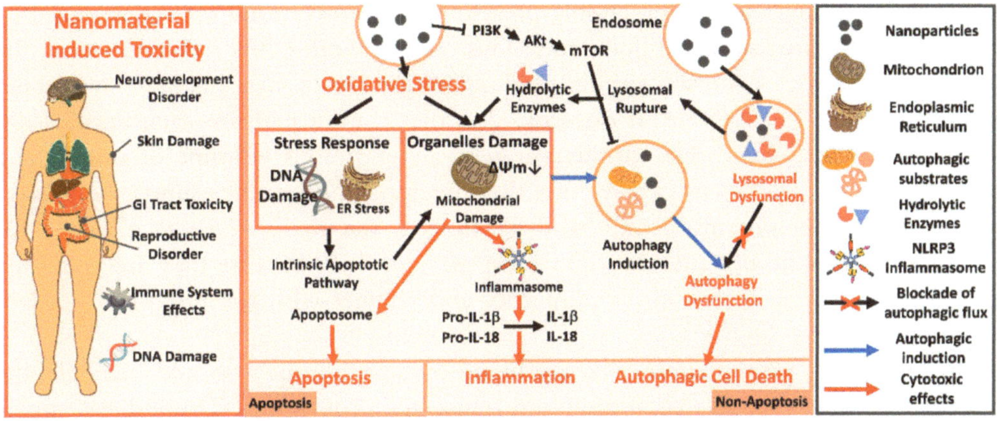

Figure 14.2 Systemic harmful consequences of autophagy-related toxicity caused by nanomaterials. *From Chen, R. J., Chen, Y. Y., Liao, M. Y., Lee, Y. H., Chen, Z. Y., Yan, S. J., Yeh, Y. L., Yang, L. X., Lee, Y. L., Wu, Y. H., & Wang, Y. J. (2020). The current understanding of autophagy in nanomaterial toxicity and its implementation in safety assessment-related alternative testing strategies.* International Journal of Molecular Sciences, *21(7), 2387. https://doi.org/10.3390/ijms21072387. https://doi.org/10.3390/ijms21072387.*

(Fig. 14.2). Overloading the lysosome with nanomaterials can lead to second-stage autophagic toxicity, which can damage organelle compartments, and release hydrolases (Chen et al., 2020).

Regulation and challenges

There are no regulations specifically related to the synthesis and manipulation of NPs, except in the United States, where there is a law relating to the research and development of nanotechnologies (Public Law 108–153).

However, many countries recognize that nanotechnologies should be taken into account by the regulations because of the effects of their size, persistence in the environment.

This regulation and this directive, as well as the secondary legislation, are part of a transversal approach—health/environment. Thus, regarding worker protection, the substance will be subject to regulatory labeling, the obligation to provide a safety data sheet, and implementing general rules to prevent chemical risks.

Conclusion and future perspectives

Environmental monitoring of nanomaterials continues to be a complex field containing a wide range of contaminants, a multitude of decomposition products or secondary chemicals, and microbial infection. As a result, rapid advancements in nanotechnology and innovative nanomaterial processing present major prospects for identification, then remediation of environmental pollutants. This present work offers a description of the many methodologies for the multiplexed identification of nanomaterials in proper environments and ecosystems. If one considers that it must perform each toxicity test on a case-by-case basis, this would represent an enormous amount of testing and would generate colossal costs. However, the toxicity of NPs cannot simply be extrapolated from other systems already studied. Indeed, the toxicity results obtained for ultrafine particles are not automatically transposable to NPs because they are presented as heterogeneous aerosols and polydispersity and contact with the pulmonary cells is made directly.

In regulation, various approaches are being considered, but it should highlight the increasingly significant role of insurers and reinsurance companies. The judicial impact of the effects of asbestos encourages them to intervene now to solicit the public authorities on the regulatory framework of nanomaterials.

Acknowledgment

We thank Dr. Ravindra Pratap Singh for his assistance with Mr. Kshitij RB Singh, and Dr. Jay Singh for comments that greatly improved the manuscript.

References

Adams, L. K., Lyon, D. Y., & Alvarez, P. J. J. (2006). Comparative eco-toxicity of nanoscale TiO_2, SiO_2, and ZnO water suspensions. *Water Research*, *40*, 3527–3532. Available from https://doi.org/10.1016/j.watres.2006.08.004.

Amato, I. (1989). Making the right stuff. *Science News*, *136*, 108. Available from https://doi.org/10.2307/3973729.

Bakand, S., Hayes, A., & Dechsakulthorn, F. (2012). Nanoparticles: A review of particle toxicology following inhalation exposure. *Inhalation Toxicology*, *24*, 125–135. Available from https://doi.org/10.3109/08958378.2010.642021.

Brant, J., Lecoanet, H., & Wiesner, M. R. (2005). Aggregation and deposition characteristics of fullerene nanoparticles in aqueous systems. *Journal of Nanoparticle Research*, *7*, 545–553. Available from https://doi.org/10.1007/s11051-005-4884-8.

Brayner, R., Ferrari-Iliou, R., Brivois, N., Djediat, S., Benedetti, M. F., & Fiévet, F. (2006). Toxicological impact studies based on *Escherichia coli* bacteria in ultrafine ZnO nanoparticles colloidal medium. *Nano Letters*, *6*, 866–870. Available from https://doi.org/10.1021/nl052326h.

Brown, D. M., Wilson, M. R., MacNee, W., Stone, V., & Donaldson, K. (2001). Size-dependent proinflammatory effects of ultrafine polystyrene particles: A role for surface area and oxidative stress in the enhanced activity of ultrafines. *Toxicology and Applied Pharmacology*, *175*, 191–199. Available from https://doi.org/10.1006/taap.2001.9240.

Brown, J. S., Zeman, K. L., & Bennett, W. D. (2002). Ultrafine particle deposition and clearance in the healthy and obstructed lung. *American Journal of Respiratory and Critical Care Medicine*, *166*, 1240–1247. Available from https://doi.org/10.1164/rccm.200205-399oc.

Carranza, J. E., Fisher, B. T., Yoder, G. D., & Hahn, D. W. (2001). On-line analysis of ambient air aerosols using laser-induced breakdown spectroscopy. *Spectrochimica Acta, Part B: Atomic Spectroscopy*, *56*, 851–864. Available from https://doi.org/10.1016/s0584-8547(01)00183-5.

Cassee, F. R., van Balen, E. C., Singh, C., Green, D., Muijser, H., Weinstein, J., & Dreher, K. (2011). Exposure, health and ecological effects review of engineered nanoscale cerium and cerium oxide associated with its use as a fuel additive. *Critical Reviews in Toxicology, 41*, 213–229. Available from https://doi.org/10.3109/10408444.2010.529105.

Chen, R. J., Chen, Y. Y., Liao, M. Y., Lee, Y. H., Chen, Z. Y., Yan, S. J., Yeh, Y. L., Yang, L. X., Lee, Y. L., Wu, Y. H., & Wang, Y. J. (2020). The current understanding of autophagy in nanomaterial toxicity and its implementation in safety assessment-related alternative testing strategies. *International Journal of Molecular Sciences, 21*(7), 2387. Available from https://doi.org/10.3390/ijms21072387.

Chen, H. H. C., Yu, C., Ueng, T. H., Chen, S., Chen, B. J., Huang, K. J., & Chiang, L. Y. (1998). Acute and subacute toxicity study of water-soluble polyalkylsulfonated C60 in rats. *Toxicologic Pathology, 26*, 143–151. Available from https://doi.org/10.1177/019262339802600117.

Chen, Z., Yang, P., Yuan, Z., & Guo, J. (2017). Aerobic condition enhances bacteriostatic effects of silver nanoparticles in aquatic environment: An antimicrobial study on *Pseudomonas aeruginosa*. *Scientific Reports*, 7. Available from https://doi.org/10.1038/s41598-017-07989-w.

Colvin, V. L. (2003). The potential environmental impact of engineered nanomaterials. *Nature Biotechnology, 21*, 1166–1170. Available from https://doi.org/10.1038/nbt875.

Dale, J. G., Cox, S. S., Vance, M. E., Marr, L. C., & Hochella, M. F., Jr. (2017). Transformation of cerium oxide nanoparticles from a diesel fuel additive during combustion in a diesel engine. *Environmental Science & Technology, 51*, 1973–1980. Available from https://doi.org/10.1021/acs.est.6b03173.

Daoud, W. A., Xin, J. H., & Zhang, Y.-H. (2005). Surface functionalization of cellulose fibers with titanium dioxide nanoparticles and their combined bactericidal activities. *Surface Science, 599*, 69–75. Available from https://doi.org/10.1016/j.susc.2005.09.038.

Delfino, R. J., Sioutas, C., & Malik, S. (2005). Potential role of ultrafine particles in associations between airborne particle mass and cardiovascular health. *Environmental Health Perspectives, 113*, 934–946. Available from https://doi.org/10.1289/ehp.7938.

Dhawan, A., & Sharma, V. (2010). Toxicity assessment of nanomaterials: Methods and challenges. *Analytical and Bioanalytical Chemistry, 398*, 589–605. Available from https://doi.org/10.1007/s00216-010-3996-x.

Donaldson, K., Brown, D., Clouter, A., Duffin, R., MacNee, W., Renwick, L., Tran, L., & Stone, V. (2002). The pulmonary toxicology of ultrafine particles. *Journal of Aerosol Medicine, 15*, 213–220. Available from https://doi.org/10.1089/089426802320282338.

Dreher, K. L. (2003). Health and environmental impact of nanotechnology: Toxicological assessment of manufactured nanoparticles. *Toxicological Sciences*, 77, 3–5. Available from https://doi.org/10.1093/toxsci/kfh041.

Du, J., Wang, S., You, H., & Zhao, X. (2013). Understanding the toxicity of carbon nanotubes in the environment is crucial to the control of nanomaterials in producing and processing and the assessment of health risk for human: A review. *Environmental Toxicology and Pharmacology, 36*, 451–462. Available from https://doi.org/10.1016/j.etap.2013.05.007.

Duke, K. S., Taylor-Just, A. J., Ihrie, M. D., Shipkowski, K. A., Thompson, E. A., Dandley, E. C., Parsons, G. N., & Bonner, J. C. (2017). STAT1-dependent and -independent pulmonary allergic and fibrogenic responses in mice after exposure to tangled vs rod-like multi-walled carbon nanotubes. *Particle and Fibre Toxicology, 14*. Available from https://doi.org/10.1186/s12989-017-0207-3.

Eckhoff, R. K. (1993). Dust explosion research. State-of-the-art and outstanding problems. *Journal of Hazardous Materials, 35*, 103–117. Available from https://doi.org/10.1016/0304-3894(93)85026-b.

Elahifard, M. R., Rahimnejad, S., Haghighi, S., & Gholami, M. R. (2007). Apatite-coated Ag/AgBr/TiO_2 visible-light photocatalyst for destruction of bacteria. *Journal of the American Chemical Society, 129*, 9552–9553. Available from https://doi.org/10.1021/ja072492m.

Elliott, D. W., & Zhang, W. (2001). Field assessment of nanoscale bimetallic particles for groundwater treatment. *Environmental Science & Technology, 35*, 4922–4926. Available from https://doi.org/10.1021/es0108584.

Fang, J., Lyon, D. Y., Wiesner, M. R., Dong, J., & Alvarez. (2007). Effect of a fullerene water suspension on bacterial phospholipids and membrane phase behavior. *Environmental Science & Technology, 41*, 2636–2642. Available from https://doi.org/10.1021/es062181w.

Ferin, J., & Oberdörster, G. (1992). Translocation of particles from pulmonary alveoli into the interstitium. *Journal of Aerosol Medicine: The Official Journal of the International Society for Aerosols in Medicine*, *5*, 179–187. Available from https://doi.org/10.1089/jam.1992.5.179.

Fortner, J., Lyon, D., Sayes, C., Boyd, A., Falkner, J., Hotze, E., Alemany, L., Tao, Y., Guo, W., Ausman, K., Colvin, V., & Hughes, J. B. (2005). C60 in water – Nanocrystal formation and microbial response. *Environmental Science & Technology*, *39*, 4307–4316.

Franklin, N. M., Rogers, N. J., Apte, S. C., Batley, G. E., Gadd, G. E., & Casey, P. S. (2007). Comparative toxicity of nanoparticulate ZnO, bulk ZnO, and $ZnCl_2$ to a freshwater microalga (*Pseudokirchneriella subcapitata*): The importance of particle solubility. *Environmental Science & Technology*, *41*(24), 8484–8490. Available from https://doi.org/10.1021/es071445r.

Gaffet, E. (2011). Nanomatériaux: Une revue des définitions, des applications et des effets sur la santé. Comment implémenter un développement sûr. *Comptes Rendus Physique*, *12*, 648–658. Available from https://doi.org/10.1016/j.crhy.2011.06.002.

Galvez, M. P., & Balk, S. J. (2017). Environmental risks to children: Prioritizing health messages in pediatric practice. *Pediatrics In Review*, *38*, 263–279. Available from https://doi.org/10.1542/pir.2015-0165.

Greim, H., Borm, P., Schins, R., Donaldson, K., Driscoll, K., Hartwig, A., Kuempel, E., Oberdörster, G., & Speit, G. (2001). Toxicity of fibers and particles—Report of the workshop held in Munich, Germany, 26–27 October 2000. *Inhalation Toxicology*, *13*, 737–754. Available from https://doi.org/10.1080/089583701316941285.

Grieger, K. D., Baun, A., & Owen, R. (2009). Redefining risk research priorities for nanomaterials. *Journal of Nanoparticle Research*, *12*, 383–392. Available from https://doi.org/10.1007/s11051-009-9829-1.

Guo, L., He, N., Zhao, Y., Liu, T., & Deng, Y. (2020). Autophagy modulated by inorganic nanomaterials. *Theranostics*, *10*, 3206–3222. Available from https://doi.org/10.7150/thno.40414.

Hahn, D. W., & Lunden, M. M. (2000). Detection and analysis of aerosol particles by laser-induced breakdown spectroscopy. *Aerosol Science and Technology*, *33*, 30–48. Available from https://doi.org/10.1080/027868200410831.

He, F., Zhao, D., & Paul, C. (2010). Field assessment of carboxymethyl cellulose stabilized iron nanoparticles for in situ destruction of chlorinated solvents in source zones. *Water Research*, *44*, 2360–2370. Available from https://doi.org/10.1016/j.watres.2009.12.041.

Hillyer, J. F., & Albrecht, R. M. (2001). Gastrointestinal persorption and tissue distribution of differently sized colloidal gold nanoparticles. *Journal of Pharmaceutical Sciences*, *90*, 1927–1936. Available from https://doi.org/10.1002/jps.1143.abs.

Hoet, P. H., Brüske-Hohlfeld, I., & Salata, O. V. (2004). Nanoparticles – Known and unknown health risks. *Journal of Nanobiotechnology*, *2*, 12. Available from https://doi.org/10.1186/1477-3155-2-12.

Huang, Z., Zheng, X., Yan, D., Yin, G., Liao, X., Kang, Y., Yao, Y., Huang, D., & Hao, B. (2008). Toxicological effect of ZnO nanoparticles based on bacteria. *Langmuir: The ACS Journal of Surfaces and Colloids*, *24*, 4140–4144. Available from https://doi.org/10.1021/la7035949.

Isigonis, P., Hristozov, D., Benighaus, C., Giubilato, E., Grieger, K., Pizzol, L., Semenzin, E., Linkov, I., Zabeo, A., & Marcomini, A. (2019). Risk governance of nanomaterials: Review of criteria and tools for risk communication, evaluation, and mitigation. *Nanomaterials*, *9*, 696. Available from https://doi.org/10.3390/nano9050696.

Joo, J., Kwon, S. G., Yu, T., Cho, M., Lee, J., Yoon, J., & Hyeon, T. (2005). Large-scale synthesis of TiO_2 nanorods via nonhydrolytic sol – gel ester elimination reaction and their application to photocatalytic inactivation of *E. coli*. *The Journal of Physical Chemistry. B*, *109*, 15297–15302. Available from https://doi.org/10.1021/jp052458z.

Kagan, V. E., Tyurina, Y. Y., Tyurin, V. A., Konduru, N. V., Potapovich, A. I., Osipov, A. N., Kisin, E. R., Schwegler-Berry, D., Mercer, R., Castranova, V., & Shvedova, A. A. (2006). Direct and indirect effects of single walled carbon nanotubes on RAW 264.7 macrophages: Role of iron. *Toxicology Letters*, *165*, 88–100. Available from https://doi.org/10.1016/j.toxlet.2006.02.001.

Kamat, P. V. (2002). Photophysical, photochemical and photocatalytic aspects of metal nanoparticles. *The Journal of Physical Chemistry. B*, *106*, 7729–7744. Available from https://doi.org/10.1021/jp0209289.

Kiwi, J., & Nadtochenko, V. (2005). Evidence for the mechanism of photocatalytic degradation of the bacterial wall membrane at the TiO_2 interface by ATR-FTIR and laser kinetic spectroscopy. *Langmuir: The ACS Journal of Surfaces and Colloids*, *21*(10), 4631–4641. Available from https://doi.org/10.1021/la046983l.

Kreyling, W. G., Holzwarth, U., Hirn, S., Schleh, C., Wenk, A., Schäffler, M., Haberl, N., & Gibson, N. (2020). Quantitative biokinetics over a 28 day period of freshly generated, pristine, 20 nm silver nanoparticle aerosols in healthy adult rats after a single 1½-hour inhalation exposure. *Particle and Fibre Toxicology*, *17*. Available from https://doi.org/10.1186/s12989-020-00347-1.

Kreyling, W. G., Semmler, M., Erbe, F., Mayer, P., Takenaka, S., Schulz, H., Oberdörster, G., & Ziesenis, A. (2002). Translocation of ultrafine insoluble iridium particles from lung epithelium to extrapulmonary organs is size dependent but very low. *Journal of Toxicology and Environmental Health, Part A*, *65*, 1513–1530. Available from https://doi.org/10.1080/00984100290071649.

Król, A., Pomastowski, P., Rafińska, K., Railean-Plugaru, V., & Buszewski, B. (2017). Zinc oxide nanoparticles: Synthesis, antiseptic activity and toxicity mechanism. *Advances in Colloid and Interface Science*, *249*, 37–52. Available from https://doi.org/10.1016/j.cis.2017.07.033.

Kyriacou, S. V., Brownlow, W. J., & Xu, X.-H. N. (2003). Using nanoparticle optics assay for direct observation of the function of antimicrobial agents in single live bacterial cells. *Biochemistry*, *43*, 140–147. Available from https://doi.org/10.1021/bi0351110.

Lam, C.-W. (2003). Pulmonary toxicity of single-wall carbon nanotubes in mice 7 and 90 days after intratracheal instillation. *Toxicological Sciences*, 77, 126–134. Available from https://doi.org/10.1093/toxsci/kfg243.

Lanone, S., & Boczkowski, J. (2006). Biomedical applications and potential health risks of nanomaterials: Molecular mechanisms. *Current Molecular Medicine*, *6*, 651–663. Available from https://doi.org/10.2174/156652406778195026.

Lin, H., Bu, Q., Cen, X., & Zhao, Y.-L. (2012). Current methods and research progress in nanomaterials risk assessment. *Current Drug Metabolism*, *13*, 354–363. Available from https://doi.org/10.2174/138920012800166535.

Lok, C.-N., Ho, C.-M., Chen, R., He, Q.-Y., Yu, W.-Y., Sun, H., Tam, P. K.-H., Chiu, J.-F., & Che, C.-M. (2007). Silver nanoparticles: Partial oxidation and antibacterial activities. *JBIC Journal of Biological Inorganic Chemistry*, *12*, 527–534. Available from https://doi.org/10.1007/s00775-007-0208-z.

Lu, L., Sui, M. L., & Lu, K. (2000). Superplastic extensibility of nanocrystalline copper at room temperature. *Science (New York, N.Y.)*, *287*, 1463–1466. Available from https://doi.org/10.1126/science.287.5457.1463.

Marante, T., Viegas, C., Duarte, I., Macedo, A. S., & Fonte, P. (2020). An overview on spray-drying of protein-loaded polymeric nanoparticles for dry powder inhalation. *Pharmaceutics*, *12*, 1032. Available from https://doi.org/10.3390/pharmaceutics12111032.

Maynard, A., & Baron, P. (2004). *Aerosols in the industrial environment. Aerosols handbook* (pp. 220–259). CRC Press.

Maynard, A. D., & Kuempel, E. D. (2005). Airborne nanostructured particles and occupational health. *Journal of Nanoparticle Research*, 7, 587–614. Available from https://doi.org/10.1007/s11051-005-6770-9.

Miyani, V. A., & Hughes, M. F. (2016). Assessment of the in vitro dermal irritation potential of cerium, silver, and titanium nanoparticles in a human skin equivalent model. *Cutaneous and Ocular Toxicology*, *36*, 145–151. Available from https://doi.org/10.1080/15569527.2016.1211671.

Moghimi, S. M., Hunter, A. C., & Murray, J. C. (2005). Nanomedicine: Current status and future prospects. *The FASEB Journal*, *19*, 311–330. Available from https://doi.org/10.1096/fj.04-2747rev.

Monteiro-Riviere, N. A., Wiench, K., Landsiedel, R., Schulte, S., Inman, A. O., & Riviere, J. E. (2011). Safety evaluation of sunscreen formulations containing titanium dioxide and zinc oxide nanoparticles in UVB sunburned skin: An in vitro and in vivo study. *Toxicological Sciences*, *123*, 264–280. Available from https://doi.org/10.1093/toxsci/kfr148.

Moore, M. N. (2006). Do nanoparticles present ecotoxicological risks for the health of the aquatic environment. *Environment International*, *32*, 967–976. Available from https://doi.org/10.1016/j.envint.2006.06.014.

Moreau, J. W., Weber, P. K., Martin, M. C., Gilbert, B., Hutcheon, I. D., & Banfield, J. F. (2007). Extracellular proteins limit the dispersal of biogenic nanoparticles. *Science (New York, N.Y.)*, *316*, 1600−1603. Available from https://doi.org/10.1126/science.1141064.

Muller, J., Huaux, F., Fonseca, A., Nagy, J. B., Moreau, N., Delos, M., Raymundo-Piñero, E., Béguin, F., Kirsch-Volders, M., Fenoglio, I., Fubini, B., & Lison, D. (2008). Structural defects play a major role in the acute lung toxicity of multiwall carbon nanotubes: Toxicological aspects. *Chemical Research in Toxicology*, *21*, 1698−1705. Available from https://doi.org/10.1021/tx800101p.

Muller, J., Huaux, F., Moreau, N., Misson, P., Heilier, J.-F., Delos, M., Arras, M., Fonseca, A., Nagy, J. B., & Lison, D. (2005). Respiratory toxicity of multi-wall carbon nanotubes. *Toxicology and Applied Pharmacology*, *207*, 221−231. Available from https://doi.org/10.1016/j.taap.2005.01.008.

Neal, A. L. (2008). What can be inferred from bacterium−nanoparticle interactions about the potential consequences of environmental exposure to nanoparticles? *Ecotoxicology (London, England)*, *17*, 362−371. Available from https://doi.org/10.1007/s10646-008-0217-x.

Nel, A., Xia, T., Mädler, L., & Li, N. (2006). Toxic potential of materials at the nanolevel. *Science (New York, N.Y.)*, *311*, 622−627. Available from https://doi.org/10.1126/science.1114397.

Nemmar, A., Hoet, P. H. M., Vanquickenborne, B., Dinsdale, D., Thomeer, M., Hoylaerts, M. F., Vanbilloen, H., Mortelmans, L., & Nemery, B. (2002). Passage of inhaled particles into the blood circulation in humans. *Circulation*, *105*, 411−414. Available from https://doi.org/10.1161/hc0402.104118.

Nikula, K. J., Vallyathan, V., Green, F. H., & Hahn, F. F. (2001). Influence of exposure concentration or dose on the distribution of particulate material in rat and human lungs. *Environmental Health Perspectives*, *109*, 311−318. Available from https://doi.org/10.1289/ehp.01109311.

Nohynek, G. J., & Dufour, E. K. (2012). Nano-sized cosmetic formulations or solid nanoparticles in sunscreens: A risk to human health? *Archives of Toxicology*, *86*, 1063−1075. Available from https://doi.org/10.1007/s00204-012-0831-5.

Oberdörster, E. (2004). Manufactured nanomaterials (Fullerenes, C60) induce oxidative stress in the brain of juvenile largemouth bass. *Environmental Health Perspectives*, *112*, 1058−1062. Available from https://doi.org/10.1289/ehp.7021.

Oberdörster, G., Ferin, J., Gelein, R., Soderholm, S. C., & Finkelstein, J. (1992). Role of the alveolar macrophage in lung injury: Studies with ultrafine particles. *Environmental Health Perspectives*, *97*, 193−199. Available from https://doi.org/10.1289/ehp.9297193.

Oberdörster, G., Ferin, J., & Lehnert, B. E. (1994). Correlation between particle size, in vivo particle persistence, and lung injury. *Environmental Health Perspectives*, *102*, 173−179. Available from https://doi.org/10.1289/ehp.94102s5173.

Oberdörster, G., Finkelstein, J. N., Johnston, C., Gelein, R., Cox, C., Baggs, R., & Elder, A. C. (2000). Acute pulmonary effects of ultrafine particles in rats and mice. *Research Report (Health Effects Institute)*, *96*, 5−74, disc. 75−86.

Oberdörster, G., Oberdörster, E., & Oberdörster, J. (2005). Nanotoxicology: An emerging discipline evolving from studies of ultrafine particles. *Environmental Health Perspectives*, *113*, 823−839. Available from https://doi.org/10.1289/ehp.7339.

Oberdörster, G., Oberdörster, E., & Oberdörster, J. (2007). Concepts of nanoparticle dose metric and response metric. *Environmental Health Perspectives*, *115*, A290. Available from https://doi.org/10.1289/ehp.115-a290a, −A290.

Ostiguy, C., Asselin, P., & Malo, S. (2006). The emergence of manganese-related health problems in Quebec: An integrated approach to evaluation, diagnosis, management and control. *Neurotoxicology*, *27*, 350−356. Available from https://doi.org/10.1016/j.neuro.2005.11.001.

Padovani, S., Sada, C., Mazzoldi, P., Brunetti, B., Borgia, I., Sgamellotti, A., Giulivi, A., D'Acapito, F., & Battaglin, G. (2003). Copper in glazes of Renaissance luster pottery: Nanoparticles, ions, and local environment. *Journal of Applied Physics*, *93*, 10058−10063. Available from https://doi.org/10.1063/1.1571965.

Pareek, V., Devineau, S., Sivasankaran, S. K., Bhargava, A., Panwar, J., Srikumar, S., & Fanning, S. (2021). Silver nanoparticles induce a triclosan-like antibacterial action mechanism in multi-drug resistant *Klebsiella pneumoniae*. *Frontiers in Microbiology*, *12*. Available from https://doi.org/10.3389/fmicb.2021.638640.

Park, B., Donaldson, K., Duffin, R., Tran, L., Kelly, F., Mudway, I., Morin, J.-P., Guest, R., Jenkinson, P., Samaras, Z., Giannouli, M., Kouridis, H., & Martin, P. (2008). Hazard and risk assessment of a nanoparticulate cerium oxide-based diesel fuel additive—A case study. *Inhalation Toxicology*, *20*, 547–566. Available from https://doi.org/10.1080/08958370801915309.

Perelshtein, I., Applerot, G., Perkas, N., Wehrschetz-Sigl, E., Hasmann, A., Guebitz, G. M., & Gedanken, A. (2008). Antibacterial properties of an in situ generated and simultaneously deposited nanocrystalline ZnO on fabrics. *ACS Applied Materials & Interfaces*, *1*, 361–366. Available from https://doi.org/10.1021/am8000743.

Peters, A., Wichmann, H. E., Tuch, T., Heinrich, J., & Heyder, J. (1997). Respiratory effects are associated with the number of ultrafine particles. *American Journal of Respiratory and Critical Care Medicine*, *155*, 1376–1383. Available from https://doi.org/10.1164/ajrccm.155.4.9105082.

Peters, A., Döring, A., Wichmann, H.-E., & Koenig, W. (1997). Increased plasma viscosity during an air pollution episode: A link to mortality? *The Lancet*, *349*, 1582–1587. Available from https://doi.org/10.1016/s0140-6736(97)01211-7.

Pflücker, F., Wendel, V., Hohenberg, H., Gärtner, E., Will, T., Pfeiffer, S., Wepf, R., & Gers-Barlag, H. (2001). The human *Stratum corneum* layer: An effective barrier against dermal uptake of different forms of topically applied micronised titanium dioxide. *Skin Pharmacology and Physiology*, *14*, 92–97. Available from https://doi.org/10.1159/000056396.

Pollmann, K., Raff, J., Merroun, M., Fahmy, K., & Selenska-Pobell, S. (2006). Metal binding by bacteria from uranium mining waste piles and its technological applications. *Biotechnology Advances*, *24*, 58–68. Available from https://doi.org/10.1016/j.biotechadv.2005.06.002.

Pradell, T., Molera, J., Smith, A. D., & Tite, M. S. (2008). The invention of lustre: Iraq 9th and 10th centuries AD. *Journal of Archaeological Science*, *35*, 1201–1215. Available from https://doi.org/10.1016/j.jas.2007.08.016.

Qi, H. J., Teo, K. B. K., Lau, K. K. S., Boyce, M. C., Milne, W. I., Robertson, J., & Gleason, K. K. (2003). Determination of mechanical properties of carbon nanotubes and vertically aligned carbon nanotube forests using nanoindentation. *Journal of the Mechanics and Physics of Solids*, *51*, 2213–2237. Available from https://doi.org/10.1016/j.jmps.2003.09.015.

Qi, P., Vermesh, O., Grecu, M., Javey, A., Wang, Q., Dai, H., Peng, S., & Cho, K. J. (2003). Toward large arrays of multiplex functionalized carbon nanotube sensors for highly sensitive and selective molecular detection. *Nano Letters*, *3*, 347–351. Available from https://doi.org/10.1021/nl034010k.

Reddy, K. M., Feris, K., Bell, J., Wingett, D. G., Hanley, C., & Punnoose, A. (2007). Selective toxicity of zinc oxide nanoparticles to prokaryotic and eukaryotic systems. *Applied Physics Letters*, *90*213902. Available from https://doi.org/10.1063/1.2742324.

Reijnders, L. (2006). Cleaner nanotechnology and hazard reduction of manufactured nanoparticles. *Journal of Cleaner Production*, *14*, 124–133. Available from https://doi.org/10.1016/j.jclepro.2005.03.018.

Rtimi, S., Nesic, J., Pulgarin, C., Sanjines, R., Bensimon, M., & Kiwi, J. (2015). Effect of surface pretreatment of TiO_2 films on interfacial processes leading to bacterial inactivation in the dark and under light irradiation. *Interface Focus*, *5*20140046. Available from https://doi.org/10.1098/rsfs.2014.0046.

Sanches, P. L., Geaquinto, L. R. O., Cruz, R., Schuck, D. C., Lorencini, M., Granjeiro, J. M., & Ribeiro, A. R. L. (2020). Toxicity evaluation of TiO_2 nanoparticles on the 3D skin model: A systematic review. *Frontiers in Bioengineering and Biotechnology*, *8*, 575. Available from https://doi.org/10.3389/fbioe.2020.00575.

Schraufnagel, D. E. (2020). The health effects of ultrafine particles. *Experimental & Molecular Medicine*, *52*, 311–317. Available from https://doi.org/10.1038/s12276-020-0403-3.

Seaton, A., Tran, L., Aitken, R., & Donaldson, K. (2009). Nanoparticles, human health hazard and regulation. *Journal of The Royal Society Interface*, 7. Available from https://doi.org/10.1098/rsif.2009.0252.focus.

Semmler, M., Seitz, J., Erbe, F., Mayer, P., Heyder, J., Oberdörster, G., & Kreyling, W. G. (2004). Long-term clearance kinetics of inhaled ultrafine insoluble iridium particles from the rat lung, including transient translocation into secondary organs. *Inhalation Toxicology*, *16*(6–7), 453–459. Available from https://doi.org/10.1080/08958370490439650.

Sharma, C. S., Sarkar, S., Periyakaruppan, A., Barr, J., Wise, K., Thomas, R., Wilson, B. L., & Ramesh, G. T. (2007). Single-walled carbon nanotubes induces oxidative stress in rat lung epithelial cells. *Journal of Nanoscience and Nanotechnology*, *7*, 2466–2472. Available from https://doi.org/10.1166/jnn.2007.431.

Shinji, H., Watanabe, M., Kudo, Y., Niitsuya, M., Tsunoda, M., Satoh, T., Sakai, Y., Kotani, M., & Aizawa, Y. (2005). The cytotoxicity of microglass fibers on alveolar macrophages of Fischer 344 rats evaluated by cell magnetometry, cytochemisry and morphology. *Environmental Health and Preventive Medicine*, *10*, 111–119. Available from https://doi.org/10.1007/bf02898001.

Shvedova, A., Castranova, V., Kisin, E., Schwegler-Berry, D., Murray, A., Gandelsman, V., Maynard, A., & Baron, P. (2003). Exposure to carbon nanotube material: Assessment of nanotube cytotoxicity using human keratinocyte cells. *Journal of Toxicology and Environmental Health, Part A*, *66*, 1909–1926. Available from https://doi.org/10.1080/713853956.

Shvedova, A. A., Kisin, E. R., Mercer, R., Murray, A. R., Johnson, V. J., Potapovich, A. I., Tyurina, Y. Y., Gorelik, O., Arepalli, S., Schwegler-Berry, D., Hubbs, A. F., Antonini, J., Evans, D. E., Ku, B.-K., Ramsey, D., Maynard, A., Kagan, V. E., Castranova, V., & Baron, P. (2005). Unusual inflammatory and fibrogenic pulmonary responses to single-walled carbon nanotubes in mice. *American Journal of Physiology-Lung Cellular and Molecular Physiology*, *289*, L698–L708. Available from https://doi.org/10.1152/ajplung.00084.2005.

Sondi, I., & Salopek-Sondi, B. (2004). Silver nanoparticles as antimicrobial agent: A case study on *E. coli* as a model for Gram-negative bacteria. *Journal of Colloid and Interface Science*, *275*, 177–182. Available from https://doi.org/10.1016/j.jcis.2004.02.012.

Stoimenov, P. K., Klinger, R. L., Marchin, G. L., & Klabunde, K. J. (2002). Metal oxide nanoparticles as bactericidal agents. *Langmuir: The ACS Journal of Surfaces and Colloids*, *18*, 6679–6686. Available from https://doi.org/10.1021/la0202374.

Sunada, K., Watanabe, T., & Hashimoto, K. (2003). Studies on photokilling of bacteria on TiO_2 thin film. *Journal of Photochemistry and Photobiology A: Chemistry*, *156*, 227–233. Available from https://doi.org/10.1016/S1010-6030(02)00434-3.

US-EPA (2005). *Nanotechnology white paper, external review draft*. December 2, 2005. Available from http://www.epa.gov/OSA/pdfs/EPA

Verran, J., Sandoval, G., Allen, N. S., Edge, M., & Stratton, J. (2007). Variables affecting the antibacterial properties of nano and pigmentary titania particles in suspension. *Dyes and Pigments*, *73*, 298–304. Available from https://doi.org/10.1016/j.dyepig.2006.01.003.

Vigneshwaran, N., Kumar, S., Kathe, A. A., Varadarajan, P. V., & Prasad, V. (2006). Functional finishing of cotton fabrics using zinc oxide–soluble starch nanocomposites. *Nanotechnology*, *17*, 5087–5095. Available from https://doi.org/10.1088/0957-4484/17/20/008.

Wang, H., Wang, J., Deng, X., Sun, H., Shi, Z., Gu, Z., Liu, Y., & Zhaoc, Y. (2004). Biodistribution of carbon single-wall carbon nanotubes in mice. *Journal of Nanoscience and Nanotechnology*, *4*, 1019–1024. Available from https://doi.org/10.1166/jnn.2004.146.

Wang, X., Padture, N. P., & Tanaka, H. (2004). Contact-damage-resistant ceramic/single-wall carbon nanotubes and ceramic/graphite composites. *Nature Materials*, *3*, 539–544. Available from https://doi.org/10.1038/nmat1161.

Watanabe, M., Okada, M., Kudo, Y., Tonori, Y., Niitsuya, M., Sato, T., Aizawa, Y., & Kotani, M. (2002). Differences in the effects of fibrous and particulate titanium dioxide on alveolar macrophages of Fischer 344 rats. *Journal of Toxicology and Environmental Health, Part A*, *65*, 1047–1060. Available from https://doi.org/10.1080/152873902760125219.

Witschger, O., & Fabries, J. F. (2005). Ultra-fine particles and occupational health. 1 -Characterization of potential health effects. *INRS*, *199*, 21–35.

Wyatt, L. H., Devlin, R. B., Rappold, A. G., Case, M. W., & Diaz-Sanchez, D. (2020). Low levels of fine particulate matter increase vascular damage and reduce pulmonary function in young healthy adults. *Particle and Fibre Toxicology*, *17*. Available from https://doi.org/10.1186/s12989-020-00389-5.

Xu, X.-H. N., Brownlow, W. J., Kyriacou, S. V., Wan, Q., & Viola, J. J. (2004). Real-time probing of membrane transport in living microbial cells using single nanoparticle optics and living cell imaging. *Biochemistry*, *43*, 10400–10413. Available from https://doi.org/10.1021/bi036231a.

Yan, D., Yin, G., Huang, Z., Li, L., Liao, X., Chen, X., Yao, Y., & Hao, B. (2011). Cellular compatibility of biomineralized ZnO nanoparticles based on prokaryotic and eukaryotic systems. *Langmuir: The ACS Journal of Surfaces and Colloids*, *27*, 13206–13211. Available from https://doi.org/10.1021/la2008107.

Zhan, G.-D., Kuntz, J. D., Garay, J. E., & Mukherjee, A. K. (2003). Electrical properties of nanoceramics reinforced with ropes of single-walled carbon nanotubes. *Applied Physics Letters*, *83*, 1228–1230. Available from https://doi.org/10.1063/1.1600511.

Zhan, G.-D., Kuntz, J. D., Wan, J., & Mukherjee, A. K. (2002). Single-wall carbon nanotubes as attractive toughening agents in alumina-based nanocomposites. *Nature Materials*, *2*, 38–42. Available from https://doi.org/10.1038/nmat793.

Zhang, L., Jiang, Y., Ding, Y., Povey, M., & York, D. (2006). Investigation into the antibacterial behaviour of suspensions of ZnO nanoparticles (ZnO nanofluids. *Journal of Nanoparticle Research*, *9*, 479–489. Available from https://doi.org/10.1007/s11051-006-9150-1.

Zhang, W. (2003). Nanoscale iron particle for environmental remediation: An overview. *Journal of Nanoparticle Research*, *5*, 323–332. Available from https://doi.org/10.1023/a:1025520116015.

SECTION 2

Pharmaceuticals

CHAPTER 15

Introduction to nanotechnological utility in the pharmaceutical industry

Vanya Nayak[1], Kshitij RB Singh[1], Rishi Paliwal[2], Jay Singh[1], Mrituanjay D Pandey[1] and Ravindra Pratap Singh[3]
[1]Department of Chemistry, Institute of Science, Banaras Hindu University, Varanasi, Uttar Pradesh, India
[2]Nanomedicine and Bioengineering Research Laboratory (NBRL), Department of Pharmacy, Indira Gandhi National Tribal University, Amarkantak, Madhya Pradesh, India
[3]Department of Biotechnology, Faculty of Science, Indira Gandhi National Tribal University, Amarkantak, Madhya Pradesh, India

Introduction

Nanotechnology fabricates different functioning systems on the nanoscale dimensions. These systems show physical, electrical, and optical properties ranging from materials science to biology (Bamrungsap et al., 2012). It has revolutionized the pharmaceutical and biomedical domain by advancing traditional diagnosis practices, controlled drug, gene, and nutrient delivery, enhancing biosensors, and so on (Amoabediny et al., 2018; Tiwari et al., 2012). Nanotechnology uses nanomaterials of dimensions 10−100 nm that help them to exhibit enhanced properties like optical, electrical, mechanical, physical, biological, and chemical that the bulk material cannot exhibit. Different nanomaterials, like polymers, lipids, dendrimer, metal-based, and carbon-based, have found their profound uses in pharmaceutical industries. These nanoparticles are synthesized through various methods, and, therefore, it is important to develop an understanding of the synthesis of these nanosystems and overcome different barriers faced in biomedical applications. Recently, nanomedicine has gained considerable attention in the biomedical domain and has become one of the highly recognized research fields because it uses medicinal techniques for diseases detection, treatment, and prevention (Lobatto et al., 2011). Moreover, nanomedicines have efficiently taken the nanotechnology market to new heights with over 75% of total sales and are now ruling the nanotechnology market (Wagner et al., 2006). Nanoparticles have found their profound uses as drug delivery carriers that can be utilized in treating different types of cancer and AIDS, gene therapy, and radiation. In addition, these nanoparticles are also utilized for the transportation of antibiotics, proteins, and vaccinations and act as vesicles to cross the blood−brain barrier (Tiwari et al., 2012). These nanoparticles regulate the size of the particle, surface-based properties, and drug release to make sure that the site-targeted drug activities take place at a fixed therapeutic rate and

Nanotechnology for Drug Delivery and Pharmaceuticals
DOI: https://doi.org/10.1016/B978-0-323-95325-2.00013-4

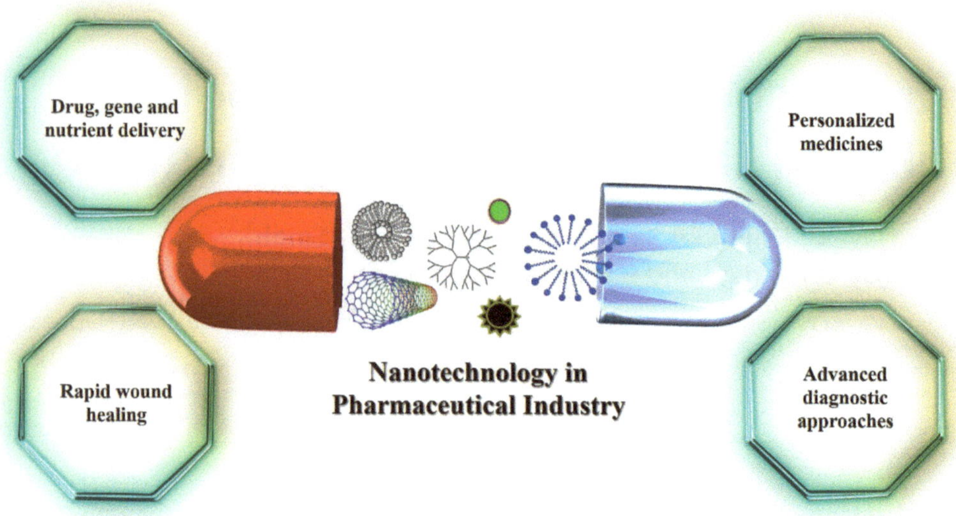

Figure 15.1 Uses of nanotechnology in the pharmaceutical industries.

dosing regimen. Moreover, advancements in the biomedical domain like personalized medicines, designing of drugs, targeted drug delivery, nanomedicines, and biomedical genetics are helping to bring sustainability to develop quality health care, as illustrated in Fig. 15.1.

Overall, the chapter entails to provide a detailed discussion on various uses of nanotechnology in the pharmaceutical industries by majorly focusing on the recent advancements in the pharmaceutical industries, the importance of nanotechnology in pharmaceutical industries, the synthesis of pharmaceutical-based nanoparticles, and their advantages and disadvantages. In addition, the chapter also briefly discusses the patents and market trends of nanotechnology in the pharmaceutical industries by highlighting different safety and legal issues on their commercial uses. Moreover, Chapter 16 of this book focuses on the recent developments in the pharmaceutical industries, followed by Chapter 17, which enhances the knowledge of different strategies to synthesize, the advantages, and disadvantages of pharmaceutical nanoparticles. Further, Chapters 18 and 19 comprehensively describe recent patents and market trends of nano-based pharmaceutical products, and perspectives, safety issues, legal factors of nano-based materials utility in pharmaceutical applications, respectively.

Nanotechnological utility in the pharmaceutical industry

The scientific world is advancing rapidly, and these advances have made nanotechnology an accepted concept. Broadly, nanotechnology consists of four generations. The first era began before the 2000s that focused on developing passive nanostructure, which can only carry out a single task at one time. Further, the second generation was marked from 2000 to 2005, in which the development of active nanostructures was focused that can perform multiple tasks like nanosensors and targeted drug delivery systems. The second generation was followed by the third and fourth generation, which was composed of different interacting elements that helped in developing advanced high-tech level state-of-the-art devices (Roco et al., 2011; Roco, 2011). However, despite rapid developments, sometimes nanotechnology is referred to as a general-purpose technology because it shows its utilities in multiple domains and is known to significantly impact the pharmaceutical industry in the coming years. A decade ago, the idea of personalized medicine was generated to solve the different limitations faced in traditional medical practices. Personalized medicines involve an enhanced patient stratification process. It reduces the number of patients by dividing them into two groups: the one in which developed drug therapy will be effective and the other population that can be affected by the side effects from the designed drug therapy. Moreover, in the industrial view, personalized medicine majorly focuses on diagnosing disease along with its risk assessment and is mainly aimed at genomic markers (Reichardt et al., 2016). The major factor that has driven the pharmaceutical industry toward developing personalized medicines is the coupling of present methods with nanotechnology by using nanoparticles to design highly specific in vivo imaging agents, which specifically target the cancer cells along with different components present in the tumor microenvironment. Moreover, estrogen receptor target pH-sensitive liposome was developed that was utilized for the site-specific intracellular delivery of doxorubicin (DOX) injected intravenously for the treatment of breast cancer. They inhibited breast tumor growth by inducing reactive oxygen species (ROS) in the tumor cells, and, therefore, it can be used as a promising nanocarrier for targeted delivery of anticancer agents with decreased cytotoxicity (Paliwal et al., 2012).

As development, globalization, and urbanization is increasing at a fast pace, the risk of getting lifestyle-related diseases is also increasing, which in turn raises the need for developing good health infrastructure, technology, and awareness among people. Therefore to handle the increasing health issues globally, lab-on-chip (LOC)-based nanodevices are used as a powerful strategy. These LOC-based nanodevices are accurate, rapid, portable, and highly sensitive that have efficiently aided in eliminating various diseases like Ebola and malaria (Kaushik et al., 2016; Kolluri et al., 2018). As the surface area increases, the diffusion distance decreases, which helps the fluid to flow through a very small channel without using any pump, increases the reaction rate by increasing the transfer of heat through decreasing heat capacity, reduces the consumption of energy, reagent, sample, and generates less waste. For instance, under suitable excitation conditions, europium nanoparticles exhibit the property of emitting stable high-intensity fluorescence; therefore these europium nanoparticles were bioconjugated and were used as probes to increase the sensitivity of microchip immunoassay without using any labile catalytic enzymes for detection of HIV-1 p24 antigen (Liu et al., 2014).

Recent developments in the pharmaceutical industry

The sudden outbreak of SARS-CoV-2 in 2020 opened many new possibilities in the pharmaceutical industry by introducing novel techniques and exploring the unexplored potentialities. SARS-CoV-2, being a major pandemic and a cause of massive destruction, upturned many traditional techniques and protocols by increasing the supply chain, increasing clinical trials to manufacturing, and introducing new projects, instruments, and protocols. Moreover, the pandemic not only fueled the research-based activities and modified regulatory norms but also forced various well-known pharmaceutical industries to enhance and reconsider their digital capabilities. Moreover, it has been assumed that around USD 2.6 billion will be utilized in discovering and developing each FDA-approved drug; therefore applied intelligence has been suggested to increase the overall research and development process, which can also improve drug discovery success rates by 8%–10%. Further, the use of applied intelligence in pharmaceutical industries can be used to search for candidate molecules for the development of drugs, develop compounds from the start, and help in synthesizing molecules with better efficacy. Currently, this technology is being used globally to form a partnership between applied intelligence firms and pharmaceutical companies. Moreover, the pharmaceutical industries have started to focus more on developing a deep understanding of patients' medical conditions and needs that are based on new knowledge sources so that the patient can get better treatments. For instance, Pfizer is now putting efforts to listen to the needs of the patient across communities, which is helping them establish communication between patients. Pfizer has developed two novel services that are available across the United States, namely, "This is Living with Cancer" and "Pfizer Oncology Together." The former includes a free app "LivingWith" that helps cancer patients to navigate their lives, and their caretakers store records, monitor about their feelings, connect with loved ones, and seek help for day-to-day related tasks. Whereas the latter is the first-of-its-kind initiative taken for cancer patients that are seeking Pfizer Oncology drugs. It includes a group of committed "Care Champions" with a social-work background that AIDS in overcoming different challenges, like transportation, emotional support ad adjustment, and financial assistance, faced during the treatment (Seven Emerging Pharma Industry Trends to Watch for in 2021, 2021).

Moreover, the concerns related to the environment have increased, which has resulted in development of more sustainable drugs or medicines that carry good medicinal value but is also safe for the environment. Therefore to minimize their impact and increase their biomedical sustainability, the optimization of designing, preparation, and usage of the nanomedicines plays a vital role. To attain sustainability a perfect balance among pharmaceuticals, the environment, and health care is necessary. Therefore nowadays, pharmaceutical industries have started to use nanotechnology to create nanomaterials-based medicines that help to provide the patient with a healthy, productive, and long life. In addition, the pharmaceutical industries have tried to enhance productivity, reduce waste, improve quality, and control research and development areas. Overall, it has led to cost-cutting and has increased the speed toward achieving sustainable development goals (Jiménez-González et al., 2011). In addition, the American Chemical Society (ACS) Green Chemistry Institute (GCI), along with various different global pharmaceutical corporations have founded the ACS GCI Pharmaceutical Roundtable (GCIPR) with a mission to increase the use of green chemistry in the drug discovery business. Therefore various methods have been proposed by different chemists and engineers to design green, safe, and sustainable protocols for drug development (Jiménez-González et al., 2013).

Role of pharmaceutical nanoparticles

Nanoparticles serve as a customized tool for several pharmaceutical applications, including solubility and bioavailability enhancement, controlled drug release, targeted drug/gene delivery, selective diagnosis, and as an adjuvant in vaccine delivery. Some nanoparticles-based marketed products like Doxil and Abraxane have improved chemotherapy among cancer patients (Ma & Mumper, 2013). In fact, nanoparticles offer altered pharmacokinetics and improved drug distribution due to their unique size and surface characteristics making them suitable for several pharmaceutical applications. Nanoparticles are broadly classified as inorganic nanomaterials, carbon-based nanoparticles, liposome-based, micelles, quantum dots, dendrimer-based, and metal-based nanoparticles. Nowadays, nanoparticles are more considered in the pharmaceutical industry than bulk matter because the extremely small size, improved size distribution, and high surface-to-volume ratio help them to show enhanced chemical, electrical, mechanical, biological, physical, and optical properties. Historically, metals show broad-spectrum biomedical properties, but their nanoforms have made them gain potentiality in the biomedical domain for effective and rapid disease diagnosis and their efficient treatment. Among all the other metal-based nanoparticles, silver and gold nanoparticles have gained their highest utility in the pharmaceutical domain. The surface of metal-based nanoparticles can easily bind with biomolecules and ligands (Nguyen et al., 2020; Selvasembian & Paramasivan, 2018a,b). Moreover, these days pharmacological applications have diverted their attention toward the biogenic synthesis of nanoparticles as they provide more biocompatibility and decrease cytotoxicity, which gives them more opportunity to explore their potentialities in medicines. For instance, leaves of *Mappia foetida*, an evergreen tree, were utilized to synthesize spherical gold nanoparticles of size 10–20 nm. The characterization analysis revealed that these synthesized gold nanoparticles were coated with different phytochemicals present in the plant extract, and this bio-capping was found to be helpful in linking folic acid (FA) and DOX, forming an *N*-hydroxysuccinimide (NHS)-activated FA and DOX gold nanoparticle (AuNPs–FA–NHS–DOX) carrier (Fig. 15.2). These developed nanocarriers were found to effectively release drugs at pH 5.3, which is considered a suitable condition for the delivery of intravenous drugs. Moreover, this designed drug carrier was found to be safe when tested against normal epithelial cells (Vero), and human cancer cells (MDA-MB-231, HeLa, SiHa, and Hep-G2) as it exhibited less toxicity toward normal cells and high toxicity toward cancer cells (Yallappa et al., 2015).

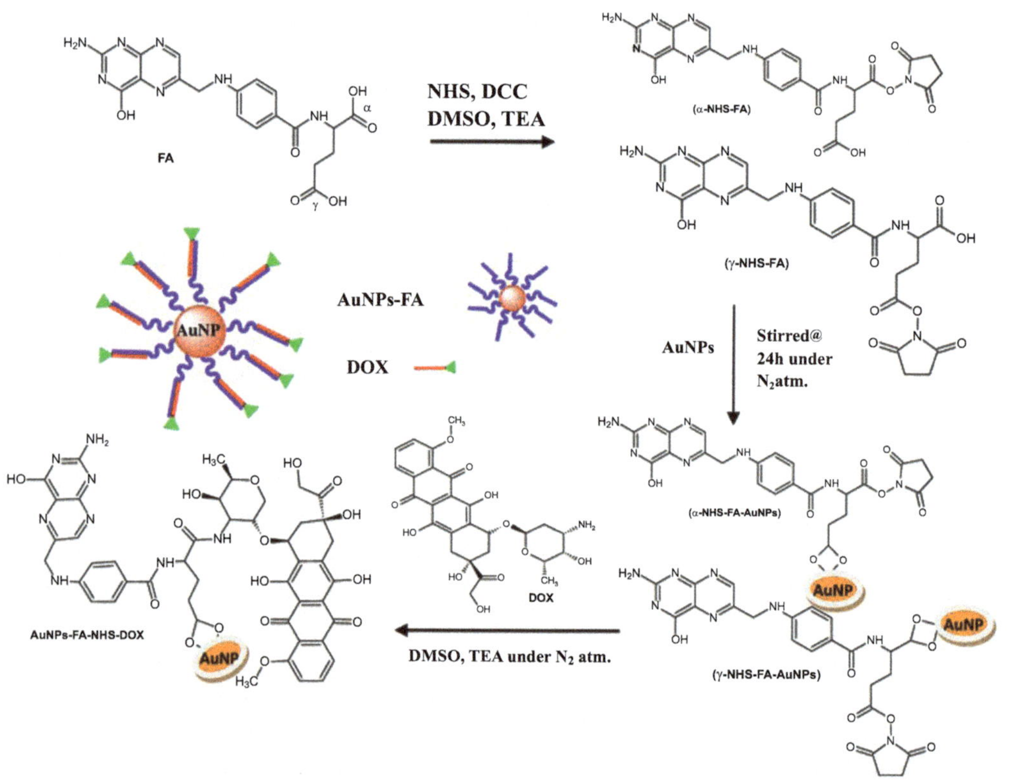

Figure 15.2 Synthesis steps for the activation of FA that are conjugated with AuNPs and DOX. *DOX*, Doxorubicin; *FA*, folic acid. *Reproduced with permission from Yallappa, S., Manjanna, J., Dhananjaya, B. L., Vishwanatha, U., Ravishankar, B., & Gururaj, H. (2015). Phytosynthesis of gold nanoparticles using Mappia foetida leaves extract and their conjugation with folic acid for delivery of doxorubicin to cancer cells.* Journal of Materials Science: Materials in Medicine, *26(9). https://doi.org/10.1007/s10856-015-5567-3.*

Apart from metal nanoparticles, other nanoparticles like nanodiamonds are also in the spotlight in the pharmaceutical industry. For instance, when nanodiamonds were conjugated with DOX, it enhanced the acute apoptotic responses and retention of drug in MDCK-MDR drug-resistant cells, therefore, proving that these nanodiamonds can be used to combat multidrug resistance cancer cells (Chow et al., 2011). Moreover, nanodiamonds have been found useful in treating leukemia cells, and in addition, when these nanodiamonds were combined with the daunorubicin complex, they showed anticancer activity against drug-resistant K562 leukemia cells and, therefore, can be used as an effective chemotherapeutic treatment (Man et al., 2014). It becomes very important to develop a deep understanding of the tumor microenvironment in order to create effective therapeutic agents using nanoparticles because different cells like immune and stromal cells, blood vessels, and extracellular fluid are also present in the environment of cancer cells (Del Vecchio et al., 2010). Moreover, functionalized nanoparticles are more considered in pharmaceutical industries as they can effectively act as a therapeutic agent and are able to withstand abnormal physiological conditions like acidic pH and hypoxia generated by the tumor cells and, therefore, can be used to design personalized treatment strategies. In addition, fluorescent carbon nanoparticles were combined with anticancer drugs that were shown to effectively treat different cancer because carbon nanoparticles exhibit high water solubility, biocompatibility, cell permeability, photostability, easy surface modifications, and low cytotoxicity as compared to traditional cancer drug therapy (Baker & Baker, 2010; Ding et al., 2014; Kumar et al., 2013). Moreover, nanoparticles as imaging agents show many benefits like it help in the complete eradication of tumors by enabling noninvasive imaging when coupled with multiple imaging modalities, possess high carrying capacities that increase the sensitivity of modalities, and can also act as an efficient theragnostic agent (Shin et al., 2013).

Moreover, the demand for nanoparticles has increased in subsequent years because the bulk materials cannot be easily modified, which limits their utilities in different domains, but on the other hand, nanomaterials can be easily modified according to desirable utilities, making them more desirable for utilizing in different domains. Further, researchers have started to focus on developing smart materials that can be used in the pharmaceutical domain to deliver drugs at the targeted site, act as efficient therapeutic agents, and be used to diagnose different diseases. Nanoparticles were found as a suitable material for preparing smart materials, as they possess the capability to respond to external stimuli, and their biomimetic activity can also be employed for the delivery of drugs and designing of specific materials having self-healing properties (Yoshida & Lahann, 2008). Based on their interactions with the environment, these smart nanoparticles are divided into two types: environment-primed nanoparticles that can change the environment of the host by introducing radiations, which help in establishing host–nanoparticles and nanoparticle–nanoparticle interactions, and environment-responsive nanoparticles that can sense and respond to the environment of the host (Kwon et al., 2015). Further, the pharmaceutical industry also uses nanodevices that can be used for monitoring quality control during the drug development process. These nanodevices use different nanocatalysts that can improve the reaction rate at low temperatures and can also increase the enantioselectivity. For instance, organic reactions widely use ferrite nanoparticles as nanocatalysts that can be easily recovered from reaction systems because they possess high chemical stability and narrow size distribution, which are considered important for designing a drug (Abu-Dief & Abdel-Fatah, 2018; Kralj et al., 2011).

Advantages

The nanoparticles lie in the nanometer range and show a high surface-to-volume ratio that aids in increasing the absorption of drug molecules. In addition, the presence of a hydrophilic and hydrophobic environment helps to improve the solubility of the nanodrug (Nagy et al., 2012). Moreover, as technology is expanding, nanobiosensors are grabbing all the attention in modern pharmaceutical applications. Hydrogels are cross-linked polymers that get swollen in water when nanoparticles are present and are highly used in fabricating biosensors. The applications of hydrogels are not just limited to the biomedical, agriculture, or environment domain but also find their utilities in pharmaceutical industries. These are generally used in developing cost-effective electrochemical biosensors to enhance their sensitivity (Hasanzadeh et al., 2014). Moreover, three-dimensional (3-D) based nanomaterials give various benefits in fabricating biosensors. The interconnected porous structure is composed of nanoscale pores that help them provide more surface area and show outstanding conducting properties of polymers as π-conjugate backbone elevates the rapid transfer of electrons. Moreover, these 3-D nanomaterials show biocompatibility that immobilizes biomolecules and keeps their bioactivity intact. Furthermore, high processability results in the desired shape on gelation and does not require additional surfactant or templating agents.

Moreover, owing to the small size and high surface area, using nanoparticles for drug delivery imparts various benefits as it has been revealed that medication delivery methods majorly depend on the size of the particle and exhibit increased bioavailability and solubility (Rizvi & Saleh, 2018). In addition, their extremely small size tricks the body's immune system and helps them to easily cross the blood–brain barrier, pulmonary system, and endothelium of tumors. Overall, these nanoparticles can be easily absorbed by different cells, enabling the delivery of different drugs at the targeted location (Kohane, 2007; Panyam & Labhasetwar, 2003). Nanoparticles synthesized using synthetic or natural biodegradable polymer enhances the bioavailability, continuous release of medications from a single dose, and adaptation to the system

(Zhang & Marksaltzman, 2013). Furthermore, different oral or injectable medicines have grown, but they are not necessarily composed of the most suitable formulation, which results in developing an opportunity to create good knowledge on carriers containing proteins or nucleic acids that can enhance their efficacy and simultaneously avoid any instability (Vo et al., 2012).

Disadvantages

Before using nanotechnology in the pharmaceutical industry, one should acquire full knowledge of the domain as well as always look for its disadvantages too. However, nanotechnology is considered the biggest boon to science and technology, but on the other hand, it can be harmful and toxic to living beings. The studies on nanotechnology's safety are not yet completed and are still in the juvenile stage and a detailed toxicological evaluation of nanoparticles to be utilized for targeted drug delivery is always required. Moreover, it has been observed that during the transition from microparticles to nanoparticles, the size range decreases. As a result, surface area increases, which creates problems like increased interarticular friction and significant sticking. Moreover, the increased surface area increases the chemical reactivity of these particles resulting in developing uncertainty in the reaction of these particles under different conditions. Further, this increased chemical reaction also generates ROS that damage DNA, cell membranes, and proteins and induce oxidative stress, and inflammation in the cells, hence leading to the generation of neurodegenerative diseases like Alzheimer's disease. Additionally, the extremely small size of nanoparticles increases their clearance rate from the body, which can create hurdles during diagnosis and drug delivery (Singh & Nehru, 2008).

Synthesis

One of the crucial steps in nanotechnology is the synthesis step as the route of synthesis majorly defines the properties of nanoparticles as the study of size, morphology, geometry, homogeneity, surface area, dispersion, the chemical composition of nanoparticles become crucial factors in determining their applications. From a broader perspective, nanoparticles can be synthesized using two methods, namely, the top-down and bottom-up methods. The top-down method involves breaking bulk materials into nanoforms and generally employs physical techniques like ball milling, sol–gel, and lithography. On the other hand, in the bottom-up method, nanoparticles are synthesized by assembling molecules, atoms, and so on. Instead of removing materials to create a structure, the bottom-up approach selectively adds an atom to create the nanoform. Biological approaches and chemical vapor deposition methods are examples of synthesizing nanoparticles of the bottom-up approach. But, nanoparticles synthesized using chemical and physical routes were costly, composed of harsh chemicals, and were highly toxic for living tissues; therefore the biological routes of nanoparticle synthesis were suggested as a better alternative as it utilizes different biological substances like enzymes, microorganisms, plants, nutrient media, and proteins. The biologically synthesized nanoparticles exhibit better tunable properties, sharp morphology, high yield, better biocompatibility, and low toxicity. Overall, biological routes are economical and eco-friendly; therefore they have gained their utility in pharmacology industries and have come out as a better alternative to traditional pharmacological techniques. In the pharmaceutical industry, metal-based nanoparticles like selenium, cerium, iron, copper, silver, platinum, palladium, zinc, and magnesium have found their broad-spectrum utilities, and nowadays researchers have started to lay their focus on biologically synthesized metal-based nanoparticles (Nayak et al., 2021; Singh et al., n.d., 2020, 2021). For instance, aqueous stem extract of *Maytenusroyleanus* was used to synthesize hexagonal gold nanoparticles of size 30 nm, and these synthesized gold nanoparticles showed effective pharmaceutical activities by exhibiting antileishmanial activity and, therefore, can be used to develop (Ahmad et al., 2016). Similarly, zinc nanoparticles also find their immense potentialities in pharmaceutical industries as an efficient antimicrobial agent (Bhuyan et al., 2015). Further, it has been observed that fabricated metal nanoparticles show enhanced properties that help them to find their utilities in different domains. Silver nanoparticles were synthesized from glucuronoxylan (GX), which is considered one of the potential hydrogel-forming polysaccharides and has been widely used to deliver several drugs as it has good pH-responsive on—off switching. These synthesized silver nanoparticles were used to prepare wound healing dressings. These bandages rapidly healed the wound because they consisted of cross-linked collagen fibers making them a potential pharmaceutical agent (Muhammad et al., 2017).

Carbon quantum dots are considered a precious gift to nanotechnology as they are very small in size, less than 10 nm, and have more enhanced optical, electrical, mechanical, and biological properties. Therefore they are considered the youngest in the family of the nanoworld. The preparation of carbon dots are rather considered easy as compared to other nanoparticles, as they only require carbon-containing precursors, which can be easily found like cellulose-, phenolic compounds—, glucose-, chitosan-, and carboxylic acid—containing compounds. Apart from these, fruit juices, lignin, domestic wastes, silk, wool, and so on can also be used to prepare carbon quantum dots, making them cost-effective and eco-friendly nanomaterials (Liu et al., 2019). Different bottom-up and top-down methods are used to synthesize carbon dots, like biomass synthesis, microwave irradiation, electrochemical methods, hydrothermal and solvothermal methods, laser ablation, surfactant extraction, and electrochemical methods. Moreover, carbon dots possess charismatic properties, like high permeability, high biocompatibility, low toxicity, good optical properties, and can easily interact with biomolecules, which helps them find their utilities in pharmaceutical industries (Wang et al., 2019). Other carbonaceous nanomaterials like graphene nanomaterials have also found their wide utility in biomedical and pharmaceutical domains (Shukla et al., 2022).

Other nanoparticles like polymer-based nanoparticles are synthesized using various different methods like extrusion, nanocrystallization, sonication, and salting out. All these methods are exclusive and produce a high yield of nanoparticles with desirable morphologies. For instance, a nanoporous membrane extrusion method was used for the synthesis of hydrophobic drugs as it initiates the precipitation of drug-loaded nanoparticles at the ends of nanopores (Guo et al., 2013). In addition, ionic gelation techniques are utilized to synthesize nanoparticles by cross-linking biodegradable hydrophilic polymers like sodium alginate, chitosan, and gelatin, like, chitosan was cross-linked with tripolyphosphate to synthesize nanosized coacervates (Fàbregas et al., 2013). Moreover, lipid nanoparticles have also gained significant recognition in pharmaceutical industries (Paliwal et al., 2011, 2009). There are various methods to synthesize lipid nanoparticles like microemulsion, high-pressure homogenization, ultrasonication, membrane contact, and solvent emulsification evaporation. However, high-pressure homogenization possesses several limitations as the risk of losing drug in the aqueous phase is always high, and since it uses a high temperature; therefore it becomes unsuitable for synthesizing thermolabile drugs. Hence, to overcome these limitations, an alternative approach was selected, known as the cold homogenization method, where lipid microparticles are synthesized by melting the lipid and drug together, which is quickly followed by solidifying the mixture. Further, these microparticles are then processed in cold aqueous surfactant and then are homogenized below room temperature to convert them into nanoparticles. The cold homogenization method gives a high yield, broad size distribution, and large-sized nanoparticles (Hou et al., 2003). Recently, a quality by design (QbD)-based approach is being used in the development and optimization of nanoparticles for desired therapeutic responses where one can tailored input variables to get nanoparticles with the desired pharmaceutical characteristics like size, surface charge, loading capacity, and drug release pattern. In addition, different routes of synthesis of different nanoparticles utilized as nanomedicine are illustrated in Fig. 15.3.

Patents and market trends of nano-based pharmaceutical products

The dominance of nanoparticles in the industrial and market domains has tremendously increased as it consists of unique properties that were realized later. However, from the economic perspective, it has been observed that adding new characteristics by fabricating it with substances attracts attention in the market. Furthermore, it has also greatly influenced academic research (Stark et al., 2015). In addition, the

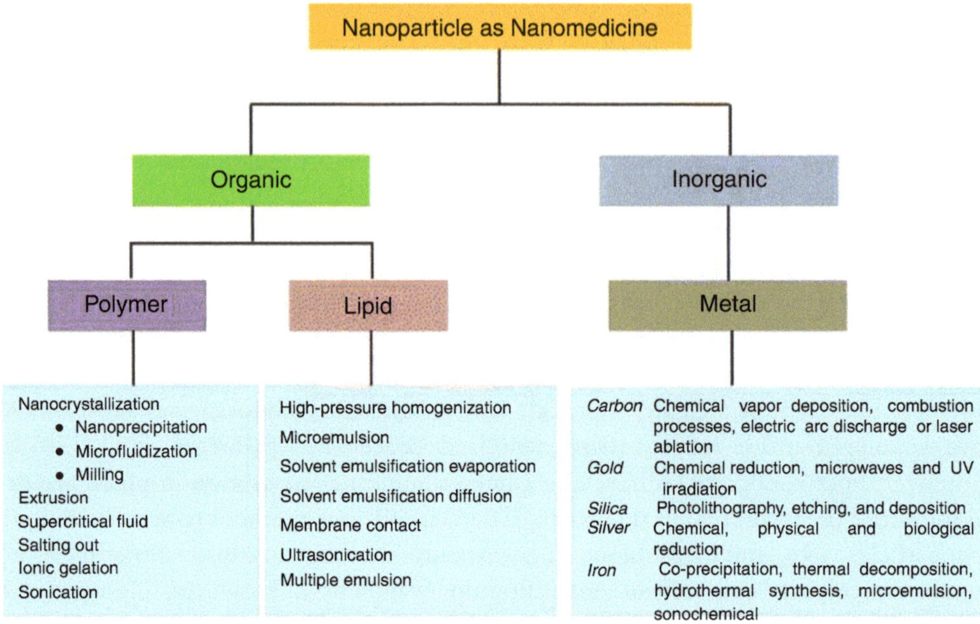

Figure 15.3 Various synthetic techniques to synthesize different nanomedicines. *Reproduced with permission from Paliwal, R., Babu, R. J. & Palakurthi, S. (2014).* AAPS PharmSciTech, *15(6), 1527–1534.*

productions of nanomaterials in large quantities are considered one of the important factors to increase the country's economy (Diallo et al., 2013). Nanomaterials are highly utilized in different industrial sectors, but apart from all, the pharmaceutical industry has emerged at a very fast speed. Moreover, booming innovative technologies have enhanced targeted drug delivery applications, cost-effective therapies, and several health-care utilities and are also claimed to increase the global nanomedicine market that revolutionized traditional disease diagnostic and treatment. In 2016 the global market for nanomedicine is recorded at $111,912 million, which is expected to reach $261,063 million by 2023, with a CAGR of 12.6% from 2017 to 2023. By looking at the significant advancements in nanosciences and nanotechnology the National Institute of Health (NIH) encouraged a National Nanotechnology Initiative (NNI) program in 2000 that promoted research on nanoscience in Health Science. In addition, interdisciplinary research has started with the help of extensive financial support from the government sector. The novel concept of "nanomedicine," was quickly taken up by pharmaceutical scientists and created a new domain, named nanopharmaceuticals (Weissig et al., 2014). It has been suggested that by 2025, the projects related to nanorobotics for the treatment of cancer will increase rapidly. Moreover, in current times 40% of products are in phase II of clinical development and are expected to be on market shelves in the coming decades (Nanomedicine Market Analysis By Products

Therapeutics, Regenerative Medicine, Diagnostics, By Application Clinical Oncology, Infectious diseases, By Nanomolecule Gold, Silver, Iron Oxide, Alumina, & Segment Forecasts, 2018-2025, 2017). Some commercially available nanomedicine-based products that are used in therapeutics are Daunoxome (Gilead), Abraxane (Abraxis Bioscience), Doxil (Bridgewater, USA), Triglide (SkyPharma), Ambisome (Gilead), MegaceES (Elan), Tricor (Elan), and Estrasorb (Novavax) Emend (Elan). Apart from this, some current nanoparticles-based formulations used for in vivo imaging involve Resovist (Schering), Feridex (Advanced Magnetics), and Gastromark (Advanced Magnetics) (Paliwal et al., 2014).

Safety and legal factors

To make nanotechnology a sustainable technology, it is very crucial to carefully check all the products' quality and safety concerns before launching in the market. Therefore specific categorization schemes are required to help the regulators and industries to foretell the potential risks so that considerable importance to the testing, decrease in the consumption of time, and reduction in the cost of in vivo studies can take place (Stone et al., 2014). Further, characterization techniques can be linked with certain alternative testing strategies for the analysis of the risk patterns and hazardous properties, which can be further used to take decisions for synthesizing nanoparticles. Moreover, Environmental Protection Agency (EPA) has classified carbon nanotubes (CNTs) under the category of "Respirable, Poorly Soluble Particulate;" therefore if any CNTs come under this category, then a request for a 90-day inhalation study is implemented. Moreover, both single-walled CNTs (SWCNTs) and multiwalled CNTs (MWCNTs) are governed by Significant New Use Regulation (SNUR). Hence, if any company desires to utilize CNTs differently, they must provide 90-days prior notice to EPA before starting its desired use. In the meantime, the EPA critically evaluates its utilization and decides if there are any chances of developing any unreasonable risk, and, therefore, suitable actions should be taken immediately. However, this approach is still challenging because it fails to give an accurate protocol for the determination of similarities between the new CNT and the existing CNT to both producer and regulator. Therefore through this method, it is hard to confirm whether the risk of using a new CNT (Godwin et al., 2015). Many factors affect the large-scale process of nanomedicines, like the nature of the material, which is regarded as safe (GRAS) status, toxicological characteristics related to the morphology of nanoparticles (Buzea et al., 2007), the biodegradability of nanocarriers in vivo, and the balance of multicomponent system in large scale. Therefore the selection of materials, method of preparation, expenses, and acceptability of the final product by patients and physicians are very important.

In addition, during the large-scale production of nanoparticles, the risk of losing the major properties of nanoparticles is always high. For instance, when nanoparticles were produced on a large scale through the emulsion method, the size of the nanoparticle decreased as the speed of the impeller and agitation time increased (Colombo et al., 2001). Moreover, the selection of the synthesis method of nanoparticles during pilot batch production is crucial to saving time from a scale-up point of view. Since a few decades, it has been observed that nanomedicine has efficiently taken over the market of biomedical and pharmaceutical industries and has set new standards in the diagnosis and therapeutics of disease. But, their market, economic value, and areas of utilities are still not clear and require comprehensive analysis. European Scientific Foundation has identified five major domains of nanomedicines as analytical tools, nanoimaging, nanomaterials and nanodevices, new therapeutic and targeted drug delivery systems, and clinical, regulatory, and toxicological assessments (Bowman & Gatof, 2015). Moreover, the commercialization of new nanomedicine in the market faces various hurdles like intellectual property landscape, regulatory issues, availability of capital, and technology transfer management issues. In addition, to analyze safety issues of engineered nanomaterials, within the EU FP7 project, Managing Risks of Nanoparticles (MARINA) has been developed that consists of two-phase risk assessment strategies, namely, problem framing (phase 1) and risk assessment (Phase 2). Phase 1 considers a base set of information that helps to identify relevant exposure scenarios (RESs) and establishes the aim for Phase 2. The importance of RES is shown by the exposure, kinetics, and hazard, in which, all three domains are exclusive of each other and contain their specific tools. Further, Phase 2 is made up of repeated methods of characterization of risk, identification of data, and combined collection and continuous analysis of data on the three domains, until adequate information is acquired to summarize possible risks in a RES. Apart from the three pillars, another (fourth) pillar, namely, risk characterization, also exists, which is composed of risk assessment tools. This strategy comprises flexible and efficient methods for collecting data and assessing risk, which is important to ensure the safety of engineered nanomaterials. However, more developments are needed to give guidance and make the MARINA Risk Assessment Strategy operational (Bos et al., 2015).

Conclusion and prospects

Modernization has changed the lifestyle of people and technologies are now creating novel tools to ease human lives. But, as the lifestyle is changing risk of getting lifestyle-related disorders has increased, which has resulted in the rapid development of healthcare and pharmaceutical facilities. In addition, the recent outbreak of the coronavirus pandemic has challenged the global public health services, but at the same time, it has effectively revolutionized the biomedical and pharmaceutical domains.

The introduction of nanotechnology in the biomedical domain is considered the biggest boon to mankind, as nanotechnology uses nanoparticles, the dimensions of which lie in the 1−100-nm range. The extremely small size of nanoparticles helps them to exhibit enhanced properties like optical, physical, chemical, and biological that cannot be obtained by bulk materials. Currently, nanomedicine has become one of the recent trends in the biomedical domain and has become one of the highly recognized research fields as it utilizes different medicinal techniques for the detection and treatment of various diseases. In addition, they are now ruling the nanotechnology market and have almost over 75% of total sales. Nanoparticles in pharmaceutical industries are majorly used as drug delivery carriers that are useful in treating different types of cancers and AIDS, used to transport antibiotics, proteins, and vaccines. With this speed, it has been assumed that nanotechnology will rule over the pharmaceutical and biomedical market in the coming decade as by that time almost 40% of products that are currently under clinical trials will be on the market shelves. Apart from this projects related to nanorobotics for the treatment of cancer will be completed by 2025. However, safety and legal issues related to the use of nanoparticles on human are still undergoing that limits their broad and long-term use, so in coming decades, it has been suggested that the studies related to biosafety, bioregulation, and ethics will be more advanced, which will ultimately result in increasing utilities of nanomedicines. Therefore this chapter aims to provide detailed knowledge on the potentialities of nanotechnology in pharmaceutical industries.

References

Abu-Dief, A. M., & Abdel-Fatah, S. M. (2018). Development and functionalization of magnetic nanoparticles as powerful and green catalysts for organic synthesis. *Beni-Suef University Journal of Basic and Applied Sciences*, 7(1), 55−67. Available from https://doi.org/10.1016/j.bjbas.2017.05.008.

Ahmad, A., Syed, F., Imran, M., Khan, A. U., Tahir, K., Khan, Z. U. H., & Yuan, Q. (2016). Phytosynthesis and antileishmanial activity of gold nanoparticles by *Maytenus royleanus*. *Journal of Food Biochemistry*, *40*(4), 420−427. Available from https://doi.org/10.1111/jfbc.12232.

Amoabediny, G., Haghiralsadat, F., Naderinezhad, S., Helder, M. N., Akhoundi Kharanaghi, E., Mohammadnejad Arough, J., & Zandieh-Doulabi, B. (2018). Overview of preparation methods of polymeric and lipid-based (niosome, solid lipid, liposome) nanoparticles: A comprehensive review. *International Journal of Polymeric Materials and Polymeric Biomaterials*, *67*(6), 383−400. Available from https://doi.org/10.1080/00914037.2017.1332623.

Baker, S. N., & Baker, G. A. (2010). Luminescent carbon nanodots: Emergent nanolights. *Angewandte Chemie - International Edition*, *49*(38), 6726−6744. Available from https://doi.org/10.1002/anie.200906623.

Bamrungsap, S., Zhao, Z., Chen, T., Wang, L., Li, C., Fu, T., & Tan, W. (2012). Nanotechnology in therapeutics: A focus on nanoparticles as a drug delivery system. *Nanomedicine: Nanotechnology, Biology, and Medicine*, 7(8), 1253−1271. Available from https://doi.org/10.2217/nnm.12.87.

Bhuyan, T., Mishra, K., Khanuja, M., Prasad, R., & Varma, A. (2015). Biosynthesis of zinc oxide nanoparticles from *Azadirachta indica* for antibacterial and photocatalytic applications. *Materials Science in Semiconductor Processing*, *32*, 55−61. Available from https://doi.org/10.1016/j.mssp.2014.12.053.

Bos, P. M. J., Gottardo, S., Scott-Fordsm, J. J., van Tongeren, M., Semenzin, E., Fernandes, T. F., Hristozov, D., Hund-Rinke, K., Hunt, N., Irfan, M. A., Landsiedel, R., Peijnenburg, W. J. G. M., Jiménez, A. S., van Kesteren, P. C. E., & Oomen, A. G. (2015). The MARINA risk assessment strategy: A flexible strategy for efficient information collection and risk assessment of nanomaterials. *International Journal of Environmental Research and Public Health, 12*(12), 15007–15021. Available from https://doi.org/10.3390/ijerph121214961.

Bowman, D. M., & Gatof, J. (2015). Reviewing the regulatory barriers for nanomedicine: Global questions and challenges. *Nanomedicine: Nanotechnology, Biology, and Medicine, 10*(21), 3275–3286. Available from https://doi.org/10.2217/nnm.15.169.

Buzea, C., Pacheco, I. I., & Robbie, K. (2007). Nanomaterials and nanoparticles: Sources and toxicity. *Biointerphases, 2*(4), MR17–MR71. Available from https://doi.org/10.1116/1.2815690.

Chow, E. K., Zhang, X. Q., Chen, M., Lam, R., Robinson, E., Huang, H., Schaffer, D., Osawa, E., Goga, A., & Ho, D. (2011). Nanodiamond therapeutic delivery agents mediate enhanced chemoresistant tumor treatment. *Science Translational Medicine, 3*(73). Available from https://doi.org/10.1126/scitranslmed.3001713.

Colombo, A. P., Briançon, S., Lieto, J., & Fessi, H. (2001). Project, design, and use of a pilot plant for nanocapsule production. *Drug Development and Industrial Pharmacy, 27*(10), 1063–1072. Available from https://doi.org/10.1081/DDC-100108369.

Del Vecchio, S., Zannetti, A., Iommelli, F., Lettieri, A., Brunetti, A., & Salvatore, M. (2010). Molecular imaging of tumor microenvironment: Challenges and perspectives. *Quarterly Journal of Nuclear Medicine and Molecular Imaging, 54*(3), 249–258.

Diallo, M. S., Fromer, N. A., & Jhon, M. S. (2013). Nanotechnology for sustainable development: Retrospective and outlook. *Journal of Nanoparticle Research, 15*(11). Available from https://doi.org/10.1007/s11051-013-2044-0.

Ding, C., Zhu, A., & Tian, Y. (2014). Functional surface engineering of C-dots for fluorescent biosensing and in vivo bioimaging. *Accounts of Chemical Research, 47*(1), 20–30. Available from https://doi.org/10.1021/ar400023s.

Fàbregas, A., Miñarro, M., García-Montoya, E., Pérez-Lozano, P., Carrillo, C., Sarrate, R., Sánchez, N., Ticó, J. R., & Suñé-Negre, J. M. (2013). Impact of physical parameters on particle size and reaction yield when using the ionic gelation method to obtain cationic polymeric chitosan–tripolyphosphate nanoparticles. *International Journal of Pharmaceutics, 446*(1–2), 199–204. Available from https://doi.org/10.1016/j.ijpharm.2013.02.015.

Godwin, H., Nameth, C., Avery, D., Bergeson, L. L., Bernard, D., Beryt, E., Boyes, W., Brown, S., Clippinger, A. J., Cohen, Y., Doa, M., Hendren, C. O., Holden, P., Houck, K., Kane, A. B., Klaessig, F., Kodas, T., Landsiedel, R., Lynch, I., & Nel, A. E. (2015). Nanomaterial categorization for assessing risk potential to facilitate regulatory decision-making. *ACS Nano, 9*(4), 3409–3417. Available from https://doi.org/10.1021/acsnano.5b00941.

Guo, P., Hsu, T. M., Zhao, Y., Martin, C. R., & Zare, R. N. (2013). Preparing amorphous hydrophobic drug nanoparticles by nanoporous membrane extrusion. *Nanomedicine: Nanotechnology, Biology, and Medicine, 8*(3), 333–341. Available from https://doi.org/10.2217/nnm.12.119.

Hasanzadeh, M., Shadjou, N., & de la Guardia, M. (2014). Electrochemical biosensing using hydrogel nanoparticles. *TrAC Trends in Analytical Chemistry, 62*, 11–19. Available from https://doi.org/10.1016/j.trac.2014.06.011.

Hou, D. Z., Xie, C. S., Huang, K. J., & Zhu, C. H. (2003). The production and characteristics of solid lipid nanoparticles (SLNs). *Biomaterials, 24*(10), 1781–1785. Available from https://doi.org/10.1016/S0142-9612(02)00578-1.

Jiménez-González, C., Ollech, C., Pyrz, W., Hughes, D., Broxterman, Q. B., & Bhathela, N. (2013). Expanding the boundaries: Developing a streamlined tool for eco-footprinting of pharmaceuticals. *Organic Process Research and Development, 17*(2), 239–246. Available from https://doi.org/10.1021/op3003079.

Jiménez-González, C., Poechlauer, P., Broxterman, Q. B., Yang, B. S., Am Ende, D., Baird, J., Bertsch, C., Hannah, R. E., Dell'Orco, P., Noorman, H., Yee, S., Reintjens, R., Wells, A., Massonneau, V., & Manley, J. (2011). Key green engineering research areas for sustainable manufacturing: A perspective from pharmaceutical and fine chemicals manufacturers. *Organic Process Research and Development*, *15*(4), 900–911. Available from https://doi.org/10.1021/op100327d.

Kaushik, A., Tiwari, S., Dev Jayant, R., Marty, A., & Nair, M. (2016). Towards detection and diagnosis of Ebola virus disease at point-of-care. *Biosensors and Bioelectronics*, *75*, 254–272. Available from https://doi.org/10.1016/j.bios.2015.08.040.

Kohane, D. S. (2007). Microparticles and nanoparticles for drug delivery. *Biotechnology and Bioengineering*, *96*(2), 203–209. Available from https://doi.org/10.1002/bit.21301.

Kolluri, N., Klapperich, C. M., & Cabodi, M. (2018). Towards lab-on-a-chip diagnostics for malaria elimination. *Lab on a Chip*, *18*(1), 75–94. Available from https://doi.org/10.1039/c7lc00758b.

Kralj, S., Drofenik, M., & Makovec, D. (2011). Controlled surface functionalization of silica-coated magnetic nanoparticles with terminal amino and carboxyl groups. *Journal of Nanoparticle Research*, *13*(7), 2829–2841. Available from https://doi.org/10.1007/s11051-010-0171-4.

Kumar, V., Toffoli, G., & Rizzolio, F. (2013). Fluorescent carbon nanoparticles in medicine for cancer therapy. *ACS Medicinal Chemistry Letters*, *4*(11), 1012–1013. Available from https://doi.org/10.1021/mL400394a.

Kwon, E. J., Lo, J. H., & Bhatia, S. N. (2015). Smart nanosystems: Bio-inspired technologies that interact with the host environment. *Proceedings of the National Academy of Sciences of the United States of America*, *112*(47), 14460–14466. Available from https://doi.org/10.1073/pnas.1508522112.

Liu, J., Du, B., Zhang, P., Haleyurgirisetty, M., Zhao, J., Ragupathy, V., Lee, S., DeVoe, D. L., & Hewlett, I. K. (2014). Development of a microchip europium nanoparticle immunoassay for sensitive point-of-care HIV detection. *Biosensors and Bioelectronics*, *61*, 177–183. Available from https://doi.org/10.1016/j.bios.2014.04.057.

Liu, M. L., Chen, B. B., Li, C. M., & Huang, C. Z. (2019). Carbon dots: Synthesis, formation mechanism, fluorescence origin and sensing applications. *Green Chemistry*, *21*(3), 449–471. Available from https://doi.org/10.1039/c8gc02736f.

Lobatto, M. E., Fuster, V., Fayad, Z. A., & Mulder, W. J. M. (2011). Perspectives and opportunities for nanomedicine in the management of atherosclerosis. *Nature Reviews. Drug Discovery*, *10*(11), 835–852. Available from https://doi.org/10.1038/nrd3578.

Ma, P., & Mumper, R. J. (2013). Paclitaxel nano-delivery systems: A comprehensive review. *Journal of Nanomedicine and Nanotechnology*, *4*(2), 6. Available from https://doi.org/10.4172/2157-7439.1000164.

Man, H. B., Kim, H., Kim, H. J., Robinson, E., Liu, W. K., Chow, E. K. H., & Ho, D. (2014). Synthesis of nanodiamond-daunorubicin conjugates to overcome multidrug chemoresistance in leukemia. *Nanomedicine: Nanotechnology, Biology, and Medicine*, *10*(2), 359–369. Available from https://doi.org/10.1016/j.nano.2013.07.014.

Muhammad, G., Hussain, M. A., Amin, M., Hussain, S. Z., Hussain, I., Abbas Bukhari, S. N., & Naeem-Ul-Hassan, M. (2017). Glucuronoxylan-mediated silver nanoparticles: Green synthesis, antimicrobial and wound healing applications. *RSC Advances*, 7(68), 42900–42908. Available from https://doi.org/10.1039/c7ra07555c.

Nagy, Z. K., Balogh, A., Vajna, B., Farkas, A., Patyi, G., Kramarics, Á., & Marosi, G. (2012). Comparison of electrospun and extruded Soluplus®-based solid dosage forms of improved dissolution. *Journal of Pharmaceutical Sciences*, *101*(1), 322–332. Available from https://doi.org/10.1002/jps.22731.

Nanomedicine Market Analysis By Products (Therapeutics, Regenerative Medicine, Diagnostics), By Application (Clinical Oncology, Infectious diseases), By Nanomolecule (Gold, Silver, Iron Oxide, Alumina), & Segment Forecasts, 2018–2025. *Grand View Research*. (2017).

Nayak, V., Singh, K. R., Singh, A. K., & Singh, R. P. (2021). Potentialities of selenium nanoparticles in biomedical science. *New Journal of Chemistry*, *45*(6), 2849–2878. Available from https://doi.org/10.1039/d0nj05884j.

Nguyen, V. H., Do, H. H., Van Nguyen, T., Singh, P., Raizada, P., Sharma, A., Sana, S. S., Grace, A. N., Shokouhimehr, M., Ahn, S. H., Xia, C., Kim, S. Y., & Le, Q. V. (2020). Perovskite oxide-based photocatalysts for solar-driven hydrogen production: Progress and perspectives. *Solar Energy*, *211*, 584–599. Available from https://doi.org/10.1016/j.solener.2020.09.078.

Paliwal, R., Babu, R. J., & Palakurthi, S. (2014). Nanomedicine scale-up technologies: Feasibilities and challenges. *AAPS PharmSciTech*, *15*(6), 1527–1534. Available from https://doi.org/10.1208/s12249-014-0177-9.

Paliwal, R., Paliwal, S. R., Agrawal, G. P., & Vyas, S. P. (2011). Biomimetic solid lipid nanoparticles for oral bioavailability enhancement of low molecular weight heparin and its lipid conjugates: In vitro and in vivo evaluation. *Molecular Pharmaceutics*, *8*(4), 1314–1321. Available from https://doi.org/10.1021/mp200109m.

Paliwal, R., Rai, S., Vaidya, B., Khatri, K., Goyal, A. K., Mishra, N., Mehta, A., & Vyas, S. P. (2009). Effect of lipid core material on characteristics of solid lipid nanoparticles designed for oral lymphatic delivery. *Nanomedicine: Nanotechnology, Biology, and Medicine*, *5*(2), 184–191. Available from https://doi.org/10.1016/j.nano.2008.08.003.

Paliwal, S. R., Paliwal, R., Pal, H. C., Saxena, A. K., Sharma, P. R., Gupta, P. N., Agrawal, G. P., & Vyas, S. P. (2012). Estrogen-anchored pH-sensitive liposomes as nanomodule designed for site-specific delivery of doxorubicin in breast cancer therapy. *Molecular Pharmaceutics*, *9*(1), 176–186. Available from https://doi.org/10.1021/mp200439z.

Panyam, J., & Labhasetwar, V. (2003). Biodegradable nanoparticles for drug and gene delivery to cells and tissue. *Advanced Drug Delivery Reviews*, *55*(3), 329–347. Available from https://doi.org/10.1016/S0169-409X(02)00228-4.

Reichardt, N. C., Martín-Lomas, M., & Penadés, S. (2016). Opportunities for glyconanomaterials in personalized medicine. *Chemical Communications*, *52*(92), 13430–13439. Available from https://doi.org/10.1039/c6cc04445j.

Rizvi, S. A. A., & Saleh, A. M. (2018). Applications of nanoparticle systems in drug delivery technology. *Saudi Pharmaceutical Journal*, *26*(1), 64–70. Available from https://doi.org/10.1016/j.jsps.2017.10.012.

Roco, M. C. (2011). The long view of nanotechnology development: The national nanotechnology initiative at 10 years. *Journal of Nanoparticle Research*, *13*(2), 427–445. Available from https://doi.org/10.1007/s11051-010-0192-z.

Roco, M. C., Mirkin, C. A., & Hersam, M. C. (2011). Nanotechnology research directions for societal needs in 2020: Summary of international study. *Journal of Nanoparticle Research*, *13*(3), 897–919. Available from https://doi.org/10.1007/s11051-011-0275-5.

Selvasembian, R., & Paramasivan, B. (2018a). Performance of novel biosorbents prepared using native and NaOH treated peltophorum pterocarpum fruit shells for the removal of malachite green. *Bioresource Technology Reports*, *3*, 75–81. Available from https://doi.org/10.1016/j.biteb.2018.06.004.

Selvasembian, R., & Paramasivan, B. (2018b). Utilization of unconventional lignocellulosic waste biomass for the biosorption of toxic triphenylmethane dye malachite green from aqueous solution. *International Journal of Phytoremediation*, *20*(6), 624–633. Available from https://doi.org/10.1080/15226514.2017.1413329.

Seven emerging pharma industry trends to watch for in 2021. *Netscribes*. (2021).

Shin, S. J., Beech, J. R., & Kelly, K. A. (2013). Targeted nanoparticles in imaging: Paving the way for personalized medicine in the battle against cancer. *Integrative Biology (United Kingdom)*, *5*(1), 29–42. Available from https://doi.org/10.1039/c2ib20047c.

Shukla, M. K., Dong, W.-L., Azizov, S., Singh, K. R., Kumar, D., Singh, R. P., & Singh, J. (2022). Trends of bioderived carbonaceous materials for futuristic biomedical applications. *Materials Letters*, *311*, 131606. Available from https://doi.org/10.1016/j.matlet.2021.131606.

Singh, K. R. B., Nayak, V., Sarkar, T., & Singh, R. P. (2020). Cerium oxide nanoparticles: Properties, biosynthesis and biomedical application. *RSC Advances*, *10*(45), 27194–27214. Available from https://doi.org/10.1039/d0ra04736h.

Singh, K. R., Nayak, V., Singh, J., Singh, A. K., & Singh, R. P. (2021). Potentialities of bioinspired metal and metal oxide nanoparticles in biomedical sciences. *RSC Advances*, *11*(40), 24722–24746. Available from https://doi.org/10.1039/d1ra04273d.

Singh, K., Nayak, V., Singh, J., Adetunji, C., & Singh, R.P. (n.d.). Introduction: Potentialities of biona-nomaterials towards the environmental and agricultural domain. In *Bionanomaterials for environmental and agricultural applications* (Vol. 2021). IOP Publishing.

Singh, O. P., & Nehru, R. M. (2008). Nanotechnology and cancer treatment. *Asian Journal of Experimental Sciences*, *22*(2).

Stark, W. J., Stoessel, P. R., Wohlleben, W., & Hafner, A. (2015). Industrial applications of nanoparticles. *Chemical Society Reviews*, *44*(16), 5793–5805. Available from https://doi.org/10.1039/c4cs00362d.

Stone, V., Pozzi-Mucelli, S., Tran, L., Aschberger, K., Sabella, S., Vogel, U., Poland, C., Balharry, D., Fernandes, T., Gottardo, S., Hankin, S., Hartl, M. G., Hartmann, N., Hristozov, D., Hund-Rinke, K., Johnston, H., Marcomini, A., Panzer, O., Roncato, D., & Scott-Fordsmand, J. J. (2014). ITS-NANO – Prioritising nanosafety research to develop a stakeholder driven intelligent testing strategy. *Particle and Fibre Toxicology*, *11*(1), 9. Available from https://doi.org/10.1186/1743-8977-11-9.

Tiwari, G., Tiwari, R., Bannerjee, S., Bhati, L., Pandey, S., Pandey, P., & Sriwastawa, B. (2012). Drug delivery systems: An updated review. *International Journal of Pharmaceutical Investigation*, *2*(1), 2. Available from https://doi.org/10.4103/2230-973x.96920.

Vo, T. N., Kasper, F. K., & Mikos, A. G. (2012). Strategies for controlled delivery of growth factors and cells for bone regeneration. *Advanced Drug Delivery Reviews*, *64*(12), 1292–1309. Available from https://doi.org/10.1016/j.addr.2012.01.016.

Wagner, V., Dullaart, A., Bock, A. K., & Zweck, A. (2006). The emerging nanomedicine landscape. *Nature Biotechnology*, *24*(10), 1211–1217. Available from https://doi.org/10.1038/nbt1006-1211.

Wang, X., Feng, Y., Dong, P., & Huang, J. (2019). A mini review on carbon quantum dots: Preparation, properties, and electrocatalytic application. *Frontiers in Chemistry*, 7. Available from https://doi.org/10.3389/fchem.2019.00671.

Weissig, V., Pettinger, T. K., & Murdock, N. (2014). Nanopharmaceuticals (part 1): Products on the market. *International Journal of Nanomedicine*, *9*, 4357–4373. Available from https://doi.org/10.2147/IJN.S46900.

Yallappa, S., Manjanna, J., Dhananjaya, B. L., Vishwanatha, U., Ravishankar, B., & Gururaj, H. (2015). Phytosynthesis of gold nanoparticles using *Mappia foetida* leaves extract and their conjugation with folic acid for delivery of doxorubicin to cancer cells. *Journal of Materials Science: Materials in Medicine*, *26*(9). Available from https://doi.org/10.1007/s10856-015-5567-3.

Yoshida, M., & Lahann, J. (2008). Smart nanomaterials. *ACS Nano*, *2*(6), 1101–1107. Available from https://doi.org/10.1021/nn800332g.

Zhang, J., & Marksaltzman, W. (2013). Engineering biodegradable nanoparticles for drug and gene delivery. *Chemical Engineering Progress*, *109*(3), 25–30. Available from http://www.aiche.org/system/files/cep/20130325.pdf.

CHAPTER 16

Recent development in the pharmaceutical industries

Ekta Poonia[1], Narender Ranga[2], Rohit Ranga[1] and Krishan Kumar[1]
[1]Physical Chemistry Research Laboratory, Department of Chemistry, D.C.R. University of Science and Technology, Sonipat, Haryana, India
[2]Nanomaterials Research Laboratory, Department of Physics, D.C.R. University of Science and Technology, Sonipat, Haryana, India

Introduction

The pharmaceutical sector has a number of peculiar traits that distinguish it from the traditional industry. It is also a sector filled with contradictions. For example, although the industry has made a significant contribution to human well-being and to reducing poor health and suffering for more than a century, it is undeniable that it is still seen as one of the least trusted industries by the general public often likened to the detriment of the nuclear industry. It is undoubtedly one of the riskiest businesses to invest in, but the public perceives it as too profitable. Most people believe that major pharmaceutical corporations spend more money on marketing than on research, despite the fact that they portray themselves as research-based enterprises. Although the danger and expenses connected with drug development are recognized, people believes that the development of drugs carried out to meet all human necessity and should be given away to everyone as needed when developed.

Note that, depending on the context, the term "drug" can refer to both an illogical substance and medicine. The term "pharmaceutical" is used in this chapter to refer to the pharmaceutical industry's end-products that are used by patients. The term "drug" is mostly applied to potential pharmaceuticals that are still in the development stage (Taylor, 2015). Development of the new product is the major need for pharmaceutical industry to achieve the desired levels of financial benefits. As a result, examining the factors that contribute to the success of new products in the pharmaceutical industry can assist the industry to develop more successful new products. Regardless of the innovative level, which might be incremental innovation by releasing new brand products or upgrading existing products, new product creation is the most important sign of continuous firm performance (Gatignon & Xuereb, 1997). In this study, new product development is assigned to any changes in the product portfolio that includes macrolevel (new to market) or at the microlevel (new product for firm). This chapter

Nanotechnology for Drug Delivery and Pharmaceuticals
DOI: https://doi.org/10.1016/B978-0-323-95325-2.00017-1

provides the recent development in the pharmaceuticals industry, that is, the cost of producing a new drug, developments of new drugs, polymer-based drug delivery systems, drug carrier systems, tissue engineering, recent nanocarrier approach for targeted drug delivery in cancer therapy, and the role of nanoparticles in the pharmaceuticals industry.

Development of new drugs

The cost of research and development for each new drug is different. The cost of developing a medicine is determined by the type of drug being developed, the risk of failure (DiMasi et al., 2003), and whether the drug is based on a chemical that has never been used in a pharmaceutical product before or is an incremental modification of an existing drug.

New drugs/medicines

The nature of products produced and sold by the innovative biopharmaceutical business has changed dramatically during the last decade (Arora et al., 2004). Today's worldwide biopharmaceutical portfolio reflects better treatment competition, the proliferation of large molecular drugs, and a growth in the number of individual or targeted therapeutic products, all of which are helping the treatment of many orphan illnesses.

As a consequence of these trends, biopharmaceutical products with small production runs, high specific production needs, and genotype-specific products have emerged. This fundamental shift in the entire product mix, combined with a constant focus on efficiency and effectiveness, is driving advancements in the technologies and processes needed to support advanced biopharmaceutical manufacturing. Construction technology innovation is assisting in the improvement of quality, flexibility, and economics, all while potentially benefiting patients both indirectly and directly. Some of these are improvements, and others are innovations. These are shown in Fig. 16.1. Drugs in each category have aided and improved people's lives. However, due to expensive prices, their reach to the general public is limited.

New drug technologies

With the development of new drugs a lot of new drug technologies were discovered such as:

- *Gene therapy* is the process of putting genes into a patient's cells in order to replace genetic defects with new, functional genes (Anderson, 1984). Although the area of research is still in its early stage of clinical trials, it has progressed tremendously since the initial clinical studies in 1990.

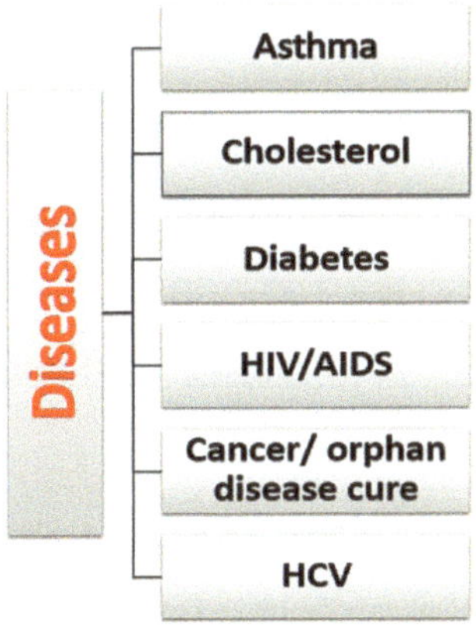

Figure 16.1 Various diseases.

- *Stem cells* are specialized cells that have the ability to mature into a range of different types of functional cells. Before being physically transplanted into patients, stem cells can be cultured in the lab and manipulated to produce the desired cell type (Fiegel et al., 2008). The goal is to remove damaged tissue and replace it with newer, healthier tissue.
- *Nanomedicine* involves the manipulation of molecules and structures at the nuclear level. The experimental use of nanoshells to transform infrared light into thermal energy to attack cancer cells is one example (Logothetidis, 2012).
- *New drug delivery systems* include finer particles called microspheres that have enough holes to deliver drugs to their targets. Various tumors and disorders are being studied using microsphere therapy treatment (Tibbitt et al., 2016).

Biopharmaceutical manufacturers are generally investing in the following areas as shown in Fig. 16.2.

New products that display improvement in drug device blend products, and drug delivery systems are coming to the market which can help to enhance drug effectiveness and support patient compliance (Verma & Garg, 2001).

Many of the existing bioinformatics technologies have a long history of their origin. These include stem cell technology, perfusion techniques, single-use bags, microbial production platforms, innovative chromatography approaches, and more. While this indicates that the biopharma industry requires an unusually long development period to develop a new product, it also suggests that innovation may not always be an opportunity. These decades-old technologies are increasingly being reevaluated as feasible options for high-quality bioprocessing, low cost, and high efficiency. Many believe regulators are examining new materials, testing product interactions, and looking at them differently from genuine equipment. The most important trend in this industry over the last 5 years has been the demand for improved process

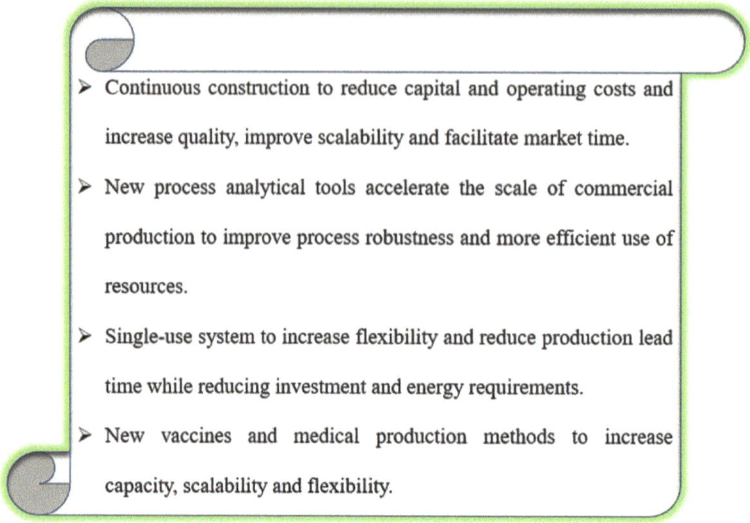

Figure 16.2 Investing areas for biopharmaceutical manufacturers.

efficiency; every new production technology must demonstrate efficiency and be regulatory-friendly.

Development of drug delivery systems

Polymer-based drug delivery systems

In medication delivery systems, degradable and nondegradable polymers are used as carriers in various ways. Injectable polymeric drug delivery systems are formulated as nano or tablets or microcapsules or micelle-forming or soluble polymer formulas (Abasian et al., 2020). Implantable drug delivery systems are made up of single or multifilament fibers, membranes, or knitted fabrics, woven or nonwoven, or things of various shapes (such as needles, buttons, and disks). Fig. 16.3 shows the different forms of polymer-based drug delivery systems. For application in the internal system an ideal polymer carrier system should be able to shown in following ways:

- be compatible with the blood;
- to circulate in the blood stream without causing embolization at capillaries;
- to prevent excretion into the kidneys;
- nonselective progression by the reticuloendothelial system to quit the drug, preferably at the desired rate in the target area and degrading in vivo during or after drug withdrawal.

The most significant aspect when a polymer-based medication delivery method is injected or delivered extravascular is tissue adaption. The foreign matter in the tissues

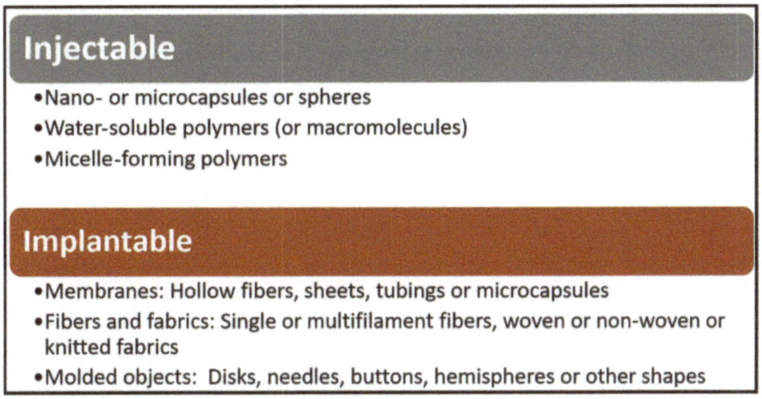

Figure 16.3 Forms of polymer-based drug delivery systems.

always produces a reaction. The inflammatory process is the most common tissue reaction in a dysfunctional system. Inflammation can be triggered by chemical, biological, or physical factors (Abasian et al., 2020).

Polymers

Polymers should exhibit the biomechanical properties (in stress, shear, and compression) required for a particular application. Therefore, they must have the required physical structure and other required qualities, such as elasticity and transparency (Ikada, 2011). Polymers should also be biocompatible. In other words, polymer and their degradation products should not induce unwanted host reactions such inflammatory reactions, toxicity, allergic reactions, and carcinogenesis. All of these characteristics depend on environmental conditions, temperature, and time and may change in the physical environment while using the system. The drug delivery system must be efficient and safe during delivery. Drug delivery techniques involve both degradable and nondegradable polymers. Some examples of nondegradable and biodegradable polymers are shown in the following section.

Nondegradable polymers

Both hydrophobic and hydrophilic polymers are used in the drug delivery system. Hydrogels are primarily a 3D structure of water-soluble polymers. They do not dissolve in water, although they can absorb more than 30% of water (Srivastava et al., 2015). They swell to a certain extent depending on their weight and, therefore, the degree of cross-linking. The key advantage of hydrogel matrix is their high biocompatibility. These polymeric metrics can be used with medications that are not only predominantly hydrophilic but also hydrophobic. Polyhydroxyethylmethacrylate and other hydrogels are widely used in drug delivery systems and medical applications (Kim et al., 2014). Fig. 16.4 shows the major nondegradable polymers for drug delivery systems.

Biodegradable polymers

Biodegradable polymers are also used in drug delivery systems, which disintegrate in the body during or after drug administration. Biodegradation is an unwanted phenomenon that causes changes in physical properties in many medicinal applications of polymeric biomaterials (Piskin, 1995). However, biodegradation, on the other hand, is generally seen as a key feature in drug delivery, because many implanted or injectable drug delivery technologies are only effective in vivo for a limited term. The accumulation of residual polymer is reduced considerably when a biodegradable matrix is used, eliminating the need for further surgery for removal of implant (Dash & Cudworth, 1998). "Hydrolytic degradation," in which enzymes may also play a part, is the major process of the in vivo degradation of polymers used in drug delivery systems (Piskin, 1995). There are several parameters that affect the hydrolytic degradation of polymers in vivo, as described in Fig. 16.5. Therefore it is a very high complex phenomenon.

Biodegradable polymers, both synthetic and natural, are briefly discussed in drug delivery formulations and shown in Fig. 16.6.

Other natural polymers

Other polymers are derived from various natural sources, such as antibody, casein, alginate, dextran, cellulose, and starch, which have also been examined as carrier metrics for drug delivery systems. Biological refining of polymer surfaces is one of the new trends (Mano, 2007). Physical and chemical modification of polymer surfaces can significantly increase their bio-adaptability. Organic modification can be considered

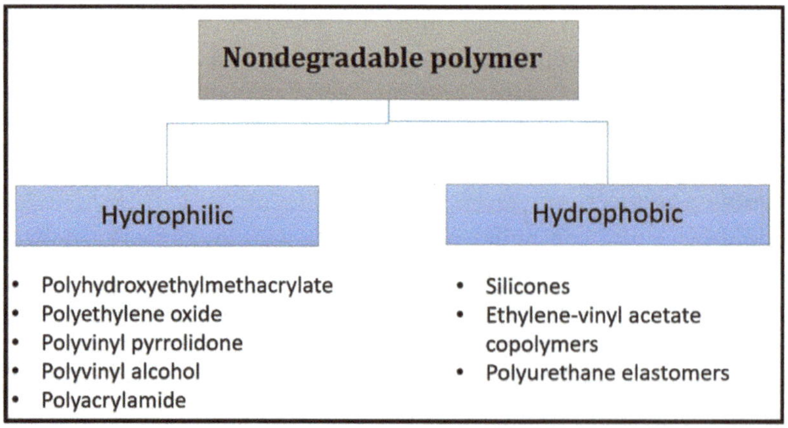

Figure 16.4 Major nondegradable polymers for drug delivery systems.

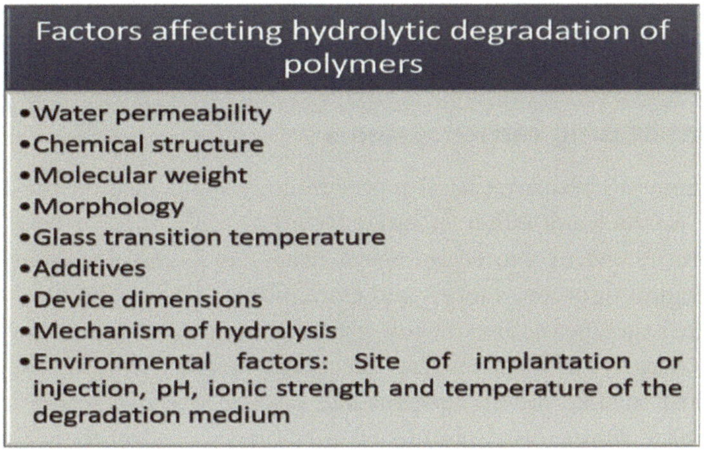

Figure 16.5 Important factors effective on hydrolytic degradation of polymers.

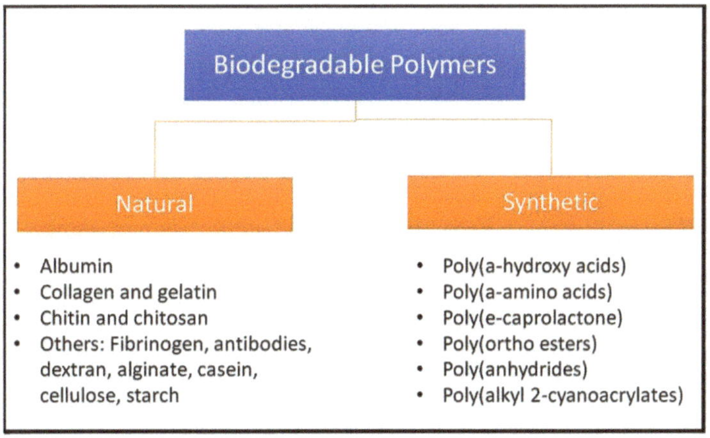

Figure 16.6 Major biodegradable polymeric biomaterials.

another step to improve their bio-adaptability and also add bio-functionality to the respective surfaces (El-Hadad, 2012).

Another important emerging trend is the manufacture of stimulant-responsive polymers. These polymers can be synthesized in the organic environment with the ability to react to biological, chemical, or physical signals. Therefore the release characteristics of these reactive systems can be better controlled, and, therefore, drugs can be delivered at in vivo at approximate release rates.

All of these emerging trends are in their infancy. However, given the significant improvements that have already been published, the most appealing path in the research and development of innovative drug delivery systems with superior in vivo performance is predicted to remain this way.

Development of drug carrier systems

There are roughly 30 pharmaceutical biotechnology medicines on the market today, and over 400 products are either in human clinical trials or have been approved by regulatory agencies. Many biotechnological drugs are being developed for diseases, such as neurological disorders, cancer, and cystic fibrosis (Bawa, 2008).

The potential therapeutic uses of this growing number of substances derived from biotechnology largely depend on the successful delivery to the sites and organs required by their suitable routes. Proteins and peptides are big, readily degraded, and easy to metabolize substances that mucosal membranes cannot easily absorb (Segura-Campos, 2011).

Peptide–protein drugs derived from biotechnology are available in approximately parenteral dosage forms, some of which are administered by the mucous membranes, and some problems are required to overcome the parenteral forms of peptides and proteins (Antosova et al., 2009). These problems are treated with manufacturing, processing, and sterilization. Alternative delivery routes, such as mouth, nose, buckle, anus, vagina, dermal, transdermal, and pulmonary, are being examined expeditiously.

Oral delivery

The most traditional path is oral administration, which is always the first option of patients. Administration of the drug by oral route can regulate blood levels, improve patient adherence, and reduce side effects, although oral delivery of proteins and peptides is available. The first pass effect, on the other hand, results in the inactivation of peptides and proteins by hepatic enzymes, as well as reduced mucosal absorption due to their large molecular size (Prasanna et al., 2012). There are a few ways to optimize protein and peptide oral intake. This can be summed up as follows:

- Protection of the molecule by enzyme inhibitors and by enteric coating.
- Improving the molecular uptake with lipid carriers.
- Increasing the absorption by enhancers.

Vaccines

Among the biotechnological products, vaccines are the second most popular products. They are being developed to prevent infectious diseases, such as herpes, influenza, hepatitis B, and more. Therapeutic vaccines have also been developed to treat cancer, psoriasis, peptic ulcer, rheumatoid arthritis, AIDS, and other diseases (Singh & O'Hagan, 1999). Traditional vaccines are made from organisms that inactivate or kill.

Traditional vaccinations are created from live organisms that have been attenuated or destroyed. Unlike traditional vaccines the new generation of vaccines can contain synthetic peptides, DNA, antigens, or recombinant DNA-derived antigens. Most of these novel vaccinations cause a poor immunological response, necessitating adjuvants (Ghattas et al., 2021).

Gene therapeutics

The recent use of genes as therapeutic agents implies that they have a lot of potential for treating disorders that are either inherited or acquired. Foreign DNA delivery and expression in eukaryotic cells is becoming increasingly significant, necessitating the use of effective carrier technologies (Han, 2000). The development of safe and effective synthetic nonviral gene delivery systems that shield RNA or DNA from nuclear breakdown and transport it to target cells is one of the primary difficulties in gene therapy. Increased translation or transcription can have negative consequences that can be mitigated with proper targeting. DNA must target the nucleus, and the cytoplasm must be targeted to reveal RNA. Thus large and heavily charged DNA and RNAs have to overcome many obstacles before reaching their target (Yu et al., 2020).

Recent research shows that innovative drug carrier systems can be used to deliver recombinant proteins—peptides, genes, and vaccines (Öner, 1998). Pharmaceutical researchers are striving to build carriers for these unique biological molecules that are safe, effective, and stable. More research is needed to hasten the release of many new biotechnology-derived therapeutic molecules.

Tissue engineering: the development of a novel composite bone substitute

Stem cells, such as induced pluripotent stem cells, embryonic stem cells, and mesenchymal stem cells, can all be used to regenerate tissue. Single stem cell transplantation into injured tissues demonstrated little therapeutic efficacy due to the restricted survivability and low regeneration activity of transplanted cells (Kwon et al., 2018).

A well-known traditional way of influencing the biological activity of stem cells "from within" is gene therapy using viral expression systems. Although, viral expression systems have been shown to trigger immunological and inflammatory responses in host tissues, and host DNA alterations may be present. As a result, nonviral expression systems with high efficiency are critical for stem cell research. Reprogramming or direct transformation of somatic cells utilizing a nonviral gene expression system, for example, has the potential to be used in clinical settings. It is possible to limit tumor growth by replacing the virus with exogenous drugs or delivery mechanisms. Electrophoreses of the cell membrane or gene delivery using liposomes or cationic polymers are examples of nonviral approaches. For the nonviral delivery of reprogramming factors into cells a number of nanoparticles have been produced (Hajj & Whitehead, 2017). Magnetic nanoparticles (MNPs), cationic polymer, chitosan, calcium phosphate, and mesoporous silica are used to make these nanoparticles. The graphene oxide–polyethylenemine combination has recently been reported as an efficient and safe route for mRNA delivery in somatic cells for direct reprogramming into induced neurons. As a result, employing nanoparticles to improve gene delivery efficiency could be highly advantageous for the direct conversion or reprogramming of somatic cells. Grafting or organ transplantation is not a new concept. In India the first skin grafting dates back to 3000 BCE (Ozhathil, 2021). However, the foundation of tissue engineering was laid by Dr. Ross in 1907 (Landecker, 2002). Ross studied the development of nerve fibers from fetal tissue. The first artificial kidney was made four decades later in 1948 (Murray et al., 1948). Although this was a failure, it envisioned the idea of tissue engineering for the production of prostheses. A number of studies on tissue assembly were published in the early 1950s and 1960s, laying the groundwork for today's regenerative medicine and tissue engineering. Tissue engineering can be defined as the process of replacing damaged tissue or organs with new tissue or working organs: There are three ways by which it can be achieved (Table 16.1).

The Inkjet Bioprinter was introduced in 2003. A bio-inkjet printer resembles a desktop printer, but instead of ink, it uses bioink in a cartridge (He et al., 2020). Bioinks are ECM materials that are printed in layers and stored in cells, such as hormones, growth factors, and fibrin (Góra, 2016). To store the cells, it also necessitates the use of computer-assisted software. Preprocessing, processing, and postprocessing are the three steps in the bioprinting process. Organ blueprints and tissues are computer produced during the preprocessing phase (Huang et al., 2017). Processing takes place after design. Cell layers are printed on the ECM using the bioprinter. The bioreactor is utilized for tissue maturation and differentiation in the final step. The growth factors essential for cell diversity (Derakhshanfar et al., 2018), the development of branched vascular networks where new blood vessels sprout with identical shape and biological function, and a lack of method are the key hurdles in 3D bioprinting. Three-dimensional printing technology provides the cell with more cells and mimics the indigenous microenvironment for tissue growth (Zhu et al., 2016).

Table 16.1 Three ways for tissue engineering.

1. Injecting specific growth factors, such as nerve growth factor, brain-derived neurotrophic factor, neutrophin-3, and recombinant human bone morphogenetic protein 2 as the differentiation marker
2. Damaged cells can be replaced with the new cells
3. Growing entire organ artificially in vitro

Recent nanocarrier approaches for targeted drug delivery in cancer therapy

Cancer is one of the most significant health concerns of the 21st century, and it has an uncontrollable spread that can damage any region of the body. Existing chemotherapy treatment options are associated with harmful effects on the immune system and other organs, as well as a lack of selectivity for tumors (Schirrmacher, 2019). Smart nanocarrier technologies for target-specific drug delivery against a range of cancers, including intracellular gene-specific targeting, have made steady progress over the last few decades. These nanocarriers are capable of recognizing and transporting tumor cells. Therapeutic agents, to a certain extent, do little or no harm to healthy cells. Nanosystems have prolonged retention in the blood, increasing their potency, improved bioavailability, and improved physicochemical properties (Navya et al., 2019). Many nanocarrier-based compositions have been developed and are being tested in clinical trials. Gold nanoparticles, carbon nanotubes, dendrites, liposomes, polymeric micelles, and other nanocarrier systems are among them. Quantum dots, metal–organic framework, and mesoporous silica nanoparticles are examples of recent advances in nanocarrier systems (Kenchegowda et al., 2021).

Nanoparticles employed in medical treatments often have a specified form, surface features, and size since these three factors have a significant impact on the efficiency of nanodrug delivery and, as a result, the treatment's success. Nanoparticles with a diameter of 10–100 nm are commonly used in cancer therapy because they can efficiently distribute drugs and have improved transparency and retention (EPR) effects (Sunderland, 2006). Polymer-based nanoparticles are another type of NP, the structural management of which is specific to medicine. Partition is formed by different monomers. The copolymerization of lactic acid and glycolic acid results in polylactic-*co*-glycolic acid (PLGA), a common polymeric NP. PLGA is commonly employed as a drug delivery carrier because of its strong bio-adaptability and biodegradability, as well as its EPR effect.

For drug delivery, MNPs, mainly metal or metal oxide nanoparticles, are utilized. To improve stability and bio-adaptability, organic substances, such as polymers and fatty acids, are commonly coated on magnetic NPs. In chemotherapy, they have been demonstrated to be very effective. Cancer treatment can be performed using gene therapy (Alfuraiji et al., 2021). In addition, magnetic hyperthermia using MNPs can achieve a thermal ablation of the tumor, offering alternative cancer treatments.

The development of immunotherapy has ushered in a new era of cancer treatment. NPs not only serve a significant role in the delivery of chemotherapy, but they also have a lot of potential in immunotherapy.

Various forms of NPs, including inorganic and organic nanoparticles, have already been employed in the clinical treatment of various cancers (Aghebati-Maleki et al., 2020).

Unlike conventional drugs, NP-based drug delivery systems are associated with better tumor targeting, stabilization, biocompatibility, and pharmacokinetics, as well as reducing systemic toxicity and overcoming drug resistance.

Hyperthermia, gene therapy, radiotherapy, targeted therapy, and chemotherapy can all benefit from NP-based drugs (Sharma et al., 2018). Different types of hybrid NPs have exhibited superior features for delivery and more attention as research has progressed. More research into the biological features of specific tumors will lead to more precise research guidelines for these medications. Furthermore, designing hybrid nanoparticles that are better suited to cancer therapy and designing NPs that target cancer cells using particular targeting opportunities merit additional investigation.

Conclusion

Recent studies have shown that recombinant genes, vaccines, proteins, and recombinant peptides have potential applications in new drug carrier systems. The challenge for pharmaceutical scientists is to create safe, stable, and effective carriers for these new organic molecules. The toxicity of nanocarriers, especially for quantum dots, is a significant impediment to the development of a successful antitumor drug delivery system. Research is still ongoing to reduce the toxicity of existing nanocarriers and to find advanced nanocarriers with low toxic profiles. The pharmaceutical sector spends a lot of money on research and development, but it is a development activity that is dominated by costs, notably in clinical trials that follow preclinical development. In short, the future of research and developments depends on adopting a comprehensive approach, which will include more actors and increasingly optimized solutions.

References

Abasian, P., Ghanavati, S., Rahebi, S., Khorasani, S., & Khalili, S. (2020). Polymeric nanocarriers in targeted drug delivery systems: A review. *Polymers for Advanced Technologies*, *31*(12), 2939–2954.

Aghebati-Maleki, A., Dolati, S., Ahmadi, M., Baghbanzhadeh, A., Asadi, M., Fotouhi, A., Yousefi, M., & Aghebati-Maleki, L. (2020). Nanoparticles and cancer therapy: Perspectives for application of nanoparticles in the treatment of cancers. *Journal of Cellular Physiology*, *235*(3), 1962–1972.

Alfuraiji, N., Hameed, R., & Kadhim, W. (2021). Application of Nano-particulate drug delivery systems to deliver therapeutic agents into cancer cells. *Karbala journal of medicine*, *14*(2), 2496–2512.

Anderson, W. F. (1984). Prospects for human gene therapy. *Science (New York, N.Y.)*, *226*(4673), 401–409.

Antosova, Z., Mackova, M., Kral, V., & Macek, T. (2009). Therapeutic application of peptides and proteins: Parenteral forever? *Trends in Biotechnology*, *27*(11), 628–635.

Arora, A., Fosfuri, A., & Gambardella, A. (2004). *Markets for technology: The economics of innovation and corporate strategy*. MIT Press.

Bawa, R. (2008). Nanoparticle-based therapeutics in humans: A survey. *Nanotechnology Law & Business*, *5*, 135.

Dash, A. K., & Cudworth, G. C. (1998). Therapeutic applications of implantable drug delivery systems. *Journal of Pharmacological and Toxicological Methods*, *40*(1), 1–12.

Derakhshanfar, S., Mbeleck, R., Xu, K., Zhang, X., Zhong, W., & Xing, M. (2018). 3D bioprinting for biomedical devices and tissue engineering: A review of recent trends and advances. *Bioactive Materials*, *3*(2), 144–156.

DiMasi, J. A., Ronald, W. H., & Henry, G. G. (2003). The price of innovation: New estimates of drug development costs. *Journal of Health Economics*, *22*(2), 151–185.

El-Hadad, A.A.-S. An approach to design new coatings for biomedical applications. (2012).

Fiegel, H. C., Kaufmann, P. M., Bruns, H., Kluth, D., Horch, R. E., Vacanti, J. P., & Kneser, U. (2008). Hepatic tissue engineering: From transplantation to customized cell-based liver directed therapies from the laboratory. *Journal of Cellular and Molecular Medicine*, *12*(1), 56–66.

Gatignon, H., & Xuereb, J.-M. (1997). Strategic orientation of the firm and new product performance. *Journal of Marketing Research*, *34*(1), 77–90.

Ghattas, M., Dwivedi, G., Lavertu, M., & Alameh, M. G. (2021). Vaccine technologies and platforms for infectious diseases: Current progress, challenges, and opportunities. *Vaccines*, *9*(12), 1490.

Góra, A. (2016). Tubular tissues and organs of human body—Challenges in regenerative medicine. *Journal of Nanoscience and Nanotechnology*, *16*(1), 19–39.

Hajj, K. A., & Whitehead, K. A. (2017). Tools for translation: Non-viral materials for therapeutic mRNA delivery. *Nature Reviews Materials*, *2*(10), 1–17.

Han, S.-o (2000). Development of biomaterials for gene therapy. *Molecular Therapy*, *2*(4), 302–317.

He, Y., Gu, Z., & Fu, J. (2020). Why choose 3D bioprinting? Part II: Methods and bioprinters. *Bio-Design And Manufacturing*, *3*(1), 1–4.

Huang, Y., Gao, G., Yonezawa, T., & Cui, X. (2017). 3D bioprinting and the current applications in tissue engineering. *Biotechnology Journal*, *12*(8), 1600734.

Ikada, Y. (2011). *Tissue engineering: Fundamentals and applications*. Elsevier.

Kenchegowda, M., Rahamathulla, M., Hani, U., Begum, M. Y., Guruswamy, S., Alshlowi, A., & Gowda, D. V. (2021). Smart nanocarriers as an emerging platform for cancer therapy: A review. *Molecules (Basel, Switzerland)*, *27*(1), 146.

Kim, J. K., Kim, H. J., Chung, J. Y., Lee, J. H., & Young, S. B. (2014). Natural and synthetic biomaterials for controlled drug delivery. *Archives of Pharmacal Research*, *37*(1), 60–68.

Kwon, S. G., Kwon, Y. W., Lee, T. W., Park, G. T., & Kim, J. H. (2018). Recent advances in stem cell therapeutics and tissue engineering strategies. *Biomaterials Research*, *22*(1), 1–8.

Landecker, H. (2002). New times for biology: Nerve cultures and the advent of cellular life in vitro. *Studies in History and Philosophy of Science Part C: Studies in History and Philosophy of Biological and Biomedical Sciences*, *33*(4), 667–694.

Logothetidis, S. (2012). *Nanomedicine: The medicine of tomorrow. Nanomedicine and Nanobiotechnology* (pp. 1–26). Berlin, Heidelberg: Springer.

Mano, J. F. (2007). Natural origin biodegradable systems in tissue engineering and regenerative medicine: Present status and some moving trends. *Journal of the Royal Society Interface*, *4*(17), 999–1030.

Murray, G., Delorme, E., & Thomas, N. (1948). Artificial kidney. *Journal of the American Medical Association*, *137*(18), 1596–1599.

Navya, P. N., Kaphle, A., Srinivas, S. P., Bhargava, S. K., Rotello, V. M., & Daima, H. K. (2019). Current trends and challenges in cancer management and therapy using designer nanomaterials. *Nano Convergence*, *6*(1), 1–30.

Öner, F. (1998). *Drug carrier systems for biotechnology derived products. Biomedical science and technology* (pp. 97–108). Boston, MA: Springer.

Ozhathil, D. K. (2021). A narrative review of the history of skin grafting in burn care. *Medicina*, *57*(4), 380.

Piskin, E. (1995). Biodegradable polymers as biomaterials. *Journal of Biomaterials Science, Polymer Edition*, *6*(9), 775–795.

Prasanna, J., Lakshmi, B., Deepthi., & Rama Rao, N. (2012). Rectal drug delivery: A promising route for enhancing drug absorption. *Asian Journal of Research in Pharmaceutical Science*, *2*(4), 143–149.

Schirrmacher, V. (2019). From chemotherapy to biological therapy: A review of novel concepts to reduce the side effects of systemic cancer treatment. *International Journal of Oncology*, *54*(2), 407–419.

Segura-Campos, M. (2011). Bioavailability of bioactive peptides. *Food Reviews International*, *27*(3), 213–226.

Sharma, A., Amit, K. G., & Rath, G. (2018). Recent advances in metal nanoparticles in cancer therapy. *Journal of Drug Targeting*, *26*(8), 617–632.

Singh, M., & O'Hagan, D. (1999). Advances in vaccine adjuvants. *Nature Biotechnology*, *17*(11), 1075–1081.

Srivastava, A., Yadav, T., Sharma, S., Nayak, A., & Mishra, N. (2015). Polymers in drug delivery. *Journal of Biosciences and Medicines*, *4*(1), 69–84.

Taylor, D. (2015). The pharmaceutical industry and the future of drug development. 1–33.

Sunderland, C. J. (2006). Targeted nanoparticles for detecting and treating cancer. *Drug Development Research*, *67*(1), 70–93.

Tibbitt, M. W., Dahlman, J. E., & Langer, R. (2016). Emerging frontiers in drug delivery. *Journal of the American Chemical Society*, *138*(3), 704–717.

Verma, R. K., & Garg, S. (2001). Drug delivery technologies and future directions. *Pharmaceutical Technology*, *25*(2), 1–14.

Yu, A.-M., Choi, Y. H., & Tu, M.-J. (2020). RNA drugs and RNA targets for small molecules: Principles, progress, and challenges. *Pharmacological Reviews*, *72*(4), 862–898.

Zhu, W., et al. (2016). 3D printing of functional biomaterials for tissue engineering. *Current Opinion in Biotechnology*, *40*, 103–112.

CHAPTER 17

Strategies to synthesize, advantages, and disadvantages of pharmaceutical nanoparticles

A Inobeme[1], CO Adetunji[2], M Maliki[1], BI Onyeachu[1], T Kelani[1], CA Eziukwu[1], E Olori[1], JT Mathew[3] and MO Bamigboye[4]

[1]Department of Chemistry, Edo State University Uzairue, Edo State, Nigeria
[2]Applied Microbiology, Biotechnology and Nanotechnology Laboratory, Department of Microbiology, Edo State University Uzairue, Edo State, Nigeria
[3]Department of Chemistry, Ibrahim Badamasi Babangida University, Lapai, Niger State, Nigeria
[4]Department of Chemical Sciences, Kings University, Odeomu, Osun State, Nigeria

Introduction

The health sector has grown enormously and continues to expand. As a result of the increasing demands, the pharmaceutical industries therefore continually respond to these rising needs through the introduction and advancement of various technologies. As the level of complexities and toxicity of drugs continue to increase, new approaches are required for efficient drug delivery that would aid in the transport of these drugs to the targeted sites. Novel methods are therefore being introduced, and one of the prominent is the pharmaceutical nanotechnology (Soares et al., 2018). Nanotechnology is a fast-advancing field that involves the production and utilization of nanosized materials that is materials that measure in nanometers. Nanotechnology involves the characterization, manipulation, and organization of matter in a systematic way at the nanoscale level. Pharmaceutical nanomaterials include various smart drugs that show their activity only when they get to the targeted site (Prestinaci et al., 2015). Pharmaceutical nanotechnology is made of two major components: the first is nanomaterials, while the other is nanodevices. The various pharmaceutical nanomaterials are produced from biomaterials that have different applications in various products. The surfaces of these nanoparticles (NPs) could be modified using various groups or suitable coatings so as to enhance their biocompatibility. The nanomaterials are further grouped into nanostructure and nanocrystalline materials. The sizes of nanocrystals could be reduced through the process of grinding using some specialized mills making it possible to use the resulting drugs as inhalers, nanosuspensions, and for intravenous application in solutions. Their small sizes enhance the surface area and bioavailability of various insoluble pharmaceuticals. The nanostructured are the nanomaterials in their

Nanotechnology for Drug Delivery and Pharmaceuticals
DOI: https://doi.org/10.1016/B978-0-323-95325-2.00006-7

processed form, which highly specialized functions and shape. Some of these include carbon nanotubes, quantum dots, fullerenes and dendrimers (Jeevanandam et al., 2018). There are various novel drugs that have been developed based on pharmaceutical nanomaterials that discharge antibiotics whenever they notice infections. This technique provides novel and remarkable tools, scopes, and avenues in therapeutic and diagnosis. This is now fully established as a novel area of drug delivery, prognosis, diagnosis, and treatment of various diseases that involve the utilization of various nanoengineered tools. The application of nanotechnology in the pharmaceutical field makes it possible for improved as fast treatments of various diseases. The usage of pharmaceutical nanotechnology makes it possible for the delivery of drugs with a remarkable level of precision and accuracy and highly minimized side effects (Dhand et al., 2015). This has also paved way for the early detection of various diseases. It is a highly challenging task developing a reliable drug delivery system that can optimize the pharmaceutical activity of the drugs while eliminating the side effects of the drugs. It is possible to control this challenging task through the use of various pharmaceutical nanomaterials. Pharmaceutical NPs (PNPs) are widely employed in drug delivery where they can improve the solubility of the drugs and could additionally bring about a moderated discharge of drugs. They have therefore been used for anticancer treatments, vaccine delivery, gene delivery, miniature nanodevices amongst others (Singh et al., 2017).

This chapter discusses the types and synthesis of PNPs, advantages, and disadvantages of the synthetic processes. Some of the areas of application of PNPs are also highlighted. Also, the roles and features of PNPs in drug delivery are further emphasized. Fig. 17.1 summarizes the scope of this chapter.

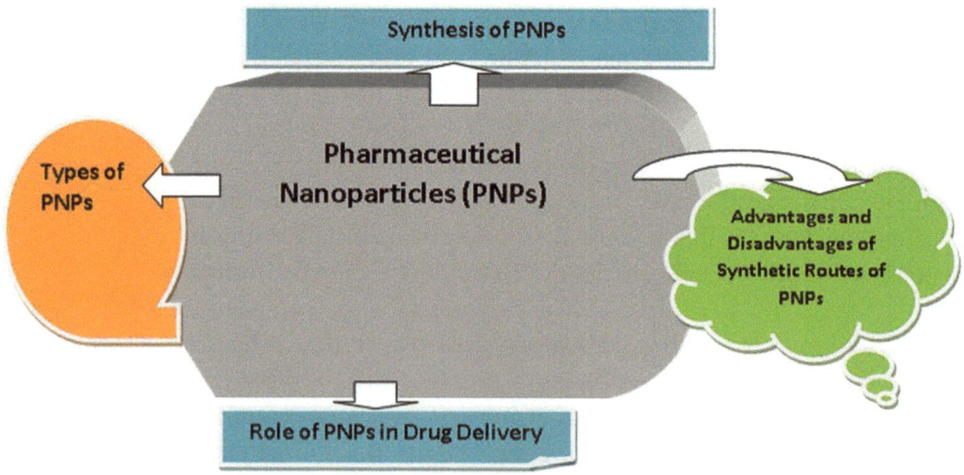

Figure 17.1 Synthesis, advantages, and applications of PNPs. *PNPs*, Pharmaceutical nanoparticles.

Pharmaceutical nanoparticles-based drug designing and drug delivery process and mechanism

Types of pharmaceutical nanoparticles

Polymeric micelles

These are produced from molecules that are spontaneous or amphiphilic surfactants. A micelle has an inner core that is hydrophobic in nature and surrounded by a covering of polymers that are hydrophilic. Their highly hydrophobic core acts as a suitable reservoir for drugs that are poorly soluble in water. Their hydrophilic shells also aid in the stabilization of the core. There are several drug molecules that have been introduced into polymeric micelles (Hanafy et al., 2018).

Hydrogel nanoparticles

Hydrogel NPs have gained remarkable attention more recently. They are one of the most prominent PNPs known for drug delivery. They are hydrophilic polymers with networks that are cross-linked. They are capable of absorbing and retaining more than 20% of their weight in water and maintaining a unique 3D structure of the polymer. Alteration of various physiological features can be used in the control of permeability, swelling properties, network structure, and mechanical stability of the hydrogels. They have been investigated comprehensively for the controlled discharge of therapeutics (Pavlovic et al., 2018).

Superparamagnetic nanoparticles

Magnetic NPs have been put forward as reliable drug carriers with a shift toward clinical assessment. The properties of iron (III) oxide could be utilized for guiding microcapsules in place for release through external magnetic field. Metallic NPs also have the advantage in that they can be heated on internalization, a phenomenon known as hyperthermia effect. Aside their uses for raising temperature and targeted discharge, they can also be used for affecting the permeability of microcapsules through the introduction of external field (Wu et al., 2014).

Ceramic nanoparticles

These are fabricated from inorganic compounds having porous properties, such as titania, alumina, and silica. They have attracted serious attention more recently due to their biocompatibility and the ease of synthesizing them together with their surface modification. These NPs are also known to show remarkable applicability in various fields (Wu et al., 2014).

Carbon-based pharmaceutical nanoparticles

These have gained much attention due to their ease of surface functionalization for the purpose of grafting nucleic acids, proteins, and peptides. Fullerene, carbon nanotubes, and nanodiamonds have been reported in this regard for the purpose of drug delivery. Multiwalled and single-wall nanotubes have become much appealing in the aspect of delivery due to their geometry, size, and surface properties (Whitlow et al., 2017).

Integrated nanocomposites

These involve the combination of various nanomaterials, taking advantage of their unique properties for the fabrication of novel NPs. Polymeric NPs and liposomes have been combined in this regard. Also, dendrimers and liposomes have also been combined giving rise to outstanding results (Debnath & Srivastava, 2021).

Liposomes

These are artificial vehicles that are self-assembled formulated from phospholipid that are amphiphilic. Such vehicles are made up of spherical bilayer structures that surround an aqueous core domain, and their sizes usually vary from 50 nm to micrometers. Liposomes have biological properties that are highly attractive such include among others, their biocompatibility, biodegradability, and its potential in entrapping both hydrophilic and hydrophobic. Other alteration of the nature of surface could be achieved through surface modification. The liposomes are the system of drug delivery that are most established clinically.

Polymeric nanoparticles

They are colloidal particles that have sizes that range from 10 to 1000 nm and could be branched, core shell structure, or spherical in shape. The nanomaterials have been produced through the use of synthetic polymers that are biodegradable. Examples of such synthetic polymeric materials that are employed for their fabrication include polyacrylates, polylactide, and polycaprolactone. There are other naturally occurring polymers that include alginate, chitosan, gelatin, and albumin. This kind of NPs has been synthesized through various methods that include solvent diffusion, emulsification, utilization of supercritical carbon dioxide, and polymerization. Recent advancement in the field of polymer science has further resulted in the fabrication of smart polymeric materials.

Polymer drug conjugates

There are various polymer drugs conjugates that have been formulated. The conjugation of large molecular polymers with drugs can bring about a remarkable improvement of the circulation of blood. Drugs that are based on protein peptides are easily digested within the body of humans (Debnath & Srivastava, 2021).

Synthesis of pharmaceutical nanomaterials, advantages, and disadvantages

There are various strategies that have been employed for the synthesis of PNPs. There are two major synthetic approaches that are the top-down and bottom-up strategies. The top-down approach involves milling, repeated quenching, and lithography. This method, however, does not have a reliable control of the structure and particle sizes of the NPs. The top-down approach for the synthesis of NPs is not good for samples that are soft. Also, it is expensive. It is also not suitable for a large scale production but good for laboratory experimentation. The bottom up is one of the most commonly employed approach used by scientists for the synthesis of NPs, and this involves the building up of the material from beneath: that is, cluster by cluster, molecule by molecule and atom by atom. There are various approaches for the production of nanoscale pharmaceutical nanomaterials that contribute to the improvement of relatively novel and poorly explored area of study. Several methods have been employed for the synthesis of PNPs. Basically, they are grouped into physical, chemical, and biological approaches (Whitlow et al., 2017). The various methods for the synthesis of PNPs are summarized in Fig. 17.2. Table 17.1 provides the features and advantages of some of the methods.

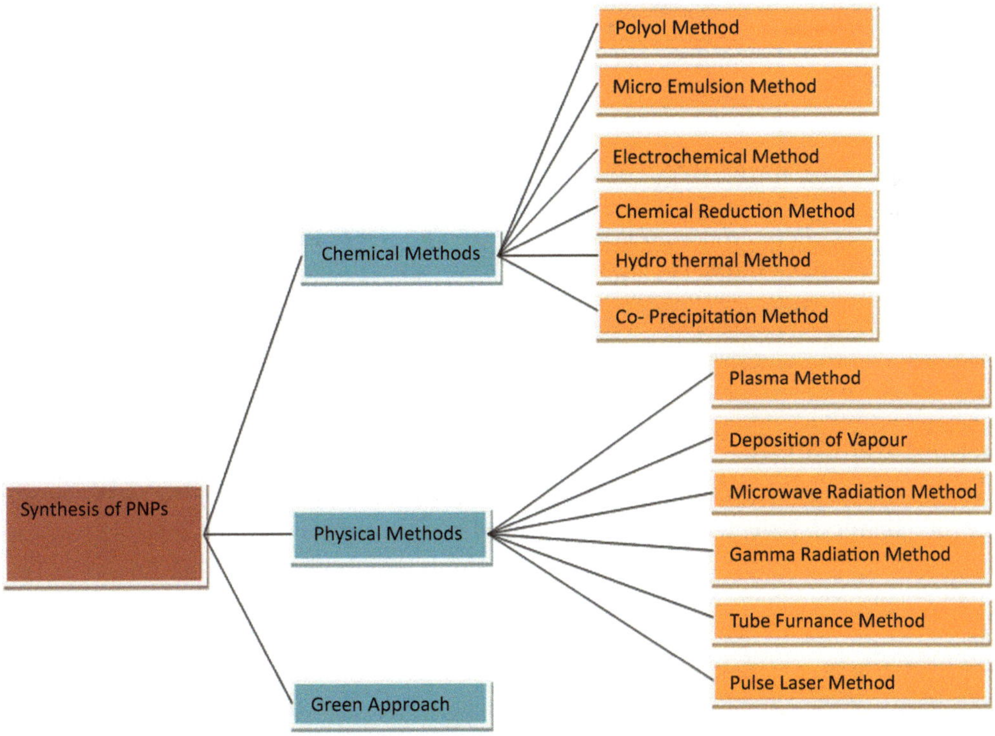

Figure 17.2 Methods for the synthesis of pharmaceutical nanoparticles.

Table 17.1 Methods for synthesis of pharmaceutical nanoparticles, features, and advantages.

Methods	Features	Advantages
Chemical methods		
1 Polyol method	Makes use of a nonaqueous liquid known as polyol as the solvent and reducing agent	Efficient in the minimization of agglomeration and surface oxidation
2 Microemulsion method	Involves the combination of two microemulsions containing a reducing agent and a metal salt	Permits flexibility with regards to texture, shape, and size control in the nanoparticle
3 Electrochemical method	Involves the use of electrochemical cells	There is a high possibility of accurately tuning the desired potential
4 Sonochemical method	This reaction occurs in the presence or absence of organic additives	Presence of organic stabilizer such as citric acid enhance the efficient control of the sizes of nanoparticle formed
Deposition of chemical vapor	Involves volatile precursor, during which the substrate is allowed to come in contact with the precursors	Suitable for the synthesis of ultrafine particles that are less than 1 μm
Physical methods		
5 Microwave irradiation	Synthesis of various inorganic, organic, and organic–inorganic blends	Improved purity, faster rates of reactions, ease of work, and higher yields
6 Pulsed laser method	Used for the synthesis of silver nanoparticles	There is complete absence of chemicals
7 Gamma radiation	It is efficient for the control of shape, overall yield of the nanoparticle	It is simple to execute and use precursors that do not constitute harm
8 Biosynthesis	It involves the use of plant materials, microorganisms, bacteria, algae amongst other as essential substrates	Involves the utilization of safe, nontoxic, and environmentally friendly materials

Chemical methods

There are various chemical pathways for the synthesis of various PNPs, involving the use of chemical reductants in solvents. Some of the prominent chemical methods include polyol method, photochemical method, electrochemical method, radiolytic method, and sonochemical method.

Polyol method

This is one of the chemical methods for the synthesis of NP. It makes use of a nonaqueous liquid known as polyol as the solvent as well as reducing agent. The use of these nonaqueous solvents has the advantage of helping in the minimization of agglomeration and surface oxidation. This method permits flexibility with regards to texture, shape, and size control in the NP. This approach also has the advantage of enhancing the production of NPs in a large scale. The most commonly employed solvent in the polyol method for the synthesis of metallic oxide is ethylene glycol due to its remarkable reducing potential, high boiling point, and dielectric constant. The ethylene glycol plays the role of a cross-linking agent for linkage with metal ions so as to form metal glycolate resulting to oligomerization. Polyol synthetic process could also be employed in the synthesis of core shell NPs and bimetallic alloys (Afolalu et al., 2019).

Microemulsion approach

This is widely employed in the production of inorganic NPs. When water and oil are combined, they do not form a single liquid but rather separate into two different phases. There is, therefore, the need for energy so as to ensure the mixing of the two phases for the formation of water–oil. The synthesis of metallic NPs in oil–water emulsion basically involves the combination of two microemulsions containing a reducing agent and a metal salt. There is a formation of Brownian motion after the collision between the different micelles on mixing the different microemulsion. The sizes and morphology of the NPs produced using this method is depended on the shape and size of the nano droplets and the nature of the surfactant. The surfactant is useful for the stabilization of the NP. One of the major disadvantages of this method is that it involves the use of toxic organic solvents (Cele, 2019).

Electrochemical method

This is the production of chemical substances through the use of an electrochemical cell. The major merit of using this approach over the conventional chemical method is the possibility of accurately tuning the desired potential. Various types of counter electrodes have been employed for studying the impact of varying electrochemical parameters on the final particle sizes. Silver NPs have been synthesized through the electroreduction of the anodically solved ions of silver in acetonitrile. The preparation of silver NPs using silver powder and aqueous solutions in electrochemical method has been well documented (Dhand et al., 2015).

Chemical reduction

This is one of the most common approaches for the synthesis of PNPs. It involves the use of various inorganic and organic reducing agents. Some of the reducing agents include elemental hydrogen, tollen reagents, poly ethylene glycol, sodium borohydride, and sodium citrate. The reducing agents have the potential of converting metallic ions into their corresponding metal NP. The reduced specie is then converted into agglomerated clusters (Afolalu et al., 2019).

Hydrothermal method

This is a chemical-based method. This synthesis involves a broad range of temperature from room to high temperature for the production of NP. It has numerous advantages when compared to physical and chemical methods. The NPs produced could be unstable when temperature is very high (Cele, 2019).

Coprecipitation method

This is a wet process. It is also known as solvent displacement approach. The polymer phase can be natural or synthetic. The polymer solvents employed are hexane, acetone and ethanol, and nonsolvent polymers. The NPs are synthesized through a rapid diffusion of the polymer solvent into the nonsolvent polymer through mixing of the polymeric solution.

Sonochemical method

This occurs through the sonochemical reduction of the corresponding metal ions. This reaction occurs in the presence or absence of organic additives. The rate of reduction is used for the control of the shape and sizes of the particles. Presence of organic stabilizer such as citric acid also helped in the control of the sizes of NP formed (Dhand et al., 2015).

Physical methods

Plasma methods

This involves the generation of the plasma through a radio frequency heat releasing coils. In this process, the original metal is embedded in a pestle and then the pestle embedded in a chamber that is evacuated. Heating of the metal above its point of evaporation is then carried out using a high-voltage coil. The gas use during this step is helium, which generate plasma of very high temperature within the regions of the coils after it has passed through the system (Cele, 2019).

Deposition of chemical vapor

This involves more than one chemical steps. This approach is mostly employed in the manufacturing of semiconductor for the deposition of thin films of various materials. This approach involves volatile precursor, during which the substrate is allowed to come in contact with the precursors. There three major steps that are involved in chemical vapor deposition approach. The first is the transport of the reactants on the growth surface through a boundary layer, a chemical reaction then take place on the growth surface. The by-products that are produced by the gas phase chemical process are then removed from the surface. The approach can be used for the synthesis of ultrafine particles that are less than 1 μm.

Microwave irradiation

This approach has been widely employed in the synthesis of various inorganic, organic, and organic–inorganic blends since it has several advantages over the traditional route of synthesis. The microwave-induced organic synthesis has been utilized widely as a result of various advantages which include improved purity, faster rates of reactions, ease of work, and higher yields (Dhand et al., 2015).

Pulsed laser method

This is commonly used for the synthesis of silver NPs. In this process a solution of silver nitrate and a reducing agent are poured into a device that looks like blender. The device is made of a solid disk that rotates with the aqueous solution. The hot spots are the portions where the reaction between reducing agent and silver nitrate take place. The control of the particle size is achieved by the presence of energy from the laser together with angular speed of the disk. The laser ablation approach has advantage over other methods during the production of the metal colloids as a result of the complete absence of chemicals. This makes it easy for the preparation of uncontaminated and pure metal colloids (Cele, 2019).

Gamma radiation

This method is very suitable for different metallic NPs. It is efficient for the control of shape, overall yield of the NP, cheap, simple to execute and use precursors that do not constitute harm. The process involves the utilization of the least number of chemical reagents when compared to the conventional approach. The reaction temperature employed in this method is close to room temperature with very few synthetic steps. Also, the number of by-products released is few.

Evaporation–condensation method

This is a vital physical approach for the synthesis of pharmaceutical NPs. This approach has certain advantages such as homogeneity in distribution of the NPs, the lack of solvent contamination in the thin film prepared amongst others.

Tube furnace method

This physical approach has some disadvantage for instance; the furnace is capable of occupying a big space, used up large amount of energy and brings about a rise in the temperature within the environment. For thermal stability to be attained a lot of time is also needed.

Green route for the biosynthesis of nanoparticles

The biosynthesis of NPs must be environmentally friendly and economically feasible with respect to cost. The best approach in the synthesis of nanomaterials in this regard is green chemistry pathway that involves the utilization of safe, nontoxic, and environmentally friendly materials. There are various methods for the extraction of the NP from its sources, which are depended on the nature of the protocol employed. The term phytomining is employ for the usage of a plant that has hyperaccumulating potential for the extraction of a metal from the biomass. Such plants have physiological processes and mechanisms that help in the regulation of the concentration of the solution of the metal. In biological method, the extracts from some living organisms act as both capping and reducing agent in the production of the NP. The reduction of the metallic ions take place through the combination of the biomolecules that are present in these extracts, such as amino acids, enzymes, polysaccharide, vitamins, and proteins, which are diverse and chemically complex. The successful synthesis of various nanomaterials using bioorganic molecules has been well documented (Zare et al., 2021). The biological methods are considered to be environmentally friendly, sustainable, cost effective, and safer for the production of NPs. Biosynthesis of PNPs has been achieved using extracts from various plants, such as *Aloe vera*, *Cinnamomum camphora*, *Emblica officinalis*, alfalfa, *Tamarindus indica*, and lemon grass. The green synthetic method of the synthesis of NPs has more advantages when compared to the traditional chemical methods in which it is cost-effective, environmentally friendly, and simple to execute. The biosynthesis of nanomaterials can be grouped into inorganic, organic, and hybrid. Most of the large molecules involved are able to form the NPs based on the treatment of samples and conditions within the environment (Debnath & Srivastava, 2021).

Various studies have already documented the synthesis of various PNPs through the use of green synthesis. Various organisms, such as fungi, yeast, bacteria, algae, yeast, and higher plants, have also been used. Green NPs could be prepared from complex molecular mixtures, proteins, carbohydrates, deoxyribonucleic acids, lipids amongst others. After the lysis of cells, the treatment of the samples could include many approaches basically employed for the fractioning of cells, including the use of salts, solvents, chaotropic agents, and homogenization in the presence of various surfactants. Inorganic bionanoparticles could be grouped into metallic and oxides. The synthesis of inorganic NPs is induced using unspecific reducing agents that are found in the medium. In hybrid green NPs, the production is propelled by various molecular precausors in the presence of some biological agents such as proteins and DNA. The use of biological templates proffers the advantages in which it provides a large diversity of three-dimensional biological structures that are available for the synthesis of the bionanoparticles (Whitlow et al., 2017).

Applications of pharmaceutical nanoparticles

PNPs have remarkable applications that have continually increased with advancement in nanotechnology. Some of the areas of application are discussed:

Chemotherapy

The conventional approach of treating cancer patients through the use of nanotechnology has saved numerous lives. These treatments, however, have their inherent side effects that are connected to the nonspecificity of the chemical substances employed. Cancer is a complex biological phenomena since the affected cells have the tendencies of rapidly dividing beyond control. The primary aim of the more recent chemotherapy is the destruction of the rapidly growing cells concerned. This approach, however, also results to the death of some other rapidly growing cells that are not cancerous hence giving rise to threatening side effects. The advancement in the aspect of PNPs has given rise to a more reliable approach. With PNPs that are smartly developed, it is possible to achieve a targeted delivery of the drugs at the affected site. Several kinds of NPs have given promising results in this regard for more efficient treatment of cancers. One of the prominent is carbon nanotube (Debnath & Srivastava, 2021).

Diagnosis and testing

PNPs are useful in the area of diagnosis. The current approaches of diagnosis and testing are restricted by the nonavailability of fluorescent markers as well as the fluorescent fading after single application. These disadvantages have been overcome through the use of fluorescent NPs. The discovery of quantum dots has further enhanced this area of diagnosis. More recently, the introduction of theranostic NPs has proven useful in the treatment and diagnosis of more serious diseases. This involves the use of drug dendrimers, drug conjugates, surfactant aggregates, carbon nanotubes, and core shells (Whitlow et al., 2017).

Treatment of HIV and AIDS

The traditional treatment of HIV and AIDs involve the administration of over 30–40 pills on daily basis. More recent advancements have been achieved through pharmaceutical nanotechnology. This has helped in the reduction of pill counts to just a few days. The development of polymeric nanomaterials that have the potential of delivering antiretroviral (ARV) drugs through intracellular means has contributed greatly to the treatment. Nanotechnology has played an indispensable role in the delivery of ARV drugs and improvement of compliance.

Nutraceutical delivery

Advancement in nanotechnology has improved the area of nutraceuticals. A larger proportion of the known nutraceuticals are lipophilic and, therefore, less soluble in water. This poses a serious limitation to their bioavailability and distribution within the biological systems. NPs have enhanced the dissolution and efficient bioavailability of these compounds. Most of the recent studies in this dimension have been targeted toward improving the dissolution processes of nutraceuticals through the formulation of NPs (Cabral et al., 2018).

The role of pharmaceutical nanoparticles in drug delivery formulations

There are numerous reasons why the utilization of NPs in the area of diagnosis and drug delivery becomes indispensable. One of the prominent reasons is the fact that the conventional drugs that are available for intravenous and oral passages are not usually produced as optimum preparations for each of the available products. Products such as those that contain nucleic acids and proteins need a more innovative and reliable kind of carrier mechanism so as to improve their effectiveness as well as ensuring they are protected from undesired biodegradation. It has been well established that the effectiveness of most systems of drug delivery is remarkably depended on the sizes of the particles aside those that are used intravenously in liquid forms. Drugs in the form of NPs have improved solubility and higher bioavailability due to their small sizes and resulting larger surface area (Zare et al., 2021). This unique physicochemical property therefore makes it easier for such drugs to pass through the blood—brain barrier (BBB) and cross through the blood systems and be taken into the tiny pathways of the dermal endothelial cells. More importantly, pharmaceutical nanomaterials that are produced from synthetic and natural polymers have gained remarkable attention due to the ease in customizing them for targeted drug delivery, controlled discharges of drugs from a unit dosage, and enhanced bioavailability of the drugs. Also, the formulation of novel systems of drug delivery has provided more advantages for the growth of commercialized pharmaceuticals. New formulations of previously existing drugs are therefore developed by various pharmaceutical industries. Such developments will further enhance the advancement of various intellectual properties from such companies. Pharmaceutical nanotechnology has further given enviable meaning to various drugs that were previously considered not to be of commercial values as a result of bioavailability and solubility (Debnath & Srivastava, 2021).

Features of pharmaceutical nanoparticles-based drug delivery

PNPs have several advantages in the area of drug delivery, which include: enhancing the stability of drugs that are hydrophobic in nature; inducing the solubility of drugs that are insoluble in aqueous media thereby making them suitable for efficient administration; improving pharmacokinetics and improved biodistribution of drugs; minimizing deleterious effects due to enhance accumulation of targeted sites; and decreasing toxicity due to the use of nanomaterials that are compatible with biological systems. It is paramount to comprehend the mechanism through which the body system manages exogenous matter for a proper understanding of the properties of drug delivery processes based on PNPs (Whitlow et al., 2017). There are three major pathways through which nanomaterials can get into the body systems. These include oral administration, inhalation, and direct intravenous administration. Once they get into the circulatory system, there is protein—particle interaction that is the first process that occurs prior to the dispersion of these materials to various organs. Once a material is identified to be foreign, such as engulfed by macrophages and passed out of the system. This is the major batter with drug delivery based on nanomaterials (Gaur et al., 2021). The removal is affected by the surface features and sizes of the particles involved. Some of the characteristics are discussed:

Size of pharmaceutical nanoparticle

The sizes and shapes of various pharmaceutical nanomaterials determine how they are viewed by cells within the body, which in turn affects their distribution pattern, targeting potential, and biotoxicity. With the introduction of PNPs, it becomes possible for such nanomaterials to pass through the BBB thus making a provision for enhanced drug delivery for illnesses that were difficult to handle previously. The introduction of PNPs also makes it possible to regulate the drug delivery processes. It is reported that 100-nm nanomaterials can show about 2.5 times ease of uptake in comparison to 1-um diameter particle. There is increase in the surface area to volume ratio as a particle gets smaller. This therefore implies a larger amount of the drugs get closer to the top of the particle when compared to bigger molecules, thereby bringing about an efficient delivery of drugs (Ansari et al., 2016).

Surface characteristics

Ideal systems of PNPs for drug delivery can be effectively enhanced through the manipulation of the surface properties. The introduction of suitable ligands, reactivity, and curvature of surface is vital in controlling aggregation, binding of receptor, stability as well as the pharmacological functioning of the drugs. As a result of the ease of the lymphatic system in recognizing PNPs, they are subjected to the natural immune systems of the body. The higher the hydrophobic nature of a nanomaterial, the higher the tendency for it to be removed due to the enhanced binding of blood components. Since the hydrophobic PNPs are easily removed, making their surfaces hydrophilic in nature could therefore enhance their duration of circulation. The creation of polymeric complexes further aid in addressing the issue of clearance but one issue of concern remains aggregation when it comes to small particles as a result of their larger surface area. Pharmaceutical nanomaterials that are more prone to aggregation include micelles, quantum dots, and dendrimers. Different techniques have therefore been put in place for the prevention of aggregation, such as coating of the NPs, alteration of their surface chargers, and the introduction of capping agents (Cabral et al., 2018).

Loading and discharge of nanoparticles

The efficient release of drugs in their nanoforms to the targeted tissue is of immense concern. Their release from formulations based on NPs is depended on various factors that include overall solubility, pH, desorption of drugs, and temperature. The release of the drugs varies depending on the nature of the NP that is used. The polymeric nanomaterial produced is either nanosphere or nanocapsules depending on their makeup. The nanospheres are uniform systems in which the polymeric chains are put together in similar pattern to the surfactant in the formation of the micelle. Nanocapsules on the other hand are heterogenous system in which the drug is inside a reservoir made of polymers (Ansari et al., 2016).

Conclusion

PNPs have attracted remarkable interest as a result of their unique physical and chemical properties. Various methods of synthesis have been put forward giving rise to various desired shapes and sizes. The synthesis of NP is affected by various factors, such as pore size, temperature, time, pressure, shape and sizes of particles, and cost of production. There are three major methods of synthesis, which are physical, chemical, and biological. The green synthesis is the most environmentally friendly and economically feasible approach for the synthesis of PNP. However, the choice of the solvent medium and the selection of a nontoxic stabilizing and reducing agent are the paramount issues that must be taken into consideration in the green synthesis of PNPs. The various approaches in the synthesis of PNPs have been well discussed as well as some of their advantages and disadvantages. This review work has made it evident that the application of pharmaceutical nanomaterials cannot be overemphasized most especially in the area of drug delivery.

References

Afolalu, S., Soetan, S. B., Ongbali, S. O., Abioye, A. A., & Oni, A. S. (2019). Morphological characterization and physio-chemical properties of nanoparticle—Review. In: *Proceedings of the IOP conference series: materials science and engineering*, *640*, 012065.

Ansari, S., Satar, R., Jafri, A., Rasool, M., Ahmad, W., & Zaidi, S. (2016). Nanodiamonds in drug delivery and stem cell therapy. *Iranian Journal of Biotechnology*, *14*(3), e1320. Available from https://doi.org/10.15171/ijb.1320.

Cabral, H., Miyata, K., Osada, K., & Kataoka, K. (2018). Block copolymer micelles in nanomedicine applications. *Chemical Reviews*, *2018*(118), 6844−6892, 14.

Cele, T. (2019). Preparation of nanoparticles. *Open Access Peer-Reviewed Chapter*. Available from https://doi.org/10.5772/intechopen.90771.

Debnath, S., & Srivastava, R. (2021). *Drug delivery with carbon-based nanomaterials as versatile nanocarriers: Progress and prospects*. Available from https://doi.org/10.3389/fnano.2021.644564.

Dhand, C., Dwivedi, N., Loh, X., & Ramakrishna, S. (2015). Methods and strategies for the synthesis of diverse nanoparticles and their applications: A comprehensive overview. *RSC Advances*, *5*(127). Available from https://doi.org/10.1039/C5RA19388E.

Gaur, M., Misra, C., Bihari, A., Swaroop, S., Maolmhuaidh, O., & Barhourm, A. (2021). Biomedical applications of carbon nanomaterials: Fullerenes, quantum dots, nanotubes, nanofibers, and graphene. *Materials (Basel)*, *14*(20), 5978. Available from https://doi.org/10.3390/ma14205978.

Hanafy, N., Elkemary, M., & Leporatti, S. (2018). Micelles structure development as a strategy to improve smart cancer therapy. *Cancers (Basel)*, *10*(7), 238. Available from https://doi.org/10.3390/cancers10070238.

Jeevanandam, J., Barhourm, A., Chan, Y., Dufresne, A., & Danquah, M. (2018). Review on nanoparticles and nanostructured materials: History, sources, toxicity and regulations. *Beilstein Journal of Nanotechnology*, *2018*(9), 1050–1074. Available from https://doi.org/10.3762/bjnano.9.98.

Pavlovic, N., GolocorbinKon, S., Danic, M., Stanimorov, B., & Mikov, M. (2018). Bile acids and their derivatives as potential modifiers of drug release and pharmacokinetic profiles. *Frontiers in Pharmacology*. Available from https://doi.org/10.3389/fphar.2018.01283.

Prestinaci, F., Pezzotti, P., & Pantosti, A. (2015). Antimicrobial resistance: A global multifaceted phenomenon. *Pathogens and Global Health*, *109*(7), 309–318. Available from https://doi.org/10.1179/2047773215Y.0000000030.

Singh, T., Shukla, S., Kumar, P., Wahla, V., Vivek, B., & Rather, I. (2017). Application of nanotechnology in food science: Perception and overview. *Frontiers in Microbiology*. Available from https://doi.org/10.3389/fmicb.2017.01501, 07 August 2017.

Soares, S., Sousa, J., Pais, A., & Vitorino, C. (2018). Nanomedicine: Principles, properties, and regulatory issues. *Frontiers in Chemistry*. Available from https://doi.org/10.3389/fchem.2018.00360.

Whitlow, J., Pacelli, S., & Paul, A. (2017). Multifunctional nanodiamonds in regenerative medicine: Recent advances and future directions. *Journal of Controlled Release: Official Journal of the Controlled Release Society*, *2017*(261), 62–86. Available from https://doi.org/10.1016/j.jconrel.2017.05.033, Sep 10.

Wu, W., Wu, Z., Yu, T., Jiang, C., & Kim, W. (2014). *Recent progress on magnetic iron oxide nanoparticles: Synthesis, surface functional strategies and biomedical applications*. Available from https://doi.org/10.1088/1468-6996/16/2/023501.

Zare, H., Ahmadi, S., Ghasemi, A., Ghanbari, M., Rabiee, N., Bagherzadeh, M., Karimi, M., Webster, T. J., Hamblin, M.R., & Mostafavi, E. (2021). *Carbon nanotubes: Smart drug/gene delivery carriers*. 16, 1681-1706. Available from https://doi.org/10.2147/IJN.S299448.

CHAPTER 18

Recent patents and market trends of nano-based pharmaceutical products

Jhansi Lakshmi Parimi[1], Nadia Razdan[2], Soumi Sadhu[2] and Padmavati Manchikanti[1]
[1]Plant Metabolic Pathway Laboratory, Rajiv Gandhi School of Intellectual Property Law (RGSOIPL), Biomaterial and Tissue Engineering Laboratory (BMTE), Indian Institute of Technology Kharagpur, Kharagpur, West Bengal, India
[2]Department of Life sciences, School of Basic Sciences and research, Sharda University, Greater Noida, Uttar Pradesh, India

Introduction

The term "nano pharmaceuticals" is defined by NIH in the year 2000, as "formulations containing 1 to 100 nanometer size, with different unique properties which are not existing and possible with their bulk counterparts" (Weissig et al., 2014). These formulations contributed to addressing the challenges and limitations of conventional drugs and diagnostic agents in multiple ways. The physical, chemical, electrical, and biological multifunctionality features of nanomaterials showed the tremendous benefit to improve bio distribution, dose manipulation, targeting, controlled release, and, most importantly, improving the half-life of the potent active pharmaceuticals to achieve overall clinical benefit. Currently, a numerous number of nanotherapeutics, nanocarriers, and nanotheranostics are serving the human and animal population (Guimarães et al., 2021). There are more than 50 varieties of nanoformulations alone (excluding biological), approved by the FDA as of today. In the past three decades, intensive research efforts in the field of nanomedicine and the products that came out as fruitful alternatives to existing modalities showed tremendous translation capacity globally. Still, there are unmet challenges in this active area. They are not only from the point of view of materials but also from the nonavailability of the testing models to how their potential clinical translatability.

Nanotherapeutics are the fruitful results of the extensive efforts to serve the diseased population by bringing a huge number of products. The innovative effort made in this prospective area has been nurtured with polymeric materials, organic and inorganic nanoparticles, lipid vesicles, and so on (Zhang et al., 2020). The major nanomaterials and their clinical and translational potential have been shown in Fig. 18.1, and global landscaping has been presented in Table 18.1. This list goes on and leads to other important sectors nanotherapeutics, nanotheranostics, nanodevices, and so on. All these are exemplified functional nanodrugs with multitargeting and stimulating

Nanotechnology for Drug Delivery and Pharmaceuticals
DOI: https://doi.org/10.1016/B978-0-323-95325-2.00004-3

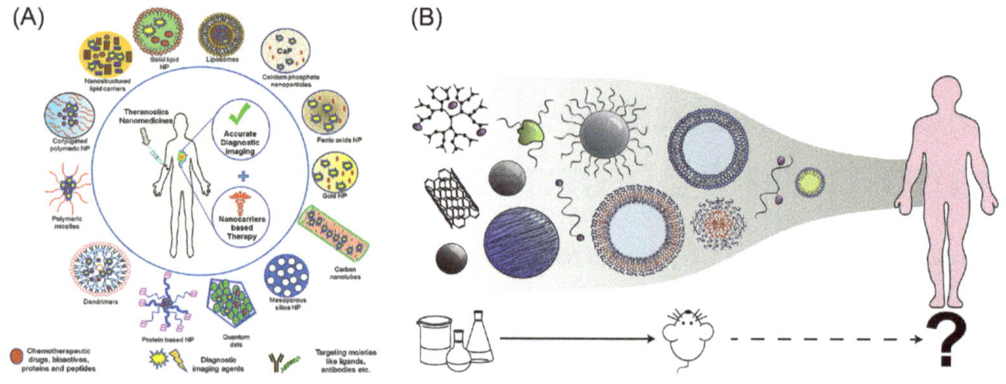

Figure 18.1 Nanomaterials used in drug delivery and pharmaceuticals with intended applications with a focus on the clinical translability. (A) Various nanocarriers used for theranostics. (B) Nanocarriers clinical translatability. *Reprinted with permission from (A) Ref Shete et al. (2022), and (B) Ref Saraf et al. (2020).*

capacity. These innovative technologies brought successful interventions in patient-centered care and individual problem and intensity-oriented treatment choices required for the treatment of various ailments. Nanomaterials with their unique properties possess the capacity to deliver, protect, and solubilize the active pharmaceutical ingredients and molecules of choice. They are not only limited to nanoparticles but also available in different shapes and forms from 1D to 3D materials and devices, for example, vesicles, fibers, tubes, rods, and wires. A detailed list of theranostic nanomedicines is presented in Fig. 18.2. This shows the collective efforts made by doctors, scientists, nano engineers, clinicians, biomedical engineers, and so on to introduce them for the best benefit of the current and future generations by bringing them available into the market (Shete et al., 2022).

All in all, "nanopharmaceutical substances," as per the existing knowledge, are drug products that must meet two prime objectives: (1) nanoengineering, which plays a primary role in fabrication or synthesis; and (2) the material itself to improve or add unique properties to the active drug entities. In this chapter, we highlight the technology domain distribution of these formulations and their market trends with a clear overview of the innovations filing trends, and exclusive materials of focus so far existing. A focus is given to detailing on the attempts made and problems associated with specific nanosystems, which provides a broad overview and the need for more product-oriented research that can foster the progress of nanomedicines from lab to clinic.

Table 18.1 Clinically approved nanoformulations for biomedical applications.

Trade name (manufacturer)	Generic name	Approved indication/ application	Approval year (drug authority)
Doxil/Caelyx (Janssen)	Liposomal DOX HCl	HIV-associated Karposi's sarcoma, ovarian cancer, multiple myeloma	1995 (FDA); 1996 (EMA)
AmBisome (Gilead Sciences)	Liposomal amphotericin B	Fungal/protozoal infections	1997 (FDA)
Visudyne (Bausch + Lomb)	Liposomal verteporfin	Macular degeneration with photodynamic therapy	2000 (FDA and EMA)
Marqibo (Acrotech Biopharma)	Liposomal vincristine sulfate	ALL	2012 (FDA)
Onivyde (Ipsen Biopharmaceuticals)	Liposomal irinotecan	Metastatic pancreatic cancer	2015 (FDA); 2016 (EMA)
Vyxeos (Jazz Pharmaceuticals)	Liposomal daunorubicin/ cytarabine	Acute myeloid leukemia	2017 (FDA); 2018 (EMA)
Diprivan (AstraZeneca)	Propofol	General anesthesia	1989 (FDA)
Cleviprex (Chiesi Farmaceutici)	Clevipidine	Hypertension	2008 (FDA), most of Europe (2011)
Cinvanti (Heron therapeutics)	Aprepitant	Prevention of acute and delayed chemotherapy-induced nausea and vomiting	2017 (FDA)
Rapamune (Pfizer)	Sirolimus	Immunosuppressant	1999 (FDA); 2001 (EMA)
Cesamet (Bausch Health)	Nabilone	Nausea and vomiting associated with cancer chemotherapy	2006 (FDA)
Tricor (AbbVie)	Fenofibrate	Hypercholesterolemia	2004 (FDA)
Abraxane (Celgene)	Albumin-bound paclitaxel	Breast cancer, NSCLC, pancreatic cancer	2005 (FDA); 2008 (EMA)
Onpattro/Patisiran (Alnylam Pharmaceuticals)	Small-interfering RNA	Polyneuropathy caused by HATTR amyloidosis	2018 (FDA and EMA)
Adagen (Leadiant Biosciences)	Pegademase bovine	Adenosine deaminase deficiency in patients with SCID	1990 (FDA)

(Continued)

Table 18.1 (Continued)

Trade name (manufacturer)	Generic name	Approved indication/ application	Approval year (drug authority)
Oncaspar (Servier Pharmaceuticals)	Pegaspargase	ALL	1994 (FDA); 2016 (EMA)
Neulasta (Amgen)	Pegfilgrastim	Neutropenia in patients with cancer receiving myelosuppressive chemotherapy	2002 (FDA and EMA)
Cimzia (UCB)	Certolizumab pegol	Crohn's disease, rheumatoid arthritis, psoriasis arthritis, and ankylosing spondylitis	2008 (FDA); 2009 (EMA)
Macugen (Pfizer)	Pegaptanib sodium	Neovascular age-related macular degeneration	2004 (FDA); 2006 (EMA)
Movantik/Moventig (AstraZeneca)	Naloxegol	Opioid-induced constipation	2014 (FDA and EMA)
Genexol-PM/Cynviloq (Samyang Biopharm)	PTX	Breast cancer, NSLC, and ovarian cancer	2007 (South Korea and other countries)
Apealea/Paclical (Oasmia Pharmaceutical)	PTX	Ovarian cancer in combination with carboplatin	2018 (EMA)
Dendrimers			
VivaGel BV (Starpharma Holdings)	SPL7013	Prevention of vaginal infection and other STD	2015 (EMA); 2017 (Australia); 2019 (Japan)
INFeD (Allergan Pharmaceuticals)	Iron dextran colloid	Iron deficiency	1974 (FDA)
Venofer (Vifor Pharma)	Iron sucrose colloid	Iron deficiency	2000 (FDA)
Ferinject (Vifor Pharma)/Injectafer (DaiichiSankyo)	Iron carboxymaltose colloid	Iron deficiency	2007 (EMA); 2009 (FDA)
Feridex/Endorem (AMAG Pharmaceuticals)	Iron dextran colloid	Imaging of liver lesions	1996 (FDA)
NanoTherm (MagForce)	Aminosilane-coated iron oxide	Hyperthermia treatment of brain tumors	2018 (EMA)

ALL, Acute lymphoblastic leukemia; *CKD*, chronic kidney disease; *DOX*, doxorubicin; *HATTR*, hereditary transthyretin-mediated amyloidosis.; *HCl*, hydrochloride; *HIV*, human immunodeficiency virus; *NSCLC*, non−small cell lung cancer; *PTX*, paclitaxel; *SCID*, severe combined immunodeficiency disease; *STD*, sexually transmitted diseases.
Source: Data from Weissig, V., Pettinger, T. K., & Murdock, N. (2014) Nanopharmaceuticals (part 1): Products on the market. *International Journal of Nanomedicine*, *9*, 4357.

Figure 18.2 Remarkable contributions of theranostic mAbs used for the hematological malignancies. *Reprinted with permission from Shete, M. B., Patil, T. S., Deshpande, A. S., Saraogi, G., Vasdev, N., Deshpande, M., Rajpoot, K., & Tekade, R. K. (2022). Current trends in theranostic nanomedicines.* Journal of Drug Delivery Science and Technology, 22, *103280.*

Patent analysis

Methodology/search strategy

Patenting trends and no. of patents in the area of nanopharmaceuticals have been done by using the Questel orbit database. We considered the last 20 years' patent applications for our analysis in this chapter.

The search strategy used for the searching was "NANOPARTICLE" "NANOPHARMACEUTICAL")/KEYW/TI/AB AND (A61K OR A61P OR B82Y OR B82B)/IPC/CPC. The number of hits we have received was 105,210. Among them, 6% of the inventions filed by the top 10 players were 6%.

The status of the inventions, including application status, assignees, and legal status has been given in detail in the following sections.

Patent filing trends

The worldwide patent database Questel orbit was searched for nanopharmaceuticals to determine the total number of patents per year. As per the number of hits, it is evident that patenting activity is on the high rise since 2001 with 11,767 applications filed between 2001 and 2005. It continued its trend until 2020 with 38,810 applications filed between 2016 and 2020. From 2020 until this year, there were only 5570 patent applications filed, which might be due to the fresh status of the applications, or many of them are still not yet published due to the patent office's publication timeline restrictions. A detailed trend of filings has been presented in Fig. 18.3A.

Geographical distribution

Patent applications in the area of nanopharmaceuticals were majorly filed by China with 31,402 applications so far, followed by the United States of America with 20,953 applications. IEP, KR, and JP also have applications filed in 5-digit numbers, that is, around 20,000 maximum. CA, IN, and DE has around 10,000 applications to their credit. India is showing an improved filing rate with 9977 applications filed so far. GB and FR have 7000 + applications to their credit, showing the potential market in those places also. Detailed depiction of the distribution has been shown in Fig. 18.3B and C. All these are the potential marketplaces for drug delivery and pharmaceutical products.

Top applicants/assignees

As per the filing trend data shown in Table 18.2, the University of California (1297) is the top leading applicant and assignee with 1297 applications to its credit, L'oreal occupies the second place with 867, followed by Samsung electronics with 837 applications, MIT—Massachusetts Institute of Technology (667), CNRS—Centre National

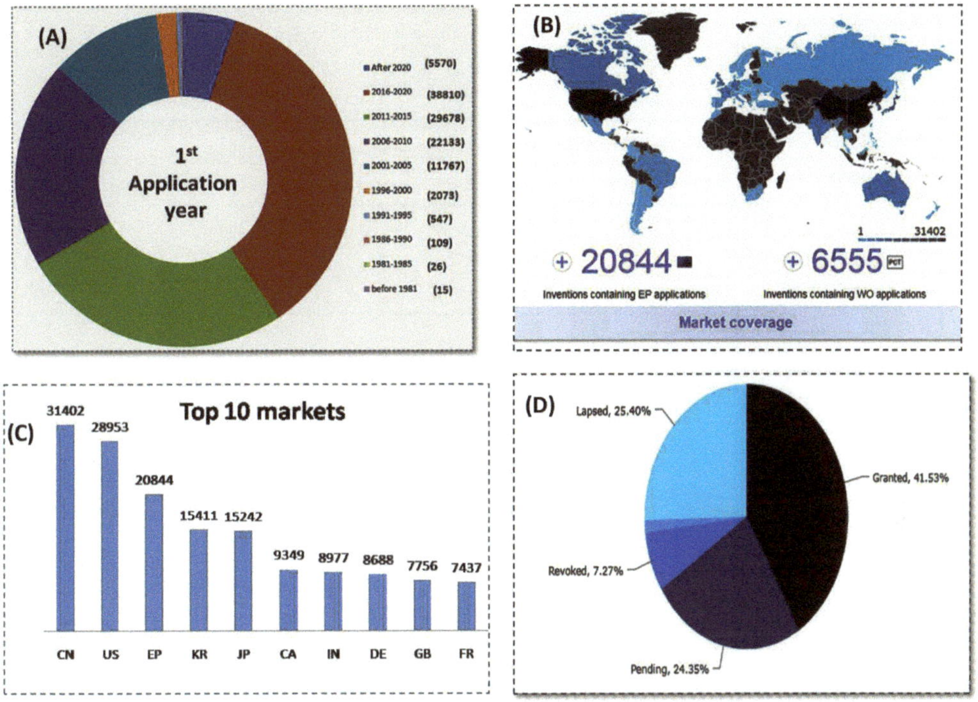

Figure 18.3 Patent analysis of nanopharmaceuticals: (A) Filing trend of the applications, (B) Market coverage, (C) Top 10 markets of nanopharmaceuticals, and (D) Status of the applications. *Data from Questel Orbit.*

de la Recherche Scientifique (652), University of Texas (601), Genentech (560), Zhejiang University (536), and Korea advanced institute of science & technology (527).

Legal status

Among the mentioned patents, 1594 patents are expired. A total of 45565 patent applications are granted so far. A total of 27,868 patents are listed as lapsed and 26,721. 7980 patents are revoked so far as shown in the Fig. 18.3D.

Technology domain distributions

The major trend in the innovations and development in the area of pharmaceuticals, especially emphasized with nanomedicine and drug delivery, is scattered with a high number of patents filed for metallic nanoparticles, followed by nanopharmaceuticals, liposomal and dendrimer-based drug delivery diagnostic devices in combination with therapeutic interventions as theranostic products and formulations as listed in Table 18.1.

Table 18.2 Key players by technical domain.

Key players by technical domain	Pharmaceuticals	Biotechnology	Medical technology	Microstructure and nanotechnology	Analysis of biological materials	Organic fine chemistry	Macromolecular chemistry, polymers	Basic materials chemistry	Chemical engineering	Food chemistry	Environmental technology	Textile and paper machines
University of California	742	150	138	97	126	69	42	48	16	7	3	2
Genentech	515	175	20	2	170	85	0	17	3	1	1	0
University of Texas	414	63	64	41	63	31	23	20	10	6	0	2
MIT—Massachusetts Institute of Technology	374	88	58	52	61	24	46	18	16	10	2	0
Johns Hopkins University	309	33	41	32	45	11	31	14	3	1	1	3
Hoffmann La Roche	267	109	8	2	73	55	2	7	4	1	2	1
CNRS—Centre National de la Recherche Scientifique	243	51	40	36	46	30	29	24	21	2	0	3
INSERM—institut national de la sante & de la recherche medicale	255	71	20	7	52	11	5	8	3	2	2	1
University of Pennsylvania	240	81	22	5	33	22	2	11	0	1	0	0
Pfizer	241	13	6	11	12	85	3	14	1	0	0	0
Massachusetts General Hospital	209	41	32	11	43	15	9	11	0	2	1	0
Us Department of Health and Human Services	203	36	12	20	45	10	5	9	1	1	0	0
Suzhou Zhiweitang Biological Technology	197	0	0	0	0	0	0	0	0	0	0	0
University of Massachusetts	183	65	8	16	28	17	17	15	3	1	0	0
Yale University	186	45	13	10	37	16	11	8	1	2	0	0
Modernatx	189	31	2	11	5	10	3	4	0	0	0	0
University of North Carolina	168	25	31	28	24	13	13	13	7	0	0	0
Novartis	174	48	11	5	21	29	8	11	2	0	0	0
Brigham and Women's Hospital	158	33	21	12	40	10	12	8	6	1	0	0
L'oreal	16	1	6	3	4	164	21	12	6	1	0	1

Nanopharmaceuticals for drug delivery

An important invention described the method of preparation and application of prodrug nanometer-sized medicine. Macromolecular prodrug nanopharmaceuticals are reduced lipoic acids that bind two hydrophobic drug molecules. The nanoparticles of the pharmaceutical composition can be used for liquid preparation, solid preparation, and semisolid preparation with low toxicity and can be used for tumor treatment (Xinsong et al., 2019). Another invention provides information on itraconazole nanocrystals and their application. The itraconazole nanocrystals help in improving the bioavailability and reduce the influence of a diet state on the bioavailability. This method has the advantages of no use of toxic solvent, simple preparation process, low cost, and easy industrialization (Yang et al., 2011). One of the inventions described the conjugation of integrin receptor antagonists to targets of the norepinephrine transporter (NET) or the catecholamine transporter. This conjugated module has a dual-targeting effect and increased targeting efficiency in the treatment and diagnostic imaging of neuroendocrine tumors (Shaker et al., 2010). Similarly, in some of the inventions, novel polymeric conjugates to a fibril disruptor agent and/or aggregates blocking agent, and additionally, a targeting moiety and/or a probe for therapy and diagnosis will provide an effective targeting of the polymer—drug conjugate to the selected diseased area for drug activity, increasing the therapeutic efficacy in the treatment of amyloidosis-related diseases, including amyloidosis related to polyneuropathic disorders and neurodegenerative diseases like FAP and AD (Floriane et al., 2019). An important invention explained the microemulsion composition comprising a herb medicine extract and omega-3-unsaturated fatty acid. This microemulsion can help in improving oral absorption of the herb medicine extract acting as an oral administration delivery system (Lin et al., 2017). A performing composition of cyclodextrin and polymeric materials designed to achieve small molecule therapeutics delivery is in the market with a good commercial value (Cheng et al., 2013). Another invention highlighted the role of thyroid hormone antagonists and their nanoparticle formulations along with antiinflammatory agents for the management of musculoskeletal disorders (Davis & Mousa, 2016).

Dendrimer nanotherapeutics

Dendrimers are the multifunctional branched polymeric nanoparticles used for the targeting and delivery of active pharmaceutical substances, growth factors, proteins, peptides, and so on. Sometimes tagging of a diagnostic moiety to the structure provides tracking and identification of the cellular responses. As shown in Fig. 18.4, the targeting groups attachment makes these materials innovative approaches for the treatment of various deadly diseases. In addition, they also provided methods of directing CRISPR complex formation in eukaryotic cells to ensure enhanced specificity for target recognition and mainly help in improving the status of the disease (MALI et al., 2015). On the contrary,

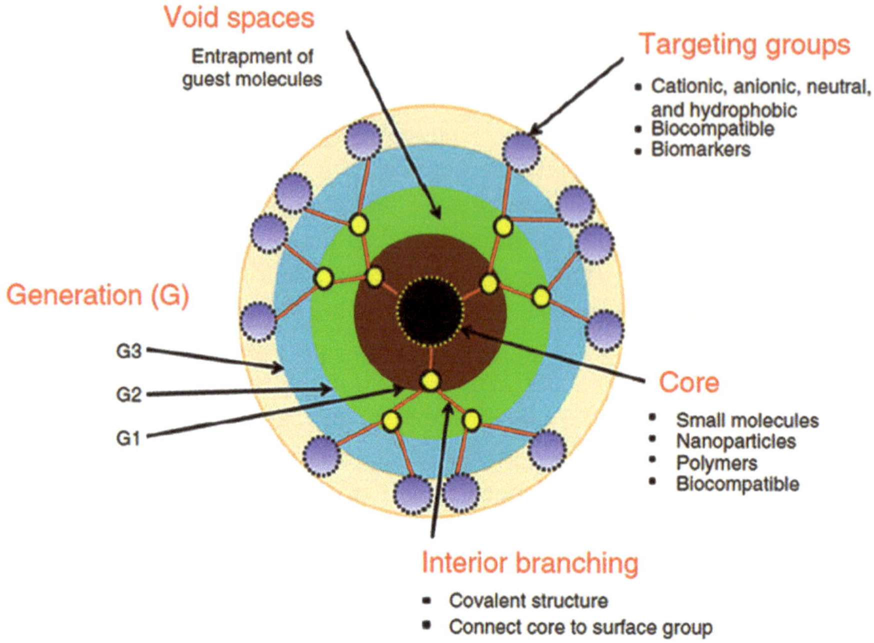

Figure 18.4 Schematic representation of dendrimers for drug delivery applications. *(Reprinted with permission from Ref. Chen et al. (2018)).*

another invention by Zhang F 2022 provided information related to the methods and compositions of nonnaturally occurring CRISPR effector proteins for DNA targeting (Zhang et al., 2022). In the list of highly performing dendrimer-based pharmaceutical preparations, an invention filed by Bancel in S2015 imparts knowledge regarding the use of polynucleotides and mRNA molecules (Bancel et al., 2015). In this direction, persistent efforts resulting from the guided nuclease systems (Quake & Wang, 2016) respiratory virus RNA-based vaccines and combinations thereof (Ciaramella & Himanshu, 2017) are in the pipeline. According to one invention by Kit S2022 amphiphilic telodendrimers have been made with customized properties for the interaction with biological membranes with hydrophilic exterior and hydrophobic core nanocarrier design (Lam et al., 2022). While another invention by Howard S2020 was about nanoparticle compositions comprising a biodegradable or biocompatible polymer arranged in a nanoparticle structure. This invention mainly provided various methods of making and using nanoparticle compositions (Howard & Michael, 2020).

Liposomes

Liposomes are the lipid carrier vesicles used for drug delivery applications with a successful history of over 50 years with active and passive targeting strategies as shown in

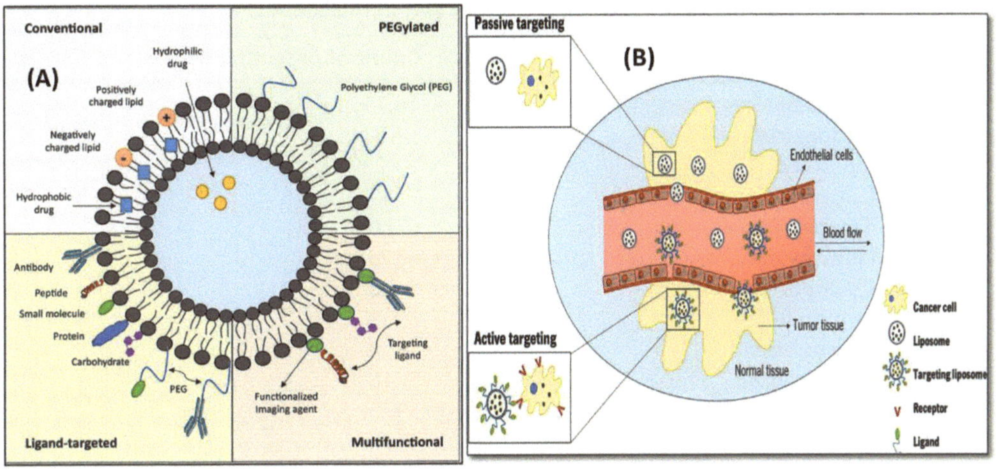

Figure 18.5 (A) Different types of liposomes used in therapeutic applications. Liposomal formulations for drug delivery, targeting, and diagnostic strategies, and (B) Schematic illustration of passive and active targeting strategies of liposomes into a tumor for enhancing the therapeutic efficacy of drugs. *Reprinted with permission from (A) Guimarães et al. (2021) and (B) Saraf et al. (2020).*

Fig. 18.5. A comprehensive list of liposomal formulations available in the market has been listed in Table 18.3. This shows the potential role played by them for the controlled and targeted drug delivery systems. In recent times, a patent application claiming the method of targeting direct CRISPR complex formation in eukaryotic cells is a liposomal-based nano-intervention used for the specific disease targeting (Guidernas, 2017). Another application claims the use of engineered targeting liposomal systems for CRISPR effector proteins for RNA guidance as a nucleic acid sequence targeting strategy (Yoo et al., 2018). Some other inventions elucidated the therapeutic application of polynucleotides, primary transcripts, and mRNA molecules (Masferrer et al., 2005). According to one invention, modified guide RNAs along with the CRISPR CAS-9 system can play an important role in modifying gene expression, particularly in mammalian cells for medical or research uses (Frederick et al., 2017). The use of nanoparticle–drug conjugates for the treatment, diagnosis, and prevention of cancer claimed by the invention (Hongli et al., 2016). These are made by using silica-based nanoparticles, which can image and target ligands and possess the capability of renal clearance. Combination therapies for treating cancer were designed by administering a topoisomerase-1 inhibitor and a PARP inhibitor. These combination therapies are useful in the treatment of human cancers with solid tumors, including cervical cancer (Dorfman et al., 2016). These are inventions claiming the novelty of the liposomal carrier systems for the therapeutic use of immunomodulatory polypeptide combinations and cytokines for eliciting an immune response (Katharina et al., 2008).

Table 18.3 Important patented molecules and formulations.

Formulation/Molecule	Count of patent families
Excipient	15,797
Nanoparticle	14,831
Liposome	10,237
Cisplatin	7139
Treating cancer	6726
Fluorouracil	6398
Cyclophosphamide	6172
Etoposide	6038
Carboplatin	5908
Methotrexate	5648
Busulfan	4575
Dacarbazine	4451
Floxuridine	3607
Azacitidine	3577
Bevacizumab	3529
Altretamine	3518
Daunomycin	3279
Amsacrine	3255
Cationic lipid	3052
Cellular uptake	2942
Estramustine	2901
Aminoglutethimide	2879
Targeted delivery	2814
Thioguanine	2772
Targeting moiety	2749
Thiophosphamide	2481
Epothilone	2414

Metallic nanoparticles

Metallic nanoparticles are the most extensively used nanomaterials with varied methods of synthesis and unique properties. Their utility is not only limited to drug delivery but also the diagnostics and devices used for the theranostic applications. In one of the recent inventions, a carbon material-based electrode can be used for detecting nicotine. This method has high sensitivity and a strong market application prospect (Thomas et al., 2007). An invention claiming the novelty and use of metallic nanocrystal suspensions made up of gold and platinum NPS complex, which is used for cancer diagnosis and treatment (Arokiasamy et al., 2011). Numerous method of producing nanoparticles has been obtained in various patents. Some inventions provided new conjugates of the bisacyloxypropylcysteine-type useful as adjuvants and/or immunomodulators as mucosal adjuvants for the prophylaxis and treatment of inflammatory diseases. An invention claims the use of anionic and amino phospholipids for targeting viral infections and tumor vasculature in different types of cancers (Crooke & Graham, 2011).

Nanodevices

Nanodevices are the nanoscale interventions used for the diagnosis and sensing-based delivery and treatment strategies of 21st-century developments. Inventions are using EXX nanosensors for the imaging of cellular biological processes within the living cells by using C-reactive proteins as antisense oligonucleotides (Christopher et al., 2009). Molecular diagnostics is another important contribution of nanoscale interventions for pharmaceutical nanodrug delivery systems. These inventions were developed with the use of liquid crystals for the quantification of the analyte. These systems perform their function by nonspecific binding with the analyte molecules.

Some inventions described the microarray method to form biodegradable polymer implant arrays in the liver tissue. This biodegradable polymer can also be loaded with the drug to form a biodegradable drug delivery array in the liver tissue (Pathak, 2021). Various methods have been invented to target nucleic acids. In this concern, novel class 1 Type IV and novel class I Type I CAS proteins and their use played an important role in modifying target sequences (Zhang et al., 2021). According to one invention, cell-based strategies involving neuroblastoma tumor-initiating cells for the patent-centered treatment of neuroblastoma (Glycotope, 2016). Other remarkable inventive strategies treating conditions, wherein there is adrenal insufficiency like cancers and psychiatric diseases. These modalities include the use of a PDE11 inhibitor for the treatment of cortisol level maintenance (Hoffman & Ceyhan, 2015).

Market trends and future perspectives

Significant therapeutic benefits achieved by the nanopharmaceuticals have been revealed, and their applicability is still limited due to scale-up, manufacturing, regulatory, and intellectual property challenges and constraints (Saraf et al., 2020). Despite the efforts to bring the laboratory research to scale up to meet the therapeutic applications still, there are very few commercially available formulations. The very first liposomal formulation, which entered the market, is Doxil, for the use for ovarian cancer and AIDS. The translation of these novel formulations requires meeting clinical trials and advanced methodologies and models for the prediction of safety and efficacy (Bulbake et al., 2017). A comprehensive list of commercially available nanoformulations has been presented in Table 18.1 which shows the successful contributions of nanopharmaceuticals for the therapeutic, diagnosis, and prophylactic purposes as shown in Fig. 18.2. Formulations even though met all the requirements of the safety and efficacy of in vitro and in vivo ethical and biological assessments only a few of them are commercially available.

All of the nanopharmaceuticals listed in the table and shown in the figure help in the timely detection, diagnosis, and treatment of diseases. Potential efficacy improvement over the conventional therapeutic strategies brought focus to these formulations globally with increased R&D efforts by pharmaceutical and biotechnology companies and institutes of eminence for the discovery of novel drugs, strategies for various disorders, cancers, and so on. Lack of regulatory guidelines and toxicity concerns associated with nanoscale materials are still unmet needs and affecting the global market growth. As per the data verified, key players in this area includes universities, and pharmaceutical and biotechnology companies. All of them are working either individually or in collaboration. The major market growth of these formulations is segmented and mainly high in North America and Europe. Nanopharmaceuticals market and development is segmented mainly into liposomes, polymeric micelles, emulsion systems, and so on. Till today, major focused diseases are cancer, autoimmune disorders, inflammatory disorders, and so on as shown in the table

By using the combinatorial approaches for the early detection and treatment strategies, nanopharmaceuticals will pave the way for deadly conditions caused due to viruses, bacteria, and other prevalent pathogens and immunological issues related to disorders, cancer, and so on as shown in Table 18.3. For these interventional approaches, the analysis of the inventive approaches through patent landscaping and analysis reduces the gray areas that need to be taken care of to avoid bottlenecks. This reduces the failures of R&D efforts and might improve the commercial applicability of these formulations.

Acknowledgments

The authors wish to thank the Department of Science and Technology (DST) for the WoS-B research fellowship—DST/WOS-B/2017/477-HFN (Dr. Jhansi Lakshmi Parimi) and IIT Kharagpur, Department of Life sciences, School of Basic Sciences and research, Sharda University (Dr. Soumi Sadhu and Dr. Nadia) for the generous support of the studies which contributed to this chapter.

References

Arokiasamy, D., Haihong, J., Zhi-Cai, S., Tunoori, A., & Wang, Y. *Selected antibodies and duramycin peptides binding to anionic phospholipids and aminophospholipids and their use in the treatment of viral infections and cancer*. European Patent. EP 2283869.16-02-2011.

Bancel, S., Chakraborty, T., Fougerolles, A.D. et al. *Modified polynucleotides for the production of proteins associated with human disease*. European Patent. EP2849799A2.25-03-2015.

Bulbake, U., Doppalapudi, S., Kommineni, N., & Khan, W. (2017). Liposomal formulations in clinical use: An updated review. *Pharmaceutics*. Available from https://doi.org/10.3390/pharmaceutics9020012.

Chen, H., Jin, Y., Sun, L., et al. (2018). Recent developments in ophthalmic drug delivery systems for therapy of both anterior and posterior segment diseases. *Colloid and Interface Science Communications*, *24*, 54–61.

Cheng, J., Davis, M.E., & Khin, K.T. *Cyclodextrin-based polymers for delivering the therapeutic agents covalently bound thereto*. European Patent.EP2277551A3.08-05-2013
Christopher, M., Barbara, I., & Abbott, N. *Uses of devices and methods for cellular assays*. European Patent. EP 2093565.26-08-2009.
Ciaramella, G., & Himanshu, S. *Respiratory virus vaccines*. WIPO Patent.WO2017070626A2.03-08-2017.
Crooke, R.M., & Graham, M.J. *Antisense modulation of C-reactive protein expression*. European Patent. EP 10176752.02-02-2011.
Davis, P.J., & Mousa, S.A. *Nanoparticle and polymer formulations for thyroid hormone analogs, antagonists, and formulations and uses*. Canada Patent. CA2673133C.30-08-2016.
Dorfman, A.R., Bryce,D.A., & Maxwell, A. et al. *Novel gold-platinum based bi-metallic nanocrystal suspensions, electrochemical manufacturing processes therefor and uses for the same*. European Patent. EP2691082B1.13-01-2016.
Floriane, S., Toni, M., Sandra, R., & Clemence, C. *Composition and method for dual targeting in treatment of neuroendocrine tumors*. US Patent. FR 1906983A 17.10.2019.
Frederick, J., HEWITT, S., Bai, A. et al. *Combinations of mRNAs encoding immune modulating polypeptides and uses thereof.* Canadian Patent. CA3024917A1. 23-11-2017.
Glycotope, G. *Cancer stem cell markers and uses thereof.* Japan Patent. JP2016047848. 07-04-2016.
Guidernas, *Methodsand uses*. European Patent.EP3 159 407 A1.26.04.2017.
Guimarães, D., Cavaco-Paulo, A., & Nogueira, E. (2021). Design of liposomes as drug delivery system for therapeutic applications. *International Journal of Pharmaceutics*, *601*, 120571, doi.org/10.1016/j.ijpharm.2021.120571.
Hoffman, C.S., & Ceyhan, O. *Inhibitors of phosphodiesterase 11 (PDE11)*. US Patent. US9173884B2.03-11-2015.
Hongli, Z., Xiaoqing, L., Minbei, L., Li, L., Libei, S., Gan, Z., & Wenbo, J. *Carbon material-based electrode for detecting nicotine and its preparation method and use*. 09-11-2016.
Howard, S., & Michael, C. *Novel nanoparticle compositions*. Japan Patent. JP2019073525A.16-09-2020.
Katharina, L., Clemens, W., & Julie, K. *Two step miniemulsion process*. European Patent. EP 1876188 A1.09-01-2008.
Lam, K.S., Li, Y., & Pan, C.-x *Porphyrin modified telodendrimers*. US Patent. US20200046841A1.11-1-2022.
Lin, H., Drusano, G., Louie, A., & Paul D. *In vitro pharmacokinetics/pharmacodynamics bellows perfusion system for enhancing effectiveness of cancer chemotherapy*. US Patent. US 36383110.19-04-2017.
Mali, P.G., George, M., & Yang, C.L. *RNA-guided human genome engineering via Cas9*. US Patent. US9023649B2.05-05-2015.
Masferrer, J., Parul, D., & Cherrigton, J. *Combination therapy for cancer treatment*. Columbia Patent. CO5560544A2.30-09-2005.
Pathak, C.P. *Method of making an in situ sustained biodegradable drug delivery implant by filling an artificial tissue cavity*. US Patent. US11045433B2.26-06-2021.
Quake, S., & Wang, J. *Compositions and methods to treat latent viral infections*. US Patent. US9487802B2.08-11-2016.
Saraf, S., Jain, A., Tiwari, A., Verma, A., Panda, P. K., & Jain, S. K. (2020). Advances in liposomal drug delivery to cancer: An overview. *Journal of Drug Delivery Science and Technology*, *56*, 101549. Available from https://doi.org/10.1016/j.jddst.2020.101549, Apr 1.
Shaker, M., Paul, D., & Faith D. *Thyroid hormone analogs and methods of use in angiogenesis*. US Patent. US50272103.22-04-2010.
Shete, M. B., Patil, T. S., Deshpande, A. S., Saraogi, G., Vasdev, N., Deshpande, M., Rajpoot, K., & Tekade, R. K. (2022). Current trends in theranostic nanomedicines. *Journal of Drug Delivery Science and Technology*, 103280, Mar 22.
Thomas, E., Guzman, C.A., & Morr, M. *New adjuvants on the basis of bisacyloxypropylcysteine conjugates and their uses in pharmaceutical compositions*. European Patent. EP 1787660A23-05-2007.
Weissig, V., Pettinger, T. K., & Murdock, N. (2014). Nanopharmaceuticals (part 1): Products on the market. *International Journal of Nanomedicine*, *9*, 4357, doi.org/10.2147/IJN.S46900.
Xinsong L., Longbing L., Wei H. *Macromolecular prodrug nanometer medicine, preparation method and application*. University of South east.CN 201811079938 A.18-01-2019.

Yang, X., Mou, D., Zhou, X., Wan, J., Chen, H., & Hui, X. *Itraconazole nanocrystals and preparation method and application*. University of Wuhan Huazhong. CN 200910063819 A.02-02-2011.

Yoo, B., Bradbury, M., Wiesner, W., & Ma, K. *Nanoparticle drug conjugates*. US Patent. US10111963B2.30-10-2018.

Zhang, C., Yan, L., Wang, X., Zhu, S., Chen, C., Gu, Z., & Zhao, Y. (2020). Progress, challenges, and future of nanomedicine. *Nano Today, 35*, 101008. Available from https://doi.org/10.1016/j.nantod.2020.101008, Dec 1.

Zhang, F., Tran, F., & Kannan, S. *Novel type iv and type ICRISPR-CAS systems and methods of use thereof*. WIPO Patent. WO2021173734A1. 02-09-2021.

Zhang, F., Zetsche, B., Gao, L., & Slaymaker, I. *Novel CRISPR enzymes and systems*. New Zealand. NZ787373.29.04.2022

CHAPTER 19

Perspectives, safety issues, and legal factors of nano-based materials utility in pharmaceutical applications

Monika Bhattu[1], Nirmalya Pal[2], Shikha Kapil[2], Deepika Kathuria[1] and Meenakshi Verma[1]
[1]University Centre for Research and Development, Chandigarh University, Mohali, Punjab, India
[2]University Institute of Biotechnology, Chandigarh University, Mohali, Punjab, India

Introduction

The health-care implementation of nanostructural material and nanotechnology presents enormous promise for the establishment of novel remedies and a greater cure for a variety of ailments. Nanomedicine employs biochemistry, biology, biotechnology, health sciences, and clinical sciences at the nanomolecular scale to offer novel therapeutic interventions. In the 1980s the proposal of tiny robotics in medical applications fueled research into the creation of novel medications, delivery techniques, and newer treatments based on the nanoscale scale features of molecules and conjugates. Since then, the discipline of nanomedicine has increased in possibilities, and numerous novel medications or drug conjugates with improved medicinal properties have entered the shelves. Nanomedicine research has evolved and expanded to all subfields of medical sciences, with a slew of applications (Pelaz et al., 2017).

The goal of nanomedicine research is to create novel remedies by using the nanoscale aspects of molecules. The exploration of technical breakthroughs for biomedical applications using bioactive molecules at the nanometer size, as well as the generation of novel technologies exploiting nanoscale features, is referred to as nanobiotechnology. The domains of nanomedicine and nanobiotechnology are inextricably linked and indistinguishable. Both encompass the study of the other, and the phrases are often used interchangeably to describe the study of either discipline. The area of nanomedicine and nanobiotechnology development has exhibited a trend of progression in the past, and many various scientific institutions have been established by various nations as a result of the potential displayed by nanomedicine in translational medicine. As the area has expanded enormously over the last 30 years with the cooperation of chemists, biologists, biotechnologists, biomedical scientists, doctors, and clinicians, so have the application fields, notably the extension of research to difficult-to-treat disorders.

Nanotechnology for Drug Delivery and Pharmaceuticals
DOI: https://doi.org/10.1016/B978-0-323-95325-2.00019-5

Initially, the core concern of research efforts was on drug delivery employing various nanosystems, such as nanopolymeric systems, metal nanoparticles (NPs), liposomes, and lipid micelles. As the sector expanded, study on the engineering of these drug carriers has long remained an important topic of investigation.

The application of synthetic techniques for the production of single-layered and multilayered drug carriers to satisfy the necessary criteria of drug and biomolecule delivery particularly targeted distribution has continued to be the main emphasis of the field's expansion. Furthermore, with the passing years and subsequent developments in the field, the study has witnessed a diversification in the investigation of undiscovered regions, as well as the direction of creation of revolutionized futuristic technologies toward the translational medical scientific research development. The literature published in various journals and portals may be used to examine the rapid evolution in nanomedicine research in recent years and the state of current topics of inquiry. Hence, this chapter describes, in detail, the current scenario of nanomedicines, role of nanomedicines in pharmaceutical industry, and the risk associated with nanomedicine-based advancements.

Figure and facts of nanomedicine market

Nanomedicine is considered a new age phrase that covers all applications by using modern technological advances in the field of nanotechnology. It is a catch-all phrase for any technology that uses tiny molecules for medicinal or further objectives. Nanotechnology is being employed to create medications that attack and destroy cancer cells while leaving healthy cells alone. The substantial burden of chronic illnesses is likely to drive the global nanomedicine industry ahead. For example, as per the study "Cancer statistics conducted for adults aged 85 years and older, 2019," reported in US, 2019, the recorded cancer cases and deaths were ~140,690 and 103,250, respectively. Moreover, increased capital investment in nanomedicine is likely to provide appealing future growth prospects for global nanomedicine industry participants. For instance, in 2020, Clene Nanomedicine, Inc., received a net cost of worth $42.5 million in Series D funding. Nowadays, the industry's major manufacturers are focusing on collaboration methods to extend their range of products and market share. Sirnaomics, Inc. collaborated with Precision NanoSystems Inc. to R&D Sirnaomics polypeptide NP-based RNAi therapeutic product. Other parties included are Johnson & Johnson, GE Healthcare, Pfizer Inc., Sigma-Tau Pharmaceuticals Inc., CombiMatrix Corporation, Abbott Laboratories, and so on. Another company, "Evotec SE" (drug R&D business), in 2020 collaborated with "leon-nanodrugs GmbH" (focuses on the reformulation) in enhancing the effectiveness of clinical and commercial nanomedicines (Goldman & Pabari, 2021a). The worldwide nanomedicines market is being driven by factors, such as aging populations, the rising prevalence of illnesses that might be treated more effectively using nanomedicines, and expanding knowledge about the availability of alternative treatment options employing nanomedicines. The worldwide nanomedicines industry is poised to increase up to USD 232 million by 2026, at a CAGR of 6.4% during the forecast period (Goldman & Pabari, 2021b).

Current trends in nanomedicines

Nanomedicines are utilized for various therapeutics and medical applications (Fig. 19.1) that are discussed later in detail.

Drug delivery

In nanomedicine, employing NPs and nanocomposite for drug delivery has remained the primary area of study. NPs, due to their nano size, easily penetrate the cell membrane and preferentially has been opted as nanodrug-delivering agent. Therefore the attributes like easy permeability across the cell membrane as well as the long life span of NPs in blood have attracted the scientific fraternity to invest in the development of nanodrugs with enhanced pharmacological profile and easy delivering mode. Metal NPs, such as Au, Ag, and CdS, and other nanoassemblies, such as liposomes, polymers, hydrogels, carbon nanotubes, chitosan, dendrimers, and silica, have been employed to modulate the properties of the existing drug to deliver at the desired site (John et al., 2017). Many drug delivery conjugates have achieved therapeutic potential as a result of considerable evaluation and implementation, notably in the field of cancer therapy.

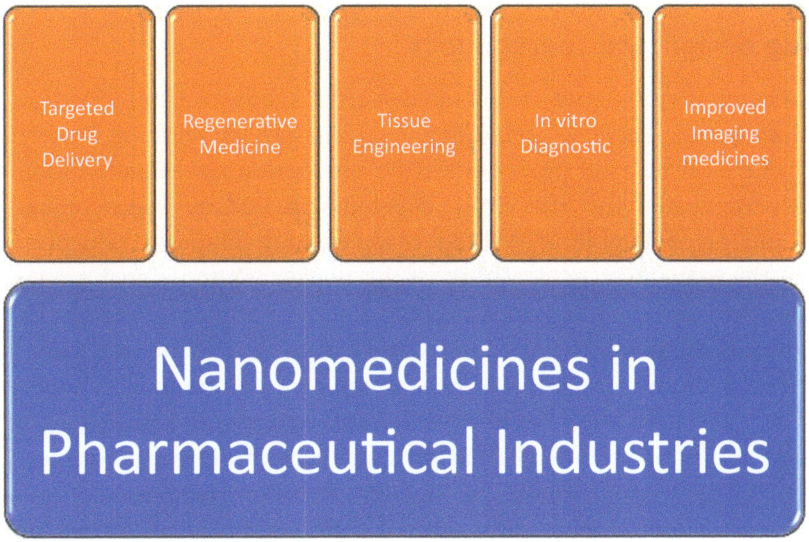

Figure 19.1 Therapeutics and medical applications of nanomedicines.

Recently the discovery of multifunctional NPs with many end applications (such as diagnostic and therapy with a single conjugation) has increased the possibility for translational nanomedicine applications. Another advancement has been the fabrication of viable pH-sensitive nanoconstructs for the applications in which the target tissue's pH differs from that of the surrounding environment (blood and serum). For instance, aptamer-based nanoconstruct and hydrogel-based delivery systems for cancer treatment were explored in this domain. Biodegradable magnetic nanoconstructs also have shown potential magnetic field–guided drug delivery applications.

NP drug delivery agents are also designed according to their mode of delivery. For instance, for oral dosages, multicomponent microemulsions are used in the case of anticancer drugs, for direct uptake nanoconjugates are used in the case of psychotropic drugs. For nasal and ocular applications, polymer, hydrogel, and hyaluronan-based nanocomposites are used to overcome static and dynamic barriers and for prolonged and sustained dosages. The intravenous nanoconjugates are designed with prolonged availability in blood and higher permeability at the desired site. Nonetheless, nanocomposites also have been synthesized to target antimicrobial-resistant strains. In the nervous system, by overcoming the blood–brain barrier (BBB), nanocomposites have become an active concept of research and development to treat various brain-related disorders. For drug delivery applications the impact of NP shape, size, and surface chemistry should be emphasized in the near future. Better drug delivery systems would be provided by size control (uniformity of nanoconjugate formulation) and mechanism research. The mechanistic aspect of nanodrug delivery system's investigations, as well as the influence of individual nanoconjugate on the target, should be emphasized.

Nanodrug design and therapeutics

Complex chemical techniques are required for the synthesis and fabrication of nanomaterial conjugates. There is continuing research into establishing better and more repeatable chemical reaction processes for the production of several existing as well as novel nanoconjugates for nanodrug development. Many nanoconjugates (both inorganic and organic molecules) need complex and tedious production processes, concerning the prevention of depletion of the precursor's functional groups, prompting the discovery of novel and conventional chemical processes. Fabrication of cyclic and linear nanopeptides is a time-consuming task as it demands additional chemical processes due to the incorporation of new amino acid compounds. A variety of cyclic and linear peptides have lately been identified and explored in research laboratories for the covalent and noncovalently bound drug delivery of diverse medicines (Sowinska et al., 2017). The improvement of surface chemistry (addition of new organic moieties) for the fabrication of carbon-based nanoconjugates (single and multiwalled carbon nanotubes, fullerene, graphene, etc.) has aided in the advancement of several novel hybrid conjugates for various applications (physical and chemical) in a biological system.

Moreover, the toxicology study of nanomaterials and nanoconjugates utilized in nanomedicine is important to know the toxicity of nanomaterials on humans as well as the hazardous effect of used or discarded nanomaterials on biosphere/biological lives. Over the last decade, nanotoxicology has emerged as a well-established topic of both nanoscience and toxicology on a global scale. The features of nanomaterials are determined by their size, shape, surface characteristics, including charge, and other factors of their physical nature; therefore their toxicological effects are comparable (Rösslein et al., 2017).

For drug development, biological macromolecules, such as proteins, antibodies, and their fragments, in combination with nanomolecules, are used in this field (Wrobeln et al., 2017) Combination studies were also reported for the already-existing drugs with nanosystems, NPs, and nanoconjugates (Bastogne, 2017) . Moreover, nanophytopharmaceuticals is found to have a prominent profile in combination with nanosystems (Singh et al., 2016). Nonetheless, nanotechnology has spread its vitality in clinical medicines and green nanoscience (using plant extracts) (Jang et al., 2016; Satalkar et al., 2016; Singh et al., 2016).

Nanoinformatics

The drug affinity and binding of nanodrugs conjugates to the desired site varies with modification in shape and size (as group orientation varies). The molecular modeling approaches are constantly investigated for in silico assessment of nanodrug conjugates and are increasing in many nanomedical sectors. The advancements in nanovector designing and nanoassemblies prediction are beneficial in furthering research for in vivo applications (Erkimbaev et al., 2016).

Nanomedicines in pharmaceutical industries

The development of superior therapies and the profitability of the pharmaceutical industries depends upon innovation. However, it has become a key issue to provide high-quality products and to maintain the profit of the industries simultaneously. U.S. drug authorities are putting continuous efforts in order to generate high-quality products while reducing the research and development, time, and cost. Drug development, and its introduction to the market, is a very tedious process (Adams & Van Brantner, 2006; DiMasi et al., 2003). Typically, it takes 10–15 years to introduce a drug to market after its discovery. The cost of research and development involved in drug development has been increasing and according to a survey; only 30% of the manufactured drugs are able to return their R&D cost after commercialization. The second foremost challenge of the pharmaceutical industry is the solubility of the drug products as they exhibit very little solubility in aqueous solutions. The decrease in the size of the particles present in the drug has been considered an effective alternative to increase solubility. Keeping all these into consideration, it has become an important issue to overcome all these hurdles, and nanotechnology has been found to be the best alternate for the same. Nanotechnology offers various advantages: (1) speed, (2) automation, (3) reliability, and (4) miniaturization (Bawa & Johnson, 2009). Among all the applications of nanotechnology in pharmaceutical industries, nanotechnology-enabled drug delivery systems (NDDSs) are of higher importance as the economical and societal benefit of NDDS is connected with high expectations. NDDSs are predicted to help with key concerns in healthcare, like enabling novel therapeutics medicines that exclusively target the illness location and lowering healthcare expenditures. Approximately greater than two dozen NDDSs have been industrialized into commercial goods to date, with many more in the works. The market for these technologies is predicted to expand from US$ 1 billion in 2010 to US$ 136 billion in 2021, according to market predictions (Te Kulve & Rip, 2013).

The global nanomedicine industry grew from $53 billion in 2009 to $138.8 billion in 2016, with anticancer drugs accounting for the most money ($33 billion in 2014). Abraxane is a paclitaxel-encapsulated human serum albumin NP. In 2019 revenue was expected to total $967 million (Miele et al., 2009). The worldwide nanomedicine marketplace is expected to approach $351 billion by 2025 billion, especially given the expected expansion in developments in targeted medicine, surgery, or diagnostic delivery using nanorobotics (Tinkle et al., 2014). With a market share of around 59%, the United States is the largest market for nanopharmaceuticals. Europe is a latecomer, with a market share of around 33% (Nance, 2019). The rise in R&D of therapeutic vaccines is one of the primary factors driving the nanopharmaceuticals market growth over the next few years, according to the nanopharmaceuticals market. Expanded illness diagnostic techniques, as well as improved research on combination medicines, will drive the market demand.

Risks associated with nanomedicines advancements

Undoubtedly, nanotechnology has the potential to revolutionize medicine in a variety of ways, from diagnostic to therapeutic, and everything in between. Various kinds of NPs are employed for the production of different types of medicines, some of which are depicted in Fig. 19.2. Nanomedicine, like nanotechnology in general, is a very new field with minimal experimental data on unintended and negative consequences. The challenges of the nanomedicines begin with their characterization to the scale-up and manufacturing process. Nanomedicine products are challenging to characterize due to their variable features. For example, polydispersity (PD) is a critical quantity that evaluates the heterogeneity of particles in terms of size, structure, and mass. If a

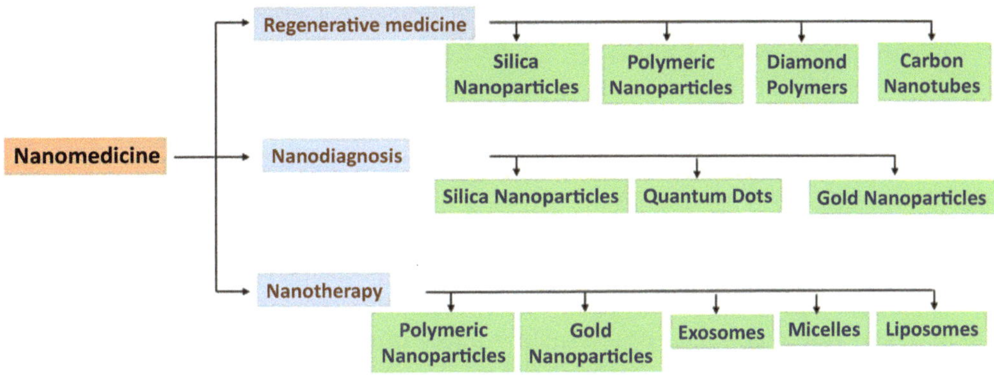

Figure 19.2 Various kinds of nanoparticles are utilized for nanomedicines.

nanomedicine has a similar average size but a dissimilar PD, secondary features, such as drug release rate, targeting, toxicity, biocompatibility, and in vivo behaviors, may alter dramatically (Aillon et al., 2009; Dobrovolskaia & McNeil, 2009; Nel et al., 2009). Further, during the nanoformulation process, various steps consisting of homogenization, sonication, emulsification, milling, organic solvent evaporation, lyophilization, centrifugation, and filtering are used (Feng et al., 2004). The improper conditions could cause the therapeutic reagents' chemical structure to change, as well as other accessories and unanticipated contaminants. As a result, making nanomedicine products entails more than just adding and mixing individual components; it necessitates definite development steps, precise investigation, and stringent quality analysis (Desai, 2012). Also, the high charges of raw ingredients and the requirement of a wacky multistep development protocol are also barriers to scaling up and producing nanomedicine, making nanotherapeutics exceedingly expensive to produce (Wu et al., 2020). The lack of understanding of how NPs could alter or interfere with the human body's biochemical pathways and activities is particularly troubling. Toxicity and exposure pathways are the main concerns of scientists (Wicki et al., 2015). The challenge for nanomedical developers and users is to strike a balance between the medical and societal benefits and risks connected with nanotechnology. The suitability of existing techniques, such as physiologically-based pharmacokinetic models and predicted structure-activity connections; utilized for the analysis of the toxicity and the dangers of the nanomedicines are quite uncertain. The issue of safety is one that affects the entire world. Along with the safety concerns, Oberdorster et al. also emphasized the regulatory issues. The author claimed that the FDA should emphasize the relevant risk assessment before the approval of any nanodrug. The ethical use of nanodrugs has also become a burning issue in today's society. Just a few of the ethical considerations include risk assessment, human enhancement, toxicity, and informed consent. Another concern is the blurry border between medicinal and nonmedicinal applications of nanotechnology in therapeutic, diagnostic, and preventive medicine. Another heated area in the extensive list of concerns is whether nanotechnology must be utilized to employ purposeful alterations in or to the body when the variation is not medically essential. The difficulties (for example, building devices to monitor nanomaterial exposure in the environment; to develop and validating methodologies to assess nanomaterial toxicity; producing new nanomaterials, models for estimating the environmental impact of NPs utilized are and human health; and creating strategic programs that allow for applicable risk-focused initiatives) were chosen to promote strategic research on a topic that was important to nanotechnology's safety (Maynard et al., 2006). These aforementioned issues, such as safety issues, regulatory issues, utilized are utilized and ethical issues (Fig. 19.3) related to nanomedicines.

Safety issues related to nanomedicines

Although the growing topic of nanomedicine is generating a lot of interest, there is presently a dearth of management in this area. Numerous nanomedicines function in a direct manner, that is, interaction with genetic materials or with biomolecule interaction; necessary for the regular functioning of the genome and cell division. These abovementioned processes can result in genotoxicity and mutagenicity (Singh et al., 2009). The hazardous effects of nanomedicines are mediated through the neutrophils and macrophages' inflammatory response, which further results in the formation of reactive oxygen and nitrogen species. These species are responsible for oxidative and nitrosative stresses (Smolkova et al., 2017). The body can be severely harmed by the accumulation of such free radicals (Lobo et al., 2010). Fig. 19.4 shows the mechanism of generation of free radicals in the body by C_{60} fullerene. Along with these, the modifications in surface and charge of particles result in increasing the toxicity of nanomedicines (Vinardell, 2005).

The calamitous impacts of the nanomaterials are reflected from the exceptional physical and chemical characteristics. The basic generalization is that the smaller the

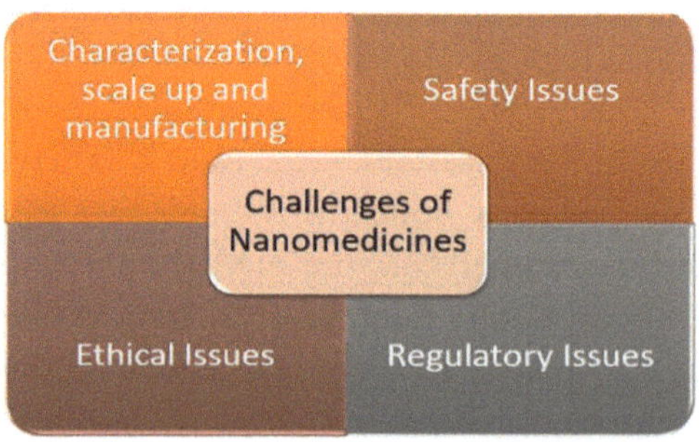

Figure 19.3 Different kinds of issues are associated with nanomedicines.

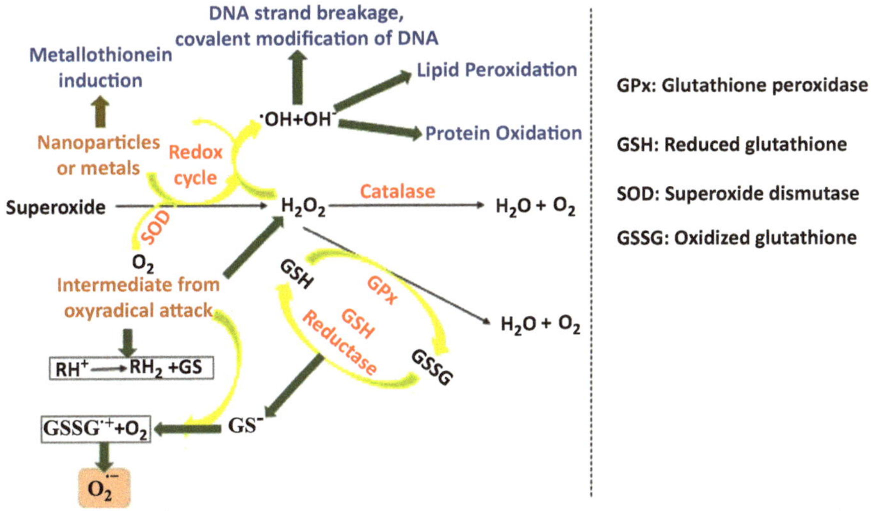

Figure 19.4 Illustration of the mechanism of free radicals' generation by C_{60} fullerene.

size of NPs, the higher will be their reactivity and, correspondingly, their toxicity due to the enhanced surface area/mass (Nighswonger, 1999). Few types of research were also reported that ultrafine NPs, such as nanoscale graphite and carbon, induce inflammatory lungs injury (Oberdörster et al., 2005). Some major changes, such as gene expression, metabolic, and apoptosis, and some cellular damages are associated with the nanomedicines are reported in the literature. NPs' interactions with the innate immune system and other tissues are still unknown. Some confirmed and potential routes of nanomedicines in the body are shown in Fig. 19.5. Due to their size, NPs can function as haptens to alter protein compositions, either by changing the functionality or making their behavior antigenic (Donaldson et al., 2004). NPs may be able to absorb proteins due to their enormous surface area. The NPs taken by the macrophages may lead to immunosuppression or immunostimulation, which are considered the unwanted interactions of NPs with the immune system (McDonald et al., 2015). Various kinds of NPs are employed to produce different kinds of drugs and exhibit different kinds of responses/toxicity in the body systems reliant upon their physical and chemical characteristics as discussed later.

The cytotoxic consequences of AgNPs are due to their size, cell absorption, tissue allocation, and infiltration competence (Khandelwal et al., 2014). AgNPs having smaller ones may be coagulated within the lungs and may reach various organs through the blood circulation (Song et al., 2013). Injuries in the brain were mentioned at high AgNPs concentrations, that is, 2.9 mg/m^3 (Kwon et al., 2012). The deposition of AgNPs in various kinds of tissues also relies upon the electric charge found on the surface of NPs' (Sharma et al., 2009). Various researches confirmed the outcomes of NPs doses, namely, weight

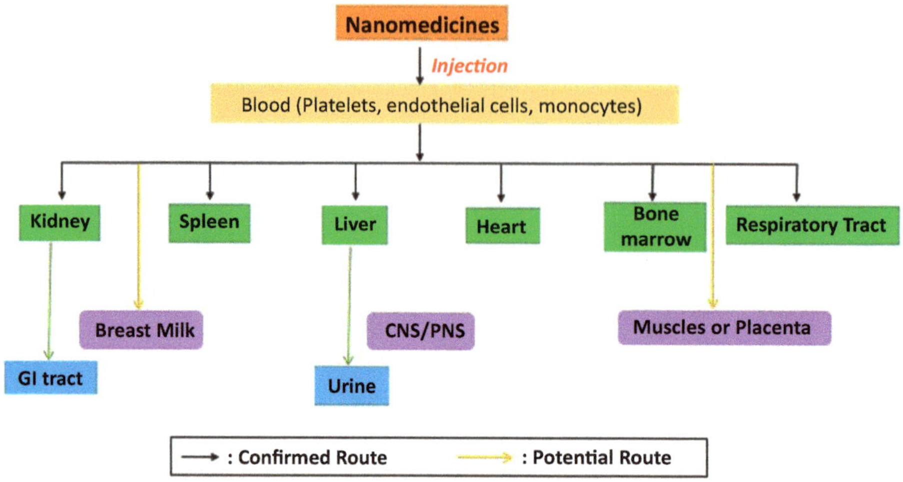

Figure 19.5 Different potential and confirmed routes of nanomedicines exposure in humans.

reduction at 10 mg/kg, liver problems at >300 mg/kg (Kim et al., 2008), and oxidative strain existed at >1000 mg/kg doses of NPs (Adeyemi & Faniyan, 2014). A study indicated that different biological entities like viruses and human cell lines had been inhibited by AgNPs within the same order, that is, 10 μg/mL, which was due to the interactions of AgNPs with cell and viral basic components (Vazquez-Muñoz et al., 2017).

Iron homeostasis plays an important role in mitochondrial respiration, DNA synthesis, and oxygen transport in the organism as a whole. It is also involved in myelin production, metabolic activities, and neurotransmitter synthesis in the CNS. Iron administration may activate and change these mechanisms, causing the upregulation of proteins involved in cell iron transport, storage, and overexpression of proteins involved in cell iron intake. Through Fenton's reaction an increase in the release of reactive oxygen species (ROS) could be caused by iron buildup. ROS may then produce oxidative stress that promotes protein aggregation, which can make contributions to neurodegeneration and cause diseases like Alzheimer's disorder and Parkinson's. Excess iron may suppress the production of occludin, a protein necessary for tight junction integrity, resulting in BBB destruction (Yarjanli et al., 2017). The surface charge is also important because excessive concentrations of anionic or cationic NPs can affect the neurovascular unit, affecting the efficacy of the BBB (Cupaioli et al., 2014). Scientific reports shed new light on the secondary poisonous outcomes that are reported in brief. Extreme allergic reactions to ferumoxytol NPs (employed intravenously) were reported along with Gell–Coombs system immune responses, nonimmune reactions, and long-term skin discoloration (Daldrup-Link, 2017).

It has been shown in research that biological and physicochemical properties are affected by the increase in surface area of NPs compared with bulk particles. For a risk analysis of NPs, three basic protocols are needed: in vivo and in vitro assays and their physicochemical analysis (Pujalté et al., 2011). Espitia et al. in 2012 examined that after consumer exposure, ZnO NPs were found to be harmful and carcinogenic to healthy eukaryotic cells. In vivo studies are morally problematic, expensive, and time-consuming to conduct without jeopardizing the efficacy and reliability of risk evaluation; as a result, in vitro testing has received a lot of attention (Espitia et al., 2012). Nanomaterials are thought to have far more harmful effects on living organisms than microscopic materials due to their particular surface area and associated reactivity. ZnO NPs have been shown to have cytotoxic effects on a variety of cell types, including human kidney cells and bronchial epithelial cells (Pujalté et al., 2011). Increased oxidative DNA damage and oxidative stress were found to be responsible for ZnO NPs' cytotoxicity in healthy cells. Zinc traces are important for a variety of biological and chemical functions in the body, including immune function, wound healing, blood coagulation, and thyroid function, but larger zinc concentrations can be hazardous to human health. Zinc poisoning is divided into two stages: acute and chronic. Lung injury occurs when zinc oxide is introduced into the human body. High zinc intakes of 60 mg/day for up to 10 weeks were required to reduce copper-containing enzymes and copper status indicators (Trumbo et al., 2001). The human body can also absorb zinc oxide through the skin. Due to the common use of zinc oxide in cosmetics, these goods may encourage its entrance.

An ocular toxicity of carbon nanotubes was tested by different groups using various in vivo or in vitro models. For example, Liu's group reported the toxicity of SWCNTs and MWCNTs to human eye cells. SWCNTs have been shown to be highly cytotoxic to ARPE19 cells with membrane integrity, reduced cell viability, altered levels of superoxide dismutase, and cell death (Yan et al., 2011). However, MWCNT leads to decreased cell viability, increased Aβ lactate in Alzheimer's disease, and α synuclein in Parkinson's disease. Various research studies showed that NPs of gold, silver, and carbon nanotubes could lead to enhanced cell apoptosis and O.S. in retinal cells of animals (Söderstjerna et al., 2014; Yan et al., 2013).

Legal factors

Incoming 5–10 years of technology of nanomedicine is likely to revolutionize the use of medicine to sustain and recover human health at the molecular and cellular levels. But the question arises here how long will nanomedicine offer valuable aids to the medical and healthcare sector (Barenholz, 2012)? Current research and development are focused on the medical application of nanotechnology neglecting the potential health and environmental risk caused by novel engineered nanomaterials. Therefore, ethical and regulatory characteristics are primitive in the applications of nanomedicine as it is applied in the field of medicine (Kagan et al., 2005). The development of nanomedicine is more challenging than other nanoproducts because it requires clinical trials, preclinical research, clinical indications, and a lot of time; also, any mistake or negative results may delay the projects (Tinkle et al., 2014). The most common challenge confronted by nanomedicine is its unsatisfactory clinical translation efficiency indicating a few problems that need to be addressed. Large-scale production of nanomedicine with high reproducibility is necessary for clinical translational. Moreover, the production of nanomedicine on large scale requires a large cost for manufacturing, preclinical tests, and high clinical cost, which stops the success of novel nanotherapeutics. Furthermore, getting regulatory permission for new nanoproducts is difficult, especially when there are similar items on the marketplace with almost the same value (Bawa et al., 2016).

Due to the lack of regulation for nanotherapeutics in quality assessment, safety control, manufacturing, and effectiveness evaluation is a fence for the production of nanomedicines. There are presently very few regulatory aspects for clinical translation of therapeutics, such as the FDA and Europeans Medicine Agency (EMA), to make available information and guidance. Presently, there is no existing regulatory test of NPs for health, safety, and ecological issues (Mühlebach, 2018). Even though FDA and EMA have approved various nanomedicines for cancer treatment, no particular rules have been implemented for the soft material containing drug items by any of the regulatory bodies. Due to the lack of direction in the assessment of nanomedicine, nanomedicine therapeutics can settle on administrative choices dependent on individual assessment of advantages and risks. Thus the regulatory process is very tedious, time-consuming, and needs expert views in new upcoming technologies resulting in regulatory delays that are important for the advancement of the new innovative technologies for the screening and characterizing the quality of nanomedicine products besides the clinical trials (Halamoda-Kenzaoui & Bremer-Hoffmann, 2018). Interestingly, the definitions, rules, and guidelines of this area are progressively being established and getting better. Additionally, the FDA and ETPN intend to work together with the NCL and European Nanomedicine Characterization Laboratory (EUNCL), respectively, for the in-depth analysis of the nanomaterials/nanomedicine to promote the regulatory reviews (Calster, 2006). Regulatory agencies play a very important role in nanomedicine therapeutics for refining and standardizing the necessities for the approval of various nanomedicines. However, there are lots of obstacles for clinical translation of nanoproducts due to inadequate regulations and knowledge about nanomedicines, and, so, the regulations implemented may not be efficient for patient security, and, therefore, the development of regulatory rules along with guidelines and technical standards are very necessary to lower the risks and regulate the usage of nanomedicines in clinical trials (Gaspar, 2007). Table 19.1 shows the lists of some nanomaterials/nanotherapeutics that have already received regulatory approval and are in clinical use or clinical trials.

Table 19.1 Few names of nanotherapeutics/nanomedicine approved for clinical use or in clinical trials.

S. No	Company name	Active molecule	Status	Year	Reference
1.	Doxil	Doxorubicin	Approved by FDA	1995	Barenholz (2012)
2.	DaunoXome	Daunorubicin	Approved by FDA	1996	Forssen (1997)
3.	Inflexal V	Virosomal influenza vaccine	Approved in Switzerland	1997	Herzog et al. (2009)
4.	Visudyne	Verteporfin	Approved by FDA	2000	Schmidt-Erfurth & Hasan (2000)
5.	DepoDur	Morphine sulfate	Approved by FDA	2004	Turan et al. (2006)
6.	Marqibo	Vincristine	Approved by FDA	2012	Bertagnolli et al. (2009)
7.	Onivyde	Irinotecan	Approved by FDA	2015	Bertagnolli et al. (2009)
8.	MBP-426	Oxaliplatin	Phase I (completed)	NA	Mita et al. (2010)
9.	ThermoDox	Doxorubicin	Phase III (completed)	NA	Poon & Borys (2009)
10.	GeneXol-PM	Paclitaxel	Approved by South Korea	2008	Kim et al. (2008)
11.	ADYNOVATE	PEGylated factor VIII	Approved by FDA	2015	Matsumura (2011)
12.	NK105	Paclitaxel	Phase III (completed)	NA	Hamaguchi et al. (2007)
13.	Pegasys	Interferon alpha-2a	Approved by FDA	2002	Cornberg et al. (2006)
14.	Opaxio	Paclitaxel	Approved by FDA	2012	Kitagawa et al. (2015)
15.	NK012	SN-38	Phase II (completed)	NA	Matsumura (2011)
16.	Emend	Aprepitant	Approved by FDA	2003	Coleman et al. (2019)
17.	RYANODEX	Dantrolene sodium	Approved by FDA	2014	Datta Gupta et al. (2019)
18.	Rapamune	Rapamycin	Approved by FDA	2000	Kendrew et al. (2013)
19.	Focalin XR	Dexmethyl phenidate HCl	Approved by FDA	2005	Coleman et al. (2019)
20.	Abraxane	Paclitaxel	Approved by FDA	2005	Miele et al. (2009)
21.	Nab-paclitaxel	Paclitaxel	Phase II (completed)	NA	Min et al. (2015)
22.	Ontak	Interleukin-2 receptor diphtheria toxin	Approved by FDA	1999	Foss et al. (2001)
23.	Kadcyla	Trastuzumab emtansine	Approved by FDA	2013	Barok et al. (2014)
24.	Feridex	Iron oxide NPs	Approved by FDA	1996	Wang (2011)
25.	Feraheme	Iron oxide NPs	Approved by FDA	2009	Feng et al. (2010)
26.	NanoTherm	Iron oxide	Approved by Europe	2010	Maier-Hauff et al. (2011)
27.	NBTXR3	Hafnium oxide NPs	Approved by Europe	2019	Bonvalot et al. (2019)
28.	CYT-6091	Tumor necrosis factor	Phase I (Completed)	NA	Libutti et al. (2010)

NPs, Nanoparticles.

Perspectives

Presently, nanomedicine/nanotherapeutics has been a global business—impacting almost every university, academic research organization, startup, and big pharma industry. Since it is a new area, there is a wide array of complex issues, including physiological, physicochemical, and molecular processes, which requires an understanding of clinical toxicities of different nanocarrier systems. In the coming years, we should have a better understanding of how to adjust NPs to minimize their poisonous, genotoxicity, and antigenicity, which will transform our industrial foundation and have a positive impact on healthcare for long-term quality of life. To effectively reflect the impacts of NPs the development of nanomedicine necessitates societal and ethical analyses, as well as exact correlations between in vitro and in vivo investigations. Although it is difficult to explain how nanomedicine will evolve in near future, lessons can be learned from advanced medical technologies, such as gene therapy and drug delivery system. As a result, the expanding number of papers in nanomedicine demonstrates that academic achievements are thriving in nanotherapeutic research. The FDA and other regulatory organizations are working hard to develop a suitable set of rules with stringent changes to benefit society. As a result, numerous nanotherapeutics have been approved for clinical use, and a small number of them, including protein-based and inorganic medicines, are currently being studied in clinical studies. When compared to standard pharmaceuticals, the commercialization of nanotherapeutics faces obstacles; thus more scientists are focusing on nanotechnologies to reduce side effects and improve efficacy. Nanotherapeutics will play a key role in fostering the widespread adoption of biotechnologies, such as gene therapy, proteomics, genomics, bioinformatics, and neuroscience, in the near future.

Conclusion

Although nanomedicine has aroused high hopes for many medical problems, it has also created scientific obstacles, owing to a lack of understanding of how nanomaterials behave inside live cells. Not all nanomaterials are equally harmful; it is critical to check the nanomaterials having unwanted characteristics that will help the nanomaterial manufacturing business to produce nanomedicines with the least amount of danger. Future nanomedical device development success and pharmaceuticals necessitate a consolidated data set in order to identify the best nanomaterial in a given situation. In these considerations, understanding the toxicity and probable negative effects of a candidate in a certain context material for medical applications, product life cycle awareness, and effective communication personnel, stakeholders, and regulators are all involved. It has also become a question of great concern, will nanomedicine make a significant contribution to medicine and healthcare in the long run? It is difficult to say if nanomedicine will bring about a series of relatively incremental enhancements to existing technologies or whether it will serve as a catalyst for a massive technical and health-care transformation. While fascinating in and of itself, the current state of nanomedicine is clearly simply a stepping stone on the path to bringing truly new solutions. Given the difficulty of clinical trials and the skepticism with which novel technologies are regarded and adopted by the general population, these will only happen over decades. However, because of basic research focusing on these difficulties, we are now closer to solving them and developing "true" nanomedicine-based medical solutions. To pick the best nanomaterial in a specific situation—understanding the toxicity and probable side effects associated with prospective nanomaterials—successful development of future nanomedical devices and medications requires a cohesive information base.

Acknowledgment

The author acknowledges Chandigarh University to provide all the essential infrastructures.

References

Adams, C. P., & Van Brantner, V. (2006). Market watch: Estimating the cost of new drug development: Is it really $802 million? *Health Affairs, 25*(2), 420–428. Available from https://doi.org/10.1377/hlthaff.25.2.420.

Adeyemi, O. S., & Faniyan, T. O. (2014). Antioxidant status of rats administered silver nanoparticles orally. *Journal of Taibah University Medical Sciences, 9*(3), 182–186. Available from https://doi.org/10.1016/j.jtumed.2014.03.002.

Aillon, K. L., Xie, Y., El-Gendy, N., Berkland, C. J., & Forrest, M. L. (2009). Effects of nanomaterial physicochemical properties on in vivo toxicity. *Advanced Drug Delivery Reviews, 61*(6), 457–466. Available from https://doi.org/10.1016/j.addr.2009.03.010.

Barenholz, Y. (2012). Doxil® – The first FDA-approved nano-drug: Lessons learned. *Journal of Controlled Release, 160*(2), 117–134. Available from https://doi.org/10.1016/j.jconrel.2012.03.020.

Barok, M., Joensuu, H., & Isola, J. (2014). Trastuzumab emtansine: mechanisms of action and drug resistance. *Breast Cancer Res, 16*(2), 209. Available from https://doi.org/10.1186/bcr3621. PMID: 24887180.

Bastogne, T. (2017). Quality-by-design of nanopharmaceuticals - a state of the art. *Nanomedicine, 13*(7), 2151–2157. Available from https://doi.org/10.1016/j.nano.2017.05.014. PMID: 28579437.

Bawa, R., Audette, G. F., & Reese, B. E. (2016). *Handbook of clinical nanomedicine: Law, business, regulation, safety, and risk. Handbook of clinical nanomedicine: Law, business, regulation, safety, and risk* (Vol. 2, pp. 1–1448). Pan Stanford Publishing Pte. Ltd. Available from https://doi.org/10.4032/9789814669238.

Bawa, R., & Johnson, S. (2009). *Emerging issues in nanomedicine and ethics. Nanotechnology and society: Current and emerging ethical issues* (pp. 207–223). Netherlands: Springer. Available from https://doi.org/10.1007/978-1-4020-6209-4_11.

Bertagnolli, M. M, Niedzwiecki, D., Compton, C. C., Hahn, H. P., Hall, M., Damas, B., Jewell, S. D., Mayer, R. J., Goldberg, R. M., Saltz, L. B., Warren, R. S., & Redston, M. (2009). Microsatellite instability predicts improved response to adjuvant therapy with irinotecan, fluorouracil, and leucovorin in stage III colon cancer: Cancer and Leukemia Group B Protocol 89803. *J Clin Oncol, 27*(11), 1814–1821. Available from https://doi.org/10.1200/JCO.2008.18.2071. PMID: 19273709.

Bonvalot, S., Rutkowski, P. L., Thariat, J., Carrère, S., Ducassou, A., Sunyach, M.-P., Agoston, P., Hong, A., Mervoyer, A., Rastrelli, M., Moreno, V., Li, R. K., Tiangco, B., Herraez, A. C., Gronchi, A., Mangel, L., Sy-Ortin, T., Hohenberger, P., de Baère, T., ... Papai, Z. (2019). NBTXR3, a first-in-class radioenhancer hafnium oxide nanoparticle, plus radiotherapy versus radiotherapy alone in patients with locally advanced soft-tissue sarcoma (Act.In.Sarc): a multicentre, phase 2-3, randomised, controlled trial. *Lancet Oncol*, *20*(8), 1148–1159. Available from https://doi.org/10.1016/S1470-2045(19)30326-2. PMID: 31296491.

Calster. (2006). Regulating nanotechnology in the European union. *Nanotechnology Law & Business*, *15*, 8–9.

Coleman, D. M., Adams, J. B., Anderson, A. L., & Frye, R. E. (2019). Rating of the effectiveness of 26 psychiatric and seizure medications for autism spectrum disorder: results of a national survey. *J Child Adolesc Psychopharmacol*, *29*(2), 107–123. Available from https://doi.org/10.1089/cap.2018.0121. PMID: 30724573.

Cornberg, M., Hadem, J., Herrmann, E., Schuppert, F., Schmidt, H. H.-J., Reiser, M., Marschal, O., Steffen, M., Manns, M. P., & Wedemeyer, H. (2006). Treatment with daily consensus interferon (CIFN) plus ribavirin in non-responder patients with chronic hepatitis C: a randomized open-label pilot study. *J Hepatol*, *44*(2), 291–301. Available from https://doi.org/10.1016/j.jhep.2005.10.021. PMID: 16360972.

Cupaioli, F. A., Zucca, F. A., Boraschi, D., & Zecca, L. (2014). Engineered nanoparticles. How brain friendly is this new guest? *Progress in Neurobiology*, *119–120*, 20–38. Available from https://doi.org/10.1016/j.pneurobio.2014.05.002.

Daldrup-Link, H. E. (2017). Ten things you might not know about iron oxide nanoparticles. *Radiology*, *284*(3), 616–629. Available from https://doi.org/10.1148/radiol.2017162759.

Datta Gupta, A., Visvanathan, R., Cameron, I., Koblar, S. A., Howell, S., & Wilson, D. (2019). Efficacy of botulinum toxin in modifying spasticity to improve walking and quality of life in post-stroke lower limb spasticity - a randomized double-blind placebo controlled study. *BMC Neurol*, *19*(1), 96. Available from https://doi.org/10.1186/s12883-019-1325-3. PMID: 31078139.

Desai, N. (2012). Challenges in development of nanoparticle-based therapeutics. *AAPS Journal*, *14*(2), 282–295. Available from https://doi.org/10.1208/s12248-012-9339-4.

DiMasi, J. A., Hansen, R. W., & Grabowski, H. G. (2003). The price of innovation: New estimates of drug development costs. *Journal of Health Economics*, *22*(2), 151–185. Available from https://doi.org/10.1016/S0167-6296(02)00126-1.

Dobrovolskaia, M. A., & McNeil, S. E. (2009). *Immunological properties of engineered nanomaterials. Nanoscience and technology: A collection of reviews from nature journals* (pp. 278–287). World Scientific Publishing Co. Available from https://doi.org/10.1142/9789814287005_0029.

Donaldson, K., Stone, V., Tran, C. L., Kreyling, W., & Borm, P. J. A. (2004). Nanotoxicology. *Occupational and Environmental Medicine*, *61*(9), 727–728. Available from https://doi.org/10.1136/oem.2004.013243.

Erkimbaev, A. O., Zitserman, V. Y., Kobzev, G. A., & Trakhtengerts, M. S. (2016). Nanoinformatics: Problems. *methods, and technologies. Scientific and Technical Information Processing*, *43*(4), 199–216. Available from https://doi.org/10.3103/S014768821604002X.

Espitia, P. J. P., Soares, N. d F. F., Coimbra, J. S. d R., de Andrade, N. J., Cruz, R. S., & Medeiros, E. A. A. (2012). Zinc oxide nanoparticles: Synthesis, antimicrobial activity and food packaging applications. *Food and Bioprocess Technology (Elmsford, N.Y.)*, *5*(5), 1447–1464. Available from https://doi.org/10.1007/s11947-012-0797-6.

Feng, J., Liu, H., Zhang, L., Bhakoo, K., & Lu, L. (2010). An insight into the metabolic responses of ultra-small superparamagnetic particles of iron oxide using metabonomic analysis of biofluids. *Nanotechnology*, *21*(39), 395101. Available from https://doi.org/10.1088/0957-4484/21/39/395101. PMID: 20820093.

Feng, S. S., Mu, L., Win, K. Y., & Huang, G. (2004). Nanoparticles of biodegradable polymers for clinical administration of paclitaxel. *Current Medicinal Chemistry*, *11*(4), 413–424. Available from https://doi.org/10.2174/0929867043455909.

Forssen, E. A. (1997). The design and development of DaunoXome® for solid tumor targeting in vivo. *Advanced Drug Delivery Reviews*, *24*(2-3), 133–150. Available from https://doi.org/10.1016/S0169-409X(96)00453-X, In this issue.

Foss, D. L., Zilliox, M. J., & Murtaugh, M. P. (2001). Bacterially induced activation of interleukin-18 in porcine intestinal mucosa. *Vet Immunol Immunopathol*, *78*(3-4), 263–277. Available from https://doi.org/10.1016/s0165-2427(00)00266-x. PMID: 11292528.

Gaspar, R. (2007). Regulatory issues surrounding nanomedicines: Setting the scene for the next generation of nanopharmaceuticals. *Nanomedicine: Nanotechnology, Biology, and Medicine*, *2*(2), 143–147. Available from https://doi.org/10.2217/17435889.2.2.143.

Goldman, I., & Pabari, M. (2021a). *Current & future scope for nanomedicines market by forecast to 2021 to 2027 with Covid-19 impact analysis* | Abbott Laboratories, CombiMatrix Corporation WWW Document.

Goldman, I., & Pabari, M. (2021b). *Nanomedicines market size, trends 2021 - global impact of COVID-19 on industry share, explosive factors of key players, progress status, and recent trends forecast to 2027*.

Halamoda-Kenzaoui, B., & Bremer-Hoffmann, S. (2018). Main trends of immune effects triggered by nanomedicines in preclinical studies. *International Journal of Nanomedicine*, *13*, 5419–5431. Available from https://doi.org/10.2147/IJN.S168808.

Hamaguchi, T., Kato, K., Yasui, H., Morizane, C., Ikeda, M., Ueno, H., Muro, K., Yamada, Y., Okusaka, T., Shirao, K., Shimada, Y., Nakahama, H., & Matsumura, Y. (2007). A phase I and pharmacokinetic study of NK105, a paclitaxel-incorporating micellar nanoparticle formulation. *Br J Cancer*, *97*(2), 170–176. Available from https://doi.org/10.1038/sj.bjc.6603855. PMID: 17595665.

Herzog, C., Hartmann, K., Künzi, V., Kürsteiner, O., Mischler, R., Lazar, H., & Glück, R. (2009). Eleven years of Inflexal V-a virosomal adjuvanted influenza vaccine. *Vaccine*, *27*(33), 4381–4387. Available from https://doi.org/10.1016/j.vaccine.2009.05.029. PMID: 19450630.

Jang, H. L., Zhang, Y. S., & Khademhosseini, A. (2016). Boosting clinical translation of nanomedicine. *Nanomedicine: Nanotechnology, Biology, and Medicine*, *11*(12), 1495–1497. Available from https://doi.org/10.2217/nnm-2016-0133.

John, A. A., Jaganathan, S. K., Ayyar, M., Krishnasamy, N. P., Rajasekar, R., & Supriyanto, E. (2017). Folic acid decorated chitosan nanoparticles and its derivatives for the delivery of drugs and genes to cancer cells. *Current Science*, *113*(8), 1530–1542. Available from https://doi.org/10.18520/cs/v113/i08/1530-1542.

Kagan, V. E., Bayir, H., & Shvedova, A. A. (2005). Nanomedicine and nanotoxicology: Two sides of the same coin. *Nanomedicine: Nanotechnology, Biology, and Medicine*, *1*(4), 313–316. Available from https://doi.org/10.1016/j.nano.2005.10.003.

Kendrew, S. G., Petkovic, H., Gaisser, S., Ready, S. J., Gregory, M. A., Coates, N. J., Nur-E-Alam, M., Warneck, T., Suthar, D., Foster, T. A., McDonald, L., Schlingman, G., Koehn, F. E., Skotnicki, J. S., Carter, G. T., Moss, S. J., Zhang, M.-Q., Martin, C. J., Sheridan, R. M., & Wilkinson, B. (2013). Recombinant strains for the enhanced production of bioengineered rapalogs. *Metab Eng*, *15*, 167–173. Available from https://doi.org/10.1016/j.ymben.2012.11.001. PMID: 23164580.

Khandelwal, N., Kaur, G., Kumar, N., & Tiwari, A. (2014). Application of silver nanoparticles in viral inhibition: A new hope for antivirals. *Digest Journal of Nanomaterials and Biostructures*, *9*(1), 175–186. Available from http://www.chalcogen.ro/175_Khandelwal.pdf.

Kim, Y. S., Kim, J. S., Cho, H. S., Rha, D. S., Kim, J. M., Park, J. D., Choi, B. S., Lim, R., Chang, H. K., Chung, Y. H., Kwon, I. H., Jeong, J., Han, B. S., & Yu, I. J. (2008). Twenty-eight-day oral toxicity, genotoxicity, and gender-related tissue distribution of silver nanoparticles in Sprague-Dawley rats. *Inhalation Toxicology*, *20*(6), 575–583. Available from https://doi.org/10.1080/08958370701874663.

Kitagawa, R., Katsumata, N., Shibata, T., Kamura, T., Kasamatsu, T., Nakanishi, T., Nishimura, S., Ushijima, K., Takano, M., Satoh, T., & Yoshikawa, H. (2015). Paclitaxel Plus Carboplatin Versus Paclitaxel Plus Cisplatin in Metastatic or Recurrent Cervical Cancer: The Open-Label Randomized Phase III Trial JCOG0505. *J Clin Oncol*, *33*(19), 2129–2135. Available from https://doi.org/10.1200/JCO.2014.58.4391. PMID: 25732161.

Kwon, J. T., Minai-Tehrani, A., Hwang, S. K., Kim, J. E., Shin, J. Y., Yu, K. N., Chang, S. H., Kim, D. S., Kwon, Y. T., Choi, I. J., Cheong, Y. H., Kim, J. S., & Cho, M. H. (2012). Acute pulmonary toxicity and body distribution of inhaled metallic silver nanoparticles. *Toxicological Research*, *28*(1), 25–31. Available from https://doi.org/10.5487/TR.2012.28.1.025.

Libutti, S. K., Paciotti, G. F., Byrnes, A. A., Alexander, H. R., Jr., Gannon, W. E., Walker, M., Seidel, G. D., Yuldasheva, N., & Tamarkin, L. (2010). Phase I and pharmacokinetic studies of CYT-6091, a novel PEGylated colloidal gold-rhTNF nanomedicine. *Clin Cancer Res, 16*(24), 6139–6149. Available from https://doi.org/10.1158/1078-0432.CCR-10-0978. PMID: 20876255.

Lobo, V., Patil, A., Phatak, A., & Chandra, N. (2010). Free radicals, antioxidants and functional foods: Impact on human health. *Pharmacognosy Reviews, 4*(8), 118–126. Available from https://doi.org/10.4103/0973-7847.70902.

Maier-Hauff, K., Ulrich, F., Nestler, D., Niehoff, H., Wust, P., Thiesen, B., Orawa, H., Budach, V., & Jordan, A. (2011). Efficacy and safety of intratumoral thermotherapy using magnetic iron-oxide nanoparticles combined with external beam radiotherapy on patients with recurrent glioblastoma multiforme. *J Neurooncol, 103*(2), 317–324. Available from https://doi.org/10.1007/s11060-010-0389-0. PMID: 20845061.

Matsumura, Y. (2011). Preclinical and clinical studies of NK012, an SN-38-incorporating polymeric micelles, which is designed based on EPR effect. *Adv Drug Deliv Rev, 63*(3), 184–192. Available from https://doi.org/10.1016/j.addr.2010.05.008. PMID: 20561951.

Maynard, A. D., Aitken, R. J., Butz, T., Colvin, V., Donaldson, K., Oberdörster, G., Philbert, M. A., Ryan, J., Seaton, A., Stone, V., Tinkle, S. S., Tran, L., Walker, N. J., & Warheit, D. B. (2006). Safe handling of nanotechnology. *Nature, 444*(7117), 267–269. Available from https://doi.org/10.1038/444267a.

McDonald, T. O., Siccardi, M., Moss, D., Liptrott, N., Giardiello, M., Rannard, S., & Owen, A. (2015). *The application of nanotechnology to drug delivery in medicine. Nanoengineering: Global approaches to health and safety issues* (pp. 173–223). Elsevier. Available from https://doi.org/10.1016/B978-0-444-62747-6.00007-5.

Miele, E., Spinelli, G. P., Miele, E., Tomao, F., & Tomao, S. (2009). Albumin-bound formulation of paclitaxel (Abraxane® ABI-007) in the treatment of breast cancer. *International Journal of Nanomedicine, 4*(1), 99–105. Available from http://www.dovepress.com/getfile.php?fileID = 4728.

Min, S. Y., Byeon, H. J., Lee, C., Seo, J., Lee, E. S., Shin, B. S., Choi, H.-G., Lee, K. C., & Youn, Y. S. (2015). Facile one-pot formulation of TRAIL-embedded paclitaxel-bound albumin nanoparticles for the treatment of pancreatic cancer. *Int J Pharm, 494*(1), 506–515. Available from https://doi.org/10.1016/j.ijpharm.2015.08.055. PMID: 26315118.

Mita, A. C., Takimoto, C. H., Mita, M., Tolcher, A., Sankhala, K., Sarantopoulos, J., Valdivieso, M., Wood, L., Rasmussen, E., Sun, Y.-N., Zhong, Z. D., Bass, M. B., Le, N., & LoRusso, P. (2010). Phase 1 study of AMG 386, a selective angiopoietin 1/2-neutralizing peptibody, in combination with chemotherapy in adults with advanced solid tumors. *Clin Cancer Res, 16*(11), 3044–3056. Available from https://doi.org/10.1158/1078-0432.CCR-09-3368. PMID: 20501621.

Mühlebach, S. (2018). Regulatory challenges of nanomedicines and their follow-on versions: A generic or similar approach? *Advanced Drug Delivery Reviews, 131*, 122–131. Available from https://doi.org/10.1016/j.addr.2018.06.024.

Nance, E. (2019). Careers in nanomedicine and drug delivery. *Advanced Drug Delivery Reviews, 144*, 180–189. Available from https://doi.org/10.1016/j.addr.2019.06.009.

Nel, A. E., Mädler, L., Velegol, D., Xia, T., Hoek, E. M. V., Somasundaran, P., Klaessig, F., Castranova, V., & Thompson, M. (2009). Understanding biophysicochemical interactions at the nano-bio interface. *Nature Materials, 8*(7), 543–557. Available from https://doi.org/10.1038/nmat2442.

Nighswonger, G. (1999). *A medical device link MD& DI column: New polymers and nanotubes add muscle to prosthetic limbs*. WWW Document.

Oberdörster, G., Oberdörster, E., & Oberdörster, J. (2005). Nanotoxicology: An emerging discipline evolving from studies of ultrafine particles. *Environmental Health Perspectives, 113*(7), 823–839. Available from https://doi.org/10.1289/ehp.7339.

Pelaz, B., Alexiou, C., Alvarez-Puebla, R. A., Alves, F., Andrews, A. M., Ashraf, S., Balogh, L. P., Ballerini, L., Bestetti, A., Brendel, C., Bosi, S., Carril, M., Chan, W. C. W., Chen, C., Chen, X., Chen, X., Cheng, Z., Cui, D., Du, J., & Parak, W. J. (2017). Diverse applications of nanomedicine. *ACS Nano, 11*(3), 2313–2381. Available from https://doi.org/10.1021/acsnano.6b06040.

Poon, R. T. P., & Borys, N. (2009). Lyso-thermosensitive liposomal doxorubicin: a novel approach to enhance efficacy of thermal ablation of liver cancer. *Expert Opin Pharmacother, 10*(2), 333–343. Available from https://doi.org/10.1517/14656560802677874. PMID: 19236203.

Pujalté, I., Passagne, I., Brouillaud, B., Tréguer, M., Durand, E., Ohayon-Courtès, C., & L'Azou, B. (2011). Cytotoxicity and oxidative stress induced by different metallic nanoparticles on human kidney cells. *Particle and Fibre Toxicology*, *8*. Available from https://doi.org/10.1186/1743-8977-8-10.

Rösslein, M., Liptrott, N. J., Owen, A., Boisseau, P., Wick, P., & Herrmann, I. K. (2017). Sound understanding of environmental, health and safety, clinical, and market aspects is imperative to clinical translation of nanomedicines. *Nanotoxicology*, *11*(2), 147–149. Available from https://doi.org/10.1080/17435390.2017.1279361.

Satalkar, P., Elger, B. S., Hunziker, P., & Shaw, D. (2016). Challenges of clinical translation in nanomedicine: A qualitative study. *Nanomedicine: Nanotechnology, Biology, and Medicine*, *12*(4), 893–900. Available from https://doi.org/10.1016/j.nano.2015.12.376.

Schmidt-Erfurth, U., & Hasan, T. (2000). Mechanisms of action of photodynamic therapy with verteporfin for the treatment of age-related macular degeneration. *Surv Ophthalmol*, *45*(3), 195–214. Available from https://doi.org/10.1016/s0039-6257(00)00158-2. PMID: 11094244.

Sharma, S., Mukkur, T. K. S., Benson, H. A. E., & Chen, Y. (2009). Pharmaceutical aspects of intranasal delivery of vaccines using particulate systems. *Journal of Pharmaceutical Sciences*, *98*(3), 812–843. Available from https://doi.org/10.1002/jps.21493.

Singh, N., Manshian, B., Jenkins, G. J. S., Griffiths, S. M., Williams, P. M., Maffeis, T. G. G., Wright, C. J., & Doak, S. H. (2009). NanoGenotoxicology: The DNA damaging potential of engineered nanomaterials. *Biomaterials*, *30*(23–24), 3891–3914. Available from https://doi.org/10.1016/j.biomaterials.2009.04.009.

Singh, P., Kim, Y. J., Zhang, D., & Yang, D. C. (2016). Biological synthesis of nanoparticles from plants and microorganisms. *Trends in Biotechnology*, *34*(7), 588–599. Available from https://doi.org/10.1016/j.tibtech.2016.02.006.

Smolkova, B., Dusinska, M., & Gabelova, A. (2017). Nanomedicine and epigenome. Possible health risks. *Food and Chemical Toxicology*, *109*, 780–796. Available from https://doi.org/10.1016/j.fct.2017.07.020.

Song, K. S., Sung, J. H., Ji, J. H., Lee, J. H., Lee, J. S., Ryu, H. R., Lee, J. K., Chung, Y. H., Park, H. M., Shin, B. S., Chang, H. K., Kelman, B., & Yu, I. J. (2013). Recovery from silver-nanoparticle-exposure-induced lung inflammation and lung function changes in Sprague Dawley rats. *Nanotoxicology*, 7(2), 169–180. Available from https://doi.org/10.3109/17435390.2011.648223.

Sowinska, M., Morawiak, M., Urbanczyk-Lipkowska, Z., & Solecka, J. (2017). *Nanochemistry in drug design. Beta-lactams: Novel synthetic pathways and applications* (pp. 311–334). Springer International Publishing. Available from https://doi.org/10.1007/978-3-319-55621-5_10.

Söderstjerna, E., Bauer, P., Cedervall, T., Abdshill, H., Johansson, F., Johansson, U. E., & Rozhkova, E. A. (2014). Silver and gold nanoparticles exposure to in vitro cultured retina – Studies on nanoparticle internalization, apoptosis, oxidative stress, glial- and microglial activity. *PLoS One*, *9*(8), e105359. Available from https://doi.org/10.1371/journal.pone.0105359.

Te Kulve, H., & Rip, A. (2013). Economic and societal dimensions of nanotechnology-enabled drug delivery. *Expert Opinion on Drug Delivery*, *10*(5), 611–622. Available from https://doi.org/10.1517/17425247.2013.770467.

Tinkle, S., Mcneil, S. E., Mühlebach, S., Bawa, R., Borchard, G., Barenholz, Y. C., Tamarkin, L., & Desai, N. (2014). Nanomedicines: Addressing the scientific and regulatory gap. *Annals of the New York Academy of Sciences*, *1313*(1), 35–56. Available from https://doi.org/10.1111/nyas.12403.

Trumbo, P., Yates, A. A., Schlicker, S., & Poos, M. (2001). Dietary reference intakes: Vitamin A, vitamin K, arsenic, boron, chromium, copper, iodine, iron, manganese, molybdenum, nickel, silicon, vanadium, and zinc. *Journal of the American Dietetic Association*, *101*(3), 294–301. Available from https://doi.org/10.1016/S0002-8223(01)00078-5.

Turan, A., White, P. F., Karamanlioglu, B., Memis, D., Tasdogan, M., Pamukçu, Z., & Yavuz, E. (2006). Gabapentin: an alternative to the cyclooxygenase-2 inhibitors for perioperative pain management. *Anesth Analg*, *102*(1), 175–181. Available from https://doi.org/10.1213/01.ane.0000184824.43411.63. PMID: 16368826.

Vazquez-Muñoz, R., Borrego, B., Juárez-Moreno, K., García-García, M., Mota Morales, J. D., Bogdanchikova, N., & Huerta-Saquero, A. (2017). Toxicity of silver nanoparticles in biological systems: Does the complexity of biological systems matter. *Toxicology Letters*, *276*, 11–20. Available from https://doi.org/10.1016/j.toxlet.2017.05.007.

Vinardell, M. P. (2005). In vitro cytotoxicity of nanoparticles in mammalian germ-line stem cell. *Toxicological Sciences*, *88*(2), 285–286. Available from https://doi.org/10.1093/toxsci/kfi340.

Wang, Y.-X. J. (2011). Superparamagnetic iron oxide based MRI contrast agents: Current status of clinical application. *Quant Imaging Med Surg*, *1*(1), 35–40. Available from https://doi.org/10.3978/j.issn.2223-4292.2011.08.03. PMID: 23256052.

Wicki, A., Witzigmann, D., Balasubramanian, V., & Huwyler, J. (2015). Nanomedicine in cancer therapy: Challenges, opportunities, and clinical applications. *Journal of Controlled Release*, *200*, 138–157. Available from https://doi.org/10.1016/j.jconrel.2014.12.030.

Wrobeln, A., Laudien, J., Groß-Heitfeld, C., Linders, J., Mayer, C., Wilde, B., Knoll, T., Naglav, D., Kirsch, M., & Ferenz, K. B. (2017). Albumin-derived perfluorocarbon-based artificial oxygen carriers: A physico-chemical characterization and first in vivo evaluation of biocompatibility. *Eur J Pharm Biopharm*, *115*, 52–64. Available from https://doi.org/10.1016/j.ejpb.2017.02.015. PMID: 28232105.

Wu, L.-P., Wang, D., & Li, Z. (2020). Grand challenges in nanomedicine. *Materials Science and Engineering: C*, *106*, 110302. Available from https://doi.org/10.1016/j.msec.2019.110302.

Yan, L., Zhang, S., Zeng, C., Xue, Y., Zhou, Z., Lu, F., Chen, H., Qu, J., Dai, L., & Liu, Y. (2011). Cytotoxicity of single-walled carbon nanotubes with human ocular cells. *Advanced materials research*, *287–290*, 32–36. Available from https://doi.org/10.4028/http://www.scientific.net/AMR.287-290.32, Vols.

Yan, Lu, Li, G., Zhang, S., Sun, F., Huang, X., Zhang, Q., Dai, L., Lu, F., & Liu, Y. (2013). Cytotoxicity and genotoxicity of multi-walled carbon nanotubes with human ocular cells. *Chinese Science Bulletin*, *58*(19), 2347–2352. Available from https://doi.org/10.1007/s11434-013-5800-8.

Yarjanli, Z., Ghaedi, K., Esmaeili, A., Rahgozar, S., & Zarrabi, A. (2017). Iron oxide nanoparticles may damage to the neural tissue through iron accumulation, oxidative stress, and protein aggregation. *BMC Neuroscience*, *18*(1). Available from https://doi.org/10.1186/s12868-017-0369-9.

Index

Note: Page numbers followed by "*f*" and "*t*" refer to figures and tables, respectively.

D

J

K

L

S

T

U

V

FSC
www.fsc.org
MIX
Papier | Fördert gute Waldnutzung
FSC® C083411

Kolibri 360 GmbH
Ferdinand-Jühlke-Straße 7
99095 Erfurt, Deutschland
produktsicherheit@kolibri360.de